For George

'Love one another'

November 2001

AUTOCOURSE ™

THE WORLD'S LEADING GRAND PRIX ANNUAL

HAZLETON PUBLISHING

contents

Photograph: Clive Mason/Allsport-Getty Images

AUTOCOURSE 2001–02

is published by:

Hazleton Publishing Ltd, 3 Richmond Hill,
Richmond, Surrey TW10 6RE.

Colour reproduction by
Barrett Berkeley Ltd, London.

Printed in England by
Butler and Tanner Ltd,
Frome, Somerset.

Hazleton Publishing Ltd is a member of
Profile Media Group Plc.

ISBN: 1-903135-06-0

DISTRIBUTORS

UNITED KINGDOM
Haynes Publishing plc
Sparkford
Near Yeovil
Somerset BA22 7JJ
Telephone: 01963 442030
Fax: 01963 440001

NORTH AMERICA
Motorbooks International
PO Box 1
729 Prospect Avenue
Osceola
Wisconsin 54020, USA
Telephone: (1) 715 294 3345
Fax: (1) 715 294 4448

REST OF THE WORLD
Menoshire Ltd
Unit 13
Wadsworth Road
Perivale
Middlesex UB6 7LQ
Telephone: 020 8566 7344
Fax: 020 8991 2439

Acknowledgements

The Editor of AUTOCOURSE wishes to thank the following for their assistance in compiling the 2001–2002 edition:
Eire: Jordan Grand Prix (Eddie Jordan, Ian Phillips, Trevor Foster, Tim Holloway, Giselle Davies, Mark Gallagher, Christine Goreham, Fiona Cole and Lindsay Haylett); France: ACO, Asiatech (David Waldron); Fédération Française du Sport Automobile, FIA (Max Mosley, Bernie Ecclestone, Francesco Longanesi-Cattani, Agnes Kaiser, Anne-Marie Guichon, Charlie Whiting, Herbie Blash and Pat Behar); Michelin (Pierre Dupasquier and Severine Ray), Prost Grand Prix (Alain Prost and Virginie Papin); Germany: Formula 3 Vereinigung, BMW Motorsport (Gerhard Berger, Mario Theissen and Guido Stalman), Sabine Kehm, Mercedes-Benz (Norbert Haug, Wolfgang Schattling, Frank Reichert, Tania Severin and Kay Oliver Langendorff); Great Britain: Arrows (Tom Walkinshaw, Daniele Audetto, Lindsay Morle, Michael Ainsley-Cowlishaw, Emily Taylor and Mike Coughlan), Autocar, British American Racing (Craig Pollock, Malcolm Oastler, Tracy Novak and Suzanne Yong), Martin Brundle, Colin Burr, Timothy Collings, Bob Constanduros, Cosworth Engineering, Peter Foubister, Maurice Hamilton, Nick Henry, Ian Hutchinson, Ilmor Engineering (Mario Illien), Jaguar Racing (Niki Lauda, Bobby Rahal, Steve Nichols, Nav Sidhu, James Thomas and Lucy James-Green), McLaren International (Ron Dennis, Adrian Newey, Martin Whitmarsh, Justine Blake, Beverley Keynes, Ellen Kolby, Jo Ramirez, Bob McMurray, Simon Points, Neil Oatley, Steve Hallam and Peter Stayner), Stan Piecha, Nigel Roebuck, Eric Silbermann, Sir Jackie Stewart, Simon Taylor, Professor Sid Watkins, WilliamsF1 (Patrick Head, Dickie Stanford, Ann Bradshaw, Silvia Hoffer, Liam Clogger, Jonathan Williams and Sir Frank Williams); Italy: Benetton Formula (Flavio Briatore, Mike Gascoyne, Pat Symonds and Sophia Claughton-Wallin), Commissione Sportiva Automobilistica Italia, Scuderia Ferrari (Ross Brawn, Claudio Berro, Antonio Ghini, Stefania Bocci, Simone Piatello and Jean Todt), Minardi Team (Paul Stoddart, Rupert Manwaring, Giancarlo Minardi, Stefania Torrelli and Graham Jones), Giorgio Piola; Japan: Bridgestone (Hirode Hamashima, Yoshihiko Ichikawa and Sarah French); Switzerland: Sauber (Peter Sauber and Agnes Carlier); USA: CART, Daytona International Speedway, Indianapolis Motor Speedway, Indy Lights, NASCAR, Roger Penske, SportsCar.

photographs published in AUTOCOURSE 2001–2002 have been contributed by:
Allsport-Getty Images UK (Clive Mason, Mark Thompson, Mike Hewitt, Ker Robertson), Allsport-Getty Images US (Robert Laberge, Jon Ferrey, Adam Pretty, Jamie Squire, Darrell Ingham), Paul-Henri Cahier, Steve Etherington/EPI, LAT Photographic (Jeff Bloxham, Malcolm Griffiths), Peter Nygaard/GP Photo, Matthias Schneider, Bryn Williams/crash.net.

Dust-jacket photograph:
World Champion: Michael Schumacher, Ferrari.

Title page photograph:
Hungary, 19 August 2001. Michael Schumacher wins the World Championship for the fourth time, and is congratulated by Jean Alesi and brother Ralf after the race.
Both photographs: Paul-Henri Cahier

publisher
RICHARD POULTER

editor
ALAN HENRY

managing editor
ROBERT YARHAM

art editor
STEVE SMALL

production manager
STEVEN PALMER

business development manager
SIMON SANDERSON

sales promotion
ANNALISA ZANELLA

marketing and
new media manager
NICK POULTER

results and statistics
DAVID HAYHOE
NICK HENRY

f1 illustrations
IAN HUTCHINSON
NICOLA CURTIS
MARK STEWARD

chief photographer
PAUL-HENRI CAHIER

chief contributing photographers
ALLSPORT-GETTY IMAGES
BRYN WILLIAMS/crash.net
MATTHIAS SCHNEIDER

AUTOCOURSE
www.autocourse.com

foreword
by MICHAEL SCHUMACHER

FOR the first time in my career I was lucky to win the title in Europe. Celebrating on the podium together with so many fans really moved me a lot. When you stand there and see all these people crying for joy and waving the flags, it's amazing, and I am glad I could experience this. What I also liked was the fact that I managed to finish my last three championships with a victory. This is very important to me.

Now I dare to say: We are in the middle of a Ferrari era, a period we dreamed of creating for a long time. We started it two years ago, and I hope we can keep it up for some more time.

Everybody asks me how I would compare these two titles I have won with Ferrari? But I cannot compare them, and I believe nobody could. When we won last year, it was just pure relief after all the pressure, after all the expectations and all that had happened in the past for those 21 years before.

This year it was less the fact that we achieved it, but more how we achieved it which was so enjoyable. It was a perfect demonstration of team strength and team effort. I can only repeat myself: We have such a great crew at the Scuderia, such a wonderful, passionate team that it's just fun to work with them.

It's their achievement and I'm more than thankful to all of them. But as I said in Hungary: I am probably not a bad racing driver but I'm quite bad at finding the right words for such enormous emotions.

CRÉATEUR D'AUTOMOBILES

RENAULT recommend elf

Clio **RENAULT** *sport v6*

For details about the Clio V6's performance please call 0800 52 51 50 or visit www.renault.co.uk

Clio
v6

Some like it hot.

Best of times, worst of times...

Above: Michael Schumacher took his second successive drivers' title for Ferrari, overtaking Alain Prost's record victory tally in the process.
Photograph: Paul-Henri Cahier

FORMULA 1 continued to flourish throughout 2001 although the understandable signs were there by the end of the season that this high-profile sport would certainly not remain insulated from the turbulent events of the wider world.

It was not simply the fact that a prospect of a round of belt-tightening must be anticipated across the board, but the tragic events of 11 September could well have a profound effect in shaping the future of the FIA F1 World Championship calendar. Both Bernie Ecclestone and Max Mosley would like to see the Grands Prix more widely spread throughout the world and not concentrated so much in Europe.

The Middle East was one target area for possible expansion, but by the end of the year the prevailing view in the paddock was that such new events would probably appear later rather than sooner. It seemed a difficult one to call.

Of course, worrying about the future is a fruitless and nerve-wracking task in such a political environment. For the moment it is perhaps appropriate to pause for breath and reflect on another season of domination from Michael Schumacher and the Ferrari team. Maranello provided another brilliant machine in the form of the F2001 and Michael used it to superb effect, demolishing record after record. Memorably, he has broken Alain Prost's record of Grand Prix victories, adding two to the previous record total of 51, and set a new benchmark for his career tally of World Championship points.

He became the first Ferrari driver to win back-to-back championship titles since Alberto Ascari in 1952–'53 and shows no signs of easing up. The metronomic perfection of his driving scales such pinnacles of precision that he makes the whole process of driving an F1 car look so simple and unruffled.

Paradoxically that apparent ease of achievement, the economy of effort, tends to undermine his image as one of the greatest drivers in the sport's history. If it looks that simple, surely it can't be that difficult? But all the great drivers have made it look easy.

That is the secret behind their genius and nobody in their right mind would bet against Michael breaking the one remaining statistical barrier ahead of him, namely the record of five World Championship titles won by the legendary Juan Manuel Fangio between 1950 and '57. Michael has now won 53 of the 162 races in which he has competed and his strike rate of 32.7 per cent is only surpassed by Fangio who won a remarkable 24 of his 51 Grands Prix.

While it is obviously unrealistic to expect every season to culminate in a nail-biting championship cliffhanger at the final race, this year has signalled an urgent need for some consistent opposition to the Schumacher steamroller.

For the first time since Nigel Mansell won the title for the Williams-Renault squad in 1992, the title battle was resolved as early as the Hungarian GP in mid-August. That left four races for the F1 fraternity to mark time as it contemplated plans for 2002.

The failure of the McLaren-Mercedes team to fulfil its traditional role as Ferrari's most formidable opponent has only in part been mitigated by the emergence of the BMW Williams team as a front-line force. Put simply, one is bound to wonder what everyone else has been doing allowing Schumacher to waltz away to his fourth title largely unchallenged.

David Coulthard drove his best season ever, but was let down by uncharacteristic unreliability on the part of his machinery. Mika Häkkinen had a patchy year, then took a sabbatical.

By contrast, the BMW Williams squad was on the up. Ralf Schumacher won three races, his dynamic new team-mate Juan Pablo Montoya just one. Yet Montoya was probably the most exciting new talent to emerge on the F1 scene since Michael himself in 1991.

Generally one would have to say F1 remained in a pretty healthy state. There were other issues, of course, most notably the car companies' assertion that they would start their own independent series after the expiry of the current Concorde Agreement in 2007 unless they could be guaranteed a bigger slice of the commercial cake.

This underlying warning ran in parallel with F1 commercial rights holder Bernie Ecclestone's sale of his business to the German Kirch media group, a complex and protracted transaction the fine detail of which baffled many commentators within the sport.

The bottom line, however, is that Bernie still remains the man who calls the shots, the F1 supremo par excellence. Quite how the car makers proposed to administer their proposed new series without the autocratic efficiency of He-Who-Must-Be-Obeyed remains a matter of relaxed speculation. If, of course, they are still in the motor racing business at all by that point.

Sadly, this latest edition of AUTOCOURSE contains a regrettable number of obituaries. Those who died in action included Michele Alboreto and NASCAR giant Dale Earnhardt. Freak accidents claimed Bob Wollek and Ilmor co-founder Paul Morgan, while age or infirmity robbed us of Ken Tyrrell, John Cooper, Walter Hayes, Vittorio Brambilla, Fondmetal boss Gabriele Rumi and former Williams ADC Charlie Crichton-Stuart. Mention of their names inevitably triggers affectionate memories within this complex tapestry which is international motor racing.

Increasingly there is concern that the tactical nature of contemporary F1 racing passes over the heads of the paying spectator, the lack of overtaking on the circuit offering questionable value for money. This is a matter which has been a subject for debate ever since refuelling was reintroduced in 1994 and many believe a root-and-branch review of the F1 business is now called for, particularly set against the backdrop of the reintroduction of electronic driver aids which we saw in 2001. There was also continued concern on the safety front that speeds should be reduced in the wake of the terrible accident which claimed the life of a track marshal in the Australian Grand Prix at Melbourne.

In that connection, some suggested that perhaps it might be time to reconsider the 2-litre V6 engine rules which have been discussed from time to time over the last five years, but the car makers firmly vetoed such moves, making the point that they would not compromise on the stability of the current 3.5-litre V10 regulations.

This means any further reductions in lap speeds decided on by the FIA will put the onus on the chassis designers agreeing to and successfully implementing further modifications. The governing body spent much of the year carefully monitoring lap speeds, particularly on tracks containing fast corners, and will legislate for change if it believes things are getting out of hand.

For those fans really hooked on speed, Champ car racing came to Europe in the autumn for two races on the ambitious new bespoke oval tracks, the Lausitzring near Dresden and Rockingham in the UK. The German race was marred by a horrifying accident to former CART Champion Alex Zanardi, but both events were otherwise regarded as a great success.

Quite what the future holds for CART is less certain, for its administrators have shown questionable judgement in changing the engine rules for 2003, thereby persuading Honda to quit the field. It now seems only a matter of time before CART has to capitulate to Tony George's Indy Racing League and the whole fabric of US single-seater racing submits itself to a shake-up with more emphasis on oval track events rather than road and street circuits.

Further down the motor racing ladder, both F3 and F3000 thrived with Justin Wilson becoming the first British driver to win the latter title since the series' inception in 1985. Wilson tested a Jordan F1 car and proved a hugely talented performer, but his 6 ft 4 in. frame posed too difficult a packaging challenge and he didn't get the drive for 2002 alongside Giancarlo Fisichella.

His place instead went to the Japanese rising star Takuma Sato who dominated the British F3 championship in fine style and looks possibly the best driver from the home of Honda to emerge as a potential F1 candidate. His progress will be followed with huge interest.

The immediate future of F1 promises more of the same. Whether the television audiences will continue to hold up in the face of the continued domination of a single team remains a matter for speculation. Yet Michael Schumacher and Ferrari are simply doing their job. The onus is on their rivals to raise their game. With the minimum of delay.

Alan Henry,
Tillingham,
Essex
November 2001

A telling index of the generally unremarkable performances delivered by most of the teams can be gauged from the fact that the Sauber-Petronas squad finished fourth in the constructors' championship behind Ferrari, McLaren and Williams.

Sauber, a staid and normally somewhat average mid-ranking team, have benefited from a decent chassis and two motivated young drivers in Kimi Räikkönen and Nick Heidfeld. But their apparent upsurge in performance was certainly due in part to the disappointing level of under-achievement displayed by Jordan, British American Racing, Benetton and Jaguar, all teams which in the normal course of events one might have expected to give their Swiss rivals a brisk run for their money.

By the end of the season the chill winds of financial reality certainly seemed to be blowing through the ranks of the F1 teams. Prost Grand Prix finished the season on the commercial ropes, battling against the spectre of huge debts for its very survival. Toyota might have been looming large on the horizon for 2002, but even the top team principals conceded there could be bumpy times ahead.

The 2001 season was also marked by the reintroduction of electronic control systems, most notably traction control. Ferrari had raised their rivals' suspicions by insisting that the reintroduction of such systems be deferred until the fifth race of the season in Spain. Dark motives were attributed to those objections, the implication perhaps being that Maranello was interpreting the wheel-spin control rules in a uniquely imaginative manner.

When it came to it, nothing changed in terms of F1's status quo and it was clear that Ferrari had no problems adapting to the new rules. Their rivals' hoped-for advantage under this new technical initiative simply didn't materialise. In fact nothing changed at all, and Ferrari effected a seamless transition into the second-generation world of electronic driver aids without a ripple.

Above, from top:
Ralf Schumacher returned Williams to the winners' circle with three strong wins.

Mika Häkkinen looks for the secrets of Ferrari's success. The Finn would decide to take some time off from Formula 1 in 2002.

The reintroduction of electronic driver aids such as traction control may have reduced wheelspin, but did not upset the established order.

Juan Pablo Montoya put a smile back on the faces of even the most world-weary Formula 1 fans.
All photographs: Paul-Henri Cahier

We spend 3 months formulating a perfect

▶ To the uninitiated, they're just cars racing around a track. But to those who know, Formula One is a game of high-speed chess.

▶ For months before, the best brains in motorsport have argued over every possible scenario. And then every possible permutation of every possible scenario. What tyres, how much fuel, how many pit-stops? What happened last year? And if it rains? Of course, we must also assume that o
be shrewd e
our strategy.
mid-race, we
when to su
something co

▶ This is v

...rategy. At a moment's notice, we change it.

...npetitors may   a race. Confusing? Yes. Obsessive?
...to anticipate   Most certainly. It's this passionate
...is why, even   commitment that helps perfect
...know exactly   our race cars. And also the
...them with   Mercedes-Benz you drive.
...ely different.   ▶ Visit us at www.mercedes-
...takes to win   benz.com/motorsport

Mercedes-Benz

The Future of the Automobile.

FIA FORMULA 1 WORLD CHAMPIONSHIP
TOP TEN DRIVERS
Chosen by the editor, taking into account their racing performances and the equipment at their disposal

Photography by **MATTHIAS SCHNEIDER**

MICHAEL SCHUMACHER

Date of birth: **3 January 1969**

Team: **Scuderia Ferrari Marlboro**

Grand Prix starts in 2001: **17**

World Championship placing: **1st**

Wins: **9**; Poles: **11**; Points: **123**

IN his tenth full season of F1 competition, Michael Schumacher shows not the slightest hint of losing his edge, interest or motivation. That in itself is the most remarkable facet of his razor-sharp competitive character which propelled him through to his second straight drivers' World Championship at the wheel of a Ferrari, his fourth overall. Michael was unquestionably the driver of the year working for the team of the year. His remarkable run of successes has depended in no small measure on the seamless transition into the new season by all involved in the Maranello F1 operation. Yet for all the precision engineering and imaginative race strategies offered by Ferrari, it is Michael who makes the key difference.

Perhaps curiously, many of Michael's fans believe his inadvertent absence from F1 for three months in the summer of 1999 after breaking his leg at Silverstone may have given fresh impetus to his career, perhaps offering an impromptu taste of the kind of sabbatical which his arch-rival Mika Häkkinen has teed up for 2002. Michael's personal fourth title bid was built off the back of Ferrari's early season mechanical reliability to the point where closest challenger David Coulthard rarely stemmed the German driver's momentum which had come from winning the Australian and Malaysian GPs in quick succession.

In fairness, however, it was a cushion Michael hardly needed even when Coulthard beat his poorly set-up Ferrari to victory in Brazil and an overheating wheel rim broke at Imola. After four races he still tied for the lead of the Championship and although Coulthard offered a strong early-season challenge, that was as bad as it got. Michael's season also served to remind one that the really great drivers in history seem to manufacture their own luck. In both Malaysia and Brazil he preserved what would eventually translate into a first and second place respectively despite lurid slides off the road which could have cost him everything. Off days were not something generally part of the Schumacher grand plan, but a distant second place to Häkkinen at Silverstone was largely down to the wrong refuelling strategy and his drive to fourth at Monza proved a rare moment of nervous disinterest. Exercising his droit de seigneur within the team, team-mate Rubens Barrichello handed him a last-corner second place in Austria but he paid his colleague back by supporting the Brazilian's unfortunately fruitless bid for second place in the championship during the last two races of the year. Decisively the best of the bunch.

2

THIS was David Coulthard's best shot at the World Championship so far and somehow encapsulated the poignant dilemma in which the popular Scot has so frequently found himself over the past few years. In the past, he has compromised his success with the occasional crucial driving error at a time when his McLaren-Mercedes has offered him bullet-proof reliability.

This year the situation has been reversed. Coulthard has not made a slip, but time and again he has been let down by his machinery. Anybody who witnessed his mature, seasoned performance in winning the Austrian Grand Prix would have concluded that here was a man capable of taking the title. It would have been laughable to suggest he would not win another race all season. But that's how it worked out.

A fortnight after that Austrian win came the crucial moment when everything went wrong. Having qualified on pole position at Monaco, a supreme achievement by any standards ahead of Michael Schumacher's Ferrari, Coulthard's McLaren-Mercedes then suffered an electrical problem on the starting grid prior to the parade lap which meant that he had to start from the back of the pack. It was genuinely a moment when one's heart ached for Coulthard as this was a race he had the chance of winning going away. As it was, his technical woes handed Schumacher a relaxed walk in the park. And from then on, David's season became unravelled.

From the Canadian Grand Prix it was almost as if Coulthard was fighting a rearguard damage limitation exercise. The rival Ferrari F2001 technical package had more of everything than the McLaren MP4/16: handling, speed and reliability. Silverstone offered a great opportunity for him to redress the balance, particularly with Häkkinen pledged to help if necessary, but Coulthard's consistency briefly slipped when he collided with Jarno Trulli's Jordan on the first corner.

Trulli, coming from behind, was the one who could have avoided the accident, but by the same token the onus was on 'DC' as a title contender not to trip over outsiders. From then on it was a question of picking up points as best he could as the title slipped further from his grasp. Coulthard deserved more from 2001 than the season delivered. Certainly he drove better than at any time previously in his career. If the McLaren-Mercedes MP4/17 is up to scratch, there is absolutely no reason why this popular and reserved Scot should not challenge strongly for the championship again in 2002.

Date of birth: **27 March 1971**

Team: **West McLaren Mercedes**

Grand Prix starts in 2001: **17**

World Championship placing: **2nd**

Wins: **2**; Poles: **2**; Points: **65**

DAVID COULTHARD

JUAN PABLO MONTOYA

3

Date of birth: 20 September 1975

Team: BMW WilliamsF1 Team

Grand Prix starts in 2001: 17

World Championship placing: 6th

Wins: 1; Poles: 3; Points: 31

ONE can always tell when an F1 newcomer has really made an impact from the chorus of doubters who seek to play down his achievements. In Juan Pablo Montoya's case the words were attributed to Michael Schumacher who suggested that the Colombian new boy in the Williams squad hadn't really done anything remarkable and that it was his brother who'd really produced the results during the course of the season.

Well, yes and no. If one scrutinises the statistical balance sheet there is no doubt that Ralf Schumacher has had an outstanding year. Yet this is a simplistic assessment of the way in which events have developed within the BMW Williams camp. What we're talking about here is how drivers adapt and respond to their environment, the set of circumstances with which they are faced. Whatever one likes to say about Montoya's established pedigree in F3000, CART, or as an F1 test driver, this was his debut World Championship season. And he carried it off with a style and delightful laid-back insouciance which mark him out as somebody really special.

Montoya first rang the F1 bell when he muscled his Williams FW23-BMW ahead of Michael Schumacher's Ferrari to take an early lead in the Brazilian Grand Prix. Granted, the Ferrari wasn't on top form that day, but Montoya came close to winning in his third Grand Prix. He finished second in Spain on a day his team-mate inexplicably spun off and achieved the same result at Nürburgring. In Austria he perhaps pushed too hard in an early defence of his lead, but rattled Michael Schumacher into making a mistake in response to that frustration. He should have won the German Grand Prix where he was running ahead of the younger Schumacher, but eventually posted his first win at Monza where he displayed a canny knack of conserving and nursing his blistered first set of tyres.

There were downside moments, of course. Montoya perhaps pushed too hard on some of the tight tracks where the Williams-BMW was not quite au point from the handling standpoint. But at the end of the day, Juan Pablo twice overtook Michael Schumacher successfully in the heat of F1 battle and Michael never managed to reverse that situation.

The second time came at Indianapolis where viewers of Bernie's digital TV could see him take his hands off the wheel on the start/finish straight in order to tighten his seat belts that last notch before squaring up to the World Champion. Great stuff. Whatever one feels about his ultimate potential, Montoya certainly helped put some fizz back into F1 during 2001. And F1 is much the better for it.

RALF Schumacher scored three outstanding victories for the BMW Williams team and had to be a strong contender for third place in our ratings, yet somehow there was something missing from his overall make-up to give him the advantage over his Colombian team-mate. On the one hand, the younger Schumacher could feel well satisfied with his performance in proving that the Williams FW23-BMW could get the job done, yet on the other hand it could be argued that he made too many slips for a driver of such experience and proven calibre.

Ralf began the season with quite a shaking after Jacques Villeneuve's BAR-Honda ploughed into the back of his car early on during the Australian Grand Prix. He then had to sit and watch two races later as his new team-mate Juan Pablo Montoya jousted with his elder brother Michael for the lead of the Brazilian GP at Interlagos. It must have been a rather unsettling experience.

However, Ralf underscored his experience and racecraft by putting the Williams-BMW alliance on the top spot of the winners' circle with a flawless victory in the San Marino GP at Imola. Similarly, in Montreal he would win decisively ahead of his brother after capitalising on a bolder refuelling strategy and his third win came at Hockenheim, although only after team-mate Montoya suffered engine failure while leading.

Disappointments included squandering a possible victory in the European GP at Nürburgring after receiving a ten-second stop-go penalty for crossing the white line separating the main track from the pit exit lane. He also suffered the embarrassment of being left on the line, his car supported on stands, after a rear wing change was needed on precautionary grounds prior to the restart at Spa.

The paradox to Ralf Schumacher's season was that in the year he finally confirmed his status as a world class F1 driver, his performances raised as many questions about his temperament as they answered about his potential quality. He didn't seem to hit it off with the thrusting Montoya and made a tactical error of criticising certain members of the Williams team in the wake of the Belgian GP debacle.

Finally, at Monza and Indianapolis, he became so bound up in the political problems which existed in the USA at the time that he simply took his eye off the ball. At the end of 2000 he had allowed himself to be wrong-footed by Jenson Button and now the same had occurred with Montoya. It left people wondering whether Ralf has what it takes to string together a consistent, season-long title challenge.

4

Date of birth: **30 June 1975**

Team: **BMW WilliamsF1 Team**

Grand Prix starts in 2001: **17**

World Championship placing: **4th**

Wins: **3**; Poles: **1**; Points: **49**

RALF SCHUMACHER

MIKA HÄKKINEN

5

Date of birth: **28 September 1968**

Team: **West McLaren Mercedes**

Grand Prix starts in 2001: **16***

World Championship placing: **5th**

Wins: **2**; Poles: **0**; Points: **37**

*failed to start French Grand Prix

MIKA Häkkinen's victory in the US Grand Prix at Indianapolis was probably the best winning drive of the entire F1 season, yet it was also psychologically the most demanding. The 1998 and '99 World Champion experienced a catalogue of frustrations starting with engine failure during Friday free practice, an accident in the warm-up and then the disappointment of being dropped from second to fourth on the grid when his best qualifying time was disallowed after missing the red pit lane exit light during that same half-hour session on race morning.

Despite this, Häkkinen got his head together and drove a hugely disciplined race to pop out in the lead after a one-stop refuelling strategy which harnessed a dauntingly long opening stint. In no way did he look like a man who was heading for a sabbatical in 2002 — even though it is his self-confessed intention to return to the F1 scene after a year's break.

Häkkinen's season started on an uncomfortable note, his McLaren MP4/16 crashing out of the Australian GP at Melbourne following a front suspension failure. He was running second at the time and the team believed his pit-stop strategy was on course to deliver him a win ahead of Michael Schumacher's Ferrari.

Make no mistake about it, Mika was badly shaken by this shunt which saw him winged by flying tyres from the trackside barrier. It somehow set the tone for the opening races of the season where a combination of flagging motivation and frustrating technical problems left him trailing in the title points table long before he bounced back to win the British GP at Silverstone.

Even as early as the Monaco GP he began thinking in terms of taking a year off and started to discuss the matter with team principal Ron Dennis. Two races earlier he had lost victory in the Spanish GP on the final lap after a hydraulic fluid leak triggered a massive clutch failure. Monaco was his low point, however, where he retired from the race after being spooked by the handling of his car. The omens hardly looked promising for the balance of the season.

Victory at Silverstone restored his morale, but from thereon McLaren was fighting something of a defensive role, short on both power and the crisp handling edge needed to run consistently at the front of the F1 pack. Nevertheless Häkkinen managed to restore his reputation by the end of the year and the question 'why is he stopping?' had replaced 'why doesn't he stop?' on most people's lips.

THE role of Ferrari number two is never the easiest of jobs in F1, particularly in a situation where Michael Schumacher's towering genius dominates every facet of the legendary Italian team's operation. Yet Rubens Barrichello continued the tricky balancing act which he carried off to good effect in 2000, fulfilling the role of obliging team player whilst at the same time managing to totally subjugate his personal ambition to the Maranello cause.

Barrichello has an even-tempered, sensible and popular personality, qualities which have enabled him to fit in well at Maranello. Ross Brawn thinks he is perhaps a more rounded talent than Eddie Irvine, who pre-dated him in that challenging role from 1996–'99 and there is certainly no question that Barrichello drove extremely well on several occasions throughout the past season.

Rarely was he genuinely quicker than Michael Schumacher, but he certainly seemed to have the upper hand in the Austrian GP where he was asked to stay behind the German driver in the early phase of the race rather than be given the chance to show whether or not he had the pace to challenge David Coulthard's winning McLaren. In the closing stages he found himself ahead of Michael and gave the Ferrari management on the pit wall a nervous few laps before finally conceding second place by slowing very pointedly only yards from the chequered flag.

There was absolutely no doubt that Barrichello was extremely upset at having his own chances reined in so publicly at this early stage of the season but Ferrari soothed his wounded feelings by announcing that it would be renewing his contract for 2002.

In the latter half of the year Barrichello's consistency was admirable and he came close to winning the Italian Grand Prix, being frustrated only by a refuelling glitch as he battled closely with Juan Montoya's Williams. He finished second on a day when Michael Schumacher's mind wasn't on the job and the World Champion wound up two places further back at the chequered flag.

For the last two races of the season Ferrari got firmly behind Barrichello in a bid to help him to second place in the World Championship, but an untypical Ferrari engine failure at Indianapolis undermined these gallant efforts.

Not yet 30, but with nine years of F1 competition under his belt, Barrichello is one of the most seasoned and consistent performers on the grid. Perhaps there isn't quite a World Championship in this likeable Brazilian, but the best of his career could still be yet to come.

6

Date of birth: **23 May 1972**

Team: **Scuderia Ferrari Marlboro**

Grand Prix starts in 2001: **17**

World Championship placing: **3rd**

Wins: **0**; Poles: **0**; Points: **56**

RUBENS BARRICHELLO

NICK HEIDFELD

7

Date of birth: **10 May 1977**

Team: **Red Bull Sauber Petronas**

Grand Prix starts in 2001: **17**

World Championship placing: **7th=**

Wins: **0**; Poles: **0**; Points: **12**

FOR a long time regarded as the most promising of Germany's new generation, Heidfeld won the Formula 3000 Championship in 1999 and was taken under Mercedes' wing in the role of McLaren test driver. He made his F1 debut with Prost in 2001 and suffered a bruising first season as Jean Alesi's team-mate, despite which he was given a chance to restore his reputation with Sauber this season.

Armed with the splendid Sergio Rinland-designed C20, Heidfeld did an excellent job although it was somehow inevitable that he would be shaded by his dynamic, high-profile team-mate Kimi Räikkönen. Even so, given Nick's relative low level of F1 racing experience, he did a fine job, opening the season with fourth place in Melbourne and then a strong third at Interlagos where he never put a wheel wrong in treacherous conditions which claimed several more seasoned competitors.

After sixth place in Spain he didn't score points again until France where he also took a single point, then repeated that in Britain and Hungary. At Indianapolis he drove well to take sixth place despite having to grapple with gearchange problems. He also qualified an excellent sixth in both the Austrian and US Grands Prix and the fact that he outqualified Räikkönen 10-7 over the season seemed an even more accurate index of this calm, introverted and very serious-minded young man's underlying potential.

At the end of the year Heidfeld clearly felt slightly indignant that the excitement over Räikkönen's admittedly impressive performance resulted in the young Finn earning the chance of promotion to the McLaren-Mercedes squad. It was almost as if the under-promoted Heidfeld had been deliberately overlooked and some F1 insiders wondered whether McLaren had perhaps been a little too speculative in their selection of Räikkönen over Heidfeld.

For the moment, however, Heidfeld will have to live with the disappointment and knuckle down to another two years with the Sauber squad before his contract comes up for renewal. Next season he will have to fend off the challenge of the unproven 19-year-old Felipe Massa as Räikkönen heads for glory with McLaren. Ironically, if the young Finn really does shine as David Coulthard's team-mate some of the positive gloss will rub off on Heidfeld. Deservedly so.

TO score a championship point on your F1 debut after only 23 car races in your entire career is a quite remarkable achievement, no matter how lucky one might be or how competitive the car is that you are driving. Kimi Räikkönen is quite clearly a remarkable talent, although the very nature of contemporary F1, with its raft of driver aids available to the men behind the wheel, inevitably gives rise to cynical speculation that it is perhaps easier than one might believe to drive one of these machines. Up to a point.

By mid-season, with McLaren facing the prospect of life without Mika Häkkinen, it was quite understandable that this front-line team should carefully consider Räikkönen as a potential successor to the senior Finn. The interesting thing here is that McLaren and Mercedes are not given to making impulsive driver selections. They analyse and number-crunch their way through the lap times and race performances of potential candidates before coming to a reasoned and justifiable decision. At the end of this process they opted for Räikkönen in a bold and ambitious strategy.

Räikkönen proved to be an astute and instinctive racer, but his freshman F1 season was not without its problems. He crashed badly on his first flying lap at a mid-season test session held at Magny-Cours and there were signs of a slight performance drop-off following his strong fourth place at Montreal. That said, he outpaced Heidfeld at Silverstone to take fifth place in the British Grand Prix where his confidence on the fast swerves of the Silverstone circuit was genuinely impressive.

At the end of the day rating Räikkönen eighth in our top ten may be regarded as reflecting a conservative and pessimistic assessment of his F1 potential. In reality, it is more a matter of measured caution. F1 history is strewn with examples of bright young stars who have shone brightly during their first season only to become mired down in the challenge of sustaining that form into a more demanding second year.

Räikkönen clearly has what it takes to flourish in F1. Yet it is far too early to say with certainty whether he has the winning touch.

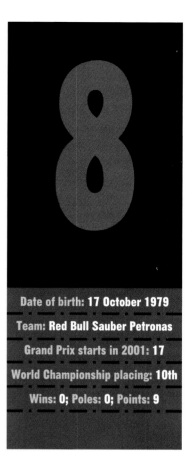

8

Date of birth: **17 October 1979**

Team: **Red Bull Sauber Petronas**

Grand Prix starts in 2001: **17**

World Championship placing: **10th**

Wins: **0**; Poles: **0**; Points: **9**

KIMI RÄIKKÖNEN

GIANCARLO FISICHELLA

9

Date of birth: 14 January 1973

Team: Mild Seven Benetton Renault

Grand Prix starts in 2001: 17

World Championship placing: 11th

Wins: 0; Poles: 0; Points: 8

GIANCARLO Fisichella was always quick, but there were those in the F1 paddock who doubted his ability to pull something extra out of the bag when under real pressure in close company. His supporters would argue that he's never had a sufficiently competitive car which would enable him to do that on a regular basis, but this year we have seen the best of the Italian driver who is now one of the most experienced performers in the business.

At the start of the year Fisichella found himself bogged down in the development of a seemingly complex and ambitiously engineered Benetton B201 which initially seemed so far away from a competitive pace that the season looked virtually a lost cause. Yet he knuckled down methodically to the task of developing the new car in a manner which consolidated the respect felt for him by the team's engineering staff.

In Brazil he wrestled his way to a sixth-place finish from 18th on the grid, an excellent performance in terrible weather conditions, but then had to wait until Hockenheim before a measure of mechanical reliability helped him to fourth place ahead of team-mate Jenson Button. Yet the best was yet to come in the Belgian Grand Prix at Spa where he vaulted up to second place at the restart and confidently held off a challenge from David Coulthard's McLaren-Mercedes before eventually losing the place after being wrong-footed while lapping a backmarker in the closing stages of the race.

At the end of the day Fisichella outqualified his new team-mate Jenson Button 13-4 over the course of the 17-race season. It was inevitably difficult to draw firm comparisons between the two men as the Benetton's reliability was generally poor and gaining any sort of consistency was always an uphill struggle for them both.

Next year Fisichella starts a three-year term back at Jordan where he first drove in 1997. In his place Jarno Trulli moves to the newly branded Renault squad where he may well benefit from the legacy of Fisichella's determined efforts this season.

JARNO Trulli only managed to finish seven of the season's 17 races in his disappointingly unreliable Jordan-Honda, this record including a disqualification in the Austrian GP where he exited the pit lane against the red light. He was also initially disqualified from fourth place in the US GP at Indianapolis, but the Jordan team appealed against the decision and the FIA Court of Appeal reinstated the Italian in his original position after it became clear that the race stewards had been guilty of procedural error.

Yet Trulli finished the season with his reputation as a promising prospect more or less intact, even though the one-time kartist from Pescara made his F1 debut as long ago as Melbourne in 1997. He consistently displayed excellent qualifying pace throughout the 2001 season although his race speed was sometimes questionable.

On several occasions he was in sight of another helping of championship points when his car let him down, but Trulli is not short on self-belief even though he has shown signs of being a touch moody in conditions of acute adversity. Towards the end of the season he was hard pressed to conceal his frustration with the succession of car problems to which he had been subjected and did not stint when it came to advising Eddie Jordan of his concerns.

Trulli gradually asserted an edge over Heinz-Harald Frentzen during the early races of the season and it was the Italian's qualifying pace which really unsettled his genial colleague. This eventually led to Frentzen attempting to persuade Jordan to pursue a line of car development which he mistakenly believed would put him on terms with Trulli. Instead, the exasperated Jordan fired Frentzen and replaced him with Jean Alesi.

The Frenchman was widely expected to show formidable pace in the Jordan but it says much for Trulli's talent that he managed to keep the upper hand. Next year he swaps places with Giancarlo Fisichella at the Renault (Benetton) team. In the long run Trulli may have got the better end of that deal.

10

Date of birth: **13 July 1974**

Team: **Benson & Hedges Jordan Honda**

Grand Prix starts in 2001: **17**

World Championship placing: **7th=**

Wins: **0**; Poles: **0**; Points: **12**

JARNO TRULLI

AHO 811

The art of performance | JAGUAR

WHEN Niki Lauda was edged off the board of directors of the airline which carried his name late in 2000, it was clear that the 51-year-old was ripe for a fresh challenge. Austrian Airlines may have settled an old score with the former F1 ace who originally provoked them by starting his own business in the late 1970s, but it was ironic that by the time Niki was subtly out-voted, Lauda-air was an associate company of its one-time arch-rival.

It was a blow for Niki, a consummate politician in his own right and by any standards a wily old bird. Yet almost within weeks he was recruited by Ford as Chairman of the Premier Performance Division, a sub-division of Wolfgang Reitzle's Premier Automotive Group which controls Jaguar, Volvo, Lincoln, Land Rover and Aston Martin.

Lauda's new role effectively mirrored that of former F1 racer Gerhard Berger at BMW. The PPD's remit is to control and coordinate the activities of Jaguar Racing, Cosworth and the Pi electronics division. On paper it looked pretty straightforward, yet it would soon become perceived in some quarters as a somewhat unwieldy package.

Ford has made a tradition of over-complicating its F1 involvement over the past two decades or more and Lauda's relationship with Jaguar Racing initially seemed to be no exception. The Austrian former triple World Champion's new role was, on the face of it, to give a broad-brush helping hand to the team's newly appointed Chief Executive Officer Bobby Rahal.

'It is not my job to interfere with the way Bobby runs the team,' said Lauda at a January media conference during which many scribes got the strong impression that this was a dream-team partnership. In reality, it would turn out to be F1's equivalent of Jack Lemmon and Walter Matthau starring together in a bizarre re-make of that famous movie, *The Odd Couple*.

The original idea was that Rahal would run the team while Lauda would deal with wider issues such as the team's position within the PAG structure and matters involving the FIA and the F1 constructors. Yet it was clear from the outset that wires had been badly crossed in the appointment of the two men.

Rahal accepted the offer to run the F1 operation from Ford director Neil Ressler on the basis that he would be free to continue running his own CART team. But this was never going to work. Jaguar Racing was desperate for direction and firm management. And what it got was management by committee with Rahal finding himself second-guessed by Lauda at every turn. Within three or four races, it became apparent that the set-up couldn't last in its original form.

Yet Lauda on the face of it seemed supportive. As this curious partnership grappled with the challenge of squeezing the best out of the Jaguar R2, a deliberately conservative design intended to provide a performance baseline after the team's traumatic first season under the Coventry brand, positive plans were being laid for the future.

Early in the year, Lauda was asked if it might not be a good idea to strengthen the engineering team by signing up Sergio Rinland, the designer of the promising Sauber C20 who'd unaccountably been dropped by the Swiss team almost before the season had started.

TALKING LAUDA

INTERVIEWED BY ALAN HENRY

unwise to take anything for granted in a situation where Lauda is prepared to do anything to guarantee the long-term success of a team which has so far attracted so much criticism.

Eventually the split with Rahal came just after the Hungarian GP. In an officially agreed form of words which certainly did little for Jaguar's credibility, the parting of the ways was touted as an 'amicable split' — something it quite clearly was not.

Yet brushing that aside, it left Lauda confident in the belief that he could steer the Jaguar F1 ship into more tranquil waters after this so-painful round of blood letting.

Niki clearly thinks it's going to be an easier job that running Lauda-air, with its huge unionised workforce in excess of 2000 people, although he is certainly mindful of the need to motivate and carry the factory-floor personnel at Milton Keynes with him if he's going to have a hope of long-term success.

Yet Niki admits he is an impatient man and one is tempted to wonder whether that impatience might eventually catch him out.

'No, it won't catch me out,' he said, 'because on the other side I know how long it takes to make a new car. You're dreaming to say it can happen tomorrow.'

So have Ford and Jaguar got the patience to see a long-term F1 programme through to a successful conclusion? 'From this side I have no problem,' he said. 'Our real problem is the Ferrari-type teams at the moment. They are so far ahead of all of us. You need a group of better people, more motivated drivers than Michael [Schumacher], and this is what I'm pushing for, although I can't give you any answers.'

Niki undertook to run the team on a day-to-day basis, at least until the end of the 2001 season. 'My decision is that I will stay as team principal,' he said. 'But for sure I need somebody to assist me running the technical side of the factory. This is in the long run what I'm going to look for. I will try and reorganise things for 2001. That is the plan.' It now appears that Günther Steiner, the technical mastermind behind Ford's WRC Focus programme, is the man who will take this role. Lauda also firmly believes that he can speed up the development tempo of the Jaguar F1 programme by leasing Cosworth CR3 V10s to the rival Arrows squad. 'We need to know where we are in comparative terms,' he insisted.

'Unless you're talking Adrian Newey, I'm not interested in any other designer,' snapped Niki. Seasoned Jaguar watchers should have taken more notice. Immediately after the Monaco Grand Prix it was announced that Newey would, after all, be recruited as technical director thanks to an initiative masterminded by Rahal, a close personal friend of the British engineer.

Of course, Newey changed his mind, much to Rahal's embarrassment and Bobby's position in the team inevitably became weakened. So did, as the conspiracy theorists suggested, Lauda deliberately leak details of the forthcoming Newey deal in order that it would be scuppered — in a bid to avert a situation which would see Rahal's power base strengthened to the point where Bobby would be beyond any sort of challenge?

'Are you completely crazy?' replied Lauda in response to such a suggestion. 'Bobby did most of the up-front negotiations with Adrian, but I was closely involved — spoke with him on several occasions. It was all coordinated and done in a proper way, an overall team effort to get Adrian on board.

'I was totally behind Bobby's efforts in trying to recruit Newey. And remember, he had absolutely and totally committed himself to Jaguar Racing before he changed his mind.'

For all that, however, Lauda eventually tired of having Rahal around. An apparent alliance between Niki and the team's number one driver Eddie Irvine emerged on one side of the divide, although Lauda's personal views about the Ulsterman have remained concealed. On the face of it they seem soulmates, but Irvine would be

Opposite: Man under pressure to deliver — Niki Lauda's enduring credibility rests on his making a success of the Jaguar F1 operation.
Photograph: Paul-Henri Cahier

This page, clockwise from top right:
The Jaguar R2 was intended to be a conservative, reliable design. It was certainly the former, hardly the latter.
Photograph: Clive Mason/Allsport-Getty Images

No fence sitter — the Jaguar team knows precisely where it stands with its no-nonsense principal.
Photograph: Bryn Williams/crash.net

Irvine proved an unpredictable blend of uncomfortable candour and practical technical input.

Rahal never had much of a chance thanks to the complexities of Jaguar/Ford transatlantic intrigue.

The Jaguar crew worked tirelessly, but the frustrations were always plain to see.
All photographs: Paul-Henri Cahier

'Anything I can do to increase the speed at which we become competitive I will do and the Arrows partnership will be positive from this standpoint.' Sceptics say it's more likely that Jaguar needs the additional funds generated by the £15 million lease fees due to be paid by Arrows.

'Trouble is, Jaguar is trying to perform like Ferrari on a Minardi budget,' said one well-placed Ford insider.

Yet Lauda is determined for the moment to shrug aside the predictions of such doomsayers.

'I am fully responsible for the entire programme,' he explained. 'The only person I am reporting to is Dr Reitzle if I think I need to speak to anybody. When I started I asked "how many people do I speak to? Ten people? It doesn't work." I asked this as the first thing when I took the job. I am here definitely for three years. At the very least.'

By the end of the three years we will know whether Niki Lauda has been able to bring to bear the necessary resourcefulness to get the job done. As *AUTOCOURSE* went to press Jacques Nasser retired as President of the Ford Motor Company after a long-running confrontation with William Clay Ford Jr, great grandson of company founder Henry Ford. It is far too early to judge how the impact of these seismic changes in Detroit will filter down to affect the Jaguar F1 programme. But it is certainly an additional potential complication to an already complex scenario.

Translating power into

AP Racing clutches win 500 Grands Prix – and counting

ENSCONCED deep within the 'hot end' of a Formula 1 car, the clutch is hidden from view and largely overlooked. Yet it is the vital link between engine and racetrack – the key to channelling all that horsepower to the tyres. The single most important test of a clutch is at the start of a race, when the red lights go out and the car accelerates from a standstill to breakneck speeds with savage force. As the entire power of the engine is transmitted through them, the clutch plates are jolted from rest to rotational speeds as high as 18,000 rpm almost instantaneously, subjecting them to temperatures as high as 600°C.

Starts today in Formula 1 are arguably the most important stage in the race, providing an opportunity for drivers to gain places in a few seconds that might otherwise take two hours of painstaking work during the course of the rest of the race.

One company has dominated Formula 1 clutch development for over three decades. It is AP Racing, based in Coventry, England. Every Formula 1 World Championship since 1967 has been won using AP Racing equipment. Setting the seal on its success, Ralf Schumacher's win in the Williams-BMW at the Canadian Grand Prix marked the 500th Grand Prix victory by an AP Racing clutch.

No two teams share an identical clutch specification. Each team demands a slightly different variation to suit its own very precise requirements. But what every Formula 1 clutch unit has in common is outstanding compactness and efficiency. Its outer casing, machined from titanium for lightness combined with strength, measures less than five inches in diameter and less than four inches in length. It weighs just 1.2 kg (2.6 lb), yet it can transmit up to 800 horsepower.

Clutch plates glow red-hot in a good start. The design of the clutch must be such that this heat is dissipated before it can be conducted to the less hardy components surrounding it. As well as the start itself, the clutch must perform super-efficiently during the practice start off the dummy grid, and during pitstop departures, and also if a restart is called for.

The first recorded Grand Prix win by an AP Racing clutch was Jim Clark's historic victory in a Ford-Cosworth DFV-powered Lotus 49 at Zandvoort in 1967. Prior to that, clutches manufactured for the mainstream market by the Automotive Products company, based at Leamington Spa, had been making their way from street to racetrack use, and AP Racing sprang forth to satisfy that demand, and to tailor clutches for the more specific requirements of competition.

Clark's Dutch Grand Prix triumph was immortalised as the DFV's maiden win, and as that legendary engine gained prominence – eventually powering almost every car on Formula 1 grids – so the AP Racing clutch gained popularity alongside it. The clutch installed in Clark's car had twin 7.25 in.-diameter driven plates made from steel with sintered surfaces (sintering is a process whereby a bronze-based powder is turned into a solid material by the application of intense heat and pressure, creating excellent friction surfaces). This unit evolved somewhat over the ensuing years as power and torque levels increased, but it was not superseded until a 'heavy duty' clutch was introduced in the mid-1980s to cope with the voracious demands of the turbocharged era's most spectacular engines.

The new clutch was a response to the fashionable start procedure of the day, in which the turbo boost pressure was built up, then power suddenly unleashed in an enormous surge. Clutches were being subjected to intolerable strains, and if the start was aborted for any reason – giving rise to a restart before clutches could cool down – there were anxious people on the pit wall, wondering if the letters 'DNF' would appear on the results sheet against their entries!

In 1986, AP Racing won a Design Council Award for this clutch, which reflected improvements in materials technology, incorporated thicker plates, and had a greater clamping (spring) load.

Formula 1 clutches got smaller after this. Honda started the trend in 1987 (though its origins can be traced back to 1983, to the Spirit-Honda driven by Stefan Johannsson) by adopting an earlier Formula 2 unit manufactured by AP Racing, with 5.5 in.-diameter (140 mm) plates, to benefit from its lower weight. Lower weight means reduced inertia, which improves engine power and responsiveness. AP Racing rapidly

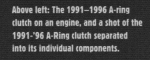

AP RACING

Top left: The unique six-wheel Tyrrell P34 which was driven by Jody Scheckter and Patrick Depailler to an historic 1-2 in the 1976 Swedish Grand Prix.

Above centre: A brilliant first Grand Prix victory for Ayrton Senna who overcame terrible weather conditions to win the 1985 Portuguese Grand Prix in the Lotus 97T-Renault.

Above: Nelson Piquet became World Champion for a third time in 1987, this time behind the wheel of the Williams FW11B powered by a turbocharged Honda engine.

Right: The 1967 7 1/4-in. sintered clutch shown behind the 1988—'92 5 1/2-in. carbon clutch.

Below right: A modern F1 brake caliper.

Above: The 2001 range of AP carbon clutches.

Left: 115 mm pull-type carbon clutch (2000).

Centre left: The magical Ayrton Senna wins the 1990 Monaco Grand Prix in his McLaren MP4/5B-Honda on the way to his second World Championship.

Near left: Mansell finally clinched his World Championship in 1992, this time aboard a Renault-powered Williams aided by the AP 5 1/2-in. carbon clutch.

Left: The compact dimensions of AP Racing's 97 mm clutch bely its immense strength.

website: www.apracing.com

stepped in with a development programme to optimise the unit for Formula 1 use — initially in the all-conquering Williams-Hondas of Piquet and Mansell — and it became the new standard for some time to come.

The 1987 season saw the widespread introduction of carbon-carbon clutch plates, which are universal in Formula 1 today. Carbon-carbon is fundamentally a better clutch material, being considerably lighter than sintered steel, and much more tolerant to high temperatures. When subjected to extreme heat, it does not melt, distort, or expand. Another advantage of carbon-carbon is that its friction levels do not degrade when it gets very hot. On the contrary, its friction generally increases with temperature, so the harder it is used the better it performs!

Carbon-carbon clutch plates did not become all-pervading until after the turbo era ended, because some teams – having initially adopted them – reverted to sintered plates. That was because some drivers felt sintered plates offered a greater degree of control during the highly demanding, turbo-driven starts.

Formula 1 clutches got smaller yet in 1994, with AP Racing's introduction of a new unit with 5 in.-diameter (127 mm) plates. In 1996, it went a step further with 4.5 in.-diameter (115 mm) plates. That year also marked the emergence of the gearbox-mounted clutch. This development was driven primarily by engine designers eager to shed the unwelcome weight and inertia of the clutch from the ultra-lightweight crankshafts they were so painstakingly crafting. It did, however, offer significant benefits for clutch performance. For one thing, the gearbox is a much kinder environment than the engine for housing a clutch, because heat and vibration are the primary causes of clutch failure. Even more importantly, though, the new arrangement facilitated a 'pull-type' clutch engagement mechanism akin to those found on motor cycles, rather than the 'push-type' mechanism still found on most road-going cars.

The result was a 15-20% improvement in clutch efficiency, and a 20% reduction in weight for a given size of clutch.

In 1999, another technological breakthrough allowed a further reduction in clutch size. A key constraining factor, prior to the reintroduction of automatic traction control, was that the smaller a clutch became, the less sensitivity it offered the driver during the crucial start procedure. AP Racing developed a 'cushion' mechanism that introduced artificial 'feel'. The result, in 2000, was the introduction of a clutch with 4-in.-diameter (97 mm) plates.

Many engineers believe that these represent the pinnacle of Formula 1 clutch development, insofar as compactness is concerned, with the materials currently available. This is partly because reducing the diameter of the clutch plates reduces their 'leverage' capability – known as effective radius – and partly because plates must have a certain amount of mass in order to absorb, and then dissipate, the enormous heat levels generated during race starts. More plates can be added to compensate, but that in turn increases the length and weight of the clutch, so a compromise must be reached. Clutch designers undertake a lot of very detailed design work and intricate machining in an effort to reintroduce lost mass and regain durability.

So materials technology is the pacing factor in Formula 1 clutch development, in spite of the fact that the FIA does not prohibit the use of 'special' materials from clutches in the way it does for engines and brakes. Plates are not the only constraining factor, for diaphragm springs are also a potential Achilles Heel. They are made from steel – albeit a very special type of steel – so there would appear to be some scope for improvement, but a lighter material has yet to emerge that will out-perform it. Increasing the clamping load is one way of compensating for smaller plates, so some current-generation Formula 1 clutches have as many as three diaphragm springs, and none have less than two. For comparison, the clutch in Clark's Lotus 49 had just one spring.

A great deal of the development in Formula 1 clutch design over the years has been to combat vibration-induced breakages. The vibration characteristics of different engine types vary considerably, imposing very different stresses and strains on clutches. Even a change in the firing order of an engine, or alterations made to the electronic mapping for traction control, can transform the clutch's operating environment to the point where its reliability is compromised.

Teams purchase a quantity of clutches before the coming season. Throughout the course of race meetings and test sessions, the teams' technicians monitor clutch plate wear levels and make adjustments by changing the main pressure plate to compensate for wear. However, performance degrades very rapidly once the wear has gone beyond a certain point so, typically, after a clutch has done a couple of races, teams return them to AP Racing's Coventry base for reconditioning.

Although other manufacturers have come and gone down the years, some even achieving Grand Prix wins, none have come close to emulating AP Racing's sustained success. At the start of the 2001 season, all but two of the eleven Formula 1 teams employed AP Racing clutches. By season's end, only one team was using a competitor's clutch. Proof that the best is hard to beat.

Furthermore, the majority of Formula 1 teams were using AP Racing's braking systems as well. With Grand Prix wins for that product rapidly approaching the 250 mark, another celebration next season is very much on the cards!

WHEELS OF FORTUNE

By ALAN HENRY

MICHAEL Schumacher's battle for a second straight Ferrari World Championship was in many ways a sub-text to the main events of the 2001 season. How come? Truth be told, what could prove to be the most significant F1 battle of all was being waged away from the circuits and could have the most far-reaching effects on the sport's future commercial development.

This has all unfolded in the wake of F1 commercial rights holder Bernie Ecclestone's decision to start cashing in his investment in the business which had been built up over more than two decades in his role as the commercial mastermind behind the sport's growth and expansion.

Ecclestone's strategy was given a boost at the start of 2001 when the FIA reached the end of what had been a tortuously confrontational battle with the European Union by agreeing a package of measures it believed would satisfy the competition commissioner Mario Monti.

The EU had been deeply concerned that the business of motor racing in general — and the ultra-lucrative FIA F1 World Championship in particular — was administered in an anti-competitive manner. Now its anxiety appeared to be allayed.

In order to satisfy the EU, Ecclestone relinquished his role as FIA vice president promotional affairs, which in truth was a rather nebulous title meaning precious little apart from putting a formal tag on the sport's commercial overlord. Yet from a day-to-day administrative standpoint, it seemed that little had changed in F1's lavishly funded eco-system.

It took Ferrari president Luca di Montezemolo to sound a cautionary note early in the 2001 season, alerting Ecclestone to the fact that the car makers now wanted a bigger share of the commercial pie than was currently provided for under the terms of the Concorde Agreement which expires in 2007. Montezemolo is a man with a keen appreciation of Ferrari's position at the epi-centre of F1 politics and commerce. He appreciates that his team is the sport's biggest box-office draw and knows how to harness that influence to get his way.

In particular, he had his own firm perspective on the commercial future of F1 at a time when Ecclestone was in negotiation with German media companies Kirch and EM.TV about selling a controlling interest in the business.

Di Montezemolo clearly favoured the alternative of Ecclestone selling a stake in the business to the major international car makers, including Fiat, Ferrari's parent company. He specifically warned that he will have nothing to do with any deal which may shift the emphasis of F1 television coverage from terrestrial channels to a pay-to-view basis, something which Kirch, who had gained control of these rights via its stake in EM.TV, seemed to be considering. In his mind, there was a clear obligation to race fans who revere the Ferrari name on a global basis. 'We will never accept pay-to-view-only television coverage of F1,' he said vehemently. 'It is absolutely against the future interest of both Ferrari and F1 as a whole. It is unbelievable. I will never accept it for Ferrari.'

For its part, the FIA, which in 2000 leased its commercial rights to Ecclestone's Formula One Management empire until the next century, had been able to satisfy the EU that it no longer has a commercial interest in the success of F1. The FIA received a $300 million one-off payment for these rights, enabling it to establish a foundation dedicated to automotive safety on both road and track.

'Over the past six months the FIA has changed its rules and commercial arrangements and will now take further measures to carry out its role as regulator of international motor sport without any commercial involvement,' said FIA president Max Mosley.

Left: Crown jewels — The combination of Monaco, Michael Schumacher and Ferrari symbolises the high-octane image of the F1 business.

Below: Bernie remains F1's ultimate powerbroker.
Both photographs: Paul-Henri Cahier

Far left: Key players — Norbert Haug, Bernie and Jean Todt.
Photograph: Bryn Williams/crash.net

Left: The hunger for Grand Prix racing seems undiminished for the moment, with massive crowds attending most circuits.
Photograph: Paul-Henri Cahier

'This will eliminate all possibility of future conflicts of interest. The constructive dialogue we have been able to establish with the European commission brings to an end a long-running and difficult dispute and will provide stability for all international motor sport, including F1. This is good for motor sport enthusiasts worldwide and for all those who work in one of the most popular of modern sports.'

Amongst other steps, the FIA also pledged to remove any obstacles to other motor sports series competing with F1. Ecclestone's Formula One Management empire also sold its interests in all forms of motorsport apart from F1, including international rallying.

This was hardly a significant move. Ecclestone neither understood rallying nor considered it sufficiently lucrative a televised spectacle and was only too willing to sell off its TV coverage rights to David Richards, owner of the Prodrive rally preparation company, for a reputed $35 million late last year.

Not that Ecclestone needed to worry either way, of course. At the age of 70 he opted to cash in a large percentage of his chips when he floated a bond which raised $1.5 billion for family trusts benefiting his wife Slavica and daughters Tamara and Petra.

He also stood to make another $1 billion if he exercised his 'put option' to oblige Thomas Haffa's EM.TV organisation, who last year purchased a stake in SLEC — his F1 holding company — to buy another 25 per cent of that company.

In reality, the concessions offered by the FIA reflected a clever and astute reading of the road ahead by Mosley and his advisors. It also endorsed the image of the now-61-year-old barrister as a streetwise operator for whom the rough and tumble of European Union politics is as much an intellectual exercise as a personal contest. Moreover, Mosley's political dexterity in clarifying the governing body's role as nothing more than a regulatory body did him no harm when it came to the FIA presidential elections in October. He was re-elected without challenge for an unprecedented third term.

As the 2001 season unfolded it was clear that Kirch was never going to earn enough from the commercial rights it had purchased from Ecclestone to make the project fully viable. Unless, of course, it could extend the Concorde agreement.

Ecclestone may have negotiated the F1 commercial rights until 2011, but in practical terms these were no good for Kirch if the teams were not bound into the system beyond 2007. Then, mid-season, the car makers raised the stakes.

Prior to the Monaco GP, Fiat chief executive officer Paolo Cantarella indicated that the European car manufacturers would organise their own series as they were worried about the commercial implications of Kirch's recent acquisition of a controlling interest in Bernie Ecclestone's SLEC empire.

The car makers in effect reaffirmed Montezemolo's concerns that Kirch's commitment to pay-to-view broadcasting would undermine the global appeal of F1 by depriving terrestrial viewers of free access which is regarded as crucial in promoting their products.

However, Kirch has now assured the manufacturers that it would continue its commitment to terrestrial television coverage beyond the expiry of the current Concorde agreement at the end of 2007. The current Concorde agreement contains a key requirement from the sport's governing body committing the commercial rights holder — currently Ecclestone — to provide free television access.

Kirch spokesman Hartmut Schultz explained: 'There are no plans to let F1 slip into pay TV.' He also explained that Kirch wanted to keep F1 attractive to a large audience.

Kirch offered a 25 per cent stake in its business to the car manufacturers, although at what price it was not revealed. Kirch has also offered veto rights to prevent it moving broadcasting of F1 to pay TV.

However, such assurances seemed to offer only a limited solution. Having shown their hand, the manufacturers now seemed determined to exact as much as possible in terms of concessions while Kirch was apparently making heavy weather of the deal.

The car makers, and the F1 teams with whom they are in partnership, will demand an increase in the 47 per cent of the commercial rights income which is currently shared with them by Ecclestone. As a pre-condition of agreeing terms to a revised

Above: **Thomas Haffa.**

Opposite: **Shutters away. Millions of F1 images are sent worldwide after every Grand Prix, providing sponsors with lasting exposure.**

Below: **The top ten teams share 47 per cent of the television income, crucial to the existence of tail-enders such as the Prost squad.**
All photographs: Paul-Henri Cahier

Top: The F1 roadshow crams the pit lane at Monza.

Above: The ultimate cosmopolitan sport — Italy's Jarno Trulli climbs aboard his British-built Jordan, powered by a Japanese Honda engine and fielded by an Irish team.

Right: Mercedes-Benz is a long-established McLaren partner.
All photographs: Paul-Henri Cahier

WHEELS OF FORTUNE

Concorde agreement from the start of 2008, they will want Kirch to increase their stake in Formula 1's lucrative cashflow.

Cantarella elaborated on the decision to start an independent series, explaining that the manufacturers also wanted more control over the sport and saw it essential to keep it in the public eye.

'It is quite simple really,' he told a meeting of the confederation of Italian industrialists in Rome. 'The constructors are the protagonists in F1, they provide the material for the sporting event and the spectacle. And so they would like to be able to run everything more directly with greater overall guarantees.

'We want F1, together with its entire heritage, to continue with order, technological development, clarity of rules and maximum visibility. As you can see, the guarantees also involve the general public.'

Thus the clock continues to tick towards the 2007 expiry of the current Concorde agreement. Yet the teams who are in partnership with the car makers are far from united. Fiat, BMW, Toyota, Mercedes-Benz and Ford all might like the notion of an independent series, but it's unlikely that all their partners will sign up. When push comes to shove, the likes of Frank Williams, Eddie Jordan, Tom Walkinshaw — and even perhaps Ron Dennis — could side with what might best be described as 'traditionalist' Ecclestone-style F1.

Yet there is still speculation about Ecclestone's ultimate stance in all this in a situation where he retains only 25 per cent of the commercial rights. What will he do now? Buy back all the Kirch/EM.TV shares at a bargain-basement price and sell them on to the car makers? Possibly.

By the end of the 2001 season Ecclestone had sold a total of 75 per cent of SLEC to Kirch media, but Bernie remains in control of the business under a shareholders' agreement which runs until the end of 2005.

Yet the car makers are still driven by concerns that the spectre of selling F1 rights in a lucrative pay-to-view deal could end up marginalising the FIA F1 World Championship.

Put simply, pay TV would be a disaster — even though it might initially yield more in cash terms for whoever might be holding, and selling, those rights. Yet the sponsors and manufacturers justify their F1 investments on the basis of 366 million terrestrial viewers worldwide for each Grand Prix on the calendar.

The bottom line is that F1 is the third-largest televised sporting event in the world after the Olympic Games and the World Cup, but takes place on 17 weekends a year. The process by which that situation evolved was masterminded by Ecclestone. At the end of the day, nobody can see him jeopardising that legacy to the F1 business.

MASERATI SPYDER - V8 - 4244cc - 390BHP - 176MPH

Maranello Sales Ltd.
The Home of Maserati.

SALES   SERVICE   PARTS   BODY REPAIRS   FINANCE

DON'T LOOK BACK IN ANGER

Above: **Team principal Craig Pollock's desire for success reflects the keen motivation of the whole team.**

S INCE its conception in 1998, British American Racing has set its standards high. Very high. Last year, major up-grades to their prestigious Technical Centre in Brackley, Northamptonshire brought them on a level with the likes of Ferrari, McLaren and Williams. The new multi-million dollar wind tunnel, and similar commitments in research and development laid a strong foundation for the 2001 season. A new engine deal secured works Honda power, linked to the strengths of the 1997 World Champion, Jacques Villeneuve. Winners both, with a total commitment to success.

The 350-strong B.A.R staff are now both highly respected and motivated. Their race budget from the generous British American Tobacco sponsorship ensures a seat at Formula 1's top table. So with all the elements seemingly in place, what are we to make of a season of such mixed fortunes?

Following an indifferent start to their GP career, Lucky Strike B.A.R Honda got their collective heads down in 2000 to produce some excellent results and fully justify their place in the GP paddock. The portents were good. The team was buoyant. Apparently, the only way was up.

On the back of that second term's success, Lucky Strike B.A.R Honda billed year three — or 2001 — as the 'quality evolution'. What transpired was a year of digging deep; re-engineering both its product and its goals. The BAR003, as the 2001 package was known, lacked the necessary development required to compete at the highest echelon of the sport and in a sport that is played out so close to the margins, such small differences proved to be key. No single aspect of the BAR003 was actually 'off the mark', but the sum of its parts just wasn't competitive enough to mount a serious challenge to the likes of Ferrari, McLaren and Williams as had been hoped.

Lucky Strike B.A.R Honda is packed with perfectionists — and bad losers. They take their lead from managing director and team principal, Craig Pollock. Only wins and podiums were ever going to be good enough this year. But no matter how quick Lucky Strike B.A.R Honda set their personal fast-track, those sort of targets are a big ask for any infant team. Perhaps then, expectations were running just too high?

Above: **Ready to race — the hi-tech world of the Formula 1 cockpit.**

Above right: **Jock Clear continued his strong engineer/driver partnership with Jacques Villeneuve.**

Right: **Villeneuve sits patiently whilst adjustments are made to his BAR003.**

Top right: **Olivier Panis was unlucky to have a hard-won fourth place taken away from him on his debut for the team in Melbourne.**

Far right: **The experienced Frenchman was a perfect foil for Villeneuve.**

'Yes — but this only became clear towards mid-season.' explains Pollock. 'We agreed objectives based upon the results of last season but we believe that every team should start the season with lofty ambitions. We certainly underestimated how much other teams were going to develop; particularly how much the older and more experienced teams would raise their game in 2001. The introduction of manufacturers and the injection of huge funding have made a big difference to the sport. All the more reason to fight and continue to develop. It gives me no satisfaction in saying this, but it became apparent that by Silverstone we were midfield runners with a slightly stronger showing in the races. Yes, it is only year three and yes, we were reliable but we came to win.'

So why didn't they? Well, Lucky Strike B.A.R Honda sent out the right messages at the start of the year by strengthening the team line-up with some high-calibre additions. On the driver front, Olivier Panis breezed into Brackley as a high-quality, highly experienced replacement for Ricardo Zonta. The 1996 Monaco GP winner brought much-needed on-track knowledge to both race and test teams and as Pollock openly declared he would do, put the pressure on Jacques Villeneuve for much of the season. JV reacted well to the Frenchman's arrival though. The duo shared language, driver styles and racing philosophy and formed an excellent relationship throughout the year. All this despite the fact that Panis proved to be JV's most competitive team-mate since Damon Hill in 1996.

The test driver line-up was expanded too. Stalwarts Darren Manning and Patrick Lemarié were retained, although their own duties were split between testing and development respectively. Two very hot newcomers — Takuma Sato and Anthony Davidson — assisted them and together this gang-of-four formed one of the better balanced test teams in Formula 1. The Lucky Strike B.A.R Honda young guns also teamed up in the prestigious British Formula 3 Championship for good measure, which they completely dominated. First and second going away. And although it was Sato who took the title and plaudits, time may show that the maturity of 22-year-old Davidson, in only his first year in F3, has the edge for success in F1.

Meanwhile, inside the garage, the highly respected James Robinson joined the team as Chief Race Engineer from Williams. His vast experience would also be vital to the team throughout a difficult year and his addition completed an intriguing reunion (with Jock Clear and Grant Tuff) of Jacques Villeneuve's 1997 World Championship-winning team.

So with two GP winners in the cockpit and many seasoned campaigners within the team, the crux of the problem for Lucky Strike B.A.R Honda in 2001 was clearly the performance of the car. The BAR003 combined two years of development by the team and Honda's considerable Formula 1 nous. Allied to a far greater emphasis on detail, the quality of finish and a new Lucky Strike livery, the BAR003 certainly looked the part and should have been very good. But like a lot of marriages, it needs time to mature. Something the team had to learn the hard way in 2001.

The year started with spring testing in Barcelona, and even

then Jacques Villeneuve had suspicions that things were not at the required level. Performance was lacking and he took no prisoners and no pleasure in letting the team know. By the time the team arrived in Australia for the first race of the season, many revisions had already been made to the car. From the Barcelona and Kyalami tests and onto Melbourne, development was the name of the game for the team. Those back at home at Brackley worked hard to find it. The wind tunnel personnel, in particular, worked overtime.

Come the opening race in Australia, the laconic and extremely likeable Olivier Panis, who had already settled easily into the team, almost grabbed a podium visit first time out. The 1996 Monaco GP winner was eventually edged into fourth by Rubens Barrichello, then knocked further back by the FIA after the race. They ruled he'd overtaken Nick Heidfeld's Sauber under yellow flags. A 25-second penalty meant his well-earned fourth place became a hard-to-swallow seventh and no points.

Never one for chucking toys out of the pram, Olivier just shrugged his shoulders at the disappointment and went on to grab the team's first points of the year two races later in Brazil, despite a problematic pit stop. This time the result stood and gave Olivier his first score since the 1999 German GP. Equally significant that day was the fact that Panis went faster than his illustrious team-mate in practice, qualifying and the race. The team had achieved the improvement they were looking for with a completely new front wing and revised aerodynamics. A brand new

upswept exhaust was also introduced to increase downforce and reduce the internal blockage around the rear suspension.

The first major overhaul to the BAR003 came in time for the return to Europe. The San Marino and Spanish GPs witnessed the arrival of a completely new aerodynamic package and a revised exhaust system. This improved the power delivery while reducing the operating temperatures of the rear suspension and lower rear wing. The results were good.

Jacques Villeneuve hadn't fared quite as well as his teammate from the kick-off. He suffered six DNFs all season, but half of them came in his first four races. But with all the style and gusto we have come to expect from the Canadian, he bounced back to take his first points of the season with a podium in Barcelona. Okay, it was a really lucky strike — Mika Häkkinen's McLaren packing up on the final lap allowed JV through to gate-crash the rostrum — but it was reward at last for Villeneuve's perseverance and the hard-working Lucky Strike B.A.R Honda team. After all the cynicism and criticism that had gone before, no one could deny the B.A.R boys and girls their moment. Celebrations were well deserved and lasted long into the morning. 'It is great,' said Villeneuve. 'Everybody in the team has worked extremely hard over the last three years and this result was much needed for all of us.'

Visibly lifted by his return to eminence, JV followed up an overly determined effort for no points in Austria with probably the best Lucky Strike B.A.R Honda performance of the season. The

team, looking to capitalise on this upturn in fortunes and to meet the unique challenge of Monte Carlo's streets, took a new front wing and diffuser to Monaco. Again the changes worked well. Villeneuve was able to throw the car around the tight street circuit with great aplomb. On a track that had plagued Villeneuve in 2000, he looked very good all afternoon and came home fourth, stuck to the tail of Irvine's Jag. It was a masterly display of driving around the toughest GP circuit of them all and a reminder, if any was needed, of why he became a World Champion in the first place. Class is permanent and all that.

But while this patch of the season was tinted purple, it didn't last. The races from Canada through to Britain all proved problematic and despite the best efforts of Lucky Strike B.A.R Honda's overworked team of technicians, engineers and mechanics, the car just wouldn't play ball. The competition was hotting up and it was proving difficult to forge such a pace. Further updates in Montreal, Nürburgring, Magny-Cours and Silverstone all helped, but were not enough to make a quantifiable difference. The car was proving less competitive and the drivers

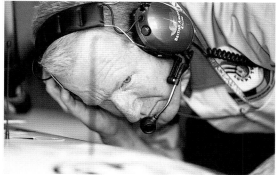

Left: Chief designer Malcolm Oastler listened to feedback from the drivers to make improvements to the BAR003 throughout the season.

Below left: A well earned swig of champagne for Villeneuve after his third place in the Spanish Grand Prix.

Bottom left: B.A.R's first podium, and a delighted Craig Pollock with the steering wheel trophy after Jacques' success in Spain.

Below: The BAR003 represented the next evolution for the three-year-old team.

Above: **Thumbs up from Jacques Villeneuve after another strong drive to third place in the German Grand Prix.**

Below right: **They also serve — members of B.A.R's pit crew watch and wait before being called to action.**

were feeling the pressure. Villeneuve's first corner lunge that dismissed his team-mate at the British GP summed up the mid-season malaise perfectly.

Understandably then, the team arrived for the German GP on a real downer. But although there were only a few technical tinkerings made to the car, they found a superb race set-up — over-winged, but ideally suited to Hockenheimring on race day. Lucky Strike B.A.R Honda went on to secure their second podium of the year, thanks to another vintage Jacques Villeneuve performance. Tenacious, quick and off the cuff, he came home in third to defy the form book. Spare a thought too for the charging Panis who, on a two-stop strategy, was desperately unlucky to finish a place outside the points after a similarly sublime drive. Time to smile again though. Time to celebrate.

Unfortunately, that success proved to be only a temporary respite and the following races proved to be character-building for the whole team. No matter what the team introduced throughout the remainder of the season and no matter how many hours they put in behind the scenes, Jacques Villeneuve and Olivier Panis were unable to scale such heights again. The competition was piling on the pressure and although the team responded for the Hungarian and Belgian Grands Prix with a huge '24-7' effort to upgrade the car, further success was not to be. In Hungary, JV finished in a lowly eighth spot, while Olivier was afflicted by electrical problems at three-quarter distance. At Spa, both cars finished, but they were well away from picking up any points.

The Italian Grand Prix at Monza went ahead despite the terrorist attacks on America only a few days before. Minds were understandably elsewhere, but JV retained his focus to grab what proved to be the team's last point of the season. He also stole the headlines for defying Michael Schumacher and his attempted driver's coup that sought to ban overtaking through the notorious Prima Variante chicane on lap one. 'I'm a racing driver and I'm going to race.' said Villeneuve. 'It was a question of principles I've had since I was a boy dreaming of being a racing driver. I believe you have to go flat out from the start and give 100 per cent to the chequered flag.' Enough said.

The penultimate race of the year at an obviously sombre Indianapolis proved to be the season's real nadir for Lucky Strike B.A.R Honda. The team did try out new rear wing formations but you felt they were already looking ahead and developing next year's car. Jacques Villeneuve looked like he would rather be somewhere else; he qualified in a career-low 18th place and finished his race in the pits after a coming-together with Pedro de la Rosa. Not even the consistent Olivier Panis managed to find a scrap in the dog's dinner that day.

'The US Grand Prix was our worst racing performance of the last three seasons and I was embarrassed,' admitted Craig Pollock afterwards. Villeneuve took most of the criticism on the chin and acknowledged a lot of it was justified.

Such frankness and honesty are rare commodities in today's F1 paddock and there is no doubt that this rallying cry stirred his troops into action for the seasonal finale at Suzuka. Despite a customary difficult qualifying session Villeneuve, in particular, drove like a man possessed.

In the end his efforts couldn't secure valuable championship points, but for Pollock, it was exactly the reaction he was looking for. There is no doubt that in the overall scheme of things, this was much more important to him than beating Jordan for the Honda laurels — a battle that would eventually be lost not on the racetrack, but in an FIA courtroom two weeks after the end of the season. Craig Pollock had cracked the whip and got an immediate response. Now he has something to work with over the winter.

So the end-of-year report for Lucky Strike B.A.R Honda reads of a team who soldiered diligently all season to make the most of a car that was not as developed as it needed to be to compete at the level expected. In mitigation, the car was always a very reliable machine in race trim. But it badly needed a boost in qualifying guise, because the best Villeneuve and Panis could extract from it all year was sixth on the grid. Moreover, the two Lucky Strike B.A.R Honda drivers' average qualifying spot slipped into double figures as the year unfolded and that is a considerable handicap to carry into any race.

However, the lowest point of this and any other year came of course at the first race in Australia, when Jacques Villeneuve collided with Ralf Schumacher's Williams at 300 km/h. Villeneuve's number 10 car was sent skyward, then cartwheeled before coming to a halt. Incredibly he was uninjured. However, track marshal Graham Beveridge was less fortunate. The 51-year-old Queenslander was tragically killed.

The terrible accident was the worst possible beginning to the

Left: Clever tactics and a well set up car brought dividends at Hockenheim for Jacques Villeneuve as the B.A.R scored its second podium finish of the year.

Below: Olivier Panis worked hard throughout the season but was unfortunate to gain little tangible reward.

year for all in Formula 1 and goes a long way to describe JV's own tardy start. This time there was no sign of the grinning Canadian emerging unscathed from another high-speed prang. Make no mistake; Beveridge's death affected him and the Lucky Strike B.A.R Honda team very badly indeed.

But after all the problems of 2001, what is needed to really turn things around? What can Pollock do to boost the Lucky Strike B.A.R Honda effort again and finally deliver on his promise of success?

Judging from the rhetoric emerging from Brackley at the end of the year, Pollock will be adopting a more hands-on role to inspire his staff to greater things in 2002. He will make whatever changes are necessary to succeed and insist on greater efforts from his drivers, staff, technical partners and suppliers.

As a team, British American Racing itself knows it must deliver in 2002. In a year when Honda look likely to choose bed partners for the foreseeable future, and co-owners and title sponsors British American Tobacco will want to quantify their huge three-year investment, significant progression is a must. But with the promised technical support, earlier development of the new car and without the distraction of the many mid-season technical introductions we

saw this year, it is a challenge Lucky Strike B.A.R Honda are up for and seem capable of making.

Craig Pollock acknowledges that the team's credibility may have slipped towards the end of 2001 and that may or may not be justified — after all every team has tough times, especially in their formative years. However, whatever the outside perspective is of Lucky Strike B.A.R Honda, Pollock's own determination remains undiluted.

'No one person in any team can turn things around themselves — it is a "team" effort. I fully intend to ensure that we have a strengthened package in place well in advance of the start of the next season. I will not accept anything less than a race-winning package. I expect to get the best from the team and the drivers at each and every race. We are a team full of youthful energy and expertise with a huge passion for what we do. Lucky Strike B.A.R Honda wants to be successful — the team wants to win. The buck stops with every single individual. We are all accountable — especially me — and no stone will be left unturned to make sure we act like a team with Championship ambitions.'

No more Mr Nice Guy then. This is a man on a mission; king of a team still hurting for success.

Above left: After a bad weekend at Indianapolis, Villeneuve produced a typically gritty performance in the Japanese Grand Prix.

Above: Don't look back in anger. The B.A.R team pose for the cameras at season's end, looking forward to more progress in 2002.

Patrick Head, Ralf Schumacher and Sir Frank Williams seem pleased with life as the Williams-BMW partnership forged its way to the sharp end of the grid during 2001.
Photograph: Paul-Henri Cahier

By ALAN HENRY

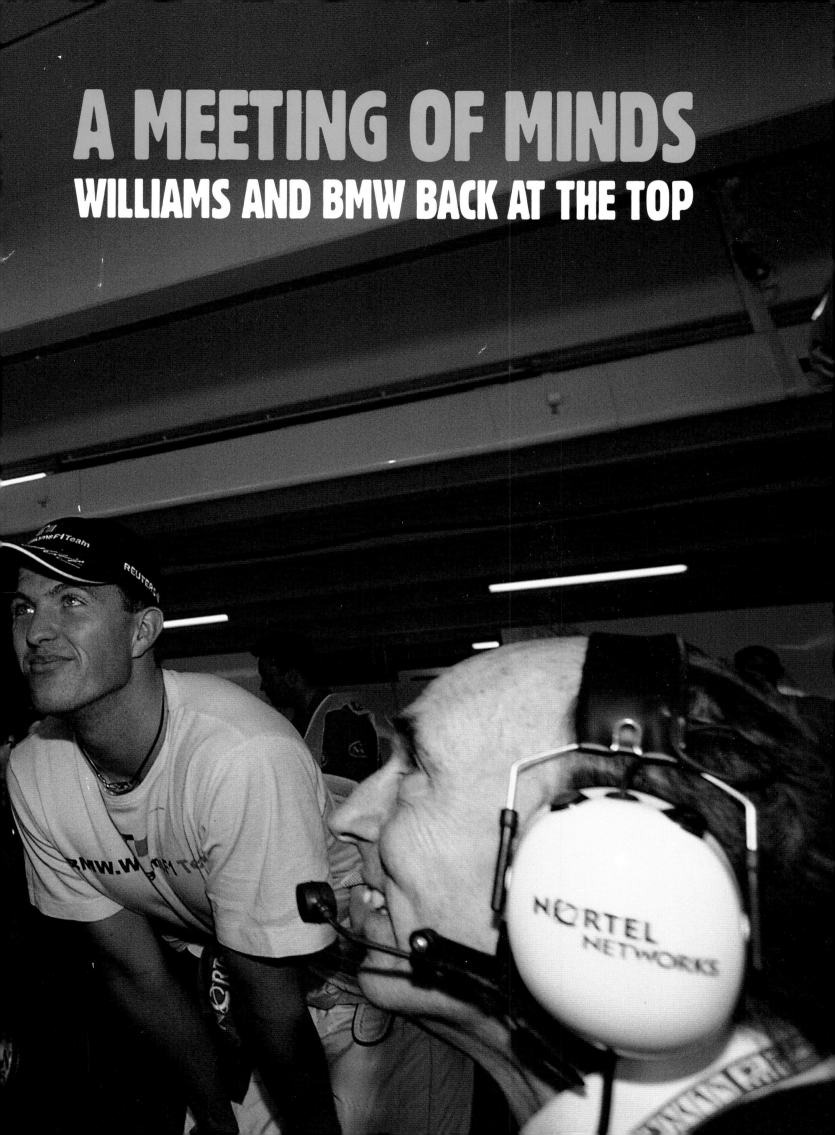

A MEETING OF MINDS
WILLIAMS AND BMW BACK AT THE TOP

WHEN Ralf Schumacher crossed the finishing line to win this year's San Marino Grand Prix at Imola it was an achievement which represented the first step in the restoration of two of the most famous names in motor sports history. For Williams Grand Prix Engineering it marked the end of the longest drought in the company's annals. No fewer than 54 Grands Prix had passed since Jacques Villeneuve triumphed in the 1997 Austrian Grand Prix and the lengthy process of recovery served as a graphic reminder of just how challenging it is to make up ground in the ferociously competitive F1 environment.

For BMW, it also represented a remarkable technical tour de force. 19 years before it had achieved another technical breakthrough when Nelson Piquet's Brabham BT50 raced to victory in the 1982 Canadian Grand Prix at Montreal, using the Munich company's remarkable 1.5-litre turbocharged four-cylinder engine.

The production-based BMW four — derived from the block of the 2002 sports saloon — went on to power Piquet to the 1983 World Championship. Yet five years later BMW bowed off the F1 stage, content for the moment with the level of its achievement and technical prowess.

Over the next decade, of course, the character of the F1 business would alter beyond belief. In the early 1980s Grand Prix racing was a worthwhile technical showcase, sure enough, but the commitment of the motor manufacturers was set against a backdrop of essentially privately owned teams.

'In that connection, I would have to say that the arrangement by which McLaren commissioned Porsche to build the TAG turbo V6 in 1983 was an extremely advanced collaboration for its time,' recalled Williams technical director Patrick Head.

'John Barnard — McLaren's technical director — gave Porsche a very specific brief as to what he wanted. Dimensions, weight, performance requirements. It was very much an arrangement ahead of its time. A bit of a contrast to Honda who initially just gave us one of its V6 engines and told us to get on with it.'

In fact, Head could be said to be diplomatically understating Honda's low-key approach. The first engine arrived at the team's headquarters in a box, together with two turbochargers. There was nothing else. Crucial ancillaries such as the radiators, and the plumbing for the turbos and exhaust systems, would have to be designed, manufactured and developed by Williams.

At the same time that Honda was starting its involvement with Williams, Renault, BMW and Ford had a presence, but they were ultimately only engine suppliers. By the mid-1990s, the depth of collaboration involved in the partnership between a team and a car maker was much more closely defined. Engine suppliers and teams became partners in the truest and most literal sense of the word.

Mercedes-Benz purchased a 40 per cent stake in the TAG McLaren Group, owners of the McLaren International F1 team. Renault purchased Benetton lock, stock and barrel. Honda became closely involved with BAR and Jordan, and Toyota decided to go it alone and establish its own F1 operation from its competition headquarters in Germany.

Of the front-line F1 teams, Williams was forced to spend two frustrating seasons marking time. After Renault Sport ceased its factory-backed programme at the end of 1997, Williams had to manage in 1998 and '99 using their old engines under a fixed-spec lease deal, supplied by Renault's satellite company Supertec.

In the years since Clay Regazzoni posted the team's maiden Grand Prix win at Silverstone in 1979, only one of the following 18 seasons would see a Williams fail to win at least one race. That was in 1988 when Nigel Mansell struggled with an uncompetitive Judd-engined machine, scoring his best result with second in the British GP before accepting a £6 million offer from Ferrari.

Yet Villeneuve's 1997 Austrian success marked the end of an era, being the final victory for the superbly successful Williams-Renault partnership. But further help was at hand.

As long ago as the 1997 British Grand Prix there had been senior BMW personnel present in the paddock as guests of the Williams team as the German car maker considered and assessed precisely what a return to F1 might offer.

Of course, by this stage the image of F1 was accelerating rapidly, helped no end by dramatically expanding global television coverage. It was almost getting to the stage when car makers could not afford to pass up the opportunity of being involved in

Top: Ralf takes his first Grand Prix win, and Williams's first in 54 races, at Imola.

Above: Frank Williams (top) and BMW Motorsport's Gerhard Berger.
All photographs: Paul-Henri Cahier

such a high-profile activity which had all the right marketing and promotional images.

Yet BMW obviously wanted to win, to do it properly. There was little interest on their part in simply participating. Some car makers seemed to think that just being in the F1 pit lane was enough, certainly better than nothing. But BMW wanted to win and judged that Williams offered the best chance of vaulting their way into the spotlight of F1 attention.

'I think it is fairly clear that Frank spent much of 1997 trying to persuade Renault not to quit F1 and, that if they were going to quit, that they would supply us engines on a customer basis,' said Patrick.

'That turned out to be the Supertec deal, but until that was arranged Renault was going to stop completely at the end of 1997. Finished, out, completely. In the event they helped us out.

'At the same time BMW had taken the decision that it wanted to become involved in F1 again. We did not persuade them as such, but they were obviously good prospects as partners for us. So they duly came back and the partnership has worked well for us.'

Patrick admits that he has been impressed with the progress the partnership has made. 'Ultimately the best alliances between engine makers and constructors in F1 today are where the engine technicians listen to the chassis engineers and vice versa,' he said.

'In that respect the BMW Williams partnership works very well. Both sides do a lot of listening.'

BMW is an extremely high-technology road car maker, yet the prime reason for its involvement in F1 remains the marketing dimension.

Underpinning this huge multi-million dollar investment is also a belief that some of the manufacturing techniques and technologies which have been employed on the latest V10 engine — all new this season — can offer positive benefits for future road car development.

It is also clear that Gerhard Berger's role alongside Mario Theissen at the head of the BMW Motorsport operation has worked extremely well. Theissen is responsible for the technical side while Berger effectively handles the Munich company's relationship with the Williams team, coaxing and cajoling wherever necessary.

At the start of the partnership there were those outside the team who felt that Berger was too much of a playboy to apply himself conscientiously to such a task, but they seriously underestimated the Austrian. Insiders have described him as 'astute and extremely intelligent — very capable at looking after the political side of BMW's involvement in the programme.'

His experience behind the wheel also enabled him quickly to assess the potential of both Jenson Button and Juan Pablo Montoya from their very first test outings for the team in 2000 and 2001 respectively.

Berger also gets on very well with Frank Williams, effectively being his opposite number at BMW while Patrick Head and Mario Theissen collaborate on the technical side.

At the end of the day the BMW-Williams alliance has thrived because both parties to the overall equation have a high regard for each other and complete faith that the other is performing its side of the bargain to the absolute best of its ability.

Ultimately, the blend of seasoned racing team and perfectionist engine specialist is the best recipe for F1 success. In contrast, projects such as British American Racing where the sponsor has bankrolled the entire infrastructure since the outset, and Toyota, which has decided to buck the trend and go it entirely alone, may find life much more difficult in the longer run.

There is no magic about achieving success in F1. It is about harnessing and applying well proven techniques and having a workforce with as much experience in the business as is conceivably possible. In that respect, the BMW-Williams combo has established itself as a textbook F1 partnership which promises even greater things in the future.

At the start of the 2001 season Sir Frank Williams predicted that the team might pick up one or two wins 'if the red or grey cars faltered.' That turned out to be a conservative assessment, but neither he nor Patrick Head are privately satisfied with the level of technical reliability the team has displayed.

They know that competitive speed is just part of the equation, but that World Championships are also won on reliability and consistency. Don't bet against the BMW-Williams alliance improving dramatically in those areas for 2002.

WILLIAMS AND BMW BACK AT THE TOP

Below: Montoya on the grid in preparation for the
US GP at Indianapolis.
Photograph: Paul-Henri Cahier

FORMULA 1 REVIEW

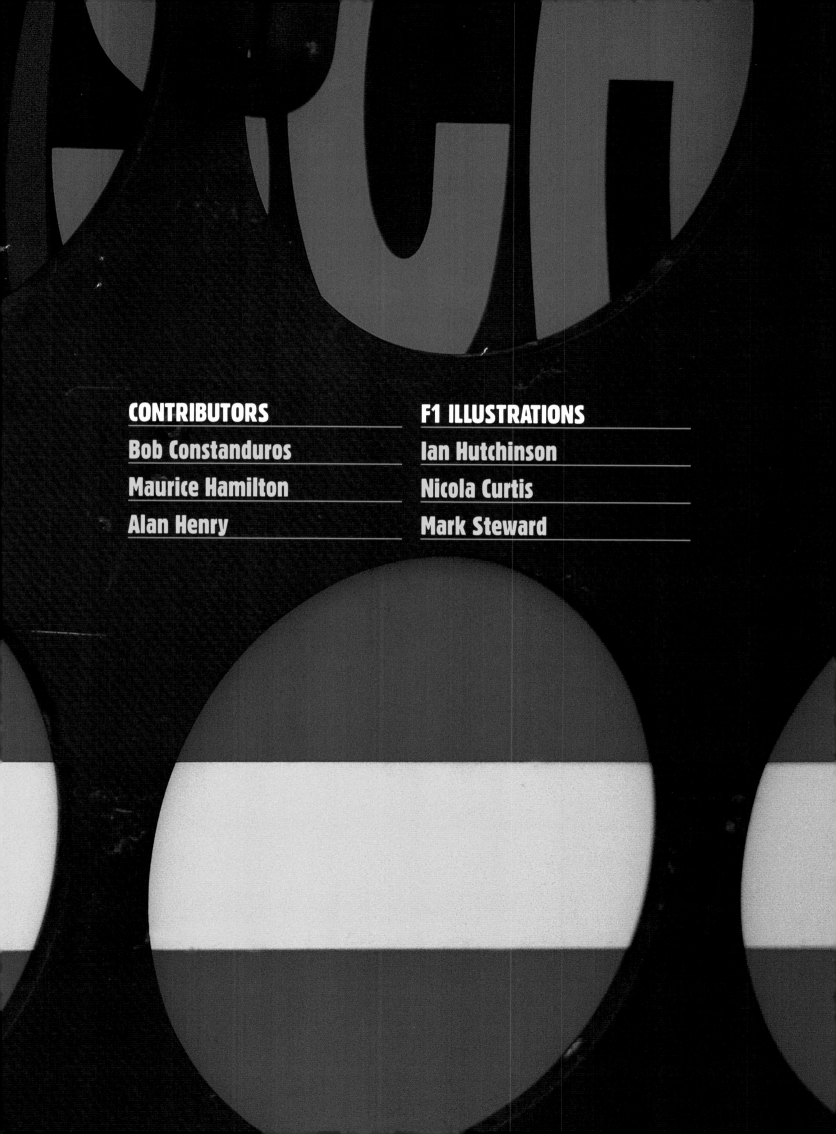

CONTRIBUTORS

Bob Constanduros

Maurice Hamilton

Alan Henry

F1 ILLUSTRATIONS

Ian Hutchinson

Nicola Curtis

Mark Steward

MICHAEL SCHUMACHER

RUBENS BARRICHELLO

SCUDERIA FERRARI MARLBORO

FERRARI effected a seamless transition into the 2001 season to the point where the last two years appeared to be little more than a 34-race series dominated by Michael Schumacher. This year Michael added another nine wins to his tally out of 17 races and, if anything, looked more composed and assured than he had done at any time in the past.

Continuity was the absolute key to the season's success with Jean Todt not only continuing to fulfil his role as sporting director with great efficiency and attention to detail, but also insulating the team's personnel from any disruptive influences which might threaten to permeate in from the outside.

'He is great at creating a glass ceiling between the senior Fiat management and the team personnel,' said one insider. 'He knows that the the racing department needs to concentrate 100 per cent unhindered on its prescribed tasks. He's very good at that.'

Against this backdrop Schumacher was defending his third title crown, paired for the second year with the pleasant and easy-going Brazilian Rubens Barrichello. They were armed with the new Ferrari F2001, an aerodynamically further refined version of the previous year's car, now powered by the type 050, 90-degree V10 engine developing around 820 bhp.

Michael started off winning at Melbourne and Malaysia, building up a psychologically advantageous points cushion which was only briefly challenged when David Coulthard fleetingly drew level at Imola. That advantage lasted as long as the next race when Schumacher was gifted second place in the Austrian GP by Barrichello, after which it was all plain sailing for the German ace.

The manner in which Barrichello, apparently faster than Schumacher on that particular day, was instructed to move over for the senior driver inevitably drew much media criticism. But the clear-sighted Todt had no doubts where his priorities lay, nor that he had done the right thing. 'For me, you run a company or you don't run a company,' he said firmly. 'You just let things go. For me it's not the case. My dream would have been to see Rubens winning in front of David and Michael. If it could not happen, then in this case David was in front, Rubens was behind, Michael was just right behind. I don't see a difference for a driver to finish second or to finish third.

'They work for a team. If you take Michael's results over one year and Rubens's results over one year, we feel — maybe wrongly — that Michael has more chances to win the championship.

'So, in this case, why give away two points? What happens if at the end of the season we lose the championship by those two points?'

Ferrari had a brilliant year technically, with only a handful of mechanical failures on their aerodynamically excellent F2001s. A fuel pump failure sidelined Schumacher at Hockenheim while Barrichello suffered a rare, and very spectacular, piston failure at Indianapolis which caused the engine to seize with just a lap and a half to run.

Yet the strangest failure of all came at Imola where both drivers were told to take it easy on the brakes. Ross Brawn explained: 'What we had with the drivers was an agreement that we would monitor the brake temperatures [via the telemetry] and give them guidance as to what they should do.

'The race started and Michael's telemetry system stopped working. Then on lap 10 or lap 15, the telemetry comes on and we were in meltdown on the brake system. We advised him to ease off, but by then we'd damaged a front wheel. We overheated the front wheel so badly that when he hit a kerb with the front left corner, the wheel collapsed and that was it.'

Brawn is a huge Schumacher fan and finds it difficult to pin down his most outstanding race of the season. 'Nürburgring and Magny-Cours were both outstandingly good races,' he reflected at Budapest on the eve of his title clincher.

'We were competitive, but he drove 100 per cent for the entire race. That's the whole thing about Michael, but in fairness Rubens is quite good at that as well. He's been a bit up and down this year in terms of qualifying, but at the start of the season he was probably getting as close to Michael as anybody has ever been.

'Then there was a period when he fell back a bit. Traffic problems and some problems with the car, to be fair to him. Having said all that, his performances in the races have been very good. He gets the bit between his teeth in races. He can overtake and he rarely makes a mistake during a race. He is a very talented racing driver, but obviously in the shadow of Michael.

'You know where you are with Rubens; he wears his heart on his sleeve. He's never been

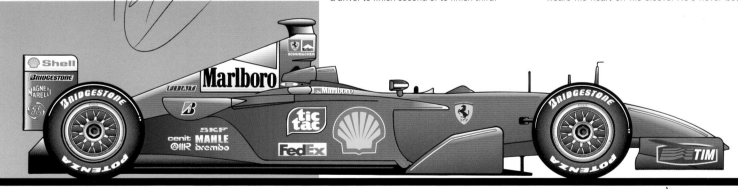

FERRARI F2001

SPONSORS	Marlboro, Shell, TIM, Tic Tac, FedEx, Bridgestone, Magneti Marelli, Fiat, SKF, GE, Tommy Hilfiger, Brembo, Mahle, OMP
ENGINE	Type: Ferrari 050 No. of cylinders (vee angle): V10 (90°) Sparking Plugs: NGK Electronics: Magneti Marelli Fuel: Shell Oil: Shell
TRANSMISSION	Gearbox: Ferrari seven-speed longitudinal semi-automatic sequential Clutch: AP Racing/Sachs hand-operated
CHASSIS	Front suspension: independent, pushrod-activated, torsion spring Rear suspension: independent, pushrod-activated, torsion spring
	Wheel diameter: front: 13 in. rear: 13 in. Wheels: BBS Tyres: Bridgestone Brake pads: Brembo Brake discs: Brembo Brake calipers: Brembo
	Steering: power-assisted Battery: Magneti Marelli Instruments: Magneti Marelli
DIMENSIONS	Wheelbase: 3010 mm Track: front: 1470 mm rear: 1405 mm Formula weight: 1322.8 lb/600 kg including driver

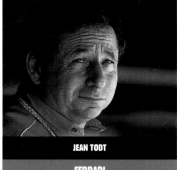

Photograph: Paul-Henri Cahier

JEAN TODT

FERRARI
Jean Todt - Sporting Director
Ross Brawn - Technical Director
Rory Byrne - Chief Designer
Paolo Martinelli - Engine Technical Director
Nicholas Tombazis - Chief Aerodynamicist
Stefano Domenicali - Team Manager
Nigel Stepney - Chief Mechanic
Luca Baldisserri - Race Engineer Car No. 1, Michael Schumacher
Carlo Cantoni - Race Engineer Car No. 2, Rubens Barrichello

ROSS BRAWN   **RORY BYRNE**

PAOLO MARTINELLI   **NIGEL STEPNEY**

LUCA BALDISSERRI   **CARLO CANTONI**

Photographs courtesy of Scuderia Ferrari Marlboro

Top left: Michael Schumacher, unchallenged on his way to another Monaco victory.

Centre left: Michael celebrates a lucky win in Spain.
Both photographs: Paul-Henri Cahier

Centre right: Barrichello lets Schumacher through in Austria, where the Brazilian believed he was capable of running quicker than his team leader.
Photograph: Clive Mason/Allsport-Getty Images

Above left: Barrichello on the podium at Monza, a race which he oh-so-nearly won.

Left: Barrichello at the A1-Ring.
Both photographs: Paul-Henri Cahier

Right: Michael Schumacher (left) together with Luca Badoer and Rubens Barrichello starring as a Jeffrey Archer lookalike.
Photograph: Mark Thompson/Allsport-Getty Images

Far right: Telling it as it was — Michael faces the microphones yet again.
Photograph: Paul-Henri Cahier

Above: Barrichello prepares for action prior to the start of the Austrian Grand Prix.
Photograph: Paul-Henri Cahier

malicious. He's got emotionally upset and disagreed with the team, but that's always been the end of it. If we've got a bad car, then Rubens is just as capable as Michael as getting a [decent] race out of it. But on one lap Michael has the edge.'

There were few entries in the debit column for Schumacher. At Silverstone the team filled his car up with fuel for a one-stop strategy, incorrectly guessing that key title rival Coulthard would be going for the same strategy. In fact David had opted for a two-stop run like team-mate Mika Häkkinen, but it all became academic when the Scot tangled with Trulli on the first corner.

That left Michael handicapped in his efforts to fend off the victorious Häkkinen, but he didn't need to fight too hard as second place was good enough once DC had dropped out. Michael eventually clinched his fourth World Championship with an unobtrusively efficient run to victory at the Hungaroring in August. His only other downside performance came at Monza where, shaken by the events of 11 September and perhaps not believing that Grands Prix should be taking place in such an atmosphere, he settled for fourth almost from the start.

Once Michael had clinched the title, Ferrari made it a priority to try vaulting Barrichello into second place and Schumacher played his role fully here. He was quite prepared to relinquish victory at Suzuka if it would help Rubens, but that depended on the Brazilian getting through into second place during the opening sprint. He failed to do so — with the result that Coulthard held on to runner-up slot.

Ferrari's early-season success, notably in Australia and Malaysia, prompted cynics to suggest they had an illegal traction control system and their advantage would evaporate once those systems became legal at the fourth race of the season.

In fact, Ferrari's 'wheelspin avoidance' systems in the first four races were judged quite legal and gave them a dramatic boost in the wet/dry conditions at Sepang. But when full closed-loop systems were readmitted from Barcelona onwards there was no obvious disruption to the F1 pecking order.

'The pressure of building a new car when you are still developing the existing car, like McLaren and probably Williams, right through to the last race of the current year is quite demanding,' said Ross Brawn.

'The F2001 is I believe the best car we've produced since I've

Tower Garage, Egham 2001

Maranello Sales Ltd.
The Home of Ferrari.

APPROVED PRE-OWNED CARS

SALES   SERVICE   PARTS   BODY REPAIRS   FINANCE

Maranello Sales Ltd. Tower Garage, Egham, Surrey TW20 0AX Telephone 01784 436431
www.maranellosales.com   sales@maranellosales.com

An Inchcape
Company

Above: Schumacher makes a routine refuelling stop at Barcelona.

Right: Suitably sombre note struck by Barrichello's car at Monza.

Far right: Ferrari worked hard all season to keep details of its braking systems secret.

Below right: 'Schuey' in casual mode, as suggested by his specially made Nike shoes.
All photographs: Paul-Henri Cahier

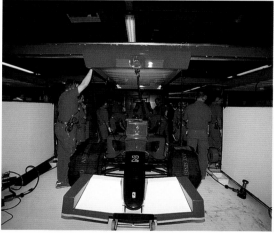

been at Maranello, along with an effort which went right to the end of the previous season. We have great stability with the likes of Rory Byrne, Aldo Costa and Giorgio Ascanelli, Paolo Martinelli — all of them have been there for five years or more. And I think the fact that we have all agreed to stay for several more years has helped the situation.'

The F2001 was regarded as 'a good evolution' from what went before, facing the challenge of lifting the front wing and imposing a size constraint on the rear wing. That said, by the middle of 2001 the team was back to the sort of downforce levels it had achieved the previous year.

Breaking the cycle of Ferrari domination in the forseeable future looks a tall order for the opposition. Schumacher simply delights in the tactile pleasure of driving a racing car, and is always cajoling, encouraging and worrying the team over how future developments are progressing. He finished the season driving a heavily revised F2001 chassis at Suzuka fitted with a selection of development components designed specifically to give the 2002 car a flying start once it is unveiled.

'Michael earns the respect and gets the commitment from all the people around him,' said Brawn. 'He's motivated, doing the best job he can, and the people around him naturally try to do the same. So you don't have to motivate the people very much when Michael is around.' It would be a brave man indeed to bet against more than the same in 2002.

TEAM-BY-TEAM REVIEW • FERRARI

Alan Henry

GET YOUR BROCHURE
FOR MORE INFORMATION ABOUT THE PRODUCTLINES PERFORMANCE, RACING AND FORMULA, NOW.

SETUP, RACE AND WIN.

SACHS RACE ENGINEERING

Official Supplier

Scuderia Ferrari

Shock absorber systems from Sachs Race Engineering help racers become champions in all categories - from amateur sport to the Rallye scene and the best in Formula 1. These winning systems are developed, designed and produced in our state-of-the-art facility in Schweinfurt, Germany by a highly qualified and motivated engineering team. Utilizing the most advanced materials, ultra-modern equipment and an ample dose of sporting spirit. Sachs expertise in racing offers our drivers a track-proven advantage.

From race to race, from triumph to triumph: Engineered to race.

Sachs Race Engineering GmbH
Ernst-Sachs-Strasse 62
D-97424 Schweinfurt
++ 49 97 21 98 43 00
katja.deutscher@sachs.de
www.sachs-race-engineering.de

SACHS
RACE **ENGINEERING**

MIKA HÄKKINEN

DAVID COULTHARD

THE McLaren-Mercedes team won four of the season's 17 races, although it should certainly have been seven. Melbourne, Barcelona and Monaco all slipped through their fingers, but even so they didn't have a technical package consistently capable of taking on the Ferrari head-to-head.

It says much for McLaren's scrupulously high standards that they regarded the 2001 season as a disappointment, even though the team finished second in the constructors' championship for the third straight season. In truth, they beat themselves even more than Ferrari did.

Mika Häkkinen and David Coulthard continued to provide the seasoned driver line-up, entering their sixth successive season as team-mates. This was an all-time record partnership since the start of the official World Championship in 1950 and matched the 1934–'39 pairing of Rudolf Caracciola and Manfred von Brauchitsch in the Mercedes-Benz team.

Their hopes rested on the well tested McLaren MP4/16 chassis and uprated Mercedes F0110K, 72-degree V10 reputedly developing around 800 bhp. There were also significant changes to the engineering staff at the races designed to enhance the team's operational efficiency.

Technically the priority for the MP4/16 was to improve the feel for the men behind the wheel while enhancing the aero package as compared with the MP4/15, albeit within the revised regulations. Unfortunately mechanical unreliability was McLaren's big handicap, ranging from a front suspension failure on Häkkinen's car at Melbourne which pitched him into an unsettling high-speed accident and a series of electronic glitches with the traction and launch control systems which left the cars stranded on the grid in Spain and Monaco (Coulthard) and Austria (Häkkinen).

The evolutionary Mercedes V10 was probably 20 bhp down on the Ferrari/BMW opposition and this was the cause of a degree of concern between McLaren and Ilmor Engineering behind the scenes. Ilmor's problems were also tragically exacerbated by the death of company co-founder Paul Morgan in a flying accident in the middle of the season.

Not that the Mercedes V10 was the root of the problem, far from it. The MP4/16 chassis was certainly not an unqualified success.

'We picked up an aerodynamic problem when we first tried to run the car [at Valencia],' said McLaren managing director Martin Whitmarsh, 'and we were trying to analyse why were having some different results when we ran on the circuit to that which we would expect in the wind tunnel.

'We didn't detect certain elements of what the front wing design was doing to the rest of the car and we had to work hard to evolve a front wing which was more sympathetic to the rest of the car package.

'By the time we got to the fifth race we felt we were probably where we ought to have been at the start and from that point on we were into the normal race-to-race improvements with smaller aerodynamic increments.'

There was an acceptance on both sides of the McLaren-Mercedes partnership that each could have done better. 'We had top speed and acceleration issues during the course of the year, which can be a question of aerodynamic drag as well as power,' continued Whitmarsh.

'But by mid-season I think that, within the partnership, both DaimlerChrysler and McLaren were conceding that neither had done as good a job as we should be doing. DaimlerChrysler accepted they needed to work harder on the engine and obviously we knew that we needed to work harder on the chassis.'

Certainly McLaren did not gain the performance advantage they'd been hoping for when traction control became permissible again as from the Spanish GP. Whitmarsh acknowledges that this was an area in which the team – including the drivers – did not do a good enough job of getting to grips with the new electronic regulations.

'From Barcelona onwards we were disappointed and highly embarrassed by our performance in the area of launch control,' he continued. 'The drivers played a part in that as well, but we have to develop a system which is robust and foolproof. We clearly had a system which was neither.'

Against this backdrop, Coulthard produced a superb year's endeavour, his best F1 season yet. The fact that his efforts were blighted by so much unreliability in the latter half of the season tended to blur memories when it came to recalling just how superbly he drove to win at Interlagos and Austria, in the latter racing through from seventh on the grid.

McLAREN MP4/16-MERCEDES-BENZ

SPONSORS	West, Mobil 1, Hugo Boss, SAP, Schüco, TAG Heuer, Warsteiner, The Advanced Composites Group, Canon, Charmilles Technologies, Enkei, GS Battery, Yamazaki Mazak, Sports Marketing Surveys, Targetti, BAE Systems, Bridgestone, Catia Solutions, Computer Associates, Kenwood, Loctite, Siemens Mobile, Sun Microsystems, TD-1, TNT
ENGINE	Type: Mercedes-Benz F0110K No. of cylinders (vee angle): V10 (72°) Electronics: TAG Electronic Systems Fuel: Mobil Unleaded Oil: Mobil 1
TRANSMISSION	Gearbox: McLaren longitudinal semi-automatic sequential Driveshafts and CV assemblies: McLaren
CHASSIS	Front suspension: double wishbone, inboard torsion bar/damper system, pushrod and bell crank-activated Rear suspension: double wishbone, inboard torsion bar/damper system, pushrod and bell crank-activated Dampers: McLaren/Penske Wheels: Enkei Tyres: Bridgestone Brake discs: Hitco Brake calipers: AP Racing Steering: McLaren power-assisted Fuel tank: ATL Battery: GS Instruments: TAG Electronic Systems
DIMENSIONS	Formula weight: 1322.8 lb/600 kg including driver

Photograph: Paul-Henri Cahier

RON DENNIS

McLAREN
Ron Dennis - Team Principal
Martin Whitmarsh - Managing Director
Adrian Newey - Technical Director
Neil Oatley - Chief Designer
Dave Ryan - Team Manager
Mike Negline - Chief Mechanic

Yet his supreme moment of the year came at Monaco when he beat Michael Schumacher to pole in a straight fight only for a launch control glitch to relegate him to the back of the grid.

Meanwhile, Häkkinen's accident at Melbourne profoundly affected the Finn's whole approach to the season. He later admitted that he found it difficult to get his head round the notion of a major suspension breakage considering just how much testing is carried out by today's front-line F1 teams. It also raised in his mind the spectre of his terrible accident in Adelaide back in 1995 when he was badly hurt following a tyre deflation during a free practice session.

It is difficult to assess just how much the effects of this accident impacted on Häkkinen's season-long performance, but he certainly had some lacklustre races, particularly in the first part of the year. He trailed home sixth, albeit with fastest race lap to his credit, in Malaysia, stalled on the grid at Interlagos and then drove an unremarkable race to fourth place at Imola.

In Spain, he drove a terrific race only for an hydraulic fluid leak to trigger a massive clutch failure while he was leading the last lap, then in Austria again his MP4/16 stalled on the grid and he was out of it from the start. At Monaco he spooked himself into believing there was something wrong with the car and withdrew from the race.

Perhaps significantly, this was the weekend when he first broached the subject of taking a sabbatical with team chief Ron Dennis. He then finished third in Canada, taking his first podium of the season, before producing a lacklustre run to sixth at the Nürburgring where he again convinced himself that he'd damaged his car after an off-track excursion at the chicane.

The McLaren stalled on the grid at Magny-Cours, but we had a flash of vintage Häkkinen at Silverstone where a two-stop strategy saw him dominate the British Grand Prix. We would see a repeat of that at Indianapolis where he scored possibly the best tactical victory of the entire F1 season.

There was also the issue of how much momentum was taken out of McLaren's development programme by technical director Adrian Newey's spending four months in negotiation to join the rival Jaguar team. Newey stayed put in the end, but even Ron Dennis the McLaren chairman conceded recently that the 'Adrian thing' was a definite setback.

'The best springboard we can provide into next season is a strong finish to this one,' said Whitmarsh. 'We will certainly win more Grands Prix. But we will have definitely failed David if we do not make him World Champion before he stops racing.' Next year perhaps?

Alan Henry

Clockwise from top:
Mika Häkkinen's victory in the British Grand Prix at Silverstone confirmed what the Finn could still do if he sensed a whiff of a winning opportunity.
Photograph: Bryn Williams/crash.net

Coulthard (left) and engineer Pat Fry (right) listen attentively.

Norbert Haug reports in to the Mercedes HQ.

Bells and whistles — a McLaren steering wheel is not just for turning.

Mika and Adrian Newey, the technical director who toyed with a switch to Jaguar, at around the time Häkkinen was toying with taking a break.
All photographs: Paul-Henri Cahier

Coulthard sits tight in the McLaren-Mercedes cockpit as the crew swarm around him in the Suzuka pit garage.
Photograph: Paul-Henri Cahier

RALF SCHUMACHER

JUAN PABLO MONTOYA

THE reputations of Williams and BMW were such that Ferrari and McLaren were keeping an anxious eye on the blue and white cars as the season began. This would be the second year of a liaison that had shown much promise in 2000. Everyone knew that BMW WilliamsF1 (to use the convoluted marketing-speak title) would improve even further in 2001. The question was, by how much?

Perhaps the greatest unknown had been created by a switch from Bridgestone to Michelin as the French tyre firm made a return to F1. It could make Williams or it could, not necessarily break them, but have the Anglo-German package effectively motoring nowhere.

Then there were the drivers. Ralf Schumacher had been made to look a touch second rate by Jenson Button at epic tracks such as Spa and Suzuka at the end of the previous year. Williams had taken some stick from the British press over driver policy (nothing new there) when Sir Frank Williams slid Button sideways to Benetton in preference for Juan Pablo Montoya, the former Williams test driver. Would the former CART Champion struggle to make the transition? And had Button undermined Ralf's confidence?

By the end of the season, Williams-BMW had won four of the 17 races. Schumacher's victory at Imola was the first for Michael's younger brother and the first for Williams since 1997. Schumacher went on to score maximum points in Canada and Germany, Montoya fulfilling his simmering promise with a maiden win in Italy; the first, you suspected, of many victories for the Colombian. All told, Williams had taken third in the championship. So a good season, then?

Well no, actually. Not by the exacting standards of Williams and BMW.

'We went into 2001 with a determination to close the gap to McLaren and Ferrari after our first year with BMW,' said Patrick Head. 'In 2000 we had reckoned we would be able to pick up the small points. We did that reasonably successfully so, obviously, the aim for 2001 was to try and get to a position where we could, in certain races, challenge for wins.

'We had this background idea that we would be disappointed if we hadn't won two or three races. We have won four races so, to some extent, it's mission accomplished. But it's like anything. When you get there, you think to yourself: 'Why haven't we done better?'

'Going into the final race, out of 32 car starts, we'd had 18 retirements, of which eight had been driver inspired — not necessarily always our drivers thanks to impacts from behind and such like — with the rest shared between car and engine. In total, that's greater than 50 per cent. If you look at Ferrari's situation, they're nothing like that. They are less than ten percent in that area, from their drivers as well as from their car.'

Apart from sorting out the reliable running of the FW23, the technical team — spearheaded by Gavin Fisher (chief designer), Geoff Willis (chief aerodynamicist) and bolstered by the arrival from Jordan of Sam Michael (chief operations engineer) — had been working closely with Michelin. The French firm did an exceptional job considering their lack of experience with grooved slicks (Bridgestone having three seasons of feedback with McLaren and Ferrari) as well as no running time on several F1 tracks.

Williams-BMW became the French firm's flag carriers in the absence of pace from the remaining Michelin runners. While four wins will have been satisfying, Michelin's shrewd motor sport director, Pierre Dupasquier, was just as aware of one or two shortcomings, the most serious being the need to scrub new tyres over a considerable period of time. Unlike Bridgestone, Michelin rubber had not been race-competitive when brand new.

'We did realise fairly early on that the front tyres particularly had a habit of graining badly,' said Head. 'The more you ran them, the more they would then clean up and come back to you. But I don't think we realised how much we had to prepare the tyres beforehand. Nor did we fully understand why, when preparing two sets of tyres, they would feel identical when you first went out and ran them but, when it came to the race, they would no longer feel identical. We were getting comments after the race such as: 'The first set were great. But what the hell did you do to the second?'

'Having said that, Michelin are making progress. They have always been a very good

WILLIAMS FW23-BMW

SPONSORS	BMW, Compaq, Allianz, Veltins, Nortel Networks, WorldCom, Reuters, Accenture, Petrobras, Castrol, Michelin
ENGINE	Type: BMW P80 No. of cylinders (vee angle): V10 (90°) Capacity: 2998 cc Electronics: WilliamsF1/BMW Fuel: Petrobras Oil: Castrol
TRANSMISSION	Gearbox: WilliamsF1 seven-speed longitudinal semi-automatic sequential Driveshafts: WilliamsF1 Clutch: AP Racing hand-operated
CHASSIS	Front suspension: WilliamsF1 double wishbone, torsion bar, pushrod Rear suspension: WilliamsF1 double wishbone, coil spring, pushrod Dampers: WilliamsF1
	Throttle: WilliamsF1 Pedals: WilliamsF1 Wheel diameter: front: 13 in. rear: 13 in. Wheels: OZ Racing Tyres: Michelin Brake discs: Carbone Industrie
	Brake pads: Carbone Industrie Steering: WilliamsF1 power-assisted Radiators: Secan/IMI Fuel tank: ATL Instruments: WilliamsF1
DIMENSIONS	Track: front: 1460 mm rear: 1410 mm Formula weight: 1322.8 lb/600 kg including driver

WILLIAMS
Sir Frank Williams - Team Principal
Patrick Head - Technical Director/Team Principal
Gavin Fisher - Chief Designer
Geoff Willis - Chief Aerodynamicist
Dickie Stanford - Team Manager
Sam Michael - Chief Operations Engineer
Carl Gaden - Chief Mechanic
Craig Wilson - Race Engineer Car No. 5,
Ralf Schumacher
Tim Preston/Tony Ross -
Race Engineers Car No. 6, Juan Pablo Montoya

PATRICK HEAD   GAVIN FISHER

GEOFF WILLIS   DICKIE STANFORD

SAM MICHAEL   CARL GADEN

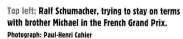

CRAIG WILSON   TIM PRESTON

Photographs courtesy of BMW WilliamsF1 Team

Top left: Ralf Schumacher, trying to stay on terms
with brother Michael in the French Grand Prix.
Photograph: Paul-Henri Cahier

Centre left: End of a long drought — Ralf wins
the San Marino Grand Prix at Imola.
Photograph: Mark Thompson/Allsport

Centre right: Primed for exciting times —
Montoya and Schumacher at the Silverstone
launch of the Williams FW23-BMW.
Photograph: Mark Thompson/Allsport-Getty Images

Left: Montoya on the grid in Austria, ultimately a
disappointing race for the team.
Photograph: Paul-Henri Cahier

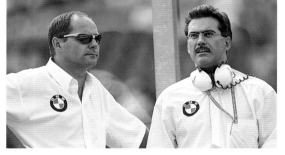

company and I think the remarkable thing is how well they have done in their first year.'

As for the Williams engine partner, BMW produced a new V10 for 2001, one which was supremely powerful but prone to six failures, a couple of which cost Montoya possible victories.

'Last year, we were deliberately conservative,' says Dr Mario Theissen, motor sport director at BMW. 'The engine was overweight, though powerful, and the main thing was that it gave our engineers the experience they needed to allow them to operate at the cutting edge of motor sport once more.

'The P80 engine of 2001 has been significantly different, markedly lighter and 90 degrees compared to the 72 degrees on the P41. For sure, we have a good power unit, probably one of the most powerful this season. But it's not just the engine that counts; it's the car and the drivers and the tyres as well. Only if you get everything right have you a chance to win. We managed that. But not often enough.'

At least Williams-BMW went into the winter break confident that they had two drivers capable of rising to the occasion. Before the season, Head had said he expected Ralf's experience to see him lead the way but, once Juan Pablo began to find his way around the team, the car and the workings of a Grand Prix weekend, there would be little to choose. Right enough, ten races into the season and Schumacher had out-qualified Montoya nine to

one. By the finish, the ratio was eleven to six with Montoya having scored his first win and generally been the faster of the two.

'I think Juan entered F1 with a very high expectation of the sort of impact he could make in the early races,' says Head. 'The way he overtook Michael in Brazil fed his view of where he should be. Then he had a rather sobering time with two silly accidents which gave him something to think about. Since then I'd say he has had a pretty strong season with quite a lot of disappointments on the reliability side.

'As for Ralf, I think having Jenson outqualify him at Spa and Suzuka – really, Ralf-type circuits — must have knocked his confidence a bit. But Ralf has liked this year's car and he was focused and calm, right from the beginning of the season. I don't think there have been too many blips in his performance, he's been pretty strong everywhere.

'But taking everything into account, there is still a long way to go to be a seriously competitive team, one which could consider entering 2002 in a position to challenge for the championship. Between us, we've got to work out how to cross that divide.'

Maurice Hamilton

Australian GP
04.03.2001

Malaysian GP
18.03.2001

Brazilian GP
01.04.2001

San Marino GP
15.04.2001

Spanish GP
29.04.2001

Austrian GP
13.05.2001

Monaco GP
27.05.2001

Canadian GP
10.06.2001

BMW Motorsport

Formula 1
BMW WilliamsF1
Team

French GP
01.07.2001

British GP
15.07.2001

German GP
29.07.2001

Hungarian GP
19.08.2001

Belgian GP
02.09.2001

Italian GP
16.09.2001

United States GP
30.09.2001

Japanese GP
14.10.2001

BMW recommends Castrol

We got a result in all 17 races.
Even if we didn't always finish first.

The engine, the engineering, and the teamwork: almost everything went like clockwork in the 2001 season.
Each and every one of the 17 races we started brought us a little closer to our ultimate goal. Of course
picking up world championship points matters, but gaining experience matters more. And in this respect,
an early retirement can sometimes be as valuable as a first-place finish.

Race by race, the BMW WilliamsF1 Team has shown what BMW Power can do. We are as surprised as
anyone by how many races we have managed to win in what is only our second season; we are proud
of what we have achieved, and now we aim to build on it. We were quick in our first season. Even quicker
this year. And we just can't wait for 2002. www.bmw-motorsport.com

GIANCARLO FISICHELLA

JENSON BUTTON

MILD SEVEN BENETTON RENAULT

YOU might have been forgiven for thinking that the Benetton-Renault squad had a pretty disappointing season, but in truth they were laying the foundations for an ambitious upsurge in performance for 2002. By the end of the year they scraped home seventh in the constructors' championship ahead of Jaguar, but in reality they were the fourth fastest team at Suzuka where Giancarlo Fisichella split the McLaren-Mercedes of Mika Häkkinen and David Coulthard in qualifying.

The purchase by Renault of the Benetton F1 team at the start of the 2000 season was part of a long-term project to mesh the French car maker's pedigree as a leading-edge F1 engine specialist with Benetton's high-technology chassis capability.

Having raced with a Supertec V10 in 2000, a direct derivation of the Renault Sport V10 which powered Jacques Villeneuve to the 1997 World Championship, Benetton went up a gear for its final season carrying the name of the famous Italian knitwear company. No longer were customer Supertec engines the order of the day, but instead an ambitious wide-angle 111-degree RS21 V10 developed by Jean-Jacques His and his team at Renault Sport.

After years of familiarity with the old 90-degree Renault V10, this was a whole new challenge facing Benetton technical director Mike Gascoyne and his team at Enstone. Not only was it a big challenge to package the new engine, but dramatic technical compromises had to be made all down the line to compensate for acute lack of power from the early V10s.

It was no joke trying to race the established runners with a power deficit initially approaching 100 bhp, but gradually the team successfully developed this integrated design and began to close the performance gap as the season progressed.

However, what became clear was that Renault Sport had great faith in the new engine. It was behind on development, not because they were struggling with the concept, but early development problems, particularly with the cylinder blocks, effectively put them about eight races behind. As the season unfolded they gradually caught up in parallel with an aggressive

programme of aerodynamic improvement from the chassis department.

Gascoyne had joined Benetton in September 2001 at a time when the team seemed on a gentle downward slide. Their 1994 and '95 World Championship successes had now faded to flickering memories. The spark had gone out. 12 months later at Suzuka, you could detect a spring in their step and huge optimism for the future.

'At the start of the season I made a point of telling the press to judge us by where we were at the end of the season rather than at the start,' said Gascoyne. 'We knew that the first part of the year would be a struggle. It would have been all-too-easy to opt for another season with the old Supertec V10 and we might well have ended up with fifth place in the constructors' championship.

'Trouble is, if we'd done that and not invested in the new, long-term programme, we'd have been facing 2002 knowing that — again — the best we could hope for would be fifth again.

'We had to accept compromises early in the season to guarantee we'd make progress at the end. Sure, as racers it was very frustrating to turn up to those early season races knowing we were going to qualify 18th or 19th. But we really didn't want to waste time on short-term fixes.'

The 2001 driver line-up saw Jenson Button moving into the team as successor to Alexander Wurz alongside Giancarlo Fisichella. The young British driver had been transferred from the BMW Williams squad after his freshman year and was theoretically on loan from Williams for two seasons, Frank's squad having the option of reclaiming him for 2003 if they so wished.

Fisichella outqualified Button 13-4 over the course of the full season and the Italian driver certainly impressed Gascoyne with the way he refused to allow short-term disappointments to overwhelm him.

Fisichella proved that there were early signs of promise when he qualified tenth at Monaco, proving that the low centre of gravity afforded by the new Renault V10 really offered worthwhile slow-corner traction benefits.

'Giancarlo did an absolutely fantastic job,' said Gascoyne. 'I simply couldn't praise him highly enough. In particular, that point he gained

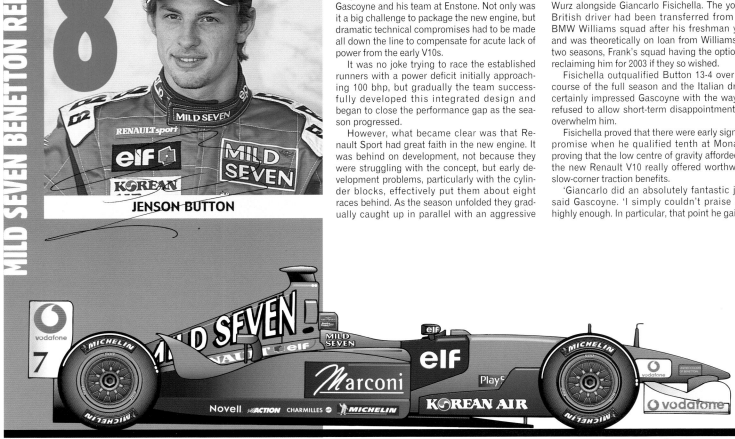

N. Curtis 2001

BENETTON B201-RENAULT

SPONSORS	Benetton, Mild Seven, Renault, Marconi, Vodafone, Michelin, Korean Air, Elf, PlayStation
ENGINE	**Type:** Renault Sport RS21 **No. of cylinders (vee angle):** V10 (111°) **Sparking plugs:** Champion **Electronics:** Magneti Marelli **Fuel:** Elf **Oil:** Elf
TRANSMISSION	**Gearbox:** Benetton six-speed longitudinal semi-automatic sequential **Driveshafts:** Benetton **Clutch:** AP Racing hand-operated
CHASSIS	**Front suspension:** double wishbone, pushrod **Rear suspension:** double wishbone, pushrod **Dampers:** Koni **Wheel diameter: front:** 13 in. **rear:** 13 in. **Wheels:** BBS
	Tyres: Michelin **Brake pads:** Hitco **Brake discs:** Hitco **Brake calipers:** AP Racing **Steering:** Benetton **Radiators:** Marston/Benetton **Fuel tank:** ATL
	Battery: Panasonic **Instruments:** Benetton
DIMENSIONS	**Wheelbase:** 3100 mm **Formula weight:** 1322.8 lb/600 kg including driver

Left: High hopes. The Benetton B201-Renault is launched in the dramatic surroundings of St. Mark's Square in Venice.
Photograph: Mark Thompson/Allsport-Getty Images

Below left: Fisichella rose to the challenge brilliantly throughout 2001.
Photograph: Paul-Henri Cahier

Below: Low profile — the Renault RS21 V10 sits snugly in the B201 chassis.
Photograph: Peter Nygaard/GP Photo

Bottom left: Jenson Button had a challenging second season in F1 fighting against the odds.
Photograph: Paul-Henri Cahier

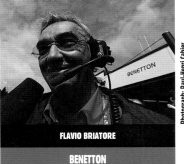

Photograph: Paul-Henri Cahier

FLAVIO BRIATORE

BENETTON
Flavio Briatore - Team Principal
Mike Gascoyne - Technical Director
Tim Densham - Chief Designer
Steve Nielsen - Team Manager
Pat Symonds - Chief Engineer
Jonathan Wheatley - Chief Mechanic
Alan Permane/Nicholas Chester -
Race Engineers Car No. 7, Giancarlo Fisichella
Paul Monaghan/Rod Nelson -
Race Engineers Car No. 8, Jenson Button

Left: Mild Seven remained title sponsors for the 11th straight season.

Below: Fisichella showed tremendous flair and control, racing to a fine third place in the Belgian Grand Prix.
Both photographs: Paul-Henri Cahier

us for sixth place in Brazil was worth its weight in gold. He carried us when we were down and, when things began to look up, at Spa he never put a wheel wrong on his run to third place.'

The Benetton-Renault upsurge effectively began with a heavily revised aerodynamic package which was introduced in time for the Hungarian Grand Prix. This really was a major step forward, but rather masked by the fact that the twisting Hungaroring was not one of Michelin's best circuits.

'We went to a Barcelona test immediately after Budapest and from the input we gathered there, we knew the car would be good at Spa,' said Gascoyne. And so it proved. Both Benettons ran strongly with Fisichella holding second place for much of the distance, eventually finishing third after Coulthard's McLaren nipped past in the closing stages.

It was a hugely encouraging result and one which raised expectations for the season's finale in Japan. 'Both Spa and Suzuka were crucially aerodynamic handling tracks and Giancarlo did really well to qualify sixth in Japan,' said Gascoyne.

'Sure, he spun, but he was trying to keep up with Ralf Schumacher at the time and running absolutely flat out. If he hadn't had mechanical problems in the closing stages I think he could have recovered to fifth, perhaps fourth, which would have been a great achievement.'

Gascoyne also has sympathy with the dilemma in which Button found himself, having inherited the 'Boy Wonder' tag from the media and now in a team with what Benetton's technical director believes was basically a quicker team-mate than he'd had with Ralf Schumacher at Williams.

'Fisi is quicker than Ralf,' said Gascoyne, 'but it was difficult for Jenson switching teams and he had to work hard to adapt. He did knuckle down in the second half of the season and got his head down much better once we had the two-car test team up and running. But he needs to continue working hard next season when he will be measuring himself against Jarno Trulli.'

Next year the Renault R202s will carry official identification from their new owners. Yet the team will remain to F1 insiders Benetton by another name. The technical team at Enstone will be working flat out to capitalise on their efforts this season and have targeted fourth place in next year's constructors' championship.

They also believe they can win the occasional race in the 2002 season, emphasising the fact that F1 endeavour is really nothing without lashings of self-belief. And they might just be right in their predictions.

Alan Henry

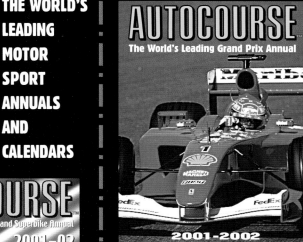

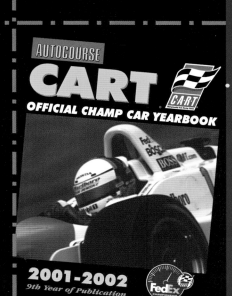

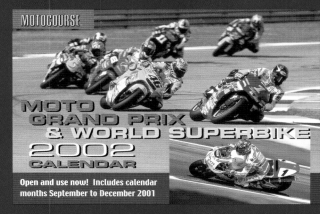

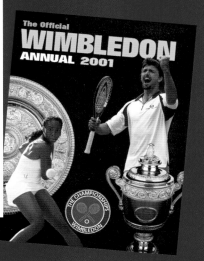

OLIVIER PANIS

JACQUES VILLENEUVE

BY their own admission, BAR took a step backwards in 2001. The car started off 'slow and difficult to drive' according to technical director Malcolm Oastler and never really improved, in spite of attempted development. This was hard to take for team principal Craig Pollock. 'We are considered one of the big teams, but a big team this year that has not produced,' he said. 'The car doesn't merit fifth in the championship.'

It wasn't for lack of trying, or resources. The budget rose and so did the personnel. 'We're up at 400 people now,' explained Pollock. 'We started the year with about 300 and we will have 450 people by the start of next season. They're nearly all in technical, testing, design, a lot in R and D, a lot in production, operational. We're bulging at the seams in the factory.' Among the new personnel was James Robinson, joining from Williams, who shared engineering duties with Steve Farrell.

Also among the new boys was Olivier Panis, joining Jacques Villeneuve after a year's sabbatical at McLaren. And the team wasn't short of test drivers either: Patrick Lemarie, Darren Manning, Anthony Davidson and Takuma Sato were all on hand although there was only one test team. This was, however, occasionally split, so that the team quite often tested in two locations. They needed to…

The initial car had a chequered career. It was soon crashed, and then had reliability problems. They were largely solved to make a car which retired seven times with mechanical problems, not reliable enough for Oastler. But when the team set about making it competitive, they hit a brick wall.

'To use a term used in the paddock, it was a badly born car,' says Pollock. 'Every time we put on a development part, instead of that part helping performance, it didn't seem to do anything at all, and the other teams, a lot of them doing less development, overtook us with flying steps. So the season, in reality, has been very, very bad.'

The car was flexible enough to make that development work. 'One of the design targets with this year's car was to achieve a substantially higher ballast figure, lower weight than last year, which we did,' says Oastler. They felt that they

BRITISH AMERICAN RACING BAR 003-HONDA

SPONSORS	British American Tobacco, Honda, Tiscali SpA, Bee-Trade, Intercond, Sonax, Multimoda Network, Bridgestone, Reynard Motorsport
ENGINE	**Type:** Honda RA001E **No. of cylinders (vee angle):** V10 (90°) **Fuel:** Nisseki **Oil:** Nisseki
TRANSMISSION	**Gearbox:** BAR/Xtrac six-speed longitudinal semi-automatic sequential **Clutch:** AP Racing hand-operated
CHASSIS	**Front suspension:** independent, pushrod-activated, inboard spring **Rear suspension:** independent, pushrod-activated, inboard spring
	Wheel diameter: front: 13 in. **rear:** 13 in. **Wheels:** OZ Racing **Tyres:** Bridgestone **Brake pads:** AP Racing **Brake discs:** AP Racing **Brake calipers:** AP Racing
DIMENSIONS	**Wheelbase:** 3050 mm **Track: front:** 1460 mm **rear:** 1420 mm **Formula weight:** 1322.8 lb/600 kg including driver

Left: Villeneuve and Panis at the launch of the new car... well, the new livery anyway. The launch machine was a mock-up using the previous year's car.
Photograph: Mark Thompson/Allsport-Getty Images

Above: Panis leads Villeneuve in the Austrian Grand Prix where the Frenchman finished fifth.
Photograph: Bryn Williams/crash.net

Right: Villeneuve seemingly found it hard to motivate himself consistently throughout the 2001 season.

Bottom: Villeneuve's best drive was a strong run to fourth place at Monaco, chasing down Irvine's Jaguar in the closing stages.
Both photographs: Paul-Henri Cahier

CRAIG POLLOCK

BRITISH AMERICAN RACING

Craig Pollock - Team Principal
Malcolm Oastler - Technical Director
Andy Green - Head of Design
Ron Meadows - Race Team Manager
Andrew Alsworth - Test Team Manager
Steve Farrell - Chief Engineer
James Robinson - Chief Race Engineer
Alistair Gibson - Chief Mechanic
David Lloyd - Senior Race Engineer
Car No. 9, Olivier Panis
Jock Clear - Senior Race Engineer
Car No. 10, Jacques Villeneuve

MALCOLM OASTLER

STEVE FARRELL   **ALISTAIR GIBSON**

ANDY GREEN   **JOCK CLEAR**

DAVID LLOYD   **ANDREW ALSWORTH**

Top left: **Suspension detail showing sensor.**

Top right: **Panis's return to F1 racing was judged a huge success.**
Both photographs: Paul-Henri Cahier

Above: **Villeneuve at speed through the Hockenheim pine forests on his way to third place in the German Grand Prix.**
Photograph: Clive Mason/Allsport-Getty Images

Below: **Villeneuve — absorbed and preoccupied.**

Following pages: **The BAR-Honda 003 was beautifully prepared, but its performance was disappointing.**
Both photographs: Paul-Henri Cahier

didn't need to change the suspension either. 'We have some geometry adjustment on the car; in the last race we were running slightly different geometry to Melbourne, but we haven't designed loads and loads of different geometries. We've done sufficient geometry experiments to satisfy ourselves that that is not where the problem lies.'

In fact Oastler pushed his guys hard. 'My approach is that I tell the guys that unless we're qualifying one-two and finishing one-two we need to improve everything. It's not like there's a key area that's got us nailed to the ground; we're working on every performance aspect that affects the car's performance. We've done four aero updates during the year. There are probably eight or ten different configurations but you break it up into big chunks. We had an update kit for Imola like most people, then another significant step for the European Grand Prix, the low-downforce package for Hockenheim and Monza, and then a big update for Hungary and Spa, and a bit more for Suzuka.

'But a huge amount of effort has gone into all sorts of areas, from the aerodynamics obviously with stiffness, weight, centre of gravity, ride. Undoubtedly we've improved since Melbourne but we haven't kept pace with the grid, hence in our last three races, our average qualifying positions are about 14th or 15th which is appalling given our resources and potential.'

For the second year, BAR were using Honda's V10 engine, developed from the previous year with more power and revs but lighter. There were continual development steps during the year, but Kazutoshi Nishizawa, technical director, would admit that 'the rate of development was not as fast as we wanted.' It was carried out in Japan, and engine rebuilds for BAR and Jordan were undertaken both in Japan and by Honda's 40-strong Bracknell-based team in England.

Honda continued to place personnel at BAR, particularly in the joint chassis development programme. Some 30 Honda people were working in design, R and D, electronics, hydraulics, throughout the factory. Pollock admitted that 'Honda is bitterly disappointed because they had high hopes for this season. But I think they also realised it's shown how bad their engine is this year, compared to what they thought it was going to be. They've under-produced, I would say… or they've under-estimated what it takes to make a winning Formula 1 engine today. Having said that, they are certainly putting in the work, a lot of work, to make sure they are going to step up and I think they are now starting to make the right decisions such as stopping Champ car and focusing on Formula 1.'

Race by race, the team didn't have a very good start to the season, with a penalty for Panis and Villeneuve's dreadful accident with Ralf Schumacher. There were two retirements in Malaysia, and then Panis's fourth place in Brazil began to turn the results around. Villeneuve was on the podium in Spain thanks to Häkkinen's last-gasp retirement, and had a good race to fourth in Monaco. Canada, however, was predictably disastrous. It was also the last time that either car qualified in single figures, apart from Villeneuve in Belgium. Lack of progress hit hard, and Villeneuve's podium from 12th on the grid in Germany and sixth from 15th in Italy were the only points-scoring positions in the last ten races.

Looking back, Pollock might have scrapped the car after the second race. It's a season that he won't go through again. 'I've told Malcolm very, very clearly and in no uncertain terms that it will not be tolerated and it will not be accepted next year.' But he also accepts 'I have to be the first to go if it doesn't work.'

Bob Constanduros

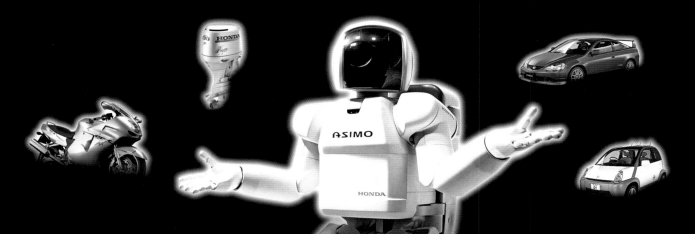

Honda Power.

The Total Power of Honda

Honda operates globally through its worldwide activities in the development, production and sales of motorcycles, automobiles and power products. Honda is also actively involved in developing advanced technologies in robotics, motor sports, and the environment. Honda Power is the total combined power of Honda as a whole. In its third era of F1 participation, Honda has undertaken innovative, challenging development in not only engine but also chassis technology. The power to challenge — this, too, is part of Honda Power. Honda's challenge goes on.

www.hondaf1.com

Photo : Jordan Honda EJ11
No.11 Jarno Trulli

Photo : BAR Honda 003
No.10 Jacques Villeneuve

www.JV-world.com

J.VILLENEUVE
0- 10

LUCKY STRIKE

E

LUCKY
STRIKE

HONDA

LUCKY STRIKE

PULL

PULL

0- 10
J.VILLENEUVE

www.JV-world.com

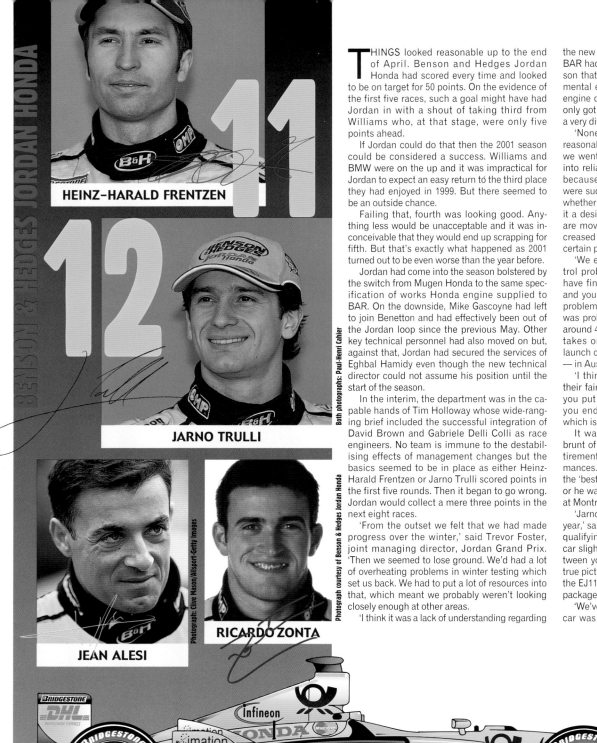

HEINZ-HARALD FRENTZEN

JARNO TRULLI

JEAN ALESI

RICARDO ZONTA

T HINGS looked reasonable up to the end of April. Benson and Hedges Jordan Honda had scored every time and looked to be on target for 50 points. On the evidence of the first five races, such a goal might have had Jordan in with a shout of taking third from Williams who, at that stage, were only five points ahead.

If Jordan could do that then the 2001 season could be considered a success. Williams and BMW were on the up and it was impractical for Jordan to expect an easy return tó the third place they had enjoyed in 1999. But there seemed to be an outside chance.

Failing that, fourth was looking good. Anything less would be unacceptable and it was inconceivable that they would end up scrapping for fifth. But that's exactly what happened as 2001 turned out to be even worse than the year before.

Jordan had come into the season bolstered by the switch from Mugen Honda to the same specification of works Honda engine supplied to BAR. On the downside, Mike Gascoyne had left to join Benetton and had effectively been out of the Jordan loop since the previous May. Other key technical personnel had also moved on but, against that, Jordan had secured the services of Eghbal Hamidy even though the new technical director could not assume his position until the start of the season.

In the interim, the department was in the capable hands of Tim Holloway whose wide-ranging brief included the successful integration of David Brown and Gabriele Delli Colli as race engineers. No team is immune to the destabilising effects of management changes but the basics seemed to be in place as either Heinz-Harald Frentzen or Jarno Trulli scored points in the first five rounds. Then it began to go wrong. Jordan would collect a mere three points in the next eight races.

'From the outset we felt that we had made progress over the winter,' said Trevor Foster, joint managing director, Jordan Grand Prix. 'Then we seemed to lose ground. We'd had a lot of overheating problems in winter testing which set us back. We had to put a lot of resources into that, which meant we probably weren't looking closely enough at other areas.

'I think it was a lack of understanding regarding the new Honda engine — from our point of view. BAR had a better handle on it for the simple reason that they had worked with the same fundamental engine the previous year. But when the engine doesn't arrive until early January, you've only got five weeks to get it in and sort it. That's a very difficult deadline.

'Nonetheless, we seemed to be performing reasonably well in the first five races. But then we went through a period of getting ourselves into reliability issues. Things were complicated because parts that had not caused problems were suddenly going wrong. So you start asking whether this is because of traction control, or is it a design fault, or is it because developments are moving on at such a fantastic rate that increased or different loads are starting to affect certain parts of the car?

'We eventually realised it was a quality control problem with certain suppliers. Then you have finishes at Magny-Cours and Silverstone and you think you have it sorted — only for the problem to come back and haunt you again. It was probably only two or three suppliers out of around 450. The rest do a fantastic job, but it just takes one to stop you finishing races. Plus, launch control caught out us — and other teams — in Austria.

'I think it's fair to say that Honda have had their fair share of reliability issues as well so, if you put that together with our own problems, you end up with an average finishing record which is below our target.'

It was Trulli who seemed to shoulder the brunt of the misfortune, a mid-season run of retirements negating excellent qualifying performances. On 12 occasions, the Italian was either the 'best of the rest' outside the top three teams, or he was in among them with second row slots at Montreal and Silverstone.

'Jarno did an exceptional job in qualifying all year,' said Foster. 'When a driver is that strong in qualifying, there is a danger he may flatter the car slightly. You should average the lap time between your two drivers in order to ascertain the true picture of where the car is. If we do that with the EJ11, then there were times when the overall package has not been competitive enough.

'We've had concerns about our race pace. The car was better than last year but we found we

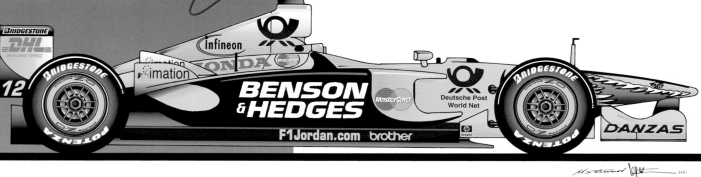

JORDAN EJ11-HONDA

SPONSORS	Benson & Hedges, Deutsche Post World Net, Danzas, DHL, Infineon, MasterCard, Lucent Technologies, LeggMason Investors, Brother, Imation, Hewlett Packard, Lubrax, Schroth, Puma, Esat Digifone, PowerMarque, Grundig, OMP, Laurent-Perrier
ENGINE	Type: Honda RA001E No. of cylinders (vee angle): V10 (90°) Sparking plugs: NGK Electronics: Honda Fuel: Elf Oil: Mitsubishi
TRANSMISSION	Gearbox: Lubrax seven-speed longitudinal semi-automatic sequential Driveshafts: Pankl Clutch: Jordan/Sachs hand-operated
CHASSIS	Front suspension: composite pushrods activating chassis-mounted dampers and torsion bars Rear suspension: composite pushrods activating gearbox-mounted dampers Dampers: Jordan/Penske Wheel diameter: front: 13 in. rear: 13 in. Wheels: OZ Racing Tyres: Bridgestone Brake pads: Brembo/Hitco Brake discs: Brembo/Hitco Brake calipers: Brembo Steering: Jordan power-assisted Radiators: Jordan Fuel tank: ATL Battery: Honda Instruments: Jordan
DIMENSIONS	Wheelbase: over 3000 mm Track: front: 1500 mm rear: 1418 mm Formula weight: 1322.8 lb/600 kg including driver Fuel capacity: approx. 100 kg

EDDIE JORDAN

JORDAN

Eddie Jordan - Team Principal/Chief Executive
Trevor Foster - Joint Managing Director
John Putt - Chief Operating Officer
Eghbal Hamidy - Technical Director
John McQuilliam - Chief Designer
John Iley - Chief Aerodynamicist
Tim Holloway - Head of Engineering
Jim Vale - Team Manager
Tim Edwards - Test Team Manager
Phil Spencer - Chief Mechanic
Gabriele Delli Colli - Senior Race Engineer
Car No. 12/11, Jarno Trulli
David Brown - Chief Engineer/Senior Race Engineer
Car No. 11/12, Heinz-Harald Frentzen/Ricardo
Zonta/Jean Alesi
Nick Burrows - No. 1 Mechanic
Car No. 12/11, Jarno Trulli
Matt Deane - No. 1 Mechanic Car No. 11/12,
Heinz-Harald Frentzen/Ricardo Zonta/Jean Alesi

EGHBAL HAMIDY   **TIM HOLLOWAY**

JIM VALE   **GABRIELE DELLI COLLI**

DAVID BROWN   **NICK BURROWS**

MATT DEANE   **TIM EDWARDS**

Photographs courtesy of Benson & Hedges Jordan Honda

Top left: Jarno Trulli qualified well at Monza, but was taken out by Jenson Button at the start of the race.

Above left: Jean Alesi switched from Prost to brighten up the second half of the Jordan season.
Both photographs: Bryn Williams/crash.net

Left: Test driver Ricardo Zonta had two race outings for the team: in Canada and here at Hockenheim.
Photograph: Paul-Henri Cahier

Above: Heinz-Harald Frentzen parted company with the team mid-season after Eddie Jordan decided he wasn't sufficiently competitive.

Top: Three distinctive detailed shots of the Jordan cockpit, nose treatment and exhaust exits.
All photographs: Paul-Henri Cahier

Opposite: Jarno Trulli finished his tenure with Jordan at Suzuka where he finished a disappointed eighth.
Photograph: Clive Mason/Allsport-Getty Images

still needed to do more work looking after the tyres. We have been putting a lot of effort into trying to understand what caused that. Also, Honda acknowledged that they needed to do a lot more work regarding engine power.'

The increased importance of electronics, thanks to the introduction of launch and traction control, tended to hurt Jordan more than other teams. Unlike, say, Sauber who plugged into Ferrari's technology, Jordan did everything in-house. There was no TAG or Pi to take care of such a complex and important issue, the Jordan technicians doing a remarkable job considering the limited resources that were typical of the team as a whole.

As if Jordan did not have enough problems, matters were made much worse at the end of July when Eddie Jordan sacked Frentzen. The reason was never made entirely clear although politics (and money) appeared to be at play, particularly when Jordan signed the Japanese driver, Takuma Sato, for 2002.

Frentzen had made a good start to the season but his performances appeared to suffer the effect of Trulli dominating qualifying. Frentzen's races were solid and reliable, but not good enough to withstand the effects of Eddie Jordan's tactical game plan.

In the meantime, test driver Ricardo Zonta filled the breach at Hockenheim (as he had done in Montreal when Frentzen had to withdraw as the result of a crash during practice). Then Jean Alesi

moved from Prost to see out his F1 career with Jordan during the final five races.

'The sudden change of driver was a big influence on the workload,' said Foster. 'It takes eight or nine days to make a new seat, plus we had to make pedals and cater for Jean not being a left-foot braker. Suddenly you find you have another week and a half's work just for the composite guys, never mind the drawing office. And this when we were chasing fourth in the championship and working on improving the car.'

It was a close-fought thing between British American Racing and Jordan as they stumbled along, each as bad as the other even if Jordan showed far more potential. The team had seven finishes in the first ten starts. Extrapolating that average over the rest of the season, they would not have reached 50 points any more than they had a hope of beating Williams. But fourth place would have been easy.

The fact that fourth slipped from their grasp indicated the continuous increase of pace in F1. Both Jordan and Honda need to move up a gear in terms of manpower and resources. As 2001 proved, mere potential is not enough.

Maurice Hamilton

JOS VERSTAPPEN

ORANGE ARROWS ASIATECH

ENRIQUE BERNOLDI

As far as Tom Walkinshaw was concerned, 2001 was a blip in Arrows's form. 'I'm quietly confident that we'll do a much better job next year than we did this year,' he explained. 'It should be the follow-on from last year.'

Then, Arrows had finished seventh in the constructors' championship but had under-performed according to technical director Mike Coughlan. That was definitely true of 2001: they would finish tenth, only ahead of non-scoring Minardi, with a single point from the Austrian Grand Prix. 'We threw away so many points at the beginning of the season, third in Austria, we were good in Brazil, Jos was in line for fifth in Monaco, other races where we could have scored significant points and been much better off,' admitted Coughlan.

But the season was short and fraught with handicaps. Firstly, for the fourth time in as many years, there was a new engine. 'We need five designers to design a new installation, a new gearbox, new hydraulics,' says Coughlan, 'so it takes an awful big chunk of your design resources when you change engines. You have to start reasonably early to be able to complete that without having a big design team.'

After Supertec the previous year, they had teamed up with Asiatech. This was the previous year's Peugeot engine, 20–25 per cent developed by the same staff but with a new modular organisation and investment from Asia, a budget of $95–100 million. In charge of an expanded staff, up from 165 to 220, was former Williams designer Enrique Scalabroni.

Scalabroni and his seven departmental heads worked hard, justifiably on reliability, development and temperatures. 'The life of our engine is fixed at 550 km,' he explained. 'It can run to 700 km but we do not want to take risks. There was big pressure on me from Japan to try to do something that is stable and works. I know that our power is not the same as the top engines but we are working in the order of 800–805 bhp.'

From late spring onwards, however, performance slipped. The engine weighed 108 kilos, excluding the exhaust, clutch and the electronics; when taken from the car, it was 120 kilos, about eight kilos heavier than the lightest. Major developments during the year were the quality of castings — the block and heads were

changed at each rebuild, 240 blocks in all; the treatment of the cylinders, two or three of which failed; a redesign of conrods which were too flexible; and a change of inlet admission and valve control systems.

Another problem was the need to run at low temperatures, which means bigger radiators causing greater aerodynamic drag. 'We were always working at 105 degrees before Monte Carlo,' explained Scalabroni. 'We did a lot of work so that engines would run at 120 degrees. It forced us to work on clearances and tolerances in the engine and work with new piston rings.'

But early season lack of reliability cost the team testing time. Coughlan was happy with the team's reliability but there were nearly 40 unscheduled engine changes. Furthermore, the engine was less fuel efficient than the Supertec, and Arrows had taken a major decision early on to run with a small fuel tank. It meant that they would usually have to make two stops for fuel and tyres.

The reason for this was that they believed everyone would have to make two stops, due to the tyre war. 'We talked to Bridgestone when Michelin were confirmed to return and we felt that the move would be towards huge tyre degradation and massive grip,' explained Coughlan. 'In the end, Michelin came along with a tyre that had good grip and low degradation and Bridgestone changed their philosophy.' Arrows were caught in the middle, having opted for a small fuel tank, thinking that there would be more fuel stops everywhere.

'We could have finished third or fourth in Malaysia for a slightly bigger tank,' said Coughlan ruefully.

This philosophy meant that Jos Verstappen, in his third year with the team, but so unable to use the tyres properly in qualifying that he was preceded on the grid by new team-mate Enrique Bernoldi 10-7 during the year, would be much lighter on fuel than those around him at the start of a race, and would overtake some 80 times during the year, usually in the first two laps.

There were many other problems. 'The power delivery, and the traction control that was on it, ended up compromising the package each time,' explained Walkinshaw. 'We really struggled to run anything like the downforce we would normally want to run and the traction control that

ARROWS A22-ASIATECH

SPONSORS	Orange, Asiatech, Red Bull, Chello, Eurobet, Lost Boys, Bridgestone, RG Tecq, Paul Costelloe, TCC, Trust, SGI, Morgan Grenfell, Catia Solutions, Dell
ENGINE	**Type:** Asiatech 001 **No. of cylinders (vee angle):** V10 (72°) **Sparking plugs:** NGK **Electronics:** TAG Electronics **Fuel:** Elf **Oil:** Elf
TRANSMISSION	**Gearbox:** Arrows carbon-fibre six-speed longitudinal semi-automatic sequential **Driveshafts:** Metalore/Arrows **Clutch:** Arrows hand-operated
CHASSIS	**Front suspension:** inboard-operated independent, carbon-fibre wishbones **Rear suspension:** inboard-operated independent, carbon-fibre wishbones
	Wheel diameter: front: 13 in. **rear:** 12 in. **Wheels:** BBS **Tyres:** Bridgestone **Brake pads:** AP Racing/Hitco **Brake discs:** AP Racing/Hitco **Brake calipers:** AP Racing
	Steering: Arrows power-assisted **Fuel tank:** Arrows/ATL **Battery:** Arrows **Instruments:** Arrows
DIMENSIONS	**Wheelbase:** 2995 mm **Track: front:** 1465 mm **rear:** 1410 mm **Formula weight:** 1322.8 lb/600 kg including driver

TOM WALKINSHAW

ARROWS
Tom Walkinshaw - Team Principal
Mike Coughlan - Technical Director
Sergio Rinland - Chief Designer
Rob Taylor - Head of Design
Nicolo Petrucci - Head of Aerodynamics
Mick Ainsley-Cowlishaw - Team Manager
Graham Taylor - Chief Engineer
Stuart Cowie - Chief Mechanic
Greg Wheeler - Race Engineer
Car No. 14, Jos Verstappen
Stefano Sordo - Race Engineer
Car No. 15, Enrique Bernoldi

MIKE COUGHLAN   **GRAHAM TAYLOR**

Top left: Enrique Bernoldi proved an extremely competent performer during his first season in F1.
Photograph: Paul-Henri Cahier

Left: Jos Verstappen is a seasoned professional with huge experience on which to draw.
Photograph: Bryn Williams/crash.net

Below: The overall Arrows package suffered from having to change engines since 2001.
Photograph: Paul-Henri Cahier

was on it was relatively crude and we were losing a huge amount of time out of slow corners; whenever wheelspin cut in it just would never control it properly.'

'We didn't have good aero balance,' continued Coughlan. 'We got understeer from our front wing and while we picked up aero efficiency, we were only keeping pace. We had efficient downforce, but not enough.'

The aerodynamic situation wasn't helped by the departure of aerodynamicist Eghbal Hamidy late the previous year, to be replaced by Nicolo Petrucci. Otherwise, to Coughlan's relief, the staff was relatively stable, up 20 to around 300.

Overall, the budget was about the same as the previous year's with further input from Red Bull to add to that of Orange and Lost Boys, but Coral Eurobet proved a fly in the ointment and caused a financial crisis which partially precipitated the sale of the team's 60 per cent ex-DERA wind tunnel at Bedford to Jaguar — although not before the 2002 challenger had taken shape. With Cosworth confirmed as early as May 2001, the team looked forward to a better future in 2002.

Bob Constanduros

NICK HEIDFELD

KIMI RÄIKKÖNEN

IN 2000, Sauber had been in a massive mid-field bunch comprising Jordan, Williams, BAR, Arrows, Benetton and Jaguar. With what was estimated as the third smallest budget in Formula 1, in 2001 they hauled themselves out of that bunch to give best only to Ferrari, McLaren and Williams, but to beat the factory-powered teams of Benetton, Jaguar, Jordan and BAR. Their fourth place in the constructors' series was the surprise of the season.

By the time the lights went out in Melbourne, there had been many changes in the 300-strong Sauber team in comparison to the previous year. Gone were Mika Salo and Pedro Diniz, the latter taking his valued Parmalat sponsorship to Prost. It was replaced by Credit Suisse chez Sauber, but to a less generous extent and although Red Bull contributed a bit more, the budget was down a fraction. Sauber were only poorer than Minardi and Prost. They could only afford a one-car test team.

The drivers were replaced by two virtual newcomers: Nick Heidfeld, with only a depressing survival season at Prost although schooling at McLaren before that, and Kimi Räikkönen, who had done just 23 Formula Renault races plus karting. Within a race or two, asked what had changed and Peter Sauber would say no more than 'we have two young and talented drivers.'

But there were other changes. Former technical director Jost Capito was shuffled off from the race to the engine department and would leave in mid-season. Sergio Rinland, the new chief designer, had gone by the time his department's car was unveiled and Leo Ress, former technical director, was now in R and D. Firmly in charge of all things technical, but delegating, was Willy Rampf. Rinland's replacement, Peter Taylor, never came due to personal reasons, and was never replaced.

'The basic car was quite good,' says Rampf who reported it was designed light. 'We had to do a lot of small modifications pre-season to improve reliability because we saw in the first test that the reliability wasn't that great. It's very important in the first races so we covered this in the pre-season tests. We made a very lightweight car, and we had to reinforce a lot of components to be back on track. Starting with a light car was done on purpose, because then

you can reinforce it and make it heavier. It's impossible to do it the other way round.

'Then we started with a very tight development programme and we kept this going throughout the whole season with the target to have new components and improvements for each event.'

This was an area in which the team had been lacking in years past. They would score points in early races, then slip back as other teams appeared with developments. Rampf was determined this shouldn't happen again. 'The major improvements were always on the aerodynamic side. We have changed everything on the car. The car which we ran in Suzuka was aerodynamically completely different to the car which we were running at the beginning of the season.'

This was the work of Seamus Mullarkey, chief aerodynamicist, who has a staff of 15 people who use a military wind tunnel at Emmen, around an hour's drive from the team's base at Hinwil. He has some 40 weeks there — but they are five-day weeks and less than 20 hours per day, unlike some teams who have three eight-hour shifts for seven days a week in their own tunnel — or tunnels.

'We had a completely different front wing at Magny Cours,' continues Rampf, 'then the floor, a lot of internals basically, and also the rear wing. But we also changed the front flap a few times and the end plates. There was a huge development programme on brake cooling, front and rear. We had new components three or four times during the season, and they always gave an improvement.' Even though they eventually ended their development at Monza, they still found steps forward in testing, and brought further modifications to the last race at Suzuka.

The team had its own gearbox, which they were very happy with and proud of. Ferrari, they suggested, were a bit jealous of it, because it's very neat.

Except for Spa, they had no problems with it. It was the only major reliability problem. Similarly, their Ferrari-bred Petronas engines were very reliable, with only one failure — in a straightline test. There was a single development on the engine at Montreal in qualifying, and raced from France onwards.

Although the team would pay tribute to its

SAUBER C20-PETRONAS

SPONSORS	Red Bull, Petronas, Credit Suisse, Bridgestone, Compaq, Walter Meier AG, Magneti Marelli, Emil Frey AG, BBS, Italdesign-Giugiaro, Toshiba, Microsoft, MAN, Sparco, Catia Solutions, MSC, Ericsson, MCM
ENGINE	**Type:** Petronas 01A **No. of cylinders (vee angle):** V10 (90°) **Sparking Plugs:** NGK **Electronics:** Magneti Marelli **Fuel:** Petronas **Oil:** Petronas
TRANSMISSION	**Gearbox:** Seven-speed longitudinal semi-automatic sequential **Clutch:** AP Racing/Sachs hand-operated
CHASSIS	**Front suspension:** independent, pushrod-activated, inboard spring **Rear suspension:** independent, pushrod-activated, inboard spring
	Wheel diameter: front: 13 in. **rear:** 13 in. **Wheels:** BBS **Tyres:** Bridgestone **Brake pads:** Brembo **Brake discs:** Brembo **Brake calipers:** Brembo
	Steering: power-assisted **Battery:** Magneti Marelli **Instruments:** Magneti Marelli
DIMENSIONS	**Wheelbase:** 3040 mm **Track: front:** 1470 mm **rear:** 1405 mm **Formula weight:** 1322.8 lb/600 kg including driver

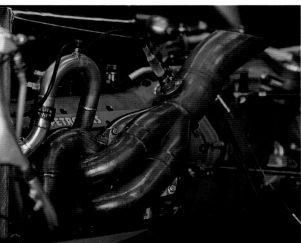

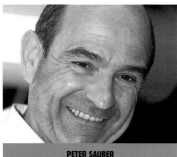

PETER SAUBER

SAUBER
Peter Sauber - Team Principal
Willy Rampf - Technical Manager
Osamu Goto - Engine Director
Beat Zehnder - Team Manager
Urs Kuratle - Chief Mechanic
Rémi Decorzent - Race Engineer
Car No. 16, Nick Heidfeld
Jacki Eeckelaert - Head of Test Team/
Race Engineer Car No. 17, Kimi Räikkönen

WILLY RAMPF   **OSAMU GOTO**

BEAT ZEHNDER   **RÉMI DECORZENT**

JACKI EECKELAERT   **URS KURATLE**

drivers, they were also more than capable of sorting out problems internally, as Rampf explains. 'Monaco is a good example. In Monaco our performance was not very good [15th and 16th in qualifying] and we really didn't know why. The car didn't feel particularly bad, but we were very slow compared to our competitors. Then we analysed everything, we went to Valencia with a big package of possible solutions, we worked it out and the next race where we ran a similar downforce configuration was Budapest where we were back on track. We performed quite well there [7th and 9th in qualifying]. That's the only time we got lost.'

While Rampf and his team were obviously good at identifying and analysing the problems, Peter Sauber was also right to praise his drivers. 'The drivers reported very accurately about the balance of the car, what the major problem was in the handling,' explained Rampf. Räikkönen would drive around problems quite happily, but Heidfeld 'doesn't give up unless he knows how to make the car fast and how to set it up as well as possible' an engineer explained. 'He works very well with engineers. His comments about the car, like what to change and how the car behaves are very precise.'

Heidfeld outqualified Räikkönen 10-7 with a best of two sixths, and got on the podium in Brazil having finished fourth in Australia. Four times he finished sixth, but he also had five collisions with other cars. His team-mate scored a point in his first Grand Prix, finished fourth in Austria and Canada with a best of two sevenths in qualifying. There were just four mechanical retirements in races. Nick made three mistakes in the year, Kimi none in races, if you assume his terminal spin at Suzuka was mechanically-induced.

It was a tremendous record, and one that will be hard to reproduce, given the circumstances. As those other midfielders use their resources, Sauber may be hard-pushed to keep up.

Bob Constanduros

Top left: The wraps come off the new Sauber-Petronas C20 at its official launch in January. Even the most optimistic team members could hardly have imagined just how effective it would be.
Photograph: Allsport-Getty Images

Centre left: The Petronas-badged V10 engine was the late-spec 2000 engine from Ferrari.

Centre right: Kimi Räikkönen was the find of the season and has been snapped up by the McLaren-Mercedes squad as Mika Häkkinen's successor.
Both photographs: Paul-Henri Cahier

Above left: Nick Heidfeld realised all his early promise during his second season in F1.

Bottom left: Kimi Räikkönen at speed — 2002 will show whether he really has the Midas touch.
Both photographs: Bryn Williams/crash.net

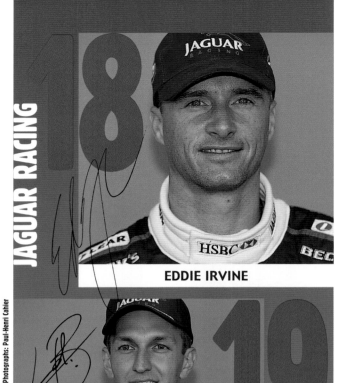

EDDIE IRVINE

LUCIANO BURTI

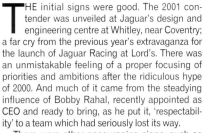

PEDRO de la ROSA

Photographs: Paul-Henri Cahier

THE initial signs were good. The 2001 contender was unveiled at Jaguar's design and engineering centre at Whitley, near Coventry; a far cry from the previous year's extravaganza for the launch of Jaguar Racing at Lord's. There was an unmistakable feeling of a proper focusing of priorities and ambitions after the ridiculous hype of 2000. And much of it came from the steadying influence of Bobby Rahal, recently appointed as CEO and ready to bring, as he put it, 'respectability' to a team which had seriously lost its way.

There were other encouraging signs, such as the signing of Mark Handford as head of aerodynamics, and the appointment Steve Nichols to oversee the technical department and liaise with John Russell, chief designer of the R2. Cosworth Racing, meanwhile, were ready to roll with the latest version of the Nick Hayes-inspired V10 and maintain a very respectable presence in the bhp league table thanks to reliable running and a planned series of useful developments.

Eddie Irvine would continue to be the driving force in every sense, the Ulsterman bringing his forceful views to bear while, at the same time, keeping an eye on Luciano Burti as the Brazilian made his debut after a one-off drive in 2000. Jaguar Racing may not have been about to win races but the programme appeared to be on a more sensible footing.

The reality was to be quite different. Jaguar created more headlines off the track than on it thanks, in large part, to the arrival of Niki Lauda at the behest of Dr Wolfgang Reitzle, the chairman of Premier Automotive Group (responsible for Aston Martin, Jaguar, Land Rover, Volvo and Lincoln). The precise nature of Lauda's role was to be just as politically suspect as the link between PAG and Jaguar *Racing*.

It was soon clear that Lauda had his shovel under Rahal. By August he was gone, the American's departure perhaps on the cards from the moment Adrian Newey reneged on a firm agreement to leave McLaren and become Jaguar's technical chief.

Photograph: Bryn Williams/crash.net

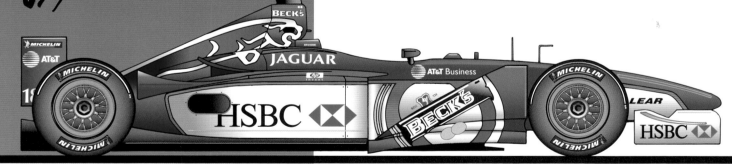

N. Christ Wher 2001

JAGUAR R2-COSWORTH

SPONSORS	HSBC, Beck's, AT&T, HP, Lear, Texaco, Michelin
ENGINE	Type: Cosworth CR3 No. of cylinders: V10 Sparking plugs: Champion Electronics: Pi/Cosworth Fuel: Texaco Oil: Texaco
TRANSMISSION	Gearbox: Jaguar seven-speed longitudinal semi-automatic sequential Driveshafts: Pankl Clutch: AP Racing hand-operated
CHASSIS	Front suspension: Double wishbones, pushrod, torsion bar, ARB, third spring Rear suspension: Double wishbones, pushrod, torsion bar, ARB, third spring
	Wheels: BBS Tyres: Michelin Brake pads: Brembo Brake discs: Brembo Brake calipers: AP Racing Radiators: Marston Fuel tank: ATL
	Steering: Jaguar power-assisted Battery: Fiamm Instruments: Pi/Jaguar
DIMENSIONS	Formula weight: 1322.8 lb/600 kg including driver

Far left: Eddie Irvine scored the team's best finish with a third at Monaco.
Photograph: Paul-Henri Cahier

Left: The Ulsterman was never backwards in coming forwards when it came to painfully candid criticism.

Centre left, above and below: Niki Lauda with Irvine — seemingly soulmates, both struggling to get the best out of the Jaguar R2.

Below: Pedro de la Rosa was drafted in to replace Luciano Burti after the first four races.
All photographs: Bryn Williams/crash.net

Bottom left: Irvine on the grid at Malaysia's Sepang circuit, ready to go.
Photograph: Paul-Henri Cahier

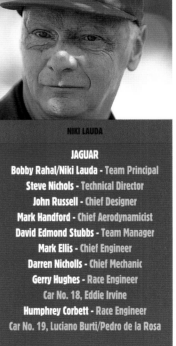

Photograph: Bryn Williams/crash.net

NIKI LAUDA

JAGUAR
Bobby Rahal/Niki Lauda - Team Principal
Steve Nichols - Technical Director
John Russell - Chief Designer
Mark Handford - Chief Aerodynamicist
David Edmond Stubbs - Team Manager
Mark Ellis - Chief Engineer
Darren Nicholls - Chief Mechanic
Gerry Hughes - Race Engineer
Car No. 18, Eddie Irvine
Humphrey Corbett - Race Engineer
Car No. 19, Luciano Burti/Pedro de la Rosa

Top: Irvine and Rahal never saw eye-to-eye.

Main photograph: Irvine gets down to business.

Above: Eddie focuses on the future.
All photographs: Paul-Henri Cahier

All of this was deeply unsettling for team members already worn down by politics getting in the way of racing. It was just as well that Nichols, calm and ego-free, was in charge. The former Ferrari and McLaren man had enough on his plate as it was.

'When I came along at the beginning of December,' says Nichols, 'the car was under manufacture. So there wasn't really any opportunity to change anything. Instability had been a problem on R1 and they had gone a long way towards trying to cure that. We had the inevitable teething troubles at the first tests, plus time lost with the weather and we had a throttle problem as well. But the initial feeling was that the car was stable. Unfortunately, it wasn't terribly quick!

'There was the perception that the car had not been reliable the previous year. To overcome that, there had been a laudable directive that the engine and gearbox package had to be running by 1 December. But the problem is, if you do that, then it means your rear suspension and a lot of your aero characteristics have to be fixed by late July or August.

'The double whammy came when, having paid a pretty serious price for reliability, we didn't get enough payback. We suffered on the performance side because so much had been fixed early and we didn't really gain as much as we should have done with the reliability.'

It was realistic to expect that Jaguar might mix it with whoever was running in the midfield but even that proved to be a touch optimistic. Irvine's excellent third place at Monaco (which coincided with the first major aero development) was a lone high point in the first two-thirds of the season.

Nichols cites the Nürburgring as an unnoticed example of an excellent job by the team, Irvine claiming a strong seventh on a day when the top three teams had a 100 per cent finishing record. Conversely, the use of the wrong grease during assembly of the fuel collector caused the filter to block just as Irvine was poised to score points at Hockenheim. On that day, Pedro de la Rosa (who replaced Burti after four races) added to the team's frustration by colliding with a Sauber. Overall, though, Nichols has no complaints about his drivers.

'I have always been a big Eddie fan,' says Nichols. 'His strengths are that he is very intelligent and he's naturally quick. A lot of people don't like him but I just think he's kinda fun-loving and a good guy to be around. He has a lot of experience and I think he's a great asset.

'Pedro is a more quiet character! His results weren't brilliant to start with but we didn't do a good job for him in the beginning — there were several reliability issues; several that were safety related — and I'm sure that detuned him. But, once he got his confidence back, he began to turn in some very reasonable performances indeed.'

Despite a very impressive late-season surge as potentially the 'best of the rest', Jaguar had to accept eighth in the constructors' championship, a pathetic return relative to the budget.

After the highly-paid Lauda had expended so much energy getting rid of Rahal, it was tempting to ask: 'Okay Niki. Now what?' That question remained unanswered at the end of another muddled season.

Maurice Hamilton

AS YOU CAN SEE,
WE PUT ALL OUR
EFFORTS INTO
POWERING RACE AND
RALLY CHAMPIONS,
NOT INTO
CREATING ADS.

POWER BY
COSWORTH
www.cosworthracing.com

ASTRA COUPE. *Handles life beautifully*

Congratulations
Jason Plato
British Touring Car
Champion 2001

VAUXHALL
Raising the Standard

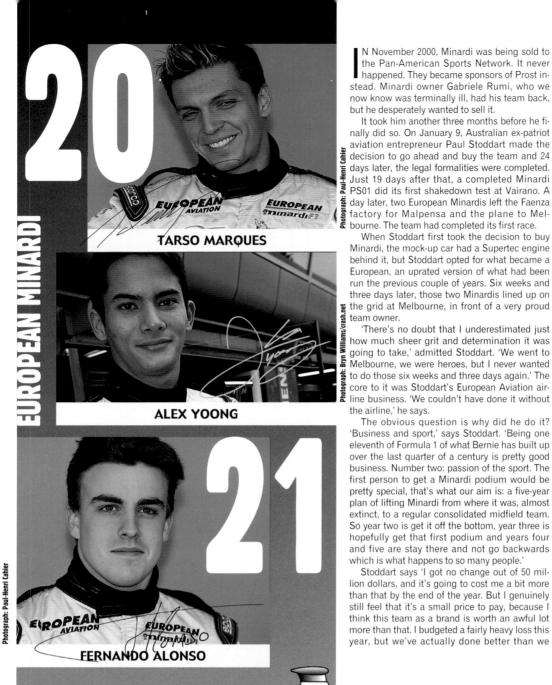

20

TARSO MARQUES

Photograph: Paul-Henri Cahier

ALEX YOONG

Photograph: Bryn Williams/crash.net

21

FERNANDO ALONSO

Photograph: Paul-Henri Cahier

IN November 2000, Minardi was being sold to the Pan-American Sports Network. It never happened. They became sponsors of Prost instead. Minardi owner Gabriele Rumi, who we now know was terminally ill, had his team back, but he desperately wanted to sell it.

It took him another three months before he finally did so. On January 9, Australian ex-patriot aviation entrepreneur Paul Stoddart made the decision to go ahead and buy the team and 24 days later, the legal formalities were completed. Just 19 days after that, a completed Minardi PS01 did its first shakedown test at Vairano. A day later, two European Minardis left the Faenza factory for Malpensa and the plane to Melbourne. The team had completed its first race.

When Stoddart first took the decision to buy Minardi, the mock-up car had a Supertec engine behind it, but Stoddart opted for what became a European, an uprated version of what had been run the previous couple of years. Six weeks and three days later, those two Minardis lined up on the grid at Melbourne, in front of a very proud team owner.

'There's no doubt that I underestimated just how much sheer grit and determination it was going to take,' admitted Stoddart. 'We went to Melbourne, we were heroes, but I never wanted to do those six weeks and three days again.' The core to it was Stoddart's European Aviation airline business. 'We couldn't have done it without the airline,' he says.

The obvious question is why did he do it? 'Business and sport,' says Stoddart. 'Being one eleventh of Formula 1 of what Bernie has built up over the last quarter of a century is pretty good business. Number two: passion of the sport. The first person to get a Minardi podium would be pretty special, that's what our aim is: a five-year plan of lifting Minardi from where it was, almost extinct, to a regular consolidated midfield team. So year two is get it off the bottom, year three is hopefully get that first podium and years four and five are stay there and not go backwards which is what happens to so many people.'

Stoddart says 'I got no change out of 50 million dollars, and it's going to cost me a bit more than that by the end of the year. But I genuinely still feel that it's a small price to pay, because I think this team as a brand is worth an awful lot more than that. I budgeted a fairly heavy loss this year, but we've actually done better than we

thought, so I've got a smile on my face in that department as well.'

Survive is what Minardi did — and more. 'We started off on a high. We went to Malaysia, got both cars home against all the odds. We went to Brazil, got a top-ten finish. This year was just survival and to compete with the professionals and, by God, we've done that.'

The team had two bases: 111 people at Minardi's traditional home in Faenza and 68 in Ledbury, England. Stoddart places huge stock in the race team in Italy, but also gradually developed Ledbury. 'Now it does production, two-seater, F3000, R and D, test team and there's a wind tunnel coming on line. What Minardi has lacked in the past has been resources; it's always had a nice tidy group of people who have done a fantastic job given the resources that they had, but they didn't have the facilities nor the budget. They were doing 20 per cent in-house, 80 per cent out — we're now doing 80–90 per cent in-house between the two production facilities and 10 per cent out.'

That included engine development and some rebuilds in Ledbury, although the main rebuilds were done by Langford and Peck. The engine was crying out for development and Stoddart warned of early-season failures. 'From Imola we had a new bottom-end package which eliminated our somewhat public demonstrations of blow-ups through pistons grabbing, a small gain but a big reliability issue. The next development was a few horsepower and a lot better reliability at the top end before Hockenheim and I am proud to say that for the first time over the past six years one of those engines didn't explode at Hockenheim.'

One down side was the departure of long-time faithful Minardi technical director Gustav Brunner to Toyota, ostensibly made an offer he couldn't refuse, breaking his contract. Stoddart is very bitter about it, but preferred not to comment.

Gabriele Tredozzi took over, producing developments throughout the season. However, the team didn't have a test chassis until the start of the European season, when everyone was working on traction and launch control anyway. 'We were playing catch-up all year,' says Stoddart. 'We had to recruit an aerodynamic team to work what little wind tunnel time we had and get productivity from it. Obviously we shut off like everybody else halfway through the year on this year's car and started on next year's.'

MINARDI PS01-EUROPEAN

SPONSORS	European Aviation, Magnum Corporation, Berhad, Leaseplan, C2C, Sebring Exhausts, Gericom, PDP, Magneti Marelli, Michelin
ENGINE	**Type:** European **No. of cylinders (vee angle):** V10 (72°) **Sparking Plugs:** Champion **Electronics:** Magneti Marelli **Fuel:** Elf **Oil:** Elf
TRANSMISSION	**Gearbox:** Minardi six-speed longitudinal semi-automatic sequential **Driveshafts:** Minardi **Clutch:** AP Racing hand-operated
CHASSIS	**Front suspension:** pullrod-activated torsion springs, carbon-wrapped titanium wishbones **Rear suspension:** pushrod-activated torsion springs and rockers,
	carbon-wrapped titanium wishbones **Suspension dampers:** Sachs **Wheel diameter: front:** 13 in. **rear:** 13 in. **Wheels:** OZ Racing **Tyres:** Michelin
	Brake pads: Brembo/Hitco **Brake discs:** Brembo/Hitco **Brake calipers:** Brembo six-piston **Steering:** Minardi unassisted rack and pinion **Radiators:** Secan
	Fuel tank: ATL **Battery:** Fiamm **Instruments:** Magneti Marelli
DIMENSIONS	**Wheelbase:** 3031 mm **Track: front:** 1480 mm **rear:** 1410 mm **Gearbox weight:** 11.45 kg **Chassis weight (tub):** 75 kg
	Formula weight: 1322.8 lb/600 kg including driver and camera **Fuel capacity:** 25.3 gallons/115 litres

MINARDI
Paul Stoddart - Team Principal
Gustav Brunner/Gabriele Tredozi -
Technical Director
George Ryton - Chief Designer
Loïc Bigois - Chief Aerodynamicist
Tony Lees - Team Manager
Andy Tilley - Chief Engineer
Nigel Steer - Chief Mechanic
Gianvito Amico - Race Engineer Car No. 20,
Tarso Marques/Alex Yoong
Alex Varnava - Race Engineer Car No. 21,
Fernando Alonso

Top left: Fernando Alonso in the Minardi PS01;
the young Spaniard was a protégé of Flavio
Briatore's management company and an
outstanding prospect for the future.
Photograph: Bryn Williams/crash.net

Left: Alex Yoong replaced Tarso Marques for the
Italian Grand Prix, the young Malaysian struggling
to get to grips with F1.
Photograph: Paul-Henri Cahier

Below: Tarso Marques has a rare moment ahead
of Fernando Alonso early in the season.
Photograph: Bryn Williams/crash.net

'We've had two significant upgrades of aero and they've both worked, one much better than the other. We had a small one for Monaco which didn't do us a lot of good and then we had the big one which was supposed to come at Silverstone with the new gearbox, which didn't happen, and we ended up having it at Hockenheim. That was a complete rear end, it was effectively next year's gearbox, next year's rear-end package.' As before, the team built a new titanium gearbox, and in spite of some gremlins, it would figure strongly for the following year.

It would be wrong not to mention the drivers, particularly Fernando Alonso, the young Spaniard who did a fantastic job in his first year, ending the year racing ahead of a Prost, a BAR and both Arrows. His great strength, says Stoddart, is his fantastic recall of every lap.

Tarso Marques was a disappointment, given his experience, while Alex Yoong did the final three races, becoming south-east Asia's first ever Grand Prix driver, but without a ringit's support from the Malaysian government, says Stoddart.

So having more than survived the first year, Stoddart has his sights firmly set on getting off the bottom in the second. The fact that the team had already decided on Asiatech engines as early as September was a recent record in itself for Minardi.

Bob Constanduros

Photograph: Charles Coates/LAT Photographic

HEINZ-HARALD FRENTZEN

PROST ACER

JEAN ALESI

Photograph: Paul-Henri Cahier

GASTON MAZZACANE

Photograph: Paul-Henri Cahier

LUCIANO BURTI

TOMAS ENGE

Photograph: Bryn Williams/crash.net

Photograph: Paul-Henri Cahier

'IT was like a cold shower,' admitted Prost managing director Joan Villadelprat. It had looked so good: pre-season testing times looked very promising, even if the car had been on low fuel. But when it failed to break into the top 12 in qualifying for the first race — and didn't improve — the writing was on the wall. 2001 was a year of survival.

Not that the team didn't know all about that. The previous year had been just the same, with the famously temperamental Peugeot engines. They went and Alain Prost signed up to take Ferrari's engine, gearbox and whole rear end.

Meanwhile the AP04 was designed by Alan Jenkins's predecessor, before Henri Durand took charge of the technical team in January — after the 2001 car had had its first test.

Prost himself had wisely signed up a new management structure, with Villadelprat coming in to take over the day-to-day management, leaving Alain as president. The Spaniard had five directors beneath him: finance, marketing, sporting, operations and technical. They, in turn, had heads of departments reporting to them. The staff was still around 250 people strong, with another 40 at John Barnard's establishment in England. Everything was in place.

What wasn't in place was the finance. Several major sponsors defected at the end of 2000, including Gauloises, PlayStation, Yahoo, Total and Agfa. This lack of stability prompted several members of the technical staff to leave as well. It caused Alain to comment 'I would prefer to have a lower budget but to know what is happening in the next five years rather than having a big budget one year and then dropping down the next. That's where we are this year.'

There was no point in closing the doors; they would just have to make do with what they could get. Pan-American Sports Network were tempted to support Prost rather than buy Minardi, bringing with them Gaston Mazzacane, albeit until the second European Grand Prix when he was replaced by Luciano Burti.

Pedro Diniz and family had become shareholders, bringing with them Parmalat support and paying for the Ferrari engines, but before the end of the season, that interest had waned.

So the testing times looked good, and might have tempted other sponsors. But by race two, the team knew that it was going to struggle. They were badly affected by Michelin's lack of

knowledge when it came to circuits at which they hadn't tested. Furthermore, their Ferrari rear suspension had been designed to work with Bridgestones. Development was needed, but there wasn't the money available, and nor did they have, in Jean Alesi, the greatest test driver in the world.

However, while Jean was qualifying on average around 15th, he was finishing, usually in the top ten. Reliability was good, and they were battling with Jaguar and Benetton, two teams infinitely better financed than they were. When Alesi scored a point in Monaco, it was like a victory for anyone else.

And in the next race, he scored two more. But two races later, it all turned sour.

Prost had done a fair amount of development. They had worked on the rear suspension, there had been brake problems early on which had been solved, to Jean's satisfaction — and he's hard on brakes. There were little bits on the aerodynamic side, including a new front wing and engine cover. At Magny-Cours, Alesi was impressed by the new aero package.

But for financial reasons, it had been tested in a straight line and not on a circuit. In short, it didn't work. Alesi had a massive spin in the first corner and, in true Alesi style, was furious. He failed to turn up for a de-brief altogether and, after the race, went to the press. Alain, in turn, warned him that he would be receiving a letter about his professional conduct and performance. It was the last straw. After scoring another point in the German Grand Prix, the Frenchman announced that he was quitting the team.

It was a strange quirk of fate for both drivers that Heinz-Harald Frentzen had received his marching orders at the same time from Jordan. They did a direct swap — although while Alesi's was financially more rewarding, Frentzen's was considerably more beneficial to his team from a technical point of view. 'Jean can do 200 laps and spend five, ten minutes with you on the behaviour of the car, he can summarise it in one minute,' said an engineer. 'Frentzen can do five laps and spend two hours going around and around identifying more little things, more problems and I think that, as a young team that we are, that's what we need, somebody to push us in the right direction and make us work and think.'

Frentzen virtually redesigned the rear suspension. He even put the car fourth on the grid in

PROST AP04-ACER

SPONSORS	PSN, Acer, Adecco, Parmalat, Dark Dog, Brastemp, Catia Solutions, Altran, New Man, Michelin, Magneti Marelli
ENGINE	Type: **Acer** No. of cylinders (vee angle): **V10 (90°)** Electronics: **Magneti Marelli** Fuel: **Shell** Oil: **Shell**
TRANSMISSION	Gearbox: **Ferrari titanium and carbon seven-speed longitudinal semi-automatic sequential** Driveshafts: **Metalore/Pankl** Clutch: **AP Racing hand-operated**
CHASSIS	Front suspension: **torsion bars, dampers** Rear suspension: **torsion bars, dampers** Suspension dampers: **Sachs** Wheel diameter: front: **13 in.** rear: **13in.**
	Wheels: **BBS** Tyres: **Michelin** Brake pads: **Carbone Industrie/Brembo/Hitco** Brake discs: **Carbone Industrie/Brembo/Hitco** Brake calipers: **Brembo**
	Steering: **Prost unassisted** Radiators: **Secan/Marston** Fuel tank: **ATL** Battery: **Fiamm** Instruments: **Prost**
DIMENSIONS	Wheelbase: **3160 mm** Track: front: **1450 mm** rear: **1420 mm** Formula weight: **1322.8 lb/600 kg including driver** Fuel capacity: **140 litres/103 kg**

ALAIN PROST

PROST

Alain Prost - Team Principal
Joan Villadelprat - Managing Director
Henri Durand - Technical Director
Jean-Paul Gousset - Deputy Technical Director
Vincent Gaillardot - Chief Engineer
Gabriele Pagliarini - Chief Mechanic
John Barnard - Exclusive Consultant
John Walton - Team Manager
Andy Le Fleming - Race Engineer Car No. 22,
Jean Alesi/Heinz-Harald Frentzen
Jean-François Sinteff - Race Engineer Car No. 23,
Gaston Mazzacane/Luciano Burti/Tomas Enge

HENRI DURAND   **JOAN VILLADELPRAT**

JOHN WALTON   **ANDY LE FLEMING**

GABRIELE PAGLIARINI   **JEAN-FRANÇOIS SINTEFF**

Belgium and went on to outqualify the driver he replaced in Italy as well. By this time, however, team-mate Burti, who had been quietly making his own progress, had suffered a huge accident in the Belgian Grand Prix in which he had suffered such serious concussion that he had been advised to take the rest of the year off.

His replacement was Czech driver Tomas Enge, who had been the team's test driver, although by this stage testing had been abandoned for the year. Enge did the last three races and, apart from a big practice accident at Suzuka, certainly didn't disgrace himself.

But the year ended as it had started, with Alain trying to secure his team's financial future as the technical team got its head down to prepare for another year.

Bob Constanduros

Top left: Alesi scored valuable points for the team before his mid-season departure.
Photograph: Paul-Henri Cahier

Centre: Luciano Burti switched from Jaguar to Prost but his season would end dramatically with a high-speed smash in the Belgian Grand Prix.

Centre left: Prost and Villadelprat confer.
Both photographs: Bryn Williams/crash.net

Above left: Heinz-Harald Frentzen brought experience and an analytical approach to the AP04's development in the second half of the season.
Photograph: Paul-Henri Cahier

Left: Gaston Mazzacane in Malaysia — he was replaced with Burti after just four races.
Photograph: Clive Mason/Allsport-Getty Images

MICHELE ALBORETO

MICHELE Alboreto very nearly became one of the greatest of Italian sporting heroes in the summer of 1985 when he seemed set to win the World Championship at the wheel of the purposeful Ferrari 156/85. In the event, a spate of late-season engine failures helped hand the title to the

McLaren-mounted Alain Prost.

Alboreto was a fine Grand Prix driver. Yet motor racing meant more to him than simply the glitz and hype of the F1 pit lane. Put simply, the curly-haired Italian was addicted to driving racing cars and that addiction cost him his life when he crashed fatally in April 2001 testing an Audi R8 at the Lausitzring in preparation for Le Mans.

Alboreto's great hero was the brilliant Swedish Lotus star Ronnie Peterson. He painted his helmet the same yellow and

blue colours as Ronnie's and admitted that, as a teenager, he was the one waving a Swedish flag in the grandstand at Monza, isolated in a sea of Ferrari fans.

Happily, it didn't work against him. Having come to prominence on the European F2 scene, Alboreto was promoted to the F1 Tyrrell team in time for the 1981 San Marino GP.

Michele spent just under three years with Tyrrell, honing his talents to the point where he was ripe for the big time. He also came to Maranello with two Grand Prix victories already under his belt. The first came in the baking heat of Las Vegas at the end of 1983, through the car park of the Caesars Palace casino.

My colleague Eoin Young saw some favourable betting odds for Alboreto and immediately invested a fistful of dollars. Alboreto duly delivered an outside — but perhaps not totally unexpected — victory when the superstars hit trouble.

Michele won again for Ken through the streets of Detroit the following summer before signing up with the Prancing Horse.

Enzo Ferrari put aside his reservations about employing his native drivers and hired Alboreto, the first Italian to drive an F1 Ferrari since Arturo Merzario more than a decade earlier. The Commendatore reckoned Italian drivers were not generally worth the extra aggravation he received in the country's national press, but Alboreto looked a rather special proposition.

There was also the unspoken possibility that here might be the first home-grown star to win a title at the wheel of one of the famous Italian machines since Alberto Ascari's double championship victories of 1952–'53. Close, as they say, but no cigar.

As it turned out, 1984 proved to be the year of the dominant Michelin-shod McLaren-TAGs which won 12 of the season's 15 races. Michele sneaked a win for Ferrari and Goodyear in the Belgian GP at Zolder, but otherwise it was thin milk for the popular Milanese.

At the end of that season Michelin quit F1 and McLaren ran head-to-head against Ferrari on Goodyear rubber for 1985. Michele really caught his stride, storming to wins at Montreal and Nürburgring to consolidate his lead at the head of the championship table. Then it all went wrong and Prost inexorably closed the gap.

Alboreto remained with Ferrari for another three years, driving variously alongside team-mates René Arnoux, Stefan Johansson and Gerhard Berger. Finally, he was dropped from the team and replaced with Nigel Mansell for 1989.

He went back to Tyrrell briefly, but quit mid-way through the season due to clashing sponsorship interests. Thereafter Alboreto's F1 career went into gentle decline and he drove for Larrousse, Footwork Arrows and Minardi, second-division operations all. He finally quit F1 at the end of 1994, scoring his last point for Minardi that year at Monaco after a respectable showing.

Yet he wasn't just an F1 driver. Michele Alboreto was a racing driver. For him, to participate was first and foremost his driving passion. Berger said of their last meeting:

'He loved just driving racing cars. He said to me "Hey, Gerhard, you shouldn't be doing what you're doing now. Come with me. We'll ring up Stefan [Johansson] and all go sports car racing together."

'I told him that wasn't for me, and I never saw him again. When I joined him at Ferrari in 1987 I suppose I added to the pressure he was already under, but he never showed any signs of resentment. For me, Michele was always the perfect Italian gentleman.'

Alboreto was far from a soft touch, though. Lurking beneath the surface was a volatile streak. After Ayrton Senna put his Ferrari on the grass at Hockenheim in 1987 at 190 mph, he paid the Brazilian back at the following race by 'brake testing' his Lotus-Honda, knocking off its nose section.

Perhaps one of Alboreto's great disappointments came in the '88 Italian GP where he had to take second place behind Berger in this classic event which all too rarely had been won by an Italian driver.

After F1, Michele raced on in touring cars and sports cars, sharing the winning Porsche at Le Mans in 1997. This unbridled enthusiasm for cars and motor racing made it somehow easier for Alboreto to come to terms with the fact that he was an ex-Ferrari driver, all too often a tag which attracts a rather unforgiving response in Italian motor racing circles.

Overwhelmingly, Michele Alboreto was a man who radiated charm and style. British fans saw him for the last time in the summer of 2000 when he drove the Type D Auto Union at the Goodwood Festival of Speed. They will have identified with him and shared from afar the sadness of his wife Nadia and his two daughters, Alice and Naomi, of whom he was so proud. *Alan Henry*

He was 44 years old.

Photograph: Paul-Henri Cahier

VITTORIO BRAMBILLA

IT is often the way that sportsmen who spectacularly distinguish themselves in their own particular field of endeavour die in a manner ironically far from their chosen calling. So it was with Vittorio Brambilla, the wild man of the Italian motor racing milieu in the 1970s, who succumbed to a heart attack while gardening at his home in Monza on the afternoon of the Monaco Grand Prix.

It was the least likely fate imaginable for the 63-year-old who, in his competitive heyday, took considerable delight in facing down all manner of high-speed risks at the wheel of a single-seater racing car.

Brambilla's defining achievement was his victory in the 1975 Austrian Grand Prix, a rain-soaked race which was flagged to a halt at half-distance. Vittorio, brimming over with delight at his achievement in the cockpit of his bright orange works March 751, took the chequered flag and began punching the air with delight — only to spin into the guard rail a few hundred yards after the finishing line. Undaunted, he completed the slowing down lap with the nose of his car virtually hanging off.

Brambilla came to racing prominence in the wake of his elder brother Ernestino — always known as 'Tino' — and, like his brother, had been something of a dab hand in motor cycle racing before switching to four wheels. He drove first in F3 and then graduated to F2, making quite a name for himself at the wheel of a Brabham BT30 entered by Scuderia Alla D'Oro and later continuing with a March-BMW into the 1973 season by which time he was beginning to temper his enthusiasm with a degree of judgement and emerged as quite a consistent, reliable performer.

With sponsorship from the Beta tools company, he eventually graduated to F1 with the March team, not only highlighting the '75 season with his Austrian victory but also claiming pole for the Swedish GP at Anderstorp. Nobody ever knew quite how he managed it — and there was much speculation that the timing beam might have been 'helped' by a timely swipe with a pit signalling board — but he led for a healthy distance in the opening stages. Whether it was through sheer merit or the reluctance of his rivals to try and overtake him was difficult to conclude.

After his Austrian GP victory, Vittorio remained with March until the end of 1975 after which a three-year stint with Team Surtees produced a succession of stirring performances, but all too frequently he overdrove the machinery and paid the price with accidents and mechanical retirements.

He also drove for the Alfa Romeo sports car team in 1977 helping the famous Milan-based marque win the World Championship for Sportscars with the T33SC/12. Vittorio was a huge fan and later drove for the F1 Alfa Romeo team. He suffered serious head injuries in the Monza startline accident which claimed the life of Ronnie Peterson at the 1978 Italian GP, but happily recovered to race again until the end of 1980.

An old-fashioned racer with a keen mechanical knowledge, Vittorio Brambilla was nevertheless far removed from the technocrats of the new millennium. His abiding qualities were a lack of complexity and overwhelming enthusiasm. He loved his sport, and it always showed. *Alan Henry*

Photograph: LAT Photographic

BOB WOLLEK

Photograph: LAT Photographic

FIRST we knew him as 'Smiling Bob', because he so seldom did. Then he was 'Brilliant Bob', because in a Group C Porsche he invariably was. Latterly, he became 'Uncle Bob'. That, too, was a fitting description of Bob Wollek and explains why his death in a senseless road accident on the eve of what should have been his 11th participation in the Sebring 12 Hours was so keenly felt in a branch of the sport in which he was truly a legend.

At the age of 57, he was a mentor to many, a friend to yet more. And those who didn't warm to this sometimes prickly character couldn't help but admire him. After a career spanning more than 30 years, the Frenchman was more than just a driver, he was part of the family of sports car racing.

The legend of Wollek owes as much to his longevity at the top of the sport as it does to an impressive record that included four victories in the Daytona 24 Hours and numerous more big wins on both sides of the Atlantic. What set him apart from fellow sports car superstars, the likes of Jacky Ickx and Derek Bell, was that he continued to race at the highest level into his late 50s.

Some of his best years were after he had passed his half-century, nowhere more so than at Le Mans, the race he spent 30 years unsuccessfully trying to win. Every year from 1994 to 1998 he was a genuine contender for victory and finished an unlucky second no fewer than three times in that period.

His wasn't a conventional racing career, which Wollek reckoned went a long way to explaining why he continued to compete into his late 50s. A former member of the French ski team, he didn't take up motor sport until he was 24. What's more, it didn't become his full-time job until the mid-1990s. Only then did he sell the car dealership in Strasbourg.

Wollek began his career in sports cars and apart from a brief flirtation with Formula 2 competed almost exclusively in the long-distance discipline. He enjoyed three separate stints as a factory Porsche driver in the 1970s, '80s and '90s, but he also drove for Matra, Lancia and Jaguar down the years.

Most reckon Wollek was at his zenith in the Group C era. He was something special in a Porsche 956 and its close cousin, the 962. He could mix it on sheer pace with anyone and, just as importantly, was unsurpassed in his ability to eke out a tank of gas in the new 'fuel formula'.

This skill, which even Wollek couldn't explain, helped the Joest Porsche team to an unexpected victory over the works cars when the 956 first appeared in private hands at Monza in 1983.

The partnership between Wollek and Joest was a special one. Together they won the European Endurance Championship in 1983 and at the end of the decade they were still at the forefront of the Porsche challenge with the ageing 962.

In between times, Wollek moved to Lancia for a two-year stint that coincided with Joest's back-to-back Le Mans victories in 1984–'85. It must have been preordained.

Bob Wollek will always be remembered as the man who never won Le Mans. *Gary Watkins*

Photograph: Paul-Henri Cahier

KEN TYRRELL

KEN Tyrrell's death in the early hours of 25 August, after a long battle against cancer, deprived motor racing of one of its most significant bedrock personalities of the post-war motor racing era.

As a team owner, he stumbled into the role of constructor almost unintentionally. He only built the first Tyrrell-Ford 001 in 1970 because he was so disappointed with the performance of the customer March 701s which future FIA president Max Mosley had sold him after it became clear that he couldn't continue with the French Matra chassis which had carried Jackie Stewart to the 1969 World Championship.

As a man, he was a straight-talking, no-nonsense individual who lived for his family and his motor racing. Pragmatic and unfussed, his career was highlighted by his great partnership with Jackie Stewart which yielded three World Championships in 1969, '71 and '73. Yet there was much more to the Tyrrell motor racing CV than those glory days with the brilliant Scottish driver who would remain steadfast as a close friend and respectful admirer to the very end of Ken's life.

Amazingly, Ken became embroiled in motor racing by accident. In 1951 the local football club at Ockham, in rural Surrey, for whom he used to play, organised a trip to Silverstone. 'It could just as easily have been the seaside at Brighton or Bognor,' he later remembered.

'The supporting race was for 500 cc F3 cars and one of the competitors was a guy called Alan Brown who I saw from the programme came from Guildford, where I lived at that time. So when I got home, I went round and knocked on Alan Brown's door and said "I saw you racing at Silverstone, sir — could I see your car?"'

'Well, he kept his car in a large garage in the garden of a nursery which his mother ran. So he showed me round the car, told me a little bit about it, and at the end of the year I bought it from him.'

Ken raced through much of the 1950s, eventually going into partnership with Alan Brown and Cecil Libowitz in 1958 to run a pair of Cooper F2 cars on an international basis. 'When eventually I discovered I could only finish fifth, sixth or seventh at this level, it didn't satisfy me,' he said.

'Then on one occasion I loaned the car to Michael Taylor at Aintree and he drove much better than I did. So I decided that team management was my particular slot.'

Tyrrell remained self-effacing about his perceived reputation as a talent spotter, but he didn't quite see it that way. 'In the early 1960s, most of the people we were racing against were owner-drivers competing for fun, but I was free to sign up whoever I thought was the best driver.'

Most memorably, he recruited Jackie Stewart after giving the young Scot a test drive at Goodwood in his F3 Cooper-BMC during which he outpaced established F1 star Bruce McLaren in the same machine. It was the start of a hugely successful professional and personal relationship.

After Stewart's glory years, Ken had hoped to sustain the momentum of that great partnership into 1974, promoting Jackie's team-mate François Cevert to the team leadership after Stewart's retirement. Sadly, Cevert was killed practising for the 1973 US Grand Prix at Watkins Glen and the crucial continuity was broken.

'François absolutely worshipped Jackie as his absolute idol,' recalled Ken. 'I remember Jackie's last F1 win, in the '73 German GP at Nürburgring, where they finished in 1-2 formation. At the end of the race he stepped out of the car and said "François could have passed me any time he liked. He was flat quicker than I was."

'But the point was that François stayed in his wheel tracks because he still felt he had a lot to learn from Jackie. And, of course, he knew that Jackie was retiring at the end of the year, and that his time would come.'

There would be no more World Championships for the Tyrrell team, but Ken's cars would continue their business in the F1 pit lane for another 25 years before he sold up to British American Racing in 1998. Jody Scheckter, Stefan Bellof, Martin Brundle, Patrick Depailler and Jean Alesi were just a handful of the rising stars who passed through the Tyrrell academy.

Racing for Ken Tyrrell was always very much a family affair. His wife Norah scarcely ever missed a race and their younger son Bob also became deeply involved in managing the business.

Ken Tyrrell had a rough-hewn dignity and reassuring sense of perspective in a sport which had been transformed from an essentially amateur pastime to a hard-nosed professional business during his half-century's involvement. He was a giant of a man and will be sorely missed. *Alan Henry*

APPRECIATIONS

JOHN COOPER

JOHN Cooper, the junior half of the famous father-and-son partnership which revolutionised Grand Prix racing in the 1950s, died on 24 December last at the age of 77.

John Cooper was born on 17 July 1923. His father Charles, an industrious and hard-working man, had an instinctive nose for business and managed successfully to combine this with a growing interest in motor racing.

In 1946 the Coopers built a 500 cc motor cycle-engined hillclimb special that would lay the foundations for their commercial racing car business. By 1948 they were in serious production making 500 cc F3 cars.

Cooper Cars steadily went from strength to strength. Mike Hawthorn, later to become Britain's first World Champion driver in 1958, cut his international racing teeth in a Formula 2 Cooper-Bristol in 1952. But it was in 1958 that Cooper was propelled into the spotlight when Stirling Moss won the Argentine Grand Prix at Buenos Aires in privateer Rob Walker's 2.2-litre Cooper-Climax.

It was a seminal turning point in post-war F1 history and, within two years, virtually all the cars on the starting grid would mimic Cooper's rear-engined layout.

The Cooper works at Surbiton, in Surrey, were dark, dank and dingy, his staff underpaid and often grumbling. Yet the genial, pipe-smoking John Cooper was always straining at the harness of Charles's penny-pinching ways.

Rows between father and son were therefore predictable and numerous. Yet by 1959 they had recruited the rugged Australian Jack Brabham to lead their own F1 team and stormed to two consecutive World Championship titles.

In the summer of 1963 John Cooper was badly injured in a terrible road accident in his prototype twin-engined Mini-Cooper saloon. He took many months to recover and Ken Tyrrell obligingly took over as Cooper team manager while he recuperated.

The following year was marked by Charles Cooper's death at the age of 71, after which the dwindling fortunes of his F1 team caused the son to sit back and take stock. He therefore proved particularly receptive to an offer for his company from the Chipstead Garages group — controlled by entrepreneur Mario Tozzi-Condivi and Marks and Spencer heir Jonathan Sieff — to buy out the company for around £200,000.

Although now out of John Cooper's immediate control, John Surtees drove a Cooper-Maserati to victory in the 1966 Mexican GP and the late Pedro Rodriguez followed that up with victory in the 1967 South African Grand Prix at Kyalami.

The company also received royalties from the British Motor Corporation for each of the Mini-Cooper saloons sold during the 1960s when they became one of the most familiar fashion items, a touchstone for their time.

In 1969 John Cooper retired to Ferring, on the Sussex coast, where he opened a small garage business. A genial, gregarious man with a wry sense of humour, he would happily reminisce about his great days in motor racing without a hint of regret at potential missed opportunities. *Alan Henry*

Photograph: LAT Photographic

WALTER HAYES

Photograph courtesy of Ford Motor Company

WALTER Hayes, who died on 26 December 2001 at the age of 76, was the driving force behind Ford's emergence as a Formula 1 power during the 1960s. Just as John and Charles Cooper revolutionised Grand Prix chassis design with their rear-engined concept, so Hayes proved the father of the most impressive F1 engine of all time, the Ford-Cosworth DFV.

The son of a printer, Walter Hayes became the editor of the now-defunct *Sunday Dispatch* newspaper at the age of 32. He left to join Ford in 1962, starting a glittering career which ended with his retirement as a Vice President of Ford of Europe in 1989.

Stuart Turner, the former Director of Motorsport for Ford of Europe and a shrewd observer of human nature, described Hayes as 'one of the giants of the game — a man who had an unconventional approach, yet an outstandingly mature man.'

He recalled their times together when they shared adjoining offices at Ford's headquarters at Warley, near Brentwood, on the eastern fringes of London.

'A number of times I went into his office and found Walter with his feet up on the desk, staring at the ceiling, just thinking,' said Turner. 'He spent a lot of time thinking and had a broad, adult and mature view of all the issues he dealt with as a result.'

Hayes was also the mastermind behind the foundation of Ford's AVO (Advanced Vehicles Operation) which produced a variety of high performance variants of their road cars in the early 1970s. He later became Vice President of Public Affairs for Ford worldwide, based in Detroit, and was one of the few European high-flyers to have made his mark inside the Ford empire on its home turf.

Hayes also became Henry Ford II's biographer and, although officially retiring in 1989, was tempted out of retirement when Ford purchased the tottering Aston Martin sports car company.

Hayes persuaded company founder Sir David Brown to return as honorary life president and he agreed, at Hayes's suggestion, to lend his initials to the company's commercially life-saving DB7 coupé. It revived a tradition stretching back to the original immediate post-war Aston Martin DB1 and was yet another feather in Walter Hayes's cap.

Possibly Hayes's greatest triumph was a victory of sheer diplomacy. Originally the Cosworth DFV V8 was developed exclusively for Lotus, but after the sensational Type 49 won first time out with Jim Clark in the 1967 Dutch Grand Prix, Walter realised that he would have to persuade Colin Chapman to agree that the engine be made available to be purchased by other teams.

'Otherwise, there is no reason why anyone else should ever win,' he said. Chapman shrugged, muttered 'oh well, what a pity.' And immediately agreed. It took a man of Walter Hayes's sheer calibre and confidence to pull off a deal like that. *Alan Henry*

GRANDS PRIX
2001

Photograph: Paul-Henri Cahier

FIA WORLD CHAMPIONSHIP • ROUND 1

AUSTRALIAN
grand prix

1st - M. SCHUMACHER • 2nd - COULTHARD • 3rd - BARRICHELLO

Above: Starting as he means to continue. Michael Schumacher takes the chequered flag to get his title defence off to a flying start.
Photograph: Paul-Henri Cahier

Right: The podium ceremony was an understandably low-key affair after the drivers were told about the death of a marshal due to flying debris. Schumacher, flanked by second- and third-placemen Coulthard and Barrichello, look immersed in thought.
Photograph: Mark Thompson/Allsport-Getty Images

THE 2001 FIA Formula 1 World Championship opened on a tragic note in Melbourne with the death of a trackside marshal taking the gilt off Michael Schumacher's dominant demonstration at the wheel of the new Ferrari F2001 which led from pole position to a convincing victory.

Graham Beveridge, a 52-year-old volunteer official, was killed by flying debris from an early race collision, just six months after his Italian contemporary Paolo Ghislimberti died under almost identical circumstances at Monza.

The tragedy at Melbourne was triggered when Jacques Villeneuve's BAR-Honda was launched into the scenery after it ran into the back of Ralf Schumacher's Williams-BMW at around 170 mph under braking for the third turn as they battled for sixth place on only the fifth lap of the race.

The Canadian driver's machine came within an ace of clearing the double-height spectator fence, but fortunately finished its crazy flight embedded in a gravel trap. Beveridge was killed by a flying wheel which, by cruel chance, managed to sneak through a tiny access aperture in the sturdy chain-link fencing.

Ralf Schumacher was amazed by the incident, BMW Williams computer traces confirming to the team's satisfaction that he went onto the brakes at precisely the same point as he had on previous laps. 'I got the feeling that he [Villeneuve] wasn't even trying to brake,' said Schumacher. 'I don't know what he was doing, to be honest.'

Below: **BAR boss Craig Pollock — visions of Gilles Villeneuve's fatal accident went through his mind after Jacques crashed into the back of Ralf Schumacher.**
Photograph: Bryn Williams/crash.net

Below centre: **Ralf Schumacher (left) and Jacques Villeneuve (separated by a marshal) look ashen-faced after their tangle, reflecting the realisation of their fortunate escape.**
Photograph: Robert Cianflone/Allsport-Getty Images

The ferocity of the accident understandably shook BAR team chief Craig Pollock back on the pit wall. 'It's the first time I've seen Jacques in an accident when I was worried,' he said.

'The reason is that I studied the accident his father [Gilles, who was killed practising for the 1982 Belgian GP] had and it was exactly the same.

'The only thing is that Gilles didn't go into the barriers and his seat belts gave in. In this one, I saw Jacques going straight towards the wall and then I thought about Greg Moore [the Canadian Champ car driver killed at Fontana in 1999]. The cars can hold up perfectly but the guys inside just cannot sustain the shock.'

The accident understandably cast a huge cloud over the event and while delighted Ferrari fans invaded the circuit to celebrate Michael Schumacher's success, unaware of the tragedy which had unfolded elsewhere on the circuit, the top three drivers clearly took very little pleasure from their achievements.

'We are all very shocked about this,' said a visibly shaken David Coulthard, runner-up in the McLaren-Mercedes MP4/16. 'We must once again have a long look at track safety and make

Inset, above left: **Ferrari fans cheer their heroes.**

Inset, centre left: **The safety car had its first deployment of the season earlier than most were expecting.**
Both photographs: Bryn Williams/crash.net

Right: Juan Pablo Montoya accelerates away to start the first weekend of his career as an F1 driver.

Below: New man at Jaguar, Niki Lauda.

Below right: Jenson Button certainly didn't have an easy time getting to grips with his new mount, the Benetton-Renault B201.
All photographs: Paul-Henri Cahier

Diary

November 2000

FIA changes course as it recommends acceptance of F1 technical working group's wish to legalise traction control for the start of the 2001 season.

Doubts cast over whether Kimi Räikkönen will be granted a super licence for the new season.

December 2000

Ferrari vetoes introduction of traction control until the fifth race of 2001.

Walter Hayes, driving force behind Ford's F1 involvement from the 1960s, dies.

John Cooper, F1 pioneer and the man who popularised rear-engined Grand Prix technology, dies.

January 2001

Niki Lauda appointed president of Ford's Premier Automotive Group with special responsibility for Jaguar F1 team.

February 2001

NASCAR legend Dale Earnhardt killed in Daytona 500.

Ross Brawn, Rory Byrne, Jean Todt and Paolo Martinelli extend their contracts with the Ferrari F1 team until 2004.

FIA threatens to re-negotiate long-term F1 commercial rights unless Bernie Ecclestone speeds up payments due under deal to extend those rights for 100 years from 2011.

MELBOURNE QUALIFYING

Michael Schumacher warmed up for qualifying by flipping his Ferrari F2001 into a gravel trap during Friday's first free practice session, the World Champion walking away from the episode with characteristic reserve after the battered, but repairable car landed back on its wheels.

The car was repaired in time for Saturday practice, although it seemed ironic that the accident occurred the day after Schumacher had been ordered by a Belgian court to wear a specific brand of crash helmet or face the prospect of paying thousands of dollars in fines. The Belgian distributors of the US Bell helmets company had ruled that he would have to pay $110,000 a day in penalties if he did not revert to wearing their products.

The case arose after Schumacher was spotted wearing a Schuberth Helme helmet during testing in Spain the previous month and Sports Europe claimed that this breached a contract he had with them to wear their Bell helmets in all sporting events in 2001. Thankfully, he had to put neither product to the test when his Ferrari flipped over.

Come qualifying, however, there were no such setbacks. Michael surged to pole position with Rubens joining him on the front row, the reigning World Champion cutting a best lap in 1m 26.892s — the pressure of F1's new tyre war contributing to his slicing an amazing 3.7s off Mika Häkkinen's 2000 pole position best.

Häkkinen qualified the McLaren third on the inside of the second row with a 1m 27.461s, frustrated that his best lap had been interrupted when the session was red flagged when Luciano Burti's Jaguar R2 slammed into a barrier after a left rear suspension breakage.

Fourth place on the grid fell to a delighted Heinz-Harald Frentzen (1m 27.658s). 'The cat is now out of the bag,' he grinned. 'This is one of the best Jordans I have ever driven.' Team-mate Jarno Trulli was, by contrast, left baffled that the handling balance he'd enjoyed in free practice had ebbed away and he had to settle for seventh on 1m 28.377s.

The BAR-Hondas of Jacques Villeneuve (1m 28.435s) and Olivier Panis (1m 28.518s) wound up eighth and ninth fastest, the Canadian steaming slightly after losing a bargeboard on his third run when he was chopped by Montoya.

Heidfeld did a super job placing the Sauber tenth and although Räikkönen was 0.3s slower in 13th place, the young Finn had achieved his best time on a lap which saw him forced to overtake two other cars. He looked born to the F1 business.

Juan Montoya struggled slightly with excessive understeer and was angry when Enrique Bernoldi's Arrows baulked him on his fourth run. The Colombian managed a 1m 28.738s best on his first F1 qualifying attempt for 11th fastest, just ahead of Eddie Irvine who did a respectable job in the Jaguar R2 on 1m 28.965s.

Behind Räikkönen, Jean Alesi struggled for aero balance with the new Prost AP04 ahead of Jos Verstappen's Arrows and the embattled Benetton B201s of Jenson Button (1m 30.035s) and Giancarlo Fisichella (1m 30.209s). Button's car needed a gearbox change after the morning free practice session and Fisichella's race car suffered a water leak, forcing him to switch to the spare car which developed a brake problem.

Bernoldi, Alonso and the struggling Mazzacane were next with Luciano Burti, bruised and battered after a big shunt when a left rear suspension pushrod broke, lining his Jaguar up on the back row of the grid alongside pay-driver Tarso Marques in the other Minardi PS01.

improvements to help the situation of those who give their time to enable us to go racing.

'That said, I had a very straightforward race and was happy to pick up six points, but that seems very insignificant when there is a loss of life involved.'

In pure racing terms, it had been business as usual at the front of the field, although the only man who seemed genuinely capable of getting on terms with Schumacher's Ferrari was his old sparring partner Mika Häkkinen. The Finn's McLaren-Mercedes was just over 4s behind when it crashed out of the race on the 26th lap after the failure of a lower right front wishbone joint.

McLarens don't often break, and what made this so frustrating was the fact that the British team reckoned it had struck just the right strategy to win the race. Häkkinen was happily unhurt despite being lightly winged by flying debris as he slammed into the tyre barriers, leaving team chief Ron Dennis and his crew to watch as Coulthard at least salvaged something from the day with a strong second place.

'Mika was carrying more fuel than Michael,' said Dennis, 'so we were planning to stop later than the Ferrari. I believe this was a winning strategy and I'm satisfied that we will be even more competitive at the second race in Malaysia.'

Into third place, Rubens Barrichello rounded off a very satisfying day for Maranello, vaulting Ferrari into a decisive early lead of the constructors' championship.

For his part, Coulthard had survived a lurid moment when he was squeezed between the impressive Jordan-Honda of Heinz-Harald Frentzen and Ralf Schumacher's Williams as they accelerated away from the grid.

'It was the worst scenario with my front wheels in front of their rear wheels as we made contact, but thankfully they moved apart and made room for me,' said Coulthard who performed strongly to lead briefly for four laps later in the race as Schumacher ducked in for fuel.

In the opening stages the Scot ran fourth, but took full advantage of a lucky break to vault ahead of Barrichello to take second place on lap 34. As the two cars slammed over the timing line, new boy Fernando Alonso accelerated out of the pits and Barrichello was momentarily baulked by the young Spaniard's Minardi going through the first corner.

With perfect timing, Coulthard took a run at him down towards the third turn, neatly outfumbling him for the place and then leaving him in the dust as he chased off after Schumacher.

Barrichello had earlier scuppered Frentzen's chances when he nudged the Jordan driver into a spin on lap 3, dropping the hapless Heinz-Harald back to 16th. Both drivers were lucky to get away without damage, although Frentzen's right rear wheel rim was bent as a result. Frentzen's subsequent recovery to finish sixth, hard on the heels of Nick Heidfeld's impressive Sauber C20, would thereafter be one of the strongest single drives of the race.

For his part, Barrichello struggled for the rest of the race. 'The impact with Frentzen affected the toe-in on the left front wheel,' he

explained, 'and from then on I couldn't keep on the pace. In fact, at the end of the race my left front tyre was ruined.

'Then Alonso probably did not notice the blue flags as he is a new boy and I had no space, so I had to go on the grass and David got past me. Finally, towards the end, Ross Brawn told me to back off because I had a slight oil problem.'

Frentzen's view of the incident was a little less benign. 'I was pleased with my start, although Coulthard and I touched wheels before the first corner,' he said.

'The car was very well balanced and I was enjoying the race, but then on my racing line Barrichello hit me from behind while trying to overtake me and pushed me into a spin. That ruined the race for me.

'After these two incidents the car was suffering with understeer. I chased [Nick] Heidfeld for the last ten laps and did everything I could, but was not able to close the gap.'

In fourth place, Olivier Panis drove a measured race in the promising BAR-Honda 003 only to have 25s added to his overall race time as a penalty for passing under a yellow flag and demoted out of the points. Heidfeld proved his F1 stature by scoring the first points of his career, barely a second ahead of the hard-charging Frentzen.

The Sauber C20, designed by Sergio Rinland prior to his abrupt replacement on the Swiss squad's engineering team late in the car's development, proved outstandingly competitive, comprehensively shading the unpromising Prost AP04 with which it shares the same 'customer spec' 90-degree type 049 Ferrari V10s used by the Maranello works team the previous season.

Heidfeld's performance came as a long-overdue public vindication of his quality as a rising star, that reputation having taken an understandable beating after his troubled freshman F1 season with the beleaguered Prost-Peugeot squad.

'Scoring my first World Championship points is excellent, and this one race has wiped away my 2000 season,' said the delighted former F3000 champion. 'I avoided the traffic in the first corner, and later got safely through the big accident when thousands of pieces seemed to be falling from the sky. I had real pressure from Heinz-Harald, but I was able to keep cool and keep pushing.'

Panis's penalty enabled new boy Kimi Räikkönen to take sixth place by just 2.7s on corrected times, the Sauber novice certainly proving wrong those sceptics who felt that he was too inexperienced to be accorded an F1 super licence.

'I made a pretty bad start, which didn't help,' said the young Finn, 'but then I got into my rhythm. My only problem was some initial understeer on my second set of tyres which prevented me from going after Heinz-Harald. But gradually the balance came back and I could keep pushing hard to the end.'

After his shake-up during qualifying, Luciano Burti drove well to finish eighth, the best-placed Jaguar R2 on this occasion, three places ahead of team-mate Eddie Irvine.

'I was pleased with my start, because I managed to overtake a few people on the first lap,' said Burti. 'We changed the brakes

GOVERNING BODY THREAT TO REDUCE F1 LAP SPEEDS

Motor racing's governing body threatened to make drastic moves to prevent F1 lap speeds spiralling dangerously out of control in the wake of the fatal accident in the Australian Grand Prix which resulted in the death of a track marshal.

FIA president Max Mosley expressed concerns that the effects of the tyre war in F1, triggered when the French Michelin company returned to racing this year to compete against rivals Bridgestone, was in danger of more than cancelling out technical changes introduced on the cars for 2001.

Mosley said that cornering speeds would be monitored in detail from the next two races in Malaysia and Brazil, the results analysed and steps taken to curb them.

'We knew that competition between the two tyre makers might increase the speed and that is why the technical commission worked on the aerodynamic regulations to reduce it,' he said.

'The impression is that the sums were not right. We don't want to jump the gun but if Malaysia and Brazil were to confirm, as I fear, the position in Melbourne, then the FIA must act quickly.'

The huge increases in speeds have stemmed from the softer rubber compounds used by the rival tyre makers as they battle for supremacy, enabling the cars to corner faster and brake later. Last year, when Bridgestone had a tyre supply monopoly, tyres were harder and more durable as every team was given the same compounds. It was particularly unfortunate that the issue of cornering speeds was set against the unrelated question of the fatal accident which befell the marshal during the course of the race because the two issues inevitably became blurred in the heat of the moment.

'The dynamics of an accident at that sort of speed are just horrendous,' said former World Champion Jackie Stewart, one of the sport's original safety campaigners more than a generation ago. However Williams technical director Patrick Head emphasised that the increased speed of the cars was not a contributory factor in the race accident.

'It was not related to car speed,' he said. 'It was related to differential in speed. One car braked and the other one following it didn't. I don't think slowing the cars down further would have made any difference to the causes of that accident.'

TECHNICAL CHANGES AIM TO KEEP LID ON LAP SPEEDS

With the prospect of a relentless tyre war between Bridgestone and F1 returnees Michelin, the FIA evolved a set of revised technical regulations for the 2001 season intended not only to ease lap speeds but also to make the cars safer.

The most significant change to this package involved the raising of front wings, ground clearance from the end plates now being increased to 50 mm. Although it was anticipated that this would lead to a slight increase in top speeds, the reduced downforce was intended to trim cornering speed sufficiently to compensate for the additional cornering abilities of the anticipated softer tyre compounds.

There were also strict modifications to the rear wing regulations, a maximum of three 'blades' now being permitted in the upper plane and just a single blade on the lower plane. The diameter of rain tyres was increased by 10 mm to 670 mm, although the dry tyre maximum dimension remained unchanged.

Most teams at Melbourne estimated that the reduction in aerodynamic downforce yielded by the new regulations had slowed up the cars by about a second a lap. However, it did not quite work out as intended at this opening race of the season.

It unfortunately turned out that the Michelin-versus-Bridgestone tyre war had effectively sliced almost 5s a lap off the best Melbourne times — and Schumacher was even 2.5s quicker than Jacques Villeneuve's '97 pole with the Williams-Renault, the last time slick rubber was used in F1.

From the safety standpoint, the requirements of impact/deformation tests on the chassis structure had been uprated to newly demanding levels. The roll-hoop loading test was dramatically increased with a requirement that it should now withstand a force of 90 kN (previously 60 kN) from above and a lateral test of 50 kN (previously 12 kN). The rearward longitudinal test was up from 45 kN to 60 kN for the new season.

In addition, it was ruled that the 25 mm thick cockpit padding should be extended to protect the drivers' legs. The cockpit opening was enlarged and moved rearwards while universal seat mountings became mandatory to aid rapid evacuation of the driver in an emergency.

In a bid to reduce the likelihood of wheels breaking off a car in a major accident, the 8 mm diameter wheel-restraining cables — each anchored independently to wheel and internal suspension mountings — had to be doubled up for 2001. Sadly, even these rigorous safety demands failed to restrain wayward wheels in the Villeneuve/Ralf Schumacher disaster which marred the first race of the season.

Top left: Michelin was back in F1 for the first time since Niki Lauda won the '84 title using their products.

Top: Ralf Schumacher straightlines a corner early in the race while, in his wake, Jarno Trulli's Jordan battles to fend off David Coulthard's McLaren.

Above: Nick Heidfeld impressed in his first race for Sauber, finishing the race in fourth place.
All photographs: Paul-Henri Cahier

Left and below left: Former Minardi pay-driver Gaston Mazzacane secured a seat with Alain Prost's team, but only subject to a review after the first four races.
Both photographs: Bryn Williams/crash.net

after the morning warm-up and they felt much better and I was very pleased to have found a workable chassis set-up from which we can now move forward.'

Irvine, muscled off the circuit by Juan Pablo Montoya's Williams-BMW at the third corner of the opening lap, dropped to the back of the pack. That was all he needed after a late switch to the spare car after his race chassis suffered a power steering failure.

'I drove round an engine misfire for the latter part of the race,' he shrugged. This was caused by a fuel pressure problem which also involved him coming in for a splash-and-dash eight laps from the end, dropping from eighth to 11th as a result.

Separating the two Jaguars at the finish were Jean Alesi's Prost-Ferrari and the Arrows-Asiatech of Jos Verstappen. The Frenchman admitted: 'To finish the race is an important first step for us. However, the result is well below my expectations.'

'I thought we could be more competitive here but from free practice on Friday it was clear that we wouldn't be able to find a satisfactory set-up for this track.'

Fernando Alonso survived to post 12th for Minardi on his F1 debut while Giancarlo Fisichella had a dismal run to 13th in the uncompetitive Benetton B201 which lost even more of its Renault RS21's modest 700 bhp power output with a broken exhaust in the closing stages.

A similar problem left Jenson Button retiring with six laps to go but in his case the cracked exhaust eventually caused the wiring loom to burn through, causing him to stop. Earlier he had been obliged to submit to a 10s stop-go penalty after his mechanics had remained too long on the grid prior to the final formation lap.

Although Räikkönen's name was deservedly up in lights by the end of the afternoon, former Indy 500 winner Juan Pablo Montoya was the best-placed novice — and heading for a top-six finish — when his Williams FW23 suffered engine failure 18 laps from the end just as he was poised to make a tactically astute late refuelling stop.

'Juan has unbelievable natural car control,' said an admiring BMW Motorsport manager Gerhard Berger. 'He still needs to channel it and get the hang of F1, but he's going to be just fine.'

The jaunty Colombian strolled back to the pits, waving to the crowd. He'd done a pretty good job with his 1m 29.606s fourth-fastest race lap. Over the next few weeks it would become clear that this performance was probably the most significant pointer for the future to emerge from the Australian Grand Prix.

On four significant counts: car, tyres, engine and drivers.

Below: Best of the rest. David Coulthard was hoping for better than third in Australia, but his McLaren-Mercedes simply couldn't match the Ferrari pace.
Photograph: Bryn Williams/crash.net

RUNNERS AND RIDERS

SCUDERIA FERRARI MARLBORO
Michael Schumacher defending his World Championship, paired for the second year with Brazil's Rubens Barrichello. New Ferrari F2001, aerodynamically further refined version of last year's car, powered by type 050, 90-degree V10 developing reputed 820 bhp. Early-season promise buttressed by announcement that Philip Morris would be extending its Marlboro title sponsorship of the team until 2006.

WEST McLAREN MERCEDES
Mika Häkkinen and David Coulthard entering their sixth successive season as team-mates, an all-time record partnership since the start of the official World Championship in 1950 and matching the 1934–'39 pairing of Rudolf Caracciola and Manfred von Brauchitsch in the Mercedes-Benz team. Hopes resting on well tested McLaren MP4/16 chassis and uprated Mercedes F0110K, 72-degree V10 developing 815 bhp. Changes to the at-circuit administration of the race team intended to boost pit-wall strategy and prompt arrival at optimum chassis set-up.

BMW WILLIAMS
Potentially formidable partnership with second-generation type P80 90-degree BMW V10 propelling aerodynamically much-improved Williams FW23. New deal as F1 returnee Michelin's prime flag carrier a calculated gamble to gain a significant performance edge in the medium-to-long term. Jenson Button replaced in driver line-up by former CART Champion and Indy 500 winner Juan Pablo Montoya with Ralf Schumacher remaining as de facto team leader for the third successive year.

MILD SEVEN BENETTON RENAULT SPORT
Jenson Button switching from BMW Williams to Renault-owned Benetton squad alongside Giancarlo Fisichella to drive Mike Gascoyne-developed B201 contender. Initially under-developed wide-angle 111-degree Renault RS21 engine left team with potential 100 bhp deficit against established runners, forcing compromises with car set-up in an attempt to make up ground.

LUCKY STRIKE BAR HONDA
Third season for BAR Squad, second as Honda partner now using Japanese company's promising RA100E V10 developing 800 bhp at 17,900 rpm. Ricardo Zonta replaced as Jacques Villeneuve's team-mate by the highly motivated former McLaren test driver Olivier Panis who team principal Craig Pollock had originally wanted in 2000, only for his choice to have been vetoed by part-owners BAT.

BENSON & HEDGES JORDAN HONDA
Head-to-head with BAR as the second official Honda factory team, Jordan started the year in upbeat mood with the new EJ-11 which highly impressed regular drivers Heinz-Harald Frentzen and Jarno Trulli at first acquaintance. Former BAR teamster Ricardo Zonta signed as test driver.

ORANGE ARROWS
Ditched customer Supertec (née Renault) V10s in favour of new partnership with Asiatech (née Peugeot) to use French-made V10s previously used to little effect by Prost. Mike Coughlan-designed Arrows A22s showed good winter testing form in the hands of Jos Verstappen now partnered by Enrique Bernoldi instead of Pedro de la Rosa. F1 winner and veteran Johnny Herbert signed as test driver.

RED BULL SAUBER PETRONAS
Best F1 Sauber yet in the form of Sergio Rinland-designed C20 now under technical direction of former McLaren engineer Stephen Taylor who joined as chief designer just prior to start of season. Customer type 049, 90-degree 2000-spec Ferrari V10s to power new car driven by all-new line-up of former F3000 champ Nick Heidfeld and boy wonder Kimi Räikkönen.

JAGUAR RACING
Major administrative changes since the end of previous season with Bobby Rahal now running team with help from former F1 champion Niki Lauda, now employed by Ford's Premier Automotive Group. New, uprated Cosworth CR3, 72-degree V10 developing 790 bhp powering R2 chassis originally penned by Gary Anderson but now developed by technical team of Steve Nichols, John Russell and aerodynamicist Mark Handford. Eddie Irvine remains as team leader partnered by former F3 star Luciano Burti.

EUROPEAN MINARDI
Saved from oblivion at 59th minute of 11th hour by European Aviation boss Paul Stoddart, Minardi continued to survive using uprated Ford Zetec-R V10 engines developing a modest 750 bhp. Another promising chassis from technical director Gustav Brunner and driver line-up headed by 19-year-old rising star Fernando Alonso plus Tarso Marques. Team operations now split between Minardi HQ in Faenza and European Aviation base at Ledbury, Herefordshire.

PROST GRAND PRIX
Attempting to shrug aside memories of abortive alliance with Peugeot with new Ferrari customer engine deal using same spec type 049 V10s as Sauber. Opted for Michelin tyres on which Jean Alesi and Gaston Mazzacane square up to opposition in AP04 engineered by former McLaren aerodynamicist Henri Durand.

ROUND 1
MELBOURNE 1–4 MARCH 2001

QANTAS
AUSTRALIAN
grand prix

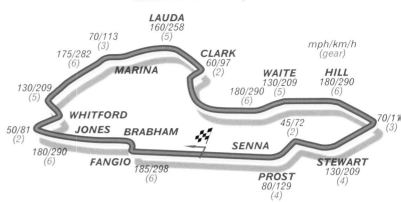

MELBOURNE – ALBERT PARK
CIRCUIT LENGTH: 3.295 miles/5.303 km

LAUDA 160/258 (5)
70/113 (3)
175/282 (6)
MARINA
CLARK 60/97 (2)
WAITE 130/209 (5)
HILL 180/290 (6)
mph/km/h (gear)
130/209 (5)
180/290 (6)
WHITFORD
JONES
BRABHAM
45/72 (2)
70/11 (3)
50/81 (2)
SENNA
STEWART 130/209 (4)
180/290 (6)
FANGIO
185/298 (6)
PROST 80/129 (4)

RACE DISTANCE: 58 laps, 191.117 miles/307.574 km   RACE WEATHER: Dry, hot and sunny

Pos.	Driver	Nat.	No.	Entrant	Car/Engine	Tyres	Laps	Time/Retirement	Speed (mph/km/h)	Gap to lea
1	Michael Schumacher	D	1	Scuderia Ferrari Marlboro	Ferrari F2001-050 V10	B	58	1h 38m 26.533s	116.485/187.464	
2	David Coulthard	GB	4	West McLaren Mercedes	McLaren MP4/16-Mercedes F0110K V10	B	58	1h 38m 28.251s	116.451/187.410	+1.7
3	Rubens Barrichello	BR	2	Scuderia Ferrari Marlboro	Ferrari F2001-050 V10	B	58	1h 39m 00.024s	115.828/186.407	+33.4
4	Nick Heidfeld	D	16	Red Bull Sauber Petronas	Sauber C20-Petronas V10	B	58	1h 39m 38.012s	115.092/185.223	+71.4
5	Heinz-Harald Frentzen	D	11	B&H Jordan Honda	Jordan EJ11-Honda RA001E V10	B	58	1h 39m 39.340s	115.067/185.182	+72.8
6	Kimi Räikkönen	SF	17	Red Bull Sauber Petronas	Sauber C20-Petronas V10	B	58	1h 39m 50.676s	114.848/184.831	+84.1
7	Olivier Panis	F	9	Lucky Strike BAR Honda	BAR 03-Honda RA001E V10	B	58	1h 39m 53.583s	114.793/184.741	+87.0
8	Luciano Burti	BR	19	Jaguar Racing	Jaguar R2-Cosworth CR3 V10	M	57			+1
9	Jean Alesi	F	22	Prost Acer	Prost AP04-Acer V10	M	57			+1
10	Jos Verstappen	NL	14	Orange Arrows Asiatech	Arrows A22-Asiatech V10	B	57			+1
11	Eddie Irvine	GB	18	Jaguar Racing	Jaguar R2-Cosworth CR3 V10	M	57			+1
12	Fernando Alonso	ESP	21	European Minardi F1	Minardi PS01-European V10	M	56			+2
13	Giancarlo Fisichella	I	7	Mild Seven Benetton Renault	Benetton B201-Renault RS21 V10	M	55			+3
14	Jenson Button	GB	8	Mild Seven Benetton Renault	Benetton B201-Renault RS21 V10	M	52	Exhaust		+6
	Juan Pablo Montoya	COL	6	BMW WilliamsF1 Team	Williams FW23-BMW P80 V10	M	40	Engine		
	Jarno Trulli	I	12	B&H Jordan Honda	Jordan EJ11-Honda RA001E V10	B	38	Misfire		
	Mika Häkkinen	SF	3	West McLaren Mercedes	McLaren MP4/16-Mercedes F0110K V10	B	25	Suspension/Accident		
	Ralf Schumacher	D	5	BMW WilliamsF1 Team	Williams FW23-BMW P80 V10	M	4	Collision with Villeneuve		
	Jacques Villeneuve	CDN	10	Lucky Strike BAR Honda	BAR 03-Honda RA001E V10	B	4	Collision with R. Schumacher		
	Tarso Marques	BR	20	European Minardi F1	Minardi PS01-European V10	M	3	Electrical		
	Enrique Bernoldi	BR	15	Orange Arrows Asiatech	Arrows A22-Asiatech V10	B	2	Accident		
	Gaston Mazzacane	ARG	23	Prost Acer	Prost AP04-Acer V10	M	0	Brakes		

Fastest lap: Michael Schumacher, on lap 34, 1m 28.214s, 134.473 mph/216.414 km/h (record).

Previous lap record: Heinz-Harald Frentzen (F1 Williams FW19-Renault V10), 1m 30.585s, 130.929 mph/210.710 km/h (1997).

Grid order	1	2	3	4	5	6	7	8	9	10	11	12	13	14	15	16	17	18	19	20	21	22	23	24	25	26	27	28	29	30	31	32	33	34	35	36	37	38	39	40	41	42	43
1 M. SCHUMACHER	1	1	1	1	1	1	1	1	1	1	1	1	1	1	1	1	1	1	1	1	1	1	1	1	1	1	1	1	1	1	1	1	1	1	1	1	4	4	4	4	1	1	1
2 BARRICHELLO	3	3	3	3	3	3	3	3	3	3	3	3	3	3	3	3	3	3	3	3	3	3	3	3	3	2	2	2	2	2	2	2	4	4	4	2	2	1	1	4	4	4	
3 HÄKKINEN	11	11	2	2	2	2	2	2	2	2	2	2	2	2	2	2	2	2	2	2	2	2	2	2	2	4	4	4	4	4	4	4	2	2	2	1	1	9	6	2	2	2	
11 FRENTZEN	5	2	4	4	4	4	4	4	4	4	4	4	4	4	4	4	4	4	4	4	4	4	4	4	4	12	12	12	12	12	9	9	9	9	9	9	9	2	2	9	9	9	
5 R. SCHUMACHER	2	4	12	12	12	12	12	12	12	12	12	12	12	12	12	12	12	12	12	12	12	12	12	12	12	9	9	9	9	9	12	16	16	16	16	6	6	6	9	16	16	16	
4 COULTHARD	12	12	5	5	9	9	9	9	9	9	9	9	9	9	9	9	9	9	9	9	9	9	9	9	9	16	16	16	16	16	16	6	6	6	6	16	16	16	16	11	11	11	
12 TRULLI	4	5	10	10	14	14	14	14	14	14	14	14	14	16	16	16	16	16	16	16	16	16	16	16	16	6	6	6	6	6	6	17	17	17	11	18	18	11	11	17	17	17	
10 VILLENEUVE	10	10	9	9	16	16	16	16	16	16	16	16	16	7	7	6	6	6	6	6	6	6	6	6	6	17	17	17	17	17	17	11	11	11	18	11	11	17	17	18	18	18	
9 PANIS	16	16	14	14	7	7	7	7	7	7	7	7	7	6	6	7	7	7	7	7	7	7	7	7	17	11	11	11	11	11	11	19	19	19	17	17	17	18	18	19	19	19	
16 HEIDFELD	9	9	16	16	6	6	6	6	6	6	6	6	8	8	8	17	17	17	17	17	17	17	11	11	19	19	19	19	19	19	22	22	18	14	14	19	19	19	22	22	22		
6 MONTOYA	14	14	7	7	8	8	8	8	8	8	8	8	22	22	17	11	11	11	11	11	11	11	7	22	22	22	22	22	18	18	14	14	14	22	22	14	14	14	21	21	21		
18 IRVINE	7	7	6	6	22	22	22	22	22	22	22	22	17	17	11	19	19	19	19	19	19	19	19	19	18	18	18	18	14	14	22	22	14	14	14	21	21	7	7				
17 RÄIKKÖNEN	6	6	8	8	17	17	17	17	17	17	17	17	11	11	19	19	22	22	22	22	22	22	21	21	21	21	21	14	14	12	12	12	12	21	21	7	7						
22 ALESI	8	8	22	22	11	11	11	11	11	11	11	11	19	19	22	18	18	18	18	18	18	18	14	14	14	14	14	21	21	21	21	21	7	7	8	8	8						
14 VERSTAPPEN	22	22	17	17	19	19	19	19	19	19	19	19	18	18	21	21	21	21	21	21	21	8	8	8	8	8	7	7	7	7	7	7	8	8									
8 BUTTON	17	17	11	11	21	21	21	21	21	21	18	18	21	14	14	14	14	14	14	14	7	7	7	7	7	8	8	8	8	8													
7 FISICHELLA	19	15	19	19	18	18	18	18	18	18	18	14	14	14	8	8	8	8	8	8																							
15 BERNOLDI	15	19	21	21																																							
21 ALONSO	21	21	18	18																																							
23 MAZZACANE	20	20	20																																								
19 BURTI	18	18																																									
20 MARQUES																																											

Pit stop
One lap behind leader

STARTING GRID

1 M. SCHUMACHER Ferrari	**2** BARRICHELLO Ferrari
3 HÄKKINEN McLaren	**11** FRENTZEN Jordan
5 R. SCHUMACHER Williams	**4** COULTHARD McLaren
12 TRULLI Jordan	**10** VILLENEUVE BAR
9 PANIS BAR	**16** HEIDFELD Sauber
6 MONTOYA Williams	**18** IRVINE Jaguar
17 RÄIKKÖNEN Sauber	**22** ALESI Prost
14 VERSTAPPEN Arrows	**8** BUTTON Benetton
7 FISICHELLA Benetton	**15** BERNOLDI Arrows
21 ALONSO Minardi	**23** MAZZACANE Prost
19 BURTI Jaguar	**20** MARQUES Minardi

47	48	49	50	51	52	53	54	55	56	57	58	•
1	1	1	1	1	1	1	1	1	1	1	1	1
4	4	4	4	4	4	4	4	4	4	4	4	2
2	2	2	2	2	2	2	2	2	2	2	2	3
9	9	9	9	9	9	9	9	9	9	9	9	
16	16	16	16	16	16	16	16	16	16	16	16	4
11	11	11	11	11	11	11	11	11	11	11	11	5
17	17	17	17	17	17	17	17	17	17	17	17	6
18	18	18	19	19	19	19	19	19	19	19		
19	19	19	14	14	14	14	14	14	14	14		
22	14	14	22	22	22	22	22	22	22	22		
14	22	22	18	18	18	18	18	18	18	18		
21	21	21	21	21	21	21	21	21	21			
7	7	7	8	8	8	7	7	7				
8	8	8	7	7	7							

TIME SHEETS

QUALIFYING

Weather: Dry, sunny and very hot

Pos.	Driver	Car	Laps	Time
1	Michael Schumacher	Ferrari	10	1m 26.892s
2	Rubens Barrichello	Ferrari	11	1m 27.263s
3	Mika Häkkinen	McLaren-Mercedes	12	1m 27.461s
4	Heinz-Harald Frentzen	Jordan-Honda	10	1m 27.658s
5	Ralf Schumacher	Williams-BMW	12	1m 27.719s
6	David Coulthard	McLaren-Mercedes	12	1m 28.010s
7	Jarno Trulli	Jordan-Honda	11	1m 28.377s
8	Jacques Villeneuve	BAR-Honda	11	1m 28.435s
9	Olivier Panis	BAR-Honda	11	1m 28.518s
10	Nick Heidfeld	Sauber-Petronas	11	1m 28.615s
11	Juan Pablo Montoya	Williams-BMW	11	1m 28.738s
12	Eddie Irvine	Jaguar-Cosworth	10	1m 28.965s
13	Kimi Räikkönen	Sauber-Petronas	12	1m 28.993s
14	Jean Alesi	Prost-Acer	11	1m 29.893s
15	Jos Verstappen	Arrows-Asiatech	11	1m 29.934s
16	Jenson Button	Benetton-Renault	12	1m 30.035s
17	Giancarlo Fisichella	Benetton-Renault	10	1m 30.209s
18	Enrique Bernoldi	Arrows-Asiatech	12	1m 30.520s
19	Fernando Alonso	Minardi-European	12	1m 30.657s
20	Gaston Mazzacane	Prost-Acer	12	1m 30.798s
21	Luciano Burti	Jaguar-Cosworth	7	1m 30.978s
22	Tarso Marques*	Minardi-European	11	1m 33.228s

107% time: 1m 32.974s   *allowed to race

FRIDAY FREE PRACTICE

Weather: Dry, hot and sunny

Pos.	Driver	Laps	Time
1	Rubens Barrichello	40	1m 28.965s
2	Jarno Trulli	35	1m 29.267s
3	Michael Schumacher	27	1m 29.284s
4	David Coulthard	37	1m 29.324s
5	Mika Häkkinen	31	1m 29.799s
6	Ralf Schumacher	41	1m 30.277s
7	Nick Heidfeld	34	1m 30.345s
8	Heinz-Harald Frentzen	31	1m 30.802s
9	Jean Alesi	23	1m 31.089s
10	Olivier Panis	42	1m 31.166s
11	Kimi Räikkönen	31	1m 31.453s
12	Jacques Villeneuve	30	1m 31.559s
13	Eddie Irvine	35	1m 31.573s
14	Jos Verstappen	39	1m 31.669s
15	Juan Pablo Montoya	37	1m 31.721s
16	Giancarlo Fisichella	32	1m 32.475s
17	Fernando Alonso	38	1m 32.587s
18	Luciano Burti	27	1m 33.011s
19	Gaston Mazzacane	31	1m 33.153s
20	Enrique Bernoldi	27	1m 33.203s
21	Jenson Button	26	1m 33.403s
22	Tarso Marques	19	1m 36.463s

SATURDAY FREE PRACTICE

Weather: Dry, hot and sunny

Pos.	Driver	Laps	Time
1	David Coulthard	30	1m 27.540s
2	Michael Schumacher	16	1m 27.561s
3	Mika Häkkinen	25	1m 27.775s
4	Heinz-Harald Frentzen	20	1m 27.940s
5	Jarno Trulli	25	1m 28.193s
6	Ralf Schumacher	21	1m 28.666s
7	Olivier Panis	30	1m 28.677s
8	Kimi Räikkönen	17	1m 28.851s
9	Eddie Irvine	27	1m 28.861s
10	Nick Heidfeld	25	1m 28.895s
11	Jacques Villeneuve	27	1m 28.962s
12	Juan Pablo Montoya	23	1m 29.184s
13	Rubens Barrichello	6	1m 29.945s
14	Jean Alesi	24	1m 29.981s
15	Fernando Alonso	28	1m 30.360s
16	Giancarlo Fisichella	27	1m 30.549s
17	Luciano Burti	17	1m 30.578s
18	Enrique Bernoldi	34	1m 30.782s
19	Jenson Button	12	1m 30.893s
20	Jos Verstappen	10	1m 31.590s
21	Gaston Mazzacane	9	1m 34.431s
22	Tarso Marques	17	1m 34.491s

WARM-UP

Weather: Overcast with light rain

Pos.	Driver	Laps	Time
1	David Coulthard	11	1m 30.099s
2	Mika Häkkinen	12	1m 30.152s
3	Jos Verstappen	14	1m 30.396s
4	Juan Pablo Montoya	11	1m 30.559s
5	Olivier Panis	13	1m 30.584s
6	Michael Schumacher	7	1m 30.839s
7	Nick Heidfeld	16	1m 30.966s
8	Eddie Irvine	13	1m 31.061s
9	Rubens Barrichello	6	1m 31.450s
10	Heinz-Harald Frentzen	13	1m 31.566s
11	Kimi Räikkönen	11	1m 31.665s
12	Jarno Trulli	13	1m 31.811s
13	Enrique Bernoldi	12	1m 32.106s
14	Jacques Villeneuve	14	1m 32.108s
15	Ralf Schumacher	13	1m 32.687s
16	Fernando Alonso	9	1m 33.717s
17	Gaston Mazzacane	11	1m 33.747s
18	Luciano Burti	14	1m 33.772s
19	Jean Alesi	9	1m 34.421s
20	Jenson Button	12	1m 34.554s
21	Giancarlo Fisichella	10	1m 34.572s
22	Tarso Marques	9	1m 35.514s

RACE FASTEST LAPS

Weather: Dry, hot and sunny

Driver	Time	Lap
Michael Schumacher	1m 28.214s	34
David Coulthard	1m 28.838s	40
Rubens Barrichello	1m 29.060s	33
Juan Pablo Montoya	1m 29.606s	40
Mika Häkkinen	1m 29.612s	25
Olivier Panis	1m 30.199s	36
Kimi Räikkönen	1m 30.229s	36
Heinz-Harald Frentzen	1m 30.266s	35
Nick Heidfeld	1m 30.317s	35
Jarno Trulli	1m 30.432s	29
Luciano Burti	1m 30.903s	31
Jean Alesi	1m 31.030s	31
Eddie Irvine	1m 31.267s	29
Jos Verstappen	1m 31.999s	56
Jenson Button	1m 32.001s	24
Fernando Alonso	1m 32.043s	56
Giancarlo Fisichella	1m 32.407s	23
Ralf Schumacher	1m 34.406s	3
Jacques Villeneuve	1m 34.432s	3
Enrique Bernoldi	1m 36.689s	2
Tarso Marques	1m 38.249s	2

CHASSIS LOG BOOK

1	M. Schumacher	Ferrari F2001/208
2	Barrichello	Ferrari F2001/206
	spare	Ferrari F2001/209
3	Häkkinen	McLaren MP4/16/3
4	Coulthard	McLaren MP4/16/1
	spare	McLaren MP4/16/2
5	R. Schumacher	Williams FW23/3
6	Montoya	Williams FW23/2
	spare	Williams FW23/1
7	Fisichella	Benetton B201/3
8	Button	Benetton B201/1
	spare	Benetton B201/2
9	Panis	BAR 03/3
10	Villeneuve	BAR 03/1
	spare	BAR 03/2
11	Frentzen	Jordan EJ11/4
12	Trulli	Jordan EJ11/3
	spare	Jordan EJ11/2
14	Verstappen	Arrows A22/1
15	Bernoldi	Arrows A22/3
	spare	Arrows A22/4
16	Heidfeld	Sauber C20/3
17	Räikkönen	Sauber C20/1
	spare	Sauber C20/4
18	Irvine	Jaguar R2/5
19	Burti	Jaguar R2/3
	spare	Jaguar R2/4
20	Marques	Minardi PS01/2
21	Alonso	Minardi PS01/1
	no spare	
22	Alesi	Prost AP04/3
23	Mazzacane	Prost AP04/2
	spare	Prost AP04/4

POINTS TABLES

DRIVERS

1	Michael Schumacher	10
2	David Coulthard	6
3	Rubens Barrichello	4
4	Nick Heidfeld	3
5	Heinz-Harald Frentzen	2
6	Kimi Räikkönen	1

CONSTRUCTORS

1	Ferrari	14
2	McLaren	6
3	Sauber	4
4	Jordan	2

FOR THE RECORD

First Grand Prix start

Fernando Alonso

Enrique Bernoldi

Juan Pablo Montoya

Kimi Räikkönen

First Grand Prix point

Kimi Räikkönen

300th Grand Prix point

David Coulthard

FIA WORLD CHAMPIONSHIP • ROUND 2

MALAYSIAN
grand prix

1st - M. SCHUMACHER • 2nd - BARRICHELLO • 3rd - COULTHARD

Michael Schumacher's Ferrari leads brother Ralf's Williams-BMW and Rubens Barrichello's Ferrari into the first corner, a split second before Ralf was tipped into a spin by the Brazilian.
Photograph: Paul-Henri Cahier

FRENTZEN RETREATS FROM TRACTION CONTROL STORM

Heinz-Harald Frentzen found himself at the centre of a storm over traction control during the Malaysian GP weekend after speculation that he'd been hinting that Ferrari's F1 engines were equipped with an illegal traction control system.

Frentzen made the comments on his personal web site after spending a frustrating time tailing Nick Heidfeld's Sauber-Ferrari in the Australian GP a fortnight earlier, noting that the Swiss machine seemed to accelerate particularly well out of slow corners and had a distinctive misfire as it did so.

Yet he was forced onto the back foot on his arrival at Sepang, making a tactical retreat from his original position rather than an unconditional withdrawal.

'After Melbourne there was some misunderstanding about my quotes,' he said. 'When people ask me "do you think it's illegal or not?" I said that I couldn't answer that question because the FIA has all the data about traction control, and whether it's illegal or not.'

Frentzen's reported remarks had originally brought forth stern criticism from Michael Schumacher who suggested that his fellow German was bringing the sport into disrepute by making these comments.

'If he gets to know this, then of course he is pissed off,' said Frentzen. 'But I did not say that the Ferrari traction control was illegal.'

Prior to the Malaysian race FIA president Max Mosley had entered the debate when he commented: 'We disagree, and we are better placed than Heinz-Harald Frentzen to know what various teams are doing.

'It is, however, a fact that some teams are able to tune their engines so that wheelspin becomes unlikely and more manageable. This is not the same thing as traction control.'

He was making the point that the current F1 technical regulations permitted pre-programmed electronic systems which anticipate the onset of wheelspin, but from the Spanish GP 'closed loop' systems — which respond to input from rear-wheel sensors — would become legal again as part of a wider package to free up engine electronic systems.

SEPANG QUALIFYING

During Friday free practice the lap times for all the leading drivers were well outside the pole position time of 1m 37.397s set by Schumacher in the 2000 Malaysian GP the previous October.

On another hot and humid day, with temperatures topping 38 degrees and a 75 per cent humidity level, the main challenge for the drivers was to remain hydrated and as comfortable as possible in the cramped and confined conditions behind the wheel. Sepang is a track which tends to promote understeer and anybody who managed to dial out that tendency from their cars certainly seemed to have an advantage in qualifying for the Malaysian Grand Prix. Nevertheless, the cars were quicker than in last year's race when it finally came to qualifying.

Yet it was Schumacher who had the real wake-up call midway through the hour-long session when brother Ralf slammed the Michelin-shod Williams-BMW FW23 round to take fastest time on 1m 35.511s. Michael had to pull out all the stops to get the Ferrari back ahead with a 1m 35.220s and, although Rubens Barrichello joined him on the front row for a Maranello 1-2, the talking point of the day was certainly the Williams.

The FW23 was clearly a well balanced chassis and, if it lacked slightly in terms of its downforce package, it certainly made up for it with its long-stroke BMW V10 engine which Gerhard Berger confirmed revs to around 18,000 rpm, thereby making it the fastest running unit on the contemporary F1 scene.

Berger and Williams tech director Patrick Head were both slightly cautious about the long-term prospects, echoing Ralf Schumacher's feelings that it could take some time to win their first race together.

'I think the car is a little bit better than in Australia,' said Head, 'and I thought that we might be able to qualify here between fifth and eighth. So I was surprised to see just how close things were at the head of the field. The Michelin tyres seemed very stable and we were happy with their wear characteristics.'

Juan Pablo Montoya also qualified well in sixth place on 1m 36.218s after losing most of Saturday practice due to a variety of technical problems. 'He is pretty good at looking at data and picking up where he's got to improve,' said Head admiringly.

Like Ferrari, Williams managed to qualify well using new tyres all round on both cars. McLaren, battling what it confidently believed to be a short-term problem, deployed worn fronts in an effort to reduce the MP4/16's incipient understeer.

Lacking sufficient front downforce, neither driver was able to pitch their car into the corners with sufficient confidence nor run as much rear downforce as they would have liked because that would have unsettled the overall balance.

This dilemma left McLaren with two options in qualifying. They could either use scrubbed front tyres with new rears, allowing them to pick up extra grip, or risk running with new tyres all round which would exacerbate the imbalance.

'Our cars are too sensitive in certain areas,' explained McLaren chief Ron Dennis. 'The basic regulations that limit the size of the tyres effectively tend to create the biggest technical challenge of making cars that don't have understeer.'

One of the associated problems with the latest generation of grooved F1 tyres was ensuring that the compounds were stable enough to sustain both lateral forces and performance. They were good after one lap, then they grained slightly, then after a few more laps became more stable until they wore down towards a slick. For his part, Coulthard reckoned the Ferrari performance was no surprise, pointing out that the intermediate tyres had been almost 5s faster than the full wets in the race-morning warm-up.

Häkkinen blitzed his way to fourth on 1m 36.040s, but Coulthard freely admitted that he made a mistake on his best run and could only line up eighth with a 1m 36.417s best.

Further back, the picture looked much as expected with Montoya splitting an on-form Jarno Trulli's Jordan EJ-11 (1m 36.180s) from Jacques Villeneuve's BAR-Honda (1m 36.397s) and Heinz-Harald Frentzen (1m 36.578s), who'd gone grass-cutting on his first run, ninth ahead of Olivier Panis (1m 36.681s).

Nick Heidfeld reckoned 11th on the grid was as good as it gets with the Sauber C20 with a 1m 36.913s, pointing out that he'd come from 10th on the grid in Australia to finish in the points. Kimi Räikkönen qualified 14th on 1m 37.728s after losing time in the morning due to a broken wishbone while — hearteningly — Jean Alesi managed 13th (1m 37.406s) behind Eddie Irvine's promising Jaguar (1m 37.140s) after a performance in the Prost-Ferrari which revived his upbeat memories of the French car's winter testing form.

Giancarlo Fisichella (1m 38.086s) and Jenson Button (1m 38.258s) were struggling for balance and grip with their Benetton B201s, lining up 16th and 17th, but at least this was ahead of Jos Verstappen's Arrows A22 in 18th even though the Dutchman would become one of the stars of the show when it came to the race.

Top left: Heinz-Harald Frentzen braked hard to avoid a controversy over the issue of traction control systems.
Photograph: Paul-Henri Cahier

Top: Niki Lauda lends a sympathetic ear to Jaguar novice Luciano Burti on the Sepang starting grid.
Photograph: Bryn Williams/crash.net

Above centre: Eddie Irvine braces himself for a difficult time with the off-the-pace Jaguar R2.

Above: A Michelin tyre technician monitors the sweltering track temperature in the pit lane during practice.
Both photographs: Paul-Henri Cahier

THE Ferrari team's ability to master chaotic and treacherously slippery track conditions was displayed to impressive effect in the Malaysian Grand Prix where Michael Schumacher and Rubens Barrichello simply left their rivals gasping for breath. At the end of the afternoon they had soared to such a commanding 1-2 success that there were — perhaps inevitably — prompted admiration and scepticism in pretty well equal order with regard to the wet-weather grip generated by the Ferrari F2001s.

It was Schumacher's 46th career victory and his sixth consecutive triumph since the 2000 Italian Grand Prix at Monza. The Malaysian success was achieved despite a last-minute switch to the spare car after traces of a possible oil leak were detected on his race machine. The first start was abandoned due to Giancarlo Fisichella missing his allocated starting place and ending up with his Benetton skewed across the track at an angle. The Italian obviously had to take the restart from the back of the grid, but the delay also enabled Heinz-Harald Frentzen to breathe again after a problem with his Jordan EJ-11.

'I was very lucky to have been able to race today,' he recounted later. 'At the start I had an electronic problem which caused the engine to misfire, but luckily there was a re-start which gave us time to reset the engine's control system and everything was fine.'

Juan Pablo Montoya was also in trouble, having to switch to the spare Williams FW23 after his race car's engine died on the starting grid. He started from the pit lane and decided to stay out just one lap longer that he'd originally banked on after the rain started pouring down. As a result he spun off and retired.

Michael Schumacher had taken an immediate 1.3s lead from Barrichello by the end of the opening lap with Jarno Trulli's Jordan-Honda third ahead of David Coulthard's McLaren-Mercedes and Heinz-Harald Frentzen in the other Jordan.

By the end of lap two Michael had extended his advantage by another 0.2s, but by then a tropical rain storm had almost flooded the circuit and the safety car was deployed to slow the field.

Even so, it was a dramatically close call. On lap 3 both Ferraris flew off the road on a patch of water at the point where Olivier Panis's BAR-Honda had spun off dramatically in a sheet of flame after its oil tank caught fire. Trulli momentarily went through into the lead on lap three as the Ferraris skidded almost out of control, but

then Coulthard led the pack in for his stop at the end of the following lap, the McLaren followed into the pit lane in quick succession by Frentzen, Barrichello, Schumacher, Jos Verstappen's Arrows A22, Trulli, Mika Häkkinen's McLaren MP4/16, Jean Alesi's Prost AP04, Ralf Schumacher's Williams FW23 and Gaston Mazzacane's Prost.

This proved to be the key strategic moment at which the outcome of the race was decided by an inspired strategic call from the Ferrari crew on the pit wall who gambled on switching their cars to intermediate tyres — rather than full wets — when they came into the pits at the end of lap four. Yet it looked as though that pit stop would effectively wipe out Ferrari's chances altogether. The drenched fans were treated to the unbelievable sight of Schumacher being forced to queue behind Barrichello for the best part of a minute before the crew could tend to his car. In the chaos surrounding this early stop, the pit crew accidentally put a full wet tyre on Rubens's right front before quickly replacing it with an intermediate to match the other three wheels; Michael then flew back into contention.

'When I went off because of the rain, I could see the barrier and thought it was over,' said a relieved Schumacher at the end of the day. 'Then [in my mirrors] I saw Rubens follow me off. I was lucky the car stayed in shape and there was no damage.

'When I came into the pits I asked them to push Rubens forward, but I could not see he had no right front tyre on. It was my decision to fit intermediate rubber and, while we knew it would be difficult at first, they would be better when the rain eased.' Immeasurably assisted by a safety car which stayed out from lap three to lap 10, enabling the Italian cars to join the tail of the queue led by David Coulthard's McLaren, the Ferraris simply stormed into fast-forward action once the pack was unleashed again.

At one point after taking the lead, Schumacher lapped an amazing 6.3s faster than Coulthard's McLaren which, even allowing for his intermediate rubber and the Scot's handling problems, seemed scarcely credible. However, Coulthard later confirmed that he'd been satisfied that at one point during the race-morning warm-up the intermediate tyres offered a huge performance advantage on a wet, but drying circuit. Nevertheless, all agreed that whatever Ferrari was legally doing to improve the grip of their cars, it was certainly outstanding.

Diary

Bob Wollek, the veteran Porsche sports car ace, is killed in a freak cycling accident while in Florida for the Sebring 12-hour race.

Jaguar Racing chief Bobby Rahal warns that F1 will never achieve nationwide television popularity in the USA until it has an American driver.

Cristiano da Matta wins the opening round of the 2001 CART championship at Monterrey, Mexico, for the Newman/Haas team.

Below: Jos Verstappen's Arrows-Asiatech started with a light fuel load, enabling the Dutchman to mix it with the leading bunch during the early stages of the race.
Photograph: Paul-Henri Cahier

Above: Mika Häkkinen's McLaren-Mercedes locks over into the first corner after the startline as, in the background, Heinz-Harald Frentzen's Jordan and Jean Alesi's Prost scramble out of the pit lane in tight formation.

Left: Rubens Barrichello stayed close to his team-mate to ensure an impressive Ferrari 1-2 in both qualifying and the race.

Right: Coulthard took another podium with third place after another convincing drive, but was unable to challenge the Ferraris in a straight fight in these conditions.

All photographs: Paul-Henri Cahier

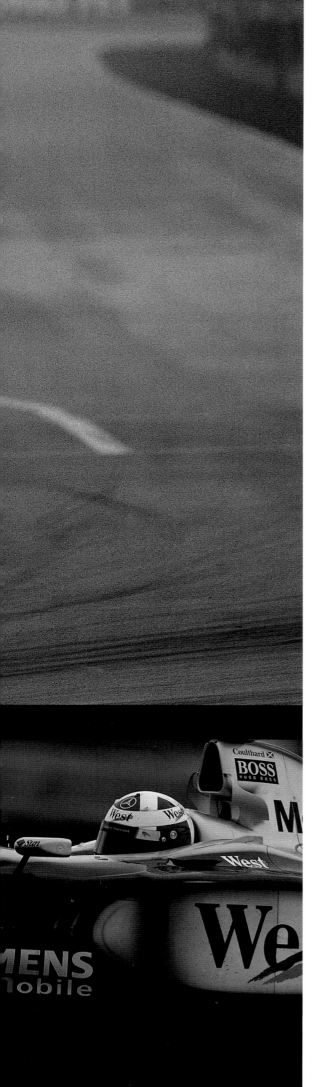

Coulthard kept manfully ahead until lap 16, but this was a lost cause. The McLaren driver was on full wets, grappling with incipient understeer, while the Ferraris were using their intermediates to brilliant effect. Barrichello went through into second at the end of lap 16 and from then on the Boys from Maranello made the whole affair a cakewalk which strengthened their vice-like grip on the title points table.

Not that the race exactly finished with unconditional fraternal greetings between the two Ferrari drivers. Rubens was extremely concerned about the uncompromising manner in which Michael had sliced ahead of him to take sixth place on lap 12. The Brazilian had just told technical director Ross Brawn over the radio that there was a lot of dirt on the circuit and that Michael needed to take care. But clearly 'Schumi' had his own ideas. 'Michael took a chance,' said Rubens. 'It was not what you would expect a teammate to do.'

Despite these oppressive conditions, the McLaren-Mercedes squad performed respectably on the face of it, David Coulthard finishing third, Mika Häkkinen a frustrated sixth. Yet scratch below the surface and McLaren admitted to problems. On a track where understeer is an incipient quality, the MP4/16s were beset by a frustrating shortage of front-end grip.

McLaren took the prudent, some would say conservative, decision to switch to full wets rather than intermediates during the scramble for tyres when the rain started. Dennis made no apologies for this: 'Should we have gone on intermediates? At the time, there was such heavy rain and running water that we took the decision that we thought was the correct one in those conditions. I am very happy with that decision.'

Schumacher also consolidated his advantage with a second stop to change onto dry weather tyres on lap 30, Barrichello having to make an unscheduled third stop later in the race to clear gravel from his undertray after an off-course excursion.

Häkkinen switched to dry-weather rubber on lap 18 but Coulthard, now running second, stayed out until lap 25 before making his change. Schumacher made his intermediates endure on the drying surface for another five laps before switching to dry tyres. From then on he was never in any sort of danger.

Frentzen successfully elbowed his way through to fourth after a great fight with Ralf Schumacher's Williams-BMW, Jos Verstappen's Arrows A22 and Häkkinen's McLaren.

'When the race started again it was a bit wet and I gained a couple of places by the first corner, but I couldn't hold my position,' said Frentzen.

'I was heavy on fuel as we had a one-stop strategy planned and I also had a clutch problem which lasted the entire race.'

In fact, Heinz-Harald did a good job coping with locking rear wheels on the downchange and was able to scramble home just 1.6s ahead of Ralf Schumacher at the flag.

Ralf spent the closing stages of the race struggling to fend off Häkkinen's McLaren after he'd been pitched into a first-corner spin by Barrichello's Ferrari and spent the rest of the afternoon playing catch-up.

'From mid-race I picked up some understeer which became bigger and bigger after my third pit stop,' said Ralf. 'My opinion is that it didn't depend on the tyre but more on the set-up of the car. But it was a good feeling anyway to keep Häkkinen behind me.'

Mika was at least satisfied to have scored his first championship point of the season, although for much of the race he had his hands full battling Jos Verstappen's Arrows-Asiatech which proved remarkably quick on the straight.

The Dutchman had made up 12 places on the opening lap from 18th on the grid thanks to diving inside Ralf Schumacher's pirouetting Williams on the first corner rather than opting for the more circuitous outside route. That gave him a clear run to mix it with the leading group where he proved extremely energetic in terms of jousting with his McLaren rival and only a late stop dropped him to seventh.

Trulli wound up eighth, struggling with difficult handling after an early spin in the rain damaged his car's bargeboards and front wing.'

Alesi was ninth for Prost ahead of Luciano Burti in the sole surviving Jaguar R2, Eddie Irvine having succumbed to a water leak after Verstappen tipped him into a spin on the opening lap.

Jenson Button's Benetton B201, Mazzacane and the Minardi PS01s of Fernando Alonso and Tarso Marques completed the 14 finishers to make it to the chequered flag.

Two down, fifteen races to go and Ferrari looked pretty well unassailable. McLaren, if not exactly struggling, knew they were not quite *au point*. There was still a long way to go, but even allowing for the obvious Williams-BMW promise, the die for the 2001 season already looked worryingly close to being cast.

Below: Malaysia offered its own unique and colourful charms.
Photograph: Bryn Williams/crash.net

ROUND 2
SEPANG 16–18 MARCH 2001

PETRONAS
MALAYSIAN
grand prix

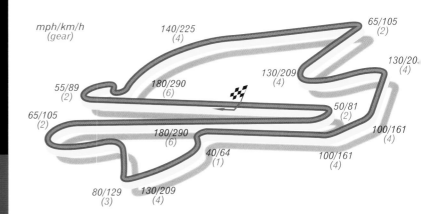

SEPANG
CIRCUIT LENGTH: 3.444 miles/5.543 km

mph/km/h (gear)

140/225 (4)
65/105 (2)
130/20. (4)
130/209 (4)
180/290 (6)
55/89 (2)
50/81 (2)
65/105 (2)
100/161 (4)
180/290 (6)
100/161 (4)
40/64 (1)
80/129 (3)
130/209 (4)

RACE DISTANCE: 55 laps, 189.434 miles/304.865 km   **RACE WEATHER:** Dry start, then heavy rain shower, followed by drying track

Pos.	Driver	Nat.	No.	Entrant	Car/Engine	Tyres	Laps	Time/Retirement	Speed (mph/km/h)	Gap to lead
1	Michael Schumacher	D	1	Scuderia Ferrari Marlboro	Ferrari F2001-050 V10	B	55	1h 47m 34.801s	105.652/170.030	
2	Rubens Barrichello	BR	2	Scuderia Ferrari Marlboro	Ferrari F2001-050 V10	B	55	1h 47m 58.461s	105.266/169.409	+23.66
3	David Coulthard	GB	4	West McLaren Mercedes	McLaren MP4/16-Mercedes F0110K V10	B	55	1h 48m 03.356s	105.186/169.281	+28.55
4	Heinz-Harald Frentzen	D	11	B&H Jordan Honda	Jordan EJ11-Honda RA001E V10	B	55	1h 48m 21.344s	104.895/168.813	+46.54
5	Ralf Schumacher	D	5	BMW WilliamsF1 Team	Williams FW23-BMW P80 V10	M	55	1h 48m 23.034s	104.868/168.769	+48.23
6	Mika Häkkinen	SF	3	West McLaren Mercedes	McLaren MP4/16-Mercedes F0110K V10	B	55	1h 48m 23.407s	104.862/168.759	+48.60
7	Jos Verstappen	NL	14	Orange Arrows Asiatech	Arrows A22-Asiatech V10	B	55	1h 48m 56.361s	104.334/167.909	+81.56
8	Jarno Trulli	I	12	B&H Jordan Honda	Jordan EJ11-Honda RA001E V10	B	54			+1
9	Jean Alesi	F	22	Prost Acer	Prost AP04-Acer V10	M	54			+1
10	Luciano Burti	BR	19	Jaguar Racing	Jaguar R2-Cosworth CR3 V10	M	54			+1
11	Jenson Button	GB	8	Mild Seven Benetton Renault	Benetton B201-Renault RS21 V10	M	53			+2 la
12	Gaston Mazzacane	ARG	23	Prost Acer	Prost AP04-Acer V10	M	53			+2 la
13	Fernando Alonso	ESP	21	European Minardi F1	Minardi PS01-European V10	M	52			+3 la
14	Tarso Marques	BR	20	European Minardi F1	Minardi PS01-European V10	M	51			+4 la
	Giancarlo Fisichella	I	7	Mild Seven Benetton Renault	Benetton B201-Renault RS21 V10	M	31	Fuel pressure		
	Jacques Villeneuve	CDN	10	Lucky Strike BAR Honda	BAR 03-Honda RA001E V10	B	3	Spun off		
	Nick Heidfeld	D	16	Red Bull Sauber Petronas	Sauber C20-Petronas V10	B	3	Spun off		
	Enrique Bernoldi	BR	15	Orange Arrows Asiatech	Arrows A22-Asiatech V10	B	3	Spun off		
	Juan Pablo Montoya	COL	6	BMW WilliamsF1 Team	Williams FW23-BMW P80 V10	M	3	Spun off		
	Eddie Irvine	GB	18	Jaguar Racing	Jaguar R2-Cosworth CR3 V10	M	3	Water leak		
	Olivier Panis	F	9	Lucky Strike BAR Honda	BAR 03-Honda RA001E V10	B	1	Oil fire		
	Kimi Räikkönen	SF	17	Red Bull Sauber Petronas	Sauber C20-Petronas V10	B	0	Clutch		

Fastest lap: Mika Häkkinen, on lap 48, 1m 40.962s, 122.811 mph/197.646 km/h.

Previous lap record: Mika Häkkinen (F1 McLaren MP4/15-Mercedes V10), 1m 38.543s, 125.826 mph/202.498 km/h (2000).

Grid order	1	2	3	4	5	6	7	8	9	10	11	12	13	14	15	16	17	18	19	20	21	22	23	24	25	26	27	28	29	30	31	32	33	34	35	36	37	38	39	40	41	42
1 M. SCHUMACHER	1	1	12	4	4	4	4	4	4	4	4	4	4	4	4	1	1	1	1	1	1	1	1	1	1	1	1	1	1	1	1	1	1	1	1	1	1	1	1	1	1	1
2 BARRICHELLO	2	2	4	11	14	11	11	11	11	11	14	14	14	14	1	2	2	2	2	2	2	4	4	4	4	2	2	2	2	2	2	2	2	2	2	2	2	2	2	2	2	2
5 R. SCHUMACHER	12	12	2	2	11	14	14	14	14	14	11	3	1	1	14	4	4	4	4	4	4	14	2	2	2	4	4	4	4	4	4	4	4	4	4	4	4	4	4	4	4	4
3 HÄKKINEN	4	4	11	1	3	3	3	3	3	3	5	3	2	2	14	14	14	14	14	14	2	12	14	14	14	14	14	14	5	5	5	5	5	5	5	14	14	14	14	14	14	14
12 TRULLI	11	11	14	14	12	12	12	12	12	12	5	11	5	3	3	3	11	11	12	12	11	3	3	3	3	5	5	14	14	14	14	14	14	14	14	11	11	11	11	11	11	11
6 MONTOYA	14	14	10	12	22	22	22	22	22	22	12	1	2	5	5	5	5	12	12	12	11	3	3	5	5	5	5	3	3	3	3	3	3	3	3	3	3	11	3	3	5	5
10 VILLENEUVE	10	10	1	3	7	7	7	7	7	7	22	2	11	11	11	11	11	11	11	12	7	3	11	11	11	11	11	11	11	11	11	11	11	11	11	3	5	5	3	3	3	3
4 COULTHARD	3	3	3	22	5	5	5	5	5	5	2	12	12	12	12	12	5	3	7	5	5	5	12	12	12	12	12	12	12	12	12	12	12	12	12	12	12	12	12	12	12	12
11 FRENTZEN	9	16	16	5	23	23	23	23	23	23	1	7	7	7	7	7	7	7	19	19	19	19	7	7	7	7	7	7	22	22	22	22	22	22	22	22	22	22	22	22	22	22
9 PANIS	16	22	22	23	2	2	2	2	2	2	7	8	19	19	19	19	19	22	5	22	22	22	23	22	22	22	22	22	19	19	19	19	19	19	19	19	19	19	19	19	19	19
16 HEIDFELD	22	7	15	7	1	1	1	1	1	8	22	22	22	22	22	22	5	22	23	8	7	7	22	20	21	21	19	8	8	8	8	8	8	8	8	8						
18 IRVINE	8	8	5	8	8	8	8	8	8	23	19	23	23	23	23	23	23	23	8	7	7	22	20	21	21	21	8	8	23	23	23	23	23	23	23	23	23					
22 ALESI	7	15	7	19	19	19	19	19	19	19	23	20	8	8	8	8	8	8	20	20	20	19	21	20	8	8	23	23	21	21	21	21	21	21	21	21	21	21				
17 RÄIKKÖNEN	15	19	23	20	20	20	20	20	20	20	20	8	20	20	20	20	20	7	8	8	21	23	8	8	23	21	21	20	20	20	20	20	20	20	20	20						
19 BURTI	19	20	8	21	21	21	21	21	21	21	21	21	21	21	21	21	8	21	21	21	21	21	8	8	23	23	20	20	20													
7 FISICHELLA	20	5	19																																							
8 BUTTON	23	23	6																																							
14 VERSTAPPEN	21	18	20																																							
23 MAZZACANE	18	6	18																																							
20 MARQUES	5	21	21																																							
21 ALONSO	6																																									
15 BERNOLDI																																										

Pit stop
One lap behind leader

STARTING GRID

1 M. SCHUMACHER Ferrari	**2** BARRICHELLO Ferrari
5 R. SCHUMACHER Williams	**3** HÄKKINEN McLaren
12 TRULLI Jordan	**6*** MONTOYA Williams
10 VILLENEUVE BAR	**4** COULTHARD McLaren
11 FRENTZEN Jordan	**9** PANIS BAR
16 HEIDFELD Sauber	**18** IRVINE Jaguar
22 ALESI Prost	**17** RÄIKKÖNEN Sauber
19 BURTI Jaguar	**7**** FISICHELLA Benetton
8 BUTTON Benetton	**14** VERSTAPPEN Arrows
23 MAZZACANE Prost	**20** MARQUES Minardi
21 ALONSO Minardi	**15***** BERNOLDI Arrows

*started from the pit lane
**started from the back of the grid
***qualifying times disallowed

All results and data © FIA 2001

46	47	48	49	50	51	52	53	54	55	●	
1	1	1	1	1	1	1	1	1	1		1
2	2	2	2	2	2	2	2	2	2		2
4	4	4	4	4	4	4	4	4			3
11	11	11	11	11	11	11	11	11	11		4
5	5	5	5	5	5	5	5	5	5		5
3	3	3	3	3	3	3	3	3			6
14	14	14	14	14	14	14	14	14			
12	12	12	12	12	12	12	12	12			
22	22	22	22	22	22	22	22	22			
19	19	19	19	19	19	19	19	19			
8	8	8	8	8	8	8	8				
23	23	23	23	23	23	23	23				
21	21	21	21	21	21	21					
20	20	20	20	20	20						

TIME SHEETS

QUALIFYING
Weather: Humid and very hot

Pos.	Driver	Car	Laps	Time
1	Michael Schumacher	Ferrari	12	1m 35.220s
2	Rubens Barrichello	Ferrari	12	1m 35.319s
3	Ralf Schumacher	Williams-BMW	12	1m 35.511s
4	Mika Häkkinen	McLaren-Mercedes	11	1m 36.040s
5	Jarno Trulli	Jordan-Honda	11	1m 36.180s
6	Juan Pablo Montoya	Williams-BMW	11	1m 36.218s
7	Jacques Villeneuve	BAR-Honda	12	1m 36.397s
8	David Coulthard	McLaren-Mercedes	12	1m 36.417s
9	Heinz-Harald Frentzen	Jordan-Honda	11	1m 36.578s
10	Olivier Panis	BAR-Honda	12	1m 36.681s
11	Nick Heidfeld	Sauber-Petronas	12	1m 36.913s
12	Eddie Irvine	Jaguar-Cosworth	12	1m 37.140s
13	Jean Alesi	Prost-Acer	12	1m 37.406s
14	Kimi Räikkönen	Sauber-Petronas	9	1m 37.728s
15	Luciano Burti	Jaguar-Cosworth	12	1m 38.035s
16	Giancarlo Fisichella	Benetton-Renault	7	1m 38.086s
17	Jenson Button	Benetton-Renault	12	1m 38.258s
18	Jos Verstappen	Arrows-Asiatech	12	1m 38.509s
19	Enrique Bernoldi*	Arrows-Asiatech	11	1m 38.708s
20	Gaston Mazzacane	Prost-Acer	12	1m 39.006s
21	Tarso Marques	Minardi-European	12	1m 39.714s
22	Fernando Alonso	Minardi-European	11	1m 40.249s

*times disallowed

FRIDAY FREE PRACTICE
Weather: Bright and sunny

Pos.	Driver	Laps	Time
1	Jarno Trulli	39	1m 38.846s
2	Michael Schumacher	34	1m 38.929s
3	Rubens Barrichello	32	1m 38.931s
4	David Coulthard	31	1m 39.300s
5	Eddie Irvine	29	1m 39.520s
6	Mika Häkkinen	26	1m 39.861s
7	Heinz-Harald Frentzen	29	1m 40.197s
8	Luciano Burti	37	1m 40.211s
9	Olivier Panis	36	1m 40.229s
10	Ralf Schumacher	33	1m 40.617s
11	Jacques Villeneuve	35	1m 41.003s
12	Nick Heidfeld	36	1m 41.027s
13	Giancarlo Fisichella	21	1m 41.375s
14	Kimi Räikkönen	37	1m 41.592s
15	Jos Verstappen	19	1m 41.794s
16	Jean Alesi	40	1m 41.834s
17	Jenson Button	23	1m 42.214s
18	Enrique Bernoldi	22	1m 42.541s
19	Gaston Mazzacane	33	1m 42.563s
20	Tarso Marques	27	1m 42.872s
21	Fernando Alonso	18	1m 43.107s
22	Juan Pablo Montoya	5	2m 13.188s

SATURDAY FREE PRACTICE
Weather: Bright and sunny

Pos.	Driver	Laps	Time
1	Rubens Barrichello	25	1m 36.188s
2	Ralf Schumacher	23	1m 36.475s
3	Mika Häkkinen	21	1m 36.519s
4	Michael Schumacher	19	1m 36.548s
5	David Coulthard	25	1m 36.814s
6	Heinz-Harald Frentzen	25	1m 37.030s
7	Jarno Trulli	19	1m 37.231s
8	Eddie Irvine	26	1m 37.360s
9	Olivier Panis	25	1m 37.391s
10	Kimi Räikkönen	17	1m 37.428s
11	Nick Heidfeld	31	1m 37.459s
12	Jacques Villeneuve	25	1m 37.463s
13	Juan Pablo Montoya	25	1m 37.502s
14	Luciano Burti	25	1m 37.636s
15	Jean Alesi	20	1m 38.130s
16	Giancarlo Fisichella	30	1m 38.548s
17	Jenson Button	23	1m 38.712s
18	Enrique Bernoldi	28	1m 38.958s
19	Jos Verstappen	26	1m 39.401s
20	Gaston Mazzacane	26	1m 39.651s
21	Fernando Alonso	23	1m 39.956s
22	Tarso Marques	24	1m 40.171s

WARM-UP
Weather: Wet track, drying. Very humid

Pos.	Driver	Laps	Time
1	Rubens Barrichello	10	1m 49.763s
2	David Coulthard	10	1m 50.846s
3	Jarno Trulli	13	1m 51.046s
4	Kimi Räikkönen	11	1m 51.265s
5	Jos Verstappen	13	1m 51.508s
6	Heinz-Harald Frentzen	10	1m 52.061s
7	Michael Schumacher	11	1m 52.316s
8	Nick Heidfeld	12	1m 53.352s
9	Olivier Panis	11	1m 53.470s
10	Jacques Villeneuve	12	1m 53.482s
11	Ralf Schumacher	7	1m 55.109s
12	Juan Pablo Montoya	12	1m 55.278s
13	Mika Häkkinen	9	1m 57.064s
14	Jean Alesi	12	1m 57.832s
15	Eddie Irvine	9	1m 58.322s
16	Gaston Mazzacane	9	1m 58.416s
17	Giancarlo Fisichella	10	1m 58.656s
18	Luciano Burti	10	2m 01.120s
19	Enrique Bernoldi	10	2m 01.630s
20	Fernando Alonso	10	2m 01.771s
21	Tarso Marques	8	2m 04.349s
22	Jenson Button	4	2m 07.047s

RACE FASTEST LAPS
Weather: Dry start, then a heavy rain shower, followed by a drying track

Driver	Time	Lap
Mika Häkkinen	1m 40.962s	48
Ralf Schumacher	1m 41.503s	54
Michael Schumacher	1m 41.833s	2
Rubens Barrichello	1m 42.037s	2
Heinz-Harald Frentzen	1m 42.119s	50
David Coulthard	1m 42.839s	47
Jos Verstappen	1m 43.029s	55
Jacques Villeneuve	1m 43.470s	2
Jarno Trulli	1m 43.559s	52
Luciano Burti	1m 43.697s	52
Jean Alesi	1m 43.853s	53
Juan Pablo Montoya	1m 43.926s	2
Gaston Mazzacane	1m 43.991s	53
Jenson Button	1m 44.891s	52
Nick Heidfeld	1m 45.328s	2
Fernando Alonso	1m 45.585s	50
Tarso Marques	1m 46.016s	50
Giancarlo Fisichella	1m 46.982s	2
Enrique Bernoldi	1m 47.294s	2
Eddie Irvine	1m 51.532s	2
Olivier Panis	1m 54.538s	1

CHASSIS LOG BOOK

1	M. Schumacher	Ferrari F2001/208
2	Barrichello	Ferrari F2001/206
	spare	Ferrari F2001/209
3	Häkkinen	McLaren MP4/16/3
4	Coulthard	McLaren MP4/16/1
	spare	McLaren MP4/16/2
5	R. Schumacher	Williams FW23/3
6	Montoya	Williams FW23/2
	spare	Williams FW23/1
7	Fisichella	Benetton B201/3
8	Button	Benetton B201/1
	spare	Benetton B201/2
9	Panis	BAR 03/3
10	Villeneuve	BAR 03/4
	spare	BAR 03/2
11	Frentzen	Jordan EJ11/4
12	Trulli	Jordan EJ11/3
	spare	Jordan EJ11/2
14	Verstappen	Arrows A22/1
15	Bernoldi	Arrows A22/3
	spare	Arrows A22/4
16	Heidfeld	Sauber C20/3
17	Räikkönen	Sauber C20/1
	spare	Sauber C20/4
18	Irvine	Jaguar R2/4
19	Burti	Jaguar R2/3
	spare	Jaguar R2/5
20	Marques	Minardi PS01/1
21	Alonso	Minardi PS01/3
	spare	Minardi PS01/2
22	Alesi	Prost AP04/3
23	Mazzacane	Prost AP04/2
	spare	Prost AP04/4

POINTS TABLES

DRIVERS

1	Michael Schumacher	20
2 =	David Coulthard	10
2 =	Rubens Barrichello	10
4	Heinz-Harald Frentzen	5
5	Nick Heidfeld	3
6	Ralf Schumacher	2
7 =	Kimi Räikkönen	1
7 =	Mika Häkkinen	1

CONSTRUCTORS

1	Ferrari	30
2	McLaren	11
3	Jordan	5
4	Sauber	4
5	Williams	2

BRAZILIAN
grand prix

1st - COULTHARD • 2nd - M. SCHUMACHER • 3rd - HEIDFELD

Main photograph: With consummate ease, Juan Pablo Montoya's Williams-BMW leads Michael Schumacher's Ferrari and the rest of the pack in the opening stages of the race. The Colombian looked unbeatable until he was accidentally punted off by Jos Verstappen.
Photograph: Paul-Henri Cahier

Left: Coulthard's victory over Schumacher was one of the most assured wins of his career, marking out the Scot as a title challenger of some calibre.
Photograph: Bryn Williams/crash.net

Below: As usual, the local Brazilian beauties graced the grid.
Photograph: Paul-Henri Cahier

INTERLAGOS QUALIFYING

In qualifying at Interlagos the brothers Schumacher wrote their own personal slice of motor racing history by buttoning up the front row together. Michael posted a 1m 13.780s with Ralf getting precariously close to his sibling on 1m 14.090s.

'We've improved the set-up and the tyres work well in the hot conditions,' said Ralf. 'The BMW engine is strong, although I'm not sure we are

yet ready to compete with Michael in the Ferrari.'

Montoya might have been on the front row had he not slammed into the tyre barriers at the start of his first run when his car momentarily bottomed out. He ran back to the pits, took the spare FW23 and qualified fourth on 1m 14.165s. 'I had a bit of an argument with a marshal who wanted me to stay where I was out on the circuit,' he said, 'and the spare certainly felt a very different car.

'It had a lot more understeer and a heat shield came off the back on the start/finish straight.'

McLaren seemed upbeat and optimistic, feeling that they had made more progress than might be immediately apparent with the handling balance of the MP4/16s. Nevertheless, the straightline speed of the new BMW V10s continued to provide them with worrying food for thought.

Häkkinen qualified third on 1m 14.122s, reporting that the car felt much improved for this race. 'I definitely thought we would be challengers this weekend,' he said with guarded satisfaction.

'We had some new bits on the car. We expected an improvement and it did happen, so we're very happy. We're certainly more competitive here than in Malaysia.'

Team-mate David Coulthard was rather disappointed to wind up fifth on 1m 14.178s. 'My first run was aborted when I hit traffic and as a result I only had three runs,' he said. 'But the balance of the car has improved and there has been a performance increase from the engine as well.'

For Rubens Barrichello, what should have been a heartening qualifying performance for Ferrari at his home Grand Prix was smothered by time-consuming understeer.

'In this morning's free practice session I ran only one set of tyres,' he said. 'In the afternoon, on new tyres, I was never able to find the ideal balance on the car which was continually understeering. Sixth place on the grid was certainly not what I was expecting here in front of my home crowd.'

Casting further down the grid, the Jordan EJ-11s of Jarno Trulli (1m 14.630s) and Heinz-Harald Frentzen (1m 14.633s) effectively emerged as best of the rest if one assumed that the leading foursome had turned into a 'sixsome', if you like, thanks to the promotion to the Premier League of the Williams-BMWs.

Losers in all this were the BAR-Hondas, both Olivier Panis (1m 15.046s) and Jacques Villeneuve (1m 15.182s) complaining of dire lack of grip and unable to squeeze any sort of decent performance from their machines. They finished the session trailing 11th and 12th.

In much the same way as Jordan embarrassed BAR, so Sauber embarrassed Prost in the customer Ferrari engine race. It was nice to hear Nick Heidfeld freely admitting that he'd taken Kimi Räikkönen's chassis settings in order to vault ahead of the young Finn in the final grid order. The German youngster consistently displayed a frankness which seems refreshingly appealing. A bit like Montoya, in many ways.

Over in the Jaguar camp, Eddie Irvine qualified his R2 in 13th place on 1m 15.192s, barely 0.2s ahead of his team-mate Luciano Burti who lined up alongside him.

'I could have done slightly better, but not by much,' confessed Irvine with his customary candour. 'We only got the car really hooked up properly in the final run and we made big steps with the steering, and that helped me a lot.'

Jean Alesi qualified his Prost-Ferrari 15th on 1m 15.437s, the Frenchman disappointed that he was still grappling excessive oversteer. He nevertheless managed to squeeze ahead of the Arrows A22s of Enrique Bernoldi (1m 15.657s) and Jos Verstappen (1m 15.704s), the Dutchman complaining that poor balance was a factor in his failing to get the upper hand over his team-mate.

Benetton had another thoroughly miserable session with its B201s. Both cars suffered from oil leaks, and while Giancarlo Fisichella muscled his way to 18th fastest on 1m 16.175s, he freely admitted 'we have no dreams for the race.'

Jenson Button struggled to 20th on 1m 16.229s, beaten by Fernando Alonso's Minardi PS01 (1m 16.184s) while Gaston Mazzacane's Prost (1m 16.520s) and Tarso Marques in the other Minardi (1m 16.784s) completed the line-up.

On another issue completely, it didn't take long to conclude that one of the safest places in São Paulo was actually the cockpit of a 180 mph F1 car.

Four Williams engineers were held up at gunpoint while leaving the track on Thursday evening, but thankfully they survived the incident without injury.

Minardi manager Tony Lees was also robbed leaving a bank where he was picking up expenses cash for the team mechanics, while there was unexpected violence of a different sort in the pit lane when an overhead moveable camera fell off its guide rails, narrowly missing Jaguar team chief Bobby Rahal as it crashed to the ground.

Top: Jenson Button doesn't want to hear any more about what might have been at Williams.
Photograph: Mark Thompson/Allsport-Getty Images

Above: Gerhard Berger was quietly confident and impressed with Montoya.
Photograph: Bryn Williams/crash.net

Right: Anxious Ferrari mechanics make a few final adjustments for Barrichello after he'd been forced to take the spare F2001 just before the start.
Photograph: Paul-Henri Cahier

Top right: Panis scored points for BAR after another strong race and this time there were no unpleasant surprises to follow.
Photograph: Bryn Williams/crash.net

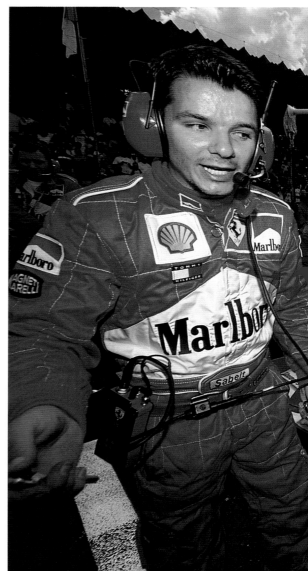

DAVID Coulthard signalled his emergence as a serious contender for the 2001 World Championship with a brilliant win in the Brazilian Grand Prix at São Paulo's bumpy and demanding Interlagos circuit. His was a decisive victory over a struggling Michael Schumacher whom he beat back into second place after a heavy shower transformed the circuit into a skating rink and fans were treated to the uncharacteristic spectacle of the Ferrari team leader first spinning and later ploughing off the road into a gravel trap.

Coulthard stamped his authority on the race with a bold overtaking manoeuvre on the Ferrari team leader going into the first corner at the start of the 50th lap. It was the second time that afternoon that Schumacher had been subjected to such treatment, the first being at the hands of Juan Pablo Montoya whose Williams-BMW surged through to take the lead at the start of the third lap.

It was a dazzling display of audacity and car control on Montoya's third F1 outing, but just as it seemed as though he had decisively out-run Schumacher, he was shunted dramatically out of the race. Jos Verstappen's Arrows A22, which he had just lapped, slammed straight into the back of his car.

Even before the cars took their place on the starting grid, a collective groan came from the passionately enthusiastic crowd as their hero Rubens Barrichello rolled to a standstill when his Ferrari's oil pressure dropped alarmingly on his first lap out of the pits.

This was the latest in a long line of frustrations for the São Paulo driver who had suffered an engine failure on Friday and then grappled with terminal understeer throughout qualifying and could only claim a disappointing sixth on the starting grid.

In sweltering temperatures of around 35 degrees, Barrichello jogged back to the pits where he slumped exhausted on the floor while the Ferrari mechanics busied themselves changing the settings on Michael Schumacher's spare car so that he could take up his position for the start.

The task of changing pedal settings, adjusting his seat harness and fitting him into the car meant that it was touch and go whether Barrichello would manage to get out onto the circuit before the pit lane exit closed 15 minutes before the start. In the event, he made it with 26s to spare, but it had certainly been an uncomfortably close call.

If this was a shaky moment for the Ferrari team, it was nothing compared with the crushing disappointment waiting for the McLaren-Mercedes team when Mika Häkkinen stalled on the grid. As Michael Schumacher led away from pole position, the pack scattered in all directions to avoid the stationary McLaren and, as the safety car was immediately sent out to slow the

Picking your moment. The Jordan-Honda EJ-11s of Heinz-Harald Frentzen and Jarno Trulli line up for attention at the same moment in the seemingly cluttered Interlagos pit lane.
Photograph: Paul-Henri Cahier

JAGUAR CANCELS SILVERSTONE F1 HQ PLANS

Jaguar's plans for a new state-of-the-art F1 headquarters at Silverstone were shelved following a failure of Ford's land management division to agree terms with the British Racing Drivers' Club, the owners of the circuit.

Team chief Bobby Rahal confirmed at Interlagos that the deal was almost certainly off and that Jaguar was looking for other alternatives.

'We have a committed capital budget for a new factory, but we certainly don't have a blank cheque,' said Rahal. 'I think the whole programme rather got ahead of itself because everybody involved wanted it to happen.

'But I have to do what's best for the company. I think we can win races from our current premises [in Milton Keynes] but we do need a new R and D department. Adrian Reynard is currently building us a new wind tunnel which will be situated at Brackley.'

It's believed that the BRDC was asking for less than a million pounds a year for the 45-year lease, on top of which Ford would have had to bear the costs of constructing the new factory.

Martin Brundle, the BRDC chairman, said that it was possible that the deal could be revived. 'We would like the Jaguar and Cosworth factories to be at Silverstone, but at a value that the [BRDC] board and its advisors can confidently put before the membership.

'The planning was already in place for a technical park before the negotiations started with Jaguar and something will be constructed there in the future.'

Above: Soccer legend Pele dwarfed all the F1 stars in terms of sporting and celebrity status.

Top right: Nick Heidfeld endorsed his F1 credentials with a strong run to third place in the Sauber-Petronas.
Both photographs: Paul-Henri Cahier

Right: Giancarlo Fisichella slogged on and survived to take a precious point for the Benetton-Renault brigade.
Photograph: Bryn Williams/crash.net

pack, the dejected Finn climbed from the cockpit and walked back to his pit.

Schumacher led the slowing field past the pits at the end of the first lap through a flurry of yellow warning flags on the start/finish line. At the end of the second lap the safety car was withdrawn and, as a rain shower doused the circuit, Montoya seized his chance to lunge down the inside of the leading Ferrari going into the first turn.

Not in the least intimidated by Schumacher's celebrity status the novice Colombian ruthlessly banged wheels with the Ferrari team leader as he forced his way ahead.

'With such a long straight from the last corner, you have to give the safety car a lot of room,' said Schumacher, 'so it is easy for the second place man to get close and slipstream by. He got it right, braking very late. He pushed me wide, but that is normal racing. We touched, but that was not a problem.' Even so, this was an extremely frustrating moment for the Ferrari ace who'd started the race on a two-stop strategy, banking on an empty track ahead which would enable him to open an early advantage. Now Montoya had undermined that finely-balanced strategy.

On the same lap the hapless Barrichello's bruising Brazilian GP ended when he slammed into the back of Ralf Schumacher's Williams-BMW under braking at the end of the long straight beyond the pits. The Ferrari's right front wheel was ripped off in the impact, but the Brazilian driver was thankfully uninjured.

'I was behind Ralf when he suddenly changed line, probably to pass another car, and he braked in front of me,' said Barrichello. 'I did not expect this and the collision was inevitable after that. These things happen in racing.'

At the end of lap four Montoya came slamming through ahead of Schumacher, leading the race in brilliant style. His Williams's Michelin tyres' wear characteristics meant that he could expect to lose grip after the first couple of laps, but if he could hang on ahead then their grip would come back after half a dozen or so laps.

Thereafter the Colombian drove with unflustered confidence and maturity, revelling in the prodigious acceleration of his powerful BMW engine to out-accelerate Schumacher time and again as they climbed the long hill up to the start/finish line.

With six laps completed Montoya was steadying his advantage over Schumacher at around 0.5s with Coulthard several lengths further back in third place keeping a watching brief. With the intention of hedging his bets in case of the forecast rain shower, David had started with a compromise chassis set-up on his McLaren. This meant that it didn't have quite the ideal, razor-sharp responsiveness in the dry, but his pay-off would come later.

Fourth and fifth were the Jordan-Hondas of Jarno Trulli and Heinz-Harald Frentzen, then Jacques Villeneuve's BAR-Honda, Nick Heidfeld's Sauber C20 and his team-mate Kimi Räikkönen.

By lap 16 jagged forks of lightning could be seen in the distance and it was clear that the forecast heavy rain was not far away. Montoya was now 0.9s ahead of Schumacher with Coulthard third and Trulli being hauled in by Panis for fourth which the Frenchman duly took from the Jordan driver going into lap 21.

On lap 25 Schumacher made his first stop in 9.6s, dropping to fourth and allowing Coulthard to close to within 2.7s of Montoya's leading Williams. Panis stopped from third on lap 28, dropping to eighth, but Montoya steadily began to open his advantage over Coulthard from 4.2s on lap 30 to 5.2s on lap 35.

At about that time the rain started to fall quite seriously, but before the track became really treacherous, Montoya had embarked on his fateful 39th lap and the collision with Verstappen came a few seconds later. The stewards later fined Verstappen $15,000, judging the accident to have been his responsibility.

The two cars pirouetted to a halt, but Montoya was cheered to the echo as he walked back to the pits, leaving Coulthard leading Schumacher by 30.5s and seemingly in a very strong position indeed for McLaren.

On lap 40 Coulthard dived into the pits for a 9.8s routine refuelling stop, just squeezing back into the race 0.7s ahead of Schumacher's Ferrari. Now the pit lane erupted into chaos as everybody scampered in for wet or intermediate rubber, but Schumacher stayed out until lap 46 before switching to intermediates.

Coulthard stayed out for another lap on dry tyres, a move which seemed to be a mistake as Schumacher made 13s on the Scot on their crucial 'in' laps prior to the stop, but immediately threw that away with a spin next time round.

That put Coulthard right back onto the Ferrari's tail and he stormed through into the lead going into lap 50, diving inside Marques's Minardi into the first corner as Schumacher opted to go round the outside of the also-ran.

From then on Coulthard had it in the bag. Schumacher, who

had chosen the same Bridgestone intermediate tyres which he had used to such good effect to win the Malaysian Grand Prix a fortnight earlier, now found his chassis set-up working against him. The net result of this was the uncharacteristic sight of the World Champion half-spinning and then sliding off the circuit as he struggled to keep touch with the McLaren, eventually dropping to second place some 16.1s behind at the chequered flag.

Schumacher took the defeat on the chin. 'David passed me when we were behind the Minardi, because at first it was on the left of the track,' he said.

'But the Minardi moved that way also. At the moment I had to make the decision, the outside line was the only option. In any case, I think David would have passed me later. The car was not working the way I liked it.'

On a day when simply to survive on the treacherous track surface was an achievement, Nick Heidfeld drove magnificently to take his Sauber-Ferrari across the line third ahead of Olivier Panis's BAR-Honda which lost time at its second stop, the Frenchman having to queue behind team-mate Villeneuve after a mix-up in radio communications. Jarno Trulli's Jordan-Honda and Giancarlo Fisichella's Benetton-Renault completed the top half-dozen.

Villeneuve came home seventh, struggling with a loose rear end after an apparent differential failure, while Alesi, Marques and Button were also classified, together with the luckless Frentzen who retired just six laps from the end with a possible third place in his sights.

Ralf Schumacher also impressed with a great drive after his Williams had been repaired following its collision with Barrichello. He climbed steadily back through the field, setting the race's fastest lap on lap 38 before spinning off at the height of the rain storm. He was not alone in this respect, sharing the experience with both Kimi Räikkönen and Eddie Irvine.

Yet it was Juan Pablo Montoya's name which was on everybody's lips at the end of the day. BMW competitions director Gerhard Berger was particularly impressed by a performance the excellence of which had been accentuated by the fact that he had sufficient fuel aboard for a single pit stop. Schumacher, running with a lighter Ferrari on a two-stop strategy, still couldn't do anything about him.

'Young drivers like to leave their calling card,' said Berger. 'And Montoya certainly did that at Interlagos.' In Michael Schumacher's top pocket.

Diary

Justin Wilson wins Interlagos supporting race to open International F3000 championship programme.

Michael Schumacher denies wild speculation that he is considering an F1 offer from Toyota.

Jaguar's F1 team has eight laptop computers stolen from its pit garage at Interlagos, while Minardi lost seven wheels.

Flavio Briatore and Eddie Jordan call for F1 racing to be better promoted to improve its flavour as a global sporting spectacle. 'At this moment we are doing absolutely nothing to increase the flavour of F1,' said the Benetton team chief. 'We know the pay TV channels are not happy with us because they are losing money.'

German broadcasting giant Kirch receives approval by the German anti-trust authorities to finalise its bid for a controlling interest in Bernie Ecclestone's SLEC F1 empire.

ROUND 3
INTERLAGOS 30 MARCH–1 APRIL 2001

grande premio MARLBORO do BRAZIL

INTERLAGOS, SÃO PAULO
AUTODROMO CARLOS PACE
CIRCUIT LENGTH: 2.677 miles/4.309 km

SUBIDA DO LAGO 80/129 (3)
CURVA DO SO 130/209 (4)
BICO DE PATO 45/72 (1)
MERGULHO 115/185 (3)
PINEIRINHO 60/97 (2)
FERRA DURA
DESCIDA DO SOL 85/137 (3)
S' DO SENNA 55/89 (2)
mph/km/h (gear)
SUBIDA DOS BOXES 160/258 (5)

RACE DISTANCE: 71 laps, 190.083 miles/305.909 km **RACE WEATHER:** Dry start, then heavy rain shower, followed by drying track

Pos.	Driver	Nat.	No.	Entrant	Car/Engine	Tyres	Laps	Time/Retirement	Speed (mph/km/h)	Gap to leader
1	David Coulthard	GB	4	West McLaren Mercedes	McLaren MP4/16-Mercedes F0110K V10	B	71	1h 39m 00.834s	115.185/185.373	
2	Michael Schumacher	D	1	Scuderia Ferrari Marlboro	Ferrari F2001-050 V10	B	71	1h 39m 16.998s	114.873/184.870	+16.16
3	Nick Heidfeld	D	16	Red Bull Sauber Petronas	Sauber C20-Petronas V10	B	70			+1
4	Olivier Panis	F	9	Lucky Strike BAR Honda	BAR 03-Honda RA001E V10	B	70			+1
5	Jarno Trulli	I	12	B&H Jordan Honda	Jordan EJ11-Honda RA001E V10	B	70			+1
6	Giancarlo Fisichella	I	7	Mild Seven Benetton Renault	Benetton B201-Renault RS21 V10	M	70			+1
7	Jacques Villeneuve	CDN	10	Lucky Strike BAR Honda	BAR 03-Honda RA001E V10	B	70			+1
8	Jean Alesi	F	22	Prost Acer	Prost AP04-Acer V10	M	70			+1
9	Tarso Marques	BR	20	European Minardi F1	Minardi PS01-European V10	M	68			+3 la
10	Jenson Button	GB	8	Mild Seven Benetton Renault	Benetton B201-Renault RS21 V10	M	64			+7 la
11	Heinz-Harald Frentzen	D	11	B&H Jordan Honda	Jordan EJ11-Honda RA001E V10	B	63	Engine		+8 la
	Kimi Räikkönen	SF	17	Red Bull Sauber Petronas	Sauber C20-Petronas V10	B	55	Spun off		
	Gaston Mazzacane	ARG	23	Prost Acer	Prost AP04-Acer V10	M	54	Clutch		
	Ralf Schumacher	D	5	BMW WilliamsF1 Team	Williams FW23-BMW P80 V10	M	54	Spun off		
	Eddie Irvine	GB	18	Jaguar Racing	Jaguar R2-Cosworth CR3 V10	M	52	Spun off		
	Juan Pablo Montoya	COL	6	BMW WilliamsF1 Team	Williams FW23-BMW P80 V10	M	38	Collision with Verstappen		
	Jos Verstappen	NL	14	Orange Arrows Asiatech	Arrows A22-Asiatech V10	B	37	Collision with Montoya		
	Luciano Burti	BR	19	Jaguar Racing	Jaguar R2-Cosworth CR3 V10	M	30	Engine water seal		
	Fernando Alonso	ESP	21	European Minardi F1	Minardi PS01-European V10	M	25	Electronics		
	Enrique Bernoldi	BR	15	Orange Arrows Asiatech	Arrows A22-Asiatech V10	B	15	Hydraulics		
	Rubens Barrichello	BR	2	Scuderia Ferrari Marlboro	Ferrari F2001-050 V10	B	2	Collision with R. Schumacher		
	Mika Häkkinen	SF	3	West McLaren Mercedes	McLaren MP4/16-Mercedes F0110K V10	B	0	Stalled on grid		

Fastest lap: Ralf Schumacher, on lap 38, 1m 15.693s, 127.342 mph/204.938 km/h.

Lap record: Michael Schumacher (F1 Ferrari F1-2000-V10), 1m 14.755s, 128.940 mph/207.509 km/h (2000).

Lap chart — Grid order (laps 1–54)

Grid order	Laps
1 M. SCHUMACHER	1 1 6 6 6 6 6 6 6 6 6 6 6 6 6 6 6 6 6 6 6 6 6 6 6 6 6 6 6 6 6 6 6 6 6 6 6 6 6 6 6 6 6 6 4 4 4 4 4 4 1 1 4 4 4 4
5 R. SCHUMACHER	6 6 1 1 1 1 1 1 1 1 1 1 1 1 1 1 1 1 1 1 1 1 1 1 1 1 1 1 1 1 1 1 4 4 4 4 4 4 4 4 4 4 4 4 1 1 1 1 1 1 4 4 1 1 1 1
3 HÄKKINEN	4 4 4 4 4 4 4 4 4 4 4 4 4 4 4 4 4 4 4 4 4 4 4 1 9 9 9 1 1 1 1 1 1 1 1 1 12 12 12 12 12 9 9 11 11 11 11 11 11 11 11 11 11 11
6 MONTOYA	12 12 12 12 12 12 12 12 12 12 12 12 12 12 12 12 12 12 12 9 9 9 9 9 12 12 12 12 12 12 12 12 12 12 12 12 11 11 11 11 12 11 18 16 16 16 16 12 12 12 12 12
4 COULTHARD	5 5 11 11 11 11 11 11 11 11 11 9 9 9 9 12 12 12 12 1 1 12 11 11 11 11 11 11 11 11 9 9 9 9 9 9 11 12 17 12 12 12 16 16 16 16 16 16
2 BARRICHELLO	11 11 10 10 10 10 10 10 10 10 10 9 9 11 11 11 11 11 11 11 11 11 11 11 11 11 16 16 16 16 16 16 16 7 7 7 16 16 16 17 17 17 17 17 17 18 22 22
12 TRULLI	2 2 16 16 16 16 9 9 9 16 16 16 16 16 16 16 16 16 16 16 16 16 17 17 17 17 17 17 17 9 9 16 16 16 7 17 17 16 12 18 18 18 18 18 22 9 9
11 FRENTZEN	10 10 17 17 17 17 9 16 16 16 17 17 17 17 17 17 17 17 17 17 17 17 17 9 9 9 9 9 9 9 17 7 17 17 17 18 18 18 22 22 22 22 22 22 9 7 7
16 HEIDFELD	16 16 18 18 18 9 9 17 17 17 17 22 22 22 22 22 22 22 22 22 22 22 14 14 14 14 19 14 14 14 14 14 14 14 17 10 10 10 10 22 22 22 7 7 9 9 9 9 7 17 17
17 RÄIKKÖNEN	17 17 22 22 22 22 22 22 22 14 14 14 14 14 14 14 14 14 14 19 19 19 19 7 7 7 7 7 7 7 10 18 18 18 18 7 23 9 9 7 7 7 7 17 23 23
9 PANIS	18 18 9 9 9 14 14 14 19 19 19 19 19 19 19 19 19 19 19 7 7 7 7 23 10 10 10 10 10 18 18 18 22 22 22 23 23 23 23 23 23 23 23 10
10 VILLENEUVE	22 14 14 14 14 19 19 19 19 19 19 10 7 7 7 7 7 7 7 7 23 10 10 10 10 18 18 18 18 18 18 22 23 23 23 23 23 10 10 10 10 10 10 10 10 20 10
18 IRVINE	9 9 19 19 19 7 7 7 7 7 7 15 15 23 23 23 23 23 23 23 23 10 20 20 20 20 18 22 22 22 22 22 22 23 20 20 20 20 20 20 20 20 20 5 5
19 BURTI	14 14 7 7 7 18 15 15 15 15 15 23 23 20 20 20 20 20 20 20 20 20 18 18 18 18 20 20 20 20 20 20 20 5 5 5 5 5 5 5 5 5 5 5 8 8
22 ALESI	19 19 8 15 15 15 23 23 23 23 23 20 20 21 21 21 21 21 21 21 21 21 10 18 22 22 23 23 23 23 23 23 23 5 8 8 8 8 8 8 8 8 8 8 8
15 BERNOLDI	7 7 15 8 8 23 20 20 20 20 20 21 15 18 18 18 10 10 10 10 21 22 22 22 22 22 5 5 5 5 5 8
14 VERSTAPPEN	8 8 23 23 23 8 21 21 21 21 21 8 8 8 10 10 10 10 8 18 18 18 5 5 5 5 8 8 8 8 8
7 FISICHELLA	15 15 20 20 20 20 8 8 8 8 8 18 18 10 18 18 18 18 18 8 8 21 5 5 5 8 8
21 ALONSO	23 23 21 21 21 18 18 18 18 18 10 10 18 5 5 5 5 5 5 5 5 5
8 BUTTON	20 20 5 5 5 5 5 5 5 5 5 5 5 5
23 MAZZACANE	21 21
20 MARQUES	

Pit stop
One lap behind leader

STARTING GRID

	1 **M. SCHUMACHER** Ferrari
5 R. SCHUMACHER Williams	
	3 **HÄKKINEN** McLaren
6 MONTOYA Williams	
	4 **COULTHARD** McLaren
2 BARRICHELLO Ferrari	
	12 **TRULLI** Jordan
11 FRENTZEN Jordan	
	16 **HEIDFELD** Sauber
17 RÄIKKÖNEN Sauber	
	9 **PANIS** BAR
10 VILLENEUVE BAR	
	18 **IRVINE** Jaguar
19 BURTI Jaguar	
	22 **ALESI** Prost
15 BERNOLDI Arrows	
	14 **VERSTAPPEN** Arrows
7 FISICHELLA Benetton	
	21 **ALONSO** Minardi
8 BUTTON Benetton	
	23 **MAZZACANE** Prost
20 MARQUES Minardi	

All results and data © FIA 2001

TIME SHEETS

QUALIFYING

Weather: Sunny and hot

Pos.	Driver	Car	Laps	Time
1	Michael Schumacher	Ferrari	11	1m 13.780s
2	Ralf Schumacher	Williams-BMW	12	1m 14.090s
3	Mika Häkkinen	McLaren-Mercedes	10	1m 14.122s
4	Juan Pablo Montoya	Williams-BMW	11	1m 14.165s
5	David Coulthard	McLaren-Mercedes	11	1m 14.178s
6	Rubens Barrichello	Ferrari	11	1m 14.191s
7	Jarno Trulli	Jordan-Honda	11	1m 14.630s
8	Heinz-Harald Frentzen	Jordan-Honda	11	1m 14.633s
9	Nick Heidfeld	Sauber-Petronas	12	1m 14.810s
10	Kimi Räikkönen	Sauber-Petronas	11	1m 14.924s
11	Olivier Panis	BAR-Honda	11	1m 15.046s
12	Jacques Villeneuve	BAR-Honda	12	1m 15.182s
13	Eddie Irvine	Jaguar-Cosworth	12	1m 15.192s
14	Luciano Burti	Jaguar-Cosworth	12	1m 15.371s
15	Jean Alesi	Prost-Acer	12	1m 15.437s
16	Enrique Bernoldi	Arrows-Asiatech	12	1m 15.657s
17	Jos Verstappen	Arrows-Asiatech	12	1m 15.704s
18	Giancarlo Fisichella	Benetton-Renault	12	1m 16.175s
19	Fernando Alonso	Minardi-European	12	1m 16.184s
20	Jenson Button	Benetton-Renault	12	1m 16.229s
21	Gaston Mazzacane	Prost-Acer	12	1m 16.520s
22	Tarso Marques	Minardi-European	12	1m 16.784s

FRIDAY FREE PRACTICE

Weather: Sunny and hot

Pos.	Driver	Laps	Time
1	David Coulthard	37	1m 15.220s
2	Jarno Trulli	42	1m 16.224s
3	Michael Schumacher	37	1m 16.598s
4	Juan Pablo Montoya	43	1m 16.851s
5	Mika Häkkinen	39	1m 16.882s
6	Ralf Schumacher	22	1m 16.929s
7	Rubens Barrichello	23	1m 16.994s
8	Heinz-Harald Frentzen	36	1m 17.072s
9	Nick Heidfeld	41	1m 17.102s
10	Eddie Irvine	35	1m 17.295s
11	Luciano Burti	47	1m 17.430s
12	Olivier Panis	40	1m 17.432s
13	Jacques Villeneuve	40	1m 17.455s
14	Jean Alesi	43	1m 17.518s
15	Kimi Räikkönen	38	1m 17.712s
16	Jos Verstappen	32	1m 17.792s
17	Giancarlo Fisichella	33	1m 18.096s
18	Fernando Alonso	40	1m 18.222s
19	Enrique Bernoldi	38	1m 18.233s
20	Gaston Mazzacane	40	1m 18.269s
21	Tarso Marques	35	1m 19.005s
22	Jenson Button	24	1m 19.585s

SATURDAY FREE PRACTICE

Weather: Sunny and hot

Pos.	Driver	Laps	Time
1	Juan Pablo Montoya	30	1m 13.963s
2	Mika Häkkinen	29	1m 14.108s
3	David Coulthard	28	1m 14.182s
4	Ralf Schumacher	33	1m 14.282s
5	Michael Schumacher	27	1m 14.652s
6	Heinz-Harald Frentzen	31	1m 14.837s
7	Rubens Barrichello	27	1m 14.895s
8	Kimi Räikkönen	23	1m 15.031s
9	Olivier Panis	29	1m 15.039s
10	Nick Heidfeld	28	1m 15.096s
11	Jarno Trulli	12	1m 15.163s
12	Eddie Irvine	31	1m 15.409s
13	Luciano Burti	33	1m 15.470s
14	Jean Alesi	28	1m 15.735s
15	Jos Verstappen	36	1m 15.972s
16	Jacques Villeneuve	16	1m 16.135s
17	Enrique Bernoldi	31	1m 16.160s
18	Gaston Mazzacane	30	1m 16.347s
19	Jenson Button	28	1m 16.411s
20	Giancarlo Fisichella	24	1m 16.439s
21	Fernando Alonso	32	1m 16.602s
22	Tarso Marques	16	1m 18.212s

WARM-UP

Weather: Sunny and hot

Pos.	Driver	Laps	Time
1	Michael Schumacher	14	1m 15.971s
2	Rubens Barrichello	13	1m 16.145s
3	Mika Häkkinen	16	1m 16.308s
4	Ralf Schumacher	13	1m 16.375s
5	Jarno Trulli	16	1m 16.449s
6	David Coulthard	15	1m 16.679s
7	Olivier Panis	14	1m 16.711s
8	Juan Pablo Montoya	16	1m 17.008s
9	Nick Heidfeld	17	1m 17.135s
10	Heinz-Harald Frentzen	15	1m 17.138s
11	Kimi Räikkönen	15	1m 17.213s
12	Jacques Villeneuve	19	1m 17.405s
13	Eddie Irvine	16	1m 17.420s
14	Luciano Burti	13	1m 17.674s
15	Gaston Mazzacane	14	1m 17.681s
16	Jean Alesi	13	1m 17.728s
17	Fernando Alonso	11	1m 18.016s
18	Jos Verstappen	17	1m 18.074s
19	Enrique Bernoldi	15	1m 18.460s
20	Giancarlo Fisichella	12	1m 18.773s
21	Tarso Marques	12	1m 19.126s
22	Jenson Button	4	1m 20.008s

RACE FASTEST LAPS

Weather: Dry start, then heavy rain shower, followed by drying track

Driver	Time	Lap
Ralf Schumacher	1m 15.693s	38
David Coulthard	1m 16.498s	44
Michael Schumacher	1m 16.545s	44
Juan Pablo Montoya	1m 16.593s	31
Olivier Panis	1m 16.732s	44
Jacques Villeneuve	1m 17.106s	41
Eddie Irvine	1m 17.132s	43
Heinz-Harald Frentzen	1m 17.522s	41
Jean Alesi	1m 17.609s	43
Jarno Trulli	1m 17.632s	41
Kimi Räikkönen	1m 17.816s	33
Giancarlo Fisichella	1m 17.830s	41
Nick Heidfeld	1m 18.064s	42
Gaston Mazzacane	1m 18.176s	23
Luciano Burti	1m 18.759s	29
Jos Verstappen	1m 18.875s	26
Enrique Bernoldi	1m 19.449s	12
Tarso Marques	1m 19.734s	34
Fernando Alonso	1m 19.765s	16
Jenson Button	1m 19.846s	38
Rubens Barrichello	1m 58.705s	2

CHASSIS LOG BOOK

1	M. Schumacher	Ferrari F2001/208
2	Barrichello	Ferrari F2001/206
	spare	Ferrari F2001/210
3	Häkkinen	McLaren MP4/16/3
4	Coulthard	McLaren MP4/16/1
	spare	McLaren MP4/16/2
5	R. Schumacher	Williams FW23/3
6	Montoya	Williams FW23/2
	spare	Williams FW23/1
7	Fisichella	Benetton B201/3
8	Button	Benetton B201/1
	spare	Benetton B201/2
9	Panis	BAR 03/3
10	Villeneuve	BAR 03/4
	spare	BAR 03/2
11	Frentzen	Jordan EJ11/4
12	Trulli	Jordan EJ11/3
	spare	Jordan EJ11/2
14	Verstappen	Arrows A22/1
15	Bernoldi	Arrows A22/3
	spare	Arrows A22/4
16	Heidfeld	Sauber C20/3
17	Räikkönen	Sauber C20/1
	spare	Sauber C20/4
18	Irvine	Jaguar R2/4
19	Burti	Jaguar R2/3
	spare	Jaguar R2/5
20	Marques	Minardi PS01/1
21	Alonso	Minardi PS01/3
	spare	Minardi PS01/2
22	Alesi	Prost AP04/3
23	Mazzacane	Prost AP04/4
	spare	Prost AP04/2

POINTS TABLES

DRIVERS

1	Michael Schumacher	26
2	David Coulthard	20
3	Rubens Barrichello	10
4	Nick Heidfeld	7
5	Heinz-Harald Frentzen	5
6	Olivier Panis	3
7 =	Jarno Trulli	2
7 =	Ralf Schumacher	2
9 =	Giancarlo Fisichella	1
9 =	Mika Häkkinen	1
9 =	Kimi Räikkönen	1

CONSTRUCTORS

1	Ferrari	36
2	McLaren	21
3	Sauber	8
4	Jordan	7
5	BAR	3
6	Williams	3
7	Benetton	1

FOR THE RECORD

First Grand Prix podium
Nick Heidfeld

10th Grand Prix win
David Coulthard

700th Grand Prix point
Michael Schumacher

58	59	60	61	62	63	64	65	66	67	68	69	70	71	●	
4	4	4	4	4	4	4	4	4	4	4	4	4	4		1
1	1	1	1	1	1	1	1	1	1	1	1	1	1		2
11	11	11	11	11	11	16	16	16	16	16	16	16	16		3
12	12	16	16	16	16	12	12	12	9	9	9	9			4
16	16	12	12	12	12	9	9	9	12	12	12	12			5
9	9	9	9	9	9	22	7	7	7	7	7				6
22	22	22	22	22	22	7	22	22	22	22	22	10			
7	7	7	7	7	7	10	10	10	10	10	10	22			
10	10	10	10	10	10	20	20	20	20	20					
20	20	20	20	20	20	8									
8	8	8	8	8	8										

FIA WORLD CHAMPIONSHIP • ROUND 4

SAN MARINO
grand prix

1st - R. SCHUMACHER • **2nd** - COULTHARD • **3rd** - BARRICHELLO

Thumbs up from Ralf on the podium. The younger Schumacher scored his first Grand Prix win in emphatic style.
Both photographs: Paul-Henri Cahier

time behind Jarno Trulli's Jordan EJ-11 (1m 23.658s). 'I had too much traffic and simply didn't find a clear lap,' said Rubens.

For his part, Trulli was delighted. 'It's almost as exciting as getting onto the front row at Monaco,' he grinned, reflecting on his previous year's achievement. 'I had the feeling from the start that this weekend was going to be good, but I just had to bide my time.'

By contrast, Heinz-Harald Frentzen (9th/1m 24.436s) was frustrated by a sudden, massive dose of understeer on his third run. He lined up just behind a moderately satisfied Olivier Panis in the BAR-Honda (1m 24.213s), the Frenchman three places ahead of team-mate Jacques Villeneuve (1m 24.769s) who'd also encountered traffic on his last run.

Kimi Räikkönen managed tenth-fastest time in the Sauber C20 (1m 24.671s), despite admitting that he'd lost three crucial tenths by braking too late at one point. Nick Heidfeld struggled with balance problems, then improved the set-up only to make two mistakes in the last sector of the lap. He wound up 12th on 1m 25.007s.

Eddie Irvine had a reasonable run to 13th on 1m 25.392s, his Jaguar R2 using a development version of the Cosworth CR3 V10 for qualifying. Team-mate Luciano Burti was two places further back on 1m 25.572s, a decent enough performance considering he had a misfire and a slow downshift mechanism. 'The engine was also pushing on in the corners,' he reported, 'which caused me one moment when I slid onto the grass.'

The two Jaguars were split by Jean Alesi's Prost AP04 (1m 25.411s), the Frenchman complaining of poor handling balance, while in the Arrows camp Enrique Bernoldi just got the upper hand over team-mate Jos Verstappen for 16th and 17th respectively.

Fernando Alonso embarrassed the Benetton lads by posting 18th in his Minardi, just ahead of Giancarlo Fisichella's Benetton B201 while Jenson Button shared the final row of the grid with Tarso Marques. 'The qualifying set-up is not too good,' said Fisichella with masterly understatement.

Alonso added: 'For us, 18th place on the grid is like pole position!'

Above: Ferrari chief designer Rory Byrne (left) chats with BMW Williams technical director Patrick Head.

Right: David Coulthard squats by his McLaren MP4/16 after kerbing it heavily during Friday practice. The car had to be rebuilt around a replacement monocoque for the following day's qualifying session.

Below, from top: Mika Häkkinen, Jarno Trulli and Nick Heidfeld.
All photographs: Paul-Henri Cahier

David Coulthard and Mika Häkkinen buttoned up the front row at Imola for the McLaren-Mercedes team, their MP4/16s getting the upper hand over the brothers Schumacher who shared row two, with Ralf (Williams FW23) just squeezing ahead of Michael's Ferrari F2001.

On this rare occasion, Schumacher and Ferrari seemed all fingers and thumbs after opting for the harder Bridgestone tyre choice. On the face of it this seemed rather surprising given the low track temperatures, but Maranello's team leader clearly believed he could benefit from the supposed extra consistency of performance conferred by the harder tyres while at the same time seeing off the McLarens.

It was an assumption which missed its target. A modified aero package, including revised bargeboards, significantly reduced the McLarens' incipient understeer to the point where Coulthard had a net advantage of 0.2s a lap over Schumacher's Ferrari, even discounting the fact that the softer tyres were 0.3s a lap quicker.

Ferrari and McLaren had both arrived at Imola convinced that they were going to make a significant step forward in terms of track performance. Maranello's technical director Ross Brawn explained that Ferrari was poised to raise the rev limit of the type 050 V10 — reputedly from 17,700 to 18,100 rpm — which would possibly unlock around an extra 30 bhp.

'We operated them quite conservatively during the first three races of the year because we'd been worried by pre-season unreliability,' he said.

During wet free practice the advantage swung back and forth between Ferrari and McLaren. Coulthard suffered something of a setback on Friday when he kerbed his MP4/16 so badly straightlining the Variante Alta that its monocoque needed replacing, a task which took the McLaren mechanics until 4.00 am on Saturday morning.

The front ends of the other two MP4/16s were also beefed up as a result of this incident, but Coulthard put smiles on everybody's face come Saturday qualifying by taking pole on 1m 23.054s.

'I have to say I'm a little surprised,' said Coulthard. 'We made changes to the set-up before the session, then again prior to the last run. It wasn't an eventful enough lap to know I was on the limit. I didn't really feel confident.'

Häkkinen joined him on the front row with a 1m 23.282s, reporting that it was damp to start with going down to Acque Minerali. 'This is a great achievement for the team.'

Ralf Schumacher was pretty happy with third, but made the point that he might have been even quicker if the track temperatures had been higher.

Team-mate Juan Pablo Montoya lost most of Friday due to an engine problem, but still reckoned he was on for a second-row start. He was thwarted when he dropped one tyre on the grass at the Variante Alta on his best lap. 'That cost me six-tenths,' he shrugged, 'and dropped me to seventh.'

Michael Schumacher acknowledged that a best of 1m 23.593s reflected the fact that 'we have paid for the choice of tyres' then added 'but it was also my fault as I lost 0.4s on the final sector and on a previous run locked up at Tamburello and went over the kerb.'

Rubens Barrichello (1m 23.786s) had to be satisfied with sixth-fastest

RALF Schumacher confirmed the BMW Williams team's rebirth as a credible World Championship contender with a dominant run to victory in the San Marino Grand Prix, leading every one of its 62 laps to the chequered flag.

It was a success which put McLaren-Mercedes and Ferrari firmly on notice that F1 again has a serious third force to be reckoned with. It was an achievement which ended Williams's streak of 54 races since 1997 without a win and established the Schumacher brothers as the only siblings to win Grands Prix in the 52-year history of the official World Championship.

David Coulthard finished second to move into the joint World Championship lead together with Michael Schumacher, the Ferrari driver posting a rare retirement with a damaged brake caliper after a disappointing qualifying performance.

In reality, it was virtually all over on the run down to the first corner. Coulthard got a touch too much wheelspin — this being the final Grand Prix prior to the reintroduction of traction control — as he moved away from pole position, allowing Ralf Schumacher first to edge alongside, then squeeze ahead of the McLaren as they went down to the first chicane.

'I moved a little bit just before the start and had to stop the car, and that's when the lights changed, so then I got too much wheelspin,' said Coulthard.

'To be honest I thought I was going to be swamped at the start, but I presume Mika must have made a bad start as well. I sensed Ralf was on the inside. I was getting ready to move that way but obviously I had to move to make sure there was enough space for us all.'

At the end of the opening lap Ralf's Williams was already 0.9s ahead of Coulthard with Jarno Trulli's Jordan-Honda EJ11 third, having edged ahead of a too-tentative Häkkinen as they jostled into that first turn. Second time round Ralf extended his lead to

1.4s with Michael — fifth behind Häkkinen — already 4.9s down on his brother.

Michael was clearly under pressure from the outset. Weighed down with fuel for a long opening run, he dropped behind Juan Pablo Montoya's Williams FW23 on lap three by which time he was 8.03s behind Ralf. Things were clearly not going to plan.

Olivier Panis's BAR-Honda and Rubens Barrichello in the other Ferrari nipped past on lap four, by which time Michael was in trouble with a gearchange glitch. Now he was 11.6s behind his brother.

On lap six Fernando Alonso was posted as the race's first retirement, slamming off the track and removing one of his Minardi's front wheels against the barrier on the outside of the Variante Alta. Next time round Jos Verstappen's Arrows also bowed out.

'I had an exhaust failure and once that happens all the underbody temperatures start going up,' shrugged the Dutchman. 'The hydraulics, the electrics and everything else heats up until the car stops. I think this is a weekend I will quickly forget.'

By lap seven Ralf had eased open his lead to 2.2s over the dogged Coulthard. But David wasn't giving up and three laps later had trimmed it back to 1.9s. By this time Trulli — losing 1.2s a lap to the leader — had dropped back to over 12s behind the best-placed McLaren and Häkkinen seemed content just to follow the Jordan round, never making a serious bid to overtake.

On lap 18 Kimi Räikkönen's Sauber speared off the road accelerating up the hill from Tosa while running ninth. The steering wheel had apparently worked loose on its splines, triggering the frightening incident.

Next time round, another F1 youngster was in trouble when Jenson Button brought his Benetton B201 into the pits from 17th place for a 7.4s refuelling stop. Unfortunately a rig malfunction

Diary

Ferrari and McLaren object to proposals to shorten a planned 11-week F1 testing ban from the middle of October 2001 until the end of December.

Allan McNish resumes the Toyota F1 test programme at Paul Ricard after Mika Salo crashed the development car a few days earlier.

Austria's agriculture minister Eric Poetl hints that the Austrian Grand Prix could be cancelled if a single outbreak of foot and mouth disease is confirmed anywhere in the country.

The Indy Racing League agrees a new set of engine regulations for the start of 2003. The rules call for 3.5-litre non-turbocharged V8s with a rev limit. CART continues to consider changes to its own engine regulations for 2003.

CAR MAKERS THREATEN INDEPENDENT RACING SERIES

In what was being regarded in motor racing circles as a calculated bluff, Europe's top car makers issued a specific threat to establish an independent F1 championship unless they receive long-term guarantees about the commercial future of the current series in the wake of Bernie Ecclestone's controversial sell-out to Kirch, the German media group.

Despite assurances to the contrary, the car makers remained acutely concerned that, long-term, Kirch will attempt to transfer the F1 championship onto pay-to-view television.

Kirch responded by offering them a 25 per cent stake in its F1 business, although no price was mentioned. The Kirch management also said the constructors could have veto rights to prevent it moving broadcasting of F1 to pay TV.

Kirch spokesman Hartmut Schultz explained: 'There are no plans to let F1 slip into pay TV.' He also explained that Kirch wanted to keep Formula 1 attractive to a large audience.

Paolo Cantarella, CEO of Fiat and chairman of the European Car Manufacturers' Association which also includes DaimlerChrysler (Mercedes), Renault, BMW and Ford (owners of Jaguar), had earlier confirmed that the decision had been made to start a new formula. They would be joined by Japanese car makers Toyota and Honda in setting up the new series for the 2008 season, after the end of the current Concorde agreement which governs the manner in which Formula 1 is operated.

'It is quite simple really,' said Cantarella at a meeting of the confederation of Italian industrialists in Rome. 'We want Formula 1, together with its entire heritage, to continue with order, technological development, clarity of rules and maximum visibility. As you can see, the guarantees also involve the general public.'

'This is obviously a high-risk game of poker,' said a highly placed source in another of the car companies.

Above: Heinz-Harald Frentzen's Jordan-Honda EJ-11 sped to sixth place immediately behind team-mate Jarno Trulli, strengthening the Silverstone-based team's perceived edge over Honda-propelled rivals BAR.
Photograph: Paul-Henri Cahier

meant that no fuel went into the car and he had to come in again next time round, dropping him virtually to last.

Lap 23 marked the beginning of the end for Michael Schumacher's San Marino GP as he limped round to the pits with an apparent left front puncture. The tyre was changed and he resumed, a 12.8s refuelling stint theoretically giving him sufficient fuel to run non-stop to the finish. But he was back next time round and retired with a faulty front-brake caliper, which in turn had damaged the wheel rim.

In reality, Coulthard was very nearly holding onto the flying Ralf in the opening stages, but as race lap times dipped into the 1m 26s bracket, the Williams's Michelin rubber certainly gave it a perceptible performance edge.

Once Ralf had led through the first round of refuelling stops, he consolidated his advantage. The Michelins seemed to be instantly quick on their return to the race while the rival Bridgestones used by McLaren and Ferrari seemed to take a couple of laps to get up to speed.

David brought his McLaren in for an 8.6s refuelling stop at the end of lap 28 while Ralf came in next time round for a 6.9s stop. Häkkinen also made an 8.2s stop from third place, having moved ahead of Trulli when the Jordan stopped on lap 24. Mika's stop allowed Barrichello through to third, but Montoya was up to fourth ahead of Trulli on lap 29 when he forced his way in front of the Jordan round the outside going into the first chicane.

Schumacher made 1.8s over Coulthard's McLaren on his out lap from their first refuelling stops and from then on controlled the pace of the race with unflustered confidence. By the time it came to his second stop on lap 46 (8.2s), he could afford to drop a second to the McLaren driver as by then the Michelins' superior track performance had clinched the day for Williams and BMW. Coulthard had made his second stop in 7.1s one lap earlier, but was still 10.6s adrift as they settled down for the run to the chequered flag.

'The FW23 responded well to set-up changes and we have to give a lot of credit to our race engineers on what is a medium-to-high downforce circuit,' said Williams aerodynamicist Geoff Willis.

Technical director Patrick Head added: 'Ralf took the lead at the start with a superb getaway, helped by the fact that David Coulthard was a gentleman from the point of view of not putting him off the track, as other people might have done.'

Coulthard later confirmed that his Bridgestones were less consistent than he would have liked. 'It was the most uneventful race I have driven this season,' he shrugged, 'but as a result of inconsistency in my tyres, also the most difficult.'

Rubens Barrichello came through to take third to give the Italian fans some measure of consolation. 'I think we had a great strategy, to be honest,' said the Brazilian. 'I was losing time behind Mika but luckily I had three more laps when he came into the pits, so I could go fast and my race was decided then.'

He finished ahead of a frustrated Häkkinen who'd made a poor

Unfortunately for the Italian driver, he had a problem when he found himself struggling on a poor second set of tyres.

Elsewhere, Benetton certainly looked as though they were on the ropes, but in a business where yesterday's Minardi can be tomorrow's Williams, it would be a brave man indeed to write off what is, after all, the next-generation Renault F1 squad.

Nothing could alter the reality that the latest Renault RS21 V10 was currently over 100 bhp down on the leading F1 power units. That said, Flavio Briatore appeared totally confident that the French engine development team, under the command of Jean-Jacques His, will be able to start to turn the situation in the not-too-distant future.

'At the moment we're just attempting to survive, but from the French Grand Prix onwards we hope to be upping the power and closing the performance gap,' Briatore explained.

Perhaps so, yet both Giancarlo Fisichella and Jenson Button had an absolutely dismal time at Imola. Fisichella dropped out with a misfire while Button trailed home in 12th place, hampered by his earlier refuelling difficulties and experiencing shoulder strain.

The problem in F1 today is that it is so promotionally driven that everybody expects an instant fix. It was the same at Jaguar where Niki Lauda and Bobby Rahal were grappling with pretty well identical problems to those at Benetton.

Outside the top six Nick Heidfeld finished seventh for Sauber ahead of Olivier Panis, the only BAR-Honda runner after Jacques Villeneuve's car suffered a major engine failure, and a less-than-satisfied Jean Alesi's Prost AP04. Luciano Burti's Jaguar and Button's Benetton completed the list of classified runners.

Ralf admitted that he was keeping his fingers crossed in the closing moments of the race. 'For the last three laps I was taking it pretty easy,' he said. 'I knew David was six or seven seconds behind me and I just tried to finish.

'I was pretty relaxed really, although the pressure is on us to continue like this now. Over the radio my engineer spoke to me first, then Patrick, then Frank.

'They said "good job" because while it might be a long time ago, they are certainly used to winning races!'

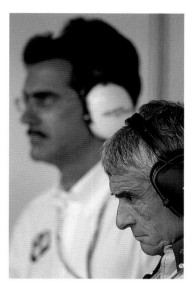

**Above: Keeping their thoughts to themselves —
BMW competitions chief Mario Theissen and
Pierre Dupasquier, his opposite number at
Michelin, watch as Ralf Schumacher heads for a
memorable victory.**
Photograph: Bryn Williams/crash.net

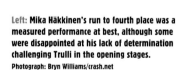

**Left: Mika Häkkinen's run to fourth place was a
measured performance at best, although some
were disappointed at his lack of determination
challenging Trulli in the opening stages.**
Photograph: Bryn Williams/crash.net

**Below: Jacques Villeneuve shades himself from
the sun in the cockpit of his BAR-Honda prior to
the start at Imola.**
Photograph: Paul-Henri Cahier

start and been forced to follow Jarno Trulli's slow Jordan in the opening phase of the race.

Trulli eventually finished fifth ahead of team-mate Heinz-Harald Frentzen, at least winning the Honda race ahead of BAR's sole survivor Olivier Panis, split from the yellow cars by Nick Heidfeld's consistently competitive Sauber C20.

Again Jaguar was thwarted in its efforts to score its first championship point of the season, even though Eddie Irvine was in ninth place on a one-stop strategy when his Cosworth V10 blew up.

'I had a good start despite carrying a heavy fuel load,' said Irvine. 'The one stop strategy I was on was absolutely right for what I believed would be a points finish.'

Interlagos star Juan Pablo Montoya qualified seventh despite not managing a lap in the dry until Saturday morning. In the race his car stuck in first gear due to a clutch problem, forcing his retirement after another very promising performance.

Häkkinen was philosophical, yet frustrated over the manner in which Jarno Trulli held him up during the early stages of the race.

'It's very difficult to overtake at Imola unless the driver in front of you makes a significant mistake, so I was stuck in fourth for most of the race,' he said. 'My current situation is very similar to the same point in the season last year.'

Trulli saw it differently 'I stayed in front of Häkkinen for 20 laps,' said the Italian. 'I was having a great race and actually pulling away from Häkkinen at one point.'

ROUND 4
IMOLA 13–15 APRIL 2001

gran premio
WARSTEINER di
SAN MARINO

IMOLA – AUTODROMO DINO E ENZO FERRARI
CIRCUIT LENGTH: 3.063 miles/4.929 km

ACQUE MINERALE 70/113 (3)
PIRATELLA 105/169 (4)
TRAGUARDO 55/89 (2)
TOSA 55/89 (2)
VARIANTE ALTA 75/121 (3)
175/281 (6)
VILLENEUVE 85/137 (3)
RIVAZZA 65/105 (2)
TAMBURELLO 100/161 (3)
mph/km/h (gear)
VARIANTE BASSA 180/290 (6)

RACE DISTANCE: 62 laps, 189.896 miles/305.609 km   RACE WEATHER: Dry, warm and sunny

Pos.	Driver	Nat.	No.	Entrant	Car/Engine	Tyres	Laps	Time/Retirement	Speed (mph/km/h)	Gap to lead
1	Ralf Schumacher	D	5	BMW WilliamsF1 Team	Williams FW23-BMW P80 V10	M	62	1h 30m 44.817s	125.555/202.062	
2	David Coulthard	GB	4	West McLaren Mercedes	McLaren MP4/16-Mercedes F0110K V10	B	62	1h 30m 49.169s	125.455/201.900	+4.35
3	Rubens Barrichello	BR	2	Scuderia Ferrari Marlboro	Ferrari F2001-050 V10	B	62	1h 31m 19.583s	124.759/200.780	+34.76
4	Mika Häkkinen	SF	3	West McLaren Mercedes	McLaren MP4/16-Mercedes F0110K V10	B	62	1h 31m 21.132s	124.723/200.723	+36.31
5	Jarno Trulli	I	12	B&H Jordan Honda	Jordan EJ11-Honda RA001E V10	B	62	1h 32m 10.375s	123.613/198.936	+85.55
6	Heinz-Harald Frentzen	D	11	B&H Jordan Honda	Jordan EJ11-Honda RA001E V10	B	61			+1 l
7	Nick Heidfeld	D	16	Red Bull Sauber Petronas	Sauber C20-Petronas V10	B	61			+1 l
8	Olivier Panis	F	9	Lucky Strike BAR Honda	BAR 03-Honda RA001E V10	B	61			+1 l
9	Jean Alesi	F	22	Prost Acer	Prost AP04-Acer V10	M	61			+1 l
10	Enrique Bernoldi	ESP	15	Orange Arrows Asiatech	Arrows A22-Asiatech V10	B	60			+2 la
11	Luciano Burti	BR	19	Jaguar Racing	Jaguar R2-Cosworth CR3 V10	M	60			+2 la
12	Jenson Button	GB	8	Mild Seven Benetton Renault	Benetton B201-Renault RS21 V10	M	60			+2 la
	Tarso Marques	BR	20	European Minardi F1	Minardi PS01-European V10	M	50	Engine		
	Juan Pablo Montoya	COL	6	BMW WilliamsF1 Team	Williams FW23-BMW P80 V10	M	48	Clutch		
	Eddie Irvine	GB	18	Jaguar Racing	Jaguar R2-Cosworth CR3 V10	M	42	Engine		
	Giancarlo Fisichella	I	7	Mild Seven Benetton Renault	Benetton B201-Renault RS21 V10	M	31	Misfire		
	Jacques Villeneuve	CDN	10	Lucky Strike BAR Honda	BAR 03-Honda RA001E V10	B	30	Engine		
	Gaston Mazzacane	ARG	23	Prost Acer	Prost AP04-Acer V10	M	28	Engine		
	Michael Schumacher	D	1	Scuderia Ferrari Marlboro	Ferrari F2001-050 V10	B	24	Brakes		
	Kimi Räikkönen	SF	17	Red Bull Sauber Petronas	Sauber C20-Petronas V10	B	17	Accident/steering wheel failure		
	Jos Verstappen	NL	14	Orange Arrows Asiatech	Arrows A22-Asiatech V10	B	6	Broken exhaust		
	Fernando Alonso	ESP	21	European Minardi F1	Minardi PS01-European V10	M	5	Accident		

Fastest lap: Ralf Schumacher, on lap 27, 1m 25.524s, 129.025 mph/207.646 km/h (record).

Previous lap record: Heinz-Harald Frentzen (F1 Williams FW19-Renault V10), 1m 25.531s, 128.936 mph/207.503 km/h (1997).

Grid order	1	2	3	4	5	6	7	8	9	10	11	12	13	14	15	16	17	18	19	20	21	22	23	24	25	26	27	28	29	30	31	32	33	34	35	36	37	38	39	40	41	42	43	44	45	46
4 COULTHARD	5	5	5	5	5	5	5	5	5	5	5	5	5	5	5	5	5	5	5	5	5	5	5	5	5	5	5	5	5	5	5	5	5	5	5	5	5	5	5	5	5	5	5	5	5	5
3 HÄKKINEN	4	4	4	4	4	4	4	4	4	4	4	4	4	4	4	4	4	4	4	4	4	4	4	4	4	4	4	4	4	4	4	4	4	4	4	4	4	4	4	4	4	4	4	4	4	4
5 R. SCHUMACHER	12	12	12	12	12	12	12	12	12	12	12	12	12	12	12	12	12	12	12	12	12	12	12	12	3	3	3	3	3	2	2	2	2	2	2	2	2	2	2	2	2	2	2	2	2	2
1 M. SCHUMACHER	3	3	3	3	3	3	3	3	3	3	3	3	3	3	3	3	3	3	3	3	3	3	3	3	6	6	6	2	2	3	3	3	3	3	3	3	3	3	3	3	3	3	3	3	3	3
12 TRULLI	1	1	6	6	6	6	6	6	6	6	6	6	6	6	6	6	6	6	6	6	6	6	6	6	2	2	2	10	10	6	6	6	6	6	6	6	6	6	6	6	6	6	6	6	6	6
2 BARRICHELLO	6	6	1	9	9	9	9	2	2	2	2	2	2	2	2	2	2	2	2	2	2	2	2	2	10	10	10	12	12	12	12	12	12	12	12	12	12	12	12	12	12	12	11	12	12	12
6 MONTOYA	9	9	9	2	2	2	2	9	1	1	1	1	1	1	1	1	1	1	1	1	10	10	11	11	12	6	12	18	18	11	11	11	11	11	11	11	11	11	11	11	11	12	16	11		
9 PANIS	2	2	2	1	1	1	1	1	9	9	9	9	9	9	9	9	9	9	9	9	9	10	11	11	12	12	18	18	18	10	11	19	16	16	16	16	16	16	16	16	16	16	11	16		
11 FRENTZEN	17	17	17	17	17	17	17	17	17	17	17	17	17	17	17	17	10	10	10	10	11	16	16	16	18	11	11	11	19	16	18	18	18	18	18	18	18	18	18	22	22	22	22			
17 RÄIKKÖNEN	10	10	10	10	10	10	10	10	10	10	10	10	10	10	10	10	11	11	11	16	18	18	18	9	9	19	19	19	16	18	22	22	22	22	22	22	22	22	22	9	9	9	9			
10 VILLENEUVE	11	11	11	11	11	11	11	11	11	11	11	11	11	11	11	16	16	16	16	9	9	9	9	19	19	16	16	16	22	22	9	9	9	9	9	9	9	9	19	19	19	19				
16 HEIDFELD	18	16	16	16	16	16	16	16	16	16	16	16	16	16	16	11	18	18	18	18	16	19	19	16	22	22	22	9	9	19	19	16	15	15	15	15	15	15	15	15	15	15	15			
18 IRVINE	16	18	18	18	18	18	18	18	18	18	18	18	18	18	18	18	22	22	22	19	1	22	22	22	22	9	9	15	15	15	15	15	15	15	15	15	15	15	15	15					
22 ALESI	22	22	22	22	22	22	22	22	22	22	22	22	22	22	22	7	7	7	7	22	22	23	23	7	7	7	15	15	7	8	8	8	8	8	8	8	8	8	20	20	20				
19 BURTI	7	7	7	7	14	14	7	7	7	7	7	7	7	7	7	19	19	19	19	23	23	7	7	15	15	15	7	7	8	20	20	20	20	20	20	20	20	20						
15 BERNOLDI	19	14	14	14	7	7	19	19	19	19	19	19	19	19	19	15	15	15	15	7	7	15	15	23	23	23	8	8	20																
14 VERSTAPPEN	14	19	19	19	19	19	15	15	15	15	15	15	15	15	15	8	8	23	23	15	15	1	8	8	8	20																			
21 ALONSO	15	15	15	15	15	8	8	8	8	8	8	8	8	8	23	23	20	20	20	20																									
7 FISICHELLA	8	8	8	8	8	23	23	23	23	23	23	23	23	23	20	20	20	20	20	20																									
23 MAZZACANE	21	21	21	21	21	23	20	20	20	20	20	20	20	20	20	20																													
8 BUTTON	20	20	20	20	23	20																																							
20 MARQUES	23	23	23	23	20																																								

Pit stop
One lap behind leader

STARTING GRID

4 **COULTHARD** McLaren	**3** **HÄKKINEN** McLaren
5 **R. SCHUMACHER** Williams	**1** **M. SCHUMACHER** Ferrari
12 **TRULLI** Jordan	**2** **BARRICHELLO** Ferrari
6 **MONTOYA** Williams	**9** **PANIS** BAR
11 **FRENTZEN** Jordan	**17** **RÄIKKÖNEN** Sauber
10 **VILLENEUVE** BAR	**16** **HEIDFELD** Sauber
18 **IRVINE** Jaguar	**22** **ALESI** Prost
19 **BURTI** Jaguar	**15** **BERNOLDI** Arrows
14 **VERSTAPPEN** Arrows	**21** **ALONSO** Minardi
7 **FISICHELLA** Benetton	**23** **MAZZACANE** Prost
8 **BUTTON** Benetton	**20** **MARQUES** Minardi

50	51	52	53	54	55	56	57	58	59	60	61	62	●
5	5	5	5	5	5	5	5	5	5	5	5	5	1
4	4	4	4	4	4	4	4	4	4	4	4	4	2
2	2	2	2	2	2	2	2	2	2	2	2	2	3
3	3	3	3	3	3	3	3	3	3	3	3	3	4
12	12	12	12	12	12	12	12	12	12	12	12	12	5
11	11	11	11	11	11	11	11	11	11	11	11	11	6
16	16	16	16	16	16	16	16	16	16	16	16	16	
9	9	9	9	9	9	9	9	9	9	9	9	9	
19	22	22	22	22	22	22	22	22	22	22	22	22	
22	19	19	19	19	19	15	15	15	15	15			
15	15	15	15	15	15	19	19	19	19	19			
8	8	8	8	8	8	8	8	8	8	8			
20													

FOR THE RECORD

First Grand Prix win
Ralf Schumacher
150th Grand Prix point
Rubens Barrichello

TIME SHEETS

QUALIFYING

Weather: Dry, cool and sunny

Pos.	Driver	Car	Laps	Time
1	David Coulthard	McLaren-Mercedes	12	1m 23.054s
2	Mika Häkkinen	McLaren-Mercedes	12	1m 23.282s
3	Ralf Schumacher	Williams-BMW	12	1m 23.357s
4	Michael Schumacher	Ferrari	12	1m 23.593s
5	Jarno Trulli	Jordan-Honda	12	1m 23.658s
6	Rubens Barrichello	Ferrari	10	1m 23.786s
7	Juan Pablo Montoya	Williams-BMW	12	1m 24.141s
8	Olivier Panis	BAR-Honda	12	1m 24.213s
9	Heinz-Harald Frentzen	Jordan-Honda	11	1m 24.436s
10	Kimi Räikkönen	Sauber-Petronas	12	1m 24.671s
11	Jacques Villeneuve	BAR-Honda	12	1m 24.769s
12	Nick Heidfeld	Sauber-Petronas	12	1m 25.007s
13	Eddie Irvine	Jaguar-Cosworth	12	1m 25.392s
14	Jean Alesi	Prost-Acer	12	1m 25.411s
15	Luciano Burti	Jaguar-Cosworth	12	1m 25.572s
16	Enrique Bernoldi	Arrows-Asiatech	12	1m 25.872s
17	Jos Verstappen	Arrows-Asiatech	12	1m 26.062s
18	Fernando Alonso	Minardi-European	12	1m 26.855s
19	Giancarlo Fisichella	Benetton-Renault	11	1m 26.902s
20	Gaston Mazzacane	Minardi-European	12	1m 27.750s
21	Jenson Button	Benetton-Renault	11	1m 27.758s
22	Tarso Marques	Minardi-European	12	1m 28.281s

FRIDAY FREE PRACTICE

Weather: Cold, wet start, drying track

Pos.	Driver	Laps	Time
1	Michael Schumacher	44	1m 25.096s
2	Rubens Barrichello	38	1m 25.372s
3	Ralf Schumacher	43	1m 25.829s
4	Mika Häkkinen	28	1m 26.341s
5	Olivier Panis	43	1m 26.535s
6	Kimi Räikkönen	41	1m 26.552s
7	Eddie Irvine	41	1m 26.599s
8	Jacques Villeneuve	35	1m 26.739s
9	Jarno Trulli	46	1m 26.923s
10	Luciano Burti	43	1m 26.933s
11	David Coulthard	24	1m 27.132s
12	Nick Heidfeld	40	1m 27.142s
13	Heinz-Harald Frentzen	44	1m 27.406s
14	Jean Alesi	37	1m 27.437s
15	Giancarlo Fisichella	39	1m 28.322s
16	Gaston Mazzacane	38	1m 28.586s
17	Jenson Button	39	1m 28.902s
18	Fernando Alonso	20	1m 28.931s
19	Enrique Bernoldi	39	1m 29.273s
20	Tarso Marques	33	1m 29.589s
21	Jos Verstappen	7	1m 29.750s
22	Juan Pablo Montoya	19	1m 39.812s

SATURDAY FREE PRACTICE

Weather: Cold, wet track, drying

Pos.	Driver	Laps	Time
1	Michael Schumacher	27	1m 30.737s
2	Rubens Barrichello	22	1m 31.003s
3	David Coulthard	26	1m 31.536s
4	Kimi Räikkönen	27	1m 31.726s
5	Heinz-Harald Frentzen	24	1m 32.164s
6	Nick Heidfeld	25	1m 32.392s
7	Ralf Schumacher	19	1m 33.025s
8	Olivier Panis	29	1m 33.071s
9	Enrique Bernoldi	19	1m 33.884s
10	Mika Häkkinen	21	1m 34.036s
11	Jean Alesi	25	1m 34.531s
12	Juan Pablo Montoya	24	1m 34.548s
13	Jacques Villeneuve	21	1m 34.789s
14	Jos Verstappen	31	1m 34.948s
15	Gaston Mazzacane	27	1m 35.056s
16	Jarno Trulli	27	1m 36.046s
17	Fernando Alonso	30	1m 36.058s
18	Tarso Marques	28	1m 36.671s
19	Jenson Button	24	1m 38.306s
20	Giancarlo Fisichella	21	1m 39.214s
21	Eddie Irvine	14	1m 41.771s
	Luciano Burti		no time

WARM-UP

Weather: Dry, bright and cool

Pos.	Driver	Laps	Time
1	David Coulthard	14	1m 26.440s
2	Ralf Schumacher	11	1m 26.727s
3	Mika Häkkinen	14	1m 26.836s
4	Nick Heidfeld	14	1m 26.929s
5	Rubens Barrichello	13	1m 26.941s
6	Michael Schumacher	14	1m 26.948s
7	Heinz-Harald Frentzen	16	1m 26.954s
8	Kimi Räikkönen	10	1m 27.492s
9	Olivier Panis	15	1m 27.534s
10	Jarno Trulli	16	1m 27.575s
11	Jos Verstappen	13	1m 27.728s
12	Jacques Villeneuve	15	1m 28.035s
13	Juan Pablo Montoya	11	1m 28.142s
14	Gaston Mazzacane	12	1m 28.404s
15	Enrique Bernoldi	13	1m 28.639s
16	Eddie Irvine	12	1m 28.655s
17	Jean Alesi	14	1m 29.347s
18	Tarso Marques	10	1m 29.480s
19	Jenson Button	5	1m 29.593s
20	Giancarlo Fisichella	16	1m 29.623s
21	Luciano Burti	6	1m 30.030s
22	Fernando Alonso	7	1m 30.150s

RACE FASTEST LAPS

Weather: Dry, warm and sunny

Driver	Time	Lap
Ralf Schumacher	1m 25.524s	27
David Coulthard	1m 25.569s	44
Rubens Barrichello	1m 26.117s	46
Mika Häkkinen	1m 26.308s	61
Juan Pablo Montoya	1m 26.385s	46
Michael Schumacher	1m 27.229s	21
Heinz-Harald Frentzen	1m 27.243s	36
Nick Heidfeld	1m 27.350s	57
Jarno Trulli	1m 27.358s	20
Olivier Panis	1m 27.582s	47
Jacques Villeneuve	1m 27.614s	27
Eddie Irvine	1m 27.854s	28
Luciano Burti	1m 27.932s	29
Jean Alesi	1m 28.369s	44
Kimi Räikkönen	1m 28.604s	17
Gaston Mazzacane	1m 28.954s	21
Enrique Bernoldi	1m 28.956s	37
Jenson Button	1m 29.096s	38
Giancarlo Fisichella	1m 29.644s	14
Jos Verstappen	1m 30.403s	4
Fernando Alonso	1m 31.671s	4
Tarso Marques	1m 31.725s	38

CHASSIS LOG BOOK

1	M. Schumacher	Ferrari F2001/208
2	Barrichello	Ferrari F2001/206
	spare	Ferrari F2001/210
3	Häkkinen	McLaren MP4/16/3
4	Coulthard	McLaren MP4/16/5
	spares	McLaren MP4/16/4 & 1
5	R. Schumacher	Williams FW23/3
6	Montoya	Williams FW23/2
	spare	Williams FW23/1
7	Fisichella	Benetton B201/3
8	Button	Benetton B201/5
	spare	Benetton B201/1
9	Panis	BAR 03/3
10	Villeneuve	BAR 03/5
	spare	BAR 03/2
11	Frentzen	Jordan EJ11/4
12	Trulli	Jordan EJ11/5
	spare	Jordan EJ11/3
14	Verstappen	Arrows A22/3
15	Bernoldi	Arrows A22/6
	spare	Arrows A22/4
16	Heidfeld	Sauber C20/3
17	Räikkönen	Sauber C20/1
	spare	Sauber C20/2
18	Irvine	Jaguar R2/4
19	Burti	Jaguar R2/3
	spare	Jaguar R2/5
20	Marques	Minardi PS01/4
21	Alonso	Minardi PS01/3
	spare	Minardi PS01/1
22	Alesi	Prost AP04/3
23	Mazzacane	Prost AP04/4
	spare	Prost AP04/2

POINTS TABLES

DRIVERS

1 =	Michael Schumacher	26
1 =	David Coulthard	26
3	Rubens Barrichello	14
4	Ralf Schumacher	12
5	Nick Heidfeld	7
6	Heinz-Harald Frentzen	6
7 =	Mika Häkkinen	4
7 =	Jarno Trulli	4
9	Olivier Panis	3
10 =	Giancarlo Fisichella	1
10 =	Kimi Räikkönen	1

CONSTRUCTORS

1	Ferrari	40
2	McLaren	30
3	Williams	12
4	Jordan	10
5	Sauber	8
6	BAR	3
7	Benetton	1

FIA WORLD CHAMPIONSHIP • ROUND 5

SPANISH
grand prix

1st - M. SCHUMACHER • 2nd - MONTOYA • 3rd - VILLENEUVE

GRAN PREMIO
MARLBORO
ESPAÑA
...UNYA

Left: Back in business — Winner Michael Schumacher celebrates his Spanish win in company with present and past Williams drivers Juan Pablo Montoya and Jacques Villeneuve.
Photograph: Bryn Williams/crash.net

Main picture: Seldom has Michael Schumacher claimed a luckier win, this time on the last lap and at the expense of a devastated Mika Häkkinen.
Photograph: Paul-Henri Cahier

Diary

Former Ferrari F1 star Michele Alboreto killed at the Lausitzring testing an Audi sports car in preparation for Le Mans.

CART threatened with multi-million dollar legal action after Texas Motor Speedway was forced to cancel its race due to safety fears created by the high g forces experienced by drivers in the high-banked super speedway.

Tomas Enge wins third round of F3000 championship at Barcelona.

Massive 11-car shunt punctuates IRL Atlanta race won by Greg Ray's Dallara.

Rusty Wallace wins NASCAR Fontana race.

Above: Luciano Burti (top) found himself transferred to the Prost squad in order to make room for F1 returnee Pedro de la Rosa in the Jaguar line-up.
Photographs: Bryn Williams (top) and Paul-Henri Cahier

Right: Schumacher went out of his way to console Mika Häkkinen after the Finn's McLaren suffered a clutch failure while leading on the last lap.
Photograph: Bryn Williams/crash.net

CATALUNYA QUALIFYING

Michael Schumacher grabbed pole position (1m 18.201s) with his Ferrari F2001, taking full advantage of the Italian car's traction control capability. Mika Häkkinen qualified second (1m 18.286s), having adjusted the traction control on his McLaren-Mercedes to the minimum setting.

The margin separating the two aces was less than one-tenth of a second and the only real surprise was the manner in which David Coulthard, the third-place qualifier on 1m 18.635s, declined to explain whether he'd turned his traction control off. Or not.

According to McLaren boss Ron Dennis, the demands on drivers with electronic control systems would mean that they would still find F1 as stimulating as they did prior to the changes in the rules.

'You have to remember that the electronic freedom encompasses every function on the engine and gearbox,' he said. 'But the more options you have, the more you have to have the ability to select those options. There are a whole range of parameters available to the drivers, and those options are variable.

'As Mika pointed out, in qualifying he had selected a configuration with fewer options available to him — I think it was a little bit too black and white to say "he switched it off" but he did switch off some of the functionality.'

Dennis sought to allay the apprehension over these developments. 'Personally, I don't think the racing will be radically different,' he said. 'perhaps unmeasurable from the viewpoint of the perception of the paying public.'

Behind Coulthard, Rubens Barrichello admitted that he was disappointed to have only managed a fourth-fastest 1m 18.674s in the other Ferrari. 'I made a few changes to the set-up during the session,' he explained, 'but they did not produce the result I was expecting. I never managed to get a perfect lap.'

Over in the Williams camp there was some disappointment that Ralf Schumacher could only manage fifth fastest with 1m 19.016s, a fortnight after scoring a decisive win at Imola.

Patrick Head and BMW motor sports chief Mario Theissen were both extremely relaxed about the effect of traction control, particularly in terms of engine unreliability. 'It is a tool to exploit the powertrain potential,' said Theissen. However, neither Ralf nor Montoya — 12th on 1m 19.660s after losing a quick lap due to traffic and a yellow flag — used it on this occasion as the team felt it required further development work.

Jarno Trulli managed 1m 19.093s for sixth-fastest time in the Jordan EJ-11, reporting that he'd encountered traffic on his best lap 'but sixth in such company is quite good.' Heinz-Harald Frentzen wound up eighth with a 1m 19.150s.

'I was one-tenth away from my aim of trying to break the 1m 19s barrier, but I got the maximum I could out of the car in the windy conditions and traffic,' he said.

The two Jordans were split by Jacques Villeneuve's BAR 003, the Canadian grappling with brake problems on his way to a 1m 19.122s, while Olivier Panis — 11th on 1m 19.479s — found himself blocked by de la Rosa and Barrichello on both his quick runs.

The Sauber C20 duo proved very well matched with Kimi Räikkönen winding up ninth (1m 19.229s) and Nick Heidfeld tenth (1m 19.232s). The young Finn reckoned he should have gone a tad quicker, but Heidfeld took the spare car after a drivetrain problem with his race chassis and complained that Coulthard baulked him on his best lap.

Further back in the field, it was felt that Eddie Irvine had been absolutely realistic in his Friday prediction that his Jaguar R2 would qualify 13th. The Ulsterman did just that with a 1m 20.326s, lining up seven places ahead of new team-mate Pedro de la Rosa (1m 21.338s) who had to take the spare car after a power steering glitch sent his race car swerving into the pit wall at the end of the morning free practice session.

Over at Prost, Jaguar refugee Luciano Burti celebrated his switch of teams by outqualifying sitting tenant Jean Alesi by just 0.02s. He dropped by the Jaguar motorhome on his way back down the paddock, admitting to Bobby Rahal that he was going to be exhausted on Sunday night as he doubted he would manage a race distance in the Prost without power steering.

The two Prosts were followed by the Arrows of Enrique Bernoldi (1m 20.696s) and Jos Verstappen (1m 20.737s). The Brazilian explained that an unexpected slide on his final run lost him time, while Verstappen spun off and damaged the floor of his car after making what he felt was a positive aerodynamic change.

Rounding off the grid was Fernando Alonso, 18th on home soil with a 1m 21.037s in the Minardi — 'very happy, a perfect lap!' — while the two struggling Benettons were 19th and 21st with Tarso Marques bringing up the rear in the other Minardi.

WHAT should have been the 19th victory of Mika Häkkinen's Formula 1 career dramatically turned into the 47th of Michael Schumacher's when the Ferrari driver emerged victorious from the battle of the walking wounded in the Spanish Grand Prix at Barcelona's Circuit de Catalunya.

As Häkkinen's McLaren-Mercedes rolled to a spectacular standstill enveloped in smoke and flame following a major clutch failure — originally triggered by a minuscule hydraulic fluid leak — less than half a mile from the finishing line, Schumacher's Ferrari, hobbled by severe tyre vibrations, surged past to take the chequered flag.

This was the fifth race of the 2001 FIA F1 World Championship season and the one where electronic driver aids were finally permitted to let rip. Launch control, traction control and fully automatic gearchange mechanisms were back, centre stage, with all the technical foibles which inevitably seemed to come hand-in-hand with their reintroduction for the first time since the end of 1993.

Objectively, it seemed a strange move to permit such a major technical rule change mid-season. Yet this was a compromise. The oppressive climate of suspicion, in which F1 had been tortured by rumour and innuendo, had prevailed for too long.

Of course, had Ferrari and its customer teams Prost and Sauber agreed, traction control could have been introduced at the start of the 2001 season. But Maranello wanted more time to develop the systems, hence this uncomfortable postponement.

Ironically, it was the presence of traction control on his McLaren MP4/16 which alerted Häkkinen to the reality that his bid for victory was doomed.

'It was on the second last corner of the second-to-last lap that I suddenly realised that the car's traction control seemed to be working harder than previously,' he explained.

'Initially I thought it was just that the rear tyres might have worn down, but then as I went round the last corner to start my last lap there was a metallic "drrrr" from the clutch. I knew that was it.'

Schumacher was genuinely sympathetic, immediately running up to Häkkinen after stopping his car in the parc fermé at the end of the race. 'I have to say I feel very sorry for Mika,' said the Ferrari ace who now found himself leading the championship by eight points from David Coulthard who finished fifth after a fraught and dramatic afternoon.

'I think we had both done a very good race, very entertaining up to the last pit stop. Then he jumped me at the last pit stop because he did a better last section and I was a bit in traffic, and having a bit of a problem on top of that.

'Seeing him retiring on the last lap, with five corners or whatever to go before the finish, was shocking. It's not the way you like to win a race, honestly. It's happened to me, and now it has happened to Mika, but that's the way it goes sometimes.'

Into second and third places came former Indianapolis 500 winners Juan Pablo Montoya and Jacques Villeneuve, in Williams-BMW and BAR-Honda respectively, with Jarno Trulli bringing his

Above: Juan Pablo Montoya earned his first visit to the podium at Barcelona, despite the Williams-BMWs running without traction control at this race which marked the return of such electronic accessories.

Overleaf: Jacques Villeneuve also managed to give BAR its first podium finish in two and a half seasons with a strong third place.
Both photographs: Paul-Henri Cahier

SLEC GETS DEAL FOR F1 RIGHTS

During the week prior to the Spanish Grand Prix, the FIA world motorsport council gave the formal green light to finalise the 100-year agreement for the commercial rights of the FIA F1 World Championship, thereby endorsing negotiations with Bernie Ecclestone which had been going on for several months.

The deal was finalised by FIA president Max Mosley, representatives of the SLEC organisation — Thomas Haffa and Dieter Hahn — and Ecclestone, on behalf of the Formula One Management organisation.

SLEC, now 75 per cent owned by German media groups Kirch and EM.TV, have paid the FIA an estimated £220 million for the rights.

An official statement from the governing body said: 'This is a further important step by the FIA towards complying with the European Commission's requirement to separate commercial and promotional activities from the sport.'

McLaren boss Ron Dennis offered qualified approval for the move. 'It is a good first step, but I don't know whether the price is right,' he said. 'But this is certainly a good baseline for the future of F1 which has defined the fact that the FIA no longer has any say in the commercial rights.'

However, the threat of an independent series being established by the manufacturers still remained as SLEC clearly had not yet offered the car makers a sufficiently generous share of the commercial rights to satisfy their ambitions.

Right: Häkkinen tries to be philosophical as he explains to the media the sequence of events which caused his retirement.
Photograph: Clive Mason/Allsport-Getty Images

Below: Stupid tangle. This moment eliminated both Pedro de la Rosa and the briefly airborne Heinz-Harald Frentzen.
Photograph: Pascal Rondeau/Allsport-Getty Images

Jordan-Honda home fourth ahead of Coulthard. As far as the Scot was concerned, even by the end of the opening lap, he had seen about as much action as the rest of the 22-car field put together.

His McLaren MP4/16 stalled prior to the parade lap, obliging him to start the race from the back of the field rather than his hard-earned third place on the second row. Then, coming out of the first corner, Enrique Bernoldi's Arrows ran into the back of him, pushing him into the car in front, Giancarlo Fisichella's Benetton.

'To come in like that and still get some points at the end of the day is very much a get-out-of jail situation,' he later admitted.

'I initiated the start sequence on the new software before the formation lap and everything was normal until I wanted to accelerate away. As a result I had to start from the back of the grid and got involved in a first-corner incident where I was hit from behind, which damaged the floor and pushed me into another car.

'I had to go into the pits for a new nosecone and could then start to catch up.'

It was easy enough for television viewers around the world to see that the McLaren had lost its nose section in this incident, but when he arrived in the pits for repairs his team mechanics realised that the rear impact had broken two stays holding on the floor section and snapped off the mounting point for the rear jack.

That meant precariously balancing the rear of the McLaren on its snapped jack stem in order to change its rear tyres, Coulthard meanwhile was shouting at his engineers that he wanted to keep the new set of Bridgestones on which he had started the race rather than switch to a set of worn tyres from qualifying.

Yet his eagle-eyed engineer Pat Fry had noticed that one of his existing tyres had been badly cut in the collision and prudently ignored his driver's requests to leave them on the car.

Meanwhile, Schumacher led Häkkinen round the opening lap ahead of Rubens Barrichello's Ferrari, Ralf Schumacher's Williams-BMW, Jarno Trulli's Jordan EJ-11 and the remarkable Juan Pablo Montoya who'd dodged through from 11th on the grid to be sixth at the end of the first lap.

Meanwhile, after his early delay, Coulthard completed the second lap in last place, 55.9s behind the leader. He was determined to get on with the programme and was down to 1m 22.5s — the fastest race lap up to that point — third time round.

Meanwhile Schumacher's Ferrari was edging away from Häkkinen. He was 1.1s ahead on lap two, but had stretched that to 1.9s with six laps completed. On the same lap Pedro de la Rosa closed the door rather too tightly on Heinz-Harald Frentzen's Jordan and the Spaniard's Jaguar joined its rival in a gravel trap, out of the race.

On lap 11 Schumacher posted a 1m 22.242s, opening the advantage over Häkkinen to 2.2s, but Mika was a match for the Ferrari and pulled it back to 1.9s next time round. By lap 13 Coulthard was up to 19th, but now 62.9s down on the leaders.

On lap 21 Trulli and Montoya came in for their first stops, the Colombian getting the jump on the Jordan driver to accelerate back into the race in fifth place. At the same time Ralf Schumacher threw away fourth place when a locking rear brake sent him pirouetting into a gravel trap, much to his abject frustration.

The balance of the race remained finely balanced between the two leading runners. On lap 23 Schumacher made an 8.7s first refuelling stop and Mika immediately picked up speed. Now he reeled off three consecutive sub-1m 22s laps before making his own 8.8s refuelling stop at the end of lap 27. It was not enough to pop him back out into the lead, and Schumacher was now 2.5s ahead.

Having charged through the second half of the field, Coulthard came in for fuel at the end of lap 28 in eighth place, taking 8.4s, and then resumed three places further back.

Above: Eddie Irvine burns rubber as he storms his Jaguar R2 back into the race after a refuelling stop.
Photograph: Paul-Henri Cahier

Gradually Michael eased open his advantage from 2.9s on lap 31 to 3.7s on lap 36 and 4.7s on lap 42. Schumacher made his second stop in 9.3s on lap 43, but Häkkinen piled on the pressure and stayed out until lap 50 before making his second stop in 8.3s. That turned the tide as Häkkinen went back into the race 3.5s in front.

By now Rubens Barrichello's Ferrari had retired from third place after an off-track excursion hinted at a technical problem which turned out to be broken rear suspension. Then Michael began slowing dramatically with that mysterious vibration on his last set of tyres and Häkkinen looked as though he would be home and dry. Until that fateful final lap.

Montoya's second place guaranteed his first visit to the victory podium in only his fifth F1 race. On a day when his team-mate, San Marino Grand Prix winner Ralf Schumacher, failed to finish, the Colombian driver saved the day for the BMW Williams team with a strong showing.

Similarly, Villeneuve posted his first podium finish in over two seasons for the BAR team just 8.8s behind the Williams. Neither of the former Indy car drivers used all the permissible electronic aids during the course of this race in the interests of mechanical reliability. Their conservatism certainly paid off.

Eddie Irvine had another disappointment when his Jaguar R2 succumbed to engine failure with 17 laps to go, possibly with his first championship points on the horizon.

After battling gamely with Olivier Panis's BAR-Honda in the opening stages, Irvine was warned over the radio that he had an oil leak with about 25 laps to run.

Rather than retire the car, the team instructed him to press on with their fingers crossed. But their audacity was not to be rewarded.

'I used less [engine] revs in the hope that the oil problem would go away,' said Irvine, 'but it was no surprise when it stopped. A shame, because the car was pretty good.'

As for Coulthard, by lap 45 back to seventh place from which he made his second stop in 7.6s, resuming 10th. By the finish he had pulled through to fifth place.

There was a slightly tetchy exchange between Coulthard and McLaren boss Ron Dennis after the race following a comment from Dennis to the effect that stalling on the grid had been his driver's fault. But he later retracted that remark.

Dennis observed: 'Based on an initial analysis we felt that David was responsible for stalling on the dummy grid. Scrutiny confirmed that a glitch in the software was at fault.'

During the course of his busy race, Coulthard had been regularly lapping at speeds which matched the pace of the leaders, even though he was having to thread a path through heavy traffic for much of the time.

The afternoon ended with Häkkinen being given a lift back to the pits on the sidepod of Coulthard's sister car. David later reported that the Finn was leaning into the cockpit, fiddling with the buttons on the centre of the steering wheel.

'I thought, if he activates the launch control mechanism, this is going to be a lot of fun for both of us,' said Coulthard later. It was reassuring that the two McLaren drivers retained their sense of humour after such a bruising afternoon.

ROUND 5
CATALUNYA 27–29 APRIL 2001

gran premio
MARLBORO de
ESPAÑA

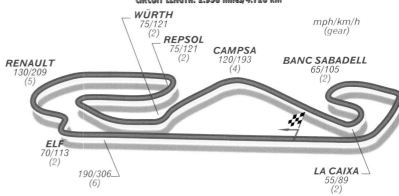

CATALUNYA CIRCUIT – BARCELONA
CIRCUIT LENGTH: 2.938 miles/4.728 km

WÜRTH 75/121 (2)
REPSOL 75/121 (2)
CAMPSA 120/193 (4)
BANC SABADELL 65/105 (2)
RENAULT 130/209 (5)
mph/km/h (gear)
ELF 70/113 (2)
190/306 (6)
LA CAIXA 55/89 (2)

RACE DISTANCE: 65 laps, 190.962 miles/307.323 km   RACE WEATHER: Dry, warm and sunny

Pos.	Driver	Nat.	No.	Entrant	Car/Engine	Tyres	Laps	Time/Retirement	Speed (mph/km/h)	Gap to lead
1	Michael Schumacher	D	1	Scuderia Ferrari Marlboro	Ferrari F2001-050 V10	B	65	1h 31m 03.305s	125.832/202.507	
2	Juan Pablo Montoya	COL	6	BMW WilliamsF1 Team	Williams FW23-BMW P80 V10	M	65	1h 31m 44.042s	124.901/201.009	+40.73
3	Jacques Villeneuve	CDN	10	Lucky Strike BAR Honda	BAR 03-Honda RA001E V10	B	65	1h 31m 52.930s	124.700/200.685	+49.62
4	Jarno Trulli	I	12	B&H Jordan Honda	Jordan EJ11-Honda RA001E V10	B	65	1h 31m 54.557s	124.662/200.625	+51.25
5	David Coulthard	GB	4	West McLaren Mercedes	McLaren MP4/16-Mercedes F0110K V10	B	65	1h 31m 54.920s	124.654/200.612	+51.61
6	Nick Heidfeld	D	16	Red Bull Sauber Petronas	Sauber C20-Petronas V10	B	65	1h 32m 05.197s	124.423/200.239	+61.89
7	Olivier Panis	F	9	Lucky Strike BAR Honda	BAR 03-Honda RA001E V10	B	65	1h 32m 08.281s	124.353/200.127	+64.97
8	Kimi Räikkönen	SF	17	Red Bull Sauber Petronas	Sauber C20-Petronas V10	B	65	1h 32m 23.112s	124.021/199.592	+79.80
9	Mika Häkkinen	SF	3	West McLaren Mercedes	McLaren MP4/16-Mercedes F0110K V10	B	64	Clutch		+1 l
10	Jean Alesi	F	22	Prost Acer	Prost AP04-Acer V10	M	64			+1 l
11	Luciano Burti	BR	23	Prost Acer	Prost AP04-Acer V10	M	64			+1 l
12	Jos Verstappen	NL	14	Orange Arrows Asiatech	Arrows A22-Asiatech V10	B	63			+2 la
13	Fernando Alonso	ESP	21	European Minardi F1	Minardi PS01-European V10	M	63			+2 la
14	Giancarlo Fisichella	I	7	Mild Seven Benetton Renault	Benetton B201-Renault RS21 V10	M	63			+2 la
15	Jenson Button	GB	8	Mild Seven Benetton Renault	Benetton B201-Renault RS21 V10	M	62			+3 la
16	Tarso Marques	BR	20	European Minardi F1	Minardi PS01-European V10	M	62			+3 la
	Rubens Barrichello	BR	2	Scuderia Ferrari Marlboro	Ferrari F2001-050 V10	B	49	Suspension		
	Eddie Irvine	GB	18	Jaguar Racing	Jaguar R2-Cosworth CR3 V10	M	48	Engine		
	Ralf Schumacher	D	5	BMW WilliamsF1 Team	Williams FW23-BMW P80 V10	M	20	Spun off		
	Enrique Bernoldi	BR	15	Orange Arrows Asiatech	Arrows A22-Asiatech V10	B	8	Fuel pressure		
	Pedro de la Rosa	ESP	19	Jaguar Racing	Jaguar R2-Cosworth CR3 V10	M	5	Collision with Frentzen		
	Heinz-Harald Frentzen	D	11	B&H Jordan Honda	Jordan EJ11-Honda RA001E V10	B	5	Collision with de la Rosa		

Fastest lap: Michael Schumacher, on lap 25, 1m 21.151s, 130.383 mph/209.831 km/h (record).

Previous lap record: Giancarlo Fisichella (F1 Jordan 197-Peugeot V10), 1m 22.242s, 128.919 mph/207.475 km/h (1997).

Grid order	1	2	3	4	5	6	7	8	9	10	11	12	13	14	15	16	17	18	19	20	21	22	23	24	25	26	27	28	29	30	31	32	33	34	35	36	37	38	39	40	41	42	43	44	45	46	47	48	49
1 M. SCHUMACHER	1	1	1	1	1	1	1	1	1	1	1	1	1	1	1	1	1	1	1	1	1	1	1	1	3	3	3	3	1	1	1	1	1	1	1	1	1	1	1	1	1	1	3	3	3	3	3	3	
3 HÄKKINEN	3	3	3	3	3	3	3	3	3	3	3	3	3	3	3	3	3	3	3	3	3	1	2	2	1	1	3	3	3	3	3	3	3	3	3	3	3	3	3	1	1	1	1	1	1	1	1		
2 BARRICHELLO	2	2	2	2	2	2	2	2	2	2	2	2	2	2	2	2	2	2	2	2	2	2	1	1	2	2	2	2	2	2	2	2	2	2	2	2	2	2	2	2	2	2	2	2	2	2	2	6	
5 R. SCHUMACHER	5	5	5	5	5	5	5	5	5	5	5	5	5	5	5	5	5	5	5	10	10	10	16		6	6	6	6	6	6	6	6	6	6	6	6	6	6	6	6	18	18	18	18		6	6	6	10
12 TRULLI	12	12	12	12	12	12	12	12	12	12	12	12	12	12	12	12	12	12	12	12	12	16	16	18	10	10	10	10	10	10	10	10	10	10	10	10	10	10	10	9	9	6	6	10	10	10	12		
10 VILLENEUVE	6	6	6	6	6	6	6	6	6	6	6	6	6	6	6	6	6	6	18	18	9	12	12	12	12	12	12	12	12	12	12	12	12	12	12	12	18	9	4	10	12	12	16	16	16	4			
11 FRENTZEN	10	10	10	10	10	10	10	10	10	10	10	10	10	10	10	10	10	10	10	16	9	9	6	16	16	16	16	16	16	16	16	16	16	16	18	9	4	4	10	12	16	16	16	4					
17 RÄIKKÖNEN	16	16	16	16	16	16	16	16	16	16	16	16	16	16	16	16	16	18	17	17	10	4	4	4	4	18	18	18	18	18	18	18	18	18	9	4	10	10	12	16	18	18	9						
16 HEIDFELD	18	18	18	18	18	18	18	18	18	18	18	18	18	18	18	18	18	18	9	6	12	18	18	18	17	17	17	17	17	17	17	17	9	9	4	12	12	12	16	9	9	9	17						
9 PANIS	17	17	9	9	9	9	9	9	9	9	9	9	9	9	9	9	9	9	9	9	17	22	12	23	17	17	17	17	9	9	9	9	9	9	17	4	16	16	16	9	4	4	4						
6 MONTOYA	9	9	17	17	17	17	17	17	17	17	17	17	17	17	17	17	17	17	17	17	22	12	22	4	9	9	9	9	4	17	17	17	17	17	17	17	17	17	17	17	17	17	22						
18 IRVINE	14	14	14	14	14	14	14	14	14	14	14	14	14	14	14	14	14	14	22	22	23	23	17	22	22	22	22	22	22	22	22	22	22	22	22	22	22	22	22	22	22	22	22	23					
23 BURTI	22	22	22	22	22	22	22	22	22	22	22	22	22	22	22	22	22	14	23	4	4	4	22	14	14	14	14	14	14	14	14	14	14	23	23	23	23	23	23	23	23	23	14						
22 ALESI	23	23	23	23	23	23	23	23	23	23	23	23	23	23	23	23	23	4	7	14	14	14	23	23	23	23	23	23	23	14	14	14	14	14	14	14	14	14	14	14	14	21							
15 BERNOLDI	7	7	7	7	7	7	7	7	7	7	7	7	7	7	7	7	4	4	4	7	14	7	21	21	21	21	21	21	21	21	21	21	21	21	21	21	21	21	21	21	21	21	7						
14 VERSTAPPEN	21	21	19	19	19	21	21	21	21	21	21	21	21	21	4	7	7	7	14	21	21	21	7	7	7	7	7	7	7	7	7	7	7	7	7	7	7	7	7	7	7	7	20						
21 ALONSO	19	19	11	11	11	19	19	19	19	19	19	19	19	19	21	20	20	20	21	20	20	20	20	20	20	20	20	20	20	20	20	20	20	20	20	20	20	20	20	20	20	20	8						
7 FISICHELLA	11	11	21	21	21	20	20	20	20	20	20	20	4	4	8	21	21	21	20	20	8	8	8	8	8	8	8	8	8	8	8	8	8	8	8	8	8	8	8	8	8								
19 DE LA ROSA	8	8	8	8	8	15	15	15	4	4	4	4	20	20	20	20	8	8	8	8																													
8 BUTTON	20	20	20	20	20	4	4	4																																									
20 MARQUES	15	15	15	15	15																																												
4 COULTHARD	4	4	4	4	4																																												

Pit stop
One lap behind leader

STARTING GRID

1 M. SCHUMACHER Ferrari	**3** HÄKKINEN McLaren
4* COULTHARD McLaren	**2** BARRICHELLO Ferrari
5 R. SCHUMACHER Williams	**12** TRULLI Jordan
10 VILLENEUVE BAR	**11** FRENTZEN Jordan
17 RÄIKKÖNEN Sauber	**16** HEIDFELD Sauber
9 PANIS BAR	**6** MONTOYA Williams
18 IRVINE Jaguar	**23** BURTI Prost
22 ALESI Prost	**15** BERNOLDI Arrows
14 VERSTAPPEN Arrows	**21** ALONSO Minardi
7 FISICHELLA Benetton	**19** DE LA ROSA Jaguar
8 BUTTON Benetton	**20** MARQUES Minardi

*started from the back of the grid

All results and data © FIA 2001

53	54	55	56	57	58	59	60	61	62	63	64	65	
3	3	3	3	3	3	3	3	3	3	3	3	1	1
1	1	1	1	1	1	1	1	1	1	1	1	6	2
6	6	6	6	6	6	6	6	6	6	6	6	10	3
10	10	10	10	10	10	10	10	10	10	10	10	12	4
12	12	12	12	12	12	12	12	12	12	12	12	4	5
16	16	16	16	16	16	16	4	4	4	4	4	16	6
4	4	4	4	4	4	4	16	16	16	16	16	9
9	9	9	9	9	9	9	9	9	9	9	9	17
17	17	17	17	17	17	17	17	17	17	17	17
22	22	22	22	22	22	22	22	22	22	22	22
23	23	23	23	23	23	23	23	23	23	23	23
14	14	14	14	14	14	14	14	14	14	14
21	21	21	21	21	21	21	21	21	21
7	7	7	7	7	7	7	7	7	7
8	8	8	8	8	8	8	8	8
20	20	20	20	20	20	20	20	20

FOR THE RECORD

First Grand Prix point	
Juan Pablo Montoya	
200th Grand Prix point	
Jacques Villeneuve	
150th Grand Prix	
Mika Häkkinen	
Michael Schumacher	

TIME SHEETS

QUALIFYING
Weather: Dry, warm and sunny

Pos.	Driver	Car	Laps	Time
1	Michael Schumacher	Ferrari	8	1m 18.201s
2	Mika Häkkinen	McLaren-Mercedes	12	1m 18.286s
3	David Coulthard	McLaren-Mercedes	12	1m 18.635s
4	Rubens Barrichello	Ferrari	11	1m 18.674s
5	Ralf Schumacher	Williams-BMW	12	1m 19.016s
6	Jarno Trulli	Jordan-Honda	12	1m 19.093s
7	Jacques Villeneuve	BAR-Honda	10	1m 19.122s
8	Heinz-Harald Frentzen	Jordan-Honda	12	1m 19.150s
9	Kimi Räikkönen	Sauber-Petronas	12	1m 19.229s
10	Nick Heidfeld	Sauber-Petronas	11	1m 19.232s
11	Olivier Panis	BAR-Honda	11	1m 19.479s
12	Juan Pablo Montoya	Williams-BMW	11	1m 19.660s
13	Eddie Irvine	Jaguar-Cosworth	12	1m 20.326s
14	Luciano Burti	Prost-Acer	12	1m 20.585s
15	Jean Alesi	Prost-Acer	12	1m 20.601s
16	Enrique Bernoldi	Arrows-Asiatech	12	1m 20.696s
17	Jos Verstappen	Arrows-Asiatech	11	1m 20.737s
18	Fernando Alonso	Minardi-European	12	1m 21.037s
19	Giancarlo Fisichella	Benetton-Renault	12	1m 21.065s
20	Pedro de la Rosa	Jaguar-Cosworth	10	1m 21.338s
21	Jenson Button	Benetton-Renault	11	1m 21.916s
22	Tarso Marques	Minardi-European	12	1m 22.522s

FRIDAY FREE PRACTICE
Weather: Overcast, then warm and sunny

Pos.	Driver	Laps	Time
1	David Coulthard	37	1m 20.107s
2	Eddie Irvine	27	1m 20.615s
3	Rubens Barrichello	27	1m 20.823s
4	Olivier Panis	28	1m 20.826s
5	Michael Schumacher	41	1m 20.880s
6	Mika Häkkinen	26	1m 20.894s
7	Pedro de la Rosa	38	1m 21.184s
8	Ralf Schumacher	33	1m 21.259s
9	Jacques Villeneuve	23	1m 21.401s
10	Jarno Trulli	28	1m 21.647s
11	Kimi Räikkönen	31	1m 21.786s
12	Nick Heidfeld	34	1m 21.808s
13	Juan Pablo Montoya	24	1m 22.020s
14	Heinz-Harald Frentzen	22	1m 22.221s
15	Jean Alesi	30	1m 22.843s
16	Enrique Bernoldi	40	1m 22.888s
17	Jos Verstappen	37	1m 22.962s
18	Giancarlo Fisichella	38	1m 22.971s
19	Jenson Button	33	1m 23.201s
20	Fernando Alonso	44	1m 23.801s
21	Luciano Burti	41	1m 23.885s
22	Tarso Marques	22	1m 25.540s

SATURDAY FREE PRACTICE
Weather: Dry, warm and sunny

Pos.	Driver	Laps	Time
1	Michael Schumacher	19	1m 18.634s
2	Rubens Barrichello	20	1m 18.674s
3	David Coulthard	29	1m 18.686s
4	Kimi Räikkönen	24	1m 18.765s
5	Nick Heidfeld	24	1m 19.010s
6	Jarno Trulli	22	1m 19.186s
7	Olivier Panis	30	1m 19.253s
8	Mika Häkkinen	22	1m 19.281s
9	Ralf Schumacher	25	1m 19.406s
10	Jacques Villeneuve	23	1m 19.577s
11	Heinz-Harald Frentzen	18	1m 19.903s
12	Juan Pablo Montoya	23	1m 20.202s
13	Jean Alesi	20	1m 20.741s
14	Luciano Burti	31	1m 20.801s
15	Enrique Bernoldi	22	1m 20.997s
16	Jos Verstappen	28	1m 21.069s
17	Eddie Irvine	26	1m 21.289s
18	Giancarlo Fisichella	28	1m 21.404s
19	Fernando Alonso	19	1m 21.493s
20	Jenson Button	23	1m 21.804s
21	Pedro de la Rosa	14	1m 22.296s
22	Tarso Marques	18	1m 24.371s

WARM-UP
Weather: Dry, warm and sunny

Pos.	Driver	Laps	Time
1	Rubens Barrichello	14	1m 20.680s
2	Mika Häkkinen	16	1m 20.901s
3	David Coulthard	11	1m 21.148s
4	Michael Schumacher	14	1m 21.211s
5	Olivier Panis	14	1m 21.558s
6	Heinz-Harald Frentzen	14	1m 21.558s
7	Ralf Schumacher	12	1m 21.886s
8	Jarno Trulli	16	1m 21.929s
9	Jacques Villeneuve	15	1m 22.120s
10	Nick Heidfeld	14	1m 22.343s
11	Juan Pablo Montoya	16	1m 22.558s
12	Kimi Räikkönen	17	1m 22.864s
13	Jos Verstappen	18	1m 23.240s
14	Eddie Irvine	12	1m 23.294s
15	Jenson Button	5	1m 23.754s
16	Jean Alesi	13	1m 23.794s
17	Pedro de la Rosa	14	1m 23.847s
18	Enrique Bernoldi	16	1m 24.138s
19	Fernando Alonso	12	1m 24.361s
20	Giancarlo Fisichella	16	1m 24.468s
21	Luciano Burti	13	1m 24.633s
22	Tarso Marques	11	1m 24.924s

RACE FASTEST LAPS
Weather: Weather: Dry, warm and sunny

Driver	Time	Lap
Michael Schumacher	1m 21.151s	25
Mika Häkkinen	1m 21.368s	49
Rubens Barrichello	1m 21.720s	27
David Coulthard	1m 22.091s	41
Ralf Schumacher	1m 22.362s	19
Olivier Panis	1m 22.475s	26
Jacques Villeneuve	1m 22.513s	22
Eddie Irvine	1m 22.568s	23
Nick Heidfeld	1m 22.738s	26
Juan Pablo Montoya	1m 22.841s	39
Kimi Räikkönen	1m 23.049s	40
Jarno Trulli	1m 23.087s	24
Jean Alesi	1m 23.668s	20
Luciano Burti	1m 23.794s	23
Jos Verstappen	1m 23.965s	17
Fernando Alonso	1m 24.423s	37
Enrique Bernoldi	1m 24.740s	4
Giancarlo Fisichella	1m 25.298s	14
Jenson Button	1m 25.406s	57
Tarso Marques	1m 25.791s	16
Pedro de la Rosa	1m 25.932s	3
Heinz-Harald Frentzen	1m 26.158s	3

CHASSIS LOG BOOK

1	M. Schumacher	Ferrari F2001/210
2	Barrichello	Ferrari F2001/206
	spare	Ferrari F2001/208
3	Häkkinen	McLaren MP4/16/4
4	Coulthard	McLaren MP4/16/5
	spare	McLaren MP4/16/3
5	R. Schumacher	Williams FW23/5
6	Montoya	Williams FW23/3
	spare	Williams FW23/1
7	Fisichella	Benetton B201/3
8	Button	Benetton B201/5
	spare	Benetton B201/1
9	Panis	BAR 03/6
10	Villeneuve	BAR 03/5
	spare	BAR 03/2
11	Frentzen	Jordan EJ11/4
12	Trulli	Jordan EJ11/5
	spare	Jordan EJ11/3
14	Verstappen	Arrows A22/6
15	Bernoldi	Arrows A22/3
	spare	Arrows A22/1
16	Heidfeld	Sauber C20/3
17	Räikkönen	Sauber C20/1
	spare	Sauber C20/5
18	Irvine	Jaguar R2/4
19	de la Rosa	Jaguar R2/3
	spare	Jaguar R2/5
20	Marques	Minardi PS01/4
21	Alonso	Minardi PS01/3
	spare	Minardi PS01/1
22	Alesi	Prost AP04/3
23	Burti	Prost AP04/4
	spare	Prost AP04/2

POINTS TABLES

DRIVERS

1	Michael Schumacher	36
2	David Coulthard	28
3	Rubens Barrichello	14
4	Ralf Schumacher	12
5	Nick Heidfeld	8
6	Jarno Trulli	7
7 =	Juan Pablo Montoya	6
7 =	Heinz-Harald Frentzen	6
9 =	Jacques Villeneuve	4
9 =	Mika Häkkinen	4
11	Olivier Panis	3
12 =	Kimi Räikkönen	1
12 =	Giancarlo Fisichella	1

CONSTRUCTORS

1	Ferrari	50
2	McLaren	32
3	Williams	18
4	Jordan	13
5	Sauber	9
6	BAR	7
7	Benetton	1

FIA WORLD CHAMPIONSHIP • ROUND 6

AUSTRIAN
grand prix

1st - COULTHARD • 2nd - M. SCHUMACHER • 3rd - BARRICHELLO

Formula 1 ™

Left: David Coulthard is immersed in thought on the podium as the national anthem celebrates his victory over Michael Schumacher at the A1-Ring. The previous afternoon, Paul Morgan, co-founder of Mercedes engine builder Ilmor Engineering, had been killed in a flying accident.
Photograph: Paul-Henri Cahier

DAVID Coulthard put his World Championship campaign firmly back on track in the Styrian sunshine with a brilliantly judged victory in the Austrian Grand Prix, out-foxing the Ferraris of Michael Schumacher and Rubens Barrichello after a strategically astute performance which saw him make his sole refuelling stop later in the race than his two rivals and emerge from it just over a second ahead of Barrichello.

It was a reassuring performance from the 30-year-old Scot who a fortnight earlier had stalled on the grid prior to the start of the Spanish Grand Prix, then collided with two other cars on the first corner and eventually finished fifth.

He finished the day just four points behind Michael Schumacher after a drive which unquestionably radiated the assurance and a maturity of a man who seemed to realise that his time had come.

Yet it was a bitter-sweet success for Coulthard and the McLaren-Mercedes team coming as it did barely 24 hours after the death of Paul Morgan, the managing director of Ilmor Engineering, the makers of Mercedes' F1 engine, in a plane crash.

Coulthard refrained from spraying champagne on the podium out of respect for the memory of the talented 52-year-old engineer who had been killed the day before the race when his vintage Sea Fury aeroplane turned over while taxiing in after landing at an aerodrome near his home. 'Paul was a genuinely popular man and you would have been hard pushed to find anybody in the business who had a hard word to say about him,' said Coulthard.

He also added: 'This must have been a great race to watch and it was definitely fun to drive. We started the race on quite a heavy fuel load to allow ourselves some flexibility with the strategy. It meant I could stay out for a few laps longer than Michael Schumacher and three more than Rubens Barrichello before my pit stop.'

Barrichello had a harsh lesson in the realities of life as a Ferrari driver when he was instructed to move over coming out of the last corner and relinquish second place to Schumacher.

The Brazilian driver finished the day feeling distinctly cool about this state of affairs. 'The team ordered me to move over,' he said at the media conference. 'I am not happy with the situation.

'I have very few things to say at this press conference. I need to speak to the team to clarify a few things. Unfortunately I cannot open my heart right now, I'm sorry.'

The start of the race saw another lurid startline incident triggered by a rash of malfunctions amongst the complex electronic launch and traction control systems which the cars have been allowed to use since the Spanish race.

On this occasion even Schumacher's pole-position Ferrari F2001 was afflicted by these gremlins, the German driver struggling to take over manual control of his start as the two Williams-BMWs of Juan Pablo Montoya and Ralf Schumacher surged into first and second places. It also left Mika Häkkinen's McLaren-Mercedes, and three other cars, seemingly glued to their starting positions.

That resulted in the safety car being deployed immediately, Mika Häkkinen's McLaren, both the Jordan-Hondas of Jarno Trulli and Heinz-Harald Frentzen, and Nick Heidfeld's Sauber C20 were left stranded on the grid.

The stricken McLaren was pushed to the pit lane before joining in briefly at the end of the third lap, then immediately came in and retired next time round. Trulli was also pushed into the pit lane.

Frentzen was similarly disappointed, but his problem was undeniably terminal. 'When I tried to move off the start I heard a grinding noise and felt the gears were jammed,' he shrugged. 'It became clear the gearbox was broken. It was a frustrating way to end a weekend where we had a good chance of scoring points.'

Trulli eventually got away behind the safety car, albeit one lap down, but was soon in trouble. After a slide into a gravel trap he pitted for attention and then found himself black flagged out of the race after ignoring a red warning light at the pit lane exit when he scampered back into the fray.

Heidfeld, who had qualified so well in sixth place, also found his Sauber's launch control glitching. 'After that, I wasn't really in the race because I was a lap behind.'

Montoya, meanwhile, had qualified brilliantly on the front row of the grid for this, only the sixth Grand Prix of his career. He surged into an immediate lead and pulled out an early 1.5s gap over team-mate Ralf Schumacher who progressively found

A1–RING QUALIFYING

Diary

Goodyear competitions chief Stu Grant visits the Austrian Grand Prix, fuelling speculation that the Akron-based tyre maker is considering an F1 return.

Bernie Ecclestone visits Moscow where he confirms that a Russian Grand Prix could take place by 2004 if the proposed circuit is ready in time.

BMW motor sport director Gerhard Berger reaffirms that the Munich company has no intention of purchasing a stake in the Williams F1 team.

There had been alarm in the McLaren-Mercedes garage on Saturday afternoon after Coulthard and Häkkinen qualified in distant seventh and eighth places on the grid, the victims of not very much in particular in terms of specific problems.

That made it even more frustrating for the front-running team which fell victim to a maelstrom of unrelated glitches. Häkkinen complained that his car's balance was adversely affected by the changing track conditions — particularly the wind — and he later also found himself grappling an apparent loss of engine power.

Despite running what technical director Adrian Newey described as almost an 'Indy speedway' wing towards the end, Häkkinen's straight line speeds bogged down frustratingly. With Coulthard complaining of poor balance and being unable to match his times from the morning session, it was an unusually poor showing all round. But as Michael Schumacher sagely observed 'never discount the McLarens, even now.'

Coulthard explained it succinctly: 'We have a very quick car but it is very tricky to balance. We didn't quite hit the sweet spot. There's really nothing more to it than that.

'We had a touch too much understeer at the end of the morning session, made a set-up change and then found there was too much oversteer in the afternoon. Nothing more.'

Meanwhile, it was get-out-of-jail day yet again for Michael Schumacher who blitzed pole position with a perfectly judged run. He admitted that he might even have been able to go slightly quicker had Jos Verstappen's Arrows not spun across in front of him on his final lap.

'But it was very tricky to get the right combination of set-up in these wind and track conditions,' added the Ferrari ace.

Second and third were the impressive Williams-BMW FW23s of Juan Pablo Montoya (1m 9.686s) and Ralf Schumacher (1m 9.769s). Montoya was obviously delighted. 'We definitely did a lot of improvements in the car and it really paid off,' he said. 'It's been very close all weekend, but it's great to be ahead of Ralf.'

The younger Schumacher took this in his stride. 'I think qualifying went relatively well,' he acknowledged. 'On one run I got held up by traffic and I made a mistake myself on the last run, which shouldn't have happened. But I think we're in a pretty promising position for tomorrow.'

Rubens Barrichello wound up a slightly disappointed fourth fastest on 1m 9.786s. 'I never had a clear lap and know I can do better,' he shrugged. 'I made three changes to the car's downforce level during the course of the session.'

Jarno Trulli was well satisfied with a fifth-fastest 1m 10.202s in the Jordan-Honda EJ-11 'considering I managed only five laps during the morning due to an engine. My first timed lap was the best, but unfortunately I couldn't improve as it felt as though the car's power was dropping away with every lap.'

Team-mate Heinz-Harald Frentzen wound up a frustrated 11th on 1m 10.923s, admitting that he had to abandon his first run when he accidentally engaged the pit lane speed limiter. 'My second run was my best,' he explained, 'but after that the balance of the car was not so good.'

Separating the two Jordans were Nick Heidfeld's Sauber on 1m 10.211s, the young German delighted with his best ever F1 qualifying effort, the two forlorn McLaren drivers, Kimi Räikkönen's Sauber (1m 10.396s) and Olivier Panis in the BAR-Honda (1m 10.435s).

Panis confessed that his best run was 'a bit messy, to be honest,' but he was much quicker than Jacques Villeneuve whose 11th place was earned by a 1m 11.058s best. Jacques spent a lot of time juggling ballast on his BAR and eventually found himself racing the spare car after suffering an engine problem during the race-morning warm-up.

Eddie Irvine (1m 11.632s) and Pedro de la Rosa (1m 11.752s) wound up a well matched 13th and 14th. 'That was a very messy qualifying session,' shrugged Irvine. 'My car didn't feel very good during the first run and Alesi also spun in front of me during my attack lap. My second was OK, but the third was a write-off.'

The Arrows A22s of Enrique Bernoldi (1m 11.823s) and Jos Verstappen (1m 12.187s) were next up ahead of Luciano Burti's Prost (1m 12.206s) and Fernando Alonso's Minardi (1m 12.640s). Jean Alesi (1m 12.910s) had a spectacular session, like Burti complaining of poor grip, and the Frenchman wound up sandwiched between the two Benettons of Giancarlo Fisichella (1m 12.644s) and Jenson Button (1m 13.459s). Fisichella suffered with an engine problem while Button had too much understeer after sustaining an oil leak in the morning.

Above: Housework. Cleaning an F1 wheel rim before it is ready to receive a new tyre.
Photograph: Clive Mason/Allsport-Getty Images

Right: Evidence. A few stones still sit on the lip of this car's diffuser, a testimony to a wheel dropped over a kerb at some point on the A1-Ring's lap.
Photograph: Paul-Henri Cahier

Above: Kimi Räikkönen drove with controlled flair to earn a strong fourth-place finish in his Sauber-Petronas C20.
Photograph: Clive Mason/Allsport-Getty Images

himself hobbled by a brake problem in the early stages, the pedal going further and further until he eventually had virtually no pressure left.

After nine laps Ralf had to retire, it later emerging that the cooling tape for the rear brake ducts had not been removed prior to the start, a somewhat embarrassing slip for this seasoned team.

Ralf's departure from the fray left brother Michael's Ferrari in second place, but Montoya was determined to prove that he wasn't about to be intimidated by the Italian car's looming presence in his Williams's mirrors.

Handicapped in the opening stages by the characteristic of his Michelin tyres which only build up their grip over the first six or seven laps, Montoya came under intense pressure from Schumacher but refused to buckle.

On lap 16 Schumacher got a run down the outside of Montoya as they climbed towards the tricky uphill Remuskurve, the second turn on the A1-Ring circuit. Schumacher attempted to outbrake Montoya, but it was a forlorn hope and the two men slid gently to the outside of the corner, allowing Barrichello through into the lead.

Behind him, Jos Verstappen's Arrows A22 had taken full advantage of its light fuel load and two-stop strategy to scramble through to second place ahead of Coulthard as the pack sorted itself out after the Montoya/Michael mêlée.

Kimi Räikkönen's Sauber C20 was now up to fourth ahead of Olivier Panis's BAR-Honda and the recovering Schumacher and Montoya, who was doing his best to clean up his Michelins after an extended excursion through the gravel trap.

Schumacher later took the opportunity to slam Juan Montoya's driving techniques.

'I was a bit upset,' said Schumacher afterwards. 'There was no way he could make that corner and all he was trying to do was take me with him. I'll have a word with him about this.

'After that I felt I would have to wait and see what happened with the pit stops. We didn't know how long everyone would go. But I had to push hard to get past the cars in front of me, so I had no chance to save fuel and came in a bit early.'

Montoya was dismissive of Schumacher's complaints. 'What happened with Michael was just a racing incident,' he shrugged. 'He braked quite late, I braked late as well, I locked the rear tyres and ran wide.'

As the World Champion recovered his composure, Panis did a great job holding off his Ferrari for several laps and Montoya held the gap to Schumacher at around 5s. Meanwhile, Verstappen made his first refuelling stop in 8.6s on lap 23, allowing Coulthard through into second place. But Barrichello was looking really confident, holding his Ferrari at just over 2s ahead of Coulthard for lap after lap.

Eventually Schumacher worked his way ahead of Panis and then made short work of the relatively obliging Räikkönen, the Ferrari customer car's team owner presumably knowing which side its bread was buttered in such circumstances.

By lap 28 Michael was back in third place with 5.9s covering the first three. By lap 38 Montoya was back to fourth place, having slipped ahead of Panis when the Frenchman ran wide at the last corner completing the previous lap. But by this time the

Colombian was in trouble and four laps later his Williams-BMW pulled off with terminal hydraulic problems.

By lap 39, Barrichello, Coulthard and Schumacher were covered by 2.9s and four laps later the trio were covered by just 1.7s. On lap 46 Schumacher brought the Ferrari in for an 8.7s stop, followed into the pits by Heidfeld who was stationary for a frustrating 18.1s after experiencing difficulties with his clutch to add to his earlier problems.

Michael resumed third, then Barrichello came in for a 9.2s stop on lap 47. This was the signal for DC to slam his foot down. On lap 48 he set the race's fastest lap in 1m 10.843s, then did a 1m 10.983s next time round.

On lap 50 Coulthard came in for a slick 8.0s refuelling stop, just scrambling back into the race 1.3s ahead of Barrichello. The McLaren team strategy had worked to perfection and now all that David had to do was keep his cool through to the chequered flag, a task he managed admirably.

Schumacher was appreciative of Barrichello's efforts in letting him through on the final corner, although he stopped short of thanking his team-mate. 'I am very happy he did that,' he said.

'Did I deserve six points [for second place] today? Maybe not. But imagine if at the end of the season I lost the World Championship by two points. Ferrari has a different philosophy [to other teams] and some will disagree with it.'

Into fourth place came the very promising Räikkönen's Sauber-Petronas ahead of Panis's BAR-Honda while Jos Verstappen prevented Eddie Irvine from scoring the Jaguar team's first point, taking sixth by 4.1s ahead of the Ulsterman.

'This point is very important for the team and for me as well,' said Verstappen. 'They all did a fantastic job. The strategy worked well for us as we could overtake at the beginning of the race and I think it was there that we earned the point. I took a lot of people into the first corner, a couple more on the straight and then two more after the safety car went in.'

Irvine was moderately satisfied. 'I made a mega start but it was a very close call in that I missed Villeneuve by inches,' he said. 'We may even have touched slightly. The car was off the line in a flash and it felt very good all afternoon, albeit not fast enough to grab points.'

Jacques Villeneuve wound up a lapped eighth after incurring a 10s stop-go penalty for speeding in the pit lane, followed by Heidfeld and the Prost AP04s of Jean Alesi and Luciano Burti.

Jenson Button trailed round at the back with his uncompetitive Benetton-Renault, probably not even allowing himself to think what he might have been achieving had he still been at the wheel of a Williams-BMW. The only thing he shared with Montoya was that neither of them completed the race distance, Button spinning off on his own oil as his Renault's engine expired.

PAUL MORGAN KILLED IN AIR ACCIDENT

Paul Morgan, the managing director of Ilmor Engineering, makers of the Mercedes-Benz F1 engines, was killed on the eve of the Austrian Grand Prix after his vintage Sea Fury aircraft tipped over after landing at Sywell airstrip, Northamptonshire.

Morgan founded Ilmor in partnership with Mario Illien back in 1983 after they both left rivals Cosworth Engineering where they had worked together.

While Illien is the technical brain behind the engine development programmes, Morgan gained a reputation as a practical down-to-earth engineer who organised the factory at Brixworth, near Northampton, presiding over the production facility with huge passion and enthusiasm. He was typical of those practical, down-to-earth, no-nonsense engineers who for the past two generations have formed the bedrock of the British motor racing industry.

Paul Morgan was born on 29 July 1948. He attended Aston University in Birmingham and graduated as a Bachelor of Science in Mechanical Engineering. In 1970, he joined Cosworth and worked on many development projects.

He owned 25 per cent of the Brixworth-based business, equal stakes also being held by Illien, the US Penske Corporation and DaimlerChrysler.

His death left a gaping hole in the McLaren-Mercedes F1 programme which would prove hard to fill on a personal basis, for Morgan was highly regarded as a man who knew the 400-plus Ilmor company employees by name.

Very much a back-room boy who liked to keep out of the limelight, Paul Morgan's great hobby was restoring and flying a small collection of historic aircraft, a passion which absorbed him to the last day of his life.

Above left, top to bottom:
Jarno Trulli climbs into the cockpit of his Jordan-Honda.
Photograph: Paul-Henri Cahier

Eddie Irvine, still struggling for points, brought his Jaguar R2 home in seventh.
Photograph: Paul-Henri Cahier

Michael Schumacher — the team had to pull rank on Barrichello to let him past into the lead.
Photograph: Clive Mason/Allsport-Getty Images

Left: Jos Verstappen ran well in the leading bunch with a light fuel load in his Arrows-Asiatech.
Photograph: Paul-Henri Cahier

ROUND 6
A1-RING 11–13 MAY 2001

grösser
A1 PREIS von
ÖSTERREICH

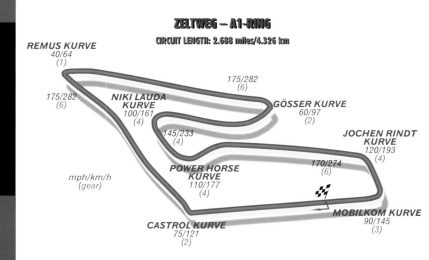

ZELTWEG – A1-RING
CIRCUIT LENGTH: 2.688 miles/4.326 km

REMUS KURVE
40/64
(1)

175/282
(6)

NIKI LAUDA
KURVE
100/161
(4)

GÖSSER KURVE
60/97
(2)

JOCHEN RINDT
KURVE
120/193
(4)

175/282
(6)

145/233
(4)

170/274
(6)

mph/km/h
(gear)

POWER HORSE
KURVE
110/177
(4)

MOBILKOM KURVE
90/145
(3)

CASTROL KURVE
75/121
(2)

RACE DISTANCE: 71 laps, 190.852 miles/307.146 km   RACE WEATHER: Dry, warm and sunny

Pos.	Driver	Nat.	No.	Entrant	Car/Engine	Tyres	Laps	Time/Retirement	Speed (mph/km/h)	Gap to lead
1	David Coulthard	GB	4	West McLaren Mercedes	McLaren MP4/16-Mercedes F0110K V10	B	71	1h 27m 45.927s	130.473/209.977	
2	Michael Schumacher	D	1	Scuderia Ferrari Marlboro	Ferrari F2001-050 V10	B	71	1h 27m 48.117s	130.419/209.890	+2.19
3	Rubens Barrichello	BR	2	Scuderia Ferrari Marlboro	Ferrari F2001-050 V10	B	71	1h 27m 48.454s	130.411/209.876	+2.52
4	Kimi Räikkönen	SF	17	Red Bull Sauber Petronas	Sauber C20-Petronas V10	B	71	1h 28m 27.520s	129.451/208.331	+41.59
5	Olivier Panis	F	9	Lucky Strike BAR Honda	BAR 03 –Honda RA001E V10	B	71	1h 28m 39.702s	129.154/207.854	+53.77
6	Jos Verstappen	NL	14	Orange Arrows Asiatech	Arrows A22-Asiatech V10	B	70			+1 la
7	Eddie Irvine	GB	18	Jaguar Racing	Jaguar R2 –Cosworth CR3 V10	M	70			+1 la
8	Jacques Villeneuve	CDN	10	Lucky Strike BAR Honda	BAR03-Honda RA001E V10	B	70			+1 l
9	Nick Heidfeld	D	16	Red Bull Sauber Petronas	Sauber C20-Petronas V10	B	69			+2 la
10	Jean Alesi	F	22	Prost Acer	Prost AP04-Acer V10	M	69			+2 la
11	Luciano Burti	BR	23	Prost Acer	Prost AP04-Acer V10	M	69			+2 la
	Jenson Button	GB	8	Mild Seven Benetton Renault	Benetton B201-Renault RS21	M	60	Engine		
	Pedro de la Rosa	ESP	19	Jaguar Racing	Jaguar R2-Cosworth CR3 V10	M	48	Transmission		
	Juan Pablo Montoya	COL	6	BMW WilliamsF1 Team	Williams FW23-BMW P80 V10	M	41	Hydraulics		
	Fernando Alonso	ESP	21	European Minardi F1	Minardi PS01-European V10	M	38	Engine		
	Tarso Marques	BR	20	European Minardi F1	Minardi PS01-European V10	M	25	Gearbox		
	Enrique Bernoldi	BR	15	Orange Arrows Asiatech	Arrows A22-Asiatech V10	B	17	Hydraulics		
DQ	Jarno Trulli	I	12	B&H Jordan Honda	Jordan EJ11-Honda RA001E V10	B	14	Exiting pit lane under red light		
	Ralf Schumacher	D	5	BMW WilliamsF1 Team	Williams FW23-BMW P80 V10	M	10	Brakes		
	Giancarlo Fisichella	I	7	Mild Seven Benetton Renault	Benetton B201-Renault RS21 V10	M	3	Engine		
	Mika Häkkinen	SF	3	West McLaren Mercedes	McLaren MP4/16-Mercedes F0110K V10	B	1	Electronics		
	Heinz-Harald Frentzen	D	11	B&H Jordan Honda	Jordan EJ11-Honda RA001E V10	B	0	Gearbox		

Fastest lap: David Coulthard, on lap 48, 1m 10.843s, 136.597 mph/219.832 km/h (record).

Previous lap record: David Coulthard (F1 McLaren MP4/15-Mercedes V10), 1m 11.783s, 134.808 mph/216.953 km/h (2000).

Grid order	1	2	3	4	5	6	7	8	9	10	11	12	13	14	15	16	17	18	19	20	21	22	23	24	25	26	27	28	29	30	31	32	33	34	35	36	37	38	39	40	41	42	43	44	45	46	47	48	49	50	51	52	53
1 M. SCHUMACHER	6	6	6	6	6	6	6	6	6	6	6	6	6	6	6	2	2	2	2	2	2	2	2	2	2	2	2	2	2	2	2	2	2	2	2	2	2	2	2	2	2	2	2	2	2	2	4	4	4	4	4	4	4
6 MONTOYA	5	5	5	5	5	5	5	5	1	1	1	1	1	1	14	14	14	14	14	14	14	4	4	4	4	4	4	4	4	4	4	4	4	4	4	4	4	4	4	4	4	4	4	4	4	4	2	2	2	2	2	2	2
5 R. SCHUMACHER	1	1	1	1	1	1	1	1	2	2	2	2	2	2	4	4	4	4	4	4	14	17	17	17	1	1	1	1	1	1	1	1	1	1	1	1	1	1	1	1	1	1	1	1	1	1	1	1	1	1	1	1	1
2 BARRICHELLO	2	2	2	2	2	2	2	2	14	14	14	14	14	14	17	17	17	17	17	17	17	9	1	1	17	17	17	17	17	17	17	17	17	17	17	17	17	17	17	17	17	17	17	17	17	17	17	17	17	17	17	17	17
12 TRULLI	4	4	4	4	14	14	14	14	4	4	4	4	4	4	9	9	9	9	9	9	9	1	9	9	9	9	9	9	9	9	9	9	9	9	9	6	6	6	6	9	9	9	14	9	9	9	9	9	9	9	9	9	9
16 HEIDFELD	18	18	18	14	4	4	4	4	17	17	17	17	17	17	1	1	1	1	1	1	1	6	6	6	6	6	6	6	6	6	6	6	9	9	9	9	9	14	14	9	18	14	14	14	14	14	14	14	14	14	14	14	14
4 COULTHARD	14	14	14	17	17	17	17	17	9	9	9	9	9	9	6	6	6	6	6	6	6	14	14	14	14	14	14	14	14	14	14	14	14	14	14	14	14	18	18	18	10	14	18	18	18	18	18	18	18	18	18	18	18
3 HÄKKINEN	17	17	17	18	18	18	9	9	15	15	15	15	15	15	15	18	18	18	18	18	18	18	18	18	18	18	18	18	18	18	18	18	18	18	18	18	18	10	10	10	14	14	10	10	10	10	10	10	10	10	10	10	10
17 RÄIKKÖNEN	9	9	9	9	9	9	18	18	18	18	18	18	18	18	10	10	10	10	10	10	10	10	10	10	10	10	10	10	10	10	10	10	10	10	10	10	10	22	22	23	22	22	22	22	22	22	22	22	22	22	22	22	22
9 PANIS	10	10	10	10	10	10	10	10	18	19	19	19	19	10	19	19	19	19	19	19	19	22	22	22	22	22	22	22	22	22	22	22	22	22	22	22	23	23	16	16	23	23	23	23	23	23	23	23	23	23	23	23	23
11 FRENTZEN	15	15	15	15	15	15	15	19	10	10	10	10	19	19	22	22	22	22	22	22	22	19	19	19	19	19	8	8	8	23	23	16	16	23	23	19	8	8	8	8	8												
10 VILLENEUVE	7	7	19	19	19	19	19	19	19	23	23	23	23	23	23	23	23	23	23	23	8	23	23	8	16	16	8	8	8	8	8	19	16	16	16	16																	
18 IRVINE	19	19	23	23	23	23	23	23	23	22	22	22	22	22	23	8	8	8	8	8	23	8	23	23	23	23	23	19	19	16	16	8	19	19	19	16	16																
19 DE LA ROSA	23	23	22	22	22	22	22	22	8	8	8	8	8	8	8	21	21	21	21	21	21	21	21	21	21	16	19	19	19	19																							
15 BERNOLDI	22	22	8	8	8	8	8	8	21	21	21	21	21	20	20	20	20	20	20	16	16	16	16	16	16	16	16	16	19	21																							
14 VERSTAPPEN	8	8	21	21	21	21	21	21	20	20	20	20	20	20	20	16	16	16	16	16	16																																
23 BURTI	21	21	7	20	20	20	20	20	5	16	16	16	16	16	16																																							
21 ALONSO	20	20	20	16	16	16	16	16	16	12	12	12	12																																								
7 FISICHELLA	12	12	12	12	12	12	12	12	12																																												
22 ALESI	16	16	16																																																		
8 BUTTON	3																																																				
20 MARQUES																																																					

Pit stop
One lap behind leader

STARTING GRID

1 **M. SCHUMACHER** Ferrari	**6** **MONTOYA** Williams
5 **R. SCHUMACHER** Williams	**2** **BARRICHELLO** Ferrari
12 **TRULLI** Jordan	**16** **HEIDFELD** Sauber
4 **COULTHARD** McLaren	**3** **HÄKKINEN** McLaren
17 **RÄIKKÖNEN** Sauber	**9** **PANIS** BAR
11 **FRENTZEN** Jordan	**10** **VILLENEUVE** BAR
18 **IRVINE** Jaguar	**19** **DE LA ROSA** Jaguar
15 **BERNOLDI** Arrows	**14** **VERSTAPPEN** Arrows
23 **BURTI** Prost	**21** **ALONSO** Minardi
7 **FISICHELLA** Benetton	**22** **ALESI** Prost
8 **BUTTON** Benetton	**20** **MARQUES** Minardi

57	58	59	60	61	62	63	64	65	66	67	68	69	70	71	•	
4	4	4	4	4	4	4	4	4	4	4	4	4	4	4		1
2	2	2	2	2	2	2	2	2	2	2	2	2	2	1		2
1	1	1	1	1	1	1	1	1	1	1	1	1	1	2		3
17	17	17	17	17	17	17	17	17	17	17	17	17	17	17		4
9	9	9	9	9	9	9	9	9	9	9	9	9	9	9		5
14	14	14	14	14	14	14	14	14	14	14	14	14	14			6
18	18	18	18	18	18	18	18	18	18	18	18	18	18			
10	10	10	10	10	10	10	10	10	10	10	10	10	10			
22	22	22	22	22	22	22	22	22	22	16	16	16	16			
23	23	23	23	23	16	16	16	16	16	16	22	22	22			
16	16	16	16	16	23	23	23	23	23	23	23	23	23			
8	8	8	8													

FOR THE RECORD

100th Grand Prix point
Sauber

TIME SHEETS

QUALIFYING
Weather: Dry, warm and sunny

Pos.	Driver	Car	Laps	Time
1	Michael Schumacher	Ferrari	12	1m 09.562s
2	Juan Pablo Montoya	Williams-BMW	12	1m 09.686s
3	Ralf Schumacher	Williams-BMW	11	1m 09.769s
4	Rubens Barrichello	Ferrari	11	1m 09.786s
5	Jarno Trulli	Jordan-Honda	11	1m 10.202s
6	Nick Heidfeld	Sauber-Petronas	12	1m 10.211s
7	David Coulthard	McLaren-Mercedes	12	1m 10.331s
8	Mika Häkkinen	McLaren-Mercedes	11	1m 10.342s
9	Kimi Räikkönen	Sauber-Petronas	12	1m 10.396s
10	Olivier Panis	BAR-Honda	12	1m 10.435s
11	Heinz-Harald Frentzen	Jordan-Honda	11	1m 10.923s
12	Jacques Villeneuve	BAR-Honda	11	1m 11.058s
13	Eddie Irvine	Jaguar-Cosworth	12	1m 11.632s
14	Pedro de la Rosa	Jaguar-Cosworth	12	1m 11.752s
15	Enrique Bernoldi	Arrows-Asiatech	12	1m 11.823s
16	Jos Verstappen	Arrows-Asiatech	11	1m 12.187s
17	Luciano Burti	Prost-Acer	12	1m 12.206s
18	Fernando Alonso	Minardi-European	12	1m 12.640s
19	Giancarlo Fisichella	Benetton-Renault	8	1m 12.644s
20	Jean Alesi	Prost-Acer	10	1m 12.910s
21	Jenson Button	Benetton-Renault	11	1m 13.459s
22	Tarso Marques	Minardi-European	5	1m 13.585s

FRIDAY FREE PRACTICE
Weather: Warm and overcast

Pos.	Driver	Laps	Time
1	David Coulthard	43	1m 11.245s
2	Mika Häkkinen	42	1m 11.272s
3	Rubens Barrichello	44	1m 11.401s
4	Ralf Schumacher	45	1m 11.555s
5	Michael Schumacher	32	1m 11.647s
6	Nick Heidfeld	44	1m 11.776s
7	Heinz-Harald Frentzen	28	1m 11.977s
8	Kimi Räikkönen	45	1m 12.189s
9	Olivier Panis	46	1m 12.259s
10	Jacques Villeneuve	49	1m 12.290s
11	Juan Pablo Montoya	44	1m 12.299s
12	Eddie Irvine	43	1m 12.346s
13	Jarno Trulli	45	1m 12.555s
14	Jos Verstappen	40	1m 12.705s
15	Pedro de la Rosa	48	1m 12.847s
16	Enrique Bernoldi	40	1m 12.853s
17	Luciano Burti	48	1m 13.169s
18	Jean Alesi	36	1m 13.288s
19	Tarso Marques	36	1m 14.314s
20	Fernando Alonso	34	1m 14.523s
21	Giancarlo Fisichella	37	1m 14.833s
22	Jenson Button	20	1m 15.570s

SATURDAY FREE PRACTICE
Weather: Warm and overcast

Pos.	Driver	Laps	Time
1	David Coulthard	38	1m 10.010s
2	Michael Schumacher	39	1m 10.039s
3	Rubens Barrichello	35	1m 10.103s
4	Mika Häkkinen	43	1m 10.148s
5	Juan Pablo Montoya	29	1m 10.391s
6	Ralf Schumacher	27	1m 10.397s
7	Heinz-Harald Frentzen	33	1m 10.434s
8	Jarno Trulli	15	1m 10.751s
9	Nick Heidfeld	26	1m 10.863s
10	Jacques Villeneuve	33	1m 10.935s
11	Olivier Panis	38	1m 11.351s
12	Kimi Räikkönen	17	1m 11.382s
13	Eddie Irvine	29	1m 11.543s
14	Jos Verstappen	27	1m 11.831s
15	Pedro de la Rosa	17	1m 11.994s
16	Enrique Bernoldi	25	1m 12.029s
17	Luciano Burti	34	1m 12.714s
18	Fernando Alonso	33	1m 13.333s
19	Giancarlo Fisichella	35	1m 13.345s
20	Tarso Marques	18	1m 13.368s
21	Jean Alesi	13	1m 13.485s
22	Jenson Button	28	1m 13.969s

WARM-UP
Weather: Sunny and bright

Pos.	Driver	Laps	Time
1	Mika Häkkinen	16	1m 11.647s
2	David Coulthard	16	1m 11.765s
3	Heinz-Harald Frentzen	17	1m 11.800s
4	Rubens Barrichello	13	1m 12.331s
5	Michael Schumacher	14	1m 12.790s
6	Jarno Trulli	18	1m 12.993s
7	Kimi Räikkönen	12	1m 13.005s
8	Jacques Villeneuve	15	1m 13.012s
9	Pedro de la Rosa	16	1m 13.149s
10	Nick Heidfeld	17	1m 13.201s
11	Olivier Panis	16	1m 13.221s
12	Eddie Irvine	17	1m 13.406s
13	Enrique Bernoldi	11	1m 13.543s
14	Jos Verstappen	15	1m 13.548s
15	Ralf Schumacher	13	1m 13.549s
16	Juan Pablo Montoya	13	1m 13.558s
17	Jean Alesi	17	1m 14.611s
18	Fernando Alonso	11	1m 14.745s
19	Tarso Marques	13	1m 15.265s
20	Luciano Burti	18	1m 15.487s
21	Giancarlo Fisichella	10	1m 15.662s
22	Jenson Button	9	1m 15.692s

RACE FASTEST LAPS
Weather: Dry, warm and sunny

Driver	Time	Lap
David Coulthard	1m 10.843s	48
Rubens Barrichello	1m 11.009s	68
Michael Schumacher	1m 11.030s	69
Juan Pablo Montoya	1m 11.140s	40
Kimi Räikkönen	1m 11.284s	70
Nick Heidfeld	1m 11.388s	69
Jacques Villeneuve	1m 11.718s	70
Eddie Irvine	1m 12.088s	69
Olivier Panis	1m 12.204s	39
Jos Verstappen	1m 12.423s	36
Luciano Burti	1m 12.642s	69
Jean Alesi	1m 13.130s	41
Jenson Button	1m 13.498s	38
Enrique Bernoldi	1m 13.587s	15
Ralf Schumacher	1m 13.888s	7
Pedro de la Rosa	1m 13.978s	35
Jarno Trulli	1m 14.082s	12
Fernando Alonso	1m 14.432s	36
Tarso Marques	1m 15.212s	25
Giancarlo Fisichella	1m 58.438s	2

CHASSIS LOG BOOK

1	M. Schumacher	Ferrari F2001/210
2	Barrichello	Ferrari F2001/206
	spare	Ferrari F2001/211
3	Häkkinen	McLaren MP4/16/4
4	Coulthard	McLaren MP4/16/5
	spare	McLaren MP4/16/3
5	R. Schumacher	Williams FW23/5
6	Montoya	Williams FW23/2
	spare	Williams FW23/1
7	Fisichella	Benetton B201/3
8	Button	Benetton B201/5
	spare	Benetton B201/1
9	Panis	BAR 03/6
10	Villeneuve	BAR 03/5
	spare	BAR 03/3
11	Frentzen	Jordan EJ11/6
12	Trulli	Jordan EJ11/5
	spare	Jordan EJ11/4
14	Verstappen	Arrows A22/6
15	Bernoldi	Arrows A22/3
	spare	Arrows A22/1
16	Heidfeld	Sauber C20/5
17	Räikkönen	Sauber C20/6
	spare	Sauber C20/1
18	Irvine	Jaguar R2/4
19	de la Rosa	Jaguar R2/3
	spare	Jaguar R2/5
20	Marques	Minardi PS01/4
21	Alonso	Minardi PS01/3
	spare	Minardi PS01/1
22	Alesi	Prost AP04/6
23	Burti	Prost AP04/4
	spare	Prost AP04/2

POINTS TABLES

DRIVERS

1	Michael Schumacher	42
2	David Coulthard	38
3	Rubens Barrichello	18
4	Ralf Schumacher	12
5	Nick Heidfeld	8
6	Jarno Trulli	7
7 =	Juan Pablo Montoya	6
7 =	Heinz-Harald Frentzen	6
9	Olivier Panis	5
10 =	Jacques Villeneuve	4
10 =	Kimi Räikkönen	4
10 =	Mika Häkkinen	4
13 =	Jos Verstappen	1
13 =	Giancarlo Fisichella	1

CONSTRUCTORS

1	Ferrari	60
2	McLaren	42
3	Williams	18
4	Jordan	13
5	Sauber	12
6	BAR	9
7 =	Arrows	1
7 =	Benetton	1

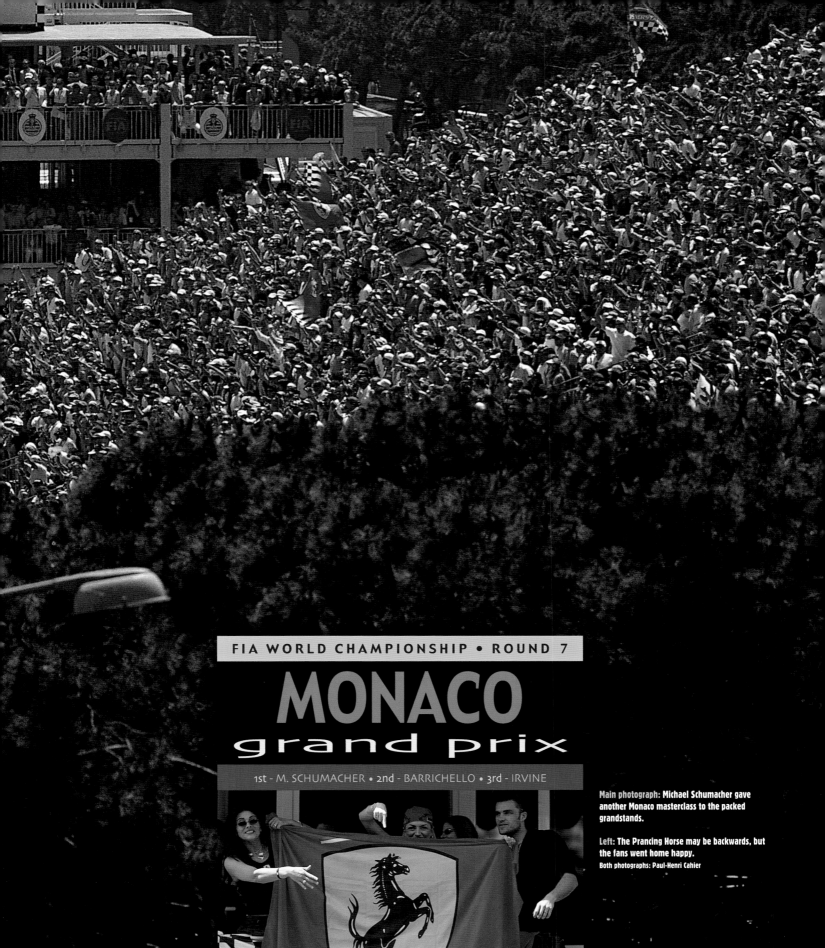

FIA WORLD CHAMPIONSHIP • ROUND 7

MONACO
grand prix

1st - M. SCHUMACHER • 2nd - BARRICHELLO • 3rd - IRVINE

Main photograph: Michael Schumacher gave another Monaco masterclass to the packed grandstands.

Left: The Prancing Horse may be backwards, but the fans went home happy.
Both photographs: Paul-Henri Cahier

MONTE CARLO QUALIFYING

David Coulthard looked every inch a World Championship contender as he qualified on pole for the 12th time in his career. He'd squeezed the most out of his McLaren-Mercedes MP4/16, opting for used front Bridgestones with new rears, thereby trading the slight diminution of ultimate braking capability for sustained front-end grip over the full lap.

It worked perfectly. Reviving his confidence after a brush with the barriers during Thursday free practice, Coulthard did the perfect job, while his two key rivals Mika Häkkinen and Michael Schumacher just failed to hit the target.

Michael wound up second on 1m 17.631s, just 0.201s shy of David's best after touching the barrier at Portier as he tried a fraction too hard on his final lap.

'I must admit that the mistake on Thursday rather took my confidence away,' said Coulthard. 'The time all came in the final segment of the lap and I hadn't really gone through that section really fast until qualifying.

'I overdid it slightly on my third run, but I knew I'd got pole in me today. I actually think we improved the car quite significantly in last week's test at Valencia and we're a little bit closer than we were at the start of the season. Of course, Monaco is less to do with aerodynamics, more with mechanical grip.'

Coulthard's performance impressed many people, notably BMW competitions chief Gerhard Berger who admitted he would have to recalibrate his assessment of the Scot. 'He looked bloody strong,' he said. 'I'm going to have to change the way I think about him.'

The Finn, confident that he could get the job done, made a minuscule change to the set-up for his final run and found a touch too much understeer blighting his efforts. He had to be satisfied with third fastest on the grid with a 1m 17.749s.

Rubens Barrichello's fourth place on 1m 17.856s was as good as the Brazilian could expect. Similarly Ralf Schumacher bagged fifth for BMW Williams (1m 18.029s) but Juan Pablo Montoya admitted he struggled slightly with set-up and tyre choice, frankly acknowledging that he'd been way off on his settings at the start of the weekend.

'I think if we had started qualifying with the car's set-up the way it was when we finished we would have been much better off,' said the Colombian after qualifying seventh on 1m 18.751s. 'We have been a bit behind, so it was difficult to catch up.'

Irvine described his sixth-fastest 1m 18.432s as 'the perfect day' but Pedro de la Rosa was playing catch-up after hitting the wall at the start of Thursday's free practice session and losing much track time as a result. Jarno Trulli's Jordan-Honda EJ-11 qualified eighth on 1m 18.921s, the Italian reporting that he was disappointed with the handling. 'The car lacked balance,' he shrugged. Still, it was better than teammate Heinz-Harald Frentzen whose 13th-fastest 1m 19.316s reflected track time lost during the morning with hydraulic problems after which he spun and stalled at Portier with seven minutes of qualifying still to go.

Jaguar was not the only team to raise its game. Giancarlo Fisichella's superb 10th place on the grid (1m 19.220s) endorsed Benetton Technical Director Mike Gascoyne's view that slow track performance was always going to be the B201's strongest card.

'On a low-speed track aerodynamic grip is less important, and the low, wide Renault engine helps a bit as well' said Gascoyne.

'I just wish we'd had the engine modifications which are due at Magny-Cours, because with those we'd have been looking pretty competitive. The performance has given the team a nice lift.'

Fisichella was sandwiched on the grid by Jacques Villeneuve's BAR-Honda (1m 19.086s) — the Canadian reporting the car as 'not too bad, although we could do with more downforce' — and Jean Alesi's Prost-Ferrari (1m 19.245s).

The Prost team had quite a stormy weekend with Luciano Burti crashing heavily at Ste. Devote following a brake failure in Saturday morning's free practice. He took the spare to qualify 21st, reporting that it didn't feel too bad.

'We made quite good progress, but we were upset that on his last lap Jean was quicker than Irvine through the first sector, but then lost his rhythm,' said Prost technical director Henri Durand.

Very disappointed were both Sauber drivers, Kimi Räikkönen (1m 20.081s) and Nick Heidfeld (1m 20.261s) qualifying 15th and 16th. The young Finn complained about traffic and nervous handling, while Heidfeld had electrical problems on his second run and had to take the spare car.

Both the Arrows and Jordan teams tried front-mounted secondary wings during Thursday free practice, but they were banned by the race stewards on safety grounds.

MICHAEL Schumacher had an easier ride than he could have ever expected to his fifth victory through the sun-kissed streets of Monte Carlo, heading a Ferrari 1-2 after key rivals McLaren-Mercedes could only salvage two Championship points from David Coulthard's distant fifth place.

The Scot's hopes of taking the World Championship lead were thwarted before the start when his McLaren-Mercedes developed an electrical problem which stalled the engine prior to the final formation lap.

As a result, he was obliged to start at the back of the 22-car field and spent a frustrating afternoon battling back to fifth place at the chequered flag.

Ironically, the pole-position McLaren was the only car to have problems getting away from the grid at the start of a race which had been viewed with acute apprehension by many teams. They had been understandably worried about the prospect of a collision on the narrow circuit caused by a repeat of the launch control glitches which had blighted the previous race in Austria. Thankfully, their fears were misplaced.

Schumacher admitted that he had to work hard to keep Mika Häkkinen at bay during the opening stages of the race, but when the Finn's McLaren MP4/16 slowed and then retired with a mysterious handling imbalance, the Ferrari ace was left to spend the rest of the afternoon simply keeping out of trouble and conserving his machinery.

It was hardly the most momentous of victories for the cool German driver. 'Honestly, I don't feel that emotional because it has been a very straightforward win,' he said.

'It wasn't anything exceptional, nothing exceptionally happened through the race which could make you emotional.' Eddie Irvine brought a welcome splash of British racing green to the Principality's podium rostrum after bringing his much-improved Jaguar R2 home a strong third.

Above: Ferrari president Luca di Montezemolo was one of the high rollers who put in an appearance at Monaco.
Photograph: Clive Mason/Allsport-Getty Images

Top: Jacques Villeneuve produced his best ever Monaco performance to take fourth place in the BAR-Honda.

Left: Enrique Bernoldi drove a very disciplined race to fend off David Coulthard for many laps, but the McLaren-Mercedes driver was not amused.
Both photographs: Paul-Henri Cahier

Far left: David Coulthard's pole-winning efforts seemed to have set him up for a Monaco victory, but his car stalled prior to the parade lap.
Photograph: Steve Etherington/EPI

Rubens Barrichello plunges down towards the harbour in his Ferrari on his way to second place.
Photograph: Paul-Henri Cahier

RENAULT BOSS BACKS BREAKAWAY GRAND PRIX SERIES

Renault Sport president Patrick Fauré joined Fiat boss Paolo Cantarella during the run-up to the Monaco Grand Prix by insisting that the world's major car makers will start their own independent racing series in 2008.

However, FIA president Max Mosley stated his firm belief that a deal would soon be struck between the Kirch media group — as F1 commercial rights holder — and the car makers for a say in how the sport is run.

Fauré reaffirmed the ACEA (European Car Makers' Association) members' fear that the prospect of the World Championship increasingly being screened on pay TV channels will damage their interests. This was despite assurances from Kirch and Bernie Ecclestone, who sold 75 per cent of his SLEC empire to the German company, that terrestrial channels will remain the priority.

'The ACEA cannot leave F1 to be run by someone else,' said Fauré. 'We will be appointing our own chief executive officer to oversee our championship.'

Fauré also added that he and the association accepted they would not be able to own and regulate their own series. 'You cannot be the players and the referee at the same time,' he said. 'It may seem a long time to 2008, but it will arrive like tomorrow.'

Mosley expressed his confidence that SLEC, Kirch and the car makers would eventually resolve their differences, whatever short-term problems might appear to be frustrating their efforts.

'Don't underestimate the car manufacturers' resources and ability,' he warned. 'But I do think the most sensible solution will be for the three groups to be involved and come to an agreement.'

It was a major boost to the fortunes of the hitherto beleaguered British team, proving that the aerodynamic and suspension modifications tested on the Jaguar the previous week at Spain's Valencia circuit were well worth their development effort.

'It was fantastic to get onto the rostrum here in Monaco,' said Irvine who had qualified an impressive sixth on the grid and just scraped home 1.7s ahead of Jacques Villeneuve's fourth-place BAR-Honda.

'We were quick all weekend and I hope we can carry that speed through to the Canadian Grand Prix in a fortnight's time.'

Coulthard had qualified brilliantly on pole position only for his efforts to be squandered when his car failed to move away at the start of the formation lap. It was another electronic glitch, not his fault.

On his return to the grid, Schumacher could hardly believe his luck, suddenly faced as he was with a clear run towards Ste. Devote. He made a copybook getaway and edged into the first right-hander ahead of Häkkinen, Barrichello, the Williams-BMWs of Ralf Schumacher and Juan Pablo Montoya and Eddie Irvine's Jaguar.

All the front runners successfully negotiated the tricky uphill right-hander, but further back Jos Verstappen's Arrows got slightly out of shape and touched Luciano Burti's Arrows. Both cars continued, although Burti would pit for a replacement nose section at the end of the third lap. Nick Heidfeld, meanwhile, got his Sauber out of shape on the run down to Portier, also after a tangle with Verstappen, hit the barrier and was out of the race.

Schumacher led from Häkkinen by 1.1s at the end of the opening lap with Coulthard still last, 19.0s behind the Ferrari team leader. Second time round saw Montoya set the fastest lap, but on the third lap he glanced the wall with the left rear of his Williams going into the swimming pool esses and crashed out of the race at the next corner.

Montoya, at least, made no bones about what caused his accident. 'I made a mistake and paid for it,' he said. 'My accident happened when I changed down [a gear], lifted off, had understeer and crashed into the barrier.

'The car was good and I have nothing to complain about.' In that respect, the relaxed Colombian was very much in the minority by the end of this most gruelling of races on the F1 calendar.

This promoted Irvine to fifth ahead of Jarno Trulli's Jordan EJ-11. On lap four Schumacher turned the fastest lap of the race so far in 1m 23.8s, moving 1.9s clear of Häkkinen, and that trend continued for another couple of laps by which time he had opened a 2.4s advantage.

At this point Häkkinen seemed to get seriously into his stride. On lap seven he took his McLaren round in 1m 22.76s, followed by a 1m 22.325s, trimming his deficit to 1.6s. On lap ten Schumacher replied with a 1m 21.709s, then Mika came back with a 1m 21.682s.

The McLaren team was confident that Häkkinen had slightly more fuel aboard than the rival Ferrari and felt Mika was in good shape. Yet suddenly the Finn slowed dramatically and came into the pits at the end of lap 14, complaining of a strange handling imbalance.

The access hatch on the top of the monocoque above his legs was removed to enable mechanics to check the steering rack and Mika resumed after a long stop, now running 17th behind Coulthard. After another slow lap he retired for good, apparently having convinced himself that there was something wrong with the car even though the team could not pinpoint the problem.

Barrichello, now running a safe second, was in fact not comfortable at all. From the physical point of view, at least.

'I had quite a lot of trouble since lap nine or ten because I started having cramp on my foot,' he later reported. 'Something happened to the pedals because they were vibrating quite a lot and actually Ross [Brawn] became a physiotherapist, because I was asking him if he knew something I could do inside the car because it was really bad.

'At one time I could hardly feel my right foot. He [Brawn] was saying "drink water, drink water" and at one stage it was gone, but I was having quite a lot of problems inside the car.'

Barrichello, who would briefly lead the race from Schumacher's 7.0s refuelling stop on lap 55 to his own 6.9s stop on lap 60, could be well satisfied with his supporting role through the streets of the Principality in a week when the Ferrari team confirmed that his contract had been renewed for 2002.

Back in the thick of the traffic, meanwhile, Coulthard found himself boxed in behind the determined Enrique Bernoldi's Arrows battling for what was initially 17th place early in the race. Despite relentlessly pressuring his rival, the young Brazilian refused to give way and Coulthard only got a free run after Bernoldi came into the pits at the end of lap 43.

However, what some people regarded as a legitimate piece of motor racing on Bernoldi's part attracted the disapproval of McLaren team principal Ron Dennis who buttonholed the Arrows driver immediately after the finish.

'It's one thing to be defending your position when you are in a challenging position,' said Dennis, 'but not when you are 16th and have a World Championship contender behind you in a quicker car.

'Some will say this is motor racing, but I don't think this is very sporting. Perhaps Bernoldi's team was looking for television exposure.'

Needless to say, Arrows team principal Tom Walkinshaw was incensed at Dennis's attitude. 'McLaren are in the state they are in today because one car failed on the line and the other failed in the race,' he said.

'He should take his anger out on himself rather than venting it on everyone else.'

Once Coulthard got ahead of the Arrows he was the fastest car on the circuit, setting the fastest race lap on his way to two valuable championship points ahead of Jean Alesi's Prost and the Benetton-Renault of Jenson Button. Yet it was far from what he had been hoping for.

'It is difficult to draw much satisfaction from this race,' he said. 'At the moment I feel absolute, total frustration. If we have technical problems, then we will have to pay the price. It's only one race.

'I had to be patient. I was concerned that if I became too aggressive I could have been in the barriers. The positive thing is that on a bad day [like this] we still scored championship points.'

Elsewhere in the pack, retirements continued at a steady rate. Pedro de la Rosa's Jaguar rolled to a halt on lap 19 while running tenth with an apparent hydraulic problem which caused his gearchange to pack up, while Jordan had a disappointing time losing Jarno Trulli from fifth place with a reported hydraulic problem and Frentzen to a high-speed accident.

Heinz-Harald was fortunate to escape with no more than a severe shaking after losing control approaching the exit of the tunnel at 170 mph. 'From the apex of the tunnel I experienced understeer and then the car inexplicably steered to the left, hitting the armco on the exit and sliding right down to the chicane,' he said.

'The impact was quite hard and I hit my head. Starting from 13th was clearly unlucky for me today.'

For much of the race distance, Ralf Schumacher's Williams-BMW held onto third place ahead of Irvine, but eventually came into the pits to retire at the end of lap 58 with what turned out to be an hydraulics problem.

'All of a sudden a warning light came on,' he reported, 'and shortly after that the power steering failed. Then as I came into the pits the gearshift packed up and the engine cut out.'

That handed Irvine a strong third place which he held onto in the face of a persistent challenge in the closing stages of the race from Jacques Villeneuve's BAR-Honda.

The Ulsterman, who had not scored a top-three finish since being replaced by Barrichello at Ferrari at the start of the previous year, couldn't resist reminding Jaguar just how much further they had to progress.

'To be honest, we deserved to have the rough time we've had,' he said. 'Our infrastructure compared with other teams is negligible.

'Having said that, in all my four years at Ferrari I never had a development which made half as much difference as the improvements we've made to this car for today's race.'

Behind Villeneuve and Coulthard, Jean Alesi's Prost AP04 claimed the final point of the afternoon despite a late race stop to replace a punctured rear tyre. The Frenchman just squeezed back into the race ahead of Jenson Button, the Englishman missing out on his first championship point of the season by 28s.

Button was the sole surviving Benetton driver after Giancarlo Fisichella hit the wall for the second time and retired at Ste. Devote after 43 laps, having earlier proved the B201's strength by getting away with a glancing blow against the barrier in the same place and continued at unabated speed.

Completing the list of classified finishers were the Arrows A20s of Jos Verstappen and Bernoldi, the Dutchman having lost crucial time when he stalled at his refuelling stop due to a fuel pressure problem, and Räikkönen's Sauber.

'Enrique did well to cope with the pressure of having Coulthard behind him for nearly half the race without making a mistake,' said Walkinshaw, summing up the team's performance.

'But we're disappointed that we have got two cars home at one of the toughest races of the year but were not rewarded with any points.'

Diary

Adrian Newey tipped to leave McLaren to join Jaguar.

Mark Webber scores his second F3000 victory of the season in the Monaco GP supporting race.

Helio Castroneves wins Indy 500 for the Penske team.

Italian F1 veteran Vittorio Brambilla, winner of the 1975 Austrian Grand Prix, succumbs to a heart attack at the age of 63.

Far left: Jean Alesi claimed a precious championship point with sixth place at the wheel of his Prost AP04.

Below: Eddie Irvine harnessed the Jaguar R2's slow-circuit edge to superb effect and produced a strong third place at the end of the day.
Both photographs: Paul-Henri Cahier

grand prix de MONACO

ROUND 7
MONTE CARLO 24–27 MAY 2001

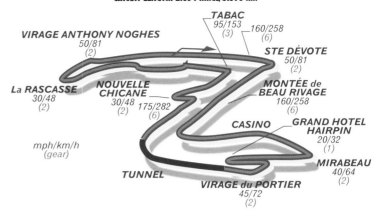

MONACO – MONTE CARLO GRAND PRIX CIRCUIT
CIRCUIT LENGTH: 2.094 miles/3.370 km

TABAC 95/153 (3)
160/258 (6)
VIRAGE ANTHONY NOGHES 50/81 (2)
STE DÉVOTE 50/81 (2)
La RASCASSE 30/48 (2)
NOUVELLE CHICANE 30/48 (2) 175/282 (6)
MONTÉE de BEAU RIVAGE 160/258 (6)
CASINO
GRAND HOTEL HAIRPIN 20/32 (1)
mph/km/h (gear)
TUNNEL
VIRAGE du PORTIER 45/72 (2)
MIRABEAU 40/64 (2)

RACE DISTANCE: 78 laps, 163.333 miles/262.860 km   RACE WEATHER: Dry, hot and sunny

Pos.	Driver	Nat.	No.	Entrant	Car/Engine	Tyres	Laps	Time/Retirement	Speed (mph/km/h)	Gap to lead
1	Michael Schumacher	D	1	Scuderia Ferrari Marlboro	Ferrari F2001-050 V10	B	78	1h 47m 22.561s	91.268/146.881	
2	Rubens Barrichello	BR	2	Scuderia Ferrari Marlboro	Ferrari F2001-050 V10	B	78	1h 47m 22.992s	91.262/146.872	+0.43
3	Eddie Irvine	GB	18	Jaguar Racing	Jaguar R2-Cosworth CR3 V10	M	78	1h 47m 53.259s	90.835/146.185	+30.69
4	Jacques Villeneuve	CDN	10	Lucky Strike BAR Honda	BAR03-Honda RA001E V10	B	78	1h 47m 55.015s	90.810/146.145	+32.45
5	David Coulthard	GB	4	West McLaren Mercedes	McLaren MP4/16-Mercedes F0110K V10	B	77			+1 la
6	Jean Alesi	F	22	Prost Acer	Prost AP04-Acer V10	M	77			+1 la
7	Jenson Button	GB	8	Mild Seven Benetton Renault	Benetton B201-Renault RS21 V10	M	77			+1 la
8	Jos Verstappen	NL	14	Orange Arrows Asiatech	Arrows A22-Asiatech V10	B	77			+1 l
9	Enrique Bernoldi	BR	15	Orange Arrows Asiatech	Arrows A22-Asiatech V10	B	76			+2 la
10	Kimi Räikkönen	SF	17	Red Bull Sauber Petronas	Sauber C20-Petronas V10	B	73			+5 la
	Ralf Schumacher	D	5	BMW WilliamsF1 Team	Williams FW23-BMW P80 V10	M	57	Hydraulics		
	Tarso Marques	BR	20	European Minardi F1	Minardi PS01-European V10	M	56	Transmission		
	Fernando Alonso	ESP	21	European Minardi F1	Minardi PS01-European V10	M	54	Gearbox		
	Heinz-Harald Frentzen	D	11	B&H Jordan Honda	Jordan EJ11-Honda RA001E V10	B	49	Accident		
	Giancarlo Fisichella	I	7	Mild Seven Benetton Renault	Benetton B201-Renault RS21 V10	M	43	Accident		
	Jarno Trulli	I	12	B&H Jordan Honda	Jordan EJ11-Honda RA001E V10	B	30	Hydraulics		
	Luciano Burti	BR	23	Prost Acer	Prost AP04-Acer V10	M	24	Slid off		
	Pedro de la Rosa	ESP	19	Jaguar Racing	Jaguar R2-Cosworth CR3 V10	M	18	Hydraulics		
	Mika Häkkinen	SF	3	West McLaren Mercedes	McLaren MP4/16-Mercedes F0110K V10	B	15	Handling problem		
	Olivier Panis	F	9	Lucky Strike BAR Honda	BAR 03-Honda RA001E V10	B	13	Steering		
	Juan Pablo Montoya	COL	6	BMW WilliamsF1 Team	Williams FW23-BMW P80 V10	M	2	Accident		
	Nick Heidfeld	D	16	Red Bull Sauber Petronas	Sauber C20-Petronas V10	B	0	Accident		

Fastest lap: David Coulthard, on lap 68, 1m 19.424s, 94.914 mph/152.749 km/h (record).

Previous lap record: Mika Häkkinen (F1 McLaren MP4/15-Mercedes V10), 1m 21.571s, 92.416 mph/148.729 km/h (2000).

Grid order (laps 1–59)

Grid order	
1	M. SCHUMACHER
3	HÄKKINEN
2	BARRICHELLO
5	R. SCHUMACHER
18	IRVINE
6	MONTOYA
12	TRULLI
10	VILLENEUVE
7	FISICHELLA
22	ALESI
9	PANIS
11	FRENTZEN
19	DE LA ROSA
17	RÄIKKÖNEN
16	HEIDFELD
8	BUTTON
21	ALONSO
14	VERSTAPPEN
15	BERNOLDI
23	BURTI
20	MARQUES
4	COULTHARD

Pit stop
One lap behind leader

STARTING GRID

	4*
1	COULTHARD
M. SCHUMACHER	McLaren
Ferrari	
	3
2	HÄKKINEN
BARRICHELLO	McLaren
Ferrari	
18	5
IRVINE	R. SCHUMACHER
Jaguar	Williams
12	6
TRULLI	MONTOYA
Jordan	Williams
7	10
FISICHELLA	VILLENEUVE
Benetton	BAR
9	22
PANIS	ALESI
BAR	Prost
19	11
DE LA ROSA	FRENTZEN
Jaguar	Jordan
16	17
HEIDFELD	RÄIKKÖNEN
Sauber	Sauber
21	8
ALONSO	BUTTON
Minardi	Benetton
15	14
BERNOLDI	VERSTAPPEN
Arrows	Arrows
20	23
MARQUES	BURTI
Minardi	Prost

*started from the back of the grid

3	64	65	66	67	68	69	70	71	72	73	74	75	76	77	78	
1	1	1	1	1	1	1	1	1	1	1	1	1	1	1	1	1
2	2	2	2	2	2	2	2	2	2	2	2	2	2	2	2	2
8	18	18	18	18	18	18	18	18	18	18	18	18	18	18	18	3
0	10	10	10	10	10	10	10	10	10	10	10	10	10	10	10	4
2	22	22	22	22	22	22	4	4	4	4	4	4	4	4	4	5
4	4	4	4	4	4	22	22	22	22	22	22	22	22			6
8	8	8	8	8	8	8	8	8	8	8	8	8	8			
4	14	14	14	14	14	14	14	14	14	14	14	14				
5	15	15	15	15	15	15	15	15	15	15	15					
7	17	17	17	17	17	17	17	17	17							

FOR THE RECORD

First Grand Prix podium
Jaguar
3500th Grand Prix point
Ferrari

TIME SHEETS

QUALIFYING

Weather: Dry, hot and sunny

Pos.	Driver	Car	Laps	Time
1	David Coulthard	McLaren-Mercedes	12	1m 17.430s
2	Michael Schumacher	Ferrari	11	1m 17.631s
3	Mika Häkkinen	McLaren-Mercedes	12	1m 17.749s
4	Rubens Barrichello	Ferrari	12	1m 17.856s
5	Ralf Schumacher	Williams-BMW	11	1m 18.029s
6	Eddie Irvine	Jaguar-Cosworth	12	1m 18.432s
7	Juan Pablo Montoya	Williams-BMW	12	1m 18.751s
8	Jarno Trulli	Jordan-Honda	12	1m 18.921s
9	Jacques Villeneuve	BAR-Honda	12	1m 19.086s
10	Giancarlo Fisichella	Benetton-Renault	11	1m 19.220s
11	Jean Alesi	Prost-Acer	12	1m 19.245s
12	Olivier Panis	BAR-Honda	12	1m 19.294s
13	Heinz-Harald Frentzen	Jordan-Honda	11	1m 19.316s
14	Pedro de la Rosa	Jaguar-Cosworth	12	1m 20.033s
15	Kimi Räikkönen	Sauber-Petronas	12	1m 20.081s
16	Nick Heidfeld	Sauber-Petronas	12	1m 20.261s
17	Jenson Button	Benetton-Renault	12	1m 20.342s
18	Fernando Alonso	Minardi-European	12	1m 20.788s
19	Jos Verstappen	Arrows-Asiatech	12	1m 20.823s
20	Enrique Bernoldi	Arrows-Asiatech	11	1m 21.336s
21	Luciano Burti	Prost-Acer	12	1m 21.771s
22	Tarso Marques	Minardi-European	12	1m 22.201s

THURSDAY FREE PRACTICE

Weather: Dry, warm and sunny

Pos.	Driver	Laps	Time
1	Mika Häkkinen	38	1m 19.853s
2	Michael Schumacher	46	1m 20.316s
3	Ralf Schumacher	45	1m 20.938s
4	Rubens Barrichello	44	1m 20.959s
5	Jarno Trulli	47	1m 21.048s
6	David Coulthard	33	1m 21.091s
7	Heinz-Harald Frentzen	46	1m 21.505s
8	Jean Alesi	40	1m 21.935s
9	Jacques Villeneuve	43	1m 22.010s
10	Juan Pablo Montoya	31	1m 22.035s
11	Giancarlo Fisichella	28	1m 22.214s
12	Eddie Irvine	35	1m 22.302s
13	Kimi Räikkönen	45	1m 22.800s
14	Nick Heidfeld	44	1m 22.807s
15	Jos Verstappen	41	1m 23.409s
16	Olivier Panis	26	1m 23.662s
17	Jenson Button	24	1m 24.026s
18	Enrique Bernoldi	42	1m 24.105s
19	Luciano Burti	51	1m 24.857s
20	Tarso Marques	36	1m 25.920s
21	Fernando Alonso	30	1m 26.393s
22	Pedro de la Rosa	9	1m 27.316s

SATURDAY FREE PRACTICE

Weather: Dry, warm and sunny

Pos.	Driver	Laps	Time
1	Mika Häkkinen	19	1m 18.282s
2	Michael Schumacher	30	1m 18.456s
3	Ralf Schumacher	22	1m 18.725s
4	David Coulthard	31	1m 19.031s
5	Eddie Irvine	31	1m 19.081s
6	Jarno Trulli	25	1m 19.307s
7	Rubens Barrichello	28	1m 19.603s
8	Juan Pablo Montoya	24	1m 19.651s
9	Jean Alesi	23	1m 20.020s
10	Heinz-Harald Frentzen	19	1m 20.064s
11	Jacques Villeneuve	34	1m 20.397s
12	Olivier Panis	33	1m 20.528s
13	Giancarlo Fisichella	21	1m 20.591s
14	Jenson Button	19	1m 21.316s
15	Kimi Räikkönen	16	1m 21.621s
16	Fernando Alonso	27	1m 21.670s
17	Jos Verstappen	17	1m 21.827s
18	Enrique Bernoldi	13	1m 22.024s
19	Nick Heidfeld	25	1m 22.207s
20	Pedro de la Rosa	38	1m 22.316s
21	Tarso Marques	27	1m 23.313s
22	Luciano Burti	13	1m 25.795s

WARM-UP

Weather: Dry, hot and sunny

Pos.	Driver	Laps	Time
1	David Coulthard	12	1m 20.944s
2	Mika Häkkinen	15	1m 21.017s
3	Michael Schumacher	14	1m 21.650s
4	Rubens Barrichello	16	1m 22.502s
5	Heinz-Harald Frentzen	14	1m 22.566s
6	Ralf Schumacher	14	1m 22.650s
7	Eddie Irvine	14	1m 22.816s
8	Jos Verstappen	17	1m 23.066s
9	Pedro de la Rosa	14	1m 23.200S
10	Giancarlo Fisichella	9	1m 23.407s
11	Jarno Trulli	14	1m 23.574s
12	Juan Pablo Montoya	14	1m 23.950s
13	Olivier Panis	14	1m 23.595s
14	Jacques Villeneuve	15	1m 23.747s
15	Nick Heidfeld	15	1m 23.842s
16	Kimi Räikkönen	16	1m 24.042s
17	Jean Alesi	15	1m 24.046s
18	Jenson Button	8	1m 24.137s
19	Fernando Alonso	12	1m 24.941s
20	Enrique Bernoldi	11	1m 25.328s
21	Luciano Burti	12	1m 25.938s
22	Tarso Marques	8	1m 26.325s

RACE FASTEST LAPS

Weather: Dry, hot and sunny

Driver	Time	Lap
David Coulthard	1m 19.424s	68
Michael Schumacher	1m 19.770s	50
Rubens Barrichello	1m 20.329s	57
Jacques Villeneuve	1m 20.417s	75
Eddie Irvine	1m 20.681s	76
Kimi Räikkönen	1m 20.705s	60
Heinz-Harald Frentzen	1m 20.810s	46
Ralf Schumacher	1m 20.975s	47
Jean Alesi	1m 21.151s	73
Jenson Button	1m 21.580s	65
Giancarlo Fisichella	1m 21.646s	37
Mika Häkkinen	1m 21.682s	12
Jos Verstappen	1m 21.732s	74
Enrique Bernoldi	1m 22.053s	75
Jarno Trulli	1m 22.345s	30
Fernando Alonso	1m 22.956s	28
Pedro de la Rosa	1m 23.483s	18
Luciano Burti	1m 24.206s	18
Tarso Marques	1m 24.570s	33
Olivier Panis	1m 24.719s	10
Juan Pablo Montoya	1m 25.773s	2

CHASSIS LOG BOOK

1	M. Schumacher	Ferrari F2001/210
2	Barrichello	Ferrari F2001/206
	spare	Ferrari F2001/208
3	Häkkinen	McLaren MP4/16/4
4	Coulthard	McLaren MP4/16/5
	spares	McLaren MP4/16/3 & 1
5	R. Schumacher	Williams FW23/5
6	Montoya	Williams FW23/2
	spare	Williams FW23/3
7	Fisichella	Benetton B201/6
8	Button	Benetton B201/5
	spare	Benetton B201/1
9	Panis	BAR 03/6
10	Villeneuve	BAR 03/3
	spares	BAR 03/5 & 4
11	Frentzen	Jordan EJ11/5
12	Trulli	Jordan EJ11/6
	spare	Jordan EJ11/4
14	Verstappen	Arrows A22/6
15	Bernoldi	Arrows A22/3
	spare	Arrows A22/1
16	Heidfeld	Sauber C20/5
17	Räikkönen	Sauber C20/6
	spare	Sauber C20/1
18	Irvine	Jaguar R2/4
19	de la Rosa	Jaguar R2/6
	spares	Jaguar R2/5 & 3
20	Marques	Minardi PS01/4
21	Alonso	Minardi PS01/3
	spares	Minardi PS01/1 & 2
22	Alesi	Prost AP04/6
23	Burti	Prost AP04/4
	spare	Prost AP04/2

POINTS TABLES

DRIVERS

1	Michael Schumacher	52
2	David Coulthard	40
3	Rubens Barrichello	24
4	Ralf Schumacher	12
5	Nick Heidfeld	8
6 =	Jacques Villeneuve	7
6 =	Jarno Trulli	7
8 =	Juan Pablo Montoya	6
8 =	Heinz-Harald Frentzen	6
10	Olivier Panis	5
11 =	Eddie Irvine	4
11 =	Kimi Räikkönen	4
11 =	Mika Häkkinen	4
14 =	Jos Verstappen	1
14 =	Jean Alesi	1
14 =	Giancarlo Fisichella	1

CONSTRUCTORS

1	Ferrari	76
2	McLaren	44
3	Williams	18
4	Jordan	13
5 =	Sauber	12
5 =	BAR	12
7	Jaguar	4
8 =	Arrows	1
8 =	Benetton	1
8 =	Prost	1

FIA WORLD CHAMPIONSHIP • ROUND 8

CANADIAN
grand prix

1st - R. SCHUMACHER • 2nd - M. SCHUMACHER • 3rd - HÄKKINEN

Previous spread: Ralf Schumacher celebrates not only his second F1 victory, but also the first sibling 1-2 in Grand Prix history, beating his brother Michael and McLaren's Mika Häkkinen.

Below: Eddie Jordan reflects on a continuing season of disappointments.
Both photographs: Bryn Williams/crash.net

Bottom: In the dark. Jaguar's Pedro de la Rosa readies himself for practice.
Photograph: Paul-Henri Cahier

MONTREAL QUALIFYING

Coulthard did a superb job on the final lap of the hour-long session to vault up to third place in the final starting order, moving ahead of a frustrated Jarno Trulli's Jordan on the last lap after the rhythm of the afternoon had been frustrated by two red-flagging episodes due to accidents.

Yet it was Michael Schumacher's Ferrari F2001 which took an easy pole, over 2s quicker than the previous year's qualifying best on 1m 15.782s.

Ralf Schumacher joined his brother on the front row with a 1m 16.297s. 'I was surprised how good the time was, to be honest,' he said after squeezing the best he could out of the harder-compound Michelins. 'I had expected a 1m 16.8s!'

Team-mate Juan Pablo Montoya had a less rewarding time. He lost most of Friday practice with a gearbox failure, after which he was always playing catch-up. He wound up tenth on 1m 17.123s.

Fourth on the grid in 1m 16.459s left Trulli extremely frustrated. Together with a handful of rivals he was mistakenly shepherded into parc fermé at the end of the pit lane after the session was red flagged for the second time when Nick Heidfeld's Sauber hit the wall with just 1m 35s of the session left to run.

Marshals told Trulli that the session was over, but then he realised that the green light at the end of the pit lane was back on. He accelerated back onto the track, but it was too late to complete another flier.

Jordan's hopes were resting on Trulli's shoulders after Heinz-Harald Frentzen withdrew from the meeting following a shunt in Friday free practice. Still groggy from his Monaco shunt, he'd withdrawn from the previous week's test at Magny-Cours and now had to miss the Canadian race, complaining of dizziness and headaches.

Frentzen's place was taken by test driver Ricardo Zonta who got into the swing of things very well, qualifying respectably on 1m 17.328s to take 12th on the grid.

Fifth on the grid was Rubens Barrichello on 1m 16.760s, the Brazilian having rumpled his Ferrari F2001 against the wall on the outside of the final turn. That obliged him to take the spare car which was set up for Schumacher. Under the circumstances, it wasn't a bad showing.

Olivier Panis did a storming job to qualify the BAR-Honda sixth on 1m 16.771s, his best grid position of the year so far. Jacques Villeneuve wound up ninth on 1m 17.035s. Jacques had switched to the spare BAR-Honda after crashing in Friday free practice and this had suffered an hydraulics problem on Saturday morning.

Mika Häkkinen's run of desperate misfortune continued. In the morning the Finn shot-blasted his car so comprehensively after a high-speed detour through a gravel trap that its front suspension members and aerodynamic deflectors had to be replaced.

In qualifying, he kerbed the MP4/16 so hard that the right-hand radiator was smashed by a dislodged lump of carbon-fibre ballast, then switched to the spare car — set-up for Coulthard — only to find that it was suffering from a misfire on its first run. He wound up eighth fastest with a 1m 16.979s, one place behind his young compatriot Kimi Räikkönen.

However, it was the off-track confrontation between Juan Pablo Montoya and local hero Villeneuve which really hit the headlines.

The BAR-Honda driver had come up behind his BMW Williams rival during the first free practice session and, having overtaken Montoya, slowed abruptly right in front of him.

Villeneuve claimed that Montoya was at fault in the incident, the Colombian vehemently disagreed and stated that the 1997 World Champion was trying to brake-test him.

The two men were later involved in a physical confrontation at the drivers' meeting, resulting in a warning from FIA race director Charlie Whiting that they risked a possible three-race suspension if there was any repeat of their on-track antics.

Behind Montoya, Heidfeld qualified eleventh on 1m 17.165s despite his accident, ahead of Zonta, Jos Verstappen's Arrows A20 (1m 17.903s) and Pedro de la Rosa's Jaguar 1m 18.015s which edged out team-mate Eddie Irvine's machine by 0.001s after backing off abruptly after a lurid moment and spoiling one of the Ulsterman's quick laps.

Jean Alesi wound up 16th for Prost on 1m 18.178s ahead of Enrique Bernoldi's Arrows (1m 18.575s) while the two Benetton B201s of Giancarlo Fisichella (1m 18.622s) and Jenson Button (1m 19.033s), neither of which were equipped with power steering as had originally been planned, sandwiched Luciano Burti in 19th place. At the tail of the field were both Minardi PS01s.

Above: David Coulthard's World Championship hopes took another dip when his McLaren-Mercedes suffered an engine failure while he was heading for another helping of championship points.
Photograph: Paul-Henri Cahier

THE Schumacher brothers made history at Montreal's Circuit Gilles Villeneuve by becoming the first siblings ever to finish first and second in a World Championship Grand Prix. It may have been against the historical odds, but Ralf was the one to come out on top, his Williams FW23-BMW decisively outperforming brother Michael's Ferrari F2001.

At the end of the afternoon Michael was left trailing by 20.2s as Ralf raced on to the second win of his career, a result achieved in the same torrid conditions which played to the strengths of his car and its Michelin tyres as when he won the San Marino Grand Prix two months earlier.

He relentlessly shadowed his elder sibling from the start, harrying the Ferrari at every turn. Michael kept his cool, but after he brought the Ferrari in for its sole refuelling stop at the end of lap 46, Ralf slammed through into the lead and reeled off a succession of fastest laps before stopping himself at the end of lap 51.

That five-lap window was the crucial period in which Ralf Schumacher snatched the advantage, emerging from the pits 6.4s ahead of the Ferrari and never thereafter being challenged all the way to the chequered flag.

By the end of the afternoon, David Coulthard's World Championship hopes were looking increasingly forlorn after his McLaren-Mercedes retired in a spectacular cloud of smoke and steam which signalled a major engine failure while holding a strong third place. There were only 13 of the race's 68 laps to go when the Scot's latest helping of dire mechanical misfortune was dealt out, a bitter blow only a fortnight after his car stalled on pole position at Monte Carlo.

Ralf was feeling really confident after qualifying his Williams-BMW second behind his brother on the front row of the grid and almost out-ran the pole-position Ferrari to the first tricky left-hander.

He nosed ahead of his elder sibling but had to drop back as Michael had the better inside line. However, he was right behind as the pack streamed successfully out onto the back straight without any of the undue incidents which have so often characterised the opening lap at this event in the past.

Despite this, at the start of the race British hopes took a major dive. At the end of the first lap Jenson Button accidentally swerved into his Benetton team-mate Giancarlo Fisichella, knocking the Italian's right front wheel askew and sending him straight into the pits to retire.

As Button, who was already in trouble after creeping at the start and in line for a 10s stop-go penalty, explained: 'I came alongside Giancarlo on the straight and he braked early. I then moved over because Bernoldi came across as well, and then Giancarlo ran into the back of me which unfortunately destroyed his race.'

Fisichella, who'd already touched Bernoldi at the hairpin and damaged his Benetton's nose wing, then broke his right front suspension against the back of Button's car under braking for the chicane.

Second time round and Michael opened his advantage to 0.7s over his brother, while Eddie Irvine's hopes of making up ground from a lowly 15th grid position by means of a two-stop strategy on the softer Michelin tyres came to an abrupt end when he collided with Nick Heidfeld's Sauber and both cars were out on the spot.

Michael Schumacher piled on the pressure over the first few laps, opening a slight gap to his brother as the Williams's Michelin tyres displayed their characteristic lag in warming up to operating temperatures compared with the Ferrari's rival Bridgestone rubber.

David Coulthard, meanwhile, was in serious trouble and was dropping away from the leaders. He ran second for the first couple of laps but then had to give best to Barrichello, his McLaren clearly not handling either well or predictably.

It had all started to go wrong for David before the start, the Scot being understandably concerned when he found a locking washer from the front suspension rolling around in his MP4/16's footwell as he negotiated the formation lap.

He threw it overboard when he arrived back on the starting grid and debated what to do over the radio link with his team during the early laps, worried that the car seemed to be handling differently on right- and left-hand corners.

'As the race progressed it got worse, but having discussed it with the team,' he explained. 'I decided to continue and go for the points which I would have been capable of achieving.'

After squeezing past Coulthard, Barrichello quickly closed in on Ralf Schumacher only to spin exiting the old hairpin on lap six as he homed in on the Williams-BMW.

'Right from the start, I had problems with the traction control,' said Rubens. 'On lap three I had to switch it off as it was causing a misfire and that was what caused me to spin. After that, the car was not as competitive as it had been at the start of the race.'

Barrichello resumed in 14th place, but by lap 20 had moved up

Diary

Honda denies rumours that they might pull out of the CART series at the end of the 2001 season.

Indy Racing League boss Tony George says he would consider expanding the series outside the USA provided it continued to grow in strength at home.

F1 team principals agree that a contract recognition board for senior personnel would be almost impossible to administer and would be unlikely to prevent disputes such as the Newey/Jaguar saga from erupting.

NASCAR reveals photographs which they claim show conclusively that Dale Earnhardt's lap seatbelt did break during his fatal accident in the 2001 Daytona 500 classic.

onto the tail of Juan Pablo Montoya's 10th-place Williams-BMW as they swept through the fast ess-bends on the return leg of the circuit. Montoya slid slightly wide, vaulting up into the barrier after clipping a kerb and skidding to a halt at the side of the track. Barrichello slammed on his brakes and spun in avoidance, also being eliminated on the spot.

That little episode resulted in the safety car being deployed to slow the field while the Ferrari and Williams were cleared away from the circuit.

The safety car was withdrawn at the end of lap 23 and Michael slowed the field to near-walking pace as he came up to take the restart, a strategy which had the effect of cooling Ralf's Michelins and allowing his elder brother to open out a 2.5s advantage by the end of lap 25.

Thereafter Ralf stabilised the advantage and the Williams driver reduced his deficit from 2.0s on lap 29 to 0.5s on lap 32, after which there was nothing to choose between the two brothers at the head of the pack.

Coulthard was still labouring in third to keep Trulli at bay while Olivier Panis's BAR-Honda was running fifth, albeit now struggling with a long brake pedal which would result in his retirement after 38 laps.

'I made a very good start and the car was really quick,' shrugged the Frenchman afterwards. 'We had a good strategy, but we had a problem with the brakes and couldn't stop the car.' An attempt to bleed the brakes failed to rectify the problem, so Panis was forced to retire.

At least he'd managed to complete four laps more than his team-mate Jacques Villeneuve who called it a day on lap 34. 'I think we used up all our bad luck for the year,' he said. 'During the race the anti-stall kicked in so I lost a lot of time. The car was running strong after that, but then we started having brake problems and eventually a driveshaft problem finished my race.'

On lap 42 Coulthard made a 9.7s refuelling stop from third place, dropping back to fifth and allowing Häkkinen through to third. The Finn had spent most of the early laps boxed in amongst competitors he usually only sees when he is lapping them.

On lap 46 Michael made his 8.4s sole refuelling stop and Ralf stayed out for those extra, decisive five laps before making his own stop. He emerged in the lead and from then on the outcome was never in doubt.

Prior to that, Ralf only had minor problems. Shadowing Michael, he periodically moved out of the Ferrari's slipstream to keep his water temperature under control. Several times he attempted to outbrake his brother into the chicane before the pits, but the Williams had a slightly short seventh gear and was just fluttering against the rev limiter.

Coulthard's misery came to an end on lap 55 when his McLaren coasted into the pit lane with engine failure while running fifth.

Stoic as ever, Coulthard refused to acknowledge that his battle for the Championship was over. 'Michael has got a big lead, but that can turn around in two races,' he said.

'The Championship is still achievable and I can only do what I can do. This was not a good weekend, in fact it was a terrible weekend.'

Yet if Coulthard was disappointed, Trulli would be heartbroken

SETTLEMENT BETWEEN JAGUAR AND McLAREN AFTER NEWEY CHANGES HIS MIND

The run-up to the Canadian GP had been monopolised by a major controversy over the future plans of McLaren technical director Adrian Newey after he agreed to join Jaguar Racing as from August 2002 — and then abruptly changed his mind.

On the evening of Tuesday 29 May, Newey committed himself to joining Jaguar Racing. Two days later he decided to change his mind and committed to staying with McLaren until 2005.

Jaguar then had the validity of its documentation endorsed by a QC. 'I don't want to get into semantics,' said Jaguar Racing CEO Bobby Rahal, 'but it is a legally binding agreement, very specific in detail.'

McLaren challenged this, although they made it very clear that they were unaware of Newey signing a commitment to join Jaguar when they negotiated a new contract with him.

'Adrian changed his mind,' said McLaren chairman Ron Dennis in Canada last weekend. 'Everybody in life changes their mind. All the issues stemming from that need to be resolved in the correct forum, which is not the media and the pit lane.'

The court hearing in London was set for the Wednesday following the Montreal race where McLaren intended to challenge an injunction which Jaguar had obtained the previous week seeking to prevent McLaren from continuing to employ Newey beyond August 2002.

However, the two teams reached a settlement, almost on the court steps, and the matter was duly resolved. It had become clear to Jaguar's lawyers that European Union employment law was weighed heavily against them. They concluded that it was unlikely the court would force an individual — in this case Newey — to work for them against his will.

Instead they settled for an apology from both Newey and McLaren chairman Ron Dennis, something which the latter was clearly willing to offer in exchange for having won the day. It is understood that McLaren also paid Jaguar a financial settlement although details of this were not made public.

'I regret that this matter has occurred but I am delighted that it has now been resolved,' said Newey. 'I apologise for any difficulties which have been caused.'

Dennis echoed those sentiments. 'I would like to apologise for any misunderstanding that has been caused over what has become a confused and complex affair,' he said.

The battle between the two teams had intensified when Jaguar released an official communiqué announcing that Newey had signed a binding contract with them, despite prior warnings from McLaren and Newey that he had changed his mind.

when his Jordan retired with a brake problem just five laps from the chequered flag while en route to a place on the rostrum. Jos Verstappen also slithered off the road due to brake problems in the closing stages after a race made additionally frustrating by the failure of his pit-to-car radio link.

After crashing in qualifying, Häkkinen lost crucial track time and seemed to be facing an uphill struggle from the start. But his team selected a strategy which saw him start the race carrying a great deal of fuel, enabling him to stay out until lap 49 before refuelling. Assisted by a spate of retirements, Häkkinen doubled his championship tally at a stroke to an admittedly modest eight points with a third-place finish.

'Thank God there aren't three of them,' he joked with some relief as he sat alongside the Schumacher brothers at the post-race media conference.

Fourth place fell to Kimi Räikkönen's Sauber ahead of Jean Alesi's Prost and the sole surviving Jaguar of Pedro de la Rosa. Such was Alesi's sheer glee at having managed to score points in two consecutive races that he threw his crash helmet — complete with radio headset — into the adoring crowd.

Frentzen's stand-in Ricardo Zonta took seventh place ahead of Luciano Burti's Prost while Tarso Marques in the Minardi was the last car running, although Verstappen and Trulli had completed sufficient laps before their retirement to be classified as finishers.

'It was a great result for Michelin which I feel, without gloating over it, had a clear advantage at this race,' said a satisfied Frank Williams. 'It was also a pleasure to watch the two brothers racing for the lead which will get great press across the world.'

ROUND 8
MONTREAL 8–10 JUNE 2001

grand prix
AIR
CANADA

MONTREAL – CIRCUIT GILLES VILLENEUVE

CIRCUIT LENGTH: 2.747 miles/4.421 km

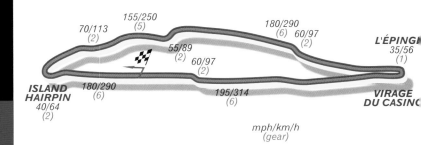

mph/km/h
(gear)

RACE DISTANCE: 69 laps, 189.549 miles/305.049 km   RACE WEATHER: Dry, hot and sunny

Pos.	Driver	Nat.	No.	Entrant	Car/Engine	Tyres	Laps	Time/Retirement	Speed (mph/km/h)	Gap to lea...
1	Ralf Schumacher	D	5	BMW WilliamsF1 Team	Williams FW23-BMW P80 V10	M	69	1h 34m 31.522s	120.315/193.629	
2	Michael Schumacher	D	1	Scuderia Ferrari Marlboro	Ferrari F2001-050 V10	B	69	1h 34m 51.757s	119.888/192.941	+20.2
3	Mika Häkkinen	SF	3	West McLaren Mercedes	McLaren MP4/16-Mercedes F0110K V10	B	69	1h 35m 12.194s	119.459/192.251	+40.6
4	Kimi Räikkönen	SF	17	Red Bull Sauber Petronas	Sauber C20-Petronas V10	B	69	1h 35m 39.638s	118.887/191.331	+68.1
5	Jean Alesi	F	22	Prost Acer	Prost AP04-Acer V10	M	69	1h 35m 41.957s	118.840/191.254	+70.4
6	Pedro de la Rosa	ESP	19	Jaguar Racing	Jaguar R2-Cosworth CR3 V10	M	68			+1
7	Ricardo Zonta	BR	11	B&H Jordan Honda	Jordan EJ11-Honda RA001E V10	B	68			+1
8	Luciano Burti	BR	23	Prost Acer	Prost AP04-Acer V10	M	68			+1
9	Tarso Marques	BR	20	European Minardi F1	Minardi PS01-European V10	M	66			+3
10	Jos Verstappen	NL	14	Orange Arrows Asiatech	Arrows A22-Asiatech V10	B	65	Brakes		+4
11	Jarno Trulli	I	12	B&H Jordan Honda	Jordan EJ11-Honda RA001E V10	B	63	Brakes		+6
	David Coulthard	GB	4	West McLaren Mercedes	McLaren MP4/16-Mercedes F0110K V10	B	54	Engine		
	Olivier Panis	F	9	Lucky Strike BAR Honda	BAR 03-Honda RA001E V10	B	38	Brakes		
	Jacques Villeneuve	CDN	10	Lucky Strike BAR Honda	BAR 03-Honda RA001E V10	B	34	Driveshaft		
	Enrique Bernoldi	BR	15	Orange Arrows Asiatech	Arrows A22-Asiatech V10	B	24	Overheating		
	Juan Pablo Montoya	COL	6	BMW WilliamsF1 Team	Williams FW23-BMW P80 V10	M	19	Accident		
	Rubens Barrichello	BR	2	Scuderia Ferrari Marlboro	Ferrari F2001-050 V10	B	19	Spun off		
	Jenson Button	GB	8	Mild Seven Benetton Renault	Benetton B201-Renault RS21 V10	M	17	Oil leak		
	Fernando Alonso	ESP	21	European Minardi F1	Minardi PS01-European V10	M	7	Transmission		
	Nick Heidfeld	D	16	Red Bull Sauber Petronas	Sauber C20-Petronas V10	B	1	Collision with Irvine		
	Eddie Irvine	GB	18	Jaguar Racing	Jaguar R2-Cosworth CR3 V10	M	1	Collision with Heidfeld		
	Giancarlo Fisichella	I	7	Mild Seven Benetton Renault	Benetton B201-Renault RS21 V10	M	0	Accident damage		

Fastest lap: Ralf Schumacher, on lap 50, 1m 17.205s, 128.094 mph/206.147 km/h.

Previous lap record: Michael Schumacher (F1 Ferrari F300-V10), 1m 19.379s, 124.586 mph/200.501 km/h (1998).

Grid order	1	2	3	4	5	6	7	8	9	10	11	12	13	14	15	16	17	18	19	20	21	22	23	24	25	26	27	28	29	30	31	32	33	34	35	36	37	38	39	40	41	42	43	44	45	46	47	48	49	50	51	5
1 M. SCHUMACHER	1	1	1	1	1	1	1	1	1	1	1	1	1	1	1	1	1	1	1	1	1	1	1	1	1	1	1	1	1	1	1	1	1	1	1	1	1	1	1	1	1	1	1	1	1	5	5	5	5	5	5	5
5 R. SCHUMACHER	5	5	5	5	5	5	5	5	5	5	5	5	5	5	5	5	5	5	5	5	5	5	5	5	5	5	5	5	5	5	5	5	5	5	5	5	5	5	5	5	5	5	5	5	5	1	1	1	1	1	1	
4 COULTHARD	4	4	2	2	2	4	4	4	4	4	4	4	4	4	4	4	4	4	4	4	4	4	4	4	4	4	4	4	4	4	4	4	4	4	4	4	4	4	4	4	3	3	3	3	3	3	3	3	3	3	3	
12 TRULLI	2	2	4	4	4	12	12	12	12	12	12	12	12	12	12	12	12	12	12	12	12	12	12	12	12	12	12	12	12	12	12	12	12	12	12	3	3	3	3	14	14	14	14	14	4	4	4	4	4			
2 BARRICHELLO	12	12	12	12	12	9	9	9	9	9	9	9	9	9	9	9	9	9	9	9	9	9	9	9	9	9	9	9	9	9	9	9	9	9	3	3	17	22	22	14	4	4	4	4	4	19	19	19	19	19	1	
9 PANIS	9	9	9	9	9	14	14	14	14	14	14	14	14	14	14	14	14	14	14	14	14	17	17	17	17	17	17	17	17	17	17	17	22	14	14	12	12	12	12	12	12	12	12	12	12	12	1					
17 RÄIKKÖNEN	14	14	14	14	14	17	17	17	17	17	17	17	17	17	17	17	17	17	17	17	17	11	11	11	11	11	11	11	11	11	3	22	22	14	14	12	19	19	19	19	19	12	17	17	17	17	17	17	17	17	1	
3 HÄKKINEN	17	17	17	17	17	11	11	11	11	11	11	11	11	11	11	11	11	11	11	11	11	3	3	3	3	3	3	3	3	3	11	14	14	12	19	19	22	17	17	17	17	22	22	22	22	22	1					
10 VILLENEUVE	11	11	11	11	11	3	3	3	3	3	3	3	3	3	3	3	3	3	3	3	3	19	19	19	19	19	19	10	10	10	22	22	19	19	19	17	17	17	22	22	22	22	22	14	14	14	14	14	14			
6 MONTOYA	3	3	3	3	3	6	6	6	6	6	6	6	6	6	6	6	6	19	19	19	10	10	10	10	10	10	10	22	22	22	22	10	14	11	11	11	11	11	11	11	11	11	11	11	11	11	11	11	11	1		
16 HEIDFELD	6	6	6	6	19	19	19	19	19	19	2	2	2	2	2	2	2	2	10	10	10	22	22	22	22	22	22	23	23	23	14	14	19	9	23	23	23	23	23	23	23	23	23	23	23	23	23	23	23	2		
11 ZONTA	16	19	19	19	10	10	10	10	10	2	19	19	19	19	19	19	19	19	22	22	22	23	23	23	23	23	23	14	14	14	19	23	20	20	20	20	20	20	20	20	20	20	20	20	20	20	20	20	2			
14 VERSTAPPEN	18	10	10	10	15	15	15	2	10	10	10	10	10	19	10	10	10	10	23	23	23	23	23	23	14	14	14	14	14	19	19	19	23	23	20	20	9	9														
19 DE LA ROSA	19	15	15	15	15	2	2	2	22	22	22	22	22	22	22	22	22	22	15	15	15	20	20	14	20	20	20	20	20	20	20	20																				
18 IRVINE	10	8	8	8	8	8	22	22	23	23	23	23	23	23	23	23	23	20	20	20	14	14																													
22 ALESI	15	20	22	22	22	22	21	23	20	20	20	20	20	20	20	20	20	20																																		
15 BERNOLDI	20	22	21	21	21	21	23	20	15	15	15	15	15	15	15	15	15	15																																		
7 FISICHELLA	8	21	20	20	20	23	20	8	8	8	8	8	8	8	8	8	8																																			
23 BURTI	22	23	23	23	23	20	8																																													
8 BUTTON	21																																																			
20 MARQUES	23																																																			
21 ALONSO																																																				

Pit stop
One lap behind leader

STARTING GRID

1 M. SCHUMACHER Ferrari	**5** R. SCHUMACHER Williams
4 COULTHARD McLaren	**12** TRULLI Jordan
2 BARRICHELLO Ferrari	**9** PANIS BAR
17 RÄIKKÖNEN Sauber	**3** HÄKKINEN McLaren
10 VILLENEUVE BAR	**6** MONTOYA Williams
16 HEIDFELD Sauber	**11** ZONTA Jordan
14 VERSTAPPEN Arrows	**19** DE LA ROSA Jaguar
18 IRVINE Jaguar	**22** ALESI Prost
15 BERNOLDI Arrows	**7** FISICHELLA Benetton
23 BURTI Prost	**8** BUTTON Benetton
20 MARQUES Minardi	**21** ALONSO Minardi

Lap chart

57	58	59	60	61	62	63	64	65	66	67	68	69	●
5	5	5	5	5	5	5	5	5	5	5	5	5	1
1	1	1	1	1	1	1	1	1	1	1	1	1	2
3	3	3	3	3	3	3	3	3	3	3	3	3	3
12	12	12	12	12	17	17	17	17	17	17	17	17	4
17	17	17	17	17	12	22	22	22	22	22	22	22	5
22	22	22	22	22	22	14	14	14	19	19	19	19	6
14	14	14	14	14	14	19	19	19	11	11	11		
19	19	19	19	19	19	19	11	11	23	23	23		
11	11	11	11	11	11	11	23	23	20				
23	23	23	23	23	23	23	20	20					
20	20	20	20	20	20	20							

FOR THE RECORD

100th Grand Prix point
Ralf Schumacher

TIME SHEETS

QUALIFYING

Weather: Dry, hot and sunny

Pos.	Driver	Car	Laps	Time
1	Michael Schumacher	Ferrari	6	1m 15.782s
2	Ralf Schumacher	Williams-BMW	8	1m 16.297s
3	David Coulthard	McLaren-Mercedes	12	1m 16.423s
4	Jarno Trulli	Jordan-Honda	10	1m 16.459s
5	Rubens Barrichello	Ferrari	11	1m 16.760s
6	Olivier Panis	BAR-Honda	10	1m 16.771s
7	Kimi Räikkönen	Sauber-Petronas	11	1m 16.875s
8	Mika Häkkinen	McLaren-Mercedes	12	1m 16.979s
9	Jacques Villeneuve	BAR-Honda	11	1m 17.035s
10	Juan Pablo Montoya	Williams-BMW	12	1m 17.123s
11	Nick Heidfeld	Sauber-Petronas	11	1m 17.165s
12	Ricardo Zonta	Jordan-Honda	11	1m 17.328s
13	Jos Verstappen	Arrows-Asiatech	10	1m 17.903s
14	Pedro de la Rosa	Jaguar-Cosworth	12	1m 18.015s
15	Eddie Irvine	Jaguar-Cosworth	12	1m 18.016s
16	Jean Alesi	Prost-Acer	10	1m 18.178s
17	Enrique Bernoldi	Arrows-Asiatech	11	1m 18.575s
18	Giancarlo Fisichella	Benetton-Renault	11	1m 18.622s
19	Luciano Burti	Prost-Acer	11	1m 18.753s
20	Jenson Button	Benetton-Renault	12	1m 19.033s
21	Fernando Alonso*	Minardi-European	11	1m 19.454s
22	Tarso Marques	Minardi-European	12	1m 20.690s

*times subsequently disallowed

FRIDAY FREE PRACTICE

Weather: Dry, hot and sunny

Pos.	Driver	Laps	Time
1	Mika Häkkinen	34	1m 17.672s
2	David Coulthard	40	1m 18.086s
3	Eddie Irvine	42	1m 18.508s
4	Rubens Barrichello	42	1m 18.570s
5	Juan Pablo Montoya	49	1m 18.639s
6	Ralf Schumacher	44	1m 18.641s
7	Nick Heidfeld	40	1m 18.967s
8	Jarno Trulli	48	1m 18.990s
9	Heinz-Harald Frentzen	39	1m 19.057s
10	Olivier Panis	47	1m 19.102s
11	Michael Schumacher	33	1m 19.166s
12	Jean Alesi	38	1m 19.209s
13	Kimi Räikkönen	32	1m 19.427s
14	Pedro de la Rosa	42	1m 19.707s
15	Giancarlo Fisichella	44	1m 20.364s
16	Jos Verstappen	24	1m 20.561s
17	Enrique Bernoldi	31	1m 21.259s
18	Luciano Burti	46	1m 21.280s
19	Jacques Villeneuve	13	1m 21.916s
20	Fernando Alonso	21	1m 22.206s
21	Jenson Button	26	1m 22.766s
22	Tarso Marques	6	1m 25.415s

SATURDAY FREE PRACTICE

Weather: Dry, hot and sunny

Pos.	Driver	Laps	Time
1	Michael Schumacher	35	1m 16.200s
2	David Coulthard	33	1m 16.707s
3	Mika Häkkinen	32	1m 16.828s
4	Rubens Barrichello	21	1m 16.986s
5	Nick Heidfeld	29	1m 17.103s
6	Kimi Räikkönen	26	1m 17.144s
7	Olivier Panis	25	1m 17.284s
8	Ralf Schumacher	31	1m 17.521s
9	Jarno Trulli	24	1m 17.618s
10	Pedro de la Rosa	28	1m 17.774s
11	Jacques Villeneuve	20	1m 17.937s
12	Eddie Irvine	23	1m 17.982s
13	Jos Verstappen	25	1m 18.030s
14	Juan Pablo Montoya	19	1m 18.216s
15	Ricardo Zonta	22	1m 18.595s
16	Enrique Bernoldi	27	1m 18.649s
17	Jean Alesi	25	1m 18.935s
18	Jenson Button	31	1m 19.213s
19	Giancarlo Fisichella	29	1m 19.347s
20	Luciano Burti	25	1m 19.693s
21	Fernando Alonso	20	1m 20.549s
22	Tarso Marques	32	1m 21.013s

WARM-UP

Weather: Dry, warm and sunny

Pos.	Driver	Laps	Time
1	Olivier Panis	12	1m 18.512s
2	David Coulthard	16	1m 18.540s
3	Ricardo Zonta	15	1m 18.545s
4	Eddie Irvine	17	1m 18.594s
5	Mika Häkkinen	14	1m 18.650s
6	Michael Schumacher	16	1m 18.663s
7	Jarno Trulli	17	1m 18.875s
8	Rubens Barrichello	15	1m 19.201s
9	Juan Pablo Montoya	15	1m 19.372s
10	Ralf Schumacher	10	1m 19.536s
11	Jacques Villeneuve	18	1m 19.572s
12	Jos Verstappen	19	1m 19.775s
13	Kimi Räikkönen	16	1m 19.876s
14	Pedro de la Rosa	15	1m 20.012s
15	Enrique Bernoldi	14	1m 20.059s
16	Nick Heidfeld	16	1m 20.062s
17	Jean Alesi	20	1m 20.943s
18	Fernando Alonso	16	1m 21.071s
19	Jenson Button	7	1m 21.114s
20	Giancarlo Fisichella	13	1m 21.344s
21	Tarso Marques	14	1m 21.415s
22	Luciano Burti	9	1m 21.563s

RACE FASTEST LAPS

Weather: Dry, hot and sunny

Driver	Time	Lap
Ralf Schumacher	1m 17.205s	50
Mika Häkkinen	1m 18.148s	45
Michael Schumacher	1m 18.176s	48
Pedro de la Rosa	1m 19.006s	50
Jos Verstappen	1m 19.257s	59
Kimi Räikkönen	1m 19.309s	63
Jean Alesi	1m 19.328s	59
Jarno Trulli	1m 19.414s	29
Rubens Barrichello	1m 19.722s	13
David Coulthard	1m 19.745s	32
Jacques Villeneuve	1m 19.782s	30
Luciano Burti	1m 19.841s	60
Olivier Panis	1m 19.856s	30
Ricardo Zonta	1m 20.078s	38
Juan Pablo Montoya	1m 20.159s	18
Enrique Bernoldi	1m 20.767s	11
Jenson Button	1m 21.124s	11
Tarso Marques	1m 22.312s	19
Fernando Alonso	1m 22.413s	4

CHASSIS LOG BOOK

1	M. Schumacher	Ferrari F2001/210
2	Barrichello	Ferrari F2001/212
	spare	Ferrari F2001/211
3	Häkkinen	McLaren MP4/16/5
4	Coulthard	McLaren MP4/16/6
	spare	McLaren MP4/16/4
5	R. Schumacher	Williams FW23/5
6	Montoya	Williams FW23/6
	spare	Williams FW23/2
7	Fisichella	Benetton B201/6
8	Button	Benetton B201/5
	spare	Benetton B201/3
9	Panis	BAR 03/6
10	Villeneuve	BAR 03/7
	spare	BAR 03/4
11	Frentzen/Zonta	Jordan EJ11/6
12	Trulli	Jordan EJ11/5
	spare	Jordan EJ11/4
14	Verstappen	Arrows A22/6
15	Bernoldi	Arrows A22/3
	spare	Arrows A22/1
16	Heidfeld	Sauber C20/5
17	Räikkönen	Sauber C20/6
	spare	Sauber C20/1
18	Irvine	Jaguar R2/6
19	de la Rosa	Jaguar R2/4
	spare	Jaguar R2/5
20	Marques	Minardi PS01/4
21	Alonso	Minardi PS01/3
	spare	Minardi PS01/1
22	Alesi	Prost AP04/6
23	Burti	Prost AP04/5
	spare	Prost AP04/1

POINTS TABLES

DRIVERS

	Driver	Points
1	Michael Schumacher	58
2	David Coulthard	40
3	Rubens Barrichello	24
4	Ralf Schumacher	22
5 =	Nick Heidfeld	8
5 =	Mika Häkkinen	8
7 =	Jacques Villeneuve	7
7 =	Kimi Räikkönen	7
7 =	Jarno Trulli	7
10 =	Juan Pablo Montoya	6
10 =	Heinz-Harald Frentzen	6
12	Olivier Panis	5
13	Eddie Irvine	4
14	Jean Alesi	3
15 =	Jos Verstappen	1
15 =	Giancarlo Fisichella	1
15 =	Pedro de la Rosa	1

CONSTRUCTORS

	Team	Points
1	Ferrari	82
2	McLaren	48
3	Williams	28
4	Sauber	15
5	Jordan	13
6	BAR	12
7	Jaguar	5
8	Prost	3
9 =	Arrows	1
9 =	Benetton	1

Michael Schumacher shaves the grass with his
Ferrari's right-hand wheels as he presses on
towards another commanding victory in the
European Grand Prix.
Photograph: Mark Thompson/Allsport-Getty Images

SILVERSTONE CONFIRMS MAJOR REBUILD FOR 2003 GRAND PRIX

The organisers of the British Grand Prix finally confirmed specific details of a major upgrade for Silverstone with an imaginative new track layout designed for better spectating and more overtaking.

World Championship rivals Michael Schumacher and David Coulthard were both consulted and apparently offered the new circuit layout their blessing. Funding for the first £40 million development phase will be provided jointly by Silverstone's owners, the British Racing Drivers' Club, race promoters Octagon Motorsports and Bernie Ecclestone's Formula One Administration company.

The circuit layout for 2003 will be significantly changed with the F1 pit complex relocated from its current site between Woodcote and Copse corner to the exit of Club corner at the opposite end of the track.

Club corner itself will be reprofiled into a banked parabolic right-hander in a bid to enhance viewing spectacle.

After the new start/finish line the circuit will dog-leg right onto a new section which completely bypasses the old Abbey chicane and Bridge corner. The revised section will rejoin the current layout just before Woodcote corner.

Apart from a more interesting track layout, better access from the soon-to-be-completed Silverstone bypass and spectator facilities up to the standards expected in the new millennium were announced as major priorities.

'All the other leisure activities which we, as motor racing, compete against have much better toilets, much better restaurants, a better experience for entire families,' said BRDC President Sir Jackie Stewart. In the longer term Silverstone will be developed into what Stewart called 'a centre of excellence' which will be undertaken in parts two and three of the development plan.

This will include educational facilities to encourage the next generation of motor racing engineers, an interactive visitors' centre, a kart circuit and a museum of British motor sport.

NÜRBURGRING QUALIFYING

Michael Schumacher took his seventh pole position of the season at the Nürburgring, although for a few fleeting laps it had looked as though it would be the Williams-BMWs of his brother Ralf and Juan Pablo Montoya which would button up the front row of the grid.

On the face of it, variations in track temperature were crucial. It rose from 22 degrees at the start of qualifying, briefly peaked at 29 degrees some 44 minutes into the session and wobbled around in between for much of that time.

Ralf Schumacher did a pole-winning run of 1m 15.335s at 1.25 pm, then improved to 1m 15.226s when the track temperature edged up to 28 degrees. But Michael performed perfectly to record a 1m 14.960s best in his Bridgestone-shod Ferrari when the temperature was at the same level.

If you factor in the statistics that the Williams-BMWs were easily first and second quickest through two of the three straightline speed-timing traps, some people reached the conclusion that the Michelins were hardly an issue. The reason that the Williams FW23s were so quick, opined these insiders, was simply down to the engine and chassis. The tyres were neither here nor there.

Yet Michelin was certainly satisfied with its efforts. 'As expected, the track is not as abrasive as it was at the start of the meeting,' said their motor sport director Pierre Dupasquier.

'We are very happy that the tyres we developed especially for the Nürburgring have worked well. It shows that we have the ability to understand circuits that are new to us.'

Under the circumstances, Michael did a great job considering he'd lost 45 minutes of the Saturday morning free practice session to a hydraulic failure and didn't get to run new tyres as a result. Team-mate Rubens Barrichello wound up fourth behind Montoya on 1m 15.622s, the Brazilian suffering with a power steering problem on his race car which was rectified in time for his runs.

David Coulthard (1m 15.717s) and Mika Häkkinen (1m 15.776s) qualified fifth and sixth, both drivers struggling to find an ideal handling balance and then also finding the cars were particularly uncomfortable riding the final chicane kerbs. Coulthard rounded off a disappointing session by sliding into the edge of the gravel trap at the final corner on his final run, bringing out a flurry of yellow flags.

Jarno Trulli wound up seventh for Jordan on 1m 16.138s, 0.2s faster than team-mate Heinz-Harald Frentzen who was making a return to the cockpit after missing the Canadian GP. The German driver was moderately satisfied with his showing, but wound up barely 0.1s ahead of Kimi Räikkönen who, together with his Sauber C20 team-mate Nick Heidfeld, was running an uprated qualifying 'B-plus' version of the Petronas-based Ferrari customer V10.

This was a very satisfying performance for the Swiss team, particularly as Heidfeld admitted he'd made a mistake at the first chicane on his best run and Räikkönen had two of his runs spoiled, one by a Benetton going off in front of him and another by the yellow flags for Coulthard.

Jacques Villeneuve had two spins during the morning's free practice session, reporting that his BAR-Honda was quite well balanced, but just too slow. In qualifying he could only manage an 11th-fastest 1m 16.439s, two places ahead of a deeply frustrated Olivier Panis (1m 16.872s) who complained 'in qualifying I couldn't match the times I was doing on full tanks in the morning.'

Eddie Irvine's Jaguar R2 (1m 16.588s) split the BAR duo, the Ulsterman admitting that he was pretty satisfied with the performance, while Pedro de la Rosa (1m 17.627s) struggled with his ultimate handling balance. 'I'm pleased with Eddie, he was damn' quick,' said team chief Bobby Rahal. 'The boys improved the car overnight and we optimised it for a good run.'

Prost also benefited from qualifying-spec Ferrari V10s in their AP04s, but the best Jean Alesi could manage was a 14th-fastest 1m 17.251s. The Frenchman complained that his car felt nervous and inconsistent, with too much oversteer. Luciano Burti did well to post a 17th-fastest 1m 18.113s after his race car developed a fuel pressure problem and he had to take the spare AP04 which was set up for Alesi.

Further back, both Arrows A22s qualified disappointingly after a session described by technical director Mike Coughlan as a 'disaster for us' and although Giancarlo Fisichella squeezed his Benetton B201 onto the grid 15th on 1m 17.378s, Jenson Button was five places further back. 'Understeer and no grip,' he shrugged.

Bringing up the rear were the Minardi PS01s of Fernando Alonso (1m 18.630s) and Tarso Marques (1m 18.689s).

Diary

Ralf Schumacher extends his contract with the BMW Williams team until the end of 2004.

Jos Verstappen and Heinz-Harald Frentzen confirmed as remaining with Arrows and Jordan respectively until the end of 2002. Frentzen, however, would have an unwelcome surprise lurking a few weeks down the road.

Max Papis wins the Portland round of the CART Championship in his Team Rahal Lola-Ford.

MICHAEL Schumacher strode to a hard-fought, but ultimately dominant victory for Ferrari in the European Grand Prix after a wheel-to-wheel battle with his brother Ralf ended when the Williams-BMW driver incurred a 10s stop-go penalty for a minor rule infringement. Michael was 0.4s ahead of his brother as he led Ralf in for their first refuelling stop in nose-to-tail formation after 28 of the race's 67 laps. They resumed in the same order, but as the siblings accelerated back onto the circuit, Ralf mistakenly placed his car too far to the left over the painted line separating the main track from the pit exit lane.

That trifling infringement incurred him what many people regarded as a draconian penalty and dropped him back to fourth at the finish. His BMW Williams team-mate Juan Pablo Montoya then took up the chase, gamely keeping some semblance of pressure on Schumacher senior's Ferrari to finish 4.2s behind at the chequered flag.

'I am extremely disappointed about the outcome of the race as I had a chance to win in front of my home crowd,' said the younger Schumacher.

'However, under the circumstances, I had to be happy with fourth. As for the white line incident, I was looking in my mirrors when I left the pits and obviously concentrated more on the traffic behind me than on the line. I have to accept the penalty.'

As always, Michael had all the luck running his way. He took the spare Ferrari F2001 out on the first parade lap and it stopped at the bottom hairpin with an apparent fuel pick-up problem. But Michael had plenty of time to hitch a lift back to the pits and take his place on pole position with his designated race car.

As the starting lights went out, Michael swerved at his brother in time-honoured fashion, almost squeezing the Williams-BMW into the pit wall as they accelerated away towards the first corner. The Williams driver declined to comment on the tense moment seconds after the start. For his part, Michael later brushed aside this apparent lack of concern for his younger sibling by explaining that he was concerned that Ralf might have been running with a lighter fuel load and therefore would pull away easily if he slipped by into the lead going into the first corner.

'I did not make a perfect start and lost a couple of metres,' said Michael. 'Then I saw Ralf up the inside of me and as I didn't know what strategy he was on, I knew I had to be first into the first corner.

'So I did the maximum you are allowed to do under the rules to tighten the line. I don't think Ralf touched the [pit] wall. It probably looked unfair from the outside, but that's the way the rules are.'

The younger Schumacher recovered his composure to slot into second place behind his brother, Ralf finishing the opening lap 1.4s behind the Ferrari. Montoya's Williams was third, then there was a gap back to David Coulthard's McLaren-Mercedes which was just ahead of Mika Häkkinen's sister car, then came Jarno Trulli's Jordan-Honda EJ-11 and the other Ferrari F2001 of Rubens Barrichello. Meanwhile, Tarso Marques had been slow away from the back of the grid in his Minardi, the Brazilian suffering a problem with his launch control which caused him to switch to a manual start.

Second time round and Michael extended his advantage to 1.5s, but the gap from the leading Ferrari to Coulthard's McLaren had opened to 4.5s.

This crucial gap opened to 5.9s on lap three, then 7.0s, 8.1s and 9.0s on consecutive laps. Coulthard and his team-mate had opted for a one-stop strategy rather than the two-stop schedule of

Top left: Jenson Button — shaded again by his team-mate.
Photograph: Mark Thompson/Allsport-Getty Images

Above left: Ralf in profile — the younger Schumacher could reflect on the Nürburgring as an opportunity missed.

Above: Nick Heidfeld took advantage of a qualifying engine to place his Sauber tenth on the grid.

Left: Giancarlo Fisichella slithers his Benetton-Renault B201 across the gravel in a lurid off-track moment.
All photographs: Paul-Henri Cahier

Far left: Tarso Marques switched off his launch control at the start, but was still last away.
Photograph: Bryn Williams/crash.net

Overleaf: On life support. Jean Alesi waits as his Prost is readied for action.
Photograph: Paul-Henri Cahier

the faster cars. In theory, a two-stop strategy at the Nürburgring would work out at around 8s quicker than a one-stopper over a race distance, but DC and McLaren reckoned this was the best way to vault him forward from his fifth place on the grid.

Marques's Minardi would prove to be the first retirement of the race, lasting until lap eight before a voltage fluctuation played havoc with the electronics, causing the gearbox to break and the engine to shut down.

In the opening phase, Michael opened an initial advantage over Ralf, but the gap stabilised on lap nine at 3.4s and remained unchanged for the next three laps. Then Schumacher junior and his Williams's Michelin rubber really began to hit their stride with track temperatures edging above the 33-degree mark and the gap came tumbling down: 2.9s, 2.3s, 2.3s, 1.7s, 1.2s and finally down to 0.8s on lap 17.

Now Ralf was all over the back of the Ferrari, looking for a gap, but Michael was unyielding in his determination to hang on ahead and was actually slowing things up a bit by lap 20 as Montoya began to close up in third place. Coulthard was now 21.3s behind in fourth place and Häkkinen had dropped even further behind after locking up and straightlining the chicane just before the entrance to the pit lane on lap 16.

On lap 26 Montoya took 0.8s out of the leaders and the Colombian posted the quickest lap so far with a 1m 18.3s on lap 27. The two Schumachers darted into the pit lane for their first refuelling stops, Michael (8.4s) gaining a slight advantage over Ralf (9.7s) which was highlighted as they rejoined with Coulthard's McLaren between them.

It was at this point that Ralf made his crucial slip. Accelerating back into the battle he allowed his Williams's left-hand wheels to cross the white line delineating the pit exit lane from the track proper. It was only a slight lapse of concentration and nobody

thought too much about it as Ralf settled down to resume the chase of his brother from 4.1s down on his Ferrari.

Ralf had slipped to 5.9s behind Michael by the time the timing screens signalled that he was being investigated for a rule infringement. Sure enough, on lap 39 he had to come in for a 10s stop-go penalty which promoted Montoya to second place ahead of Rubens Barrichello's Ferrari, the annoyed Ralf and then a long gap back to Coulthard's McLaren which had made its sole refuelling stop in 10.6s on lap 38.

'I was looking in the mirrors when I left the pits and was obviously concentrating more on the traffic behind me than the [white] line,' said Ralf Schumacher later. 'I have to accept the penalty.'

Soon afterwards, both Jordans hit trouble. Trulli had made a great start and, relishing in his car's excellent handling balance, had been all over Häkkinen's McLaren in the early stages. He'd made his sole refuelling stop on lap 30 and was running hard when his engineers noticed a loss of gearbox hydraulic pressure. Eventually the gearbox seized and he retired after 44 laps.

Team-mate Heinz-Harald Frentzen lasted only another four laps and was running eighth when his traction control suddenly failed, spinning him off the circuit as he exited the lower hairpin. 'It is clear that we are not realising our potential,' said a frustrated Eddie Jordan in masterly understatement.

Montoya, who'd momentarily led the race on lap 29 as he came in for his own first refuelling stop, duly made his second stop from second place on lap 50, following Michael Schumacher into the pit lane. They resumed 10.2s apart with Ralf holding onto a third place which he lost to Coulthard when he made his second scheduled stop two laps later.

With Mika Häkkinen struggling home sixth behind Rubens Barrichello's Ferrari after battling severe tyre vibrations for the first half of the race, Coulthard made no bones about the fact

that he was concerned about the McLaren team's current state of competitiveness.

'The reality is we're quite a bit adrift,' he said. 'About half a second a lap. How will we be at Magny-Cours next week? Well, I hope it's only four-tenths a lap there.'

Replying to a request for an assessment of the potential of the increasingly competitive Williams-BMWs, Coulthard said, tongue-in-cheek: 'They obviously have reasonable acceleration, or maybe it's low [aerodynamic] drag or sticky tyres.'

Then he added in a voice laden with irony: 'It can't possibly be the engine, because we have the best engine.' This was interpreted as an urgent signal for Mercedes-Benz to find more power from their Ilmor-built V10s.

Prior to the race, McLaren chairman Ron Dennis admitted that the recent legal tussle with rivals Jaguar over the services of top designer Adrian Newey had a definite destabilising effect.

'The thing with Adrian just threw you [us] off-balance,' he said. 'We have tremendous depth, and we know where we are going, but we've had things that unbalanced the harmony of the team.

'We don't think we're the team we have been — or will be in the future.'

Ironically, the Jaguar R2s of Eddie Irvine and Pedro de la Rosa produced extremely promising performances to take seventh and eighth places, the best team performance of their season so far.

'I couldn't have done any better today and it shows how important it is for us to qualify better,' said Irvine who started from 12th place on the grid.

'The car felt great, but we need to fully exploit the qualifying hour in an effort to grab the points that are out there for the taking. The pit-stop strategy was excellent and the Michelin tyres worked perfectly.'

At least they finished, which is more than three out of four of the Honda-engined cars managed. Aside from Jordan's woes, in the BAR-Honda camp, Olivier Panis spun off when an electrical fault affected his gearchange mechanism.

Five years earlier Jacques Villeneuve had scored his first win here at the wheel of a Williams-Renault on what was only his fourth F1 outing. This time an uncompetitive ninth at the chequered flag provided a painful reminder for the Canadian driver of just what a capricious and unpredictable business Grand Prix racing can be.

During the second half of the race a terrific battle for tenth place raged between F1's latest baby and its most seasoned veteran, Kimi Räikkönen's Sauber C20 and Jean Alesi's Prost AP04. Youth eventually triumphed in this battle of the Ferrari-engined rivals when Alesi went in too deep under braking for the hairpin at the bottom of the circuit and spun into the gravel with three laps to go as he attempted to outfox the young Finn.

Above: Patrick Head — managing a smile on BMW's home turf.
Photograph: Paul-Henri Cahier

Below: David Coulthard worked hard to squeeze third place out of his McLaren-Mercedes MP4/16.
Photograph: Bryn Williams/crash.net

Below left: Adrian Newey — the calm before the storm.

Bottom left: Ron Dennis — looking for better times.
Both photographs: Paul-Henri Cahier

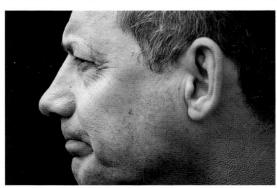

ROUND 9
NÜRBURGRING 22–24 JUNE 2001

WARSTEINER grand prix of EUROPE

NÜRBURGRING – GRAND PRIX CIRCUIT
CIRCUIT LENGTH: 2.688 miles/4.326 km

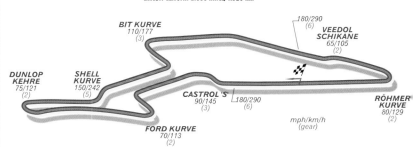

RACE DISTANCE: 67 laps, 189.664 miles/305.235 km   **RACE WEATHER:** Dry, hot and sunny

Pos.	Driver	Nat.	No.	Entrant	Car/Engine	Tyres	Laps	Time/Retirement	Speed (mph/km/h)	Gap to lead
1	Michael Schumacher	D	1	Scuderia Ferrari Marlboro	Ferrari F2001-050 V10	B	67	1h 29m 42.724s	126.848/204.143	
2	Juan Pablo Montoya	COL	6	BMW WilliamsF1 Team	Williams FW23-BMW P80 V10	M	67	1h 29m 46.941s	126.749/203.983	+4.21
3	David Coulthard	GB	4	West McLaren Mercedes	McLaren MP4/16-Mercedes F0110K V10	B	67	1h 30m 07.717s	126.261/203.199	+24.99
4	Ralf Schumacher	D	5	BMW WilliamsF1 Team	Williams FW23-BMW P80 V10	M	67	1h 30m 16.069s	126.067/202.886	+33.34
5	Rubens Barrichello	BR	2	Scuderia Ferrari Marlboro	Ferrari F2001-050 V10	B	67	1h 30m 28.219s	125.785/202.432	+45.49
6	Mika Häkkinen	SF	3	West McLaren Mercedes	McLaren MP4/16-Mercedes F0110K V10	B	67	1h 30m 47.592s	125.338/201.712	+64.86
7	Eddie Irvine	GB	18	Jaguar Racing	Jaguar R2-Cosworth CR3 V10	M	67	1h 30m 48.922s	125.307/201.662	+66.19
8	Pedro de la Rosa	ESP	19	Jaguar Racing	Jaguar R2-Cosworth CR3 V10	M	66			+1 la
9	Jacques Villeneuve	CDN	10	Lucky Strike BAR Honda	BAR 03-Honda RA001E V10	B	66			+1 la
10	Kimi Räikkönen	SF	17	Red Bull Sauber Petronas	Sauber C20-Petronas V10	B	66			+1 la
11	Giancarlo Fisichella	I	7	Mild Seven Benetton Renault	Benetton B201-Renault RS21 V10	M	66			+1 la
12	Luciano Burti	BR	23	Prost Acer	Prost AP04-Acer V10	M	65			+2 la
13	Jenson Button	GB	8	Mild Seven Benetton Renault	Benetton B201-Renault RS21 V10	M	65			+2 la
14	Fernando Alonso	ESP	21	European Minardi F1	Minardi PS01-European V10	M	65			+2 la
15	Jean Alesi	F	22	Prost Acer	Prost AP04-Acer V10	M	64	Spun off		+3 la
	Jos Verstappen	NL	14	Orange Arrows Asiatech	Arrows A22-Asiatech V10	B	58	Engine		
	Nick Heidfeld	D	16	Red Bull Sauber Petronas	Sauber C20-Petronas V10	B	54	Driveshaft		
	Heinz-Harald Frentzen	D	11	B&H Jordan Honda	Jordan EJ11-Honda RA001E V10	B	48	Spun/traction control failure		
	Jarno Trulli	I	12	B&H Jordan Honda	Jordan EJ11-Honda RA001E V10	B	44	Gearbox hydraulics		
	Enrique Bernoldi	BR	15	Orange Arrows Asiatech	Arrows A22-Asiatech V10	B	29	Transmission		
	Olivier Panis	F	9	Lucky Strike BAR Honda	BAR 03-Honda RA001E V10	B	23	Electrical/Spun off		
	Tarso Marques	BR	20	European Minardi F1	Minardi PS01-European V10	M	7	Gearbox		

Fastest lap: Juan Pablo Montoya, on lap 27, 1m 18.354s, 130.069 mph/209.326 km/h.

Previous lap record: Heinz-Harald Frentzen (F1 Williams FW19-Renault V10), 1m 18.805s, 129.325 mph/208.128 km/h (1997).

Grid order	1	2	3	4	5	6	7	8	9	10	11	12	13	14	15	16	17	18	19	20	21	22	23	24	25	26	27	28	29	30	31	32	33	34	35	36	37	38	39	40	41	42	43	44	45	46	47	48	49	50
1 M. SCHUMACHER	1	1	1	1	1	1	1	1	1	1	1	1	1	1	1	1	1	1	1	1	1	1	1	1	1	1	1	1	1	6	1	1	1	1	1	1	1	1	1	1	1	1	1	1	1	1	1	1	1	1
5 R. SCHUMACHER	5	5	5	5	5	5	5	5	5	5	5	5	5	5	5	5	5	5	5	5	5	5	5	5	5	5	5	5	5	1	4	5	5	5	5	5	5	5	6	6	6	6	6	6	6	6	6	6	6	6
6 MONTOYA	6	6	6	6	6	6	6	6	6	6	6	6	6	6	6	6	6	6	6	6	6	6	6	6	6	6	6	6	4	5	4	4	4	4	4	4	6	2	2	2	2	5	5	5	5	5	5	5	5	5
2 BARRICHELLO	4	4	4	4	4	4	4	4	4	4	4	4	4	4	4	4	4	4	4	4	4	4	4	4	4	4	5	6	6	6	6	6	6	6	4	2	5	5	5	5	4	4	4	4	4	4	4	4	4	4
4 COULTHARD	3	3	3	3	3	3	3	3	3	3	3	3	3	3	3	3	3	3	3	3	3	3	3	3	3	3	3	3	3	2	2	2	2	2	2	2	4	4	4	4	2	2	2	2	2	2	2	2	2	2
3 HÄKKINEN	12	12	12	12	12	12	12	12	12	12	12	12	12	12	12	12	12	12	12	12	12	12	12	12	12	12	12	2	2	3	18	18	10	10	10	10	12	12	3	3	3	3	3	3	3	3	3	3	3	3
12 TRULLI	2	2	2	2	2	2	2	2	2	2	2	2	2	2	2	2	2	2	2	2	2	2	2	2	2	2	2	12	16	18	10	10	10	12	12	12	12	19	19	18	18	18	18	18						
11 FRENTZEN	16	16	16	16	16	16	16	16	16	16	16	16	16	16	16	16	16	16	16	16	16	16	16	16	16	16	18	16	16	12	12	12	12	19	19	19	19	10	3	11	11	11	11	19	19					
17 RÄIKKÖNEN	17	17	17	17	17	17	17	17	17	17	17	17	17	17	17	17	17	17	17	17	17	17	17	17	18	17	17	10	19	19	19	3	3	3	3	3	18	19	19	19	10	10								
16 HEIDFELD	11	11	11	11	11	11	11	11	11	11	11	11	11	11	11	11	11	11	11	11	11	11	11	11	11	18	17	10	10	12	3	3	3	22	22	22	22	18	11	10	10	10	17	17						
10 VILLENEUVE	18	18	18	18	18	18	18	18	18	18	18	18	18	18	18	18	18	18	18	18	18	18	18	18	18	11	10	19	19	22	22	22	22	18	18	18	18	11	10	17	17	17	22	22	16	16				
18 IRVINE	10	10	10	10	10	10	10	10	10	10	10	10	10	10	10	10	10	10	10	10	10	10	10	10	14	14	14	18	18	11	11	11	11	11	11	11	11	17	17	22	22	16	16	16						
9 PANIS	7	7	7	7	7	7	7	7	7	7	7	7	7	7	7	7	7	7	7	14	14	14	19	19	19	22	22	11	17	17	17	17	17	17	17	17	16	16	22	22	16	16	7	7						
22 ALESI	14	14	14	14	14	14	14	14	14	14	14	14	14	14	14	14	14	7	19	19	19	14	22	22	22	11	11	11	17	16	16	16	16	16	16	16	22	22	14	14	7	7	23	14						
7 FISICHELLA	19	19	19	19	19	19	19	19	19	19	19	19	19	19	19	19	19	15	9	22	22	22	7	7	7	7	7	7	7	7	7	7	7	7	14	14	7	7	23	14	8									
19 DE LA ROSA	15	15	15	15	15	15	15	15	15	15	15	15	15	15	15	15	9	22	21	21	7	14	14	14	14	14	14	14	14	14	14	14	8	7	21	23	14	8	8	23										
23 BURTI	9	9	9	9	9	9	9	9	9	9	9	9	9	9	9	9	15	7	7	8	8	15	15	15	15	21	21	21	21	21	21	21	21	21	8	7	21	23	21	8	21	21	2							
15 BERNOLDI	8	8	8	8	8	8	8	8	8	8	8	8	8	8	8	8	21	21	8	15	15	15	21	21	21	21	21	21	21	21	21	21	21	21	21	21	8	21	21											
14 VERSTAPPEN	22	22	22	22	22	22	22	22	22	22	22	22	22	22	22	22	21	15	15	21	21	21	23	23	23	23	23	23	23	23	8																			
8 BUTTON	23	23	23	23	23	23	23	23	23	23	21	21	21	21	21	21	21	7	7	23	23	23	23	23																										
21 ALONSO	21	21	21	21	21	21	21	21	21	21	23	23	23	23	23	23	23	23	23																																
20 MARQUES	20	20	20	20	20	20	20																																												

Pit stop
One lap behind leader

STARTING GRID

1 **M. SCHUMACHER** Ferrari	**5** **R. SCHUMACHER** Williams
6 **MONTOYA** Williams	**2** **BARRICHELLO** Ferrari
4 **COULTHARD** McLaren	**3** **HÄKKINEN** McLaren
12 **TRULLI** Jordan	**11** **FRENTZEN** Jordan
17 **RÄIKKÖNEN** Sauber	**16** **HEIDFELD** Sauber
10 **VILLENEUVE** BAR	**18** **IRVINE** Jaguar
9 **PANIS** BAR	**22** **ALESI** Prost
7 **FISICHELLA** Benetton	**19** **DE LA ROSA** Jaguar
23 **BURTI** Prost	**15** **BERNOLDI** Arrows
14 **VERSTAPPEN** Arrows	**8** **BUTTON** Benetton
21 **ALONSO** Minardi	**20** **MARQUES** Minardi

All results and data © FIA 2001

Lap leader chart

54	55	56	57	58	59	60	61	62	63	64	65	66	67	•
1	1	1	1	1	1	1	1	1	1	1	1	1	1	1
6	6	6	6	6	6	6	6	6	6	6	6	6	6	2
4	4	4	4	4	4	4	4	4	4	4	4	4	4	3
5	5	5	5	5	5	5	5	5	5	5	5	5	5	4
2	2	2	2	2	2	2	2	2	2	2	2	2	2	5
3	3	3	3	3	3	3	3	3	3	3	3	3	3	6
18	18	18	18	18	18	18	18	18	18	18	18	18	18	
19	19	19	19	19	19	19	19	19	19	19	19	19	19	
10	10	10	10	10	10	10	10	10	10	10	10	10	10	
17	17	17	17	17	17	17	17	17	17	17	17	17	17	
22	22	22	22	22	22	22	22	22	22	7	7			
7	7	7	7	7	7	7	7	7	7	23				
16	14	14	14	14	23	23	23	23	23	8				
14	8	23	23	23	8	8	8	8	8	21				
8	23	8	8	21	21	21	21	21	21					
23	21	21	21	21										
21														

FOR THE RECORD

100th Grand Prix

Olivier Panis

75th Grand Prix

Ralf Schumacher

TIME SHEETS

QUALIFYING

Weather: Dry, warm and sunny

Pos.	Driver	Car	Laps	Time
1	Michael Schumacher	Ferrari	8	1m 14.960s
2	Ralf Schumacher	Williams-BMW	12	1m 15.226s
3	Juan Pablo Montoya	Williams-BMW	11	1m 15.490s
4	Rubens Barrichello	Ferrari	11	1m 15.622s
5	David Coulthard	McLaren-Mercedes	12	1m 15.717s
6	Mika Häkkinen	McLaren-Mercedes	12	1m 15.776s
7	Jarno Trulli	Jordan-Honda	10	1m 16.138s
8	Heinz-Harald Frentzen	Jordan-Honda	11	1m 16.376s
9	Kimi Räikkönen	Sauber-Petronas	11	1m 16.402s
10	Nick Heidfeld	Sauber-Petronas	11	1m 16.438s
11	Jacques Villeneuve	BAR-Honda	12	1m 16.439s
12	Eddie Irvine	Jaguar-Cosworth	11	1m 16.588s
13	Olivier Panis	BAR-Honda	11	1m 16.872s
14	Jean Alesi	Prost-Acer	11	1m 17.251s
15	Giancarlo Fisichella	Benetton-Renault	11	1m 17.378s
16	Pedro de la Rosa	Jaguar-Cosworth	12	1m 17.627s
17	Luciano Burti	Prost-Acer	11	1m 18.113s
18	Enrique Bernoldi	Arrows-Asiatech	12	1m 18.151s
19	Jos Verstappen	Arrows-Asiatech	11	1m 18.262s
20	Jenson Button	Benetton-Renault	11	1m 18.626s
21	Fernando Alonso	Minardi-European	11	1m 18.630s
22	Tarso Marques	Minardi-European	12	1m 18.689s

FRIDAY FREE PRACTICE

Weather: Warm and overcast

Pos.	Driver	Laps	Time
1	Mika Häkkinen	40	1m 16.408s
2	David Coulthard	38	1m 16.579s
3	Ralf Schumacher	43	1m 17.355s
4	Michael Schumacher	49	1m 17.507s
5	Rubens Barrichello	41	1m 17.665s
6	Juan Pablo Montoya	45	1m 17.737s
7	Jarno Trulli	39	1m 18.133s
8	Nick Heidfeld	38	1m 18.196s
9	Jean Alesi	47	1m 18.352s
10	Olivier Panis	50	1m 18.410s
11	Kimi Räikkönen	37	1m 18.413s
12	Jacques Villeneuve	38	1m 18.434s
13	Pedro de la Rosa	47	1m 18.473s
14	Giancarlo Fisichella	34	1m 19.339s
15	Eddie Irvine	23	1m 19.503s
16	Jos Verstappen	23	1m 19.640s
17	Enrique Bernoldi	39	1m 19.822s
18	Jenson Button	32	1m 19.978s
19	Heinz-Harald Frentzen	17	1m 19.988s
20	Luciano Burti	30	1m 20.094s
21	Fernando Alonso	45	1m 20.183s
22	Tarso Marques	21	1m 21.129s

SATURDAY FREE PRACTICE

Weather: Dry, warm and sunny

Pos.	Driver	Laps	Time
1	Ralf Schumacher	30	1m 15.355s
2	Juan Pablo Montoya	28	1m 15.749s
3	Rubens Barrichello	30	1m 15.855s
4	Mika Häkkinen	27	1m 16.038s
5	David Coulthard	32	1m 16.237s
6	Michael Schumacher	12	1m 16.308s
7	Jarno Trulli	31	1m 16.385s
8	Heinz-Harald Frentzen	29	1m 16.407s
9	Olivier Panis	33	1m 16.625s
10	Kimi Räikkönen	21	1m 16.852s
11	Nick Heidfeld	23	1m 16.941s
12	Jacques Villeneuve	28	1m 17.006s
13	Eddie Irvine	28	1m 17.609s
14	Enrique Bernoldi	25	1m 17.686s
15	Luciano Burti	37	1m 17.688s
16	Giancarlo Fisichella	31	1m 17.785s
17	Jean Alesi	24	1m 17.839s
18	Pedro de la Rosa	31	1m 18.048s
19	Jos Verstappen	28	1m 18.123s
20	Jenson Button	29	1m 18.674s
21	Fernando Alonso	29	1m 19.164s
22	Tarso Marques	22	1m 20.208s

WARM-UP

Weather: Dry, hot and sunny

Pos.	Driver	Laps	Time
1	Rubens Barrichello	13	1m 18.209s
2	Michael Schumacher	15	1m 18.371s
3	Ralf Schumacher	13	1m 18.392s
4	Eddie Irvine	15	1m 18.466s
5	David Coulthard	13	1m 18.674s
6	Juan Pablo Montoya	13	1m 18.843s
7	Jarno Trulli	14	1m 19.002s
8	Mika Häkkinen	11	1m 19.164s
9	Nick Heidfeld	14	1m 19.732s
10	Kimi Räikkönen	16	1m 19.787s
11	Pedro de la Rosa	11	1m 19.796s
12	Olivier Panis	16	1m 19.808s
13	Jean Alesi	15	1m 19.854s
14	Heinz-Harald Frentzen	17	1m 19.917s
15	Enrique Bernoldi	14	1m 20.098s
16	Jos Verstappen	17	1m 20.115s
17	Jacques Villeneuve	14	1m 20.320s
18	Luciano Burti	15	1m 20.608s
19	Tarso Marques	13	1m 20.988s
20	Fernando Alonso	13	1m 21.367s
21	Jenson Button	8	1m 21.423s
22	Giancarlo Fisichella	16	1m 21.766s

RACE FASTEST LAPS

Weather: Dry, hot and sunny

Driver	Time	Lap
Juan Pablo Montoya	1m 18.354s	27
Ralf Schumacher	1m 18.498s	54
Rubens Barrichello	1m 18.537s	59
Michael Schumacher	1m 18.612s	49
Eddie Irvine	1m 18.674s	34
David Coulthard	1m 18.883s	63
Luciano Burti	1m 19.105s	57
Mika Häkkinen	1m 19.273s	65
Jarno Trulli	1m 19.484s	32
Pedro de la Rosa	1m 19.737s	65
Jacques Villeneuve	1m 19.797s	65
Heinz-Harald Frentzen	1m 19.892s	31
Jean Alesi	1m 20.049s	48
Jenson Button	1m 20.069s	25
Kimi Räikkönen	1m 20.498s	34
Giancarlo Fisichella	1m 20.729s	26
Fernando Alonso	1m 20.937s	29
Nick Heidfeld	1m 20.976s	53
Jos Verstappen	1m 21.154s	23
Enrique Bernoldi	1m 21.188s	25
Olivier Panis	1m 21.314s	23
Tarso Marques	1m 23.778s	4

CHASSIS LOG BOOK

1	M. Schumacher	Ferrari F2001/210
2	Barrichello	Ferrari F2001/206
	spare	Ferrari F2001/211
3	Häkkinen	McLaren MP4/16/7
4	Coulthard	McLaren MP4/16/6
	spare	McLaren MP4/16/4
5	R. Schumacher	Williams FW23/5
6	Montoya	Williams FW23/6
	spare	Williams FW23/2
7	Fisichella	Benetton B201/6
8	Button	Benetton B201/5
	spare	Benetton B201/3
9	Panis	BAR 03/6
10	Villeneuve	BAR 03/7
	spare	BAR 03/4
11	Frentzen	Jordan EJ11/6
12	Trulli	Jordan EJ11/5
	spare	Jordan EJ11/4
14	Verstappen	Arrows A22/6
15	Bernoldi	Arrows A22/3
	spare	Arrows A22/1
16	Heidfeld	Sauber C20/5
17	Räikkönen	Sauber C20/6
	spare	Sauber C20/1
18	Irvine	Jaguar R2/4
19	de la Rosa	Jaguar R2/6
	spare	Jaguar R2/5
20	Marques	Minardi PS01/4
21	Alonso	Minardi PS01/3
	spare	Minardi PS01/1
22	Alesi	Prost AP04/6
23	Burti	Prost AP04/5
	spare	Prost AP04/2

POINTS TABLES

DRIVERS

	Driver	Pts
1	Michael Schumacher	68
2	David Coulthard	44
3	Rubens Barrichello	26
4	Ralf Schumacher	25
5	Juan Pablo Montoya	12
6	Mika Häkkinen	9
7	Nick Heidfeld	8
8 =	Jacques Villeneuve	7
8 =	Kimi Räikkönen	7
8 =	Jarno Trulli	7
11	Heinz-Harald Frentzen	6
12	Olivier Panis	5
13	Eddie Irvine	4
14	Jean Alesi	3
15 =	Jos Verstappen	1
15 =	Pedro de la Rosa	1
15 =	Giancarlo Fisichella	1

CONSTRUCTORS

		Pts
1	Ferrari	94
2	McLaren	53
3	Williams	37
4	Sauber	15
5	Jordan	13
6	BAR	12
7	Jaguar	5
8	Prost	3
9 =	Arrows	1
9 =	Benetton	1

FIA WORLD CHAMPIONSHIP • ROUND 10

FRENCH
grand prix

1st - M. SCHUMACHER • 2nd - R. SCHUMACHER • 3rd - BARRICHELLO

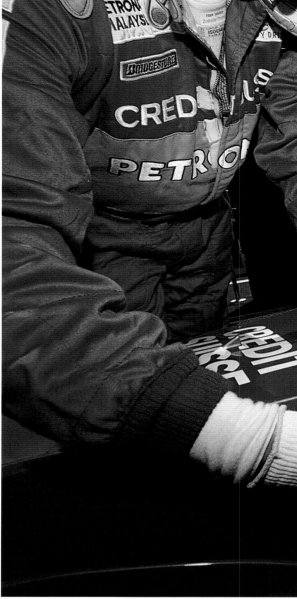

Previous spread: Michael Schumacher produced his sixth victory of the season with the Ferrari F2001 at the Circuit de Nevers.
Photograph: Paul-Henri Cahier

Below: 'Schuey' was also the quickest man around the paddock.
Photograph: Bryn Williams/crash.net

MAGNY-COURS QUALIFYING

Ralf Schumacher's pole-winning efforts at Magny-Cours were thoroughly convincing, leaving brother Michael contemplating a helping of the same medicine which he'd dished out to his young sibling a week earlier at the Nürburgring.

There Michael had once again stretched the specious FIA-approved 'one move' rule to the outer limits of acceptability by almost pushing Ralf into the pit wall. Now the boot was on the other foot.

'My mother has warned him,' said Ralf with a twinkle in his eye, knowing full well that he'd been able to exert a perceptible performance edge over his elder brother in this qualifying session which looked a closer fought affair on paper than perhaps it was in reality.

Ralf looked as though he could do pretty well what he liked with his Williams, whereas Michael was simply wringing his Ferrari F2001's neck. Ralf used the softer-option Michelin tyre which, although quicker to start with, would require 'a bit of nursing' after the first half-dozen or so race laps.

Juan Pablo Montoya used the harder Michelin compound to qualify sixth. In the 0.636s gap which separated the two Williams-BMWs were crammed Michael's Ferrari (1m 12.999s), the McLaren-Mercedes MP4/16s of David Coulthard (1m 13.186s) and Mika Häkkinen (1m 13.268s) and Jarno Trulli's Jordan EJ-11 (1m13.310s).

Coulthard was satisfied with the feel of his McLaren to gain third place, despite the fact the Scot and his team-mate Mika Häkkinen — fourth fastest on the day — were struggling when it came to straightline speed. Nevertheless, they were happy with the performance of Bridgestone's latest harder-compound tyre and David reckoned it was possible to win from the second row.

'I had a touch too much oversteer on the final sector of the lap,' he said, 'and I also found some gravel which Burti had thrown onto the track on my third run. But my fourth run was neater and quieter, while being slightly quicker. It was OK.'

Häkkinen was happy with fourth, despite complaining about a slight engine vibration, while Trulli echoed Coulthard's approval of the latest Bridgestone which enabled him to squeeze ahead of Montoya. Right behind the Colombian's Williams came the other Jordan of Heinz-Harald Frentzen (1m 13.815s), the German driver admitting he was 'pleased to have guessed the right set-up' after losing time with an electronics glitch during the morning's free practice session.

A disappointed Rubens Barrichello lined up eighth on 1m 13.867s which saw him need a torsion bar change after kerbing his F2001 quite heavily over the final chicane.

'I just could not find the right set-up today,' he admitted. 'The car was very nervous under braking and that stopped me having a good session and that caused me to abort my second run as I went straight on at a corner. Starting from the fourth row is not ideal, but with good strategy I think we can make up some places.'

Ninth fastest was Nick Heidfeld's Sauber C20 on 1m 14.095s, four places ahead of team-mate Kimi Räikkönen who could not improve on 1m 14.536s. 'My second-to-last run was pretty good until I came across some gravel that somebody had thrown onto the track,' said Heidfeld. 'My last run was clear and clean, and I'm satisfied with ninth because qualifying was very difficult here.' Räikkönen just wasn't entirely happy with his car's handling balance.

Jacques Villeneuve (1m 14.096s) and Olivier Panis (1m 14.181s) were well matched in the BAR-Honda camp, the latter complaining slightly about traffic. Overall, both drivers felt they had improved the car's feel.

For Jaguar, Eddie Irvine could not better a 12th-fastest 1m 14.441s. He set his best time on his first run, spinning off in the race car on his second and having to take the spare for his final two runs.

'The T-car was actually slightly better balanced than my race car, but into corner seven the rear of the car was very wayward, and I half spun on my last lap,' he explained.

Pedro de la Rosa, delayed in starting the session for 20 minutes due to a problem with the electrics on the overhead gantry in his garage, wound up 14th on 1m 15.020s. The two Jaguars were split by Luciano Burti's Prost AP04 (1m 15.072s) which spun and damaged a bargeboard during the course of the session, even though the Brazilian wound up four places ahead of his frustrated team-mate Jean Alesi (1m 15.774s).

In 16th and 17th places, Giancarlo Fisichella (1m 15.220s) and Jenson Button (1m 15.420s) looked much more promising than of late with the Benetton B201s. During the morning free practice session the team tried a revised aerodynamic package which caused some slight handling imbalance, but the latest Renault engine evolution specification was a definite step in the right direction.

Even so, Button admitted he had not done himself justice, even allowing for the fact that his first run was spoiled by Irvine spinning in front of him. 'My second run was better,' said Jenson, 'but I'm afraid I mucked up the next two because I was supposed to adjust the differential setting after turn two. Unfortunately, I forgot to do so on both occasions.'

Jos Verstappen's Arrows (1m 15.707s) just edged out Alesi, while Enrique Bernoldi's sister car wound up 20th ahead of the two Minardis, the usual occupants of the back row.

Diary

Jaguar F1 boss Bobby Rahal admits that he would like to give an F1 test to Indy 500 winner Helio Castroneves.

Benetton takes up its option on Mark Webber's services as test driver for 2002 on the weekend he wins the Magny-Cours round of the F3000 championship.

Top right: Dry ice is packed into a Sauber radiator ducting in a bid to keep temperatures under control prior to the start in the sweltering conditions.

Above right: Eddie Jordan certainly needed to be hard bitten to keep his resolve in the face of his team's disappointing form.

Above centre right: The message from Mika's supporters proved to be in vain.

Right: Arm raised aloft, Häkkinen signals he has problems on the grid — for the third time so far this season.

All photographs: Paul-Henri Cahier

LAUDA CONCERNED OVER F1 COMMERCIAL FUTURE

Niki Lauda, chairman of Ford's Premier Automotive Group, spoke out at the French Grand Prix of the need for urgent talks between all F1 team owners, the car manufacturers and the Kirch media group over the commercial future of F1.

Lauda was concerned that there had been hardly any contact between the teams and Kirch, who now owned 75 per cent of SLEC, the Ecclestone family umbrella which controls the British tycoon's F1 business and the commercial rights to the FIA F1 World Championship.

'It just cannot be right that we are left to read in the newspapers what is going on,' said the triple former World Champion.

'It seems to me that very little organisational strategy has been established and it is important that any talks which take place are properly coordinated.

'I do agree with the concerns of the smaller F1 teams who are worried when the big manufacturers seem to be negotiating alone on behalf of everybody.

'When Bernie made the investments in F1 which have brought about all the current TV coverage all the constructors agreed and were happy about it. He was one of us.

'As ownership [of the commercial rights] has now changed, the future needs to be discussed in detail. We just don't know what the new owner [Kirch] might do.'

Ecclestone had retained a 25 per cent stake in SLEC, but Kirch was believed to be concerned that its £700 million investment for the 75 per cent could not be recouped in the six years remaining under the present Concorde agreement which governs the F1 championship.

MICHAEL and Ralf Schumacher's apparent quest to dominate F1 as their own private domain took another decisive step forward as they raced to another commanding 1-2 victory, for Ferrari and BMW Williams respectively, in the French Grand Prix at the Circuit de Nevers.

With track temperatures soaring to 47 degrees early in the race, the elder Schumacher's latest success left him one win short of Alain Prost's all-time record of 51 victories which has endured since the French driver's retirement at the end of 1993.

Yet despite his commanding success at Magny-Cours, Michael was not about to anticipate how the balance of his admittedly extremely convincing season would ultimately unfold.

'I am a bit too realistic,' he said. Images of those two successive retirements in the 2000 Austrian and German Grands Prix clearly still lurked vividly in the World Champion's sub-conscious.

'We have seen how quickly things can turn around again,' he warned, 'and although it's a very comfortable lead, there are still seven races to go and 70 points to give away, so there is no reason to start celebrating before it's done.'

Above: Ralf Schumacher picked up second place for another 1-2 with his brother after his Williams team-mate's BMW engine failed.
Photograph: Paul-Henri Cahier

For all that, his championship rival David Coulthard had a frustrating afternoon, any satisfaction deriving from his determined run to fourth behind Rubens Barrichello's Ferrari inevitably shaded by a self-inflicted wound in the form of a 10s stop-go penalty for speeding in the pit lane.

Ralf Schumacher accelerated cleanly into an immediate lead from the first pole position of his career which had been achieved on his 26th birthday, leaving Michael to struggle momentarily with a hint of clutch trouble as his Ferrari accelerated away from the line. Coulthard very nearly squeezed through into second place, but Michael firmly defended his position and the first leading group streamed through the Estoril right-hander onto the back straight in grid order.

Well, almost. Mika Häkkinen's McLaren MP4/16 hadn't even managed to get round to take its fourth place on the grid, having been left stranded prior to setting out on the parade lap. Mechanics fell on the stricken machine in an attempt to coax it into life, but a gearbox breakage was quickly diagnosed and the Finn's race was over before it started.

He wasn't the only one in trouble. Pedro de la Rosa's Jaguar limped into the pits, rather than onto the grid, at the end of the parade lap and only got going a lap down after engineers had reset his electronics. The McLaren team subsequently confirmed that Häkkinen's failure was due to an assembly problem. 'I feel nothing,' said Häkkinen thoughtfully, 'because there is nothing to feel.'

As Häkkinen strolled back to the McLaren motorhome, Ralf Schumacher came slamming through to lead at the end of the first lap by 0.3s from his brother's Ferrari. Third was Coulthard, then Juan Pablo Montoya's Williams FW23, Rubens Barrichello's Ferrari, the Jordan-Honda EJ-11s of Jarno Trulli and Heinz-Harald Frentzen and Jacques Villeneuve's BAR-Honda.

Coulthard was hanging on as best he could and, second time round, there was already a 1.4s gap back to Montoya in fourth place. Montoya had shrewdly opted for the harder Michelin compound

which he personally felt would be a better bet over a race distance than the softer version chosen by his team-mate.

By lap four Ralf Schumacher was 0.9s ahead of Michael, but Montoya was steadying the gap to Coulthard's third-place McLaren. On lap six Villeneuve pulled off into the gravel from eighth place, retiring on the spot with an apparent electrical problem. 'A shame,' shrugged Jacques, 'the car was working really well and our strategy was to just keep attacking as we had nothing to lose.'

With 20 of the race's 72 laps completed, Ralf had eased open his advantage to 2.1s. Coulthard was still a strong third ahead of Montoya, Barrichello, the two Jordans and Nick Heidfeld's Sauber. Running strongly, Eddie Irvine's Jaguar was scrambling all over Olivier Panis's BAR for ninth while, further back, Enrique Bernoldi retired from 14th place when his Arrows succumbed to engine failure.

Barrichello had been going well and saving fuel after a good start from eighth place on the grid. Ross Brawn then came onto the radio with the suggestion that he switch to a three-stop strategy. Rubens agreed and accordingly made his first stop in 7.0s from fifth place at the end of lap 21, resuming seventh.

On lap 24 Ralf Schumacher made his first refuelling stop in 10.3s, which was 3s longer than brother Michael was at rest when he brought the Ferrari in next time round. Ralf's delay was caused when he mistakenly engaged first gear before one of the Williams's rear wheels was properly attached. Crucially, Michael's actual fuelling process took 2s less than Ralf's which meant that the Ferrari was carrying 24 litres less in its tank when it accelerated back into the fray. Add to that the fact that Ralf suddenly found his second set of soft-compound Michelins not working as well as the first and that crucial two laps saw Michael vault from 3s behind his brother to 4s ahead. Thus possession of the race changed hands.

With Coulthard making a 9.1s first refuelling stop on lap 26, Montoya was left leading by 8.9s from Michael Schumacher. Unfortunately David incurred his penalty whilst accelerating back

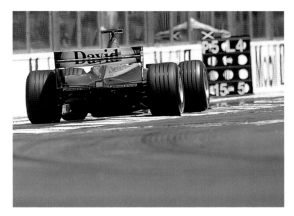

into the race which meant that he had to come in at the end of lap 32 for his stop-go, two laps after Montoya relinquished the lead with an 8.9s first refuelling stop.

'I turned off the button a little bit too early,' said Coulthard. 'It was a mistake I wasn't aware of at the time because I was being fed information by my pit crew over the radio as to precisely where the other cars were on the circuit.

'It was very frustrating, but these cars tend to accelerate pretty quickly. The car was pretty good on the final set of tyres and I was able to push Rubens [Barrichello] quite hard in the closing stages. But I couldn't quite get close enough to make an overtaking move stick.'

Thus by the end of lap 33 Michael Schumacher was leading by a decisive 8.9s from Ralf, then there was a gap to Barrichello, Montoya, Coulthard and Trulli. On lap 36 Barrichello made his second stop from third place in 8.2s, dropping to fourth behind Montoya and the Colombian really picked up the pace and began closing in on his team-mate.

On lap 43 Montoya was less than a second behind Ralf, closing all the time, the German driver seemingly oblivious to messages over the radio from the pit wall to let Juan Pablo through. Next time round Ralf came in for an 8.7s second refuelling stop, rather earlier than he'd planned due to the problems with his second set of tyres, followed by Michael in 10.7s next time round.

That left Montoya in the lead and he stayed out until lap 50 before making his second stop in 8.8s followed by Coulthard from fourth place in 7.6s on the following lap. That left Michael leading from Barrichello by 8.8s with Montoya third ahead of Schumacher, although it was only a brief moment of glory for the Indy 500 star as he retired with a big-end failure in his car's BMW engine two laps later. Even so, he'd set fourth-fastest lap of the race and proved his point as to the efficacy of his tyre choice.

Barrichello lasted in second place until lap 54 when he made his third refuelling stop in 8.6s, resuming third. Next time round Eddie Irvine retired the Jaguar R2 from seventh place with engine problems after a very promising run.

As the two Schumacher brothers headed on towards unchallenged first and second places, all that remained was to see whether Coulthard could get on terms with Barrichello and steal third from the Ferrari driver. He strained every sinew, but couldn't quite pull it off, even though Rubens later admitted that he was struggling slightly over the final stint as his fourth set of rear tyres blistered quicker than he'd expected.

'This did not affect me in terms of putting the power down or changing direction,' he explained, 'but it did affect my braking, particularly at turn five [the hairpin].

'That is how David managed to come alongside me once, because I braked at my usual point and nearly went off, and the second time was when I got held up by a backmarker.

'It was a good battle, but from where I started I knew I would have to fight today. Eighth to third is a good achievement.'

Trulli's Jordan came home fifth with the Sauber C20s of Heidfeld and Kimi Räikkönen sixth and seventh. Heidfeld was well satisfied, reporting that his car felt better in the race than it had done during testing the previous week, but Räikkönen was slightly frustrated by high-speed oversteer.

Frentzen was eighth ahead of a disappointed Panis, while the Prost AP04s of Luciano Burti and Jean Alesi sandwiched Giancarlo Fisichella's 11th-place Benetton. Burti was well satisfied, despite being frustrated by poor grip from his second set of tyres, but Alesi was extremely disappointed, having never managed to work out a decent chassis set-up all weekend.

For his part, Fisichella touched Jos Verstappen's Arrows at the start, losing a few positions. Giancarlo reckoned that must have done some damage because the B201 felt progressively odder under braking as the race wore on. Under the circumstances it was a whole lot better than Jenson Button's run which ended with a spin into a gravel trap after 68 laps, probably when the engine failed.

'The engine started to cut out before my second stop and when I pitted Giancarlo was already there,' he explained. 'Not ideal, but because I had a fuel-pressure problem I had no option but to come in at that moment.' Separating the two Benettons were Alesi, Jos Verstappen's Arrows — which lost time with a fuel rig problem at its first stop — then the delayed de la Rosa and Tarso Marques in the Minardi.

Michael Schumacher now aimed for Silverstone and the 50th anniversary of Ferrari's first World Championship Grand Prix victory, achieved by Froilan Gonzalez. Would Maranello's peerless team leader ensure that it was remembered as a very special anniversary indeed?

Left, top to bottom:
Coulthard gets the message from the McLaren pit.
Photograph: Bryn Williams/crash.net

Jarno Trulli drove well to take fifth place in the Jordan-Honda EJ-11.

Feeling wistful — McLaren's third driver Alexander Wurz was on hand until Saturday afternoon.
Both photographs: Paul-Henri Cahier

Nick Heidfeld's Sauber C20 leads Eddie Irvine's Jaguar R2 as they battle for sixth place, just before the Ulsterman's car stopped with engine problems.

Michael Schumacher and Rubens Barrichello celebrate first and third for Ferrari.
Both photographs: Bryn Williams/crash.net

FIA F1 WORLD CHAMPIONSHIP

ROUND 10
MAGNY-COURS 29 JUNE–1 JULY 2001

MOBIL 1
grand prix de
FRANCE

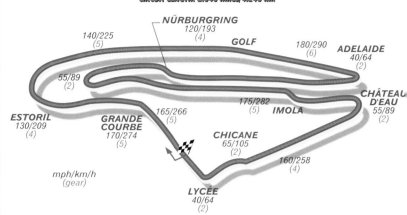

CIRCUIT DE NEVERS – MAGNY-COURS
CIRCUIT LENGTH: 2.640 miles/4.248 km

NÜRBURGRING 120/193 (4)
GOLF
140/225 (5)
180/290 (6)
ADELAIDE 40/64 (2)
55/89 (2)
175/282 (5)
IMOLA
CHÂTEAU D'EAU 55/89 (2)
ESTORIL 130/209 (4)
165/266 (5)
GRANDE COURBE 170/274 (5)
CHICANE 65/105 (2)
160/258 (4)
mph/km/h (gear)
LYCÉE 40/64 (2)

RACE DISTANCE: 72 laps, 190.069 miles/305.886 km   RACE WEATHER: Dry, hot and sunny

Pos.	Driver	Nat.	No.	Entrant	Car/Engine	Tyres	Laps	Time/Retirement	Speed (mph/km/h)	Gap to lea
1	Michael Schumacher	D	1	Scuderia Ferrari Marlboro	Ferrari F2001-050 V10	B	72	1h 33m 35.636s	121.846/196.093	
2	Ralf Schumacher	D	5	BMW WilliamsF1 Team	Williams FW23-BMW P80 V10	M	72	1h 33m 46.035s	121.621/195.731	+10.3
3	Rubens Barrichello	BR	2	Scuderia Ferrari Marlboro	Ferrari F2001-050 V10	B	72	1h 33m 52.017s	121.492/195.523	+16.3
4	David Coulthard	GB	4	West McLaren Mercedes	McLaren MP4/16-Mercedes F0110K V10	B	72	1h 33m 52.742s	121.476/195.497	+17.1
5	Jarno Trulli	I	12	B&H Jordan Honda	Jordan EJ11-Honda RA001E V10	B	72	1h 34m 43.921s	120.382/193.737	+68.2
6	Nick Heidfeld	D	16	Red Bull Sauber Petronas	Sauber C20-Petronas V10	B	71			+1
7	Kimi Räikkönen	SF	17	Red Bull Sauber Petronas	Sauber C20-Petronas V10	B	71			+1
8	Heinz-Harald Frentzen	D	11	B&H Jordan Honda	Jordan EJ11-Honda RA001E V10	B	71			+1
9	Olivier Panis	F	9	Lucky Strike BAR Honda	BAR 03-Honda RA001E V10	B	71			+1
10	Luciano Burti	BR	23	Prost Acer	Prost AP04-Acer V10	M	71			+1
11	Giancarlo Fisichella	I	7	Mild Seven Benetton Renault	Benetton B201-Renault RS21 V10	M	71			+1
12	Jean Alesi	F	22	Prost Acer	Prost AP04-Acer V10	M	70			+2
13	Jos Verstappen	NL	14	Orange Arrows Asiatech	Arrows A22-Asiatech V10	B	70			+2
14	Pedro de la Rosa	ESP	19	Jaguar Racing	Jaguar R2-Cosworth CR3 V10	M	70			+2
15	Tarso Marques	BR	20	European Minardi F1	Minardi PS01-European V10	M	69			+3
16	Jenson Button	GB	8	Mild Seven Benetton Renault	Benetton B201-Renault RS21 V10	M	68	Engine/spun off		+4
17	Fernando Alonso	ESP	21	European Minardi F1	Minardi PS01-European V10	M	65	Engine		+7
	Eddie Irvine	GB	18	Jaguar Racing	Jaguar R2-Cosworth CR3 V10	M	54	Engine		
	Juan Pablo Montoya	COL	6	BMW WilliamsF1 Team	Williams FW23-BMW P80 V10	M	52	Engine		
	Enrique Bernoldi	BR	15	Orange Arrows Asiatech	Arrows A22-Asiatech V10	B	17	Engine		
	Jacques Villeneuve	CDN	10	Lucky Strike BAR Honda	BAR03-Honda RA001E V10	B	5	Electrics		
DNS	Mika Häkkinen	SF	3	West McLaren Mercedes	McLaren MP4/16-Mercedes F0110K V10	B	0	Gearbox		

Fastest lap: David Coulthard, on lap 53, 1m 16.088s, 124.976 mph/201.130 km/h (record).

Previous lap record: Nigel Mansell (F1 Williams FW14B-Renault V10), 1m 17.070s, 123.355 mph/198.521 km/h (1992).

Grid order		
5 R. SCHUMACHER	5 5 5 5 5 5 5 5 5 5 5 5 5 5 5 5 5 5 5 5 5 5 5 1 4 6 6 6 6 1 1 1 1 1 1 1 1 1 1 1 1 1 1 1 6 6 6 6 6 1 1 1	
1 M. SCHUMACHER	1 1 1 1 1 1 1 1 1 1 1 1 1 1 1 1 1 1 1 1 1 1 1 5 1 4 6 1 1 1 1 5 5 5 5 5 5 5 5 5 6 1 1 1 1 1 1 2 2 5	
4 COULTHARD	4 4 4 4 4 4 4 4 4 4 4 4 4 4 4 4 4 4 4 4 4 4 4 4 6 1 5 5 5 4 2 2 2 2 6 6 6 6 6 6 5 2 2 2 2 2 6 5 5 2	
12 TRULLI	6 6 6 6 6 6 6 6 6 6 6 6 6 6 6 6 6 6 6 6 6 5 5 4 4 4 2 4 6 6 6 6 2 2 2 2 2 2 2 4 4 4 4 4 4 6 4 4	
6 MONTOYA	2 2 2 2 2 2 2 2 2 2 2 2 2 2 2 2 2 2 2 12 12 12 2 2 2 2 2 6 6 4 4 4 4 4 4 4 4 4 5 5 5 5 5 4 12 12	
11 FRENTZEN	12 12 12 12 12 12 12 12 12 12 12 12 12 12 12 12 12 11 11 2 12 18 12 12 12 12 12 12 12 12 12 12 12 12 12 12 12 12 12 16 16	
2 BARRICHELLO	11 11 11 11 11 11 11 11 11 11 11 11 11 11 11 11 11 11 11 2 2 11 18 12 12 16 16 16 16 16 16 16 16 16 16 16 18 18 18 18 12 16 16 16 16 18	
16 HEIDFELD	10 10 10 10 10 17 17 17 17 16 16 16 16 16 16 16 16 16 18 18 16 11 11 11 11 11 11 11 11 11 11 11 11 11 16 16 18 18 18 17 18	
10 VILLENEUVE	17 17 17 17 17 16 16 16 16 16 16 16 16 17 9 9 9 9 9 16 9 23 11 11 18 18 18 18 18 18 18 18 18 18 16 16 16 16 17 17 17 17 11 11	
9 PANIS	16 16 16 16 16 9 9 9 9 9 9 9 9 18 18 18 18 9 23 23 16 11 17 17 17 17 17 17 17 17 17 9 9 9 9 17 11 11 11 11 11 9 9	
18 IRVINE	18 9 9 9 18 18 18 18 18 18 18 23 23 23 23 23 16 16 14 17 9 9 9 9 9 9 9 9 9 17 17 17 17 23 9 9 9 9 9 7	
17 RÄIKKÖNEN	9 18 18 18 23 23 23 23 23 23 23 14 14 14 14 14 14 9 23 23 23 23 23 23 23 23 23 23 23 23 23 9 23 7 7 7 7 23 23	
23 BURTI	23 23 23 23 14 14 14 14 14 14 14 14 15 15 9 14 7 7 7 7 7 7 7 7 7 7 7 7 7 7 7 7 7 23 23 23 8 23	
7 FISICHELLA	14 14 14 14 15 15 15 15 15 15 15 8 7 17 7 22 17 14 14 14 14 14 14 14 14 14 14 14 8 22 22 22 8 22	
8 BUTTON	15 15 15 15 8 8 8 8 8 8 8 7 17 22 7 8 22 22 22 22 22 22 22 22 22 22 22 14 8 8 22 22 22 14 14	
14 VERSTAPPEN	7 8 8 8 7 7 7 7 7 7 7 7 17 17 22 8 22 8 8 8 8 8 14 14 14 14 14 14 14 8 14 14 14 14 21	
22 ALESI	8 7 7 7 22 22 22 22 22 22 22 22 22 20 20 20 20 20 20 21 21 21 21 21 21 21 21 21 21 21 21 21 21 19 19	
15 BERNOLDI	22 22 22 22 20 20 20 20 20 20 20 20 20 21 21 21 21 21 20 20 20 20 20 20 20 20 20 20 20 20 20 19 19 20 20	
21 ALONSO	20 20 20 20 21 21 21 21 21 21 21 21 21 19 19 19 19 19 19 19 19 19 19 19 19 19 19 19 19 19 19 20 20	
20 MARQUES	21 21 21 21 19 19 19 19 19 19 19 19 19	
3 HÄKKINEN	19 19 19 19 19	
19 DE LA ROSA		

Pit stop
One lap behind leader

STARTING GRID

1 **M. SCHUMACHER** Ferrari	**5** **R. SCHUMACHER** Williams
3* **HÄKKINEN** McLaren	**4** **COULTHARD** McLaren
6 **MONTOYA** Williams	**12** **TRULLI** Jordan
2 **BARRICHELLO** Ferrari	**11** **FRENTZEN** Jordan
10 **VILLENEUVE** BAR	**16** **HEIDFELD** Sauber
18 **IRVINE** Jaguar	**9** **PANIS** BAR
19 **DE LA ROSA** Jaguar	**17** **RÄIKKÖNEN** Sauber
7 **FISICHELLA** Benetton	**23** **BURTI** Prost
14 **VERSTAPPEN** Arrows	**8** **BUTTON** Benetton
15 **BERNOLDI** Arrows	**22** **ALESI** Prost
20 **MARQUES** Minardi	**21** **ALONSO** Minardi

*did not start

TIME SHEETS

QUALIFYING
Weather: Dry, hot and sunny

Pos.	Driver	Car	Laps	Time
1	Ralf Schumacher	Williams-BMW	10	1m 12.989s
2	Michael Schumacher	Ferrari	12	1m 12.999s
3	David Coulthard	McLaren-Mercedes	12	1m 13.186s
4	Mika Häkkinen	McLaren-Mercedes	12	1m 13.268s
5	Jarno Trulli	Jordan-Honda	12	1m 13.310s
6	Juan Pablo Montoya	Williams-BMW	12	1m 13.625s
7	Heinz-Harald Frentzen	Jordan-Honda	11	1m 13.815s
8	Rubens Barrichello	Ferrari	11	1m 13.867s
9	Nick Heidfeld	Sauber-Petronas	12	1m 14.095s
10	Jacques Villeneuve	BAR-Honda	12	1m 14.096s
11	Olivier Panis	BAR-Honda	12	1m 14.181s
12	Eddie Irvine	Jaguar-Cosworth	10	1m 14.441s
13	Kimi Räikkönen	Sauber-Petronas	12	1m 14.536s
14	Pedro de la Rosa	Jaguar-Cosworth	11	1m 15.020s
15	Luciano Burti	Prost-Acer	11	1m 15.072s
16	Giancarlo Fisichella	Benetton-Renault	11	1m 15.220s
17	Jenson Button	Benetton-Renault	12	1m 15.420s
18	Jos Verstappen	Arrows-Asiatech	12	1m 15.707s
19	Jean Alesi	Prost-Acer	11	1m 15.774s
20	Enrique Bernoldi	Arrows-Asiatech	12	1m 15.828s
21	Fernando Alonso	Minardi-European	12	1m 16.039s
22	Tarso Marques	Minardi-European	11	1m 16.500s

FRIDAY FREE PRACTICE
Weather: Dry, hot and sunny

Pos.	Driver	Laps	Time
1	David Coulthard	35	1m 14.935s
2	Eddie Irvine	27	1m 15.133s
3	Jacques Villeneuve	39	1m 15.224s
4	Mika Häkkinen	33	1m 15.372s
5	Ralf Schumacher	27	1m 15.537s
6	Juan Pablo Montoya	52	1m 15.582s
7	Michael Schumacher	48	1m 15.810s
8	Pedro de la Rosa	45	1m 16.140s
9	Jarno Trulli	52	1m 16.187s
10	Rubens Barrichello	47	1m 16.325s
11	Olivier Panis	20	1m 16.364s
12	Luciano Burti	50	1m 16.455s
13	Heinz-Harald Frentzen	45	1m 16.868s
14	Kimi Räikkönen	25	1m 16.906s
15	Nick Heidfeld	46	1m 17.011s
16	Jean Alesi	32	1m 17.088s
17	Jenson Button	34	1m 17.172s
18	Jos Verstappen	34	1m 17.285s
19	Enrique Bernoldi	23	1m 17.527s
20	Giancarlo Fisichella	35	1m 17.566s
21	Fernando Alonso	45	1m 17.866s
22	Tarso Marques	38	1m 18.372s

SATURDAY FREE PRACTICE
Weather: Dry, hot and sunny

Pos.	Driver	Laps	Time
1	Michael Schumacher	16	1m 13.729s
2	Ralf Schumacher	29	1m 13.953s
3	David Coulthard	23	1m 13.972s
4	Mika Häkkinen	15	1m 14.295s
5	Jarno Trulli	20	1m 14.482s
6	Rubens Barrichello	18	1m 14.515s
7	Juan Pablo Montoya	25	1m 14.652s
8	Nick Heidfeld	33	1m 14.652s
9	Eddie Irvine	38	1m 14.824s
10	Kimi Räikkönen	25	1m 14.872s
11	Heinz-Harald Frentzen	20	1m 14.992s
12	Jacques Villeneuve	28	1m 15.061s
13	Olivier Panis	32	1m 15.122s
14	Pedro de la Rosa	42	1m 15.602s
15	Jean Alesi	25	1m 15.750s
16	Jos Verstappen	28	1m 15.829s
17	Luciano Burti	38	1m 15.846s
18	Giancarlo Fisichella	28	1m 15.873s
19	Jenson Button	25	1m 16.129s
20	Enrique Bernoldi	26	1m 16.177s
21	Fernando Alonso	26	1m 17.135s
22	Tarso Marques	33	1m 17.156s

WARM-UP
Weather: Dry, hot and sunny

Pos.	Driver	Laps	Time
1	Mika Häkkinen	14	1m 15.428s
2	Michael Schumacher	16	1m 15.429s
3	Rubens Barrichello	13	1m 15.676s
4	David Coulthard	12	1m 15.780s
5	Jarno Trulli	17	1m 15.980s
6	Kimi Räikkönen	14	1m 16.136s
7	Olivier Panis	15	1m 16.184s
8	Pedro de la Rosa	15	1m 16.426s
9	Nick Heidfeld	16	1m 16.559s
10	Eddie Irvine	14	1m 16.567s
11	Juan Pablo Montoya	16	1m 16.735s
12	Enrique Bernoldi	11	1m 16.777s
13	Heinz-Harald Frentzen	16	1m 16.952s
14	Jacques Villeneuve	15	1m 17.073s
15	Jos Verstappen	14	1m 17.120s
16	Luciano Burti	16	1m 17.443s
17	Ralf Schumacher	15	1m 17.605s
18	Jean Alesi	15	1m 17.945s
19	Giancarlo Fisichella	18	1m 18.084s
20	Jenson Button	9	1m 18.431s
21	Fernando Alonso	16	1m 19.986s
22	Tarso Marques	9	1m 21.295s

RACE FASTEST LAPS
Weather: Dry, hot and sunny

Driver	Time	Lap
David Coulthard	1m 16.088s	53
Rubens Barrichello	1m 16.181s	23
Michael Schumacher	1m 16.286s	27
Juan Pablo Montoya	1m 16.355s	34
Ralf Schumacher	1m 16.585s	18
Eddie Irvine	1m 17.304s	23
Kimi Räikkönen	1m 17.311s	8
Jarno Trulli	1m 17.369s	29
Pedro de la Rosa	1m 17.508s	67
Nick Heidfeld	1m 17.538s	23
Heinz-Harald Frentzen	1m 17.540s	20
Giancarlo Fisichella	1m 17.968s	26
Jacques Villeneuve	1m 18.181s	4
Olivier Panis	1m 18.250s	68
Luciano Burti	1m 18.253s	50
Jenson Button	1m 18.359s	25
Jos Verstappen	1m 18.662s	47
Jean Alesi	1m 18.817s	14
Enrique Bernoldi	1m 19.181s	13
Fernando Alonso	1m 19.199s	62
Tarso Marques	1m 19.608s	54

CHASSIS LOG BOOK

	Driver	Chassis
1	M. Schumacher	Ferrari F2001/210
2	Barrichello	Ferrari F2001/206
	spare	Ferrari F2001/211
3	Häkkinen	McLaren MP4/16/7
4	Coulthard	McLaren MP4/16/6
	spare	McLaren MP4/16/4
5	R. Schumacher	Williams FW23/5
6	Montoya	Williams FW23/6
	spare	Williams FW23/2
7	Fisichella	Benetton B201/6
8	Button	Benetton B201/5
	spares	Benetton B201/3 & 2
9	Panis	BAR 03/6
10	Villeneuve	BAR 03/7
	spares	BAR 03/5 & 4
11	Frentzen	Jordan EJ11/4
12	Trulli	Jordan EJ11/5
	spare	Jordan EJ11/6
14	Verstappen	Arrows A22/6
15	Bernoldi	Arrows A22/3
	spare	Arrows A22/1
16	Heidfeld	Sauber C20/5
17	Räikkönen	Sauber C20/6
	spare	Sauber C20/1
18	Irvine	Jaguar R2/4
19	de la Rosa	Jaguar R2/6
	spare	Jaguar R2/5
20	Marques	Minardi PS01/4
21	Alonso	Minardi PS01/3
	spare	Minardi PS01/1
22	Alesi	Prost AP04/6
23	Burti	Prost AP04/5
	spare	Prost AP04/2

POINTS TABLES

DRIVERS

1	Michael Schumacher	78
2	David Coulthard	47
3	Ralf Schumacher	31
4	Rubens Barrichello	30
5	Juan Pablo Montoya	12
6 =	Nick Heidfeld	9
6 =	Mika Häkkinen	9
6 =	Jarno Trulli	9
9 =	Jacques Villeneuve	7
9 =	Kimi Räikkönen	7
11	Heinz-Harald Frentzen	6
12	Olivier Panis	5
13	Eddie Irvine	4
14	Jean Alesi	3
15 =	Jos Verstappen	1
15 =	Pedro de la Rosa	1
15 =	Giancarlo Fisichella	1

CONSTRUCTORS

1	Ferrari	108
2	McLaren	56
3	Williams	43
4	Sauber	16
5	Jordan	15
6	BAR	12
7	Jaguar	5
8	Prost	3
9 =	Arrows	1
9 =	Benetton	1

Lap Chart

	59	60	61	62	63	64	65	66	67	68	69	70	71	72	
	1	1	1	1	1	1	1	1	1	1	1	1	1	1	1
	5	5	5	5	5	5	5	5	5	5	5	5	5	5	2
	2	2	2	2	2	2	2	2	2	2	2	2	2	2	3
	4	4	4	4	4	4	4	4	4	4	4	4	4	4	4
	12	12	12	12	12	12	12	12	12	12	12	12	12	12	5
	16	16	16	16	16	16	16	16	16	16	16	16	16	16	6
	17	17	17	17	17	17	17	17	17	17	17	17	17		
	11	11	11	11	11	11	11	11	11	11	11	11	11	11	
	9	9	9	9	9	9	9	9	9	9	9	9	9	9	
	7	23	23	23	23	23	23	23	23	23	23	23	23	23	
	23	7	7	7	7	7	7	7	7	7	7	7	7		
	8	8	8	8	8	8	8	8	8	8	8	22	22		
	22	22	22	22	22	22	22	22	22	22	22	14	14		
	14	14	14	14	14	14	14	14	14	14	19	19			
	21	21	21	21	19	19	19	19	19	20					
	19	19	19	19	21	21	21	20	20	20					
	20	20	20	20	20	20	20								

FOR THE RECORD

First pole position
Ralf Schumacher
50th Grand Prix win
Michael Schumacher

FIA WORLD CHAMPIONSHIP • ROUND 11

BRITISH
grand prix

1st - HÄKKINEN • 2nd - M. SCHUMACHER • 3rd - BARRICHELLO

Main photograph: Back on top — Mika celebrates that winning feeling again for the first time since the 2000 Belgian GP.
Photograph: Mark Thompson/Allsport-Getty Images

Inset: Häkkinen was in a class of his own thanks to his determination and McLaren's shrewd two-stop strategy.
Photograph: Bryn Williams/crash.net

TOYOTA WILL TEST NEW F1 CAR TO LAST MOMENT

Toyota threatened to ignite a major F1 controversy in the run-up to the British Grand Prix by indicating that it would be testing right through until the end of December and was not bound by the terms of the 'test ban treaty' which prevents all existing competitors from testing for ten weeks from the middle of October.

The Japanese company, whose racing chief Ove Andersson offered the startling claim that 'we are not welcome in F1,' said it planned to continue testing its new F1 car right up until the start of the New Year. It stated that it had clarified this matter with the FIA, arguing that its agreement with the sport's governing body to enter the World Championship was made before the testing ban was introduced and that there was nothing wrong with its strategy.

Toyota also contended that, as a newcomer, it did not have to abide by these rules until the start of 2002, its first active season in the F1 business.

However, with entries for the 2002 title contest officially closing on November 11, rival teams were calling for the FIA to make it plain to Toyota that they were obliged to fall into line.

'Once Toyota's entry for next year's World Championship is accepted, they are in the same contractual situation and are obliged to abide by the same rules and obligations as everybody else,' said McLaren managing director Martin Whitmarsh.

Below: Jarno Trulli steered his Jordan EJ-11 to an impressive fourth place on the grid next to Coulthard, but tangled with the Scot at the start of the race.
Photograph: Paul-Henri Cahier

SILVERSTONE QUALIFYING

Unpredictable weather was inevitably on the menu for the British Grand Prix weekend, although thankfully the whole affair was rather more comfortable for the spectators than the sodden Easter fixture of the previous year. Nevertheless there was still plenty of rain to keep the spectators amused as well as the sight of both Schumacher brothers burying Ferrari and Williams FW23 respectively in the gravel traps during the course of free practice.

Ferrari, Jordan and BAR were also in a spot of trouble on Friday afternoon when they were each fined $2500 for running wet-weather tyres right at the end of the free practice session when rain began falling. Under FIA rules the session had not officially been declared wet, so they should have stuck to dry-weather rubber.

Heavy rain on Saturday morning also left track conditions very green early in qualifying and there was no activity for 23 minutes of the crucial hour-long session. Then Kimi Räikkönen broke the deadlock with the Sauber C20, triggering a helter-skelter of frenzied activity which came down to a shoot-out between Michael Schumacher and Häkkinen.

The Finn, delighted at having successfully dialled out any trace of frustrating understeer from his McLaren MP4/16, ran Michael a close second, but in the end it was the Ferrari star who aced pole by a wafer-thin 0.082s.

'With everybody waiting for almost half an hour before going out, it meant that there was not much time to get in four runs and improve the car,' said Michael.

'Then the timing monitors failed and although we knew the lap times, we could not see the sector times which can be useful in analysing where we needed to improve.'

For his part, Häkkinen was well pleased to be on the front row, confessing that 'the car is performing well and extremely enjoyable to drive.' Disappointingly, David Coulthard was another 0.4s down in third place, explaining that the changing track conditions made it difficult for him to find the optimum handling balance.

This left him on the second row alongside the bullish Jarno Trulli (1m 20.930s), the Italian believing that he could have squeezed another 0.003s out of his Jordan EJ-11 to beat Coulthard had he not broken a suspension pushrod after clipping a kerb at Becketts and stopping on the circuit as a result.

Heinz-Harald Frentzen was right behind on 1m 21.217s in fifth place in the other Jordan while next up was Rubens Barrichello's Ferrari F2001 (1m 21.715s) and Räikkönen's Sauber on 1m 22.023s. Rubens was very frustrated after getting tangled up in traffic — in particular

accusing Enrique Bernoldi of having baulked him twice — while Räikkönen was quite happy after squeezing some improvement out of the Sauber's latest aerodynamic upgrade.

Life was more frustrating in the Williams camp. Where Juan Pablo Montoya (1m 22.219s) and Ralf Schumacher (1m 22.283s) qualified their FW23s eighth and tenth. Schumacher set his quickest time on his second stint and failed to improve with most of the field towards the end of the session, while Montoya followed Trulli's example by clipping a kerb at Becketts, bending a pushrod and being obliged to take the spare car set for his team-mate.

'We did one run, then made some adjustments, and the spare worked out quite well,' said the Colombian. 'I managed to get by Jenson [Button] coming through the last corner and that really helped.'

The BAR-Hondas of Olivier Panis (1m 22.316s) and Jacques Villeneuve (1m 22.916s) lined up immediately behind Ralf, the Canadian driver having a niggling day which started with a gearbox problem during the morning. In qualifying a suspected electronic glitch forced him to take the spare car, but in contrast Panis reported his car 'didn't feel too bad, but we're not quite quick enough yet.'

Over at Jaguar, Eddie Irvine lost much of free practice before a pushrod failure in qualifying forced him to switch to the spare R2 which was set up for Pedro de la Rosa, the Ulsterman ending up two places behind his colleague as a result.

'Irv' managed a 1m 23.439s, but he carefully rationalised not breaking into the high 1m 22s bracket. 'There's no point in benchmarking our package to the pole position time and the best yardstick of our development has to be the top Michelin runners [Montoya],' he said.

'It could have been better if I hadn't switched to the T-car. Not only was it set up for Pedro, but it didn't have the latest elements of the aero package either. Combine that with the fact that I missed the last two tests and I'm sure I could have got into the 22-second bracket.'

In the Arrows camp, Jos Verstappen (17th on 1m 24.067s) judged that he got everything he could out of the car, steadily improving throughout the session. Team-mate Enrique Bernoldi (1m 24.606s) had a throttle problem on his first run which lost him momentum.

Jenson Button (1m 24.123s) wound up 18th just 0.1s ahead of Giancarlo Fisichella in their Benetton B201s, but over at Minardi Fernando Alonso's satisfaction at having qualified 1s faster than Rubens Barrichello's 2000 pole time was shaded by the fact that Tarso Marques failed to make the 107 per cent qualifying cut after engine problems in the other PS01 challenger.

MIKA Häkkinen arrived at Silverstone with everything to prove, in his own mind, at least. It was almost ten months since he'd last won a Grand Prix and his previous outing at Magny-Cours had seen him fail even to complete the formation lap. Just to round things off, a rare McLaren suspension failure had pitched him into a 190 mph shunt during testing the previous week at Monza. It was surely time for his luck to change.

It did just that. Qualifying second, he decisively out-ran Michael Schumacher's Ferrari F2001 to score his first ever victory in the British Grand Prix. Prior to the race, the McLaren camp had been sending coded messages to the effect that this was the payback race for David Coulthard, the day on which Häkkinen would gift a race win to the Scot in the interests of his championship hopes. But in the event, it simply didn't matter.

As Michael's Ferrari and Mika's McLaren MP4/16-Mercedes sprinted towards Copse, the seeds of Coulthard's downfall were already being sown. He'd got away cleanly from third place on the grid, but Jarno Trulli had been even faster off the mark from fourth spot in his Jordan-Honda EJ-11 and was aiming confidently down the inside of David's McLaren as they swung into the first right-hander.

Coulthard came across and Trulli suddenly began to realise there was not enough room for both of them. He tried desperately to back out of the confrontation, but David didn't give an inch.

As a result, Coulthard's McLaren was suddenly pitched into a half spin which launched him off the track to the right. Thankfully he managed to avoid making contact with any other member of the 22-car pack, but by the time he regained control his car was pointing in the correct direction but now in the pit exit lane and down in a distant 18th place.

Trulli, meanwhile, slammed off the road into the gravel on the left and retired immediately with broken left front suspension.

'I had track space and felt that I was sufficiently far ahead that he [Trulli] should have backed off, given the nature of the corner,' said Coulthard.

'He hit me ahead of my right rear wheel which showed that I was ahead. The car sustained quite serious damage to its undertray and diffuser, but I pressed on for the moment while trying to establish over the radio with the pit just how badly damaged things might be.

'The car didn't feel right, but before we reached a conclusion I'd spun off for good. This would have been a McLaren 1-2 for certain.

'I am very disappointed, but I'm determined to look on the positive side. We had the right strategy and seemed to have a bigger edge over Ferrari than they'd had over us at Nürburgring and Magny-Cours.'

For his part, Trulli was extremely annoyed, particularly as he'd believed his Jordan-Honda might have pipped Coulthard for third place on the starting grid had it not been for a suspension problem on his fastest run in Saturday's qualifying session.

'To be out of the race at such an early stage is incredibly disappointing,' said the Italian. 'I had a very good start and was next to David on the inside by the first corner.

'I don't know whether he just didn't see me, or didn't want to give up his fight, but either way, he closed the door leaving me with no more room to brake or avoid an accident, so our cars touched.

'It was a racing incident and David and I will talk about it, although generally I think the car on the outside should leave enough room for the inside car to move.'

This wasn't the only close encounter in the opening moments of the race. Braking for Copse, Jacques Villeneuve locked up the front wheels of his BAR-Honda and was unable to turn in at the appropriate moment, much to the detriment of his team-mate Olivier Panis.

'Olivier was on the outside of me and when he turned, I couldn't avoid him, so we touched, which put him off,' said an apologetic Villeneuve. 'Things like that happen at the start, but it's not good for the team or [for] Olivier so I feel very sorry about that.'

Häkkinen, meanwhile, was all over Schumacher's Ferrari as they slammed through to complete the opening lap 0.2s apart. Juan Pablo Montoya's Williams FW23 was up to third after a terrific opening lap ahead of Rubens Barrichello's Ferrari F2001, Ralf Schumacher's Williams FW23 and the Sauber C20 of Kimi Räikkönen.

It quickly became clear that Mika had more speed than his key rival, the McLaren running a two-stop strategy compared with the rather ambitious one-stop schedule on which Michael and Ross Brawn had decided.

This strategy had been adopted because the Ferrari management judged that McLaren would probably split its approach, using Häkkinen as hare on a two-stop strategy with Coulthard on a

Left: Michael Schumacher demonstrated a Ferrari 375 owned by Bernie Ecclestone, a sister car of that which won the 1951 British Grand Prix in the hands of Froilan Gonzalez.
Photograph: Clive Mason/Allsport-Getty Images

Below: Heinz-Harald Frentzen prepares for what would be his last race for the Jordan team. He was fired by fax a few days later after a string of disappointing races.
Photograph: Paul-Henri Cahier

Left: Laying down the law — Olivier Panis makes a firm point over the BAR breakfast table.
Photograph: Paul-Henri Cahier

Below: Fernando Alonso's Minardi after shedding its left front wheel.
Photograph: Clive Mason/Allsport-Getty Images

more conservative one-stop run. Not worrying too much what Mika might be up to, Schumacher and Brawn preferred to cover Coulthard's supposed strategy. Although such considerations quickly became academic.

Coulthard continued until mid-way round lap three when his damaged rear suspension pitched his mortally wounded McLaren into the gravel trap and out of the race at the Luffield left-hander.

Mid-way round the fifth lap, Häkkinen proved just how right McLaren's planned two-stop strategy would be, swooping past Schumacher's Ferrari to take the lead on the 175 mph approach to the fast Becketts section of the circuit. Michael had run slightly wide on the exit of Copse and given Mika the chance he needed. He out-accelerated the Ferrari and then chopped commandingly across Michael's nose, effectively winning the day there and then.

From then on his lighter fuel load paid dividends and the Finn streaked away from Michael, the German driver struggling slightly with his car as he worked to fend off the tenacious Juan Pablo Montoya's Williams-BMW.

However, Montoya eventually closed in and took second place from Schumacher going into Copse on lap 18. Häkkinen made his first refuelling stop on lap 21, emerging just behind the Colombian driver but ahead of Schumacher.

'My car wasn't really quite the way I would have liked it,' said Schumacher. 'I had some problems, especially at the entry to Copse corner, where I got sideways a couple of times. The car was not well balanced and I could not get the maximum out of it.'

On lap 25 Montoya made his first refuelling stop, leaving the way clear for Häkkinen to surge back into the lead. By lap 30 Mika led by 13.3s from Schumacher with Barrichello and Ralf Schumacher — who were both on one-stop strategies — next up ahead of a frustrated Montoya who was anxious to pass his unhelpful German team-mate and have a clear run at Barrichello.

Ralf, however, was to be less than accommodating when it

Above right: **Peter Sauber was certainly well pleased with his two drivers at Silverstone.**
Photograph: Bryn Williams/crash.net

Above far right: **Nick Heidfeld heads for a strong sixth place behind Sauber team-mate Kimi Räikkönen.**
Photograph: Clive Mason/Allsport-Getty Images

Right: **Michael Schumacher's fuel-heavy Ferrari tries to fend off Häkkinen's McLaren into Copse corner during the opening phase of the race.**
Photograph: Bryn Williams/crash.net

came to helping his team-mate. Immediately prior to his stop, Montoya was lapping in the mid-1m 24s bracket, but now he found himself running a second a lap slower. Ralf eventually came in for his sole refuelling stop at the end of lap 35, only for a sticking fuel nozzle to keep the Williams stationary for an over-long 12.5s.

Now Häkkinen led by 17.7s from Schumacher with Barrichello third, just 0.2s ahead of Montoya. Then there was a gap to Räikkönen, now ahead of Ralf Schumacher, and Nick Heidfeld in the other Sauber. On lap 37 Ralf Schumacher rolled to a frustrated halt out on the circuit, the result of a big-end failure. 'I heard a strange noise and the engine stopped,' said the Williams driver.

On lap 39 Häkkinen and Schumacher came in to refuel; Mika for the second time, Michael for the first and only time. They resumed over 20s apart and there was nothing Michael could do to close the gap in the 21 laps remaining to the end.

Eventually Häkkinen took the chequered flag over half a minute ahead of Schumacher, but it was a good day for Maranello overall as Barrichello survived to finish a strong third after staying ahead of Montoya through their respective first and second refuelling stops on laps 41 and 42 respectively, the Brazilian making 2.4s just on the time stationary in the pit lane.

'I am happy with this result because this is my first F1 podium at Silverstone,' said Rubens. 'I made up a few places at the start and certainly going for a long first stint was the best idea. The car did not really have the balance I like; all weekend it was different to the way it had been at the test. So I was driving carefully while still trying to be quick. Even with the heavy fuel load, I

was coping well.' In fourth place, Montoya was clearly extremely annoyed at the manner in which he had been blocked by his team-mate Ralf Schumacher immediately after his first refuelling stop, but was sufficiently diplomatic to keep his thoughts to himself, in public at least.

It fell to Patrick Head, the pugnacious technical director of the Williams team, to call a spade a spade. 'If Ralf had let Juan Pablo through as we'd asked him, he would have finished third,' he stated. He later added: 'From eighth and tenth on the grid a fourth place is probably as good as we might expect.'

That left the Sauber C20s of Kimi Räikkönen and Nick Heidfeld to pick up the final two points' scoring positions in fifth and sixth. Heinz-Harald Frentzen disappointed the Jordan team with a rather lacklustre seventh, while Jacques Villeneuve wound up eighth ahead of Eddie Irvine's Jaguar R2.

Irvine ran a two-stop strategy in contrast to team-mate Pedro de la Rosa who had to make an extra unscheduled stop after a glitch with the refuelling rig and run non-stop thereafter to a distant 12th.

Back in the McLaren garage Coulthard took it on the chin. 'Sorry to have damaged the car,' he said to his mechanics. 'No worries,' one of them replied. It was a reassuring remark intended to convey the message that there was always 2002 for the Scot successfully to complete his quest for the World Championship.

By the same token, there was an unspoken acceptance that Silverstone had marked the effective end for DC's title hopes for the current year. And the dream of scoring a hat trick of Silverstone victories was similarly shattered.

Below: **David Coulthard — pondering a first-corner mistake.**
Photograph: Clive Mason/Allsport-Getty Images

Bottom: **Häkkinen looks pensive prior to the start.**

Main photograph: **Michael Schumacher knew that he'd out-scored the right McLaren rival.**
Both photographs: Paul-Henri Cahier

ROUND 11
SILVERSTONE 13–15 JULY 2001

FOSTER'S
BRITISH
grand prix

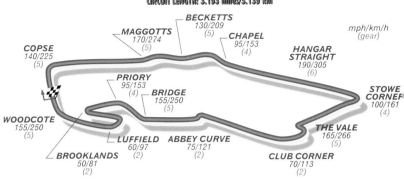

SILVERSTONE – GRAND PRIX CIRCUIT

CIRCUIT LENGTH: 3.193 miles/5.139 km

mph/km/h (gear)

BECKETTS 130/209 (5)
MAGGOTTS 170/274 (5)
CHAPEL 95/153 (4)
COPSE 140/225 (5)
HANGAR STRAIGHT 190/305 (6)
PRIORY 95/153 (4)
BRIDGE 155/250 (5)
STOWE CORNER 100/161 (4)
WOODCOTE 155/250 (5)
LUFFIELD 60/97 (2)
ABBEY CURVE 75/121 (2)
THE VALE 165/266 (5)
BROOKLANDS 50/81 (2)
CLUB CORNER 70/113 (2)

RACE DISTANCE: 60 laps, 191.603 miles/308.356 km   RACE WEATHER: Dry, warm and sunny

Pos.	Driver	Nat.	No.	Entrant	Car/Engine	Tyres	Laps	Time/Retirement	Speed (mph/km/h)	Gap to lea
1	Mika Häkkinen	SF	3	West McLaren Mercedes	McLaren MP4/16-Mercedes F0110K V10	B	60	1h 25m 33.770s	134.359/216.231	
2	Michael Schumacher	D	1	Scuderia Ferrari Marlboro	Ferrari F2001-050 V10	B	60	1h 26m 07.416s	133.485/214.823	+33.6
3	Rubens Barrichello	BR	2	Scuderia Ferrari Marlboro	Ferrari F2001-050 V10	B	60	1h 26m 33.051s	132.825/213.762	+59.2
4	Juan Pablo Montoya	COL	6	BMW WilliamsF1 Team	Williams FW23-BMW P80 V10	M	60	1h 26m 42.542s	132.583/213.372	+68.7
5	Kimi Räikkönen	SF	17	Red Bull Sauber Petronas	Sauber C20-Petronas V10	B	59			+1
6	Nick Heidfeld	D	16	Red Bull Sauber Petronas	Sauber C20-Petronas V10	B	59			+1
7	Heinz-Harald Frentzen	D	11	B&H Jordan Honda	Jordan EJ11-Honda RA001E V10	B	59			+1
8	Jacques Villeneuve	CDN	10	Lucky Strike BAR Honda	BAR 03-Honda RA001E V10	B	59			+1
9	Eddie Irvine	GB	18	Jaguar Racing	Jaguar R2-Cosworth CR3 V10	M	59			+1
10	Jos Verstappen	NL	14	Orange Arrows Asiatech	Arrows A22-Asiatech V10	B	58			+2 ▶
11	Jean Alesi	F	22	Prost Acer	Prost AP04-Acer V10	M	58			+2 ▶
12	Pedro de la Rosa	ESP	19	Jaguar Racing	Jaguar R2-Cosworth CR3 V10	M	58			+2 ▶
13	Giancarlo Fisichella	I	7	Mild Seven Benetton Renault	Benetton B201-Renault RS21 V10	M	58			+2 ▶
14	Enrique Bernoldi	BR	15	Orange Arrows Asiatech	Arrows A22-Asiatech V10	B	58			+2 ▶
15	Jenson Button	GB	8	Mild Seven Benetton Renault	Benetton B201-Renault RS21 V10	M	58			+2 ▶
16	Fernando Alonso	ESP	21	European Minardi F1	Minardi PS01-European V10	M	57			+3 ▶
	Ralf Schumacher	D	5	BMW Williams F1 Team	Williams FW23-BMW P80 V10	M	36	Engine		
	Luciano Burti	BR	23	Prost Acer	Prost AP04-Acer V10	M	6	Engine		
	David Coulthard	GB	4	West McLaren Mercedes	McLaren MP4/16-Mercedes F0110K V10	B	2	Damage from collision with Trulli/spun off		
	Jarno Trulli	I	12	B&H Jordan Honda	Jordan EJ11-Honda RA001E V10	B	0	Collision with Coulthard		
	Olivier Panis	F	9	Lucky Strike BAR Honda	BAR 03-Honda RA001E V10	B	0	Collision with Villeneuve		

Fastest lap: Mika Häkkinen, on lap 34, 1m 23.405s, 137.882 mph/221.900 km/h (record).

Previous lap record: Michael Schumacher (F1 Ferrari F310B-V10), 1m 24.475s, 136.109 mph/219.047 km/h (1997).

Grid order	1	2	3	4	5	6	7	8	9	10	11	12	13	14	15	16	17	18	19	20	21	22	23	24	25	26	27	28	29	30	31	32	33	34	35	36	37	38	39	40	41	42	43	44	45
1 M. SCHUMACHER	1	1	1	1	3	3	3	3	3	3	3	3	3	3	3	3	3	3	3	3	3	3	6	6	6	3	3	3	3	3	3	3	3	3	3	3	3	3	3	3	3	3	3	3	3
3 HÄKKINEN	3	3	3	3	1	1	1	1	1	1	1	1	1	1	1	1	1	6	6	6	6	3	3	3	6	1	1	1	1	1	1	1	1	1	1	1	1	1	1	2	2	1	1	1	1
4 COULTHARD	6	6	6	6	6	6	6	6	6	6	6	6	6	6	6	6	6	1	1	1	1	1	1	1	1	2	2	2	2	2	2	2	2	2	2	2	2	2	2	6	1	2	2	2	2
12 TRULLI	2	2	2	2	2	2	2	2	2	2	2	2	2	2	2	2	2	2	2	2	2	2	2	2	5	5	5	5	5	5	5	5	6	6	6	6	6	1	6	6	6	6	6	6	
11 FRENTZEN	5	5	5	5	5	5	5	5	5	5	5	5	5	5	5	5	5	5	5	5	5	5	5	5	6	6	6	6	6	6	6	6	5	17	17	17	17	17	16	17	17	17	17		
2 BARRICHELLO	17	17	17	17	17	17	17	17	17	17	17	17	17	17	17	17	17	17	17	16	11	11	11	11	10	10	10	10	10	10	10	10	17	17	BARRICHELLO	17	5	16	16	16	11	16	16	16	16
17 RÄIKKÖNEN	16	16	16	16	16	16	16	16	16	16	16	16	16	16	16	16	16	16	17	16	14	10	10	17	17	17	17	17	17	17	17	17	16	16	16	16	11	11	11	11	17	11	11	11	10
6 MONTOYA	11	11	11	11	11	11	11	11	11	11	11	11	11	11	11	11	11	11	11	11	10	17	17	16	16	16	16	16	11	11	11	11	11	14	14	14	14	14	10	10	11	10	10	10	11
16 HEIDFELD	22	22	22	14	14	14	14	14	14	14	14	14	14	14	14	14	14	14	14	10	17	16	16	11	11	11	11	11	11	11	11	10	19	19	14	10	10	10	18	18	18	18	18	18	
5 R. SCHUMACHER	10	10	14	22	22	22	22	22	22	22	10	10	10	10	10	10	10	10	10	17	16	22	22	22	22	22	22	19	19	19	14	14	10	10	18	18	18	14	14	14	14				
9 PANIS	14	14	10	10	10	10	10	10	10	10	22	22	22	22	22	22	22	22	22	22	19	19	19	19	22	14	14	10	18	18	22	22	22	22	22	22	22	22	22						
10 VILLENEUVE	19	19	19	19	19	19	19	19	19	19	19	19	19	19	19	19	19	19	18	18	18	18	18	18	18	18	18	18	18	19	22	8	8	15	15	15	15	19	19	19					
19 DE LA ROSA	8	8	8	8	8	8	8	8	8	8	8	8	8	8	8	8	8	8	8	15	14	14	14	14	14	14	14	22	22	22	22	8	15	15	7	7	7	7	7	7	7				
22 ALESI	15	15	15	15	15	15	15	15	15	15	15	15	15	15	15	15	15	15	18	7	7	8	8	8	8	8	8	8	15	21	8	15	21	8	19	19	19	19	15	15	15				
18 IRVINE	18	18	18	18	18	18	18	15	15	15	15	15	15	15	15	15	15	15	15	15	15	15	15	15	21	7	7	19	8	8	8	8	8												
23 BURTI	23	23	23	23	23	21	21	21	21	21	21	21	21	21	21	21	21	8	21	15	21	21	21	21	21	21	21	21	21	7	19	19	21	21	21	21	21	21	21						
14 VERSTAPPEN	7	7	7	21	21	23	7	7	7	7	7	7	7	7	7	7	7	7	7	8	21	7	7	7	7	7	7	7	7	7	7	19													
8 BUTTON	4	4	21	7	7	7																																							
7 FISICHELLA	21	21																																											
15 BERNOLDI																																													
21 ALONSO																																													

Pit stop
One lap behind leader

STARTING GRID

1 M. SCHUMACHER Ferrari	**3** HÄKKINEN McLaren
4 COULTHARD McLaren	**12** TRULLI Jordan
11 FRENTZEN Jordan	**2** BARRICHELLO Ferrari
17 RÄIKKÖNEN Sauber	**6** MONTOYA Williams
16 HEIDFELD Sauber	**5** R. SCHUMACHER Williams
9 PANIS BAR	**10** VILLENEUVE BAR
19 DE LA ROSA Jaguar	**22** ALESI Prost
18 IRVINE Jaguar	**23** BURTI Prost
14 VERSTAPPEN Arrows	**8** BUTTON Benetton
7 FISICHELLA Benetton	**15** BERNOLDI Arrows
21 ALONSO Minardi	

TIME SHEETS

QUALIFYING
Weather: Dry, warm and sunny

Pos.	Driver	Car	Laps	Time
1	Michael Schumacher	Ferrari	12	1m 20.447s
2	Mika Häkkinen	McLaren-Mercedes	12	1m 20.529s
3	David Coulthard	McLaren Mercedes	12	1m 20.927s
4	Jarno Trulli	Jordan-Honda	10	1m 20.930s
5	Heinz-Harald Frentzen	Jordan-Honda	12	1m 21.217s
6	Rubens Barrichello	Ferrari	12	1m 21.715s
7	Kimi Räikkönen	Sauber-Petronas	12	1m 22.023s
8	Juan Pablo Montoya	Williams-BMW	9	1m 22.219s
9	Nick Heidfeld	Sauber-Petronas	11	1m 22.223s
10	Ralf Schumacher	Williams-BMW	9	1m 22.283s
11	Olivier Panis	BAR-Honda	12	1m 22.316s
12	Jacques Villeneuve	BAR-Honda	11	1m 22.916s
13	Pedro de la Rosa	Jaguar-Cosworth	12	1m 23.273s
14	Jean Alesi	Prost-Acer	12	1m 23.392s
15	Eddie Irvine	Jaguar-Cosworth	11	1m 23.439s
16	Luciano Burti	Jaguar-Cosworth	12	1m 23.735s
17	Jos Verstappen	Arrows-Asiatech	12	1m 24.067s
18	Jenson Button	Benetton-Renault	12	1m 24.123s
19	Giancarlo Fisichella	Benetton-Renault	12	1m 24.275s
20	Enrique Bernoldi	Arrows-Asiatech	10	1m 24.606s
21	Fernando Alonso	Minardi-European	12	1m 24.792s
	107% time			1m 26.078s
22	Tarso Marques	Minardi-European	12	1m 26.506s

FRIDAY FREE PRACTICE
Weather: Warm and windy, then rain shower

Pos.	Driver	Laps	Time
1	Mika Häkkinen	35	1m 22.827s
2	David Coulthard	42	1m 22.894s
3	Rubens Barrichello	41	1m 23.578s
4	Michael Schumacher	46	1m 23.619s
5	Heinz-Harald Frentzen	38	1m 23.877s
6	Nick Heidfeld	42	1m 24.096s
7	Pedro de la Rosa	22	1m 24.116s
8	Ralf Schumacher	42	1m 24.222s
9	Jarno Trulli	47	1m 24.343s
10	Kimi Räikkönen	39	1m 24.387s
11	Jacques Villeneuve	37	1m 24.436s
12	Olivier Panis	37	1m 24.562s
13	Eddie Irvine	43	1m 24.733s
14	Jean Alesi	38	1m 24.832s
15	Jos Verstappen	41	1m 25.026s
16	Enrique Bernoldi	36	1m 25.209s
17	Juan Pablo Montoya	38	1m 25.267s
18	Luciano Burti	32	1m 25.448s
19	Jenson Button	35	1m 25.673s
20	Fernando Alonso	34	1m 26.695s
21	Giancarlo Fisichella	26	1m 26.730s
22	Tarso Marques	31	1m 27.203s

SATURDAY FREE PRACTICE
Weather: Wet and overcast

Pos.	Driver	Laps	Time
1	Michael Schumacher	12	1m 31.430s
2	Heinz-Harald Frentzen	28	1m 31.803s
3	Mika Häkkinen	20	1m 31.849s
4	David Coulthard	24	1m 32.014s
5	Rubens Barrichello	19	1m 32.128s
6	Nick Heidfeld	29	1m 33.837s
7	Jarno Trulli	29	1m 33.879s
8	Kimi Räikkönen	23	1m 34.069s
9	Olivier Panis	20	1m 34.097s
10	Ralf Schumacher	18	1m 34.248s
11	Juan Pablo Montoya	21	1m 34.674s
12	Pedro de la Rosa	26	1m 35.157s
13	Jos Verstappen	21	1m 35.173s
14	Enrique Bernoldi	25	1m 35.402s
15	Giancarlo Fisichella	19	1m 35.624s
16	Jacques Villeneuve	6	1m 35.690s
17	Jenson Button	23	1m 35.974s
18	Jean Alesi	18	1m 36.193s
19	Luciano Burti	20	1m 37.203s
20	Fernando Alonso	16	1m 38.748s
21	Tarso Marques	14	1m 40.199s
22	Eddie Irvine	7	1m 43.227s

WARM-UP
Weather: Dry, warm and sunny

Pos.	Driver	Laps	Time
1	David Coulthard	14	1m 22.994s
2	Jarno Trulli	14	1m 23.182s
3	Mika Häkkinen	16	1m 23.416s
4	Heinz-Harald Frentzen	17	1m 24.052s
5	Michael Schumacher	14	1m 24.407s
6	Olivier Panis	14	1m 24.598s
7	Kimi Räikkönen	17	1m 24.609s
8	Ralf Schumacher	18	1m 24.631s
9	Rubens Barrichello	13	1m 24.657s
10	Eddie Irvine	16	1m 25.147s
11	Jacques Villeneuve	18	1m 25.217s
12	Juan Pablo Montoya	15	1m 25.260s
13	Jos Verstappen	17	1m 25.581s
14	Enrique Bernoldi	15	1m 25.658s
15	Nick Heidfeld	8	1m 25.734s
16	Pedro de la Rosa	13	1m 26.463s
17	Fernando Alonso	16	1m 26.988s
18	Giancarlo Fisichella	5	1m 27.198s
19	Jenson Button	17	1m 27.987s
20	Jean Alesi	18	1m 28.060s
21	Luciano Burti	17	1m 28.240s

RACE FASTEST LAPS
Weather: Dry, warm and sunny

Driver	Time	Lap
Mika Häkkinen	1m 23.405s	34
Michael Schumacher	1m 23.928s	42
Juan Pablo Montoya	1m 24.437s	23
Rubens Barrichello	1m 24.445s	44
Eddie Irvine	1m 24.544s	59
Kimi Räikkönen	1m 24.563s	34
Nick Heidfeld	1m 24.765s	46
Heinz-Harald Frentzen	1m 25.029s	23
Ralf Schumacher	1m 25.188s	33
Pedro de la Rosa	1m 25.739s	33
Jacques Villeneuve	1m 25.809s	27
Jos Verstappen	1m 26.394s	40
Jean Alesi	1m 26.497s	29
Enrique Bernoldi	1m 26.695s	25
Giancarlo Fisichella	1m 26.798s	41
Jenson Button	1m 26.963s	24
Fernando Alonso	1m 27.091s	30
David Coulthard	1m 28.908s	2
Luciano Burti	1m 29.252s	4

CHASSIS LOG BOOK

	Driver	Chassis
1	M. Schumacher	Ferrari F2001/210
2	Barrichello	Ferrari F2001/206
	spare	Ferrari F2001/211
3	Häkkinen	McLaren MP4/16/7
4	Coulthard	McLaren MP4/16/6
	spare	McLaren MP4/16/5
5	R. Schumacher	Williams FW23/5
6	Montoya	Williams FW23/6
	spare	Williams FW23/2
7	Fisichella	Benetton B201/6
8	Button	Benetton B201/5
	spares	Benetton B201/3 & 2
9	Panis	BAR 03/6
10	Villeneuve	BAR 03/7
	spare	BAR 03/4
11	Frentzen	Jordan EJ11/4
12	Trulli	Jordan EJ11/5
	spares	Jordan EJ11/6 & 2
14	Verstappen	Arrows A22/6
15	Bernoldi	Arrows A22/3
	spare	Arrows A22/1
16	Heidfeld	Sauber C20/7
17	Räikkönen	Sauber C20/6
	spare	Sauber C20/1
18	Irvine	Jaguar R2/4
19	de la Rosa	Jaguar R2/6
	spare	Jaguar R2/5
20	Marques	Minardi PS01/4
21	Alonso	Minardi PS01/3
	spare	Minardi PS01/1
22	Alesi	Prost AP04/6
23	Burti	Prost AP04/5
	spare	Prost AP04/2

POINTS TABLES

DRIVERS

	Driver	Points
1	Michael Schumacher	84
2	David Coulthard	47
3	Rubens Barrichello	34
4	Ralf Schumacher	31
5	Mika Häkkinen	19
6	Juan Pablo Montoya	15
7	Nick Heidfeld	10
8 =	Kimi Räikkönen	9
8 =	Jarno Trulli	9
10	Jacques Villeneuve	7
11	Heinz-Harald Frentzen	6
12	Olivier Panis	5
13	Eddie Irvine	4
14	Jean Alesi	3
15 =	Jos Verstappen	1
15 =	Pedro de la Rosa	1
15 =	Giancarlo Fisichella	1

CONSTRUCTORS

	Constructor	Points
1	Ferrari	118
2	McLaren	66
3	Williams	46
4	Sauber	19
5	Jordan	15
6	BAR	12
7	Jaguar	5
8	Prost	3
9 =	Arrows	1
9 =	Benetton	1

FOR THE RECORD

400th Grand Prix point
Mika Häkkinen

Lap chart (partial)

49	50	51	52	53	54	55	56	57	58	59	60	
3	3	3	3	3	3	3	3	3	3	3	3	1
1	1	1	1	1	1	1	1	1	1	1	1	2
2	2	2	2	2	2	2	2	2	2	2	2	3
6	6	6	6	6	6	6	6	6	6	6	6	4
17	17	17	17	17	17	17	17	17	17	17		5
16	16	16	16	16	16	16	16	16	16	16		6
11	11	11	11	11	11	11	11	11	11	11		
10	10	10	10	10	10	10	10	10	10	10		
18	18	18	18	18	18	18	18	18	18	18		
14	14	14	14	14	14	14	14	14	14			
22	22	22	22	22	22	22	22	22	22			
19	19	19	19	19	19	19	19	19	19			
7	7	7	7	7	7	7	7	7				
15	15	15	15	15	15	15	15	15				
8	8	8	8	8	8	8	8	8				
21	21	21	21	21	21	21	21					

FIA WORLD CHAMPIONSHIP • ROUND 12

GERMAN
grand prix

1st - R. SCHUMACHER • 2nd - BARRICHELLO • 3rd - VILLENEUVE

Main photograph: Ralf Schumacher saved the day for the BMW Williams team, posting his third win of the season after team-mate Juan Pablo Montoya's sister car expired with engine failure while well in the lead.
Photograph: Bryn Williams/crash.net

Inset: Ralf signs autographs for his vociferous home-track fans.
Photograph: Steve Etherington/EPI

HOCKENHEIM QUALIFYING

When Jarno Trulli's Jordan-Honda stopped out on the circuit with about seven minutes of qualifying still to go at Hockenheim on Saturday afternoon, the Italian driver understandably found a degree of ambivalence from the marshals when it came to finding a lift back to the paddock.

It seemed that the track officials were as put out as the paying public over Eddie Jordan's decision to replace Heinz-Harald Frentzen in his line-up for the German Grand Prix. But that was kid's stuff compared with the race-morning warm-up.

First Trulli stopped again with another engine failure and Ricardo Zonta soon afterwards spun into a gravel trap in the other Jordan-Honda EJ-11. Frentzen, sunning himself in distant Spain, must have been choking over his breakfast with the sheer mirth of the situation.

Trulli qualified a distant 10th as a result, but however a clear run he might have enjoyed, there was never much prospect of his getting on terms with the Williams FW23-BMWs of Juan Pablo Montoya and Ralf Schumacher. Nor anybody else, come to that.

'Everybody worked so hard for this,' said Montoya after pipping his team-mate for pole with a 1m 38.117s best.

'Ralf ran me pretty close. He did four runs, I did three and my second one went so well. The car was working very well and we did a [set-up] change for the last run and I was two-tenths up already on my time. Then when Ralf crossed the line they told me to back off.'

Throughout the weekend the competing teams had to battle sweltering temperatures in addition to the punishingly long straights which exact a fierce toll on the high-revving V10s. On the tyre front, Michelin certainly seemed to have the upper hand on this occasion, the French tyre maker reacting promptly by strengthening its carcasses in the wake of a tyre failure on Ralf Schumacher's Williams in testing at Monza ten days earlier.

Over in the McLaren-Mercedes camp, Mika Häkkinen was revelling in the fine handling balance of his low-downforce MP4/16, but privately worrying that he could do with more power. He wound up third on 1m 38.811s, but team-mate David Coulthard was unaccountably and continually blistering tyres, ending up fifth on 1m 39.574s.

Turned out in ultra low-downforce trim, Häkkinen touched 224 mph on the straight during qualifying, but the overall package wasn't enough to keep the MP4/16s in play in a straight fight against Ferrari, let alone the Williams-BMWs.

Michael Schumacher's Ferrari F2001 wound up fourth on 1m 38.941s, just 0.824s away from pole. 'It wasn't such a good qualifying session for us,' admitted Maranello technical director Ross Brawn.

'We did not get the car working well on all parts of the track and had some wheel locking problems. Michael was as quick as the Williams in the third sector, so they are clearly making up time in the forest.' Barrichello wound up sixth behind Coulthard, the Brazilian managing a 1m 39.682s.

At Sauber, Nick Heidfeld (1m 39.921s) and Kimi Räikkönen (1m 40.072s) both did terrific jobs to qualify seventh and eighth. Heidfeld admitted they got the car 'just right' for qualifying, but Räikkönen complained that his car felt too nervous every time he touched a chicane kerb.

For Jaguar, Pedro de la Rosa wound up ninth on 1m 40.265s, the Spaniard very satisfied to have out-run Eddie Irvine (1m 40.371s) by two places on the grid. Irvine believed he could have done better had he not been obliged to abort his final run coming into the stadium due to waved yellow flags after Luciano Burti spun off in his Prost.

Jacques Villeneuve (1m 40.437s) and Olivier Panis (1m 40.610s) were next up, struggling for grip and grappling with lack of Honda power, in their BAR 003s. Frentzen's replacement Ricardo Zonta was next on 1m 41.174s, sandwiched between the Prost AP04s of Jean Alesi (1m 40.724s) and Burti (1m 41.213s).

Giancarlo Fisichella (1m 41.299s) and Jenson Button (1m 41.438s) in the Benetton-Renaults seemed to be struggling in 17th and 18th places with precious little indication of the promising time to come on Sunday.

Fisichella needed an engine change and had to go straight into qualifying with a race-spec V10 while Button lost crucial time in the morning with gearbox trouble.

Rounding off the grid were the two Arrows A22s of Enrique Bernoldi and Jos Verstappen, who spun on the last lap, and the Minardis of Fernando Alonso and Tarso Marques which were understandably breathless on this super-fast circuit.

Right: This five-shot sequence illustrates just what a lucky escape Luciano Burti enjoyed after rolling his Prost over the back of Michael Schumacher's stricken Ferrari as the pack accelerated away from the grid.
All photographs: Mark Thompson/Allsport-Getty Images

Below: Brazilians step out together — the hapless Burti (left) with his compatriot Rubens Barrichello walk out to the pre-race driver parade.
Photograph: Bryn Williams/crash.net

Diary

Toyota F1 boss Ove Andersson reaffirms his confidence that Allan McNish will be a member of the Japanese company's race team in 2002.

Ferrari confirms deal to continue using Bridgestone tyres until the end of 2004.

CART racer Alex Barron predicts 200-mph-plus lap speeds at the forthcoming Rockingham 500 after testing at Britain's new bespoke oval track in preparation for its first Champ car fixture.

Justin Wilson extends F3000 championship points lead after strong second place at Hockenheim.

Kenny Bräck increases CART points lead with commanding victory at Chicago ahead of Patrick Carpentier and Gil de Ferran.

Above: His time would come — Montoya dominated the race until his car overheated at a delayed refuelling stop.
Photograph: Paul-Henri Cahier

JUAN Pablo Montoya's chances of a first F1 victory were cruelly dashed as he dominated the German Grand Prix at Hockenheim, the Colombian running 9.6s ahead of his BMW Williams team-mate Ralf Schumacher when his bid for glory collapsed at his sole refuelling stop.

On lap 22 of the 45-lap race Montoya pulled into the pit lane for what should have been a routine 8s break in his run to victory. In fact a glitch in the electronic software controlling the pre-programmed refuelling rig meant that no fuel was being delivered to the waiting FW23.

The refuelling crew quickly switched to Ralf Schumacher's rig, but by the time the Colombian's car finally accelerated back into the fray it had been stationary for 29.9s. The damage had been done.

The residual heat build-up in the sweltering 32-degree ambient temperature had tipped the BMW V10 over its operating limits. Three laps later, with Montoya flying in third place, an overheated exhaust valve failed and his Williams rolled to a halt in a cloud of smoke.

'I am so disappointed,' said Montoya. 'I cannot find the words to describe how I feel. Up to the pit stop the race was going perfectly for me. We then had a problem with the refuelling rig and this lost me the lead. [Then] I had a safe second and two laps later the engine just went.'

Ralf Schumacher was thus left with an easy win in the 12th round of the World Championship, his third this season for the Williams-BMW-Michelin alliance which can be expected to duplicate this form on forthcoming high-speed circuits including Spa-Francorchamps, Monza, Indianapolis and Suzuka.

The younger Schumacher didn't miss a chance of having a dig at Montoya by suggesting that his less experienced rival had pushed too hard.

Yet Williams technical director Patrick Head certainly declined to back up that contention. 'Nothing Juan Pablo was doing in any way used his engine harder than Ralf,' he said. 'He was using no more revs. When it goes against you, it goes against you, but he had everyone covered, including his team-mate, and is very happy.'

Montoya had accelerated cleanly away from pole position only for chaos to explode in his wake as Michael Schumacher's Ferrari, starting from fourth place on the grid, suddenly slowed with gear selection problems during the sprint to the first corner.

The pack scattered to avoid him, but the hapless Luciano Burti was not so fortunate, a car immediately ahead of his Prost jinking to one side just in time to leave the young Brazilian facing the near-stationary rear wing of the World Champion's Ferrari.

In a split second, Burti's Prost was catapulted high into the air over the back of Schumacher's car, cartwheeling down the road in company with its rivals and actually bouncing on the sidepod of Enrique Bernoldi's Arrows before crashing to a halt against the tyre barrier.

Burti was thankfully unhurt, but the collision had left razor-sharp shards of carbon fibre scattered across the full width of the circuit. The safety car was initially deployed, but the race was quickly red flagged on safety grounds. Bernoldi was also shaken. 'I think I was pretty lucky at the start,' he admitted. 'I got away well from the grid, but the next thing I knew there was a car sailing over my head. The wheel landed on my car and broke the engine cover and rear wing. It was a pretty big hit, so I was glad to see the red flag.'

Schumacher and Burti were both able to take the restart, in the spare Ferrari and Prost respectively, and it was Montoya who again made a clear getaway to lead from his team-mate Ralf. Going down the first chicane, Pedro de la Rosa's Jaguar got a little

too close to Nick Heidfeld's Sauber and ran into the back of his rival under braking, eliminating both cars on the spot.

By the end of the opening lap Montoya was 2.1s ahead of Ralf Schumacher and next time round the two Williams-BMWs had opened a 1.9s advantage over Michael Schumacher in third place. Next up were Mika Häkkinen's McLaren MP4/16, Rubens Barrichello's Ferrari, David Coulthard's McLaren and Kimi Räikkönen's Sauber.

By the end of the third lap, some fancy footwork between the two Ferraris saw Barrichello vaulting up to fourth and the pack settled down with the two McLaren-Mercedes struggling to keep pace with their Italian rivals on the long straights through the pine forests.

On lap five there was an uncomfortable moment when Ricardo Zonta's Jordan tagged the rear end of Jos Verstappen's Arrows. Zonta pitted for repairs, but the collision had damaged his Jordan's left front suspension, bargeboard and brake cooling duct, so he was out a couple of laps later.

Both drivers disagreed over who was to blame and Verstappen was also winged in the collision, having to make his first refuelling stop early in order to check for damage.

With ten laps completed Montoya had eased open a 6.1s advantage. Ralf in turn was 3.3s ahead of Barrichello who had moved ahead of Michael Schumacher, while Häkkinen was next ahead of Coulthard and the rest of the pack strung out behind.

Battling for the distinction of being the best Honda runner, Olivier Panis forced his BAR ahead of Jarno Trulli's Jordan when he straightlined the first chicane on lap 12. Trulli thought he would give back the place as they braked for the Ostkurve, but Panis was having none of it and Jarno spun off trying to avoid him.

'Regulations state that he should have let me have my position back, so I tried to overtake him at the next chicane and he closed the door, which I didn't expect,' said Trulli.

'He closed the door, I had to turn in quickly to avoid an accident, and spun off.' That left Panis and his team-mate Jacques Villeneuve running eighth and ninth behind Räikkönen's Sauber.

For his part, Panis had nothing to say. He clearly didn't believe that he'd done anything wrong. 'I tried very hard to overtake him, but was losing a lot of time,' he shrugged.

Häkkinen was next to go mid-way round lap 14 while hanging onto fifth place. 'I was very confident with the car and happy with

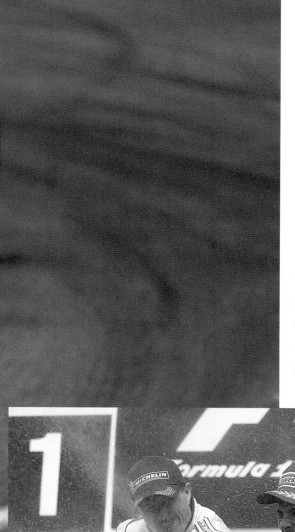

following his 8.6s refuelling stop on lap 27, DC became the latest casualty to drop out with engine failure.

The way the race was unfolding, this was clearly pay-off time for those who had reliability on their side. Ralf duly reeled off the laps to his third victory of the season and Barrichello stormed home an obviously satisfied second.

'Given that we felt the Williams was on another level, the two-stop strategy was the right decision and I was the only one who could match their pace at the start thanks to that strategy,' said Rubens who had a great fight with Coulthard as he was making up ground following his first stop.

Jacques Villeneuve's run to third place reflected an impressive use of a one-stop strategy on lap 24 in contrast to team-mate Olivier Panis who finished seventh after a two-stop run.

'We weren't very competitive all weekend,' he admitted with characteristic candour. 'But on race morning, surprisingly, in the warm-up, after a few changes on the car it was really rather good with fuel on board so we knew we had the chance to do a good race.

'When Olivier got close to me he was going a lot faster, so I let him by so he could play with Jarno a little and what I was hoping happened. Jarno went off, so then I was just trying to stay in Olivier's tow so he could carry me along.'

Fourth and fifth places were earned by the Benetton-Renault B201s of Giancarlo Fisichella and Jenson Button who had a technically untroubled afternoon for a change.

'I drove conservatively in the early stages and saved enough fuel to do a slightly longer first stint than planned,' said Fisichella. 'When I rejoined I was ahead of Jenson and things continued to go well, although I ran slightly wide near the end and lost a bit of time.'

Moreover, as Button correctly observed, the Benettons had genuinely good pace. 'My car was very well balanced and I think we were quicker than the Jordans and the BARs when we were running the same fuel load,' he said. 'I had one problem. I pulled my water bottle tube out of my mouth so it was spraying all over my face whenever I braked. It wasn't an easy race, especially with Alesi right behind, but it was good fun.'

Alesi finished sixth ahead of Panis with the Arrows of Bernoldi and Verstappen heading Fernando Alonso's Minardi home as the final finisher.

For Ralf Schumacher, of course, it was his 'Day of Days'. Not since Rudolf Caracciola's Mercedes won the 1939 race at the Nürburgring had a German driver been propelled to victory in the German Grand Prix by a German engine.

That said it all, really.

ALESI POISED TO REPLACE FRENTZEN

French veteran Jean Alesi finished the German GP weekend poised to replace Heinz-Harald Frentzen in the Jordan-Honda squad after team chief Eddie Jordan abruptly fired the German driver only four days before his home race at Hockenheim.

The plan mooted was for Alesi (37), who won the 1989 F3000 championship for Jordan, to join the Silverstone-based team as part of a complex deal which would boost the precarious finances of the cash-strapped Prost team.

With Honda's support it was being speculated that Alesi could join the team in time for the Hungarian GP on 19 August. Prost sources said there was no way Alesi could leave before the end of the season under the terms of his contract, but relations were already tense between the two Frenchman following a rather public difference of views after the French GP, a race which Alesi regarded as particularly disappointing.

Ideally, Jordan wanted to secure the services of 19-year-old Fernando Alonso, now with Minardi, but the Spaniard was contracted to Renault via Flavio Briatore's management company. So Eddie Jordan pursued the Alesi deal instead.

The decision to ditch Frentzen came after a blazing row between him and Jordan after the British GP. Frentzen was left threatening to sue Jordan for the £5 million he was due to earn under the terms of his next year's contract.

'It has been a disappointing season for both of us,' explained Eddie Jordan. 'We had an exchange of views following the British Grand Prix and this is the outcome.'

A statement from Frentzen said: 'My position in this matter is now under legal advice. Due to the current situation, I am unable to make any further comment whatsoever at this time.'

Jordan was also expected to test British F3 championship leader Takuma Sato and F3000 front-runner Justin Wilson. But for the moment, Alesi was the first choice. And would duly get the drive.

the situation,' he said. 'All of a sudden I felt a vibration behind me, saw smoke and the engine stopped.'

Lap 16 saw Barrichello make his first stop from third place in 8.9s, emerging fifth behind Michael Schumacher and Coulthard. On the same lap Eddie Irvine's Jaguar R2 succumbed with a fuel pressure problem caused by a system blockage on a day when the Ulsterman reckoned he was well on course for a finish in the points.

'Regardless of how many cars dropped out, we were always well placed to fight for points and it's very disappointing to retire in this manner,' he shrugged. 'Big shame, especially since the car felt so good and well balanced.'

Montoya's disastrous refuelling stop followed on lap 22 with Ralf surging through into the lead, leaving brother Michael to bring the Ferrari in from what was second place next time round. The red car was stationary for 10.7s, but had scarcely accelerated back into the race when it stopped by the side of the track with a rare fuel-pump failure.

With Montoya also out for good next time round, the order was now Ralf Schumacher from Barrichello and Coulthard, the Scot seemingly in with a chance of turning the tide which had run against him for so long. Alas, a few hundred yards after rejoining

grösser MOBIL 1 PREIS VON DEUTSCHLAND

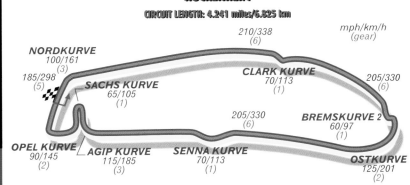

HOCKENHEIM
CIRCUIT LENGTH: 4.241 miles/6.825 km

mph/km/h
(gear)

NORDKURVE
100/161
(3)
185/298
(5)

SACHS KURVE
65/105
(1)

210/338
(6)

CLARK KURVE
70/113
(1)

205/330
(6)

205/330
(6)

BREMSKURVE 2
60/97
(1)

OPEL KURVE
90/145
(2)

AGIP KURVE
115/185
(3)

SENNA KURVE
70/113
(1)

OSTKURVE
125/201
(2)

RACE DISTANCE: 45 laps, 190.838 miles/307.125 km   RACE WEATHER: Very hot and sunny

Pos.	Driver	Nat.	No.	Entrant	Car/Engine	Tyres	Laps	Time/Retirement	Speed (mph/km/h)	Gap to lea
1	Ralf Schumacher	D	5	BMW WilliamsF1 Team	Williams FW23-BMW P80 V10	M	45	1h 18m 17.873s	146.240/235.351	
2	Rubens Barrichello	BR	2	Scuderia Ferrari Marlboro	Ferrari F2001-050 V10	B	45	1h 19m 03.990s	144.818/233.063	+46.1
3	Jacques Villeneuve	CDN	10	Lucky Strike BAR Honda	BAR 03-Honda RA001E V10	B	45	1h 19m 20.679s	144.311/232.246	+62.8
4	Giancarlo Fisichella	I	7	Mild Seven Benetton Renault	Benetton B201-Renault RS21 V10	M	45	1h 19m 21.350s	144.290/232.213	+63.4
5	Jenson Button	GB	8	Mild Seven Benetton Renault	Benetton B201-Renault RS21 V10	M	45	1h 19m 23.327s	144.231/232.117	+65.4
6	Jean Alesi	F	22	Prost Acer	Prost AP04-Acer V10	M	45	1h 19m 23.823s	144.215/232.092	+65.9
7	Olivier Panis	F	9	Lucky Strike BAR Honda	BAR 03-Honda RA001E V10	B	45	1h 19m 35.400s	143.866/231.530	+77.5
8	Enrique Bernoldi	BR	15	Orange Arrows Asiatech	Arrows A22-Asiatech V10	B	44			+1
9	Jos Verstappen	NL	14	Orange Arrows Asiatech	Arrows A22-Asiatech V10	B	44			+1
10	Fernando Alonso	ESP	21	European Minardi F1	Minardi PS01-European V10	M	44			+1
	Jarno Trulli	I	12	B&H Jordan Honda	Jordan EJ11-Honda RA001E V10	B	34	Hydraulics		
	David Coulthard	GB	4	West McLaren Mercedes	McLaren MP4/16-Mercedes FO110K V10	B	27	Engine		
	Tarso Marques	BR	20	European Minardi F1	Minardi PS01-European V10	M	26	Engine		
	Juan Pablo Montoya	COL	6	BMW WilliamsF1 Team	Williams FW23-BMW P80 V10	M	24	Engine		
	Michael Schumacher	D	1	Scuderia Ferrari Marlboro	Ferrari F2001-050 V10	B	23	Fuel pressure		
	Luciano Burti	BR	23	Prost Acer	Prost AP04-Acer V10	M	23	Spun off		
	Kimi Räikkönen	SF	17	Red Bull Sauber Petronas	Sauber C20-Petronas V10	B	16	Driveshaft		
	Eddie Irvine	GB	18	Jaguar Racing	Jaguar R2-Cosworth CR3 V10	M	16	Fuel blockage		
	Mika Häkkinen	SF	3	West McLaren Mercedes	McLaren MP4/16-Mercedes FO110K V10	B	13	Engine		
	Ricardo Zonta	BR	11	B&H Jordan Honda	Jordan EJ11-Honda RA001E V10	B	7	Accident damage		
	Nick Heidfeld	D	16	Red Bull Sauber Petronas	Sauber C20-Petronas V10	B	0	Collision with de la Rosa		
	Pedro de la Rosa	ESP	19	Jaguar Racing	Jaguar R2-Cosworth CR3 V10	M	0	Collision with Heidfeld		

Fastest lap: Juan Pablo Montoya, on lap 20, 1m 41.808s, 149.959 mph/241.336 km/h (record).

Previous lap record: Rubens Barrichello (Ferrari F1-2000-V10), 1m 44.300s, 146.376 mph/235.570 km/h (2000).

Grid order	1	2	3	4	5	6	7	8	9	10	11	12	13	14	15	16	17	18	19	20	21	22	23	24	25	26	27	28	29	30	31	32	33	34	35	36	37	38	39	40	41	42	43	44	45	
6 MONTOYA	6	6	6	6	6	6	6	6	6	6	6	6	6	6	6	6	6	6	6	6	6	6	5	5	5	5	5	5	5	5	5	5	5	5	5	5	5	5	5	5	5	5	5	5	1	
5 R. SCHUMACHER	5	5	5	5	5	5	5	5	5	5	5	5	5	5	5	5	5	5	5	5	1	2	2	2	2	2	2	2	2	2	2	2	2	2	2	2	2	2	2	2	2	2	2	2	2	
3 HÄKKINEN	1	1	1	1	2	2	2	2	2	2	2	2	2	2	2	1	1	1	1	1	2	6	4	4	4	10	10	10	10	10	10	10	10	10	10	10	10	10	10	10	10	10	10	10	3	
1 M. SCHUMACHER	3	3	2	2	2	1	1	1	1	1	1	1	1	1	1	4	4	4	2	2	2	6	4	7	10	7	7	7	7	7	7	7	7	7	7	7	7	7	7	7	7	7	7	7	4	
4 COULTHARD	2	2	3	3	3	3	3	3	3	3	3	3	4	4	4	2	2	2	4	4	4	10	22	10	7	9	9	9	8	8	8	8	8	8	8	8	8	8	8	8	8	8	8	8	5	
2 BARRICHELLO	4	4	4	4	4	4	4	4	17	17	9	10	10	10	10	10	10	10	10	10	12	9	8	9	22	22	22	22	22	22	22	22	22	22	22	22	22	22	22	22	22	22	22	22	6	
16 HEIDFELD	17	17	17	17	17	17	17	17	17	17	17	17	17	9	9	10	8	8	8	8	8	8	12	9	8	22	22	22	9	9	9	9	9	9	9	9	9	9	9	9	9	9	9	9		
17 RÄIKKÖNEN	18	18	18	18	18	18	18	18	18	18	18	18	9	10	10	8	7	7	7	7	7	7	22	9	8	22	15	12	12	12	12	12	15	15	15	15	15	15	15	15	15					
19 DE LA ROSA	12	12	12	12	12	12	12	12	12	9	9	10	8	8	7	22	22	22	22	22	22	12	8	22	12	12	15	15	15	15	15	14	14	14	14	14	14	14	14	14	14					
12 TRULLI	10	10	10	10	10	10	10	10	10	9	9	10	8	7	7	22	23	12	12	12	12	9	15	15	15	14	14	14	14	14	14	21	21	21	21	21	21	21	21							
18 IRVINE	14	14	14	14	14	9	9	9	10	10	8	7	22	22	23	12	9	9	23	23	23	14	14	14	14	21	21	21	21	21	21															
10 VILLENEUVE	11	11	11	11	9	14	8	8	8	8	7	22	7	22	22	9	23	23	23	23	23	23	14	21	21	21																				
9 PANIS		8	9	9	11	15	15	15	15	15	15	15	23	12	12	17	15	15	15	15	15	15	21	20	20																					
22 ALESI		9	9	8	8	15	8	7	7	7	7	22	12	18	18	15	14	14	14	14	14	14	20																							
11 ZONTA		7	15	15	15	8	7	23	23	22	22	23	21	15	15	18	20	20	20	21	21	21	21																							
23 BURTI	15	7	7	7	23	7	22	22	23	23	23	21	18	20	14	14	21	21	21	20	20	20	20																							
7 FISICHELLA	23	23	23	23	7	23	23	22	21	21	21	21	14	14	14	20																														
8 BUTTON	22	22	22	22	22	21	14	20	20	20	20	20	15	21	21																															
15 BERNOLDI	21	21	21	21	21	11	20	14	14	14	14	14																																		
14 VERSTAPPEN	20	20	20	20	20	20	11																																							
21 ALONSO																																														
20 MARQUES																																														

Pit stop
One lap behind leader

STARTING GRID

6 **MONTOYA** Williams	5 **R. SCHUMACHER** Williams
3 **HÄKKINEN** McLaren	1 **M. SCHUMACHER** Ferrari
4 **COULTHARD** McLaren	2 **BARRICHELLO** Ferrari
16 **HEIDFELD** Sauber	17 **RÄIKKÖNEN** Sauber
19 **DE LA ROSA** Jaguar	12 **TRULLI** Jordan
18 **IRVINE** Jaguar	10 **VILLENEUVE** BAR
9 **PANIS** BAR	22 **ALESI** Prost
11 **ZONTA** Jordan	23 **BURTI** Prost
7 **FISICHELLA** Benetton	8 **BUTTON** Benetton
15 **BERNOLDI** Arrows	14 **VERSTAPPEN** Arrows
21 **ALONSO** Minardi	20 **MARQUES** Minardi

FOR THE RECORD

First pole position
Juan Pablo Montoya

75th Grand Prix start
Jarno Trulli

TIME SHEETS

QUALIFYING
Weather: Very hot and sunny

Pos.	Driver	Car	Laps	Time
1	Juan Pablo Montoya	Williams-BMW	8	1m 38.117s
2	Ralf Schumacher	Williams-BMW	12	1m 38.136s
3	Mika Häkkinen	McLaren-Mercedes	10	1m 38.811s
4	Michael Schumacher	Ferrari	11	1m 38.941s
5	David Coulthard	McLaren-Mercedes	9	1m 39.574s
6	Rubens Barrichello	Ferrari	11	1m 39.682s
7	Nick Heidfeld	Sauber-Petronas	12	1m 39.921s
8	Kimi Räikkönen	Sauber-Petronas	12	1m 40.072s
9	Pedro de la Rosa	Jaguar-Cosworth	12	1m 40.265s
10	Jarno Trulli	Jordan-Honda	8	1m 40.322s
11	Eddie Irvine	Jaguar-Cosworth	12	1m 40.371s
12	Jacques Villeneuve	BAR-Honda	12	1m 40.437s
13	Olivier Panis	BAR-Honda	11	1m 40.610s
14	Jean Alesi	Prost-Acer	12	1m 40.724s
15	Ricardo Zonta	Jordan-Honda	12	1m 41.174s
16	Luciano Burti	Prost-Acer	11	1m 41.213s
17	Giancarlo Fisichella	Benetton-Renault	12	1m 41.299s
18	Jenson Button	Benetton-Renault	10	1m 41.438s
19	Enrique Bernoldi	Arrows-Asiatech	11	1m 41.668s
20	Jos Verstappen	Arrows-Asiatech	11	1m 41.870s
21	Fernando Alonso	Minardi-European	12	1m 41.913s
22	Tarso Marques	Minardi-European	11	1m 42.716s

FRIDAY FREE PRACTICE
Weather: Very hot and sunny

Pos.	Driver	Laps	Time
1	Eddie Irvine	32	1m 41.424s
2	Juan Pablo Montoya	43	1m 41.487s
3	Mika Häkkinen	29	1m 41.949s
4	Rubens Barrichello	22	1m 41.953s
5	Michael Schumacher	35	1m 42.255s
6	Pedro de la Rosa	39	1m 42.302s
7	David Coulthard	31	1m 42.304s
8	Jean Alesi	35	1m 42.828s
9	Jarno Trulli	34	1m 42.941s
10	Ralf Schumacher	18	1m 42.987s
11	Giancarlo Fisichella	33	1m 43.014s
12	Nick Heidfeld	37	1m 43.211s
13	Ricardo Zonta	36	1m 43.461s
14	Olivier Panis	33	1m 43.487s
15	Jenson Button	30	1m 43.496s
16	Kimi Räikkönen	26	1m 43.528s
17	Jacques Villeneuve	36	1m 43.815s
18	Jos Verstappen	22	1m 44.143s
19	Luciano Burti	39	1m 44.162s
20	Enrique Bernoldi	24	1m 44.549s
21	Fernando Alonso	27	1m 44.730s
22	Tarso Marques	33	1m 45.005s

SATURDAY FREE PRACTICE
Weather: Very hot and sunny

Pos.	Driver	Laps	Time
1	Ralf Schumacher	25	1m 39.188s
2	Juan Pablo Montoya	23	1m 39.469s
3	Michael Schumacher	22	1m 39.937s
4	Mika Häkkinen	18	1m 40.069s
5	Nick Heidfeld	24	1m 40.263s
6	Rubens Barrichello	20	1m 40.436s
7	Eddie Irvine	14	1m 40.443s
8	Olivier Panis	29	1m 40.575s
9	David Coulthard	14	1m 40.697s
10	Jarno Trulli	25	1m 40.894s
11	Pedro de la Rosa	27	1m 40.905s
12	Kimi Räikkönen	21	1m 41.153s
13	Jean Alesi	27	1m 41.428s
14	Ricardo Zonta	12	1m 41.534s
15	Jacques Villeneuve	24	1m 41.683s
16	Jenson Button	10	1m 41.771s
17	Luciano Burti	28	1m 42.136s
18	Enrique Bernoldi	24	1m 42.223s
19	Jos Verstappen	14	1m 42.580s
20	Giancarlo Fisichella	5	1m 43.256s
21	Fernando Alonso	21	1m 43.512s
22	Tarso Marques	28	1m 43.909s

WARM-UP
Weather: Very hot and sunny

Pos.	Driver	Laps	Time
1	Ralf Schumacher	13	1m 42.621s
2	Juan Pablo Montoya	7	1m 42.651s
3	David Coulthard	15	1m 42.743s
4	Michael Schumacher	13	1m 42.747s
5	Rubens Barrichello	10	1m 42.989s
6	Mika Häkkinen	13	1m 43.129s
7	Nick Heidfeld	13	1m 43.479s
8	Enrique Bernoldi	10	1m 43.512s
9	Jacques Villeneuve	15	1m 43.570s
10	Olivier Panis	11	1m 43.615s
11	Jos Verstappen	14	1m 43.704s
12	Pedro de la Rosa	8	1m 43.706s
13	Eddie Irvine	15	1m 43.851s
14	Jarno Trulli	12	1m 43.856s
15	Kimi Räikkönen	12	1m 43.986s
16	Jean Alesi	15	1m 44.300s
17	Giancarlo Fisichella	15	1m 44.601s
18	Luciano Burti	15	1m 45.004s
19	Fernando Alonso	12	1m 45.263s
20	Jenson Button	5	1m 45.653s
21	Tarso Marques	10	1m 45.981s
22	Ricardo Zonta	3	6m 35.247s

RACE FASTEST LAPS
Weather: Very hot and sunny

Driver	Time	Lap
Juan Pablo Montoya	1m 41.808s	20
Ralf Schumacher	1m 42.048s	17
Rubens Barrichello	1m 42.638s	10
Michael Schumacher	1m 42.853s	21
Olivier Panis	1m 43.329s	30
Jacques Villeneuve	1m 43.448s	21
Mika Häkkinen	1m 43.516s	4
David Coulthard	1m 43.571s	26
Jarno Trulli	1m 43.740s	33
Giancarlo Fisichella	1m 43.999s	34
Jenson Button	1m 44.051s	31
Jean Alesi	1m 44.135s	42
Kimi Räikkönen	1m 44.365s	10
Eddie Irvine	1m 44.415s	11
Jos Verstappen	1m 44.681s	35
Luciano Burti	1m 44.683s	17
Enrique Bernoldi	1m 44.785s	31
Ricardo Zonta	1m 45.591s	4
Fernando Alonso	1m 45.908s	4
Tarso Marques	1m 46.013s	12

CHASSIS LOG BOOK

1	M. Schumacher	Ferrari F2001/210
2	Barrichello	Ferrari F2001/206
	spare	Ferrari F2001/211
3	Häkkinen	McLaren MP4/16/7
4	Coulthard	McLaren MP4/16/5
	spares	McLaren MP4/16/4 & 6
5	R. Schumacher	Williams FW23/5
6	Montoya	Williams FW23/6
	spare	Williams FW23/2
7	Fisichella	Benetton B201/6
8	Button	Benetton B201/5
	spares	Benetton B201/3 & 2
9	Panis	BAR 03/6
10	Villeneuve	BAR 03/4
	spare	BAR 03/7
11	Zonta	Jordan EJ11/4
12	Trulli	Jordan EJ11/6
	spare	Jordan EJ11/5
14	Verstappen	Arrows A22/6
15	Bernoldi	Arrows A22/3
	spare	Arrows A22/1
16	Heidfeld	Sauber C20/7
17	Räikkönen	Sauber C20/6
	spare	Sauber C20/1
18	Irvine	Jaguar R2/4
19	de la Rosa	Jaguar R2/5
	spare	Jaguar R2/6
20	Marques	Minardi PS01/4
21	Alonso	Minardi PS01/3
	spare	Minardi PS01/1
22	Alesi	Prost AP04/6
23	Burti	Prost AP04/5
	spare	Prost AP04/4

POINTS TABLES

DRIVERS

1	Michael Schumacher	84
2	David Coulthard	47
3	Ralf Schumacher	41
4	Rubens Barrichello	40
5	Mika Häkkinen	19
6	Juan Pablo Montoya	15
7	Jacques Villeneuve	11
8	Nick Heidfeld	10
9 =	Kimi Räikkönen	9
9 =	Jarno Trulli	9
11	Heinz-Harald Frentzen	6
12	Olivier Panis	5
13 =	Eddie Irvine	4
13 =	Giancarlo Fisichella	4
13 =	Jean Alesi	4
16	Jenson Button	2
17 =	Jos Verstappen	1
17 =	Pedro de la Rosa	1

CONSTRUCTORS

1	Ferrari	124
2	McLaren	66
3	Williams	56
4	Sauber	19
5	BAR	16
6	Jordan	15
7	Benetton	6
8	Jaguar	5
9	Prost	4
10	Arrows	1

FIA WORLD CHAMPIONSHIP • ROUND 13

HUNGARIAN
grand prix

1st - M. SCHUMACHER • 2nd - BARRICHELLO • 3rd - COULTHARD

Previous spread: Reaching the pinnacle. Rubens
Barrichello, Jean Todt and Michael Schumacher
celebrate another World Championship secured,
while David Coulthard is left with his thoughts
which reflect his obvious disappointment.

Previous spread inset: The Ferrari F2001s of
Michael Schumacher and Rubens Barrichello
assume their familiar 1-2 placings at the start of
the race.
Both photographs: Paul-Henri Cahier

Diary

Jaguar team principal Bobby
Rahal's position in jeopardy as he
faces challenge to his authority
from Niki Lauda.

Alain Prost predicts that Michael
Schumacher could win over 60
Grands Prix before retiring from
racing.

Kenny Bräck announces he will
quit the Team Rahal CART
operation to join Chip Ganassi
Racing for the 2002 season.

Honda denies speculation that it
will supply engines to the
McLaren team in 2004, reviving
the partnership which won four
straight World Championships
from 1988–'91.

HUNGARORING QUALIFYING

Coulthard enjoyed a leisurely lunch in the sun outside the McLaren
motorhome on Friday after effectively scuttling what was left of his title
hopes with an unscheduled trip over one of the unyielding kerbs which
abound at the Hungarian track.

It certainly wasn't the scenario he'd been anticipating. Coulthard had
arrived determined to capitalise on the excellent handling of his
McLaren MP4/16-Mercedes on this circuit which should have played to
its technical and aerodynamic strengths.

Instead, a slight error saw him smash the car over that kerb, wrecking
its chassis as the undertray was pushed up through the floor. On Saturday the Scot was left to tackle second practice and qualifying in a completely new car rebuilt overnight by his mechanics around a fresh
chassis, but having lost well over an hour of crucial track time he was
set to spend the rest of the weekend making up for lost time.

The drivers all agreed that the serrated kerbing was too severe to be
placed on the outside of such a fast corner and it was duly sanded down
overnight before Saturday practice after consultation with FIA race director Charlie Whiting.

Not that this changed anything when it came to qualifying as Schumacher
bagged the 41st pole position of his career with a 1m 14.059s best.

Michael needed just two runs and six of his permitted 12 laps to push
pole position 0.8s ahead of Coulthard, although the Scot did an admittedly excellent job in his repaired McLaren to qualify second after losing
one run to an obstructive Heinz-Harald Frentzen who clearly wasn't
using the mirrors on his Prost AP04.

Third fastest was Rubens Barrichello's Ferrari on 1m 14.953s with
Ralf Schumacher's Williams FW23 a distant fourth on 1m 15.095s. Had
it not been for a slight moment with Montoya and a touch of unwanted
understeer developing during the session, Rubens reckoned he could
have joined Michael on the front row.

All in all, the performance of the first three on the grid served as a
major vindication of Bridgestone's new-construction tyre which had
been produced for this event. In really hot conditions the Michelins had
been expected to exert a worthwhile advantage, but even with track
temperatures nudging 41 degrees the Bridgestones seemed to have the
upper hand.

High-downforce aerodynamic trim was the order of the day with many
cars sprouting additional secondary wings at various points on their engine covers. Jaguar, in particular, had come to Hungary with great

hopes for a revised version of their Monaco high-downforce trim which
had worked so well for Eddie Irvine through the streets of the principality two months ago.

Yet the comparative lack of pace from the Michelins sentenced the
Jaguars to their customary 13th and 14th on the grid, on this occasion
Pedro de la Rosa getting the upper hand on 1m 16.543s. Irvine (1m
16.607s) freely confessed that he'd made a mess of things, over-driving
in his efforts to squeeze into the top ten. 'Without being there, you really
haven't got a hope,' shrugged the Ulsterman.

As far as newcomers Jean Alesi (12th for Jordan on 1m 16.471s) and
Heinz-Harald Frentzen (16th for Prost on 1m 17.196s) were concerned,
they were both feeling their way at the wheel of unfamiliar cars after
circumstances had caused them to swap teams when 'H-H' was dropped
from the Jordan squad following the British GP.

Although the effervescent Alesi was delighted finally to have returned to the team which helped him win the 1989 F3000 title, it was
clear that the veteran Frenchman was making no excuses for the gaping 1.1s interval which separated him from team-mate Jarno Trulli in
fifth place on 1m 15.394s.

'He's the benchmark for the performance of this car,' said Jean with a
disarming frankness, 'and I've got to match up to that.'

The other Michelin-shod Williams of Juan Montoya wound up eighth on
1m 15.881s, the Colombian grappling with power oversteer on the tight
little track which ended with a spin.

Montoya was thus separated from his team-mate by the impressive
Trulli, Mika Häkkinen's McLaren MP4/16 (1m 15.411s) and Nick Heidfeld's Sauber (1m 15.739s), the young German driver running wide at
one point and almost spinning as a result.

Kimi Räikkönen managed a 1m 15.906s in the other Sauber for ninth
place after being baulked by a Jordan, then came the BAR-Hondas of
Jacques Villeneuve (1m 16.212s) and Olivier Panis (1m 16.382s) both of
which displayed improved handling balance since free practice, although Panis lost time with an electrical problem and then had a spin.

Giancarlo Fisichella (1m 16.632s) and Jenson Button (1m 17.535s)
wound up 15th and 17th, the British driver suffering two engine failures
during the day which obliged him to take the spare car which had no grip.

Immediately behind Button came Fernando Alonso's Minardi on 1m
17.624s ahead of Luciano Burti's Prost (1m 18.238s), the struggling Ar-
rows-Asiatechs and Tarso Marques's Minardi bringing up the rear as usual.

MICHAEL Schumacher posted a commanding victory in the Hungarian Grand Prix to become the first Ferrari driver since Alberto Ascari in 1952–'53 to win consecutive World Championship titles. The fact that it was the most processional race of the season on the acrobatic, relatively undemanding Hungaroring could not detract from his equalling, on the same day, Alain Prost's achievements of a fourth title crown and a 51st career win.

Everybody in the F1 business knows that it's impossible to overtake on this confined little circuit, but that reality was academic as Schumacher started from pole and produced a dominant victory which his driving genius managed to project as a relaxed walk in the park to his frustrated and outclassed rivals.

It was also a day which emphasised yet again that when things go wrong for Michael, he still has luck on his side. Poised on the verge of his fourth World Championship title, the Ferrari driver's out lap prior to the start of the race saw him lock his rear brakes coming up to a tight right-hander.

Michael reckoned he could have negotiated the corner, but he chose instead to steer off the track rather than risk damaging contact with the kerbing that inflicted mortal damage to David Coulthard's McLaren-Mercedes MP4/16 during Friday's free practice session at the Hungaroring.

Even so, it was clear that the Ferrari F2001 had suffered minor damage in the impact and mechanics worked hard to change a cracked aerodynamic side deflector after he drew up on pole position prior to the final formation lap.

Schumacher shared the front row with David Coulthard's McLaren-Mercedes after the Scot produced a tremendous qualifying effort to split the two Ferraris at the head of the grid.

Ironically, even that sliver of consolation worked against the Scot who had to line up on the dusty side of the circuit and immediately slipped to third place behind Barrichello on the run to the first corner.

The Ferraris got away cleanly and at the end of the opening lap Michael was already 1.3s ahead of his team-mate with Coulthard third, the best-placed McLaren just ahead of Ralf Schumacher's Williams-BMW. Then there was a gap already opening to Jarno Trulli's Jordan EJ-11, Mika Häkkinen's McLaren, Nick Heidfeld's

Sauber C20, Juan Montoya's Williams and Kimi Räikkönen in the other Sauber.

Already the Jaguar team had taken a body blow as Eddie Irvine blotted his copybook by spinning off going into the first corner, ending his race bogged firmly down in the gravel trap.

'It was my fault completely,' he confessed. 'I was running down the dusty side of the track and simply went into the first turn too fast. I haven't been able to get the best out of the car all weekend. I made a big charge at the beginning but maybe carried too much [speed] into the corner and paid the price.'

For the first few laps, Michael kept the pace down, knowing that Barrichello was covering Coulthard in third place. Then, once his tyres had scrubbed in, he piled on the pressure and pulled commandingly away.

On lap five the timing screen flashed up a warning that Jenson Button had been given a 10s stop-go penalty for a jump start in his Benetton B201. Next time round the hapless British driver came in to take his medicine, after which he had to settle down and carve his way through from the tail of the field.

'The car moved forward, but I braked before the lights came on and stopped,' he shrugged. 'But these things happen.'

With ten laps completed Schumacher had almost 3s on Barrichello with a 6.1s gap separating Coulthard in third place from the pursuing Ralf Schumacher. Luciano Burti checked out into a gravel trap after eight laps and Enrique Bernoldi duplicated this slip when he locked his Arrows's rear brakes three laps later challenging Fernando Alonso's Minardi.

On lap 28 Schumacher's Ferrari briefly dropped to third place behind Barrichello and Coulthard as he came in for his first refuelling stop, then surged back ahead on lap 33 when both his rivals made their stops.

The scenario was repeated on lap 52 when Michael stopped for the second time and he was back ahead again on lap 55 for the 22-lap run to the finish which he completed with consummate efficiency and economy of effort.

Barrichello and Coulthard had a closely matched race, the Scot vaulting ahead of his Ferrari rival at the first round of refuelling stops only to lose his advantage by a fraction of a second when he came in for a second time.

Above: Mika Häkkinen bounces his McLaren-Mercedes MP4/16 over one of the Hungaroring kerbs. He had to make do with fifth, unable to find a way past Ralf Schumacher despite being considerably quicker than the Williams-BMW.
Photograph: Bryn Williams/crash.net

Far left: Heinz-Harald Frentzen returned to the F1 fray with the Prost-Acer team, but spun off due to a traction control problem.
Photograph: Paul-Henri Cahier

As it turned out, a sticking refuelling nozzle was the final straw for Coulthard at that second stop. As long as he continued man-handling his McLaren around ahead of Barrichello, he still had a glimmer of an outside chance. However, a refuelling stop that should have been 3s quicker finally extinguished any hope of challenging Schumacher.

With track temperatures soaring to over 40 degrees all through the weekend, the Bridgestone runners had played things safe. In this supremely high-downforce environment, Ferrari and McLaren opted for a proven tyre construction in a hard compound.

Some more ambitious runners, including Jordan and Sauber, opted for a newer construction tyre made available specifically for this race. It didn't upset the pecking order one iota.

'In the early stages of the race I was trying to preserve my tyres for later and my first set was better than Rubens's,' said Schumacher after his victory. 'But later in the race he gave me a lot of pressure. Towards the end I was worried about making a mistake because one car was dropping a thin film of oil on the track. It has been a beautiful weekend and we have done everything we could.'

Coulthard finished the afternoon dehydrated and thoroughly fed up, almost allowing his composure to slip in the post-race media conference. He'd been battling too much oversteer, he explained, and his McLaren just wasn't working as well as the rival Ferraris.

Fourth place fell to Ralf Schumacher's Williams-BMWs, its handling characteristics unsuited to this tortuous circuit, ahead of Mika Häkkinen's McLaren-Mercedes and Nick Heidfeld's Sauber C20.

Häkkinen, who had been held up by Jarno Trulli (Jordan-Honda) for 28 laps, came in on lap 38 for his 6.8s first stop, returning to the race in fifth position. On lap 51 the Finn established a new lap record in 1m 16.723s.

Mika made his second stop on lap 56, falling back from fourth to fifth, but he took less fuel than originally planned to be able to catch and overtake Ralf Schumacher. Eventually he didn't find an opportunity to pass the German and had to come in for a quick splash-and-dash stop on lap 71.

'During the first 29 laps of the race I was stuck behind Trulli who was about 1.5s slower per lap than me,' he said. 'It was only after his first pit stop that I could make inroads on Ralf Schumacher, who by then was about 30s ahead.

'We changed the strategy so I only took a little fuel load at the second stop to see whether it would be possible to overtake Ralf.

Unfortunately this didn't work because overtaking at this track is impossible if the driver ahead of you doesn't make a mistake. Then I had to come in for my additional fuel stop and that was it.'

Mika finished ahead of the Saubers of Heidfeld and Räikkönen, Montoya's Williams and Jacques Villeneuve in the sole surviving BAR-Honda, Olivier Panis's car succumbing to an electrical problem after 58 laps.

Having qualified strongly in fifth, Trulli was nothing but a mobile chicane until his first refuelling stop on lap 29 not only lost him five places due to a fuel nozzle problem, but now left Häkkinen with a clear run at the younger Schumacher's Williams.

Trulli eventually wound up retiring with hydraulic failure while his new team-mate Jean Alesi scrambled home 10th, suffused with delight to be back behind the wheel of a halfway competitive car after his transfer from the Prost squad.

'It was a really tough race for me as I was learning things about the car all the time and trying to remember which buttons to use and work with the clutch on the steering wheel as opposed to having a pedal,' said Alesi, as breathless as his driving style.

Yet these were all fragile footnotes to the main point of the afternoon, the acclamation of a multiple World Champion. And there will be more success to come.

'The whole thing about Michael is, above all else, that he absolutely loves driving racing cars,' said Ross Brawn, the Ferrari technical director. In fact he loves driving as much as he hates losing.

Yet it was all a strangely understated affair. Having matched Alain Prost's hitherto unsurpassed tally of victories, Schumacher seems hardly likely to pause for breath before steaming on to break all the remaining records in the F1 book.

Yet, asked whether he thought he would beat Fangio's record of five championships, Michael remained charmingly deferential.

'You know it's not really a target and I don't think it's really a fair comparison anyway because what this man has done in the times when he was in F1 I think is outstanding,' he said.

'All we are doing in comparison is pretty small, if you see the safety and the cars from the old days it's something unbelievable to imagine to race this fast.

'I couldn't, and I think it is not fair to compare at all.'

CLINGING TO THE WRECKAGE

As the victorious Ferrari team members hugged each other, sprayed champagne and danced jigs around the base of Michael Schumacher's victory podium, the rest of the F1 fraternity was left licking its wounds in the dusty Hungaroring paddock.

Confronting the realities of the F1 business can sometimes be an uncomfortable process. Not since Nigel Mansell clinched his World Championship crown here at the Hungaroring nine years ago, with a second-place finish behind Ayrton Senna's McLaren, had the title contest been settled so early in the season.

For Ron Dennis, the McLaren chairman, it was also a moment to reflect on a painfully disappointing season which had thus far yielded just three wins out of 13 races, two for Coulthard and one for the hapless Mika Häkkinen. 'Generally it has been a season that has got plenty of errors in it,' he said. 'Not as many as most of the other teams, but more than Ferrari, and that's what motor racing is all about.

'We're not going to whinge and moan, we'll concentrate on trying to win as many of the remaining races as possible. We will be trying to do a much better job in 2002.'

Dennis refused to lay any of the blame for the poor season on his drivers after a season in which McLaren had been expected by many observers to give Ferrari a far harder time than in fact it had done.

'I think the drivers have done a pretty good job in both cases,' he said. 'It's all too easy to question the performance of a driver at individual races, but I think, to be honest, both David and Mika have reason to question our performance.

'We haven't really been as good as we have been and we certainly haven't been as good as we're going to be, that's the most important thing. We have never been quitters and we're not going to start now. We'll be working flat out to win all the remaining races and intend to hit the ground running at the start of 2002.'

Now the challenge remaining for McLaren-Mercedes would be to fend off their rivals at BMW Williams for second place in the constructors' championship. And it promised to be a close-run thing.

ROUND 13
HUNGARORING 17–19 AUGUST 2001

MARLBORO
MAGYAR
nagydij

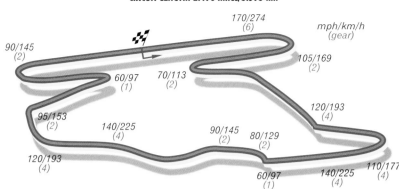

HUNGARORING
CIRCUIT LENGTH: 2.470 miles/3.975 km

170/274 (6)
mph/km/h (gear)
90/145 (2)
105/169 (2)
60/97 (1)
70/113 (2)
120/193 (4)
95/153 (2)
140/225 (4)
90/145 (2)
80/129 (2)
120/193 (4)
60/97 (1)
140/225 (4)
110/177 (4)

RACE DISTANCE: 77 laps, 190.186 miles/306.075 km   RACE WEATHER: Very hot and sunny

Pos.	Driver	Nat.	No.	Entrant	Car/Engine	Tyres	Laps	Time/Retirement	Speed (mph/km/h)	Gap to leader
1	Michael Schumacher	D	1	Scuderia Ferrari Marlboro	Ferrari F2001-050 V10	B	77	1h 41m 49.675s	112.063/180.348	
2	Rubens Barrichello	BR	2	Scuderia Ferrari Marlboro	Ferrari F2001-050 V10	B	77	1h 41m 53.038s	112.001/180.249	+3.36
3	David Coulthard	GB	4	West McLaren Mercedes	McLaren MP4/16-Mercedes F0110K V10	B	77	1h 41m 53.615s	111.991/180.232	+3.94
4	Ralf Schumacher	D	5	BMW WilliamsF1 Team	Williams FW23-BMW P80 V10	M	77	1h 42m 39.362s	111.159/178.893	+49.68
5	Mika Häkkinen	SF	3	West McLaren Mercedes	McLaren MP4/16-Mercedes F0110K V10	B	77	1h 42m 59.968s	110.788/178.297	+70.29
6	Nick Heidfeld	D	16	Red Bull Sauber Petronas	Sauber C20-Petronas V10	B	76			+1
7	Kimi Räikkönen	SF	17	Red Bull Sauber Petronas	Sauber C20-Petronas V10	B	76			+1
8	Juan Pablo Montoya	COL	6	BMW WilliamsF1 Team	Williams FW23-BMW P80 V10	M	76			+1
9	Jacques Villeneuve	CDN	10	Lucky Strike BAR Honda	BAR 03-Honda RA001E V10	B	75			+2 la
10	Jean Alesi	F	12	B&H Jordan Honda	Jordan EJ11-Honda RA001E V10	B	75			+2 la
11	Pedro de la Rosa	ESP	19	Jaguar Racing	Jaguar R2-Cosworth CR3 V10	M	75			+2 la
12	Jos Verstappen	NL	14	Orange Arrows Asiatech	Arrows A22-Asiatech V10	B	74			+3 la
	Giancarlo Fisichella	I	7	Mild Seven Benetton Renault	Benetton B201-Renault RS21 V10	M	67	Engine		
	Heinz-Harald Frentzen	D	22	Prost Acer	Prost AP04-Acer V10	M	63	Spun off		
	Tarso Marques	BR	20	European Minardi F1	Minardi PS01-European V10	M	63	Engine		
	Olivier Panis	F	9	Lucky Strike BAR Honda	BAR 03-Honda RA001E V10	B	58	Electronics		
	Jarno Trulli	I	11	B&H Jordan Honda	Jordan EJ11-Honda RA001E V10	B	53	Hydraulics		
	Fernando Alonso	ESP	21	European Minardi F1	Minardi PS01-European V10	M	37	Spun off		
	Jenson Button	GB	8	Mild Seven Benetton Renault	Benetton B201-Renault RS21 V10	M	34	Spun off		
	Enrique Bernoldi	BR	15	Orange Arrows Asiatech	Arrows A22-Asiatech V10	B	11	Spun off		
	Luciano Burti	BR	23	Prost Acer	Prost AP04-Acer V10	M	8	Spun off		
	Eddie Irvine	GB	18	Jaguar Racing	Jaguar R2-Cosworth CR3 V10	M	0	Spun off		

Fastest lap: Mika Häkkinen, on lap 51, 1m 16.723s, 115.895 mph/186.515 km/h (record).

Previous lap record: Nigel Mansell (F1 Williams FW14B-Renault V10), 1m 18.308s, 113.349 mph/182.418 km/h (1992).

Grid order	1	2	3	4	5	6	7	8	9	10	11	12	13	14	15	16	17	18	19	20	21	22	23	24	25	26	27	28	29	30	31	32	33	34	35	36	37	38	39	40	41	42	43	44	45	46	47	48	49	50	51	52	53	54	55	56	57	58
1 M. SCHUMACHER	1	1	1	1	1	1	1	1	1	1	1	1	1	1	1	1	1	1	1	1	1	1	1	1	1	1	1	1	2	2	4		1	1	1	1	1	1	1	1	1	1	1	1	1	1	1	1	1	1	1	1	1	4	4	1	1	1
4 COULTHARD	2	2	2	2	2	2	2	2	2	2	2	2	2	2	2	2	2	2	2	2	2	2	2	2	2	2	2	2	4	2	1	4	4	4	4	4	4	4	4	4	4	4	4	4	4	4	4	4	4	4	2	1	2	2	2	2
2 BARRICHELLO	4	4	4	4	4	4	4	4	4	4	4	4	4	4	4	4	4	4	4	4	4	4	4	4	4	4	4	4	1	1	2	2	2	2	2	2	2	2	2	2	2	2	2	2	2	2	2	2	2	1	2	4	4	4
5 R. SCHUMACHER	5	5	5	5	5	5	5	5	5	5	5	5	5	5	5	5	5	5	5	5	5	5	5	5	5	5	5	5	5	5	5	5	5	5	5	5	5	5	5	5	5	5	5	5	5	5	5	5	5	5	3	3	3	5	5
11 TRULLI	11	11	11	11	11	11	11	11	11	11	11	11	11	11	11	11	11	11	11	11	11	11	11	11	11	11	11	11	3	3	3	3	3	3	3	3	3	3	3	3	3	3	3	3	3	3	3	5	5	5	3	3
3 HÄKKINEN	3	3	3	3	3	3	3	3	3	3	3	3	3	3	3	3	3	3	3	3	3	3	3	3	3	3	3	3	6	6	6	17	17	17	17	17	17	17	17	17	16	16	16	16	16	16	16	16	16	16	16	16
16 HEIDFELD	16	16	16	16	16	16	16	16	16	16	16	16	16	16	16	16	16	16	16	16	16	16	16	16	16	16	16	16	6	6	11	10	17	16	16	16	16	16	16	16	17	6	6	17	17	17	17	17	17	17
6 MONTOYA	6	6	6	6	6	6	6	6	6	6	6	6	6	6	6	6	6	6	6	6	6	6	6	6	16	10	10	17	16	6	6	6	6	6	6	6	6	6	6	17	17	17	9	9	9	6	6	6	6
17 RÄIKKÖNEN	17	17	17	17	17	17	17	17	17	17	17	17	17	17	17	17	17	17	17	9	9	12	12	12	9	9	9	9	9	9	9	9	9	9	9	9	9	9	9	9	9	6	6	6	6	9	9	10	10
10 VILLENEUVE	9	9	9	9	9	9	9	9	9	9	9	9	9	9	9	9	9	9	9	17	10	17	16	11	11	11	11	11	11	11	11	11	11	11	11	11	11	11	11	10	10	12	11	11	10	10	12	12
9 PANIS	10	10	10	10	10	10	10	10	10	10	10	10	10	10	10	10	10	10	10	10	10	10	10	10	12	16	16	9	10	10	10	10	10	10	10	10	10	10	11	12	11	11	10	10	12	12	9	19
12 ALESI	19	19	19	19	19	19	19	19	12	12	12	12	12	12	12	12	12	12	12	12	12	9	11	12	12	12	12	10	12	12	12	12	12	12	12	12	12	12	10	11	12	10	19	19	19	19	19	7
19 DE LA ROSA	12	12	12	12	12	12	12	12	19	19	19	19	19	19	19	19	19	19	19	19	19	19	19	19	19	19	19	19	7	7	7	7	7	7	7	7	7	7	19	12	12	19	12	12	7	7	7	22
18 IRVINE	7	7	7	7	7	7	7	7	7	7	7	7	7	7	7	7	7	7	7	14	14	14	7	7	7	7	19	19	19	19	19	19	19	19	19	19	7	7	7	7	7	7	7	22	22	22	14
7 FISICHELLA	14	14	14	14	14	14	14	14	14	14	14	14	14	14	14	7	7	22	22	22	22	22	22	22	22	22	22	22	22	22	22	22	22	14	14	14	14	14	20
22 FRENTZEN	8	8	8	8	21	21	21	21	21	21	21	21	21	21	21	22	21	22	14	14	14	14	14	14	14	14	14	14	14	14	14	14	14	22	20	20	20	9
8 BUTTON	21	21	21	21	15	15	15	15	15	15	12	22	22	22	22	22	22	8	8	8	8	8	8	21	21	21	8	8	8	21	20	20	20	20	20	20	20	20
21 ALONSO	15	15	15	15	15	23	23	22	22	22	8	8	8	8	8	8	8	21	21	8	21	21	21	20	20	20
23 BURTI	23	23	23	23	8	22	22	20	20	20	20	20	20	20	20	20	20	20	20	20	20	20
15 BERNOLDI	22	22	22	22	22	22	20	20	8	8	8
14 VERSTAPPEN	20	20	20	20	20	20	8	8
20 MARQUES								

Pit stop
One lap behind leader

STARTING GRID

1 M. SCHUMACHER Ferrari	**4** COULTHARD McLaren
2 BARRICHELLO Ferrari	**5** R. SCHUMACHER Williams
11 TRULLI Jordan	**3** HÄKKINEN McLaren
16 HEIDFELD Sauber	**6** MONTOYA Williams
17 RÄIKKÖNEN Sauber	**10** VILLENEUVE BAR
9 PANIS BAR	**12** ALESI Jordan
19 DE LA ROSA Jaguar	**18** IRVINE Jaguar
7 FISICHELLA Benetton	**22** FRENTZEN Prost
8 BUTTON Benetton	**21** ALONSO Minardi
23 BURTI Prost	**15** BERNOLDI Arrows
14 VERSTAPPEN Arrows	**20** MARQUES Minardi

All results and data © FIA 2001

TIME SHEETS

QUALIFYING

Weather: Very hot and sunny

Pos.	Driver	Car	Laps	Time
1	Michael Schumacher	Ferrari	6	1m 14.059s
2	David Coulthard	McLaren-Mercedes	11	1m 14.860s
3	Rubens Barrichello	Ferrari	11	1m 14.953s
4	Ralf Schumacher	Williams-BMW	12	1m 15.095s
5	Jarno Trulli	Jordan-Honda	10	1m 15.394s
6	Mika Häkkinen	McLaren-Mercedes	11	1m 15.411s
7	Nick Heidfeld	Sauber-Petronas	9	1m 15.739s
8	Juan Pablo Montoya	Williams-BMW	11	1m 15.881s
9	Kimi Räikkönen	Sauber-Petronas	12	1m 15.906s
10	Jacques Villeneuve	BAR-Honda	11	1m 16.212s
11	Olivier Panis	BAR-Honda	8	1m 16.382s
12	Jean Alesi	Jordan-Honda	12	1m 16.471s
13	Pedro de la Rosa	Jaguar-Cosworth	10	1m 16.543s
14	Eddie Irvine	Jaguar-Cosworth	11	1m 16.607s
15	Giancarlo Fisichella	Benetton-Renault	11	1m 16.632s
16	Heinz-Harald Frentzen	Prost-Acer	12	1m 17.196s
17	Jenson Button	Benetton-Renault	12	1m 17.535s
18	Fernando Alonso	Minardi-European	11	1m 17.624s
19	Luciano Burti	Prost-Acer	12	1m 18.238s
20	Enrique Bernoldi	Arrows-Asiatech	11	1m 18.258s
21	Jos Verstappen	Arrows-Asiatech	12	1m 18.389s
22	Tarso Marques	Minardi-European	11	1m 19.139s

FRIDAY FREE PRACTICE

Weather: Very hot and sunny

Pos.	Driver	Laps	Time
1	Michael Schumacher	38	1m 16.651s
2	Rubens Barrichello	33	1m 16.734s
3	Mika Häkkinen	25	1m 16.789s
4	Ralf Schumacher	40	1m 17.308s
5	Eddie Irvine	31	1m 17.409s
6	Jean Alesi	20	1m 17.862s
7	Giancarlo Fisichella	33	1m 17.896s
8	Nick Heidfeld	33	1m 17.928s
9	Olivier Panis	39	1m 17.970s
10	David Coulthard	9	1m 18.182s
11	Pedro de la Rosa	29	1m 18.195s
12	Jarno Trulli	41	1m 18.277s
13	Juan Pablo Montoya	36	1m 18.524s
14	Heinz-Harald Frentzen	32	1m 18.724s
15	Kimi Räikkönen	29	1m 18.834s
16	Jacques Villeneuve	32	1m 19.238s
17	Jenson Button	31	1m 19.263s
18	Jos Verstappen	39	1m 19.368s
19	Enrique Bernoldi	37	1m 19.466s
20	Fernando Alonso	35	1m 19.992s
21	Luciano Burti	36	1m 20.615s
22	Tarso Marques	38	1m 20.981s

SATURDAY FREE PRACTICE

Weather: Very hot and sunny

Pos.	Driver	Laps	Time
1	David Coulthard	17	1m 15.263s
2	Michael Schumacher	23	1m 15.466s
3	Rubens Barrichello	16	1m 15.650s
4	Nick Heidfeld	27	1m 15.821s
5	Mika Häkkinen	17	1m 15.839s
6	Jarno Trulli	23	1m 16.021s
7	Ralf Schumacher	14	1m 16.033s
8	Juan Pablo Montoya	22	1m 16.098s
9	Eddie Irvine	29	1m 16.471s
10	Giancarlo Fisichella	28	1m 16.513s
11	Kimi Räikkönen	18	1m 16.578s
12	Olivier Panis	30	1m 16.581s
13	Jenson Button	13	1m 16.619s
14	Jacques Villeneuve	29	1m 17.087s
15	Heinz-Harald Frentzen	29	1m 17.203s
16	Jean Alesi	21	1m 17.334s
17	Pedro de la Rosa	30	1m 17.549s
18	Luciano Burti	30	1m 17.992s
19	Fernando Alonso	30	1m 18.234s
20	Enrique Bernoldi	28	1m 18.533s
21	Jos Verstappen	9	1m 18.954s
22	Tarso Marques	18	1m 19.153s

WARM-UP

Weather: Very hot and sunny

Pos.	Driver	Laps	Time
1	David Coulthard	11	1m 16.915s
2	Michael Schumacher	15	1m 17.338s
3	Rubens Barrichello	14	1m 17.360s
4	Ralf Schumacher	13	1m 17.608s
5	Mika Häkkinen	12	1m 17.704s
6	Jarno Trulli	15	1m 18.433s
7	Nick Heidfeld	15	1m 18.851s
8	Olivier Panis	12	1m 18.881s
9	Kimi Räikkönen	13	1m 19.068s
10	Eddie Irvine	16	1m 19.148s
11	Pedro de la Rosa	12	1m 19.393s
12	Juan Pablo Montoya	17	1m 19.465s
13	Jacques Villeneuve	14	1m 19.554s
14	Jean Alesi	13	1m 19.581s
15	Giancarlo Fisichella	11	1m 19.704s
16	Jos Verstappen	17	1m 19.887s
17	Enrique Bernoldi	13	1m 20.500s
18	Heinz-Harald Frentzen	17	1m 20.546s
19	Luciano Burti	15	1m 20.652s
20	Fernando Alonso	12	1m 20.965s
21	Tarso Marques	12	1m 21.354s
22	Jenson Button	8	1m 21.397s

RACE FASTEST LAPS

Weather: Very hot and sunny

Driver	Time	Lap
Mika Häkkinen	1m 16.723s	51
David Coulthard	1m 17.054s	53
Ralf Schumacher	1m 17.233s	54
Rubens Barrichello	1m 17.274s	51
Michael Schumacher	1m 17.436s	23
Juan Pablo Montoya	1m 18.030s	34
Nick Heidfeld	1m 18.165s	50
Pedro de la Rosa	1m 18.186s	51
Kimi Räikkönen	1m 18.216s	28
Jarno Trulli	1m 18.536s	50
Jean Alesi	1m 19.134s	32
Olivier Panis	1m 19.222s	29
Giancarlo Fisichella	1m 19.471s	24
Jenson Button	1m 19.475s	29
Jacques Villeneuve	1m 19.494s	75
Heinz-Harald Frentzen	1m 20.046s	50
Jos Verstappen	1m 20.401s	51
Tarso Marques	1m 21.379s	51
Fernando Alonso	1m 21.533s	18
Luciano Burti	1m 21.912s	8
Enrique Bernoldi	1m 22.045s	7

CHASSIS LOG BOOK

1	M. Schumacher	Ferrari F2001/211
2	Barrichello	Ferrari F2001/206
	spare	Ferrari F2001/210
3	Häkkinen	McLaren MP4/16/7
4	Coulthard	McLaren MP4/16/6
	spares	McLaren MP4/16/4 & 5
5	R. Schumacher	Williams FW23/5
6	Montoya	Williams FW23/6
	spare	Williams FW23/2
7	Fisichella	Benetton B201/6
8	Button	Benetton B201/5
	spares	Benetton B201/3 & 1
9	Panis	BAR 03/6
10	Villeneuve	BAR 03/4
	spare	BAR 03/7
11	Trulli	Jordan EJ11/7
12	Alesi	Jordan EJ11/6
	spares	Jordan EJ11/5 & 3
14	Verstappen	Arrows A22/6
15	Bernoldi	Arrows A22/3
	spare	Arrows A22/1
16	Heidfeld	Sauber C20/7
17	Räikkönen	Sauber C20/6
	spare	Sauber C20/1
18	Irvine	Jaguar R2/4
19	de la Rosa	Jaguar R2/7
	spare	Jaguar R2/6
20	Marques	Minardi PS01/4
21	Alonso	Minardi PS01/3
	spare	Minardi PS01/1
22	Frentzen	Prost AP04/6
23	Burti	Prost AP04/4
	spare	Prost AP04/2

POINTS TABLES

DRIVERS

1	Michael Schumacher	94
2	David Coulthard	51
3	Rubens Barrichello	46
4	Ralf Schumacher	44
5	Mika Häkkinen	21
6	Juan Pablo Montoya	15
7 =	Jacques Villeneuve	11
7 =	Nick Heidfeld	11
9 =	Kimi Räikkönen	9
9 =	Jarno Trulli	9
11	Heinz-Harald Frentzen	6
12	Olivier Panis	5
13 =	Eddie Irvine	4
13 =	Giancarlo Fisichella	4
13 =	Jean Alesi	4
16	Jenson Button	2
17 =	Jos Verstappen	1
17 =	Pedro de la Rosa	1

CONSTRUCTORS

1	Ferrari	140
2	McLaren	72
3	Williams	59
4	Sauber	20
5	BAR	16
6	Jordan	15
7	Benetton	6
8	Jaguar	5
9	Prost	4
10	Arrows	1

2	63	64	65	66	67	68	69	70	71	72	73	74	75	76	77	•
1	1	1	1	1	1	1	1	1	1	1	1	1	1	1	1	1
2	2	2	2	2	2	2	2	2	2	2	2	2	2	2	2	2
4	4	4	4	4	4	4	4	4	4	4	4	4	4	4	4	3
5	5	5	5	5	5	5	5	5	5	5	5	5	5	5	5	4
3	3	3	3	3	3	3	3	3	3	3	3	3	3	3	3	5
6	16	16	16	16	16	16	16	16	16	16	16	16	16	16	16	6
7	17	17	17	17	17	17	17	17	17	17	17	17	17			
6	6	6	6	6	6	6	6	6	6	6	6	6	6			
0	10	10	10	10	10	10	10	10	10	10	10	10	10			
2	12	12	12	12	12	12	12	12	12	12	12	12	12			
9	19	19	19	19	19	19	19	19	19	19	19	19	19			
7	7	7	7	7	7	14	14	14	14	14	14	14				
2	22	14	14	14	14											
4	14															
0	20															

BELGIAN
grand prix

1st - M. SCHUMACHER • 2nd - COULTHARD • 3rd - FISICHELLA

Main photograph: Giancarlo Fisichella's stunning drive into third place showed the dramatic upward progress made by Benetton-Renault.
Photograph: Paul-Henri Cahier

Left: Coulthard seems less than happy with his second place as he joins Schumacher and Fisichella on the podium.
Photograph: Bryn Williams/crash.net

A combination of circumstance and misfortune saw Michael Schumacher's key rivals effectively capitulate to the newly crowned World Champion in the Belgian Grand Prix at Spa-Francorchamps, allowing him an unchallenged run to an all-time record 52nd career victory. Such was his mastery of the occasion that Schumacher's immaculate driving style made the Ferrari F2001's pace seem almost slow for much of the race, but his economy of effort and delicate touch at its wheel ensured that in reality it was far from that.

Yet the strength of his domination could be judged from the fact that he set the race's fastest lap in 1m 49.758s third time round after the restart — and no other competitor got within a second of that time for the rest of the afternoon.

'I can't say I'm much motivated by statistics,' said the Ferrari driver with his characteristic directness, 'but of course it does mean something to have that number [of wins] on my account. But I will be more delighted in a few years when I am sitting on my sofa, with a beer and cigar, thinking about it.'

Yet if Schumacher had an untroubled afternoon's work at the front of the field, Alain Prost had a lot more to worry about than simply losing his previous all-time F1 record of 51 victories. His team's number two driver Luciano Burti was involved in a horrifying high-speed accident on the 175 mph, top-gear Blanchimont right-hander on the return leg towards the start/finish line.

The young Brazilian driver was taken to hospital in Liège suffering with serious bruising and concussion but, while a brain scan revealed that he had suffered internal bruising, there was no sign of any swelling. He was released from hospital later in the week but would not race again during the 2001 season.

Burti had been dicing wheel-to-wheel with his former Jaguar team-mate Eddie Irvine for 15th place when the two cars touched as they approached this high-speed corner on the fourth lap of the race.

It said much for the standards of construction of today's generation of F1 chassis that the car remained intact after hitting the protective tyre barrier at undiminished speed.

Irvine, on the outside, held to his line and, as Burti apparently tried to back out of an increasingly tight situation, he collided with the Jaguar's left rear wheel. The impact ripped off the Prost's front wing and the car speared off across the gravel trap before burying itself into the tyre barrier with a fearful impact.

Irvine, whose wrecked Jaguar spun to a halt a little further along the circuit, leaped from the cockpit and ran back to help marshals rescue Burti from the badly damaged Prost. Race officials initially deployed the safety car in order to slow the field, but when the severity of Burti's accident was fully appreciated the red flags were shown and the race halted.

Irvine was summoned to the race stewards who examined the

SPA-FRANCORCHAMPS QUALIFYING

Michael Schumacher and David Coulthard may have been destined to end up first and second in the race at Spa-Francorchamps, but both their weekends got off to potentially disastrous starts during Friday free practice.

As usual, however, when it goes wrong for Michael it invariably also goes right. Despite a slight error in heavy rain which saw him wreck the nose wing of his Ferrari against a rear wheel of Pedro de la Rosa's Jaguar R2, he finished the Friday a commanding 0.7s ahead of Jarno Trulli's Jordan and his Ferrari team-mate Rubens Barrichello.

Schumacher's skirmish with de la Rosa served as a graphic reminder of just how hazardous it can be groping through the murk on this circuit where spray tends to hang between the trees on the fast straights through the pine forests.

'Regarding the incident with Pedro, the situation was the usual one when you are running in spray,' he said. 'All you see is the spray [and] you have to hope that the driver in front behaves normally and accelerates down the straight.

'I was being careful, because I knew there was a risk of aquaplaning, so I was not going flat out. I just had a feeling that he might be going slowly, which is why, at the last moment, I moved over even though I could not see anything. By then it was already too late.'

Schumacher could count himself fortunate that his Ferrari suffered relatively little damage, rather more than could be said for David Coulthard's McLaren-Mercedes which the Scot slammed off the road into the guard rail just three laps into the morning session.

'Obviously it's not an ideal situation,' said Coulthard with masterly understatement. 'I got on the grass on the wrong side of the kerb and lost the back of the car. The mechanics worked very hard and almost succeeded in having the car ready before the end of the session.'

Unfortunately the McLaren team's remarkable efforts to rebuild Coulthard's car in a little more than an hour and a half still left the Scot unable to complete any further laps, leaving him slowest of the day.

McLaren was at the forefront of controversy after qualifying on Saturday when it lodged a protest against 17 of the competing cars after qualifying for the Belgian Grand Prix on the basis that they had ignored the rule which requires one to slow down for a waved yellow warning flag.

In the closing stages of the hour-long session, with the track drying out, the lap times came tumbling down with Juan Montoya (1m 52.072s) just pipping his team-mate Ralf Schumacher (1m 52.959s) for pole.

Mika Häkkinen (1m 57.043s) and Coulthard (1m 58.008s) were left trailing seventh and ninth, in part because their pit crew had reminded them to back off for the waved yellow flags at the Burnenville corner where Nick Heidfeld's Sauber C20 had become stranded just off the racing line when it jammed in fifth gear.

Ron Dennis pointed out that he simply wanted to know how the rules should be interpreted rather than risk wholesale disqualifications.

'If you go through a sector of the lap under a waved yellow flag and improve your time, then you will lose your previous best lap time,' said Dennis.

'If you are a disciplined team, in such circumstances you get onto the radio and tell your driver that if they exceed their previous best sector time they will be penalised.

'I just want to know how to run a racing team. We told our drivers to back off and it looks embarrassing for us, as if we got it wrong.'

Predictably, this objection was rejected by the stewards and Michael Schumacher's Ferrari F2001 (1m 54.685s) duly lined up on the second row alongside Heinz-Harald Frentzen's Prost AP04 (1m 55.223s), a protest that Frentzen had overtaken Kimi Räikkönen's Sauber C20 (12th/1m 59.050s) under yellow flags also being thrown out.

Frentzen was understandably delighted to have timed his run on the drying track to perfection, ending up just ahead of Rubens Barrichello's Ferrari (1m 56.116s), Jacques Villeneuve's BAR-Honda (1m 57.038s) and Mika Häkkinen.

The remainder of the grid was strung out behind in a somewhat haphazard order, reflecting the need to be out at precisely the right moment on the drying track. Yet Giancarlo Fisichella's eighth place on 1m 57.668s was a significant straw in the wind, reflecting very positively on Benetton's latest aero package and Renault's progress on the V10 engine. As the race would certainly prove.

Below: The ill-starred Luciano Burti photographed looking pensive before the race start.
Photograph: Paul-Henri Cahier

Below centre: The remains of Burti's Prost, its monocoque reassuringly intact, are recovered from the circuit after his accident.

Bottom: Juan Pablo Montoya really piled on the pressure in qualifying, timing his best run perfectly to produce a dazzling pole position.
Both photographs: Clive Mason/Allsport-Getty Images

Diary

Minardi confirms deal to use Asiatech V10 engines for the 2002 season.

Justin Wilson becomes the first British driver to clinch the FIA Formula 3000 title with a second-place finish to Ricardo Sperafico at Spa.

Indianapolis boss Tony George announces a new feeder series for the Indy Racing League similar to CART's Indy Lights category.

Takuma Sato clinches British F3 Championship crown with victory at Thruxton.

Right: David Coulthard makes the most of a brief sunny spell in the paddock at Spa-Francorchamps.

Opposite: After the Williams-BMW challenge self-destructed, Michael Schumacher cruised to what seemed like an unflustered 52nd career Grand Prix victory.

Both photographs: Paul-Henri Cahier

PROST BRACES HIMSELF FOR MORE PROBLEMS

As a shell-shocked Alain Prost collected together the debris of his F1 team following Luciano Burti's massive accident, the 46-year-old Frenchman may also have reflected the task of winning Grands Prix from behind the wheel is a whole lot easier than doing so as a team principal.

As the shaken Burti recovered in hospital, Prost squared up to a battle against his creditors to secure new investment in the team. More than £10 million in debt, Prost was believed to be negotiating with wealthy Saudi Arabian sources for an injection of new funds which would enable the team to continue using leased Ferrari V10 engines in 2002.

Failure would risk Prost losing control of his team to Brazilian supermarket millionaire Abilio Diniz and his son, former Formula 1 driver Pedro, who already owned an undisclosed percentage of the team.

The Diniz family had reportedly offered to buy the Prost team for one dollar in exchange for assuming its liabilities, but the former four-times World Champion was determined to thwart their ambitions.

In less stressful moments Prost acknowledged that Michael Schumacher was now poised to win many more races before finally retiring from driving.

'It could be 60, could be 70,' he said. 'One factor in his favour is the fact that there are fewer really top teams, so he will probably hang on at Ferrari, and the cars as a whole are generally more reliable which gives a driver a chance to finish more races and therefore have more chances to win.'

When Prost moved ahead in the record books after his victory in the 1987 Portuguese Grand Prix, an admiring Jackie Stewart had said: 'that drive was absolutely superb. A faultless performance. I honestly believe him to be in a class of his own amongst today's Grand Prix drivers and couldn't be happier that it was Alain who finally beat my record.'

Prost added: 'What I remember most about that day was that we did a group photograph with the McLaren mechanics and with Jackie and a board saying "28 victories" and I was embarrassed for him.'

'When you beat somebody's record, it can hardly be nice. It was a strange feeling. I also remember that Jackie said that I might even win 40 races and I was thinking "no way, I never can win 40 races" and now we see how it turned out. So you never know.'

Prost admitted to feeling philosophical about Schumacher matching — and almost inevitably beating — his achievement. 'You obviously want to keep these sorts of records,' he said, 'but when I retired at the end of 1993 Ayrton Senna had 41 wins and, had he lived, I think he would have quite obviously beaten my record first.

'I was convinced at the time that it was Ayrton who would threaten my record rather than Michael, but either way it doesn't really matter because it was going to be beaten by a top guy.'

matter in detail but eventually concluded it had simply been a racing accident.

'I was taking my line out of Stavelot and into Blanchimont and there wasn't anything unusual about my entry into the fast left-hander midway through the corner,' said the Jaguar driver.

'But midway through the corner I felt an impact on the rear and after that I was a passenger. I knew Luciano was there, but I simply didn't expect him to have a go on the inside of that corner. He hit the wall very hard indeed and I'm glad he's OK.'

After the debris had been cleared up, the race was restarted 40 minutes later over 36 laps rather than the original 43. By this point the Williams-BMW challenge had evaporated amidst a swirl of embarrassing technical problems after Juan Pablo Montoya and Ralf Schumacher had qualified commandingly in first and second places.

Montoya's Williams FW23 stalled on pole position prior to the first parade lap after which he had to start at the back. He climbed up to 15th by the time the race was stopped for Burti's accident and restarted in that position on the second grid.

Others not taking the restart as they had failed to complete the first race included Räikkönen's Sauber C20 and Fernando Alonso's Minardi PS01.

Before the restart a cracked rear wing beam had been detected and changed on Montoya's car and the team decided to do the same as a precaution on Ralf Schumacher's car, now effectively at the front of the grid in the absence of Montoya.

Unfortunately the race was restarted more promptly than the team was expecting and, as a result of this, we were treated to the bizarre sight of Ralf's FW23 left high and dry on axle stands while the mechanics vacated the grid under the 15 seconds rule prior to the start of the second parade lap.

By the time the mechanics had returned to the grid to lower the car from its stands, the younger Schumacher had to take the second start from the back of the grid.

All this drama allowed Schumacher to accelerate his Ferrari gently into the lead at the restart while his rivals sat and fumed behind Giancarlo Fisichella's Benetton which had demonstrated the effectiveness of the team's traction control system by vaulting through from sixth to second at the first turn.

By the end of the opening lap, Schumacher was 3.7s ahead of Fisichella with Barrichello third, then David Coulthard's McLaren-Mercedes, Jenson Button in the other Benetton and Mika Häkkinen's McLaren-Mercedes.

Further back Montoya banged wheels with de la Rosa before recovering and then pulling in with a terminal engine failure. By lap three Schumacher was 8.3s ahead of Fisichella, after which he stretched his advantage to 10.4s, 12.2s and 14.2s on consecutive laps. It was all over bar the shouting.

By lap seven he was 16.2s ahead as the first spate of refuelling stops began, Häkkinen coming in from fifth place for an 8.5s stop and Jean Alesi's Jordan from sixth in 8.7s. Further back Olivier Panis also brought his BAR-Honda in for fuel, but inadvertently ran over the white line on the exit as he resumed, earning the Frenchman a 10s stop-go penalty.

On lap ten Schumacher brought the leading Ferrari in for a 9.4s refuelling stop, allowing Fisichella into the lead before the Italian made his first stop next time round. The Benetton was refuelled and fresh rear tyres fitted, but the original front tyres were left on the car.

By lap 12 Schumacher was now 21.1s ahead and had precious little to help him concentrate, so it was perhaps unsurprising that his concentration lapsed briefly five laps later. Michael was fiddling with some buttons on the steering wheel when he ran wide

at Stavelot, but quickly gathered everything up and resumed without further drama.

In fact, for television viewers this was momentarily confusing. At almost exactly the same moment a tight-in shot showed a Ferrari missing its nose wing and, for a few seconds, it seemed as though Michael may have paid a high price for his fleeting inattention.

In fact, it was his team-mate Barrichello who had hit one of the rubber cones set into the kerbing on the entrance to the Bus Stop chicane immediately prior to the pits. It dropped him from fifth to ninth after a long haul round a full lap before he could pit for repairs.

At least Rubens managed to continue. Jenson Button duplicated the move in his Benetton, but crashed into the barrier on the left of the track before he could regain control of his B201. The young Englishman was understandably deeply disappointed.

'The car was fine when I turned left,' he shrugged, 'but it didn't want to turn right because the wing had fallen under my wheels, so I hit the wall.'

On lap 23 Fisichella and Häkkinen made their second stops, allowing Coulthard briefly up into second place some 30.3s behind Schumacher's Ferrari. Next time round David made his own second stop with the result that the status quo was restored by the end of lap 25 when Michael brought the leading Ferrari in, also for a second time.

By this stage his lead was up to 45s and he could easily resume with a half-minute lead over Fisichella who was now under even more pressure from the persistent Coulthard.

The Scot eventually managed to nip ahead of Fisichella — who retained his original front tyres even at his second stop — as they lapped Enrique Bernoldi's Arrows with eight laps to go.

'Second place is satisfying after the difficult start to my weekend, but I have to say Giancarlo did an amazing race,' he said.

'His Benetton was quick in all the right areas, but I've never been behind such a messy car. It was losing a lot of oil, so both my car and helmet were covered. I soon ran out of visor tear-offs and had to wipe the visor on the straights, which was a bit of a distraction.'

On this most challenging of circuits, where lap speeds regularly average around 135 mph, it seemed like a masterly piece of understatement from the phlegmatic Scot.

Häkkinen's efforts to get on terms with Fisichella in the closing stages were thwarted by a frustrating handling imbalance, but he still stayed comfortably ahead of Barrichello's delayed Ferrari to the chequered flag.

The final few laps were also enlivened by a torrid contest for sixth place between Jean Alesi's Jordan and Ralf Schumacher's Williams which had climbed steadily through the field throughout the race. Ralf did everything he could to pressure the veteran Frenchman into a mistake, but Jean simply wasn't having it.

'It was really motivating for me to see the pit board with my name and position on it with drivers such as Rubens and Ralf behind me,' he enthused. Alesi's performance came as a consolation prize for Jordan after Jarno Trulli had suffered engine failure just four laps from the finish while holding fifth place.

Behind Ralf Schumacher, Jacques Villeneuve came home eighth in his BAR-Honda ahead of a disappointed Heinz-Harald Frentzen who'd qualified fourth in his Prost AP04 only to stall on the grid at the first start. Taken in the round, it hadn't really been Prost's weekend.

Meanwhile, Michael Schumacher sauntered up to the winner's rostrum, not a bead of perspiration on his face. One was almost tempted to wonder what had everybody else in the race been doing all afternoon?

ROUND 14

SPA-FRANCORCHAMPS
31 AUGUST–2 SEPTEMBER 2001

FOSTER'S
BELGIAN
grand prix

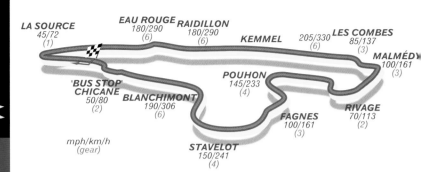

SPA-FRANCORCHAMPS
CIRCUIT LENGTH: 4.330 miles/6.968 km

LA SOURCE 45/72 (1)
EAU ROUGE 180/290 (6)
RAIDILLON 180/290 (6)
KEMMEL
LES COMBES 85/137 (3)
205/330 (6)
MALMÉDY 100/161 (3)
POUHON 145/233 (4)
'BUS STOP' CHICANE 50/80 (2)
BLANCHIMONT 190/306 (6)
RIVAGE 70/113 (2)
FAGNES 100/161 (3)
STAVELOT 150/241 (4)
mph/km/h (gear)

RACE DISTANCE: 36 laps, 155.859 miles/250.831 km   RACE WEATHER: Warm and cloudy

Pos.	Driver	Nat.	No.	Entrant	Car/Engine	Tyres	Laps	Time/Retirement	Speed (mph/km/h)	Gap to leader
1	Michael Schumacher	D	1	Scuderia Ferrari Marlboro	Ferrari F2001-050 V10	B	36	1h 08m 05.002s	137.354/221.050	
2	David Coulthard	GB	4	West McLaren Mercedes	McLaren MP4/16-Mercedes F0110K V10	B	36	1h 08m 15.100s	137.015/220.505	+10.09
3	Giancarlo Fisichella	I	7	Mild Seven Benetton Renault	Benetton B201-Renault RS21 V10	M	36	1h 08m 32.744s	136.427/219.559	+27.74
4	Mika Häkkinen	SF	3	West McLaren Mercedes	McLaren MP4/16-Mercedes F0110K V10	B	36	1h 08m 41.089s	136.151/219.114	+36.08
5	Rubens Barrichello	BR	2	Scuderia Ferrari Marlboro	Ferrari F2001-050 V10	B	36	1h 08m 59.523s	135.545/218.139	+54.52
6	Jean Alesi	F	12	B&H Jordan Honda	Jordan EJ11-Honda RA001E V10	B	36	1h 09m 04.686s	135.376/217.867	+59.68
7	Ralf Schumacher	D	5	BMW WilliamsF1 Team	Williams FW23-BMW P80 V10	M	36	1h 09m 04.988s	135.366/217.851	+59.9*
8	Jacques Villeneuve	CDN	10	Lucky Strike BAR Honda	BAR 03-Honda RA001E V10	B	36	1h 09m 09.972s	135.203/217.589	+64.97
9	Heinz-Harald Frentzen	D	22	Prost Acer	Prost AP04-Acer V10	M	35			+1
10	Jos Verstappen	NL	14	Orange Arrows Asiatech	Arrows A22-Asiatech V10	B	35			+1
11	Olivier Panis	F	9	Lucky Strike BAR Honda	BAR 03-Honda RA001E V10	B	35			+1
12	Enrique Bernoldi	BR	15	Orange Arrows Asiatech	Arrows A22-Asiatech V10	B	35			+1
13	Tarso Marques	BR	20	European Minardi F1	Minardi PS01B-European V10	M	32			+4 la
	Jarno Trulli	I	11	B&H Jordan Honda	Jordan EJ11-Honda RA001E V10	B	31	Engine		
	Jenson Button	GB	8	Mild Seven Benetton Renault	Benetton B201-Renault RS21 V10	M	17	Accident		
	Juan Pablo Montoya	COL	6	BMW WilliamsF1 Team	Williams FW23-BMW P80 V10	M	1	Engine		
	Pedro de la Rosa	ESP	19	Jaguar Racing	Jaguar R2-Cosworth CR3 V10	M	1	Accident damage		
	Nick Heidfeld	D	16	Red Bull Sauber Petronas	Sauber C20-Petronas V10	B	0	Accident		
DNS	Kimi Räikkönen	SF	17	Red Bull Sauber Petronas	Sauber C20-Petronas V10	B		Transmission		
DNS	Eddie Irvine	GB	18	Jaguar Racing	Jaguar R2-Cosworth CR3 V10	M		Accident		
DNS	Luciano Burti	BR	23	Prost Acer	Prost AP04-Acer V10	M		Accident		
DNS	Fernando Alonso	ESP	21	European Minardi F1	Minardi PS01B-European V10	M		Gearbox		

Fastest lap: Michael Schumacher, on lap 3, 1m 49.758s, 142.012 mph/228.546 km/h (record).

Previous lap record: Alain Prost (F1 Williams FW15C-Renault V10), 1m 51.095s, 140.424 mph/225.990 km/h (1993).

Grid order	1	2	3	4		1	2	3	4	5	6	7	8	9	10	11	12	13	14	15	16	17	18	19	20	21	22	23	24	25	26	27	28	29	30	31	32	33	34	35	36	
6 MONTOYA	1	1	1	1		1	1	1	1	1	1	1	1	1	1	1	1	1	1	1	1	1	1	1	1	1	1	1	1	1	1	1	1	1	1	1	1	1	1	1	1	1
5 R. SCHUMACHER	5	5	5	5		7	7	7	7	7	7	7	7	7	7	7	7	7	7	7	7	7	7	7	7	7	7	4	4	7	7	7	4	4	4	4	4	4	4	4	4	2
1 M. SCHUMACHER	2	2	2	2		2	2	2	2	2	2	2	4	4	4	4	4	4	4	4	4	4	4	4	4	7	4	4	7	7	7	7	7	7	7	7	7	7	7	7	3
22 FRENTZEN	7	7	3	3		4	4	4	4	4	4	4	2	3	3	3	3	3	3	3	3	3	3	3	3	3	3	3	3	3	3	3	3	3	3	3	3	3	3	3	4
2 BARRICHELLO	3	3	4	4		8	3	3	3	3	3	10	8	2	2	2	2	2	2	2	2	2	2	11	12	10	10	5	5	5	5	11	11	11	11	11	11	2	2	2	2	2	5
10 VILLENEUVE	4	4	7	7		3	8	11	11	11	12	10	10	8	10	11	11	11	11	11	11	11	11	12	11	12	12	11	12	12	12	12	12	12	12	12	12	12	12	12	12	6
3 HÄKKINEN	10	10	17	17		11	11	8	12	12	11	12	5	5	3	8	12	12	12	12	12	12	10	5	11	12	12	12	12	12	2	2	2	2	2	5	5	5	5	5	5	
7 FISICHELLA	17	17	10	10		12	12	12	8	8	10	8	3	11	12	10	10	10	10	10	10	10	2	5	11	12	2	2	2	2	10	10	10	5	5	5	10	10	10	10	10	
4 COULTHARD	8	8	8	12		10	10	10	10	10	8	14	11	5	10	22	22	22	22	22	8	8	5	2	2	2	10	10	10	10	5	5	5	10	10	10	22	22	22	22		
19 DE LA ROSA	19	12	12	8		14	14	14	14	14	15	5	14	12	22	8	8	8	8	8	5	5	14	14	14	14	14	22	22	22	22	22	22	22	22	22	14	14	14	14		
9 PANIS	9	19	19	19		9	9	9	9	9	9	11	12	22	5	5	5	5	5	5	22	14	22	22	22	22	22	14	14	14	14	14	14	14	14	14	9	9	9	9		
17 RÄIKKÖNEN	12	9	9	16		5	5	5	5	5	22	15	9	9	14	14	14	14	14	22	9	9	9	9	9	9	9	9	9	9	9	9	9	15	15	15	15	15	15	15		
12 ALESI	16	16	16	11		6	22	22	22	22	22	15	9	14	14	9	15	15	15	15	15	15	15	15	15	9	15	15	15	15	15	15	15	20								
16 HEIDFELD	18	18	11	9		22	15	15	15	15	15	20	14	15	15	9	9	9	9	9	20	20	20	20	20	20	20	20	20	20	20	20	20									
8 BUTTON	11	11	18	6		15	20	20	20	20	20	9	20	20	20	20	20	20	20	20	20																					
11 TRULLI	14	6	6	22		20																																				
18 IRVINE	6	23	23	14		19																																				
23 BURTI	23	14	14	15																																						
14 VERSTAPPEN	15	22	22	20																																						
21 ALONSO	22	15	15																																							
15 BERNOLDI	20	20	20																																							
20 MARQUES	21	21																																								

Pit stop
One lap behind leader

STARTING GRID

	1 **M. SCHUMACHER** Ferrari
5* **R. SCHUMACHER** Williams	
3 **HÄKKINEN** McLaren	**2** **BARRICHELLO** Ferrari
7 **FISICHELLA** Benetton	**4** **COULTHARD** McLaren
10 **VILLENEUVE** BAR	**17**** **RÄIKKÖNEN** Sauber
8 **BUTTON** Benetton	**12** **ALESI** Jordan
16 **HEIDFELD** Sauber	**19** **DE LA ROSA** Jaguar
9 **PANIS** BAR	**11** **TRULLI** Jordan
22 **FRENTZEN** Prost	**6** **MONTOYA** Williams
15 **BERNOLDI** Arrows	**14** **VERSTAPPEN** Arrows
	20 **MARQUES** Minardi

*started from the back of the grid
**did not start

TIME SHEETS

QUALIFYING
Weather: Warm, wet track, drying

Pos.	Driver	Car	Laps	Time
1	Juan Pablo Montoya	Williams-BMW	7	1m 52.072s
2	Ralf Schumacher	Williams-BMW	10	1m 52.959s
3	Michael Schumacher	Ferrari	8	1m 54.685s
4	Heinz-Harald Frentzen	Prost-Acer	10	1m 55.233s
5	Rubens Barrichello	Ferrari	7	1m 56.116s
6	Jacques Villeneuve	BAR-Honda	11	1m 57.038s
7	Mika Häkkinen	McLaren-Mercedes	12	1m 57.043s
8	Giancarlo Fisichella	Benetton-Renault	7	1m 57.668s
9	David Coulthard	McLaren-Mercedes	10	1m 58.008s
10	Pedro de la Rosa	Jaguar-Cosworth	11	1m 58.519s
11	Olivier Panis	BAR-Honda	8	1m 58.838s
12	Kimi Räikkönen	Sauber-Petronas	8	1m 59.050s
13	Jean Alesi	Jordan-Honda	10	1m 59.128s
14	Nick Heidfeld	Sauber-Petronas	9	1m 59.302s
15	Jenson Button	Benetton-Renault	7	1m 59.587s
16	Jarno Trulli	Jordan-Honda	10	1m 59.647s
17	Eddie Irvine	Jaguar-Cosworth	9	1m 59.689s
18	Luciano Burti	Prost-Acer	7	1m 59.900s
19	Jos Verstappen*	Arrows-Asiatech	10	2m 02.039s
20	Fernando Alonso*	Minardi-European	8	2m 02.594s
21	Enrique Bernoldi*	Arrows-Asiatech	10	2m 03.048s
22	Tarso Marques*	Minardi-European	10	2m 04.204s

107% time: 1m 59.917s   *allowed to race

FRIDAY FREE PRACTICE
Weather: Cool and overcast, then heavy rain

Pos.	Driver	Laps	Time
1	Michael Schumacher	28	1m 48.655s
2	Jarno Trulli	34	1m 49.404s
3	Rubens Barrichello	35	1m 49.456s
4	Giancarlo Fisichella	30	1m 50.192s
5	Mika Häkkinen	29	1m 50.239s
6	Kimi Räikkönen	34	1m 50.495s
7	Ralf Schumacher	23	1m 50.801s
8	Eddie Irvine	34	1m 51.555s
9	Jean Alesi	30	1m 51.631s
10	Jenson Button	21	1m 51.673s
11	Olivier Panis	24	1m 52.071s
12	Heinz-Harald Frentzen	33	1m 52.073s
13	Pedro de la Rosa	31	1m 52.119s
14	Nick Heidfeld	31	1m 52.436s
15	Jacques Villeneuve	20	1m 52.804s
16	Juan Pablo Montoya	24	1m 52.829s
17	Jos Verstappen	34	1m 52.955s
18	Fernando Alonso	26	1m 55.021s
19	Tarso Marques	30	1m 55.099s
20	Enrique Bernoldi	30	1m 55.491s
21	Luciano Burti	13	2m 11.037s
22	David Coulthard	3	12m 37.913s

SATURDAY FREE PRACTICE
Weather: Cool and overcast

Pos.	Driver	Laps	Time
1	Juan Pablo Montoya	12	1m 47.494s
2	Ralf Schumacher	15	1m 47.768s
3	Mika Häkkinen	12	1m 48.465s
4	David Coulthard	13	1m 48.698s
5	Rubens Barrichello	10	1m 49.071s
6	Giancarlo Fisichella	12	1m 49.511s
7	Eddie Irvine	12	1m 49.857s
8	Jacques Villeneuve	14	1m 49.953s
9	Jenson Button	12	1m 50.130s
10	Jean Alesi	13	1m 50.485s
11	Jarno Trulli	11	1m 50.494s
12	Olivier Panis	15	1m 50.501s
13	Heinz-Harald Frentzen	14	1m 50.765s
14	Pedro de la Rosa	9	1m 52.267s
15	Luciano Burti	16	1m 52.740s
16	Enrique Bernoldi	15	1m 52.906s
17	Fernando Alonso	14	1m 53.546s
18	Tarso Marques	12	1m 53.861s
19	Michael Schumacher	7	1m 57.257s
20	Jos Verstappen	7	1m 57.477s
21	Kimi Räikkönen	5	1m 58.547s
22	Nick Heidfeld	3	2m 55.816s

WARM-UP
Weather: Warm and bright

Pos.	Driver	Laps	Time
1	Michael Schumacher	11	1m 49.495s
2	Mika Häkkinen	9	1m 50.694s
3	Kimi Räikkönen	11	1m 50.738s
4	Ralf Schumacher	12	1m 50.776s
5	Eddie Irvine	11	1m 50.818s
6	Heinz-Harald Frentzen	12	1m 50.908s
7	Juan Pablo Montoya	8	1m 50.993s
8	Jarno Trulli	8	1m 51.062s
9	Nick Heidfeld	11	1m 51.317s
10	Rubens Barrichello	6	1m 51.394s
11	Pedro de la Rosa	10	1m 51.418s
12	David Coulthard	9	1m 51.750s
13	Jean Alesi	11	1m 52.338s
14	Giancarlo Fisichella	12	1m 52.436s
15	Fernando Alonso	9	1m 52.479s
16	Olivier Panis	10	1m 52.519s
17	Jacques Villeneuve	12	1m 52.903s
18	Tarso Marques	8	1m 52.908s
19	Luciano Burti	9	1m 53.083s
20	Jos Verstappen	13	1m 53.737s
21	Enrique Bernoldi	13	1m 54.472s
22	Jenson Button	3	2m 34.526s

RACE FASTEST LAPS
Weather: Warm and cloudy

Driver	Time	Lap
Michael Schumacher	1m 49.758s	3
Ralf Schumacher	1m 51.058s	21
David Coulthard	1m 51.608s	31
Giancarlo Fisichella	1m 51.725s	10
Mika Häkkinen	1m 51.741s	9
Rubens Barrichello	1m 51.776s	20
Jarno Trulli	1m 51.828s	4
Jean Alesi	1m 51.996s	5
Jacques Villeneuve	1m 52.372s	11
Olivier Panis	1m 52.533s	24
Jenson Button	1m 53.409s	17
Heinz-Harald Frentzen	1m 54.051s	15
Jos Verstappen	1m 54.095s	4
Enrique Bernoldi	1m 55.196s	4
Nick Heidfeld	1m 55.804s	4
Tarso Marques	1m 56.484s	8

CHASSIS LOG BOOK

1	M. Schumacher	Ferrari F2001/213
2	Barrichello	Ferrari F2001/206
	spare	Ferrari F2001/211
3	Häkkinen	McLaren MP4/16/7
4	Coulthard	McLaren MP4/16/6
	spares	McLaren MP4/16/4 & 5
5	R. Schumacher	Williams FW23/7
6	Montoya	Williams FW23/6
	spare	Williams FW23/2
7	Fisichella	Benetton B201/6
8	Button	Benetton B201/5
	spares	Benetton B201/3 & 1
9	Panis	BAR 03/6
10	Villeneuve	BAR 03/4
	spare	BAR 03/5
11	Trulli	Jordan EJ11/5
12	Alesi	Jordan EJ11/4
	spare	Jordan EJ11/3
14	Verstappen	Arrows A22/6
15	Bernoldi	Arrows A22/3
	spare	Arrows A22/1
16	Heidfeld	Sauber C20/7
17	Räikkönen	Sauber C20/6
	spare	Sauber C20/1
18	Irvine	Jaguar R2/6
19	de la Rosa	Jaguar R2/7
	spare	Jaguar R2/4
20	Marques	Minardi PS01B/4
21	Alonso	Minardi PS01B/3
	spare	Minardi PS01/1
22	Frentzen	Prost AP04/6
23	Burti	Prost AP04/4
	spare	Prost AP04/2

POINTS TABLES

DRIVERS

1	Michael Schumacher	104
2	David Coulthard	57
3	Rubens Barrichello	48
4	Ralf Schumacher	44
5	Mika Häkkinen	24
6	Juan Pablo Montoya	15
7 =	Jacques Villeneuve	11
7 =	Nick Heidfeld	11
9 =	Kimi Räikkönen	9
9 =	Jarno Trulli	9
11	Giancarlo Fisichella	8
12	Heinz-Harald Frentzen	6
13 =	Olivier Panis	5
13 =	Jean Alesi	5
15	Eddie Irvine	4
16	Jenson Button	2
17 =	Jos Verstappen	1
17 =	Pedro de la Rosa	1

CONSTRUCTORS

1	Ferrari	152
2	McLaren	81
3	Williams	59
4	Sauber	20
5 =	BAR	16
5 =	Jordan	16
7	Benetton	10
8	Jaguar	5
9	Prost	4
10	Arrows	1

ITALIAN
grand prix

1st - MONTOYA • 2nd - BARRICHELLO • 3rd - R. SCHUMACHER

Previous spread: **The first of many? Juan Pablo Montoya finally nailed that elusive first Grand Prix win at Monza, emerging on top from a close battle with Rubens Barrichello's Ferrari.**
Both photographs: Paul-Henri Cahier

Diary

Alex Zanardi has both legs amputated following high-speed collision with CART rival Alex Tagliani in the American Memorial 500 at Lausitzring.

Brazilian Euro F3000 champion Felipe Massa tipped strongly to land seat at Sauber in 2002 as Kimi Räikkönen's successor.

Ferrari boss Luca di Montezemolo calls for F1 teams to give more decision-making power to the FIA in order that costs can be kept down.

British manufacturers Lola and Reynard confirm plans to build cars for the Indy Racing League in 2003.

MONZA QUALIFYING

The whole mood over the Monza weekend was one of incomprehension over the events in the wider world combined with a degree of apprehensive caution over the prospect of attending the US Grand Prix at Indianapolis a fortnight later.

'The teams should all try and be positive and not just symbolic,' said McLaren boss Ron Dennis. 'We should be unified and responsible. The race promoters are partners in the F1 business. We have to strike a careful balance between continuing business as usual and taking a respectful stance in view of the events which have happened.'

Mika Häkkinen was shaken but unhurt after wrecking his McLaren-Mercedes MP4/16 against the barrier on the fast right-hander, badly damaging its monocoque. On the weekend that he had formally announced his intention to take a sabbatical in 2002, the Finn had been struggling with handling balance all weekend, qualifying a disappointed seventh on 1m 23.394s, one place behind team-mate David Coulthard (1m 23.148s).

Meanwhile, Juan Pablo Montoya did a brilliant job bagging the third pole position of his career ahead of the Ferraris of Rubens Barrichello and Michael Schumacher. 'Monty' has become a great favourite within the F1 community, in many ways reminding one of the hapless Zanardi with his genuine openness and wry sense of humour. It was a day on which it was difficult to disentangle the underlying tension from the events of the day.

Montoya admitted that he was happy with the feel of his car, although not totally confident that pole was actually within his reach. 'It's obviously very satisfying to have beaten Ferrari here on their home ground,' he acknowledged, but Ralf Schumacher certainly didn't share his optimism.

The German driver could only line up fourth on 1m 22.841s, complaining that his FW23 yawed from understeer to oversteer and that his fourth run was spoiled by a yellow flag.

Ferrari obviously had qualifying engines available for this crucial race, Barrichello completing his first run on used rubber before switching to a new set of Bridgestones which helped him nail a 1m 22.528s for the second place on the front row.

Michael Schumacher confessed to a slight mistake on the lap's first sector on his third run, ending up with a 1m 22.624s, third overall. 'I thought we could take pole, but we didn't quite manage it,' he explained thoughtfully. 'And yes, it is hard to concentrate.'

Splitting the two McLaren-Mercedes from the front-running quartet, Jarno Trulli did a superb job with his Jordan EJ-11, reporting that he was delighted with the car and very impressed with the latest Bridgestones on his way to a fifth-fastest 1m 23.126s.

Jean Alesi, by contrast, had a simply disastrous session and wound up 16th on 1m 24.198s in the other Jordan-Honda. The knock-on effect of a morning transmission problem blighted his efforts, brake balance and handling generally being well off the mark.

In the McLaren camp Coulthard was particularly frustrated. 'We've been rather struggling here,' he said. 'We knew from Hockenheim that we're a little bit off the pace at these kind of circuits.'

Right behind the McLarens came the two Sauber C20s who'd lost time on Friday with a repeat of the same strange gearbox problem which had bugged them at Spa. Heidfeld, eighth on 1m 23.417s, had a generally good day under the circumstances but Kimi Räikkönen (1m 23.595s) blamed Jenson Button for holding him up at the first chicane.

In the Jaguar squad Pedro de la Rosa was satisfied with tenth on 1m 23.693s, but Eddie Irvine spent the two days of practice and qualifying struggling with a brake balance problem which had pitched him into a gravel trap on Friday. He was still grappling with the problem on Saturday and it left him trailing 13th on 1m 24.031s.

Button was delighted with the Benetton's handling balance and particularly pleased with the 11th-place 1m 23.892s best it delivered as a result. Team-mate Giancarlo Fisichella was very unhappy in 14th place on 1m 24.090s after an hydraulic problem in the morning and an engine problem in the afternoon.

By contrast, Heinz-Harald Frentzen (1m 23.943s) rated his 12th place more significant than fourth on the grid at Spa a fortnight earlier as there were no ifs and buts about this performance. 'H-H' was getting the hang of the Prost and reckoned it was potentially a pretty respectable car, lacking only a degree of front-end grip. Tomas Enge, the Czech F3000 ace standing in for the recovering Luciano Burti, had a painful introduction to F1 with no fewer than three engine malfunctions during the course of the day.

Over in the BAR-Honda enclave, Jacques Villeneuve (1m 24.164s) and Olivier Panis (1m 24.677s) could almost be seen shaking their heads in dismay at qualifying 15th and 17th. Both reported that the car's mechanical grip was fine, but aerodynamic downforce was lacking. 'It was a frustrating session, but I think we managed to learn a few things,' shrugged Panis.

Completing the grid were the breathless Arrows of Enrique Bernoldi (1m 25.444s) and Jos Verstappen (1m 25.511s), the hapless Enge and both Minardi drivers Fernando Alonso (1m 26.218s) and new boy Alex Yoong (1m 27.463s). The last two in the line-up had a nerve-wracking time when their race cars both suffered identical gearchange actuator failures on the out lap and then had to share the spare car equipped with the earlier transmission and rear suspension package.

IT was always going to happen, and sooner rather than later. Juan Pablo Montoya had signalled his winning intent and capability almost from the very start of his F1 career with the BMW Williams team and when the opportunity came at Monza, he seized it with both hands. The Colombian rising star emerged from the Italian Grand Prix with his first F1 victory after qualifying on pole position and driving with a perfect balance of aggression and restraint throughout the 53-lap event.

The Colombian ace had qualified on pole position, but Rubens Barrichello's Ferrari F2001 was alongside him on the front row, the Brazilian driver having outqualified an off-form Michael Schumacher who was preoccupied with concerns about circuit safety and his unwillingness to compete in the forthcoming US Grand Prix due to security considerations.

Ferrari judged that a two-stop strategy for the race was the best way in which they could emerge triumphant over Montoya's Williams-BMW and it was Barrichello who set the early pace. After Montoya led for the first eight laps, Barrichello surged ahead as the Williams driver found himself grappling with blistering on his hard-option Michelin rear tyres and a heavy fuel load.

As Montoya struggled to fend off the World Champion in third place, Barrichello, aided by the slightly softer new Bridgestone compound which had been introduced for this race, opened a 9.5s lead before dodging into the pits for a first refuelling stop on lap 19. It should have been accomplished in around 10s — following Schumacher's example the previous lap — but an extraordinary glitch saw Barrichello stationary for 16.3s before accelerating back into the fray.

Schumacher had made his stop on the previous lap and the plan had been to fill Barrichello with a light fuel load for a short middle stint in a bid to put Montoya under the maximum possible pressure. Unfortunately there was a problem recalibrating the rig and it had to be manhandled aside to make way for the spare — which had Schumacher's heavier load programmed in for delivery.

Not only did this glitch cost Barrichello about 7s, but it also sent him back into the race marginally heavier than was ideal. Bearing in mind the fact that Montoya would eventually win by 5.17s, had the Brazilian enjoyed a trouble-free first stop, things might have been very close indeed.

'The two-stop strategy was definitely the right decision,' said Barrichello, 'and Ross Brawn was magic to think of this, which gave us the chance to fight the Williams.' He added diplomatically 'I am not sure what happened in the pit stop, but it cost me a lot of time. Enough to lose the race.'

Williams technical director Patrick Head reckoned that Montoya still had something in hand to fend off the Ferraris. For his part, Montoya certainly agreed.

His one-stop strategy was sufficiently effective to leave him nursing a 6.5s advantage over Barrichello when the Ferrari driver emerged from his final refuelling stop with 12 laps to run.

'I blistered a rear tyre early on,' said Montoya, 'and that left the car sliding around under braking. It took me a couple of laps to get into the groove and handle that problem. Then, at the refuelling stop, we adjusted the front wing a little too much and that left me with too much understeer. But I had the speed when I needed it to keep ahead.'

It was the fourth BMW Williams team victory of the season and one which saw Ralf Schumacher, architect of the previous three wins, trailing home third. Ralf had been out to lunch for much of the weekend, honestly admitting that he'd never got on top of the programme.

He was using the same revised-spec FW23 chassis with its stiffer monocoque and revised suspension geometry which he'd driven for the first time at Spa, but this time he'd opted for the original aerodynamic package with a different cooling system.

Whether this, or his apparent obsession with not going to the US Grand Prix, affected his performance was hardly clear but Ralf certainly reflected his elder brother's overtly gloomy outlook throughout a weekend in which the drivers had been stunned by news of Alex Zanardi's terrible accident in Germany.

Above: Chaos reigns at the first chicane after Jenson Button punted Jarno Trulli's Jordan into an impromptu pirouette. In the foreground, Schumacher's Ferrari takes a short cut.
Photograph: Mark Thompson/Allsport-Getty Images

Far left: The banner of support for Alex Zanardi from Jacques Villeneuve's fans emphasised that the Italian driver's plight was at the forefront of everybody's minds on race day at Monza.
Photograph: Clive Mason/Allsport-Getty Images

Left, above: Czech Tomas Enge, a leading light in F3000, made his F1 debut for Prost as Luciano Burti's stand-in.
Photograph: Bryn Williams/crash.net

Left, below: Minardi replaced Tarso Marques with the ambitious Malaysian driver Alex Yoong.
Photograph: Clive Mason/Allsport-Getty Images

RÄIKKÖNEN SIGNED UP AS HÄKKINEN OPTS FOR McLAREN SABBATICAL

F1 prodigy Kimi Räikkönen was confirmed as a McLaren-Mercedes driver for the 2002 season over the Italian GP weekend, amazing all those paddock insiders who believed that he'd been targeted as a long-term talent by the Ferrari squad.

Räikkönen, who was catapulted directly from the minor-league Formula Renault into F1 at the start of 2001 by the Sauber team, will replace fellow Finn Mika Häkkinen who is standing down at the end of the season after nine years with McLaren.

Officially Häkkinen is taking a one-year sabbatical to recharge his batteries and admits that he is keen to resume his career with McLaren in 2003. However the reality is that it is far from certain that the 32-year-old twice World Champion will ever race again in the sport's most senior category.

'F1 has been virtually my whole life since I started karting in 1974,' said Häkkinen. 'The intensity of my career has become increasingly difficult for those around me. I asked the team for a break which would be a good way to recharge my batteries and enjoy more time with my wife Erja and my son Hugo.

'Of course it might have been easier to retire, but that just isn't a decision I feel ready to take. [But] I know that I will have to work hard to return after my break, but I know that I want to return with the McLaren-Mercedes team.'

For his part, David Coulthard seemed not the slightest bit intimidated by Räikkönen's arrival as he confidently believes himself capable of an even stronger championship bid in 2002.

'My contract with McLaren was agreed a few months ago,' he said, 'and I am looking forward to next year's championship challenge. Thanks to Mika, I have gained a valuable insight into fast Finns, which I am sure will be useful next year.'

It was on Saturday afternoon that the news came through from the Lausitzring that the popular Zanardi, who'd driven for Williams throughout an acutely disappointing 1999 season, had suffered horrifying injuries which resulted in both his legs having to be amputated.

Perhaps for Michael Schumacher, this was the last straw. With the championship clinched and obviously deeply affected by the New York terrorist attacks, he seemed preoccupied that something might go wrong at Monza.

Prior to the start, he and his brother tried to rally the other drivers to agree a no-passing treaty for the first two chicanes on the opening lap, haunted by memories of the accident which killed marshal Paolo Ghislimberti in last year's race.

This was an issue which caused a lot of ill-feeling, for the drivers believed they had a worthwhile viewpoint while several team principals thought that if they'd wanted the Monza circuit configuration changed, they should have done it before the morning of this year's race.

Initially it was suggested that the race should be started behind the safety car, but the stewards rejected that idea after Jacques Villeneuve stood out against it. Schumacher was furious and suggested an informal arrangement, but Benetton's Flavio Briatore, BAR's Craig Pollock and Arrows boss Tom Walkinshaw insisted that their drivers got on and raced.

This prompted some drivers to become very animated about the issue, understandably perhaps. Jean Alesi didn't mince his words. 'Briatore is a bully and this is a disgrace,' he said.

'We wanted to drive safely at the start so there was nothing bad for people watching all round the world.'

Without naming names, David Coulthard added: 'You see the true colour of individuals in these situations,' he said. 'It is a sport, a hard business and we all want to win. There has to be an element of sense and clearly that did not work today.'

For his part, Frank Williams was sympathetic with the drivers. 'After the events in New York and Germany, if F1 had had a bit of carnage like last year at one of the chicanes, it would have been very bad for business,' he said.

And so they raced. Montoya led away from the start pursued by Barrichello and Ralf Schumacher, but further back future Renault team-mates Jenson Button and Jarno Trulli were involved in another contretemps when the British driver slammed his Benetton into the back of the Jordan driver going into the first corner.

'Button hit the rear of my car as he turned in and pushed me into a spin,' fumed Trulli. 'He clearly badly misjudged his braking but I was already in the corner so there was nothing I could do.'

Button was apologetic. 'I braked at the same time as everyone else, but couldn't stop in time to avoid Trulli,' he said. 'I ran into him, lost my front wing and put him out of the race, for which I was very sorry.'

Having failed to gain the support he was looking from his colleagues, Schumacher made a storming start and ran with the leading bunch before fading to a disappointing fourth. 'Luckily, everything went well and nothing happened,' he shrugged. 'I am glad that this weekend is over but it was a pity Rubens was not able to win the race.'

David Coulthard qualified sixth and Mika Häkkinen seventh with David reaching the first corner in fifth place at which point Mika was forced up the escape road avoiding a pile-up between several other cars. This dropped him back to 13th at the end of the opening lap.

On lap seven David stopped out on the circuit when the engine failed, the cause of which was still being investigated on Sunday evening.

'There is no doubt that this has been a race of attrition,' David said. 'Unfortunately this didn't work to our advantage as both Mika and I retired. It's been a difficult weekend for us with a few problems along the way, but we still hoped to get points. At least I retained my second place in the championship points standings.'

Mika, who like David was on a one-stop strategy, was up to tenth place by lap 19 when he stopped at the first chicane with a drivetrain problem.

'The pile-up at the first corner after the start caused me to go straight on at the chicane which cost me several positions and I came out 13th,' said Mika.

'This was extremely disappointing as we drivers had discussed that we should be particularly careful at the start, as the first chicane is so tight. On lap ten I got stuck in fifth gear and as I went around the chicane, I lost all the gears and that was the end of my race.'

Behind Michael Schumacher, Pedro de la Rosa brought his Jaguar R2 home a strong fifth to give the British team the boost it had been looking for. With a heavy fuel load and a one-stop strategy which took him to lap 37 of the 53-lap race before topping up, de la Rosa made the best use of his soft-compound Michelins to get the job done.

By contrast, Eddie Irvine was in trouble almost from the start in the other Jaguar R2, despite completing the opening lap in seventh place. The Ulsterman immediately detected a power loss from the Cosworth CR3 V10, but the problem didn't appear to be showing up on the team's telemetry, so 'Irv' was called in at the end of lap 14.

Close examination suggested that part of the oil breathing system worked loose, allowed some lubricant to get inside the combustion chamber and effectively caused a spark plug to fail.

'It's been a bad weekend for me from the minute I arrived at Monza,' said Irvine. 'The car hasn't really been to my liking all weekend and it was difficult achieving a good set-up. It's very disappointing not to have scored today, but Pedro has compensated the team with some well deserved points.'

Sixth place fell to Jacques Villeneuve, the BAR-Honda driver getting to within 8s of de la Rosa despite having to ease back and conserve fuel after it became clear that a rig problem had resulted in his car being under-fuelled at his sole stop on lap 33. At least the Canadian got a point to move BAR ahead of key rivals Jordan in the constructors' championship, crossing the line less than a second ahead of Kimi Räikkönen's Sauber which was the last unlapped runner.

Jean Alesi's Jordan EJ-11 took eighth ahead of Olivier Panis's BAR-Honda, while Giancarlo Fisichella at least got his Benetton B201 to the finish in tenth which made up in some small measure for Button's disappointment.

For the moment, however, the day belonged to Montoya. Interestingly, there was no outward show of congratulations from his BMW Williams team-mate as they mounted the rostrum.

On the face of it, Juan Pablo finished that sunny afternoon in Italy with Ralf Schumacher psychologically on the run. The heat was certainly building within Frank Williams's team.

Far left: Michael Schumacher, Jean Alesi and David Coulthard in deep discussion on the starting grid.

Below far left: Ferrari sported black nose cones and ran devoid of all commercial sponsorship identification in deference to the events of 11 September.
Both photographs: Paul-Henri Cahier

Below near left: Jenson Button was told by Benetton boss Flavio Briatore to race from the start and ignore the proposed first-lap ban on overtaking.
Photograph: Mark Thompson/Allsport-Getty Images

Below: Pedro de la Rosa survived to take a heartening fifth place for the increasingly stressed Jaguar team.

Overleaf: Rubens Barrichello was a strong contender for victory at Monza, but an unexpectedly long refuelling stop meant that he had to settle for second behind Montoya.
Both photographs: Paul-Henri Cahier

ROUND 15
MONZA 14–16 SEPTEMBER 2001

gran premio
CAMPARI
d'ITALIA

MONZA – GRAND PRIX CIRCUIT
CIRCUIT LENGTH: 3.596 miles/5.788 km

CURVA DI LESMO
100/161 (3)
90/145 (2)
CURVA DEL SERRAGLIO
205/330 (6)
SECONDA VARIANTE
70/113 (2)
VARIANTE ASCARI
100/161 (3)
RETTILINEO PARABOLICA
205/330 (6)
mph/km/h (gear)
210/338 (6)
CURVA GRANDE
180/290 (5)
PRIMA VARIANTE
60/97 (2)
CURVA PARABOLICA
155/250 (4)

RACE DISTANCE: 53 laps, 190.605 miles/306.749 km   RACE WEATHER: Warm and sunny

Pos.	Driver	Nat.	No.	Entrant	Car/Engine	Tyres	Laps	Time/Retirement	Speed (mph/km/h)	Gap to lea
1	Juan Pablo Montoya	COL	6	BMW WilliamsF1 Team	Williams FW23-BMW P80 V10	M	53	1h 16m 58.493s	148.571/239.103	
2	Rubens Barrichello	BR	2	Scuderia Ferrari Marlboro	Ferrari F2001-050 V10	B	53	1h 17m 03.668s	148.405/238.835	+5.1
3	Ralf Schumacher	D	5	BMW WilliamsF1 Team	Williams FW23-BMW P80 V10	B	53	1h 17m 15.828s	148.016/238.209	+17.3
4	Michael Schumacher	D	1	Scuderia Ferrari Marlboro	Ferrari F2001-050 V10	B	53	1h 17m 23.484s	147.772/237.816	+24.9
5	Pedro de la Rosa	ESP	19	Jaguar Racing	Jaguar R2-Cosworth CR3 V10	M	53	1h 18m 13.477s	146.198/235.283	+74.9
6	Jacques Villeneuve	CDN	10	Lucky Strike BAR Honda	BAR 03-Honda RA001E V10	B	53	1h 18m 20.962s	145.965/234.908	+82.4
7	Kimi Räikkönen	SF	17	Red Bull Sauber Petronas	Sauber C20-Petronas V10	B	53	1h 18m 21.600s	145.945/234.876	+83.1
8	Jean Alesi	F	12	B&H Jordan Honda	Jordan EJ11-Honda RA001E V10	B	52			+1
9	Olivier Panis	F	9	Lucky Strike BAR Honda	BAR 03-Honda RA001E V10	B	52			+1
10	Giancarlo Fisichella	I	7	Mild Seven Benetton Renault	Benetton B201-Renault RS21 V10	M	52			+1
11	Nick Heidfeld	D	16	Red Bull Sauber Petronas	Sauber C20-Petronas V10	B	52			+1
12	Tomas Enge	CZ	23	Prost Acer	Prost AP04-Acer V10	M	52			+1
13	Fernando Alonso	ESP	21	European Minardi F1	Minardi PS01-European V10	M	51			+2
	Enrique Bernoldi	BR	15	Orange Arrows Asiatech	Arrows A22-Asiatech V10	B	46	Gearbox		
	Alex Yoong	MAS	20	European Minardi F1	Minardi PS01-European V10	M	44	Spun off		
	Heinz-Harald Frentzen	D	22	Prost Acer	Prost AP04-Acer V10	M	28	Transmission		
	Jos Verstappen	NL	14	Orange Arrows Asiatech	Arrows A22-Asiatech V10	B	25	Electrics		
	Mika Häkkinen	SF	3	West McLaren Mercedes	McLaren MP4/16-Mercedes F0110K V10	B	19	Transmission		
	Eddie Irvine	GB	18	Jaguar Racing	Jaguar R2-Cosworth CR3 V10	M	14	Misfire/oil leak		
	David Coulthard	GB	4	West McLaren Mercedes	McLaren MP4/16-Mercedes F0110K V10	B	6	Engine		
	Jenson Button	GB	8	Mild Seven Benetton Renault	Benetton B201-Renault RS21 V10	M	4	Engine		
	Jarno Trulli	I	11	B&H Jordan Honda	Jordan EJ11-Honda RA001E V10	B	0	Collision with Button		

Fastest lap: Ralf Schumacher, on lap 39, 1m 25.073s, 152.323 mph/245.140 km/h (record).

Previous lap record: Mika Häkkinen (F1 McLaren MP4/15-Mercedes V10), 1m 25.595s, 151.394 mph/243.645 km/h (2000).

Grid order	1	2	3	4	5	6	7	8	9	10	11	12	13	14	15	16	17	18	19	20	21	22	23	24	25	26	27	28	29	30	31	32	33	34	35	36	37	38	39
6 MONTOYA	6	6	6	6	6	6	6	6	2	2	2	2	2	2	2	2	2	2	2	6	6	6	6	6	6	6	6	6	5	5	5	5	5	5	5	2	2	2	2
2 BARRICHELLO	2	2	2	2	2	2	2	6	6	6	6	6	6	6	6	6	6	6	5	5	5	5	5	5	5	5	5	5	2	2	2	2	2	2	2	6	6	6	6
1 M. SCHUMACHER	1	1	1	1	1	1	1	1	1	1	1	1	1	1	1	1	1	1	5	2	2	2	2	2	2	2	2	2	6	6	6	6	6	6	6	1	1	1	1
5 R. SCHUMACHER	5	5	5	5	5	5	5	5	5	5	5	5	5	5	5	5	5	5	1	1	1	1	1	1	1	1	1	1	1	1	1	1	1	1	1	5	5	5	5
11 TRULLI	4	4	4	4	4	4	14	14	14	14	14	14	14	14	12	12	12	12	12	12	12	12	19	19	19	19	19	19	19	19	19	19	19	19	19	19	19	19	19
4 COULTHARD	19	19	19	19	14	14	17	17	17	17	17	12	12	12	12	17	17	17	17	17	17	17	10	10	10	10	10	10	10	10	10	10	10	10	10	10	10	10	10
3 HÄKKINEN	18	18	14	14	17	17	12	12	12	12	12	17	17	17	17	14	14	14	19	19	19	19	12	12	12	12	12	12	12	17	17	17	17	17	17	17	17	17	17
16 HEIDFELD	14	14	17	17	12	12	19	19	19	19	19	19	19	19	19	19	19	19	10	10	10	10	15	15	15	9	9	9	9	12	12	12	12	12	12	12	12	12	12
17 RÄIKKÖNEN	17	17	18	12	19	19	10	10	10	10	10	10	10	10	10	10	10	10	3	15	15	15	9	9	9	22	22	7	7	17	17	9	9	9	9	9	9	9	9
19 DE LA ROSA	12	12	12	18	15	15	15	15	15	15	15	3	3	3	3	3	3	15	9	9	9	22	22	22	22	7	7	17	17	23	23	7	7	7	7	7	7	7	7
8 BUTTON	10	15	15	10	10	10	3	3	3	3	3	15	15	15	15	15	15	9	22	22	22	7	7	7	7	16	17	23	23	7	7	16	16	16	16	16	16	16	16
22 FRENTZEN	15	10	10	18	18	3	9	9	9	9	9	9	9	9	9	9	9	22	16	16	16	16	16	16	16	16	16	16	16	15	15	15	15	15	15	15	15	15	15
18 IRVINE	3	3	3	3	3	9	22	22	22	22	22	22	22	22	22	22	22	16	7	7	7	9	17	17	17	17	15	23	15	15	15	15	23	23	23	23	23	23	23
7 FISICHELLA	9	9	9	9	9	22	21	21	21	21	21	21	21	16	16	16	7	7	14	14	14	14	14	14	14	14	21	21	21	21	21	21	21	21	21	21	21	21	21
10 VILLENEUVE	22	22	22	22	22	18	18	16	16	16	16	16	16	16	16	16	7	7	14	23	23	23	23	21	21	21	21	20	21	20	20	20	20	21	20	20	20	20	20
12 ALESI	21	21	21	21	21	21	16	7	7	7	7	7	7	7	7	21	23	23	21	21	21	21	21	20	20	20													
9 PANIS	23	23	23	23	16	16	7	23	23	23	23	23	23	23	23	21	21	20	20	20	20	20																	
15 BERNOLDI	16	16	16	16	7	23	18	18	18	18	18	18	18	20	20	20	20	20																					
14 VERSTAPPEN	20	7	7	7	23	23	20	20	20	20	20	20	20	20																									
23 ENGE	7	20	20	20	20	20																																	
21 ALONSO	8	8	8	8																																			
20 YOONG																																							

Pit stop
One lap behind leader

STARTING GRID

6 **MONTOYA** Williams	**2** **BARRICHELLO** Ferrari
1 **M. SCHUMACHER** Ferrari	**5** **R. SCHUMACHER** Williams
11 **TRULLI** Jordan	**4** **COULTHARD** McLaren
3 **HÄKKINEN** McLaren	**16*** **HEIDFELD** Sauber
17 **RÄIKKÖNEN** Sauber	**19** **DE LA ROSA** Jaguar
8 **BUTTON** Benetton	**22** **FRENTZEN** Prost
18 **IRVINE** Jaguar	**7*** **FISICHELLA** Benetton
10 **VILLENEUVE** BAR	**12** **ALESI** Jordan
9 **PANIS** BAR	**15** **BERNOLDI** Arrows
14 **VERSTAPPEN** Arrows	**23** **ENGE** Prost
21 **ALONSO** Minardi	**20** **YOONG** Minardi

*started from the pit lane

FOR THE RECORD

First Grand Prix win
Juan Pablo Montoya
First Grand Prix start
Tomas Enge
Alex Yoong
650th Grand Prix start
Ferrari

Lap chart (partial)

43	44	45	46	47	48	49	50	51	52	53	
6	6	6	6	6	6	6	6	6	6	6	1
5	5	5	5	2	2	2	2	2	2	2	2
2	2	2	2	5	5	5	5	5	5	5	3
1	1	1	1	1	1	1	1	1	1	1	4
19	19	19	19	19	19	19	19	19	19	19	5
10	10	10	10	10	10	10	10	10	10	10	6
17	17	17	17	17	17	17	17	17	17	17	
12	12	12	12	12	12	12	12	12	12		
9	9	9	9	9	9	9	9	9	9		
7	7	7	7	7	7	7	7	7	7		
16	16	16	16	16	16	16	16	16			
23	23	23	23	23	23	23	23	23			
15	15	15	15	21	21	21	21				
21	21	21	21								
20	20										

TIME SHEETS

QUALIFYING
Weather: Warm and sunny

Pos.	Driver	Car	Laps	Time
1	Juan Pablo Montoya	Williams-BMW	12	1m 22.216s
2	Rubens Barrichello	Ferrari	11	1m 22.528s
3	Michael Schumacher	Ferrari	10	1m 22.624s
4	Ralf Schumacher	Williams-BMW	12	1m 22.841s
5	Jarno Trulli	Jordan-Honda	12	1m 23.126s
6	David Coulthard	McLaren-Mercedes	12	1m 23.148s
7	Mika Häkkinen	McLaren-Mercedes	11	1m 23.394s
8	Nick Heidfeld	Sauber-Petronas	12	1m 23.417s
9	Kimi Räikkönen	Sauber-Petronas	11	1m 23.595s
10	Pedro de la Rosa	Jaguar-Cosworth	11	1m 23.693s
11	Jenson Button	Benetton-Renault	12	1m 23.892s
12	Heinz-Harald Frentzen	Prost-Acer	12	1m 23.943s
13	Eddie Irvine	Jaguar-Cosworth	10	1m 24.031s
14	Giancarlo Fisichella	Benetton-Renault	9	1m 24.090s
15	Jacques Villeneuve	BAR-Honda	12	1m 24.164s
16	Jean Alesi	Jordan-Honda	12	1m 24.198s
17	Olivier Panis	BAR-Honda	11	1m 24.677s
18	Enrique Bernoldi	Arrows-Asiatech	12	1m 25.444s
19	Jos Verstappen	Arrows-Asiatech	12	1m 25.511s
20	Tomas Enge	Prost-Acer	9	1m 26.039s
21	Fernando Alonso	Minardi-European	9	1m 26.218s
22	Alex Yoong	Minardi-European	11	1m 27.463s

FRIDAY FREE PRACTICE
Weather: Warm and slightly overcast

Pos.	Driver	Laps	Time
1	Ralf Schumacher	43	1m 24.667s
2	Juan Pablo Montoya	37	1m 25.067s
3	Michael Schumacher	34	1m 25.131s
4	Pedro de la Rosa	43	1m 25.205s
5	Rubens Barrichello	39	1m 25.311s
6	Mika Häkkinen	37	1m 25.343s
7	David Coulthard	39	1m 25.544s
8	Nick Heidfeld	9	1m 25.740s
9	Jean Alesi	37	1m 25.849s
10	Heinz-Harald Frentzen	37	1m 25.860s
11	Giancarlo Fisichella	50	1m 25.911s
12	Jarno Trulli	39	1m 25.987s
13	Jenson Button	39	1m 26.197s
14	Olivier Panis	43	1m 26.354s
15	Jacques Villeneuve	40	1m 26.521s
16	Kimi Räikkönen	4	1m 26.701s
17	Fernando Alonso	34	1m 26.972s
18	Enrique Bernoldi	44	1m 27.217s
19	Eddie Irvine	23	1m 27.401s
20	Tomas Enge	29	1m 27.662s
21	Jos Verstappen	18	1m 27.900s
22	Alex Yoong	31	1m 28.250s

SATURDAY FREE PRACTICE
Weather: Warm and sunny

Pos.	Driver	Laps	Time
1	Michael Schumacher	14	1m 23.178s
2	Juan Pablo Montoya	19	1m 23.477s
3	Jarno Trulli	19	1m 23.762s
4	Rubens Barrichello	19	1m 23.828s
5	David Coulthard	17	1m 23.873s
6	Ralf Schumacher	19	1m 23.917s
7	Nick Heidfeld	35	1m 24.251s
8	Mika Häkkinen	18	1m 24.263s
9	Pedro de la Rosa	25	1m 24.575s
10	Kimi Räikkönen	35	1m 24.586s
11	Eddie Irvine	24	1m 24.642s
12	Giancarlo Fisichella	14	1m 24.683s
13	Jean Alesi	10	1m 24.928s
14	Olivier Panis	27	1m 24.990s
15	Jenson Button	12	1m 25.062s
16	Jacques Villeneuve	16	1m 25.258s
17	Heinz-Harald Frentzen	20	1m 25.600s
18	Jos Verstappen	24	1m 26.285s
19	Enrique Bernoldi	23	1m 27.309s
20	Tomas Enge	17	1m 28.064s
	Alex Yoong		no time
	Fernando Alonso		no time

WARM-UP
Weather: Warm and sunny

Pos.	Driver	Laps	Time
1	Michael Schumacher	14	1m 26.029s
2	David Coulthard	14	1m 26.086s
3	Juan Pablo Montoya	15	1m 26.247s
4	Rubens Barrichello	10	1m 26.296s
5	Kimi Räikkönen	12	1m 26.389s
6	Jarno Trulli	14	1m 26.446s
7	Jean Alesi	12	1m 26.778s
8	Ralf Schumacher	11	1m 26.793s
9	Mika Häkkinen	10	1m 26.825s
10	Jacques Villeneuve	12	1m 27.161s
11	Nick Heidfeld	14	1m 27.218s
12	Pedro de la Rosa	14	1m 27.351s
13	Eddie Irvine	15	1m 27.458s
14	Jos Verstappen	16	1m 27.548s
15	Olivier Panis	10	1m 27.708s
16	Enrique Bernoldi	14	1m 27.766s
17	Giancarlo Fisichella	10	1m 28.137s
18	Jenson Button	14	1m 28.633s
19	Heinz-Harald Frentzen	15	1m 28.752s
20	Fernando Alonso	8	1m 29.027s
21	Alex Yoong	11	1m 29.826s
22	Tomas Enge	7	1m 30.445s

RACE FASTEST LAPS
Weather: Warm and sunny

Driver	Time	Lap
Ralf Schumacher	1m 25.073s	39
Rubens Barrichello	1m 25.221s	39
Michael Schumacher	1m 25.525s	52
Juan Pablo Montoya	1m 25.657s	52
Jean Alesi	1m 26.365s	28
Pedro de la Rosa	1m 26.381s	34
Olivier Panis	1m 26.386s	31
Kimi Räikkönen	1m 26.656s	51
Jacques Villeneuve	1m 26.657s	31
Nick Heidfeld	1m 26.825s	52
Giancarlo Fisichella	1m 27.283s	29
David Coulthard	1m 27.323s	4
Heinz-Harald Frentzen	1m 27.394s	28
Mika Häkkinen	1m 27.627s	15
Tomas Enge	1m 27.643s	52
Fernando Alonso	1m 27.709s	50
Jos Verstappen	1m 27.945s	22
Jenson Button	1m 28.268s	4
Enrique Bernoldi	1m 28.578s	24
Eddie Irvine	1m 29.262s	2
Alex Yoong	1m 30.605s	21

CHASSIS LOG BOOK

1	M. Schumacher	Ferrari F2001/213
2	Barrichello	Ferrari F2001/206
	spare	Ferrari F2001/211
3	Häkkinen	McLaren MP4/16/7
4	Coulthard	McLaren MP4/16/6
	spares	McLaren MP4/16/4 & 5
5	R. Schumacher	Williams FW23/7
6	Montoya	Williams FW23/8
	spare	Williams FW23/2
7	Fisichella	Benetton B201/6
8	Button	Benetton B201/5
	spares	Benetton B201/3 & 1
9	Panis	BAR 03/6
10	Villeneuve	BAR 03/8
	spare	BAR 03/4
11	Trulli	Jordan EJ11/5
12	Alesi	Jordan EJ11/4
	spare	Jordan EJ11/3
14	Verstappen	Arrows A22/6
15	Bernoldi	Arrows A22/3
	spare	Arrows A22/8
16	Heidfeld	Sauber C20/7
17	Räikkönen	Sauber C20/6
	spares	Sauber C20/1 & 5
18	Irvine	Jaguar R2/5
19	de la Rosa	Jaguar R2/7
	spare	Jaguar R2/6
20	Yoong	Minardi PS01B/4
21	Alonso	Minardi PS01B/3
	spare	Minardi PS01/1
22	Frentzen	Prost AP04/6
23	Enge	Prost AP04/3
	spare	Prost AP04/2

POINTS TABLES

DRIVERS

1	Michael Schumacher	107
2	David Coulthard	57
3	Rubens Barrichello	54
4	Ralf Schumacher	48
5	Juan Pablo Montoya	25
6	Mika Häkkinen	24
7	Jacques Villeneuve	12
8	Nick Heidfeld	11
9 =	Kimi Räikkönen	9
9 =	Jarno Trulli	9
11	Giancarlo Fisichella	8
12	Heinz-Harald Frentzen	6
13 =	Olivier Panis	5
13 =	Jean Alesi	5
15	Eddie Irvine	4
16	Pedro de la Rosa	3
17	Jenson Button	2
18	Jos Verstappen	1

CONSTRUCTORS

1	Ferrari	161
2	McLaren	81
3	Williams	73
4	Sauber	20
5 =	BAR	17
5 =	Jordan	16
7	Benetton	10
8	Jaguar	7
9	Prost	4
10	Arrows	1

FIA WORLD CHAMPIONSHIP • ROUND 16

UNITED STATES
grand prix

1st - HÄKKINEN • 2nd - M. SCHUMACHER • 3rd - COULTHARD

The unique grandeur and atmosphere of
Indianapolis are captured during practice as
Jacques Villeneuve heads down the pit lane
in his BAR-Honda.
Photograph: Clive Mason/Allsport-Getty Images

Diary

Murray Walker (above) finally retires from F1 commentating after more than half a century in the business. Indianapolis chief Tony George presents him with one of the original bricks used to build the Indianapolis track in 1911 as a memento.

Tony George indicates that there will be no changes to the F1 circuit layout at least until after the 2003 race.

BMW is set to test its all-new type P82 engine at Barcelona during the week following the US Grand Prix in preparation for 2002.

The Toyota F1 team is buoyed up by testing times at Kuala Lumpur's Sepang circuit just 2s away from Mika Häkkinen's fastest race lap in the 2001 Malaysian GP.

Right: The stars and stripes flew proudly at what was an understandably emotional time for all involved at Indianapolis.

Below right: Hope springs eternal. Cap and pen in hand, a passionate Ferrari fan waits in the hope of grabbing Michael Schumacher's autograph.
Both photographs: Paul-Henri Cahier

Below: Jean Alesi celebrated his 200th — and penultimate — Grand Prix start. The veteran Frenchman would announce his retirement from F1 prior to the final race of the season.
Photograph: Clive Mason/Allsport-Getty Images

INDIANAPOLIS QUALIFYING

Despite suffering an engine oil pump failure during Saturday morning's free practice session, Michael Schumacher just eased out his old rival Mika Häkkinen for pole position with a 1m 11.708s, although the Finn would eventually have to make do with fourth on the grid on the strength of his second quickest 1m 12.309s after his controversial race-morning penalty.

'We have been strong all weekend in the final sector of the lap,' said Schumacher, 'because our straightline speed has been fastest. I didn't bother with the final run, because by then I knew we had got the best set-up on the car and I had got the most I could out of it and out of myself. You can never be sure that someone won't go quicker, but it turned out alright in the end.'

Ralf Schumacher (1m 11.986s) just pipped Juan Montoya (1m 12.252s) for what eventually turned out to be second and third on the grid, while Rubens Barrichello's Ferrari (1m 12.327s) wound up fifth ahead of Nick Heidfeld's Sauber C20 (1m 12.434s) and David Coulthard (1m 12.500s), the Scot unsettled slightly by a touch too much oversteer.

'I couldn't quite nail the car into the apex of the corners,' he explained, 'and it was actually better yesterday with more fuel, so things should be better again tomorrow.'

In the Sauber camp Nick Heidfeld (1m 12.434s) was delighted to have matched his previous best qualifying record of sixth place in Austria despite losing 0.2s on his final run when yellow flags came out for Enge's spin. Räikkönen (1m 12.881s) could not find the optimum balance and struggled with understeer and oversteer, winding up 11th.

Eighth and ninth were the Jordan-Hondas of Jarno Trulli (1m 12.605s) and Jean Alesi (1m 12.607s). Both drivers were struggling badly through the infield after trading grip for lower downforce and consequent improved straightline speed on the main straight.

'I don't always know what direction to go with the car to make it better, so that is why it always takes some time compared with Trulli,' confessed Alesi. 'But I am very happy with this result, achieving my best lap time at the end of the session.'

Jenson Button was well satisfied with a tenth-fastest 1m 12.805s in the Benetton B201, but Giancarlo Fisichella (12th/1m 12.942s) was unhappy with the balance of his car. He also caught the yellow flag on his last run and lost part of his car's engine cover which blew off on the main straight.

'I am in the top ten for the first time this year so it's fantastic,' enthused Button. 'Hopefully we can do something at the start and at the first corner as well, but I hope to make it round this time.'

In the BAR-Honda enclave, both Olivier Panis (1m 13.122s) and Jacques Villeneuve (1m 14.012s) were struggling with acute lack of grip. They were split by the two Jaguars of Eddie Irvine (14th/1m 13.189s) and Pedro de la Rosa (16th/1m 13.679s), neither of whom got the best out of their Michelin rubber.

Both Jaguar drivers complained of excessive understeer and Irvine was also hampered by a serious front-end vibration after making a set-up change for his fourth run. 'That last run was slower, but I really don't quite understand the problem there,' he reflected.

Heinz-Harald Frentzen (1m 13.281s) reckoned that the Prost team had slightly improved the handling balance of his 15th-place AP04, but the novice Tomas Enge, while admitting the grip level had improved, still had too much understeer and eventually slid into a tyre barrier thanks to a grabbing front brake. He would up 21st on 1m 14.185s.

Completing the grid were the Arrows of Enrique Bernoldi (1m 14.129s) and Jos Verstappen (1m 14.138s) while Fernando Alonso produced his best-ever qualifying effort to line up 17th on 1m 13.991s in the Minardi PS01 after what he described as the perfect session. His team-mate Alex Yoong (1m 15.247s) was still learning the ropes and wound up a not altogether unsurprising last.

Above: Scramble through the first corner with the McLaren-Mercedes of Mika Häkkinen and David Coulthard heading the midfield pack as they chase after the Ferraris and Williams-BMWs.
Photograph: Paul-Henri Cahier

MIKA Häkkinen may have committed himself to a year's sabbatical in 2002, but his performance in the US Grand Prix at Indianapolis hardly looked that of a man facing long-term retirement. The combination of a bold race strategy and considerable strategic nerve on the part of Häkkinen and the McLaren-Mercedes squad yielded the Finn his 20th career Grand Prix victory after a fascinating race of changing fortunes.

Having celebrated his 33rd birthday on Friday, Häkkinen ran the gauntlet of an engine failure in practice, demotion from second to fourth on the starting grid after a minor rule infringement and a damaging crash in the race-morning warm-up to score a highly impressive success.

A tactically astute race strategy saw him popping out into the lead beyond half-distance after running with a heavy fuel load and making a single stop with only 27 laps left to run.

'This was one of the highlights of the season for me,' said Häkkinen. 'Winning the British GP was something to put in my record book, and Indianapolis was the other. And this is it.

'All the frustrations of the morning made me go flat out after the stewards dropped me to the second row. It was disappointing, obviously, and all that frustration made me go flat out. I don't know what else to say, to be honest.'

Häkkinen emerged from the race buoyed by the prospect of the final race of the season at Suzuka where McLaren promised even more technical modifications for the MP4/16 challengers.

'We have something coming up in the pipeline in the factory and we're confident that the performance of the car will be better at Suzuka, so we can perform better and go quicker,' he said.

Michael Schumacher finished second after his team-mate Rubens Barrichello suffered a rare Ferrari engine failure with just two laps left to run. That left David Coulthard to take third place in the other McLaren-Mercedes ahead of Jarno Trulli's Jordan-Honda, although the Italian would later be excluded for a worn undercar skidplate and Eddie Irvine's Jaguar R2 promoted to fourth, temporarily, as it turned out.

There had been a cruel disappointment lying in store for

Häkkinen on race morning. A moment's inattention saw him accelerate out of the pit lane when the red warning light was still showing, a seemingly trifling offence for which the veteran Finn would receive a draconian penalty.

After deliberating on the matter the stewards decided to delete his fastest qualifying time from Saturday which had the effect of dropping him from second to fourth on the grid and moving the Williams-BMWs of Ralf Schumacher and Juan Montoya to second and third.

It was an extraordinary situation as such infringements in the warm-up have always involved fines and many people in the paddock were wondering how the stewards could penalise a driver in Saturday qualifying for an infringement which took place the following day.

'Now I understand why I'm finally giving up this bloody business,' fumed McLaren's veteran team coordinator Jo Ramirez who would retire after the race at the end of 40 years in top-line motor racing. 'This is just unprecedented.'

After days of uncertainty and speculation that the spectator attendance figures might be down, it seemed that at least 150,000 of the 170,000 who had purchased grandstand tickets turned up on the day.

Prior to the start there was inevitably speculation that Ralf Schumacher's prodigiously powerful BMW engine might propel his Williams ahead on the long half-mile run to the first corner, but when it came to it his elder brother got the jump on him in his Ferrari.

Under braking for turn one it was Juan Montoya's Williams' FW23 which pulled level with Schumacher's Ferrari on the outside, but there was no way the former Indy 500 winner could make the move stick and had to drop back into second.

By the end of the opening lap Schumacher's Ferrari was already 0.8s ahead of Montoya with Rubens Barrichello moving the other Ferrari right onto the second-place Williams's tail in a bid to move up a position.

Starting the third lap Barrichello proved his determination by

CHALLENGE FACING US DRIVERS AIMING FOR F1

As Mika Häkkinen and Michael Schumacher were cheered to the echo after finishing first and second at Indianapolis it seemed that there was only one thing missing to complete the crowd's delight, an American F1 driver.

In the 51-year history of the official FIA F1 World Championship the only Americans to have won the title were Phil Hill (1961) and Mario Andretti (1978). Andretti is also the last driver to have scored a home Formula 1 win in his native land with his victory through the streets of Long Beach, California, 24 years ago.

There is no logical reason why an American driver should not scale the upper reaches of Formula 1, but a general marked reluctance to decamp to Europe when there are so many thriving US domestic racing formulae is certainly one of the reasons why there is no American currently contesting the World Championship.

The last to give it a serious try was Mario Andretti's elder son Michael who was recruited by McLaren to partner Ayrton Senna in 1993 on the strength of consistently impressive performances in the US Champ car series.

Unfortunately Andretti junior failed in his quest to follow in his father's footsteps, at least in part due to the fact that he insisted on commuting to the GPs from his home in Nazareth, Pennsylvania, rather than moving to Europe. Before the end of the season he was dropped from the team and replaced by the young Mika Häkkinen.

McLaren team principal Ron Dennis made the point that any ambitious youngster who wishes to make a bid for Formula 1 must also race in Europe in the junior formulae.

'History shows that if an American or a driver of any other nationality wishes to take a career path with a view to coming to F1, they have to accept they are going to have to race in Europe,' he said.

'There are now three primary feeder formulae. They are F3, Formula 3000 and Formula Renault. That's where young drivers need to be if they expect to be seen and ultimately selected.'

running down the outside of Montoya to take the place as they approached the first turn.

Further back, the first skirmish of the afternoon had taken place at the end of the opening lap when the Saubers of Nick Heidfeld and Kimi Räikkönen, together with Trulli's Jordan, made it three abreast under braking for the first turn.

Trulli squeezed Räikkönen into his team-mate, the Finn's C20 sustaining frontal damage in the impact which required him to pit for a replacement nose section next time round.

'I made a reasonable start,' said Kimi, 'and was pushing close with Nick in ninth place at the end of the first lap, but under braking for the first corner Trulli tried to come round the outside and pinched me.

'I hit my nose on Nick when Trulli hit the back of my car. I stopped for a new nose, but a driveshaft had been damaged so I had to stop out on the circuit.'

On lap five Schumacher eased slightly to allow Barrichello to take over the lead, in line with the commitment to help his team-mate for the loyal supporting role which he assumed without too much complaint this season.

Yet it wasn't as simple as it looked. Barrichello was running with a lighter fuel load which made his car quicker in the early stages, but the fact that he was on a two-stop strategy became clear when he made an 8.6s first refuelling stop with only 27 of the race's 73 laps completed.

That let Schumacher's Ferrari back into the lead less than one second ahead of Montoya with the McLaren-Mercedes of Häkkinen and David Coulthard now third and fourth.

Montoya, urged on by the crowd, now got his head down and slashed Schumacher's advantage with a succession of quick laps which saw him surge ahead of the Ferrari under braking for the first turn at the start of lap 34.

Michael later admitted that it had been a pretty straightforward race for him, apart from Montoya's overtaking move. 'I don't really know where he came from,' he grinned, 'because he was a long way back when I left turn 11, but then I saw in my mirrors that he was right with me.

'I tried to make life difficult for him, but at that stage our tyres were near the end of their life and not as good as theirs.' Schumacher by this time had also concluded that the harder Bridgestone compound for which Ferrari had opted was perhaps not the optimum choice after all. McLaren, having selected the softer tyre, had made a better decision.

Once ahead Montoya easily pulled out a couple of seconds on the Ferrari before pitting for fuel two laps later. He rejoined in fifth place and, with those runners ahead still to make their stops, looked a strong contender for eventual victory.

Unfortunately the Colombian driver's hopes of winning in Formula 1 at this same venue where he triumphed in the Indianapolis 500 18 months previously were thwarted when he rolled to a halt with hydraulic failure in front of the pits on lap 38.

'We were doing well until I stopped,' shrugged Montoya

philosophically. 'It is a bit disappointing as I think we could have got a win here which would have been my second, and two back-to-back wins would have been brilliant. As for the overtaking manoeuvre on Michael, it was good fun. I was just basically going for it.'

Montoya at least had the satisfaction of having out-run his team-mate Ralf Schumacher quite decisively for the second straight race. Ralf had never been quite happy with the balance of his FW23 and, despite running much less fuel for a one-stop strategy, was unable to make a serious bid to pass the Colombian when they were running in tight formation during the race's opening stages.

'You never count your chickens in this business,' said Williams technical director Patrick Head, 'but there is no doubt that Juan would have been very strong in the closing stages.

'In the thick of his chase of Michael he was handling his car's oversteer brilliantly, even changing down a couple of gears with his left hand, so as not to lose momentum, as he piled on the opposite lock with his right hand.'

For his part, Ralf Schumacher was quite frank about his eventual error when he spun off on lap 37. 'It was nothing but driver error,' he shrugged. 'I lost the back end. I had a lot of oversteer, simply lost it and couldn't correct it. These weekends happen. We just hope we'll learn from it and do better next time.'

Häkkinen now went into the lead, the Finn running a very long opening stint on a one-stop refuelling strategy and did not come in to refuel until the end of lap 46.

The McLaren driver rejoined in second place, crucially a couple of seconds ahead of Michael Schumacher and, with Barrichello's leading Ferrari still to make its second refuelling stop, looked in very strong shape indeed.

He duly moved ahead when Barrichello stopped on lap 50 and with the Brazilian retiring with engine failure two laps from the finish, Coulthard could consolidate his second place in the title chase while Jarno Trulli's Jordan, Eddie Irvine's Jaguar and Nick Heidfeld's Sauber filled the remaining top six places in their wake.

After Trulli's later exclusion there was a sliver of consolation for the Jordan team in that Alesi was promoted to sixth, but the team immediately made it clear that they would be appealing against the exclusion. The subsequent FIA court of appeal found in Trulli's favour.

For the McLaren-Mercedes squad it was a great day in more ways than one. Häkkinen had scored the team's fourth win of the year and brought Mercedes up equal with BMW's tally of four victories, as well as securing second place in the constructors' championship.

In the drivers' contest, Coulthard was almost home and dry in second place. Barrichello would now have to win at Suzuka with David fifth or lower to turn things around. The engine failure at Indianapolis had been as bitter for Ferrari as it had been rare. But Rubens made it clear he wasn't counting anything out.

'Having the spare car at my disposal proves the team believes in the fact I can win,' he said, 'and today I showed that I have the right motivation to succeed in that.'

Above: The Indianapolis fans really seemed to have taken to F1 on its second appearance at the Brickyard.
Photograph: Paul-Henri Cahier

Above left: Jarno Trulli had the initial disappointment of losing his points after being disqualified from fourth place, but the Italian was reinstated after an appeal by the Jordan-Honda team.
Photograph: Bryn Williams/crash.net

Opposite: Mika Häkkinen rides high on the shoulders of McLaren team coordinator Jo Ramirez; both were scheduled to take a break from F1 at the end of the season. DaimlerChrysler director Jürgen Hubbert is on their left.
Photograph: Mark Thompson/Allsport-Getty Images

ROUND 16
INDIANAPOLIS 28–30 SEPTEMBER 2001

SAP
UNITED STATES
grand prix

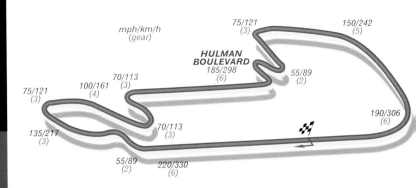

INDIANAPOLIS – GRAND PRIX CIRCUIT
CIRCUIT LENGTH: 2.605 miles/4.192 km

mph/km/h (gear)

75/121 (3)
150/242 (5)
HULMAN BOULEVARD 185/298 (6)
55/89 (2)
70/113 (3)
100/161 (4)
75/121 (3)
190/306 (6)
135/217 (3)
70/113 (3)
55/89 (2)
220/330 (6)

RACE DISTANCE: 73 laps, 190.139 miles/306.016 km **RACE WEATHER: Warm and bright**

Pos.	Driver	Nat.	No.	Entrant	Car/Engine	Tyres	Laps	Time/Retirement	Speed (mph/km/h)	Gap to lea
1	Mika Häkkinen	SF	3	West McLaren Mercedes	McLaren MP4/16-Mercedes F0110K V10	B	73	1h 32m 42.840s	123.055/198.038	
2	Michael Schumacher	D	1	Scuderia Ferrari Marlboro	Ferrari F2001-050 V10	B	73	1h 32m 53.886s	122.811/197.646	+11.0
3	David Coulthard	GB	4	West McLaren Mercedes	McLaren MP4/16-Mercedes F0110K V10	B	73	1h 32m 54.883s	122.788/197.610	+12.0
4	Jarno Trulli	I	11	B&H Jordan Honda	Jordan EJ11-Honda RA001E V10	B	73	1h 33m 40.263s	121.798/196.015	+57.4
5	Eddie Irvine	GB	18	Jaguar Racing	Jaguar R2-Cosworth CR3 V10	M	73	1h 33m 55.274s	121.473/195.493	+72.4
6	Nick Heidfeld	D	16	Red Bull Sauber Petronas	Sauber C20-Petronas V10	B	73	1h 33m 55.836s	121.461/195.473	+72.9
7	Jean Alesi	F	12	B&H Jordan Honda	Jordan EJ11-Honda RA001E V10	B	72			+1
8	Giancarlo Fisichella	I	7	Mild Seven Benetton Renault	Benetton B201-Renault RS21 V10	M	72			+1
9	Jenson Button	GB	8	Mild Seven Benetton Renault	Benetton B201-Renault RS21 V10	M	72			+1
10	Heinz-Harald Frentzen	D	22	Prost Acer	Prost AP04-Acer V10	M	72			+1
11	Olivier Panis	F	9	Lucky Strike BAR Honda	BAR 03-Honda RA001E V10	B	72			+1
12	Pedro de la Rosa	ESP	19	Jaguar Racing	Jaguar R2-Cosworth CR3 V10	M	72			+1
13	Enrique Bernoldi	BR	15	Orange Arrows Asiatech	Arrows A22-Asiatech V10	B	72			+1
14	Tomas Enge	CZE	23	Prost Acer	Prost AP04-Acer V10	M	72			+1
15	Rubens Barrichello	BR	2	Scuderia Ferrari Marlboro	Ferrari F2001-050 V10	B	71	Engine		+2
	Jacques Villeneuve	CDN	10	Lucky Strike BAR Honda	BAR 03-Honda RA001E V10	B	45	Collision damage		
	Jos Verstappen	NL	14	Orange Arrows Asiatech	Arrows A22-Asiatech V10	B	44	Engine		
	Juan Pablo Montoya	COL	6	BMW WilliamsF1 Team	Williams FW23-BMW P80 V10	M	38	Hydraulic pump		
	Alex Yoong	MAS	21	European Minardi F1	Minardi PS01B-European V10	M	38	Gearbox		
	Ralf Schumacher	D	5	BMW WilliamsF1 Team	Williams FW23-BMW P80 V10	M	36	Spun off		
	Fernando Alonso	ESP	21	European Minardi F1	Minardi PS01B-European V10	M	36	Driveshaft		
	Kimi Räikkönen	SF	17	Red Bull Sauber Petronas	Sauber C20-Petronas V10	B	2	Driveshaft		

Fastest lap: Juan Pablo Montoya, on lap 35, 1m 14.448s, 125.956 mph/202.707 km/h (record).

Previous lap record: David Coulthard (F1 McLaren Mercedes MP4/15), 1m 14.711s, 125.513 mph/201.994 km/h (2000).

Grid order	1	2	3	4	5	6	7	8	9	10	11	12	13	14	15	16	17	18	19	20	21	22	23	24	25	26	27	28	29	30	31	32	33	34	35	36	37	38	39	40	41	42	43	44	45	46	47	48	49	50	51	52	53
1 M. SCHUMACHER	1	1	1	1	2	2	2	2	2	2	2	2	2	2	2	2	2	2	2	2	2	2	2	2	2	2	2	1	1	1	1	1	1	6	6	1	1	1	3	3	3	3	3	3	3	2	2	2	3	3	3	3	3
5 R. SCHUMACHER	6	6	2	2	1	1	1	1	1	1	1	1	1	1	1	1	1	1	1	1	1	1	1	1	6	6	6	6	6	6	1	1	3	3	3	4	4	4	4	2	2	2	3	3	3	2	2	2					
6 MONTOYA	2	2	6	6	6	6	6	6	6	6	6	6	6	6	6	6	6	6	6	6	6	6	6	3	3	3	3	3	3	3	4	4	4	2	2	2	2	1	1	1	1	1	1	1	1	1	1	1	1	1	1	1	1
3 HÄKKINEN	5	5	5	5	5	5	5	5	5	5	5	5	5	5	5	5	5	5	5	5	5	3	3	3	2	4	4	4	4	4	4	2	2	1	1	1	1	4	4	4	4	4	4	4	4	4	4	4	4	4	4	4	4
2 BARRICHELLO	3	3	3	3	3	3	3	3	3	3	3	3	3	3	3	3	3	3	3	3	3	4	4	4	2	2	2	2	2	2	6	6	7	7	16	16	16	16	16	16	18	18	18	18	11	11							
16 HEIDFELD	4	4	4	4	4	4	4	4	4	4	4	4	4	4	4	4	4	4	4	4	16	16	11	11	11	11	11	11	11	11	11	11	11	16	16	18	18	18	18	18	11	11	11	11	18	18							
4 COULTHARD	11	16	16	16	16	16	16	16	16	16	16	16	16	16	16	16	16	16	16	16	11	11	12	12	12	12	12	12	12	12	7	7	18	18	22	11	11	11	11	16	16	16	16	16	16	18							
11 TRULLI	16	11	8	8	8	11	11	11	11	11	11	11	11	11	11	11	11	11	5	12	12	5	5	5	5	5	5	16	11	9	12	12	12	12	12	12																	
12 ALESI	17	8	11	11	11	11	11	8	8	8	12	12	12	12	12	12	12	12	12	5	5	16	16	16	16	16	5	5	16	18	22	11	9	12	7	7	19	19	19	7	7	7											
8 BUTTON	7	7	7	7	7	7	7	7	7	7	12	8	8	8	8	8	8	8	8	8	8	8	8	8	8	8	8	7	22	22	9	9	12	10	7	19	7	7	7	8	8	8											
17 RÄIKKÖNEN	8	18	12	12	12	12	12	12	12	12	7	7	7	7	7	7	7	7	7	7	7	7	7	7	7	7	7	18	19	9	9	12	10	19	19	8	22	8	8	8	22	22	22										
7 FISICHELLA	18	12	18	18	18	18	18	18	18	18	18	18	18	18	18	18	18	18	18	18	18	18	18	18	18	18	18	14	22	12	12	10	10	19	7	8	22	8	22	22	22	9	9	9									
9 PANIS	12	14	14	14	14	14	14	14	14	14	14	14	14	14	14	14	14	14	14	14	22	22	22	22	22	22	22	9	10	10	19	19	7	22	9	9	9	9	9	19	19	19	19										
18 IRVINE	14	9	9	9	9	9	9	9	9	9	9	22	9	9	22	9	22	22	22	22	9	22	22	22	22	22	9	22	9	8	8	8	8	8	8	15	15	15	15	15	15	15	15										
22 FRENTZEN	9	22	22	22	22	22	22	22	22	22	22	9	22	22	9	22	9	9	9	9	15	10	8	8	15	8	15	15	15	15	15	23	23	23																			
19 DE LA ROSA	22	15	15	15	15	15	15	15	15	15	15	15	15	15	15	15	15	15	15	15	10	15	15	10	19	15	14	14	14	14	14	23	10																			
21 ALONSO	15	10	10	10	10	10	10	10	10	10	10	10	10	10	10	10	10	10	10	10	19	21	14	14	23	23	23	23	23	10																							
10 VILLENEUVE	10	19	19	19	19	19	19	19	19	19	19	19	19	19	19	19	19	19	19	19	21	23	23	23																												
15 BERNOLDI	19	21	21	21	21	21	21	21	21	21	21	21	21	21	21	21	21	21	21	21	23	8	8	20	20																										
14 VERSTAPPEN	21	20	20	20	20	20	20	20	20	20	20	20	20	20	20	23	23	23	23	23	23	14																													
23 ENGE	20	23	23	23	23	23	23	23	23	23	23	23	23	23	23	20	20	20	20	20	20	20																													
20 YOONG	23	17																																																			

Pit stop
One lap behind leader

STARTING GRID

1		**5**
M. SCHUMACHER		**R. SCHUMACHER**
Ferrari		Williams
6		**4***
MONTOYA		**HÄKKINEN**
Williams		McLaren
2		**16**
BARRICHELLO		**HEIDFELD**
Ferrari		Sauber
4		**11**
COULTHARD		**TRULLI**
McLAREN		Jordan
12		**8**
ALESI		**BUTTON**
Jordan		Benetton
17		**7**
RÄIKKÖNEN		**FISICHELLA**
Sauber		Benetton
9		**18**
PANIS		**IRVINE**
BAR		Jaguar
22		**19**
FRENTZEN		**DE LA ROSA**
Prost		Jaguar
21		**10**
ALONSO		**VILLENEUVE**
Minardi		BAR
15		**14**
BERNOLDI		**VERSTAPPEN**
Arrows		Arrows
23		**20**
ENGE		**YOONG**
Prost		Minardi

*moved from second place after best qualifying time disallowed

59	60	61	62	63	64	65	66	67	68	69	70	71	72	73	
3	3	3	3	3	3	3	3	3	3	3	3	3	3	3	1
2	2	2	2	2	2	2	2	2	2	1	1	1	1	2
1	1	1	1	1	1	1	1	1	1	2	4	4	4	3
4	4	4	4	4	4	4	4	4	4	4	2	11	11	4
11	11	11	11	11	11	11	11	11	11	11	11	18	18	5
18	18	18	18	18	18	18	18	18	18	18	18	16	16	6
16	16	16	16	16	16	16	16	16	16	16	16	12		
12	12	12	12	12	12	12	12	12	12	12	12	7		
7	7	7	7	7	7	7	7	7	7	7	7	8		
8	8	8	8	8	8	8	8	8	8	8	8	22		
22	22	22	22	22	22	22	22	22	22	22	22	9		
9	9	9	9	9	9	9	9	9	9	9	9	19		
19	19	19	19	19	19	19	19	19	19	19	19	15		
15	15	15	15	15	15	15	15	15	15	15	15	23		
23	23	23	23	23	23	23	23	23	23	23	23			

FOR THE RECORD

200th Grand Prix

Jean Alesi

250th Grand Prix point

Jordan Grand Prix

TIME SHEETS

QUALIFYING

Weather: Dry and warm

Pos.	Driver	Car	Laps	Time
1	Michael Schumacher	Ferrari	9	1m 11.708s
2	Mika Häkkinen*	McLaren-Mercedes	11	1m 11.945s
3	Ralf Schumacher	Williams-BMW	11	1m 11.986s
4	Juan Pablo Montoya	Williams-BMW	11	1m 12.252s
5	Rubens Barrichello	Ferrari	12	1m 12.327s
6	Nick Heidfeld	Sauber-Petronas	11	1m 12.434s
7	David Coulthard	McLaren-Mercedes	12	1m 12.500s
8	Jarno Trulli	Jordan-Honda	11	1m 12.605s
9	Jean Alesi	Jordan-Honda	12	1m 12.607s
10	Jenson Button	Benetton-Renault	12	1m 12.805s
11	Kimi Räikkönen	Sauber-Petronas	12	1m 12.881s
12	Giancarlo Fisichella	Benetton-Renault	12	1m 12.942s
13	Olivier Panis	BAR-Honda	12	1m 13.122s
14	Eddie Irvine	Jaguar	12	1m 13.189s
15	Heinz-Harald Frentzen	Prost	11	1m 13.281s
16	Pedro de la Rosa	Jaguar	12	1m 13.679s
17	Fernando Alonso	Minardi European	12	1m 13.991s
18	Jacques Villeneuve	BAR-Honda	12	1m 14.012s
19	Enrique Bernoldi	Arrows-Asiatech	10	1m 14.129s
20	Jos Verstappen	Arrows-Asiatech	12	1m 14.138s
21	Tomas Enge	Prost-Acer	11	1m 14.185s
22	Alex Yoong	Minardi-European	12	1m 15.247s

*time disallowed

FRIDAY FREE PRACTICE

Weather: Cool and overcast

Pos.	Driver	Laps	Time
1	Mika Häkkinen	30	1m 13.387s
2	Michael Schumacher	43	1m 13.552s
3	Rubens Barrichello	44	1m 13.584s
4	David Coulthard	41	1m 13.656s
5	Eddie Irvine	52	1m 13.806s
6	Nick Heidfeld	48	1m 13.827s
7	Heinz-Harald Frentzen	37	1m 13.858s
8	Pedro de la Rosa	50	1m 13.917s
9	Ralf Schumacher	42	1m 13.919s
10	Juan Pablo Montoya	45	1m 13.983s
11	Kimi Räikkönen	45	1m 14.027s
12	Jean Alesi	33	1m 14.057s
13	Jenson Button	47	1m 14.186s
14	Jarno Trulli	38	1m 14.215s
15	Olivier Panis	52	1m 14.368s
16	Tomas Enge	40	1m 14.767s
17	Giancarlo Fisichella	21	1m 14.911s
18	Jacques Villeneuve	33	1m 14.999s
19	Fernando Alonso	48	1m 15.131s
20	Enrique Bernoldi	48	1m 15.449s
21	Jos Verstappen	26	1m 15.547s
22	Alex Yoong	47	1m 16.318s

SATURDAY FREE PRACTICE

Weather: Sunny and bright

Pos.	Driver	Laps	Time
1	Michael Schumacher	21	1m 12.078s
2	Mika Häkkinen	30	1m 12.330s
3	Nick Heidfeld	27	1m 12.407s
4	Ralf Schumacher	26	1m 12.454s
5	Rubens Barrichello	29	1m 12.463s
6	Juan Pablo Montoya	23	1m 12.668s
7	Giancarlo Fisichella	31	1m 12.672s
8	David Coulthard	29	1m 12.724s
9	Jenson Button	22	1m 12.955s
10	Kimi Räikkönen	21	1m 13.186s
11	Jarno Trulli	29	1m 13.205s
12	Olivier Panis	30	1m 13.521s
13	Jean Alesi	33	1m 13.675s
14	Pedro de la Rosa	33	1m 13.753s
15	Heinz-Harald Frentzen	25	1m 13.870s
16	Enrique Bernoldi	24	1m 13.978s
17	Eddie Irvine	39	1m 14.052s
18	Tomas Enge	31	1m 14.205s
19	Jacques Villeneuve	25	1m 14.346s
20	Fernando Alonso	32	1m 14.867s
21	Jos Verstappen	34	1m 14.902s
20	Alex Yoong	29	1m 15.604s

WARM-UP

Weather: Warm and bright

Pos.	Driver	Laps	Time
1	Ralf Schumacher	15	1m 13.912s
2	David Coulthard	13	1m 13.982s
3	Mika Häkkinen	16	1m 14.025s
4	Michael Schumacher	14	1m 14.029s
5	Jos Verstappen	15	1m 14.036s
6	Juan Pablo Montoya	19	1m 14.063s
7	Pedro de la Rosa	18	1m 14.083s
8	Kimi Räikkönen	16	1m 14.145s
9	Rubens Barrichello	12	1m 14.220s
10	Nick Heidfeld	18	1m 14.528s
11	Eddie Irvine	16	1m 14.597s
12	Jarno Trulli	17	1m 14.778s
13	Giancarlo Fisichella	8	1m 14.979s
14	Jenson Button	19	1m 15.122s
15	Olivier Panis	15	1m 15.201s
16	Jean Alesi	14	1m 15.344s
17	Tomas Enge	15	1m 15.437s
18	Enrique Bernoldi	15	1m 15.649s
19	Jacques Villeneuve	16	1m 15.958s
20	Heinz-Harald Frentzen	15	1m 16.037s
21	Fernando Alonso	14	1m 16.332s
22	Alex Yoong	14	1m 16.646s

RACE FASTEST LAPS

Weather: Warm and bright

Driver	Time	Lap
Juan Pablo Montoya	1m 14.448s	35
Mika Häkkinen	1m 14.481s	45
Rubens Barrichello	1m 14.629s	47
David Coulthard	1m 14.641s	39
Ralf Schumacher	1m 14.706s	22
Michael Schumacher	1m 14.841s	32
Eddie Irvine	1m 15.139s	58
Nick Heidfeld	1m 15.169s	29
Jarno Trulli	1m 15.199s	63
Jenson Button	1m 15.252s	71
Heinz-Harald Frentzen	1m 15.296s	38
Giancarlo Fisichella	1m 15.457s	40
Jean Alesi	1m 15.659s	67
Pedro de la Rosa	1m 15.758s	68
Olivier Panis	1m 15.919s	67
Enrique Bernoldi	1m 16.068s	68
Tomas Enge	1m 16.155s	71
Jos Verstappen	1m 16.342s	35
Jacques Villeneuve	1m 16.680s	40
Fernando Alonso	1m 16.694s	30
Alex Yoong	1m 17.079s	25
Kimi Räikkönen	1m 51.518s	2

CHASSIS LOG BOOK

1	M. Schumacher	Ferrari F2001/213
2	Barrichello	Ferrari F2001/206
	spare	Ferrari F2001/211
3	Häkkinen	McLaren MP4/16/4
4	Coulthard	McLaren MP4/16/6
	spares	McLaren MP4/16/7 & 5
5	R. Schumacher	Williams FW23/7
6	Montoya	Williams FW23/8
	spare	Williams FW23/2
7	Fisichella	Benetton B201/6
8	Button	Benetton B201/5
	spares	Benetton B201/3 & 1
9	Panis	BAR 03/6
10	Villeneuve	BAR 03/4
	spare	BAR 03/1
11	Trulli	Jordan EJ11/5
12	Alesi	Jordan EJ11/4
	spare	Jordan EJ11/3
14	Verstappen	Arrows A22/6
15	Bernoldi	Arrows A22/3
	spare	Arrows A22/1
16	Heidfeld	Sauber C20/7
17	Räikkönen	Sauber C20/6
	spare	Sauber C20/1
18	Irvine	Jaguar R2/4
19	de la Rosa	Jaguar R2/6
	spare	Jaguar R2/7
20	Marques	Minardi PS01B/4
21	Alonso	Minardi PS01B/3
	spare	Minardi PS01/1
22	Frentzen	Prost AP04/6
23	Burti	Prost AP04/4
	spare	Prost AP04/2

POINTS TABLES

DRIVERS

1	Michael Schumacher	113
2	David Coulthard	61
3	Rubens Barrichello	54
4	Ralf Schumacher	48
5	Mika Häkkinen	34
6	Juan Pablo Montoya	25
7 =	Jacques Villeneuve	12
7 =	Nick Heidfeld	12
7 =	Jarno Trulli	12
10	Kimi Räikkönen	9
11	Giancarlo Fisichella	8
12 =	Eddie Irvine	6
12 =	Heinz-Harald Frentzen	6
14 =	Jean Alesi	5
14 =	Olivier Panis	5
16	Pedro de la Rosa	3
17	Jenson Button	2
18	Jos Verstappen	1

CONSTRUCTORS

1	Ferrari	167
2	McLaren	95
3	Williams	73
4	Sauber	21
5	Jordan	19
6	BAR	17
7	Benetton	10
8	Jaguar	9
9	Prost	4
10	Arrows	1

JAPANESE
grand prix

1st - M. SCHUMACHER • 2nd - MONTOYA • 3rd - COULTHARD

The Champion and his successor? Michael Schumacher (right) and a real contender for his crown, Juan Pablo Montoya.
Photograph: Paul-Henri Cahier

F1 SQUARES UP TO PROSPECT OF ECONOMIC RECESSION

With the Prost team facing possible bankruptcy in the aftermath of the Japanese Grand Prix, F1 team chiefs freely acknowledged at Suzuka that the long-term effects of a global recession could spread out to touch the sport of motor racing and that steps must be taken to mitigate their effect.

However it became clear that team chiefs were divided over precisely how best to handle the harsh winds of economic reality in a business where even a minor-league team consumes a budget of around £35 million a year.

'Nobody is immune from what is happening,' said McLaren boss Ron Dennis. 'Share prices have gone through the floor, companies look immediately to their advertising budgets and that, ultimately, trickles into motor sport. And it does trickle.

'We [F1] tend to be the last in and last out of any recession and that's going to happen this time round. Whether all the teams will survive you will have to wait and see. Like others, we have sponsors who were on the brink of commitment and have pulled back and are re-evaluating where and how to spend their money, what they have of it.

'It's going to be a tough time. But the only way that we economise is when we are forced into economies. The teams traditionally spend all the money they've got.'

Eddie Jordan added: 'We in F1 are not recession-proof. I think there is immense responsibility on teams like McLaren, Williams and Ferrari to guide us through this time because the people who will suffer least will be them because they are the successful ones.'

At around the time of the Italian GP Prost had been expected to announce the identity of a major new sponsor, hotly tipped to be Saudi Arabia's Prince Al-Waleed who owns stakes in Citibank and Canary Wharf amongst his various diverse investments.

It was understood that his contribution would have enabled Prost to fend off what looked increasingly like a hostile bid for the team as well as help fund its continued use of Ferrari V10 customer engines in 2002.

Yet the absence of a firm sponsorship deal seemed to have left Prost on the ropes. Despite paring his budget down to what must be regarded as austerity levels by the standards of contemporary F1, Prost still spent around $20 million on running his team this season — and that was before expending almost the same figure on leasing the Ferrari engines.

SUZUKA QUALIFYING

It had been the stability of Michael Schumacher's Ferrari F2001 through the fast swerves behind the pits that was the key clue to the World Champion's 11th pole of the season, the characteristic Bridgestone efficiency through such turns giving a sufficient advantage in the first sector of the 3.640-mile circuit to keep them ahead overall despite the superior Michelin performance in the third sector where braking into and hard acceleration out of the tight pit chicane are at a premium.

Suzuka is a fascinating circuit, longer than the average GP track and offering the challenge of dramatic speed variation throughout its lap. In addition, the topography of the circuit is undulating and the surface is abrasive, which can cause potential degradation problems.

Schumacher's superiority translated into a 0.7s advantage over Montoya (1m 33.184s) who manhandled his Williams FW23 to second place ahead of Ralf Schumacher's sister car (1m 33.297s) and Rubens Barrichello's Ferrari (1m 33.323s). The strength of the Williams FW23s pushed the McLaren-Mercedes of Mika Häkkinen (5th/1m 33.662s) and David Coulthard (7th/1m 33.916s) well back from the expected scene of the main action because both drivers were complaining of excessive understeer.

Giancarlo Fisichella demonstrated just how much Renault's latest V10 had improved by using a qualifying-spec unit to bag sixth place on the grid on 1m 33.830s. Both he and Jenson Button (9th/1m 34.375s) — along with all the Michelin runners — also faced the pressing priority of having to scrub in as many sets of tyres as possible, a task which needed to be carried out gently and progressively on this abrasive track surface.

Jarno Trulli qualified his Jordan EJ-11 eighth on 1m 34.002s, reporting that his second run proved to be his personal best despite encountering traffic. Jean Alesi was 11th on 1m 34.420s, disappointed that he hadn't done better.

In the Sauber camp, Nick Heidfeld had walked away from a fearful high-speed smash during Friday free practice, but his C20 was duly rebuilt for Saturday. He reported that the set-up was not quite as good as it had been at some previous races and he was pleasantly surprised to wind up 10th on 1m 34.386s.

'On my last run I got some traffic which was not enough to hold me up although I did lose some downforce, which was a shame because I had improved in the second sector,' he said. Team-mate Kimi Räikkönen wound up 12th on 1m 34.581s.

Over at Jaguar there were no real problems and no real surprises with Eddie Irvine lining up 13th on 1m 34.851s. He surprisingly admitted that he was about one second a lap quicker than he'd expected and he had no explanation for this. De la Rosa's car was well balanced but not quick enough. 'But if we're going to beat Benetton we're going to have to be a second a lap quicker than we were today,' mused Irvine.

Like Jordan, the BAR-Hondas were equipped with revised S-spec V10 engines for this event, although frankly it didn't yield much in the way of a performance boost. Villeneuve (14th/1m 35.109s) was quite happy with the handling balance, although he made some small set-up changes which did not have the effect he'd hoped for. Panis reported his car felt a bit better than on Friday, but not by much, and was not satisfied with his 17th-fastest 1m 35.766s. 'We are just bloody slow, that's all,' he shrugged.

Heinz-Harald Frentzen managed a respectable 1m 35.132s for Prost while Tomas Enge, another to be recovering from a big shunt in Friday's free practice session, took the spare AP04 to qualify 19th on 1m 36.446s.

Fernando Alonso did a good job with his Minardi to post a 1m 36.410s (18th) while the Arrows of Enrique Bernoldi and Jos Verstappen, plus slowcoach Alex Yoong's Minardi completed the 22-car field.

MICHAEL Schumacher finished the 2001 FIA F1 World Championship season at Suzuka as he'd started seven months earlier at Melbourne. With an unchallenged victory. Starting from pole position, his Ferrari F2001 dominated the 53-lap race to notch up the German driver's 53rd Grand Prix victory and in the process burst through another of Alain Prost's records. The latest benchmark to yield to Schumacher's genius was the all-time career record of championship points scored, Michael now having posted 801 to Prost's previous best of 798.5.

Juan Pablo Montoya took a brilliant second place in the Japanese GP ahead of David Coulthard and Mika Häkkinen, the McLaren-Mercedes drivers rounding off the most successful driver partnership in F1 history as Häkkinen prepared himself for a sabbatical in 2002 from which he may or may not return to the sport.

Since they were first paired together in 1996, Häkkinen and Coulthard had between them scored 30 wins, bagged 33 pole positions and set 38 fastest race laps — as well as leading 9500 of the 25,000 km of racing laps which have taken place during that period.

Five laps from the end of this particular race Häkkinen eased up and relinquished third place to Coulthard as a nicely timed good-bye gesture.

'I reckon he really did it just so that he didn't have to come up

here and answer questions from you lot,' quipped Coulthard to the media pack at the post-race press conference.

Coulthard might have been right. Although Häkkinen told McLaren boss Ron Dennis over the radio that this was the 'pay-back' race for all the help 'DC' had given him over recent years, most observers felt that the popular Finn just wanted to slip away and start his planned year's break with the minimum of fuss.

The outcome of the race was sorted in the first five minutes with Schumacher's new set of latest-spec Bridgestone rubber powering him to an 8.2s lead after only three laps. In his wake Montoya's scrubbed Michelins took the first 20 miles or so to develop maximum grip, but by then the mathematics were so overwhelmingly stacked against the Colombian that there was no way of redressing the balance.

Schumacher surged ahead going into the first corner, moving across to block Montoya, and Ralf Schumacher just failed to get ahead of his Williams team-mate as they went through. Häkkinen got the jump on Barrichello off the line, but Rubens powered the light-tanked Ferrari round the outside to take fourth as they went through the first turn.

Approaching the daunting left-hand 130-R turn at 175 mph at the end of the opening lap, Barrichello edged inside Ralf Schumacher

to take third place as Michael led Montoya across the timing line for the first time, already 3.6s clear.

Barrichello was clearly up for more of this, knowing full well that his only chance of winning depended on his getting ahead of Montoya and into second place as early as possible. Second time round and he was right on the Williams's tail coming through 130-R, neatly dodging out to the right and outbraking 'JPM' into the chicane. Rubens led across the timing line, but Montoya came swooping back to retake the place as they slammed down into the first right-hander after the pits.

'It really surprised me,' said Montoya, 'because I pretty much closed him out under braking and suddenly I saw him sliding in. I thought "leave him enough room" and when I came out of the corner I had better speed than him.

'I managed to get a good tow out of him and go back in front through the first corner. It was pretty good after that, because I managed to pull out enough lead that when he used the new tyres and everything, we were still ahead of him.'

That effectively sunk Barrichello's outside chance of taking second place ahead of Coulthard in the championship. He needed to win and Michael was ready to help, but once he failed to make that move against Montoya stick he was history. Not that anybody

quite understood what Ferrari was up to putting him on a three-stop strategy in the first place. They tried it with Eddie Irvine two years ago and it didn't work then.

'You can do all the number crunching you like, but we've never managed to work out a way that a three-stop strategy is quicker round Suzuka,' said Williams technical director Patrick Head.

'Having said that, you wouldn't want to criticise Ferrari over that. Taken as a whole, you'd have to say that their race strategies are generally pretty impressive.'

While Häkkinen proceeded on his uneventful way to fourth, the other member of F1's retirement party, Jean Alesi, signed off his career in a frightful accident in which he was nothing more than a passenger.

Alesi was chasing Kimi Räikkönen's Sauber C20 for ninth place on lap six when the Finn's car suffered an apparent left rear suspension breakage which pitched it into a violent spin. Alesi slammed straight into his rival and the two cars piled off the track amidst a hail of flying wheels, one of which oh-so-nearly caught Eddie Irvine's passing Jaguar.

'I'm not really sure what happened,' explained a dismayed Räikkönen. 'The lap before, my car had begun to understeer in the fast left-handers behind the pits, but that lap the back end suddenly snapped round and I spun. The next thing I knew Alesi hit me and there was debris everywhere.

'It was a pretty big shunt and I have a bit of a head and neck ache. But otherwise I'm fine.'

For Alesi, it was a disappointing way to end his F1 career. 'Both Kimi and I were really lucky to get away without any injuries and I am so relieved that I did not hurt him as he spun right in front of me and there was no way I could avoid him,' said the Frenchman.

'There are just too many people I would like to thank so I can really only say that I think they know who they are and I will be seeing them again. Special thanks to Eddie and the Jordan team because we've had a lot of fun these last two races.'

It was an uncomfortable note on which to end the season, but happily both drivers survived with nothing more than a severe shaking. It was yet another testimony to the sophistication and efficiency of today's super-safe carbon-fibre F1 chassis technology.

Montoya escaped without penalty after straightlining the chicane, but his team-mate Ralf Schumacher did it twice and collected a 10s stop-go penalty, the Williams team having been warned by an e-mail from race director Charlie Whiting after the first infringement.

Michael Schumacher brought the Ferrari in for its first 8.8s refuelling stop at the end of lap 18, allowing Montoya ahead to lead through to his own 8.3s stop at the end of lap 23. On that same lap Coulthard stopped from fourth place and Irvine from seventh, the Jaguar driver frustrated that no fuel went into his car due to an electrical glitch with the controls on the rig.

He resumed and came in on the next lap only for the problem to repeat itself, forcing the Ulsterman to retire. 'What looked like a brilliant stop turned out to be a total disaster because no fuel went into the car,' said Irvine. 'I came straight back again, but the problem re-occurred on the second rig too, so I had no choice but to call it a day.

'It seems that there was a power failure on both rigs. The team tried to switch the power source, and in Pedro's case it worked. But not mine. There is no way of preparing for bizarre issues like this.'

Häkkinen made a 7.6s first stop from second place on lap 24 after which the field settled down again with Michael's Ferrari leading Montoya by 6.3s and Barrichello close behind the Williams in third. Then came Ralf Schumacher, Häkkinen and Coulthard, the Scot grappling with poor low-speed grip.

On lap 29 Ralf Schumacher came in for his stop-go penalty at the same time as Barrichello made the second of his three refuelling stops. Barrichello was slow away and Schumacher veered across the white line delineating the pit exit road from the track proper as they rejoined the circuit.

The FIA observer at that point reported to the race stewards that the Ferrari had been going 'abnormally slowly' and Ralf was permitted to proceed without further penalty.

Michael Schumacher made a second 9.0s refuelling stop on lap 36, again allowing Montoya briefly back into the lead until he made a 7.6s stop on lap 38. Thereafter the race settled down to run out to its logical conclusion, Schumacher easing up to win by 3.1s ahead of the gallant Montoya with Coulthard third from the generous Häkkinen, Barrichello a disappointed fifth and Ralf Schumacher sixth.

Jenson Button's seventh place in the Benetton B201 clinched the Enstone-based team's seventh place in the constructors' championship ahead of the dejected Jaguar squad who'd had a miserable afternoon with Pedro de la Rosa falling victim to an oil leak.

Jarno Trulli came home eighth in his Jordan-Honda EJ-11, freely admitting that the car wasn't quick enough to score points on the Italian's final race for the team prior to switching to Renault's F1 squad in 2002.

'I just was not able to go any faster,' he shrugged. 'I really don't know why we were so slow. I feel really down about finishing the season like this, but I have good memories of my two years of Jordan. They have been a very important stepping stone in my career.'

Nick Heidfeld's Sauber was ninth, having benefited from a spin by Jacques Villeneuve's BAR-Honda, while Fernando Alonso was a terrific 11th in the Minardi, 0.2s ahead of Heinz-Harald Frentzen's Prost. Olivier Panis's BAR-Honda was next up ahead of the struggling Arrows of Enrique Bernoldi and Jos Verstappen with Alex Yoong's trailing Minardi the only other car running in 16th place.

So there was the bottom line. Nine wins out of 17 races for Michael Schumacher, three wins for Ralf Schumacher, two each for David Coulthard and Mika Häkkinen and one for the dynamic Montoya. In that respect, F1 in 2001 had been very much a family affair.

Opposite page: David Coulthard was gifted third place at Suzuka by his McLaren-Mercedes team-mate Mika Häkkinen, rounding off the Scot's most successful F1 season to date.
Photograph: Paul-Henri Cahier

Below: Fernando Alonso's run to ninth place in the Minardi PS01 was the young Spaniard's best drive of the year.
Photograph: Bryn Williams/crash.net

Bottom: Goodbye to all that. Jean Alesi takes his leave of the F1 business after a spectacular collision with Kimi Räikkönen's spinning Sauber. Both men were shaken, but not stirred.
Photograph: Clive Mason/Allsport-Getty Images

Diary

British F3 champion Takuma Sato is signed to partner Giancarlo Fisichella at Jordan in 2002. Jean Alesi decides to retire as a result.

Ford rally engineer Günther Steiner, the man behind the development of the Focus WRC challenger, is tipped to join Jaguar's F1 operation as managing director.

Honda announces that it is quitting CART at the end of next season after the US series announces new engine regulations for 2003.

Max Papis wins the Laguna Seca round of the CART championship in a Team Rahal Reynard-Ford.

ROUND 17
SUZUKA 12–14 OCTOBER 2001

FUJI TELEVISION
JAPANESE
grand prix

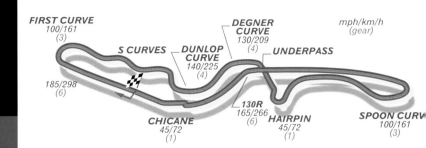

SUZUKA RACING CIRCUIT
CIRCUIT LENGTH: 3.640 miles/5.859 km

FIRST CURVE 100/161 (3)
DEGNER CURVE 130/209 (4)
mph/km/h (gear)
S CURVES
DUNLOP CURVE 140/225 (4)
UNDERPASS
185/298 (6)
130R 165/266 (6)
HAIRPIN 45/72 (1)
SPOON CURVE 100/161 (3)
CHICANE 45/72 (1)

RACE DISTANCE: 53 laps, 192.831 miles/310.331 km   **RACE WEATHER:** Dry, sunny and warm

Pos.	Driver	Nat.	No.	Entrant	Car/Engine	Tyres	Laps	Time/Retirement	Speed (mph/km/h)	Gap to leader
1	Michael Schumacher	D	1	Scuderia Ferrari Marlboro	Ferrari F2001-050 V10	B	53	1h 27m 33.298s	132.143/212.664	
2	Juan-Pablo Montoya	COL	6	BMW WilliamsF1 Team	Williams FW23-BMW P80 V10	M	53	1h 27m 36.452s	132.064/212.537	+3.1
3	David Coulthard	GB	4	West McLaren Mercedes	McLaren MP4/16-Mercedes F0110K V10	B	53	1h 27m 56.560s	131.560/211.727	+23.2
4	Mika Häkkinen	SF	3	West McLaren Mercedes	McLaren MP4/16-Mercedes F0110K V10	B	53	1h 28m 08.837s	131.255/211.235	+35.5
5	Rubens Barrichello	BR	2	Scuderia Ferrari Marlboro	Ferrari F2001-050 V10	B	53	1h 28m 09.842s	131.230/211.195	+36.5
6	Ralf Schumacher	D	5	BMW WilliamsF1 Team	Williams FW23-BMW P80 V10	M	53	1h 28m 10.420s	131.215/211.172	+37.1
7	Jenson Button	GB	8	Mild Seven Benetton Renault	Benetton B201-Renault RS21 V10	M	53	1h 29m 10.400s	129.745/208.805	+97.1
8	Jarno Trulli	I	12	B&H Jordan Honda	Jordan EJ11-Honda RA001E V10	B	52			+1
9	Nick Heidfeld	D	16	Red Bull Sauber Petronas	Sauber C20-Petronas V10	B	52			+1
10	Jacques Villeneuve	CDN	10	Lucky Strike BAR Honda	BAR 03-Honda RA001E V10	B	52			+1
11	Fernando Alonso	ESP	21	European Minardi F1	Minardi PS01-European V10	M	52			+1
12	Heinz-Harald Frentzen	D	22	Prost Acer	Prost AP04-Acer V10	M	52			+1
13	Olivier Panis	F	9	Lucky Strike BAR Honda	BAR 03-Honda RA001E V10	B	51			+2
14	Enrique Bernoldi	BR	15	Orange Arrows Asiatech	Arrows A22-Asiatech V10	B	51			+2
15	Jos Verstappen	NL	14	Orange Arrows Asiatech	Arrows A22-Asiatech V10	B	51			+2
16	Alex Yoong	MAS	20	European Minardi F1	Minardi PS01-European V10	M	50			+3
17	Giancarlo Fisichella	I	7	Mild Seven Benetton Renault	Benetton B201-Renault RS21 V10	M	47	Gearbox		+6
	Pedro de la Rosa	ESP	19	Jaguar Racing	Jaguar R2-Cosworth CR3 V10	M	45	Oil leak		
	Tomas Enge	CZE	23	Prost Acer	Prost AP04-Acer V10	M	42	Wheel bearing		
	Eddie Irvine	GB	18	Jaguar Racing	Jaguar R2-Cosworth CR3 V10	M	24	Fuel rig malfunction		
	Kimi Räikkönen	SF	17	Red Bull Sauber Petronas	Sauber C20-Petronas V10	B	5	Accident		
	Jean Alesi	F	12	B&H Jordan Honda	Jordan EJ11-Honda RA001E V10	B	5	Accident		

Fastest lap: Ralf Schumacher, on lap 46, 1m 36.944s, 133.950 mph/215.573 km/h (new record).

Previous lap record: Heinz-Harald Frentzen (F1 Williams FW19-Renault V10), 1m 38.942s, 132.576 mph/213.361 km/h (1997).

Grid order	1	2	3	4	5	6	7	8	9	10	11	12	13	14	15	16	17	18	19	20	21	22	23	24	25	26	27	28	29	30	31	32	33	34	35	36	37	38	39
1 M. SCHUMACHER	1	1	1	1	1	1	1	1	1	1	1	1	1	1	1	1	1	1	6	6	6	5	5	1	1	1	1	1	1	1	1	1	1	1	6	6	1
6 MONTOYA	6	2	6	6	6	6	6	6	6	6	6	6	6	6	6	6	6	5	5	5	3	3	6	6	6	6	6	6	6	6	6	6	3	1	6		
5 R. SCHUMACHER	2	6	2	2	2	2	2	2	2	2	2	2	2	2	5	5	5	3	3	1	1	6	2	2	2	2	3	3	3	3	3	3	1	3	4		
2 BARRICHELLO	5	5	5	5	5	5	5	5	5	5	5	5	5	5	3	3	3	1	1	4	6	2	5	5	5	4	4	4	4	4	4	4	4	2			
3 HÄKKINEN	7	7	3	3	3	3	3	3	3	3	3	3	3	3	4	4	4	4	4	6	2	5	3	3	3	5	5	5	2	2	2	2	2	3			
7 FISICHELLA	3	3	4	4	4	4	4	4	4	4	4	4	4	2	2	2	2	2	2	2	4	4	4	4	4	2	2	2	5	5	5	5	5	5			
4 COULTHARD	4	4	11	11	11	11	11	11	11	11	11	11	11	11	8	8	8	8	18	18	18	19	19	11	11	11	11	11	7	7	7	8	8	7			
11 TRULLI	11	11	8	8	8	8	8	8	7	7	7	7	11	18	18	18	18	19	19	11	11	7	7	7	7	7	10	8	7	7	8						
8 BUTTON	8	8	17	17	17	7	7	7	7	8	8	8	7	10	10	19	11	11	7	10	10	10	10	10	10	11	8	11	11	11	11						
16 HEIDFELD	17	17	12	12	12	18	18	18	18	18	18	18	18	16	16	16	11	7	7	18	10	19	8	8	8	8	8	11	10	10	10	10					
12 ALESI	12	12	18	18	10	10	10	10	10	10	10	10	19	7	8	8	10	16	16	16	16	16	16	16	16	16	16	16									
17 RÄIKKÖNEN	18	18	7	7	7	16	16	16	16	16	16	11	11	11	10	10	10	8	16	19	19	19	19	19	19	19	19	19									
18 IRVINE	10	10	10	10	10	19	19	19	19	7	7	16	16	16	16	21	21	21	21	21	21	21	21	22	22												
10 VILLENEUVE	16	16	16	16	14	14	14	14	14	14	21	21	21	21	21	23	23	22	22	22	22	22	22	21	22												
22 FRENTZEN	19	19	19	19	9	9	9	9	23	23	23	23	23	14	14	14	22	23	23	23	23	23	9	9													
19 DE LA ROSA	22	14	14	14	21	21	21	21	21	21	14	14	14	23	15	15	14	9	9	9	14	14	23	23													
9 PANIS	14	22	21	9	9	23	23	23	23	23	23	23	9	15	14	22	9	22	22	9	9	9	14	15	14	14												
21 ALONSO	21	21	9	21	21	15	15	15	15	15	15	15	15	22	22	9	15	15	15	15	15	15	15	14	15													
23 ENGE	9	9	23	23	23	20	20	20	20	20	20	20	20	9	23	15	23	20	20	20	20	20	20	20													
14 VERSTAPPEN	23	23	15	15	15	22	22	22	22	22	22	22	22	20	20	20	20	14	14	14	20																
20 YOONG	20	20	20	20	20																																
15 BERNOLDI	15	15	22	22	22																																

Pit stop
One lap behind leader

1
M. SCHUMACHER
Ferrari

6
MONTOYA
Williams

5
R. SCHUMACHER
Williams

2
BARRICHELLO
Ferrari

3
HÄKKINEN
McLaren

7
FISICHELLA
Benetton

4
COULTHARD
McLaren

11
TRULLI
Jordan

8
BUTTON
Benetton

16
HEIDFELD
Sauber

12
ALESI
Jordan

17
RÄIKKÖNEN
Sauber

18
IRVINE
Jaguar

10
VILLENEUVE
BAR

22
FRENTZEN
Prost

19
DE LA ROSA
Jaguar

9
PANIS
BAR

21
ALONSO
Minardi

23
ENGE
Prost

15*
BERNOLDI
Arrows

14
VERSTAPPEN
Arrows

20
YOONG
Minardi

*started from the pit lane

43	44	45	46	47	48	49	50	51	52	53	●
1	1	1	1	1	1	1	1	1	1	1	1
6	6	6	6	6	6	6	6	6	6	6	2
3	3	3	3	3	4	4	4	4	4	4	3
4	4	4	4	3	3	3	3	3	3	3	4
2	2	2	2	2	2	2	2	2	2	2	5
5	5	5	5	5	5	5	5	5	5	5	6
7	7	7	7	8	8	8	8	8	8	8	
8	8	8	11	11	11	11	11	11	11		
11	11	11	11	10	10	16	16	16	16		
10	10	10	10	16	16	10	10	10	10		
16	16	16	16	7	21	21	21	21	21		
19	19	19	21	21	22	22	22	22	22		
21	21	21	22	12	9	9	9	9			
22	22	22	9	14	14	14	14	15			
9	9	9	14	14	15	15	15	14			
14	14	14	15	15	20	20	20				
15	15	15	20	20							
20	20	20									

QUALIFYING
Weather: Warm, dry and sunny

Pos.	Driver	Car	Laps	Time
1	Michael Schumacher	Ferrari	9	1m 32.484s
2	Juan Pablo Montoya	Williams-BMW	12	1m 33.184s
3	Ralf Schumacher	Williams-BMW	12	1m 33.297s
4	Rubens Barrichello	Ferrari	11	1m 33.323s
5	Mika Häkkinen	McLaren-Mercedes	11	1m 33.662s
6	Giancarlo Fisichella	Benetton-Renault	11	1m 33.830s
7	David Coulthard	McLaren-Mercedes	11	1m 33.916s
8	Jarno Trulli	Jordan-Honda	12	1m 34.002s
9	Jenson Button	Benetton-Renault	12	1m 34.375s
10	Nick Heidfeld	Sauber-Petronas	12	1m 34.386s
11	Jean Alesi	Jordan-Honda	12	1m 34.420s
12	Kimi Räikkönen	Sauber-Petronas	11	1m 34.581s
13	Eddie Irvine	Jaguar-Cosworth	11	1m 34.851s
14	Jacques Villeneuve	BAR-Honda	12	1m 35.109s
15	Heinz-Harald Frentzen	Prost-Acer	11	1m 35.132s
16	Pedro de la Rosa	Jaguar-Cosworth	12	1m 35.639s
17	Olivier Panis	BAR-Honda	12	1m 35.766s
18	Fernando Alonso	Minardi-European	11	1m 36.410s
19	Tomas Enge	Prost-Acer	10	1m 36.446s
20	Enrique Bernoldi	Arrows-Asiatech	12	1m 36.885s
21	Jos Verstappen	Arrows-Asiatech	11	1m 36.973s
22	Alex Yoong	Minardi-European	11	1m 38.246s

FRIDAY FREE PRACTICE
Weather: Dry, warm and bright

Pos.	Driver	Laps	Time
1	Jean Alesi	32	1m 35.454s
2	Juan-Pablo Montoya	44	1m 35.977s
3	Pedro de la Rosa	38	1m 36.225s
4	Mika Häkkinen	34	1m 36.430s
5	Heinz-Harald Frentzen	41	1m 36.439s
6	Eddie Irvine	42	1m 36.589s
7	David Coulthard	33	1m 36.638s
8	Michael Schumacher	34	1m 36.727s
9	Ralf Schumacher	32	1m 36.874s
10	Rubens Barrichello	33	1m 36.994s
11	Jarno Trulli	34	1m 37.564s
12	Jenson Button	34	1m 37.645s
13	Nick Heidfeld	20	1m 37.665s
14	Jacques Villeneuve	30	1m 38.312s
15	Kimi Räikkönen	31	1m 38.315s
16	Giancarlo Fisichella	24	1m 38.398s
17	Fernando Alonso	30	1m 38.961s
18	Olivier Panis	33	1m 39.108s
19	Jos Verstappen	34	1m 39.511s
20	Enrique Bernoldi	33	1m 39.744s
21	Alex Yoong	32	1m 39.952s
22	Tomas Enge	18	1m 41.216s

SATURDAY FREE PRACTICE
Weather: Dry and warm

Pos.	Driver	Laps	Time
1	Ralf Schumacher	31	1m 33.969s
2	Juan-Pablo Montoya	25	1m 34.301s
3	David Coulthard	19	1m 34.562s
4	Michael Schumacher	17	1m 34.711s
5	Jenson Button	21	1m 34.735s
6	Jarno Trulli	11	1m 34.909s
7	Nick Heidfeld	18	1m 35.037s
8	Mika Häkkinen	15	1m 35.043s
9	Rubens Barrichello	16	1m 35.222s
10	Jacques Villeneuve	26	1m 35.457s
11	Heinz-Harald Frentzen	26	1m 35.483s
12	Kimi Räikkönen	15	1m 35.672s
13	Jean Alesi	13	1m 35.719s
14	Olivier Panis	26	1m 36.051s
15	Eddie Irvine	27	1m 36.060s
16	Giancarlo Fisichella	32	1m 36.114s
17	Pedro de la Rosa	25	1m 36.144s
18	Tomas Enge	28	1m 37.246s
19	Fernando Alonso	27	1m 37.429s
20	Enrique Bernoldi	23	1m 37.514s
21	Jos Verstappen	22	1m 37.805s
22	Alex Yoong	24	1m 38.839s

WARM-UP
Weather: Dry, warm and sunny

Pos.	Driver	Laps	Time
1	Michael Schumacher	10	1m 36.231s
2	David Coulthard	12	1m 36.685s
3	Nick Heidfeld	12	1m 36.966s
4	Jarno Trulli	14	1m 37.140s
5	Jean Alesi	12	1m 37.361s
6	Mika Häkkinen	13	1m 37.584s
7	Rubens Barrichello	13	1m 37.813s
8	Heinz-Harald Frentzen	14	1m 37.891s
9	Kimi Räikkönen	12	1m 37.942s
10	Pedro de la Rosa	13	1m 37.970s
11	Ralf Schumacher	13	1m 38.183s
12	Eddie Irvine	9	1m 38.183s
13	Jacques Villeneuve	15	1m 38.604s
14	Giancarlo Fisichella	15	1m 38.641s
15	Jenson Button	16	1m 38.740s
16	Olivier Panis	11	1m 39.091s
17	Juan Pablo Montoya	9	1m 39.182s
18	Enrique Bernoldi	12	1m 39.295s
19	Tomas Enge	13	1m 40.324s
20	Jos Verstappen	14	1m 40.482s
21	Alex Yoong	11	1m 41.104s
22	Fernando Alonso	12	1m 42.142s

RACE FASTEST LAPS
Weather: Dry, hot and sunny

Driver	Time	Lap
Ralf Schumacher	1m 36.944s	46
Rubens Barrichello	1m 36.970s	17
Juan Pablo Montoya	1m 37.017s	20
Michael Schumacher	1m 37.133s	29
Mika Häkkinen	1m 37.298s	40
David Coulthard	1m 37.313s	51
Heinz-Harald Frentzen	1m 38.240s	48
Giancarlo Fisichella	1m 38.361s	13
Jenson Button	1m 38.526s	36
Eddie Irvine	1m 38.620s	22
Nick Heidfeld	1m 38.647s	21
Jarno Trulli	1m 38.857s	28
Jacques Villeneuve	1m 38.887s	22
Fernando Alonso	1m 39.153s	36
Pedro de la Rosa	1m 39.182s	40
Olivier Panis	1m 39.299s	44
Tomas Enge	1m 39.827s	27
Kimi Räikkönen	1m 39.991s	4
Jean Alesi	1m 40.225s	4
Enrique Bernoldi	1m 40.940s	46
Jos Verstappen	1m 41.383s	16
Alex Yoong	1m 42.915s	42

FOR THE RECORD

50th Grand Prix start

British American Racing

	Driver	Chassis
1	M. Schumacher	Ferrari F2001/214
2	Barrichello	Ferrari F2001/206
	spare	Ferrari F2001/211
3	Häkkinen	McLaren MP4/16/4
4	Coulthard	McLaren MP4/16/6
	spare	McLaren MP4/16/5
5	R. Schumacher	Williams FW23/7
6	Montoya	Williams FW23/8
	spare	Williams FW23/2
7	Fisichella	Benetton B201/6
8	Button	Benetton B201/5
	spare	Benetton B201/1
9	Panis	BAR 03/4
10	Villeneuve	BAR 03/8
	spare	BAR 03/5
11	Alesi	Jordan EJ11/4
12	Trulli	Jordan EJ11/5
	spare	Jordan EJ11/3
14	Verstappen	Arrows A22/6
15	Bernoldi	Arrows A22/4
	spare	Arrows A22/3
16	Heidfeld	Sauber C20/7
17	Räikkönen	Sauber C20/5
	spare	Sauber C20/1
18	Irvine	Jaguar R2/4
19	de la Rosa	Jaguar R2/7
	spare	Jaguar R2/5
20	Yoong	Minardi PS01/4
21	Alonso	Minardi PS01/3
	spare	Minardi PS01/1
22	Frentzen	Prost AP04/6
23	Enge	Prost AP04/5
	spare	Prost AP04/3

POINTS TABLES

DRIVERS

	Driver	Points
1	Michael Schumacher	123
2	David Coulthard	65
3	Rubens Barrichello	56
4	Ralf Schumacher	49
5	Mika Häkkinen	37
6	Juan Pablo Montoya	31
7 =	Jacques Villeneuve	12
7 =	Nick Heidfeld	12
7 =	Jarno Trulli	12
10	Kimi Räikkönen	9
11	Giancarlo Fisichella	8
12 =	Eddie Irvine	6
12 =	Heinz-Harald Frentzen	6
14 =	Olivier Panis	5
14 =	Jean Alesi	5
16	Pedro de la Rosa	3
17	Jenson Button	2
18	Jos Verstappen	1

CONSTRUCTORS

		Points
1	Ferrari	179
2	McLaren	102
3	Williams	80
4	Sauber	21
5	Jordan	19
6	BAR	17
7	Benetton	10
8	Jaguar	9
9	Prost	4
10	Arrows	1

QANTAS
AUSTRALIAN
GRAND PRIX
MELBOURNE 2001

Formula 1™

statistics • FIA F1 WORLD CHAMPIONSHIP 2001 • DRIVERS' POINTS TABLE

Compiled by Nick Henry

Place	Driver	Nationality	Date of birth	Car	Australia	Malaysia	Brazil	San Marino	Spain	Austria	Monaco	Canada	Europe	France	Britain	Germany	Hungary	Belgium	Italy	USA	Japan	Points total
1	Michael Schumacher	D	3/1/69	Ferrari	1pf	1p	2p	R	1pf	2p	1	2p	1p	1	2p	R	1p	1f	4	2p	1p	123
2	David Coulthard	GB	27/3/71	McLaren-Mercedes	2	3	1	2p	5	1f	5pf	R	3	4f	R	R	3	2	R	3	3	65
3	Rubens Barrichello	BR	23/5/72	Ferrari	3	2	R	3	R	3	2	R	5	3	3	2	5	2		15*	5	56
4	Ralf Schumacher	D	30/6/75	Williams-BMW	R	5	Rf	1f	R	R	R	1f	4	2p	R	1	4	7	3f	R	6f	49
5	Mika Häkkinen	SF	28/9/68	McLaren-Mercedes	R	6f	R	4	9*	R	R	3	6	DNS	1f	R	5f	4	R	1	4	37
6	Juan Pablo Montoya	COL	20/9/75	Williams-BMW	R	R	R	R	2	R	R	2f	R	4	Rpf	8	Rp		1p	Rf	2	31
7=	Jacques Villeneuve	CDN	9/4/71	BAR-Honda	R	R	7	R	3	8	4	R	9	R	8	3	9	8	6	R	10	12
7=	Nick Heidfeld	D	10/5/77	Sauber-Petronas	4	R	3	7	6	9	R	R	6	6	R	6	R	11	6	9		12
7=	Jarno Trulli	I	13/7/74	Jordan-Honda	R	8	5	5	4	DQ	R	11*	R	5	R	—	—	R	R	4	8	12
10	Kimi Räikkönen	SF	17/10/79	Sauber-Petronas	6	R	R	R	8	4	10	4	10	7	5	R	7	DNS	7	R	R	9
11	Giancarlo Fisichella	I	14/1/73	Benetton-Renault	13	R	6	R	14	R	R	R	11	11	13	4	R	3	10	8	17*	8
12=	Eddie Irvine	GB	10/11/65	Jaguar-Cosworth	11	R	R	R	R	7	3	R	7	R	9	R	DNS	R	5	R		6
12=	Heinz-Harald Frentzen	D	18/5/67	Jordan-Honda	5	4	11*	6	R	R	—	R	8	7	—							6
				Prost-Acer												R	9	R	10	12		
14=	Olivier Panis	F	2/9/66	BAR-Honda	7	R	4	8	7	5	R	R	R	R	7	R	11	9	11	13		5
14=	Jean Alesi	F	11/6/64	Prost-Acer	9	9	8	9	10	10	6	5	15*	12	11	6	—					5
				Jordan-Honda												—	10	6	8	7	R	
16	Pedro de la Rosa	ESP	24/2/71	Jaguar-Cosworth	—	—	—	—	R	R	R	6	8	14	12	R	11	R	5	12	R	3
17	Jenson Button	GB	19/1/80	Benetton-Renault	14*	11	10	12	15	R	7	R	13	16*	15	5	R	R	9	7		2
18	Jos Verstappen	NL	4/3/72	Arrows-Asiatech	10	7	R	R	12	6	8	10*	R	13	10	9	12	10	R	R	15	1
19	Ricardo Zonta	BR	23/3/76	Jordan-Honda	—	—	—	—	—	—	7	—	—	R	—							0
20	Luciano Burti	BR	5/3/75	Jaguar-Cosworth	8	10	11															0
				Prost-Acer				11	11	R	8	12	10	R	R	R	DNS					
21	Enrique Bernoldi	BR	19/10/78	Arrows-Asiatech	R	R	R	R	R	9	R	R	R	R	14	8	R	12	R	13	14	0
22	Tarso Marques	BR	19/1/76	Minardi-European	R	14	9	R	16	R	9	R	15	DNQ	R	R	13					0
23	Fernando Alonso	ESP	29/7/81	Minardi-European	12	13	R	R	13	R	R	R	14	17*	16	10	R	13	R	11		0
24	Tomas Enge	CZ	11/9/76	Prost-Acer															12	14	R	0
25	Gaston Mazzacane	D	8/5/75	Prost-Acer	R	12	R	R														0
26	Alex Yoong	MAL	20/7/76	Minardi-European															R	R	16	0

KEY

p	pole position	R	retired	DNQ	did not qualify		
f	fastest lap	DQ	disqualified	EXC	excluded		
*	classified but not running at the finish	DNS	did not start	WD	withdrawn		

POINTS & PERCENTAGES

Compiled by David Hayhoe

Photograph: Paul-Henri Cahier

GRID POSITIONS: 2001

Pos.	Driver	Starts	Best	Worst	Average
1	Michael Schumacher	17	1	4	1.71
2	Ralf Schumacher	17	1	10	3.41
3	Rubens Barrichello	17	2	8	4.47
4	Mika Häkkinen	16	2	8	4.56
5	David Coulthard	17	1	9	4.76
6	Juan Pablo Montoya	17	1	12	5.41
7	Jarno Trulli	17	4	16	6.76
8	Heinz-Harald Frentzen	15	4	16	9.60
9	Nick Heidfeld	17	6	16	9.71
10	Kimi Räikkönen	17	7	15	10.41
11	Jacques Villeneuve	17	6	18	10.76
12	Olivier Panis	17	6	17	11.41
13	Eddie Irvine	17	6	17	12.82
14	Ricardo Zonta	2	12	15	13.50
15	Pedro de la Rosa	13	9	20	13.77
16	Jean Alesi	17	9	20	14.12
17	Giancarlo Fisichella	17	6	19	15.18
18	Luciano Burti	14	14	21	16.93
19	Jenson Button	17	9	21	16.94
20	Jos Verstappen	17	13	21	18.00
21	Enrique Bernoldi	17	15	22	18.53
22	Fernando Alonso	17	17	22	19.47
23 =	Gaston Mazzacane	4	19	21	20.00
23 =	Tomas Enge	3	19	21	20.00
25	Tarso Marques	13	20	22	21.77
26	Alex Yoong	3	22	22	22.00

CAREER PERFORMANCES: 2001 DRIVERS

Driver	Nationality	Races	Championships	Wins	2nd places	3rd places	4th places	5th places	6th places	Pole positions	Fastest laps	Points
Jean Alesi	F	201	—	1	16	15	11	15	13	2	4	242
Fernando Alonso	E	17	—	—	—	—	—	—	—	—	—	—
Rubens Barrichello	BR	147	—	1	11	13	13	12	4	3	3	195
Enrique Bernoldi	BR	17	—	—	—	—	—	—	—	—	—	—
Luciano Burti	BR	15	—	—	—	—	—	—	—	—	—	—
Jenson Button	GB	34	—	—	—	—	1	5	1	—	—	14
David Coulthard	GB	124	—	11	24	16	6	9	5	12	17	359
Pedro de la Rosa	E	46	—	—	—	—	1	4	—	—	—	6
Tomas Enge	CZ	3	—	—	—	—	—	—	—	—	—	—
Giancarlo Fisichella	I	91	—	—	5	4	5	5	4	1	1	75
Heinz-Harald Frentzen	D	129	—	3	3	11	12	9	13	2	6	159
Mika Häkkinen	FIN	161	2	20	14	17	13	10	9	26	25	420
Nick Heidfeld	D	33	—	—	—	1	1	1	4	—	—	13
Eddie Irvine	GB	130	—	4	6	15	10	6	6	—	1	184
Tarso Marques	BR	24	—	—	—	—	—	—	—	—	—	—
Gaston Mazzacane	RA	21	—	—	—	—	—	—	—	—	—	—
Juan Pablo Montoya	CO	17	—	1	3	—	1	—	—	3	3	31
Olivier Panis	F	108	—	1	3	1	4	5	7	—	—	61
Kimi Räikkönen	FIN	17	—	—	—	2	1	1	—	—	—	9
Michael Schumacher	D	162	4	53	29	15	7	6	4	43	44	801
Ralf Schumacher	D	83	—	3	3	8	9	12	4	1	6	135
Jarno Trulli	I	80	—	—	1	—	3	3	5	—	—	26
Jos Verstappen	NL	91	—	—	—	2	1	2	2	—	—	17
Jacques Villeneuve	CDN	99	1	11	5	7	8	6	5	13	9	209
Alex Yoong	MAL	3	—	—	—	—	—	—	—	—	—	—
Ricardo Zonta	BR	31	—	—	—	—	—	3	—	—	—	3

Note: drivers beginning the formation lap are deemed to have made a start

UNLAPPED: 2001

Number of cars on same lap as leader

Grand Prix	Starters	at 1/4 distance	at 1/2 distance	at 3/4 distance	at full distance
Australia	22	17	14	7	7
Malaysia	22	15	7	7	7
Brazil	22	18	10	5	2
San Marino	22	19	10	7	5
Spain	22	19	11	2	8
Austria	22	15	9	7	5
Monaco	22	16	11	6	4
Canada	22	17	13	10	5
Europe	22	20	14	7	7
France	21	19	12	7	5
Britain	21	17	10	5	4
Germany	22	19	14	7	7
Hungary	22	15	8	5	5
Belgium	22	16	13	10	8
Italy	22	19	13	7	7
USA	22	21	12	8	6
Japan	22	18	12	12	7

LAP LEADERS: 2001

Grand Prix	Michael Schumacher	Ralf Schumacher	Juan Pablo Montoya	Mika Häkkinen	Rubens Barrichello	David Coulthard	Jarno Trulli	Total
Australia	54	—	—	—	—	4	—	58
Malaysia	42	—	—	—	—	12	1	55
Brazil	4	—	36	—	31	—	—	71
San Marino	—	62	—	—	—	—	—	62
Spain	39	—	—	26	—	—	—	65
Austria	—	—	15	—	31	25	—	71
Monaco	73	—	—	—	5	—	—	78
Canada	45	24	—	—	—	—	—	69
Europe	66	—	1	—	—	—	—	67
France	39	23	9	—	—	1	—	72
Britain	4	—	3	53	—	—	—	60
Germany	—	23	22	—	—	—	—	45
Hungary	71	—	—	—	2	4	—	77
Belgium	36	—	—	—	—	—	—	36
Italy	—	7	29	—	17	—	—	53
USA	14	—	2	31	26	—	—	73
Japan	46	2	5	—	—	—	—	53
Total	533	141	122	110	81	77	1	1065
Per cent	50.1	13.2	11.5	10.3	7.6	7.2	0.1	100

RETIREMENTS: 2001

Number of cars to have retired

Grand Prix	Starters	at 1/4 distance	at 1/2 distance	at 3/4 distance	at full distance	percentage
Australia	22	5	6	8	9	59.1
Malaysia	22	7	7	8	8	63.6
Brazil	22	2	5	8	12	45.5
San Marino	22	2	7	8	10	54.5
Spain	22	3	4	5	7	68.2
Austria	22	6	7	10	11	50.0
Monaco	22	5	7	12	12	45.5
Canada	22	5	9	10	13	40.9
Europe	22	1	3	5	8	63.6
France	21	2	2	4	6	71.4
Britain	21	4	4	5	5	76.2
Germany	22	3	6	11	12	45.5
Hungary	22	3	5	6	10	54.5
Belgium	22	7	8	8	9	59.1
Italy	22	3	6	7	9	59.1
USA	22	1	3	7	8	63.6
Japan	22	2	3	3	6	72.7

WILSON WALKS TALL

By SIMON ARRON

SILVERSTONE, September 20. Ensconced in a quilted jacket that provides apt protection against the gathering breeze, Keith Wilson stands at Club Corner and looks on expectantly.

He is accompanied by a couple of friends who, more than quarter of a century earlier, had worked as mechanics on Keith's Jamun Formula Ford car. They were with him at Oulton Park in April 1975, when Wilson ran over — of all things — a snake's nest as he approached Lodge Corner. With a brake pipe torn asunder in one of motor racing's more unusual, and less celebrated, mishaps, Wilson was helpless and smashed headlong into the wooden sleepers. The impact shattered his lower legs and, with it, his modest motor sport ambitions. It would be 12 months before he returned to work and he never raced again. Besides, within a couple of years of regaining his mobility he had other things to occupy him, such as a young son.

At Silverstone, he is watching his 23-year-old progeny Justin completing the second day of his maiden Formula 1 test with Jordan Grand Prix — an opportunity that came his way in the wake of

an extraordinary, record-breaking campaign in the FIA Formula 3000 Championship. 'It is great,' Keith says, 'when you relive a few of your own youthful dreams through your children's success.'

Wilson Junior, the first British driver to lift the FIA F3000 title, has come a long way in recent seasons. At the end of 1997 his future prospects looked bleak. Two years in Formula Vauxhall with top team Paul Stewart Racing had produced a clutch of wins but no title. Team patron Jackie Stewart, three times Formula 1 World Champion, counselled Wilson to pursue a career in touring or sports cars. Although he appreciated the youngster's pace, he felt a 6 ft 3 in. frame would militate against his ever becoming an F1 driver. 'That was hard to take,' Justin says, 'because you respect the opinion of someone like Jackie. But with hindsight it probably made me even more determined.'

Wilson ignored the advice and turned instead to the new-for-1998 Formula Palmer Audi series, which cost less than one third of the price of a seat in F3, the alternative that was beyond his means. It was a last roll of the dice. The first prize in that inaugural FPA season was a fully-sponsored FIA F3000 drive — worth more

Inset far left: **Justin Wilson established an all-time record points tally in becoming Britain's first F3000 champion.**

Left: **Wilson's Nordic team-mate Tomas Enge managed only a single win, but had the backing to graduate into Formula 1 with Prost after Luciano Burti's accident at Spa.**

Below and below left: **Super Nova's Mark Webber's early title challenge petered out in a string of retirements, but at least the talented Australian had the satisfaction of taking a prestigious win at Monaco.**
All photographs: Paul-Henri Cahier

than Wilson could dream about raising commercially. Win the title and he could advance his career; fail and he would become just another gifted young hopeful to have evaporated from the sporting map. He won the title.

He has seldom looked back — and in 2001 he built on two promising seasons in F1's ante-chamber to put together the most devastating campaign in the series' 17-season history.

Staying with Coca-Cola Nordic Racing for a second year, Wilson scored points in 11 of the 12 races and finished in the top three 10 times. He tallied 71 points — six more than previous record-holder Juan Pablo Montoya. His contribution helped Nordic to set new standards in the championship for teams, where it became the first entrant to notch up more than 100 points in a season. Yet there was no great magic involved. Nordic had greater collective team spirit and experience than any rival. Wilson and Czech sidekick Tomas Enge were both old hands in F3000 terms and they were absolutely united in their efforts. They shared all available data and their competitive, but friendly, rivalry spurred them on. When Wilson clinched the title at Spa,

Enge was there below the podium, giving his adversary a smile and a big thumbs-up. The team motto? 'Race hard — but don't be stupid.'

Although they were usually quite evenly matched in terms of speed, only once, at Silverstone, did they trip each other up, and that didn't prove significantly costly. Of the two, however, Wilson made fewer unforced errors. In fact he didn't make any... apart from spinning shortly after taking the chequered flag in Brazil, where he braked a trifle abruptly after clinching the first of his three wins. His only retirement came at the Nürburgring, where a sheared bolt caused a brake disc to come loose.

Team boss Derek Mower says: 'Justin is an incredibly canny racer — and he's very bright. He listens, which is more than you can say for many drivers. After he started and finished sixth in the second race at Imola, we sat down and had a long talk about qualifying, because it was obvious he needed to up his game. He got away with starting seventh in Brazil because other drivers made mistakes. You can pass there, too, but that's not the case at all circuits. After that we went to Barcelona and bang, he took

Right: Wilson strolls onto the podium whilst his team-mate Tomas Enge happily contemplates his win. Second-placed Bas Leinders enjoys the banter.
Photograph: Paul-Henri Cahier

Below right: Sébastien Bourdais scored DAMS's first victory since 1997.
Photograph: Mark Thompson/Allsport-Getty Images

Below: Eventual winner Antonio Pizzonia leads Petrobras team-mate Ricardo Sperafico and Nordic's Tomas Enge at Hockenheim.
Photograph: Paul-Henri Cahier

pole position. He never had a problem after that — and the more successful he became, the more his confidence grew.

'There were other guys out there who were sometimes as quick, but they were prone to making mistakes. Justin took everything in his stride — he is brilliant at adjusting to changing conditions and finding the limit.'

Highly-rated Australian Mark Webber (Super Nova) ultimately tied with Enge on points, but took second in the series by virtue of his three wins to the Czech's two. Backed by Renault Sport, Webber won convincingly at Imola, Monaco and Magny-Cours, but his title chances suffered because he spent more time in Benetton's F1 car during the season than he did in the F3000 Lola. At times — usually after completing three Grand Prix distances in as many days — he admitted finding it hard to adapt to the slower car. His year ended with a run of four straight non-finishes, three of them the result of first-lap accidents (and at Spa he was fortunate to escape with superficial injuries after smiting the barriers at about 150 mph). In stark contrast, he was quick and consistent in the Benetton without putting a scratch on it.

Like Webber, the friendly, uncomplicated Enge waged a fast but mistake-ridden campaign. Of the top three, however, Tomas was the only one with strong personal backing as well as ability, which made him a logical target for the cash-strapped Prost GP team before the F3000 season was complete.

Defending champion team Petrobras Junior came closest to matching Nordic as a talented collective, but its rookie drivers lacked experience. Ricardo Sperafico and Antonio Pizzonia collected one win apiece and shared three pole positions between them. Of the two, Pizzonia has the edge in flair, Sperafico the upper hand in common sense. Antonio might have added wins at Interlagos and Monza to his Hockenheim success. He was unlucky to be penalised on home turf for overtaking when the safety car was running (he didn't see the warning flags because he was too close to the car ahead, which slowed unexpectedly), but he thoroughly deserved to be clobbered in Italy for a piece of startline thuggery that must be eliminated from his repertoire.

Both drivers were immensely impressive and have what it takes to win the title in 2002. Pizzonia needs to polish a couple of rough edges, however, if he is to counter Sperafico's more measured approach. And on his day the latter can be untouchable, as he proved at Spa.

Studious Frenchman Sébastien Bourdais (DAMS) and Italian firebrand Giorgio Pantano (Astromega) were the year's only other winners. In a season dominated by teams from Norfolk, England (which won 10 races between them), Bourdais and his Le Mans-based team ironically scored their lone success at a slippery Silverstone. At least one of those Norfolk teams wants to lure Bourdais away for 2002.

Left: Frenchman Sébastien Bourdais made a successful switch to DAMS after being released from Prost Junior at the start of the season.

Below left: The 2000 British F3 champion Antonio Pizzonia made mistakes, but proved his speed in the Petrobras Junior Team.

Below centre left: Astromega's Giorgio Pantano scored his only victory in the final race of the season at Monza.

Below centre: Ricardo Sperafico was closely matched with team-mate Pizzonia and took a highly impressive win at Spa.
All photographs: Paul-Henri Cahier

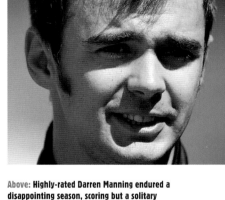

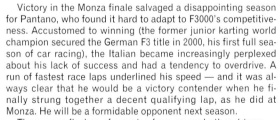

Above: Highly-rated Darren Manning endured a disappointing season, scoring but a solitary podium finish.

Left: Ricardo Mauricio bounced back in the Red Bull Junior squad at Monaco and was a consistent points scorer thereafter.

Below left: Experienced F3000 campaigner Bas Leinders looked to be a title contender at the start of the season, but ended up scratching for points.
All photographs: Paul-Henri Cahier

Victory in the Monza finale salvaged a disappointing season for Pantano, who found it hard to adapt to F3000's competitiveness. Accustomed to winning (the former junior karting world champion secured the German F3 title in 2000, his first full season of car racing), the Italian became increasingly perplexed about his lack of success and had a tendency to overdrive. A run of fastest race laps underlined his speed — and it was always clear that he would be a victory contender when he finally strung together a decent qualifying lap, as he did at Monza. He will be a formidable opponent next season.

There were flashes of promise from several other drivers — notably Patrick Friesacher (Red Bull Junior), Darren Manning (Arden Team Russia), Ricardo Mauricio (Red Bull Junior), David Saelens (European Minardi), Jaime Melo Junior (Durango), Bas Leinders (KTR) and Sperafico's twin brother Rodrigo (Coloni), plus lively one-off cameos from Stéphane Sarrazin (Prost Junior, Monaco) and Tomas Scheckter (European Minardi, Hockenheim). Although 19 of the 37 drivers who started races scored at least a point, however, the regular front-runners' consistency left only lean pickings for the rest.

While there was quality at the front of the field, strength in depth was sorely lacking. That drivers such as Jenson Button and Kimi Räikkönen have recently created an impact after bypassing F3000 has brought the formula's relevance into question, and some rising stars seem determined to avoid it. One needs, however, to take a balanced view. The F1 success of recent F3000 graduates such as Juan Pablo Montoya, Nick Heidfeld and Fernando Alonso suggests there isn't too much wrong with it as a training formula, and Wilson is a shining prospect. The tight, one-make regulations might make it fearsomely tough — but that is the kind of education drivers need. For the fortunate few that filter into F1, life will hardly become any easier.

Stunning Sato sets the pace

By MARCUS SIMMONS

Top and above right: Takuma Sato could well be the first Japanese driver to taste victory in Formula 1 following his promotion to Jordan Grand Prix for 2002. He won the British F3 championship after winning 12 of the 26 rounds for Carlin Motorsports.

Above: Anthony Davidson made an equally favourable impression and could follow team-mate Sato into the big time.
All photographs: Peter Spinney/LAT Photographic

Centre right: Leading contenders for the German F3 championship Stefan Mucke, Frank Diefenbacher and Toshihiro Kaneishi share the podium at Hockenheim.

Bottom right: Diefenbacher won four rounds of the German series, but found his title was to be decided in the court rooms rather than on track, the crown going to Kaneishi.
Both photographs: Malcolm Griffiths/LAT Photographic

WILL Takuma Sato's rise to prominence in European motor sport, culminating in the 2001 British Formula 3 Championship title, be looked upon one day as a pivotal moment to match that of Emerson Fittipaldi's early exploits more than 30 years ago?

In the same way as Fittipaldi stormed through the junior ranks and then into Formula 1 with Lotus, paving the way for a host of wannabes from his Brazilian homeland to invade Britain, Sato — whose F3 crown was rewarded with a Jordan F1 seat — seems to be doing the same for the Japanese.

Sato's decision to reject Honda's offer of a fully paid-up drive in the 1998 Japanese F3 series — his prize for winning the motor giant's Suzuka Racing School scholarship — in favour of making his way in Europe truly paid off in 2001. Entering his second season in British F3's top flight, and remaining with the Carlin Motorsport squad with which he had made such an impression in his rookie season, Sato won 12 of the 26 championship races. To those victories he added successes in the Marlboro Masters at Zandvoort (Europe's biggest F3 race) and the British Grand Prix support event.

Not even the ostriches in F1 could fail to notice, and Jordan's gain is the loss of BAR, for which Sato acted as test driver in parallel with his F3 activities.

What really stood out about the little Japanese was not so much his winning record, more the way in which he went about his racing. There is something akin to the spirit of Gilles Villeneuve encapsulated within: a never-say-die attitude which gave spectators some royal entertainment. His performance in holding off a train of cars while leading at Donington, with his left-rear tyre as flat as a pancake, was something to behold.

Likewise, his stunning drive in race two at Oulton Park, where

tyre problems in qualifying and a puncture in the first race had left him on a real mish-mash of Avons, was a revelation. Fourth on the grid, he burst through to lead by the second bend at Cascades. Adjusting his driving constantly to allow for the condition of his rubber, he then disappeared into the distance.

And with Anthony Davidson — arguably the second best driver in F3 — as team-mate, Sato even had someone from whom he could learn yet more to further boost his armoury. A stunning rookie season from the red-headed Brit provided him with six championship race wins, plus storming successes in the Pau Grand Prix and the Elf Masters at Spa. With just Macau and Korea to go at the time of writing, Carlin Motorsport was facing the distinct possibility of a total whitewash of F3's internationals.

Davidson proved himself to be a fantastic driver in 2001. He has a flowing, smooth style and is awesomely late on the brakes, yet still finds the apex with pinpoint accuracy. He can use contours in the road which no else realises exist to find a new, and quicker, line. If Sato is Villeneuve, Davidson is Prost.

The domination of these two was bad news for the rest, but did help raise the standards of the British championship so high that none of the foreign teams got a look-in at any of the European internationals. In fact, the UK squads completed an unprecedented top four in the Marlboro Masters. The quantity of runners may not be that high in Britain (around 18 regulars compared to 28 in Germany), but the quality in 2001 was something else again.

Three different drivers took it in turns to challenge the Carlin hegemony in Britain. At the start of the season it was the underfinanced Matt Davies, who struck a late deal with the promising Team Avanti just hours before qualifying for the first round. Armed with an Opel-powered Dallara (unusual among the hordes of Dallara-Mugen Hondas in Britain), he won two of the first three races.

But he was never going to keep up that momentum as long as he was having to scratch around for cash. By the time his season's budget was secured in July, Davies and Avanti were too far behind to catch up.

Derek Hayes then took up the challenge. Leading the Manor Motorsport team which had won the 1999 and 2000 titles, the Northern Irishman made a smooth transition from Formula Palmer Audi and put in some very consistent results early on. Then he really stepped up to the pace, setting three pole positions in a row in late spring and clashing controversially with Sato at Croft. After that purple patch, though, his focus seemed to wane, and despite notching up a win at Brands Hatch he never looked likely to recapture that form.

So it was that James Courtney completed the season as the most likely fly in Carlin's ointment. Teamed with Andre Lotterer at Jaguar Racing (formerly Stewart Racing), the Australian rookie impressed by winning on his debut at Silverstone. He then dropped back into the pack a little but came on strong towards the end of the year, easily outscoring Lotterer, who already had a year of German F3 under his belt.

Jaguar didn't seem to get its cars as consistently on the mark as Carlin or Manor. When things did go well, Lotterer — with his awesome commitment and car control — was a star, but it was the smoother and more consistent Courtney who proved the better season-long contender.

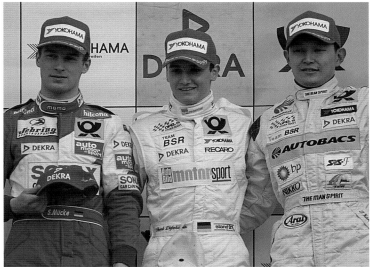

The other winners in Britain were Gianmaria Bruni and Andy Priaulx. Italian Bruni was the man who took that Donington race after Sato's tyre deflated, but otherwise it was an unhappy year in which he often complained of a lack of performance from his Fortec Dallara's Renault engine. Guernseyman Priaulx won two races for Alan Docking Racing in the wet, in which he is gaining a reputation for being an expert, but with a lack of money the team's form varied alarmingly in the dry.

Although the German championship finished in early October, the identity of its champion was not decided with the last race of th season. Frank Diefenbacher thought he'd done enough by finishing second in the final round at Hockenheim, but a protest from Team Kolles, whose driver Pierre Kaffer alleged that Diefenbacher had overtaken him under yellow flags, was upheld by the stewards. That gave the crown to Diefenbacher's Opel Team BSR team-mate Toshihiro Kaneishi.

But BSR chief Bertram Schafer saw fit to appeal that verdict, meaning that Japanese Kaneishi (who followed in Sato's wheeltracks by venturing to Europe in 2000) had to wait for the German authorities to grind their legal processes into action, and they finally confirmed the Japanese driver as champion towards the end of October.

With only two wins to his credit, Kaneishi was hardly the most exciting driver in Germany. Diefenbacher and F3 veteran Kaffer took four wins each, while Markus Winkelhock — son of the late Manfred — notched up three in an impressive rookie season.

But while the form of the others varied more greatly, and the incidents mounted up, 'Toshi' just racked up the points virtually every time out.

Winkelhock's team-mate Stefan Mucke (around whom the Mucke Motorsport team was set up) almost matched Kaneishi's consistency. Another two-time winner, he sneaked into second spot in the points ahead of Diefenbacher after the latter's yellow-flag exclusion.

Other race winners were Briton Gary Paffett (who switched from Renault to Opel power mid-season), Brazilian Joao Paulo de Oliveira (who was transformed in the middle of the season into a real contender), Japanese F3 rookie Kousuke Matsuura and Swede Bjorn Wirdheim. An incredibly international bunch. In fact, of the 32 points scorers, only five were German.

The French championship was yet another to be won by a Japanese. This time it was Ryo Fukuda, who actually pre-dated Sato in Europe by winning a competition in the mid-'90s to attend the La Filiere racing school. Since then he has risen through the ranks to become a very hot property, albeit hampered by a chronic lack of finance. For 2001 he hooked up with Serge Saulnier, who had sold his Promatecme team and re-established his squad as Saulnier Racing.

Fukuda's only real rival was Portuguese Tiago Monteiro (who drove for ASM), these two miles clear of their opposition. Both men are smart and tough contenders in the international races (both were very quick at Zandvoort) who could go far.

Which brings us to the Japanese championship, ironically dominated by Europeans! Frenchman Benoit Treluyer did the business here for the Mugen-powered Dome team, his main rival being Italian Paolo Montin at the wheel of the TOM'S team's Toyota-engined car.

South American championship honours looked set to go to Juliano Moro from his faster but wilder Amir Nasr Racing team-mate Thiago Medeiros. Notable here was the mid-season debut of Nelson Piquet Junior, who finished less than a second behind Moro in his first car race...

Other than that, the declining Italian championship finally abandoned any pretentions at being any more than club racing, the American series struggled again in its second year, the Russians witnessed an all-Italian battle between Maurizio Mediani and Alberto Pedemonte, and the Spaniards launched a one-make F3 series for Toyota-engined Dallaras. In its first year, it seems to have unearthed a very good prospect in the form of Basque Ander Vilarino.

Back in Britain, yet more Japanese hopefuls joined in before the end of the season, with the promise of more to come in 2002. Now we've found our Fittipaldi, who will be Carlos Pace?

Joest do it

By GARY WATKINS

The driver trio of Pirro, Biela and Kristensen
triumphed for Audi for the second successive year.
Photograph: Mark Thompson/Allsport-Getty Images

AN act of God. Nothing less than a miracle was going to deprive Audi of a second straight victory at the Le Mans 24 Hours. God did vent his anger on La Sarthe in the form of torrential rain that made the 2001 edition of the French enduro one of the wettest ever. Not that Audi and its Joest Racing squad took too much notice. Rain or no, their pair of R8 prototypes swept to another dominant one-two victory.

The wet conditions, which required several deployments of the safety car for no other reason than the intensity of the rain, might have acted as a leveller. In fact, no one else got a look in over the course of the 69th running of the 24 Hours. Bar a dozen or so laps early on, one of the factory Audi's topped the order all the way and the leader enjoyed a four-lap cushion over the best of the rest by one-third distance.

The opposition showed flashes of promise, but the factories ranged against the might of Audi, and the experience of Reinhold Joest's squad, were never quite in the same class. The year-old R8 design, the subject of two evolutions since winning in 2000, remained the fastest and most reliable thing in the place, their six-man squad of drivers made two serious errors between them and the Joest team proved once again it has no peers in sports car racing. Not least when they changed the complete rear end on each car in just five minutes apiece.

12 months before, the Audi that headed home a one-two-three formation finish was the one that didn't require this routine service. This time, the winner was decided not by time spent in the pits, more by seconds lost off the track.

Laurent Aïello had converted Rinaldo Capello's pole position into the lead, but when the heavens opened for the first time he opted to stay out on slicks. It was a fateful decision that effectively cost him, Capello and Christian Pescatori — the replacement for the late Michele Alboreto — victory. Aïello slewed off the track and lost two minutes to repair minor rear-end damage.

Thereafter, Aïello and co. were playing catch-up to the sister car of Tom Kristensen, Emanuele Pirro and Frank Biela, a game that wasn't aided by minor rear suspension damage sustained in the early-race off. The fightback did take the second Audi briefly into the lead, but its tenure of the top spot lasted exactly one lap before Aïello complained of problems engaging sixth gear.

According to normal Audi practice, the car was called in for a precautionary change of gearbox. Things went from bad to worse for the second-place Audi at this juncture. Capello reckoned his R8's twin-turbo V8 powerplant wasn't pulling as it had before and more time was lost in the pits while the engine management box was replaced. Ten laps later the Italian beached the car in the Dunlop Chicane gravel, losing the best part of five minutes.

'I think I was a bit nervous after the pit stops,' explained Capello after climbing from a car that was now three laps behind the leader. 'I don't think we can beat the number one car now, not unless they have a mechanical problem.'

The Kristensen-Pirro-Biela R8, which had just one off-track excursion during the race, did encounter a problem, a notchy fourth gear that required another super-quick gearbox change from the Joest squad. It was quick enough for Pirro to resume with more than a lap in hand with four hours to go. Aïello briefly got onto the same lap as the leader, but the result was never really in doubt. Pirro crossed the line a lap ahead to record only the second back-to-back triumph by a three-man driving squad in the history of the great race.

The battle for the final spot on the podium proved an interesting one. The Bentley factory, making a return to La Sarthe after an absence of 71 years, just had the measure of Chrysler and Cadillac to pull off an amazing 'debut' result. Martin Brundle led early on, but it was the second EXP Speed 8 coupé crewed by Andy Wallace, Eric van de Poele and Butch Leitzinger that claimed third place, albeit 15 laps down on the winners.

It was an impressive result for a car that hadn't run with its definitive engine — the same powerplant as found in the Audi — until the beginning of March. There were teething problems along the way: water seeped into the cars' gearbox hydraulics and precipitated the retirement of the Brundle car, while so short was the time for testing that there were no niceties as power steering or effective windscreen wipers.

Chrysler's low-key prototype assault, handled by the French ORECA team, netted fourth, though a chance of a podium looked on until a series of stops to change the starter motor late in the race. Cadillac looked good for a top-six until its sole surviving Northstar LMP broke its clutch in the final hour and limped home in 15th place.

Le Mans also witnessed the return of another famous British marque, MG pitching up at La Sarthe with two lightweight 'baby' prototypes. The project had started late and, in particular, the car's bespoke turbo engine was far from race-ready. The two Lola-built machines still made waves, out-of-work Champ car driver Mark Blundell running as high as third at one stage.

A race finish would have been a major surprise, though most recognised that to get one car past half-distance was an achievement in itself. Chevrolet dominated the GTS ranks with its Corvette C5-Rs, though its cause was aided when the two Chrysler Vipers expected to mount a challenge were both seriously damaged during the initial cloud burst.

Le Mans, once more, was Audi's race.

The US-based championship to which it has lent its name also looked like being an Audi benefit. The Joest cars dominated the first five rounds of the American Le Mans Series to extend the unbeaten run of the R8 to 14 races in all competitions.

Audi and Joest went on to clinch a second straight ALMS title but not before they came under some heavy fire from the Panoz team and its quirky front-engined cars. The US squad abandoned the radical LMP07 it had raced up to Le Mans in June in favour of the long-serving LMP Roadster S and promptly won two races with the talents of David Brabham and Jan Magnussen behind the wheel.

There could have been more, thanks in part to some disastrous luck for ALMS partners Kristensen and Capello. The latter won the

Below: The number two Joest Audi R8 of Aïello, Capello and Pescatori had to be content with second place behind the sister car.
Photograph: Mark Thompson/Allsport-Getty Images

Bottom: The third-placed Bentley EXP Speed 8 of Wallace, Leitzinger and van de Poele marked an impressive return for the famous mark after an absence of 71 years.
Photograph: Bryn Williams/crash.net

Left: **Stefan Johansson brought the evocative Gulf colour scheme back to Le Mans on his own Audi.**
Photograph: Ker Robertson/Allsport-Getty Images

Below left: **The Hawaiian Tropic girls brightened up the rain-drenched proceedings.**
Photograph: Bryn Williams/crash.net

Below: **Mark Blundell made a return to racing action with the newly formed MG team.**
Photograph: Mark Thompson/Allsport-Getty Images

first five rounds (Kristensen was paired with Pirro and Biela in round two at Sebring), yet went into the final round of the series with only a remote chance of winning the title.

More ill-fortune for Kristensen and Capello in the seasonal finale at Road Atlanta meant there was no fairy-tale ending for the faster of the two Joest crews. The end-of-season crown was Pirro's property by virtue of the eccentric ALMS scoring system that left team-mate Biela trailing four points behind.

Three cars shared the ten ALMS rounds between them, though there should have been another winner. Formula 1 refugee Johnny Herbert made an immediate impression after joining the series with the privateer Champion Audi team. Paired with Andy Wallace, he could count himself unlucky not to notch up a victory. At Mosport, he was catching race leader Pirro when an adventurous move around a slower car put him in the barriers. Less than a month later at Laguna Seca, a disputed 20-second stop-go penalty lost the British pair certain victory.

The ALMS remained the world's most prestigious sports car championship in 2001. Over in North America the Grand-American Road Racing Association's series, now in its sophomore season, catered for many of the privateers forced out of the rival championship by the domination of the factory teams. Briton James Weaver literally only had to start the season finale in November to claim the title for the Riley & Scott-equipped Dyson Racing squad.

Over in Europe, the FIA GT Championship made steady progress and could count the Spa 24 Hours among its rounds. The double points on offer for the former touring car classic were enough to give Larbre Competition Chrysler Viper drivers Christophe Bouchut and Jean-Philippe Belloc the title with four of the 11 races yet to run.

The FIA Sports car Championship, formerly the SportsRacing World Cup, also continued to grow. Grids were up and so was the quality at the front of the field. On the downside, though, the title went to the ageing Ferrari 333SP, an eight-year-old design, for the fourth straight season. Marco Zadra took the honours in the Scuderia Italia entry after a consistent season in which he won twice and finished second four times with two different team-mates.

Perhaps the 2001 season wasn't a classic for sports car racing, but the jewel in its crown, the Le Mans 24 Hours, appeared well on the way to returning to its late-1990s peak.

Above: **Chrysler just missed the final Le Mans podium place.**
Photograph: Bryn Williams/crash.net

Left: **Anthony Reid, Warren Hughes and Jonny Kane shared one of the promising new lightweight MGs.**
Photograph: Ker Robertson/Allsport-Getty Images

TOURING CARS REVIEW
Plato's republic
by Charles Bradley

Top: Jason Plato leads team-mate Yvan Muller at Knockhill. The Triple-Eight pair waged a season-long, sometimes acrimonious, battle for the crown.
Photograph: Jeff Bloxham/LAT Photographic

Above: Jason Plato proved a tough competitor and became the first British driver to hold the BTCC crown since John Cleland in 1995.
Photograph: Malcolm Griffiths/LAT Photographic

LAST year, AUTOCOURSE charted the demise of touring car racing across the globe as manufacturers tightened their collective belts or ploughed more funding into the ravenous cash-consumer that is Formula 1. This year, we are glad to report that the green shoots of recovery have begun to appear.

In Britain, a new rules package to replace the highly successful, if expensive, Super Touring formula was implemented. Although manufacturer take-up was weak, only Vauxhall, Peugeot and, belatedly, MG took the plunge, the series looks poised to blossom once again under series organiser TOCA's reign.

With a new man at the helm, Richard West, replacing outgoing series guru Alan Gow, a new broom swept through the championship with the advent of British Motorsport Promoters and Octagon taking up the reigns. In the wake of its new generation of BTC Touring cars, the championship retained its Super Production class element, under the BTC Production moniker.

Although the quantity was down on years past, the most cars entered in the top class were 11, the quality of racing at the front of the field was sufficient to keep the British tin-top fans happy. The title was fought out between works Vauxhall Astra Coupé duo Jason Plato and Frenchman Yvan Muller, as their Triple Eight Race Engineering-run Astras proved to be the class of the field.

As ever in touring cars, the battle always threatened to get out of hand in a physical sense. As the end of the year drew close, Plato and Muller clashed on numerous occasions, most notably at Silverstone in the penultimate round.

Leader Muller encountered fuel pressure problems, prompting Plato to attempt a very ambitious lunge on the final corners of the last lap. He succeeded in taking victory, but only after making solid contact with Muller which earned him a time penalty, although Yvan believed he should have been excluded altogether.

This set up a series finale at Brands Hatch which was further complicated by dismal weather conditions. Plato held a six-point

advantage, although a pending appeal against his Silverstone penalty further clouded the issue. Muller did all he could to reverse his points deficit but his car went up in flames, along with his title hopes, while leading the final race of the year. He was left to reflect that he won ten races to Plato's nine.

Plato's championship was the first for a home driver since John Cleland in 1995, underlining the international appeal of the series over the past decade. It might have lost the driving skills of the likes of former champions Alain Menu, Laurent Aïello, Rickard Rydell, et cetera, but there can be little doubt that in beating Muller — one of the most sublimely talented tin-top drivers of his generation — Plato's success was well earned.

Third in the title race was James Thompson, who secured a late deal to drive in Triple Eight's satellite team, Team Egg Sport. The financial side of the deal with the Internet bank was arranged by former Renault Spider racer Phil Bennett, who piloted the second car.

Thompson never quite got a handle on his Astra's handling, hampered by the fact his race engineer was working part-time away from his day job with British American Racing's F1 test team. But the former Honda star proved he could beat the works machinery on his day, and rued the lack of pre-season running that was afforded to Plato and Muller, and so finished the year in third.

Team-mate Bennett belied his inexperience at this level by netting a couple of race wins, albeit aided by the lack of success ballast he carried in comparison to the big three usually ahead of him. He also got in trouble on more than one occasion for his overly robust driving tactics, however, and served a one-race ban at Oulton Park after an unnecessary collision in the previous round, but was a convincing fourth in the final standings.

Besides Vauxhall, the other works team was Peugeot, its squad run by 1992 championship-winning team boss Vic Lee. Due to a shortage of bodyshells for its more suitable new 307 model, it opted for the larger 406 Coupé, but the car proved recalcitrant to sort out. Despite a likely Oulton Park win for BTCC returnee Steve Soper being wiped out by a late race engine failure, the marque failed to make the impression it had hoped for. Soper ended the season with a massive shunt at Brands Hatch which left him with concussion, while young team-mate Dan Eaves also suffered a season punctuated by accidents and poor reliability but finished ahead of his more experienced team-mate in fifth place in the championship standings.

Former Independents Cup king Matt Neal started the year with the squad, but fell out with the team after the opening round and plied his trade elsewhere. Former World Superbike star Aaron Slight made a mid-season guest appearance in Neal's old car at Donington and didn't disgrace himself, although his planned programme of races didn't extend beyond a one-off.

Making more of an immediate impact was the West Surrey Racing-run MG ZS, built by renowned single-seater chassis and sports car constructors Lola. They appeared for the final three rounds of the season, and lead driver Anthony Reid scored a surprise victory at Brands Hatch when a gamble on tyre choice paid off thanks to a fortuitous red flag. His team-mate Warren Hughes was never far behind, and scored the marque's maiden BTCC pole at Brands.

Plucky privateer efforts from Lexus and Alfa Romeo showed occasional promise, but delivered little. Former British GT champions ABG Motorsport entered a Lexus IS200 for Kurt Luby (a second car for Thomas Erdos never materialised) and solid progress was made with the rear-wheel drive car early on. Then Luby parted company, giving Brazilian Erdos his chance, and the team was renamed Total Motorsport Racing after further upheaval within its ranks.

Erdos finished the season seventh in the points table, not far behind Soper in the last of the works cars, but well clear of the plethora of drivers who drove JSM's Alfa 147s throughout the season. Chronic engine problems forced David Pinkney to split with the team, but its brace of cars began to at least finish races by the end of the season, with 1992 champion Tim Harvey, young gun Tom Ferrier (who almost scored the most unlikely victory of the season at Donington) and former Indie Cup racer Mark Blair behind the wheel at various points of the season.

In BTC Production, former works Peugeot racer Simon Harrison won the title (effectively for the third time in four years) in his HTML-run Peugeot 306. He fought out a season-long battle with Honda Accord racer James Kaye and team-mate Roger Moen. Youngsters Mat Jackson and Gareth Howell were best of the rest in their GR Motorsport Ford Focuses.

While the BTCC was starting out into a brave new world with its fresh regulations, the German DTM series was reaping the fruits of its successful rebirth in 2000. Once again, AMG Mercedes ace Bernd Schneider was the man to beat and, just like last year, no one could hold a candle to the former F1 racer.

Schneider was paired in the lead AMG squad with Scotland's Peter Dumbreck, who rued a streak of bad luck after his debut victory at Eurospeedway Lausitz which allowed Uwe Alzen to grab the runner-up spot after wins at Norisring and a real thriller at Zandvoort.

Alzen was recruited to lead AMG's B team (other candidates were Aïello and Rydell) after he was sacked by Opel for his collision with then team-mate Reuter in the 2000 finale which cost them the manufacturers' title. Behind Dumbreck, Alzen's teammate Marcel Fässler was fourth in the championship thanks to a debut win at Oschersleben. Bernd Maylander scored the other victory on offer, at Hockenheim, in his Eschmann AMG Mercedes after his multiple Porsche Supercup-winning team-mate Patrick Huisman was robbed by a sticking wheel nut.

Unlike last season, however, the privately-run Abt Sportsline Audi TT-R team was Mercedes' closest opposition, and the works Opel squads suffered a nightmare season. They built five all-new Astra V8 Coupés (Mercedes built six of its revamped CLKs) but the car was very difficult to both engineer and drive quickly. With just a narrow window of performance to work with, only one or two Opels could trouble the massed Mercs and Audis at the front of the grid at a time. Only Manuel Reuter, who finished second last year, was able to drag himself into the top ten by the season's end. No Opel driver stood on the podium all season and former BTCC champ Alain Menu didn't even score a point for his new manufacturer.

Taking full benefit was the Abt team, who proved hugely popular with the German crowd in taking the fight to the all-conquering Three-Pointed Star. In the absence of a third official manufacturer, the Kempteners played a clever political game over the winter by not accepting the initial offer of some small rule changes.

The team wanted to be allowed to stretch its TT-Rs, which were miles off the pace last season, and reposition the wings to be given a fighting chance of race wins. It paid off, and former BTCC champion Laurent Aïello rewarded them with their first DTM race win at the Nürburgring in May.

The Frenchman suffered from missing the Sachsenring round (he was busy finishing runner-up at Le Mans) and, to add insult to injury, Schneider won that race from 20th on the grid while Aïello's car was written off in the biggest shunt of the year by his understudy Kris Nissen. He also won the season's second visit to the Nürburgring, but late-season bad luck, including two big crashes at Zandvoort and Hockenheim, coupled with Merc's strength in depth dropped him to fifth in the final reckoning.

Abt's other drivers also showed flashes of inspiration, with Christian Abt and Mattias Ekström the pick of the bunch, as youngster Martin Tomczyk showed his inexperience on more than one occasion.

But although the four-litre V8s of the DTM and common component-based BTCC form a blueprint for the future, good old Super Touring wasn't quite ready to roll over and die in 2001. The Euro Super Touring series, based on the old Italian championship, was granted full FIA status to resurrect the European Touring Car Championship for the first time since 1987.

The title was battled out by Alfa Romeo and Honda, and formed part of satellite TV broadcaster Eurosport's Super Racing Weekend initiative, receiving extensive coverage as a result. Alfa's Fabrizio Giovanardi took the championship, his fifth title in five years, ahead of team-mate Nicola Larini. The pair saw off a stern challenge from Honda's Gabriele Tarquini in a title race that went down to the wire.

To highlight how seriously their teams were taking the matter, Alfa recruited Sauber-bound Felipe Massa and BTCC runner-up Yvan Muller, while Honda welcomed back James Thompson for the title crunch.

In the Super Production class, Dutchmen Peter Kox and Duncan Huisman were locked in an increasingly bad-tempered championship duel in their BMW 320s, which went to Kox after he punted off Huisman in the final race of the year.

Series organisers have been given the go-ahead by the FIA to run a new set of rules for next season called Super 2000, which are backed by Volvo, Alfa, BMW, Honda and Nissan. The regulations are based on Super Production with uprated engines and a common aerodynamic package.

Elsewhere, the remaining bastion of Super Touring was Sweden, which has become a renowned Valhalla for the ageing machinery. Italy's Roberto Colciago took the title in his Audi A4, beating off the Volvos of Jan 'Flash' Nilsson and Jens Edman.

Adding another twist to the rules conundrum, the silhouette stock car route has been taken by France and Belgium, while Germany's V8 STAR series, won by veteran racer Johnny Cecotto, has formed an effective second division to the DTM.

Touring car racing is definitely back on its feet, but questions remain over how big are the steps it can take, given the fragmentation of the regulations across Europe.

Below: Former BTCC champion Anthony Reid returned to the series with MG late in the year and took a surprise victory.

Bottom: Collisions were commonplace in a keenly contested series. James Thompson's Astra receives some rear end modifications courtesy of Yvan Muller.
Both photographs: Bryn Williams/crash.net

Year of living dangerously

US RACING REVIEW

Right: Kenny Bräck fought de Ferran all the way for the FedEx series title, and despite scoring more wins, the Swede was overhauled in the points tally by Gil de Ferran as the season came to a close.

Below: CEO Joe Heitzler presided over a stormy year for CART.

Both photographs: Jamie Squire/Allsport-Getty Images

The season got off to a troubled start with the late cancellation of the Rio meeting followed by the decision not to start at the Texas Motor Speedway on race-day morning after drivers complained of sustaining excessive g forces. Max Papis and Gil de Ferran (bottom) tackle the track during practice.

Photograph: Robert Laberge/Allsport-Getty Images

THE 2001 American racing season could not have been more turbulent. It started with the death of seven-time NASCAR champion Dale Earnhardt on the last lap of the Daytona 500 in February. Earnhardt's death focused even more interest on the booming world of NASCAR and triggered a fierce debate about safety, or the lack of it, in American stock car racing.

In recent years political turmoil in CART has overshadowed some extremely fine racing and fierce championship battles. This year we had a superb championship fight with four drivers and three teams still in the frame with three races to go, but there were so many political issues and problems that few people seemed to care.

CART's difficult year started at the Texas Motor Speedway in April with a decision to cancel the race as fans were arriving at the track on race morning. Two days of practice and qualifying confirmed everyone's worst fears about the high-banked 1.5-mile superspeedway north of Dallas as the g forces generated proved too much for the human body to withstand. Data showed the drivers were undergoing sustained vertical g loads of more than 3.3 and lateral loads of more than 5g.

Two big collisions with the wall added to everyone's worries. Cristiano da Matta and Mauricio Gugelmin crashed heavily in separate accidents with Gugelmin's massive shunt occupying more than half the track. It started in turn two where Gugelmin's car hit the wall for the first time, recording a frontal impact of 66g. The badly wrecked car continued sliding down the backstretch before striking the wall again in turn three, this time taking a 113g backwards hit. Incredibly, in a testament to the energy-absorbing crashability of the chassis, Gugelmin was badly bruised but otherwise unhurt!

The truly remarkable thing, of course, is why the problems at TMS weren't recognised in winter testing. Temperatures were much warmer in late April so that speeds were up ten mph or more over testing, but the fact is everyone in the garage area expected the 230 mph-plus lap speeds and nobody was surprised at the results.

Also, CART's retired chief steward Wally Dallenbach inspected the track when it was built four years ago and declared unequivocally that it wasn't fit for Champ cars. Dallenbach said the banked track was too steep and the corners too tight with insufficient banking to properly carry the cars off the corners and onto the straightaways.

In the end safety won out, but the cancellation resulted in a lawsuit and CART ultimately paid the Texas track around US$3.5 million in an undisclosed settlement.

CART's growing welter of problems proceeded through a series of disputes with its engine manufacturers which included an inscrutable squabble over the legality of plenum chambers and 'pop-off' valves. A firestorm erupted at Detroit in June when CART adopted a new turbo boost-limiting pop-off valve for the rest of the season. The introduction of the new valve caused relations between the governing body and its engine manufacturers — Honda in particular — to deteriorate to a new low.

CART's new pressure relief valve was three-quarters of an inch taller than the previous valve with an extended base or skirt. The extension was designed to minimise the possibility of cheating the valve as CART believed certain manufacturers had been doing.

CART was informed by Toyota a few weeks earlier that Toyota believed its competitors had discovered a way of pulling three more inches of boost pressure by accelerating the flow of air across the pressure sensor inside the plenum chamber.

Honda and Ford people said they knew nothing about the new pop-off valve until a few days before the start of practice in Detroit. Nor was the new valve formally mandated until immediately before the start of the first practice session in Detroit resulting in most Honda and some Ford teams sitting idle 'on strike' in the pit lane that morning.

An unsuccessful protest and appeal by Honda followed and after Toyota and Honda spent a month throwing mud at each other, the great pop-off valve dispute was finally resolved by everyone agreeing to revert to racing with the extended or 'spacer valve' first introduced at Detroit in June. Following the July 2 hearing of Honda's appeal however, CART partially reversed its decision, requiring the standard, pre-Detroit pop-off valve for Toronto and the next two races on the Michigan and Chicago ovals. Another configuration was supposed to have been approved for the balance of the season pending discussion between CART and its three engine manufacturers.

Despite the theoretically final decision of CART's appeals panel Toyota continued to push for CART to require the extended valve used in Detroit, Portland and Cleveland to be required for the Michigan 500. Sure enough, the day after the race in Toronto CART confirmed that the 'spacer valve' was now required wear for the rest of the season.

Leaving the Ovals Behind?

All of which brings us to CART's last hurrah at Michigan near the end of July. Over the past three or four years the crowds at Michigan have declined in inverse proportion to the unbelievably fierce racing on the track. The better and more exciting the race, it seemed, the smaller the crowd the following year.

Everyone scratched their heads over how and why this trend occurred. The last two years something like 40,000 fans have shown up on race day, resulting in CART's decision to quit the high-banked superspeedway after this past year's race to be replaced in 2002 by the IRL. CART also ran its last race at the short 0.096-mile Nazareth oval in 2001 after pulling out of the Homestead-Miami and Gateway ovals in 2000, all these desertations essentially because of dwindling crowds.

Roger Penske sold Michigan and his other tracks — Homestead-Miami, Nazareth and California — to ISC three years ago after deciding to get out of the racetrack business to focus his vast business empire on selling cars and leasing trucks, but Penske continues as the vice-chairman and a director of ISC.

ISC is an offshoot of NASCAR and the Daytona-based France family, of course, and the publicly-traded company is the world's largest racetrack business, owning 13 tracks across the United States. You would expect major races at tracks owned by such a company to be energetically promoted but at Homestead, Nazareth and Michigan — since Penske sold them — there has been little promotion of the race events. Usually, there wasn't a single billboard, nor did you hear or see any TV or radio ads, or hear much talk about the race among the locals.

Clearly, ISC decided to turn its back on CART and support Tony George and the IRL so that CART is left with just three domestic oval races — California, Milwaukee and Chicago — with the IRL picking up the pieces as CART vacates the premises. CART likes to promote the wide variety of tracks on which its cars and drivers race, yet it is steadily losing any oval racing content.

'I think it was a huge mistake for CART not to return [to Michigan],' said Penske. 'I don't understand CART's position. One minute we're talking about strategy that has differentiation, meaning road courses and ovals, and to walk away from what I consider one of the biggest tracks in the country in regard to potential, I don't understand it.

'Obviously, the [CART-IRL] split has created the problem at Michigan. CART's decision not to renew its contract with Nazareth and not to go back to Homestead certainly sent a message to ISC management, and they determined their long-term strategy was going to be the IRL on their ovals, and not CART.'

With ISC controlling most of America's major ovals and CART also falling out of bed in the wake of the Texas abandonment with ISC's only rival Bruton Smith's Speedway Motorsports, the future for CART appears to lie more and more in street races and international venues. The IRL, weak as it may be, has solidified itself in partnership with ISC as an oval racing series, filling the void as CART moves on.

Everyone's a winner! But none was certain to retain their seats in their respective teams for 2002.

Max Papis (top) took two wins which were more due to strategy than outright speed. Unfortunately the likeable Italian blotted his copybook by twice knocking team-mate Kenny Bräck out of contention for race victories.
Photograph: Robert Laberge/Allsport-Getty Images

Roberto Moreno (centre) was the oldest driver in the CART FedEx series but he was the quickest man in Vancouver.
Photograph: Adam Pretty/Allsport-Getty Images

Bruno Junqueira (above) had a tough rookie year with Ganassi but drove superbly to snatch an unlikely win at Elkhart Lake.
Photograph: Robert Laberge/Allsport-Getty Images

CART Before Horsepower

Dispiriting as this sequence of events may have been they were merely primers for the potentially organisation-busting argument that erupted near the end of the season over the proposed 2003 engine rules.

The engine rules had been fiercely debated for three or four years and in 1998 CART's four engine manufacturers — Honda, Ford/Cosworth, Mercedes-Benz and Toyota — proposed a 1.8-litre turbo formula with the boost limit set at 55 in. Hg.

The aim was to downsize the existing 2.65-litre engine and retain both turbocharging and the pop-off valve to limit turbo boost as a means of controlling increases in horsepower that would inevitably come over time. The idea made a lot of sense and also provided a way to differentiate Champ car technology from F1.

Yet CART's team owners were reluctant to make a decision. As time went on more and more of them believed they should switch to Tony George's IRL engine rules — normally-aspirated 3.5-litre engines with strict cost and development limits attached. The owners thought that by going to the IRL engine rules they could get back into bed with George and make everything right again after George's deeply damaging split with CART at the end of 1995.

The owners, unable to make a decision, missed the March 2001 deadline for determining the 2003 rules. The rulebook said the missed deadline meant new engine rules couldn't be introduced until 2004.

A month later Toyota announced it would build IRL-spec engines in 2003 and in late September the Japanese manufacturing giant issued an ultimatum to CART confirming Toyota would build only an IRL-type normally-aspirated engine in 2003. Switch to the IRL's 3.5-litre naturally-aspirated formula in 2003, was the message, or it's sayonara.

Toyota had signed up Chip Ganassi for the 2000 season, and Pat Patrick and Carl Haas for the past year. Ganassi, Patrick and Haas were paid more money in sponsorship than the cost of their annual engine lease programmes. Roger Penske was also on board having long been a proponent of a single series and common CART/IRL engine formula. On October 4, within days of Toyota's IRL-only statement, the owners voted to introduce an IRL-like engine formula in 2003. The only owners not to vote for the rule change were Jerry Forsythe, who voted against the move, and Mo Nunn who abstained.

Forsythe is the largest shareholder among CART's team owners and he was incensed by the decision. Forsythe insisted the team owners were not empowered to make a major rule change and said he would resort to all legal means to reverse the decision.

Forsythe said he believes CART must pursue its own path, entirely separate from the IRL. 'We don't need to be associated with the IRL,' Forsythe said. 'We're a separate series that is very different technically and as far as venues and so forth that has so much to offer the race fan. And you and I know that the merger of the two series will never happen.'

A Big Shake-up

On our deadline in late October, Forsythe and some of the other major shareholders in CART were attempting to take control of the company, buying the remaining shares owned by most of CART's team owners. Their plan was to remove the team owners from making any decisions by dismantling CART's franchise board and installing Long Beach promoter Chris Pook as the company's new boss.

Before any of these changes could happen Honda announced at Laguna Seca in the middle of October that it will pull out of Champ car racing at the end of 2002. 'This decision is a great disappointment to Honda as we have informed CART from the beginning of the process that it is impossible to supply a new engine conforming to their proposed specifications prior to the 2004 season,' said Honda's Tom Elliott.

Elliott said Honda was not interested in the IRL. One week later Ford's racing boss Dan Davis confirmed that Ford/Cosworth won't build an engine for CART's 2003 engine rules.

'The major obstacle for our continued participation in CART is return on investment,' said Davis, director of Ford's Racing Technology division. 'Ford is not willing to commit the massive resources required to design, develop, and produce a brand new engine and the necessary volume of parts at a significant financial loss in order to participate in a series that today has questionable marketing value.'

Davis added that Ford would continue in CART if the Champ car organising body decided to adopt a 'spec engine' for 2003. Cosworth, a wholly-owned subsidiary of Ford, proposed a 'spec' version of its current 2.65-litre turbo Ford/Cosworth XF.

The proposal was rejected by CART's team owners at the October 4 meeting where the decision was taken to switch to 3.5-litre 'atmo' engines in 2003, but Davis said in late October that the offer from Ford and Cosworth still stands.

CART's problems may be traced back many years to its start, in fact, in 1979.

CART was founded as a committee of team owners, a democratic group, all with their own interests, strengths and power bases, and from the earliest days the owners failed to find the leadership required. A Bernie Ecclestone or Bill France did not emerge from their ranks as was the case in Formula 1 and NASCAR respectively.

Instead, the team owners preferred to appoint various managers to try to run things by consensus and it never worked. From Jim Melvin to John Frasco, John Caponigro, Johnny Capels, Bill Stokkan and then Andrew Craig, the job became a true revolving door. In June of last year, of course, Andrew Craig was replaced on an interim basis by Bobby Rahal. Bobby really didn't want the job on principle, but also because he was already being lured towards Jaguar and F1.

The team owners hired Joe Heitzler to take over from Rahal on a full-time basis, but Heitzler found, as had all his predecessors, the position to be fraught with difficulties.

Helio Castroneves excelled on the road and street courses and the Marlboro Team Penske driver claimed wins at Long Beach, Detroit (above) and Mid-Ohio.

Left: Michael Andretti teamed up with Barry Green and Motorola but, despite a win at Toronto, could not sustain a championship challenge.

Both photographs: Robert Laberge/Allsport-Getty Images

Right: Gil de Ferran takes the plaudits on the Rockingham podium after a sensational last-corner manoeuvre saw him snatch victory from championship rival Kenny Bräck (left). De Ferran's Penske team-mate Helio Castroneves (right) took third place.
Photograph: Robert Laberge/Allsport-Getty Images

Below: Cristiano da Matta was the equal of anyone when his car was working well and took masterful wins in Monterrey, Surfers Paradise and Fontana to prove it.
Photograph: Darrell Ingham/Allsport-Getty Images

Below centre: Easily the most impressive young driver in CART during 2001 was PacWest's Scott Dixon. The 21-year-old became the series' youngest ever winner after a canny victory in Nazareth which belied his inexperience.
Photograph: Robert Laberge/Allsport-Getty Images

Bottom: Dario Franchitti and Team Kool Green had an up and down year with the Scots driver scoring just a single win.
Photograph: Jamie Squire/Allsport-Getty Images

A Positive European Debut

Indeed, CART made a successful debut in Europe with a pair of September races at the EuroSpeedway in Germany and Rockingham, England, ovals both. The two, brand new oval tracks gave European fans their first taste of modern American oval racing at speeds of more than 200 mph and the races were roundly well-received.

The German race drew a huge crowd of more than 80,000, bigger than the same day's Italian GP, and Rockingham proved a great tonic for both the paying public and media in England who have grown weary of the tedium and remoteness of modern F1.

While the EuroSpeedway was a delight to behold, complete and ready to go in every respect, Rockingham barely made the green flag. The track had been underbuilt, lacking the necessary layers of aggregate beneath the pavement to properly drain water. Also the pavement itself was too coarse so that despite no serious rain during the weekend the track suffered from 'weepers', essentially puddles backing up onto the track surface. There was no serious running at all on the first two days and the race finally started late in the afternoon over a shortened distance beneath a fast-setting sun.

Despite a serious lack of practice the drivers and teams put on a great race with championship rivals Gil de Ferran and Kenny Bräck passing each other twice in the last lap and a half. It was an exciting end to a tough couple of weeks for the Champ car fraternity most of whom had arrived in Germany just before the September 11 terrorist attacks on New York and Washington.

Marooned in Europe for a couple of weeks, most of them wanted desperately to get home to their families and were devastated to witness Alex Zanardi's terrible accident in the closing laps of the EuroSpeedway race. They then had to stand around for two days at Rockingham, expecting that the race might never happen.

Zanardi's freak accident with Alex Tagliani cost the popular Italian his legs but his life was saved by CART's excellent safety team and pair of quick-thinking, cool-acting doctors, Steve Olvey and Terry Trammell. Drs Olvey and Trammell put their 50 years of combined experience to best use, using Zanardi's seatbelts as tourniquets to stem the loss of blood so that he could be flown to Berlin for successful emergency surgery.

While Zanardi faces a long and difficult rehabilitation and begins to learn to walk with prosthetic legs, CART's long-time technical

chief and circuit inspector Kirk Russell was sacked the week after Rockingham. Russell had been with CART since its formation and among his many jobs also served as chief steward in 2000.

Almost lost beneath the crush of politics was the racing which was often fantastic. No fewer than 11 drivers won Champ car races in 2001, equalling the previous year's record for multiple winners. Defending champion Gil de Ferran didn't score his first win of the year until Rockingham in September, but another win in the streets of Houston two weeks later and third place at Laguna Seca the following weekend put him in command of the title chase.

De Ferran clinched his second consecutive CART driver's championship and thus became only the fourth driver to win back-to-back CART championships. The others were Rick Mears in 1981–'82, Bobby Rahal in 1986–'87 and Alex Zanardi in 1997–'98. De Ferran's second championship also marked a record-setting 11th National Championship and ninth CART Championship for Team Penske. The team has a record 110 race wins and 135 pole positions since it started competing in Indy or Champ car racing in 1968.

In his second year with the mighty Penske team de Ferran really came into his own. He began to deserve his moniker as 'The Professor' with his excellent technical and set-up skills and more often than not was able to outpace his fiery young team-mate Castroneves. Nor were there many mistakes from de Ferran in 2001 as he matured at 33 (he turned 34 on November 11) into the perfectly faultless Penske driver and multiple champion.

De Ferran's strongest challengers were Kenny Bräck with Bobby Rahal's team and his own Penske team-mate Helio Castroneves. In his second year in CART, 1998 IRL champion and '99 Indy 500 winner Bräck led the championship most of the year.

He won four oval races but wasn't able to win on a road or street circuit where the Lola chassis run by Rahal's team couldn't match Penske's Reynards. The Lola didn't put the power down as well as the Reynard and often used up its rear tyres much more voraciously than the competition. The 26-year-old Castroneves won three CART races — all on road circuits — plus the Indy 500 and was superb on occasion, always quick, but not quite as complete a driver in 2001 as his more experienced team-mate. Other drivers to win Champ car races in 2001 were Cristiano da Matta, Scott Dixon, Max Papis, Dario Franchitti, Michael Andretti, Patrick Carpentier, Bruno Junqueira and Roberto Moreno. Dixon and Junqueira did so in their rookie years, Kiwi Dixon becoming the

youngest winner in the history of a major single-seater race when he won at Nazareth in May at 20 years and nine months old.

Honda clinched CART's Maufacturer's Championship at La-guna Seca with two races still to run just two days after announc-ing its withdrawal at the end of 2002. De Ferran's back-to-back wins at Rockingham and Houston, and a third place at Laguna Seca, wrapped up Honda's fourth CART maufacturer's title and its third in the last four years. Honda's other CART championships came in 1996, '98 and '99, all three with Chip Ganassi's team. Honda-powered drivers have also won the last six consecutive CART driver's titles.

CART's Indy Lights championship came to the end of its road in 2001 after a lifespan of 16 years. With the Lights series struggling to attract much of a field in recent years, CART decided to focus on its Toyota/Atlantic series in 2002 with plans to develop a more powerful version of the formula in 2005.

A victim of the political battle over the future of Indy Lights was series boss Roger Bailey who had run the championship from its first days. Bailey is one of the most respected men in motor racing with more than 40 years' experience in all facets of the business but he did not survive the season, losing his job near year's end after a long dispute with CART boss Heitzler.

The final Lights championship was won convincingly by 26-year-old Townsend Bell who won six of 12 races. Bell also made his Champ car debut with Patrick Racing near the end of the year and is expected to drive a Champ car full-time for Patrick in 2002. Irishman Damien Faulkner and Brit Dan Wheldon battled for sec-ond in the championship, both winning races during the year.

The demise of Indy Lights opened the door for Tony George to create his own, Nissan-powered Lights series to run with IRL races in 2002. Bailey was expected to administer the new Lights series for George and, like the IRL, the new series will race strictly on ovals.

The Toyota/Atlantic championship was won easily by Brazilian Hoover Orsi who took five wins. Canadian David Rutledge finished second in the championship from impressive young American rookie Joey Hand and Argentine Martin Basso. Many Lights teams are switching to Toyota/Atlantic next year, preferring to run both road courses and ovals rather than a strictly oval series, and it will be interesting to see how Toyota/Atlantic and the IRL's new Lights series fare over the next few years.

Above: Alex Zanardi now faces the biggest challenge of his life as he recovers from his horrendous accident at Lausitzring.
Photograph: Robert Laberge/Allsport-Getty Images

Below: The EuroSpeedway in Germany provided fabulous viewing for the spectators.
Photograph: Jon Ferrey/Allsport-Getty Images

Above: Ecstatic Indy 500 winner Helio Castroneves delights the fans with his customary fence-climbing celebration.

Top right: Tony Stewart remained one of NASCAR's most exciting and sometimes unpredictable chargers.
Both photographs: Robert Laberge/Allsport-Getty Images

Centre right: Veteran Ricky Rudd continued to prove a doughty competitor.
Photograph: Donald Miralle/Allsport-Getty Images

Below right: Dale Earnhardt Jr proved he had the talent to follow in his late father's footsteps with the #8 Dale Earnhardt Inc. Chevy Monte Carlo.
Photograph: Jon Ferrey/Allsport-Getty Images

Below: Sam Hornish Jr emerged as the IRL's most talented young driver and a worthy winner of the series.
Photograph: Robert Laberge/Allsport-Getty Images

IRL Emergent?

As troubled as CART is, the IRL has its own commercial problems. It has pulled reasonable crowds at some races, usually as a result of season-ticket deals at new ISC or Bruton Smith tracks, but many of its races continue to struggle to draw much of a crowd. The IRL's biggest strength is its alliance with ISC.

The IRL puts on entertaining shows, but it still lacks credibility and glitz as well as superstar drivers and teams. The reason the cars run so close is because they are the opposite of what an F1 or Indy car is supposed to be. An F1 or Indy car should have more horsepower than grip or downforce. That's what makes an F1 or Indy car so exciting to watch, or drive.

But Tony George's formula for the IRL was to substantially cut horsepower and add downforce so that the cars are slower down the straights relative to a CART car and as quick or quicker in the corners because they generate so much downforce. This also makes them relatively easy to drive and enables them to run side-by-side, or in multiple grooves, more easily than a Champ car. As Juan Montoya says, IRL cars aren't much more than overgrown F3000 cars.

The big question about the future is whether any CART teams will defect to the IRL. The Indy 500 is one thing, but the rest of the series has yet to build the critical mass to attract major sponsors or teams. Mind you, if CART does adopt IRL-like engine rules the move may provide some momentum to gathering that critical mass and at the end of the year no less a man than Roger Penske was quietly threatening to make the switch.

Helio Castroneves and Gil de Ferran scored a stunning one-two victory for Roger Penske's team at Indianapolis as Penske recorded his 11th win in the 500 and Castroneves equalled the previous year's performance by Juan Montoya, winning the race in his rookie start. The race was a convincing demonstration for Penske's team in its first start at Indianapolis since 1994. It was also a crushing triumph for CART's teams over the IRL as CART drivers finished first through fifth with the first IRL regular a lap behind in seventh place.

De Ferran's second place completed Penske's first one-two at Indianapolis while Michael Andretti drove a very good race from near the back of the field to finish third. Jimmy Vasser, driving for Chip Ganassi on a one-off basis, was able to beat young teammate Bruno Junqueira into fourth place with NASCAR star Tony Stewart falling to sixth in one of Ganassi's other cars so that last year's winners finished fourth through sixth.

Penske was deeply satisfied with his team's 11th win at Indianapolis. The last time Penske was at Indy was 1995, the year before the CART-IRL split and both of his drivers, Emerson Fittipaldi and Al Unser Jr, failed to qualify that year. To return six years later and score his team's 11th win may have sown the seeds for the departure from CART of Penske and primary sponsor Marlboro.

The IRL championship was won convincingly by 22-year-old Sam Hornish who was in his second year racing Indy cars. A graduate of F2000 and Toyota/Atlantic, Hornish landed a top drive with Panther Racing and quickly asserted himself scoring his first IRL victory at Phoenix in April and going on to win two more races. Hornish wrapped-up the IRL title with two races to go handily beating veterans Buddy Lazier and Scott Sharp.

Earnhardt Dies, Gordon Dominates

Dale Earnhardt's death on the last lap of the season-opening Daytona 500 resulted in a lot of talk about safety.

A six-month investigation into Earnhardt's accident was supposed to be the most exhaustive in the sport's history yet no recommendations were made for improving the crash-resistance of NASCAR's antique cars, nor were there any moves by NASCAR to create a CART-style safety team. Instead, the investigation centred on the improper installation of Earnhardt's seat belts.

After the report was made public, safety maven Bill Simpson resigned from his eponymous safety equipment company rather than engage in a protracted legal battle with NASCAR. A long-time friend of Earnhardt, Simpson had frequently excoriated the NASCAR legend over the way his seat belts were mounted. There was also lots of talk about making the HANS device mandatory, something NASCAR resisted until near the end of the season.

Many believe that NASCAR should also address its tube-framed cars which have been made stiffer over the years with little regard paid to energy-absorption. The fact is most new cars manufactured in Detroit these days enjoy much more in the way of energy-absorbing extremities than a NASCAR stock car. NASCAR needs a complete rethink of its basic chassis format, a design which was abandoned 40 years ago by every other form of motor sport.

Like Ayrton Senna's death in 1994, Earnhardt's demise generated

even more media and public interest in an already booming form of racing. NASCAR also launched a new $400 million TV deal with NBC and Fox in 2001 and it is now the 600-pound gorilla of American motor sport, completely dominant in the national media and popular culture. While CART and the IRL have lost ground over the last six years NASCAR has forged ahead, pushing single-seater or open-wheel racing out of the national consciousness.

The 2001 Winston Cup championship was utterly dominated by 30-year-old Jeff Gordon who won his fourth title by the widest margin in NASCAR history aboard one of Rick Hendrick's Chevrolets. Gordon won the championship in 1995, '97 and '98 and was second in '96, winning no fewer than 40 races during those four years. He was less successful in 1999 and 2000 however, finishing sixth and ninth in the championship.

Many people attributed Gordon's decline to the departure of long-time crew chief Ray Evernham near the end of 1999 but Gordon rebounded powerfully in 2001. He won six of the 33 Winston Cup races run before AUTOCOURSE went to press, and led more than 20 per cent of the season's total laps, more than twice as many as any other driver. From the middle of the season nobody else was in the title hunt.

While Gordon ran away, the battle for runner-up was disputed by veterans Ricky Rudd, Sterling Marlin and Dale Jarrett and new star Tony Stewart. Rudd and Jarrett drove Fords for Robert Yates's team while Marlin drove a Dodge for Chip Ganassi's new NASCAR team. Dodge returned to NASCAR in 2001 after a ten-year absence

and Marlin scored the marque's first win since its return at Michigan in August.

NASCAR boasts plenty of young talent these days, led by Stewart and Dale Earnhardt Jr, the latter making his Winston Cup debut in 1999, scoring his first win in 2000 and had won three races in 2001 driving a Chevrolet for his late father's team. Other rapid risers include Kevin Harvick, Earnhardt Sr's replacement at Richard Childress Racing, as well as Matt Kenseth and Ryan Newman. Harvick showed his stuff by competing in both the Winston Cup and second division Busch Grand National series in 2001, a grand total of almost 70 races! Harvick ran away with the BGN championship, handily outpointing former champion Jeff Green.

Other American champions in 2001 included Italian veteran Emanuele Pirro who shaded Joest/Audi team-mate Frank Biela to the American Le Mans title. The Joest Audi R8s dominated the sports car series with Audi drivers Rinaldo Cappelo, Tom Kristensen and Andy Wallace finishing third, fourth and fifth in points.

Jan Magnussen and David Brabham were next in the championship driving one of Don Panoz's front-engined Panoz LMP1s. The SCCA's TransAm championship was won for the third time in four years by veteran Paul Gentilozzi who drove his own Jaguar XKR.

The Grand-Am Championship went down to the season finale at Daytona International Speedway, where Englishman James Weaver clinched the Sports Prototype class driver's title in a Dyson Racing Team's Riley and Scott.

Top: Jeff Gordon was back to his best and won the NASCAR crown by a country mile with the Rick Hendrick's Chevrolet Monte Carlo.

Above left: Matt Kenseth strapped into his Roush Racing Ford Taurus. Dale Earnhardt's tragic accident raised concerns over the simple construction of NASCAR machines.
Both photographs: Jon Ferrey/Allsport-Getty Images

Above centre: Kevin Harvick emerged as one of the series' exciting new talents behind the wheel of the Richard Childress Chevy Monte Carlo.

Above: Veteran Dale Jarrett was always a factor in the Robert Yates Ford Taurus.
Both photographs: Robert Laberge/Allsport-Getty Images

Above: **The number '3', so synonymous with the late Dale Earnhardt.**
Photograph: Donald Miralle/Allsport-Getty Images

Below: **'The Intimidator'.**
Photograph: Jon Ferrey/Allsport-Getty Images

DALE EARNHARDT

First of all he was 'Ironhead', before evolving into 'The Intimidator', the quintessential southern stock car driver of the last 20 years. Dale Earnhardt was the man so many others wanted to be. He was tough, fast, supremely confident and a brilliant racer.

Earnhardt was the acknowledged master of drafting on the superspeedways. He seemed to understand how to use the air better than any other driver and his results at Daytona and Talladega proved it. At Talladega, Earnhardt won no fewer than ten 500-miles races, and despite winning the Daytona 500 just once, in 1998, he won 33 other races at Daytona over the years, including a string of ten consecutive 125-mile qualifying race wins between 1990–'99.

He was also a grand master of 'laying a fender' on another car. Unlike most forms of motor racing, stock car racing is a contact sport. Using your car's fenders to best effect is one of the arts of the game, and nobody could do it better than 'The Intimidator'. Over the years Earnhardt crashed many people, always with a deft touch. He played the odds and won many times. He raised the ire of plenty of drivers and even more fans, emerging — until Jeff Gordon and Tony Stewart came along — as the man people loved to hate.

Earnhardt played the game to the maximum on and off the track. He got the most out of the black and silver colours of team owner Richard Childress's primary sponsor GM Goodwrench, becoming just as much 'The Man in Black', as 'The Intimidator'. The sobriquets were interchangeable. He was the menacing, dark force, the guy who was going to push to the maximum at every turn, in every situation. It was an image Earnhardt cultivated superbly, and of course he could back it up implacably on the racetrack.

Dale Earnhardt was the son of Ralph Earnhardt, a renowned short-track driver from North Carolina who won a NASCAR Late Model Sportsman championship in the late 1950s. He started racing on Carolina short tracks like his father and made his Winston Cup debut in 1975 when he was 24 years old. Earnhardt ran a handful of races over the next four years and his big break came in 1979 when Rodney Osterlund hired him to run the full NASCAR schedule for the first time. He scored his first win that year at Bristol, Tennessee, finished seventh in the championship and was NASCAR's rookie of the year.

Earnhardt continued with Osterlund in 1980 and '81, winning five races in 1980 and taking the first of his seven championships. After Osterlund's team folded in the middle of 1981 he joined Richard Childress's team for the second half of the year, then drove for veteran NASCAR team owner Bud Moore in 1982 and '83. He rejoined Childress for 1984 and the pair remained together for the next 17 years, creating the most successful combination in modern NASCAR history.

The Earnhardt-Childress pairing won the NASCAR championship in 1986, '87, '90, '91, '93 and '94. The last title was Earnhardt's seventh, equalling the record number of championships won by Richard Petty and placing him at the pinnacle of the stock car racing's pantheon. The last few years were a little less successful, although he was second to Jeff Gordon in the 1995 championship and finished second again in last season's championship to Bobby Labonte. He also won six races over the last three years.

Earnhardt won 76 Winston Cup races from 676 starts over 26 seasons and is ranked sixth on NASCAR's all-time winners list behind Richard Petty, David Pearson, Bobby Allison, Darrell Waltrip and Cale Yarborough. It's a sobering thought that all five of those other legends of stock car racing survived their driving careers and are alive and happy today.

While Earnhardt is gone, his name and spirit will remain. His son Dale Jr has proven himself a superstar in his own right in the past few years driving for Dale Earnhardt Incorporated, a three-car Chevrolet team with Earnhardt Jr, Daytona winner Waltrip and Steve Park driving. Earnhardt's wife Teresa, who was at his side when he was pronounced dead, has run the business end of the team in partnership with her late husband and she continues in this role, a very strong personality who was entirely the equal of her late husband. The memory and legacy of Dale Earnhardt will cast a very long shadow. *Gordon Kirby*

OTHER MAJOR RESULTS

Compiled by David Hayhoe

International Formula 3000 Championship

All cars are Lola B99/50-Zytek V8

FIA INTERNATIONAL FORMULA 3000 CHAMPIONSHIP, Autodromo Jose Carlos Pacé, Interlagos, São Paulo, Brazil, 31 March. Round 1. 35 laps of the 2.677-mile/4.309-km circuit, 93.731 miles/ 150.845 km.
1 Justin Wilson, GB, 53m 48.503s, 104.517 mph/168.202 km/h; 2 Jaime Melo Jr., BR, 53m 56.152s; 3 Sébastien Bourdais, F, 54m 05.962s; 4 David Saelens, B, 54m 10.418s; 5 Joël Camathias, CH, 54m 15.601s; 6 Fabrizio Gollin, I, 54m 17.070s; 7 Mark Webber, AUS, 54m 17.114s; 8 Darren Manning, GB, 54m 18.711s; 9 Antonio Pizzonia, BR, 54m 28.492s; 10 Bas Leinders, B, 54m 31.875s; 11 Andrea Piccini, I, 54m 33.616s; 12 Tomas Enge, CZ, 54m 34.908s; 13 Rodrigo Sperafico, BR, 54m 35.226s; 14 Derek Hill, USA, 54m 39.301s; 15 Gabriele Varano, I, 54m 51.430s; 16 Justin Keen, GB, 54m 52.161s; 17 Ananda Mikola, RI, 54m 59.229s; 18 Yann Goudy, F, 55m 11.001s; 19 Giorgio Pantano, I, 34 laps (DNF - spin); 20 Nicolás Filiberti, I, 34; 21 Mario Haberfeld, BR, 16 (DNF - mechanical); 22 Viktor Maslov, RUS, 10 (DNF - spin); 23 Patrick Freisacher, A, 8 (DNF - accident); 24 Antonio Garcia, E, 8 (DNF - accident); 25 Gabriele Lancieri, I, 4 (DNF - spin); 26 Ricardo Sperafico, BR, 0 (DNF - accident).
Fastest race lap: Pizzonia, 1m 27.755s, 109.839 mph/176.769 km/h.
Fastest qualifying lap: Melo Jr., 1m 26.732s, 111.135 mph/ 178.854 km/h.
Championship points: 1 Wilson, 10; 2 Melo Jr., 6; 3 Bourdais, 4; 4 Saelens, 3; 5 Camathias, 2; 6 Gollin, 1.

FIA INTERNATIONAL FORMULA 3000 CHAMPIONSHIP, Autodromo Enzo e Dino Ferrari, Imola, Italy, 14 April. Round 2. 31 laps of the 3.065-mile/4.933-km circuit, 94.875 miles/ 152.686 km.
1 Mark Webber, AUS, 56m 45.779s, 100.285 mph/161.393 km/h; 2 Darren Manning, GB, 56m 49.082s; 3 Tomas Enge, CZ, 56m 49.869s; 4 Antonio Pizzonia, BR, 56m 55.537s; 5 Patrick Freisacher, A, 56m 55.950s; 6 Justin Wilson, GB, 56m 56.712s; 7 Rodrigo Sperafico, BR, 57m 00.853s; 8 Fabrizio Gollin, I, 57m 03.022s; 9 Bas Leinders, B, 57m 14.892s; 10 Viktor Maslov, RUS, 57m 17.468s; 11 Giorgio Pantano, I, 57m 18.290s; 12 Justin Keen, GB, 57m 22.519s; 13 Gabriele Lancieri, I, 57m 24.282s; 14 Ricardo Sperafico, BR, 57m 25.067s; 15 Joël Camathias, CH, 57m 25.933s; 16 Antonio Garcia, E, 57m 36.859s; 17 Nicolás Filiberti, I, 30 laps; 18 Andrea Piccini, I, 24 laps (DNF - accident); 19 Mario Haberfeld, BR, 24 (DNF - accident); 20 Jaime Melo Jr., BR, 12 (DNF - accident); 21 David Saelens, B, 12 (DNF - accident); 22 Gianluca Calcagni, I, 7 (DNF - accident); 23 Derek Hill, USA, 7 (DNF - accident); 24 Gabriele Varano, I, 6 (DNF - accident); 25 Sébastien Bourdais, F, 0 (DNF - spin); 26 Ananda Mikola, RI, 0 (DNF - spin).
Fastest race lap: Webber, 1m 40.232s, 110.093 mph/177.177 km/h.
Fastest qualifying lap: Webber, 1m 38.518s, 112.008 mph/ 180.259 km/h.
Championship points: 1 Wilson, 11; 2 Webber, 10; 3=Manning, 6; 3= Melo Jr., 6; 5= Enge, 4; 5= Bourdais, 4.

FIA INTERNATIONAL FORMULA 3000 CHAMPIONSHIP, Circuit de Catalunya, Montmeló, Barcelona, Spain, 28 April. Round 3. 32 laps of the 2.939-mile/4.730-km circuit, 93.972 miles/ 151.233 km.
1 Tomas Enge, CZ, 52m 00.457s, 108.413 mph/174.474 km/h; 2 Bas Leinders, B, 52m 02.668s; 3 Justin Wilson, GB, 52m 03.663s; 4 Mario Haberfeld, BR, 52m 09.721s; 5 David Saelens, B, 52m 20.588s; 6 Antonio Pizzonia, BR, 52m 21.291s; 7 Mark Webber, AUS, 52m 22.695s; 8 Patrick Freisacher, A, 52m 23.013s; 9 Giorgio Pantano, I, 52m 29.713s; 10 Antonio Garcia, E, 52m 30.098s; 11 Sébastien Bourdais, F, 52m 41.308s; 12 Viktor Maslov, RUS, 52m 59.475s; 13 Andrea Piccini, I, 53m 02.405s; 14 Nicolás Filiberti, I, 53m 03.014s; 15 Gabriele Varano, I, 53m 04.444s; 16 Derek Hill, USA, 53m 07.096s; 17 Fabrizio Gollin, I, 53m 08.366s; 18 Joël Camathias, CH, 53m 09.087s; 19 Ricardo Sperafico, BR, 53m 09.925s; 20 Darren Manning, GB, 53m 10.871s; 21 Jaime Melo Jr., BR, 53m 12.386s; 22 Rodrigo Sperafico, BR, 53m 13.557s; 23 Ananda Mikola, RI, 53m 21.892s; 24 Gabriele Lancieri, I 20 laps (DNF - withdrawn following penalties).
Fastest race lap: Wilson, 1m 36.230s, 109.952 mph/176.951 km/h.
Fastest qualifying lap: Wilson, 1m 33.931s, 112.643 mph/ 181.282 km/h.
Championship points: 1 Wilson, 15; 2 Enge, 14; 3 Webber, 10; 4= Melo Jr., 6; 4= Manning, 6; 4= Leinders, 6.

FIA INTERNATIONAL FORMULA 3000 CHAMPIONSHIP, A1-Ring, Spielberg, Austria, 12 May. Round 4. 35 laps of the 2.688-mile/ 4.326-km circuit, 94.082 miles/151.410 km.
1 Justin Wilson, GB, 51m 57.144s, 108.655 mph/174.864 km/h; 2 Bas Leinders, B, 51m 57.599s; 3 Tomas Enge, CZ, 51m 58.093s; 4 Antonio Pizzonia, BR, 51m 59.211s; 5 Jaime Melo Jr., BR, 52m 08.893s; 6 Andrea Piccini, I, 52m 11.559s; 7 Dino Morelli, GB, 52m 29.999s; 8 Rodrigo Sperafico, BR, 52m 31.944s; 9 David Saelens, B, 52m 32.764s; 10 Nicolás Filiberti, I, 52m 33.420s; 11 Viktor Maslov, RUS, 52m 43.813s; 12 Gabriele Lancieri, I, 52m 44.691s; 13 Derek Hill, USA, 52m 59.059s; 14 Gabriele Varano, I, 53m 05.414s; 15 Giorgio Pantano, I, 32 laps; 16 Sébastien Bourdais, F, 1 (DNF - accident damage); 17 Patrick Freisacher, A, 0 (DNF - accident); 18 Mark Webber, AUS, 0 (DNF - accident); 19 Fabrizio Gollin, I, 0 (DNF - accident); 20 Antonio Garcia, E, 0 (DNF - accident); 21 Darren Manning, GB, 0 (DNF - accident); 22 Mario Haberfeld, BR, 0 (DNF - accident); 23 Joël Camathias, CH, 0 (DNF - accident); 24 Ricardo Sperafico, BR, 0 (DNF - accident).
Fastest race lap: Pantano, 1m 24.003s, 115.198 mph/185.393 km/h.
Fastest qualifying lap: Bourdais, 1m 23.240s, 116.254 mph/ 187.093 km/h.
Championship points: 1 Wilson, 25; 2 Enge, 18; 3 Leinders, 12; 4 Webber, 10; 5 Melo Jr., 8; 6 Pizzonia, 7.

FIA INTERNATIONAL FORMULA 3000 CHAMPIONSHIP, Monte Carlo Street Circuit, Monaco, 26 May. Round 5. 45 laps of the 2.094-mile/3.370-km circuit, 94.231 miles/151.650 km.
1 Mark Webber, AUS, 1h 13m 21.073s, 77.079 mph/124.047 km/h; 2 Justin Wilson, GB, 1h 13m 21.966s; 3 Stéphane Sarrazin, F, 1h 13m 28.320s; 4 Sébastien Bourdais, F, 1h 13m 29.810s; 5 Ricardo Sperafico, BR, 1h 13m 38.171s; 6 Ricardo Mauricio, BR, 1h 13m 45.110s; 7 Tomas Enge, CZ, 1h 13m 45.639s; 8 Fabrizio Gollin, I, 1h 14m 09.481s; 9 Rodrigo Sperafico, BR, 1h 14m 10.689s; 10 Viktor Maslov, RUS, 1h 14m 11.489s; 11 Jaime Melo Jr., BR, 1h 14m 12.394s; 12 Mario Haberfeld, BR, 42 laps (DNF - accident); 13 Patrick Freisacher, A, 42 (DNF - accident); 14 Giorgio Pantano, I, 29 (DNF - accident); 15 Bas Leinders, B, 28 (DNF - accident); 16 Joël Camathias, CH, 28 (DNF - accident); 17 Darren Manning, GB, 24 (DNF - accident); 18 Antonio Pizzonia, BR, 24 (DNF - accident); 19 Dino Morelli, GB, 23 (DNF - throttle cable); 20 Gabriele Lancieri, I, 16 (DNF - accident); 21 David Saelens, B, 7 (DNF - accident); 22 Andrea Piccini, I, 0 (DNF - accident); 23 Derek Hill, USA, 0 (DNF - accident); 24 Gabriele Varano, I, 0 (DNF - spin).
Fastest race lap: Webber, 1m 30.462s, 83.333 mph/134.112 km/h.
Fastest qualifying lap: Webber, 1m 29.643s, 84.094 mph/ 135.337 km/h.
Championship points: 1 Wilson, 31; 2 Webber, 20; 3 Enge, 18; 4 Leinders, 12; 5 Melo Jr., 8; 6= Bourdais, 7; 6= Pizzonia, 7.

FIA INTERNATIONAL FORMULA 3000 CHAMPIONSHIP, Nürburgring Grand Prix Circuit, Nürburg/Eifel, Germany, 23 June. Round 6. 33 laps of the 2.831-mile/4.556-km circuit, 93.411 miles/ 150.331 km.
1 Tomas Enge, CZ, 50m 50.598s, 110.234 mph/177.405 km/h; 2 Mark Webber, AUS, 50m 56.224s; 3 Ricardo Sperafico, BR, 50m 59.261s; 4 David Saelens, B, 51m 09.285s; 5 Ricardo Mauricio, BR, 51m 11.431s; 6 Antonio Pizzonia, BR, 51m 12.354s; 7 Darren Manning, GB, 51m 12.814s; 8 Sébastien Bourdais, F, 51m 13.747s; 9 Andrea Piccini, I, 51m 19.297s; 10 Patrick Freisacher, A, 51m 20.242s; 11 Bas Leinders, B, 51m 32.266s; 12 Rodrigo Sperafico, BR, 51m 32.788s; 13 Jaime Melo Jr., BR, 51m 33.317s; 14 Gabriele Lancieri, I, 51m 45.512s; 15 Derek Hill, USA, 51m 54.669s; 16 Jonathan Cochet, F, 51m 58.143s; 17 Viktor Maslov, RUS, 52m 07.149s; 18 Joël Camathias, CH, 52m 12.208s; 19 Zsolt Baumgartner, H, 52m 13.404s; 20 Fabrizio Gollin, I, 32 laps; 21 Giorgio Pantano, I, 30; 22 Dino Morelli, GB, 29 (DNF - accident); 23 Mario Haberfeld, BR, 29 (DNF - accident); 24 Justin Wilson, GB, 7 (DNF - brakes).
Fastest race lap: Pantano, 1m 31.669s, 111.177 mph/ 178.922 km/h.
Fastest qualifying lap: Enge, 1m 30.433s, 112.696 mph/ 181.367 km/h.
Championship points: 1 Wilson, 31; 2 Enge, 28; 3 Webber, 26; 4 Leinders, 12; 5= Melo, 8; 5= Saelens, 8; 5= Pizzonia, 8.

FIA INTERNATIONAL FORMULA 3000 CHAMPIONSHIP, Circuit de Nevers, Magny-Cours, France, 30 June. Round 7. 36 laps of the 2.641-mile/4.251-km circuit, 94.977 miles/152.850 km.
1 Mark Webber, AUS, 54m 39.769s, 104.250 mph/167.774 km/h; 2 Justin Wilson, GB, 54m 47.223s; 3 Tomas Enge, CZ, 54m 49.562s; 4 Patrick Freisacher, A, 55m 00.824s; 5 Darren Manning, GB, 55m 03.118s; 6 Sébastien Bourdais, F, 55m 03.905s; 7 Mario Haberfeld, BR, 55m 05.471s; 8 Giorgio Pantano, I, 55m 06.813s; 9 David Saelens, B, 55m 07.836s; 10 Antonio Pizzonia, BR, 55m 10.143s; 11 Jonathan Cochet, F, 55m 24.499s; 12 Fabrizio Gollin, I, 55m 37.147s; 13 Ricardo Sperafico, BR, 55m 37.494s; 14 Jaime Melo Jr., BR, 55m 52.692s; 15 Rodrigo Sperafico, BR, 55m 53.132s; 16 Derek Hill, USA, 55m 53.614s; 17 Joël Camathias, CH, 55m 54.505s; 18 Viktor Maslov, RUS, 35 laps; 19 Gabriele Lancieri, I, 35; 20 Dino Morelli, GB, 35; 21 Bas Leinders, B, 28 (DNF - spin); 22 Andrea Piccini, I, 5 (DNF - spin); 23 Ricardo Mauricio, BR, 1 (DNF - accident damage); 24 Zsolt Baumgartner, H, 0 (DNF - accident).
Fastest race lap: Webber, 1m 29.826s, 105.863 mph/ 170.369 km/h.
Fastest qualifying lap: Enge, 1m 27.436s, 108.756 mph/ 175.026 km/h.
Championship points: 1 Wilson, 37; 2 Webber, 36; 3 Enge, 32; 4 Leinders, 12; 5= Melo Jr., 8; 5= Manning, 8; 5= Bourdais, 8; 5= Saelens, 8; 5= Pizzonia, 8.

FIA INTERNATIONAL FORMULA 3000 CHAMPIONSHIP, Silverstone Grand Prix Circuit, Towcester, Northamptonshire, Great Britain, 14 July. Round 8. 30 laps of the 3.194-mile/5.141-km circuit, 95.769 miles/154.126 km.
1 Sébastien Bourdais, F, 50m 56.439s, 112.801 mph/ 181.536 km/h; 2 Justin Wilson, GB, 50m 57.365s; 3 Antonio Pizzonia, BR, 51m 00.781s; 4 Mark Webber, AUS, 51m 03.982s; 5 Tomas Enge, CZ, 51m 04.732s; 6 Darren Manning, GB, 51m 07.310s; 7 Ricardo Mauricio, BR, 51m 08.988s; 8 Bas Leinders, B,51m 10.519s; 9 Jonathan Cochet, F, 51m 10.963s; 10 Fabrizio Gollin, I, 51m 20.763s; 11 Ricardo Sperafico, BR, 51m 29.037s; 12 Jaime Melo Jr., BR, 51m 32.066s; 13 Gabriele Lancieri, I, 51m 40.349s; 14 Rodrigo Sperafico, BR, 51m 40.844s; 15 Mario Haberfeld, BR, 52m 01.065s; 16 Viktor Maslov, RUS, 52m 07.607s; 17 Joël Camathias, CH, 52m 15.440s; 18 Zsolt Baumgartner, H, 52m 20.277s; 19 Patrick Freisacher, A, 29 laps; 20 Giorgio Pantano, I, 28 (DNF - spin); 21 Andrea Piccini, I, 24 (DNF - spin); 22 Dino Morelli, GB, 18 (DNF - withdrawn); 23 Derek Hill, USA, 11 (DNF - electrics);
Did not start: David Saelens, B (accident during qualifying).
Fastest race lap: Bourdais, 1m 40.456s, 114.479 mph/ 184.236 km/h.
Fastest qualifying lap: Enge, 1m 38.312s, 116.975 mph/ 188.254 km/h.
Championship points: 1 Wilson, 43; 2 Webber, 39; 3 Enge, 34; 4 Bourdais, 18; 5= Leinders, 12; 5= Pizzonia, 12.

FIA INTERNATIONAL FORMULA 3000 CHAMPIONSHIP, Hockenheimring Grand Prix Circuit, Heidelberg, Germany, 28 July. Round 9. 22 laps of the 4.241-mile/6.825-km circuit, 93.299 miles/ 150.150 km.
1 Antonio Pizzonia, BR, 44m 47.547s, 124.975 mph/201.128 km/h; 2 Justin Wilson, GB, 44m 52.535s; 3 Ricardo Sperafico, BR, 44m 56.343s; 4 Sébastien Bourdais, F, 45m 01.751s; 5 Tomas Enge, CZ, 45m 05.363s; 6 Bas Leinders, B, 45m 06.328s; 7 Giorgio Pantano, I, 45m 07.637s; 8 Rodrigo Sperafico, BR, 45m 12.314s; 9 Joël Camathias, CH, 45m 13.772s; 10 Gabriele Lancieri, I, 45m 19.877s; 11 Patrick Freisacher, A, 45m 23.159s; 12 Jaime Melo Jr., BR, 45m 25.913s; 13 Enrico Toccacelo, I, 45m 32.637s; 14 Viktor Maslov, RUS, 45m 44.878s; 15 Jonathan Cochet, F, 45m 58.503s; 16 Zsolt Baumgartner, H, 46m 05.997s; 17 Ricardo Mauricio, BR, 46m 12.994s; 18 Tomas Scheckter, ZA, 10 laps (DNF - differential); 19 Derek Hill, USA, 5 (DNF - accident); 20 Mario Haberfeld, BR, 2 (DNF - suspension); 21 Darren Manning, GB, 1 (DNF - spin); 22 Mark Webber, AUS, 1 (DNF - accident damage); 23 Fabrizio Gollin, I, 1 (DNF - accident damage); 24 Andrea Piccini, I, 0 (DNF - spin).
Fastest race lap: Enge, 2m 00.795s, 126.388 mph/203.402 km/h.
Fastest qualifying lap: Sperafico (Ricardo), 1m 59.526s, 127.730 mph/205.562 km/h.
Championship points: 1 Wilson, 49; 2 Webber, 39; 3 Enge, 36; 4 Pizzonia, 22; 5 Bourdais, 21; 6 Leinders, 13.

FIA INTERNATIONAL FORMULA 3000 CHAMPIONSHIP, Hungaroring, Mogyorod, Budapest, Hungary, 18 August. Round 10. 38 laps of the 2.470-mile/3.975-km circuit, 93.858 miles/151.050 km.
1 Justin Wilson, GB, 58m 00.190s, 97.089 mph/156.250 km/h; 2 Ricardo Mauricio, BR, 58m 05.784s; 3 Sébastien Bourdais, F, 58m 08.683s; 4 Patrick Freisacher, A, 58m 14.718s; 5 Giorgio Pantano, I, 58m 16.941s; 6 Bas Leinders, B, 58m 21.117s; 7 Ricardo Sperafico, BR, 58m 41.542s; 8 Andrea Piccini, I, 58m 43.665s; 9 Gabriele Lancieri, I, 58m 51.317s; 10 Antonio Garcia, E, 58m 56.411s; 11 Tomas Enge, CZ, 59m 01.059s; 12 Derek Hill, USA, 59m 07.939s; 13 Joël Camathias, CH, 59m 08.676s; 14 Norberto Fontana, RA, 59m 09.213s; 15 Mark Webber, AUS, 33 laps (DNF - spin); 16 Darren Manning, GB, 28 (DNF - withdrawn); 17 Mario Haberfeld, BR, 23 (DNF - spin); 18 Enrico Toccacelo, I, 16 (DNF - spin); 19 Zsolt Baumgartner, H, 13 (DNF - accident); 20 Viktor Maslov, RUS, 10 (DNF - spin); 21 Marc Goossens, B, 3 (DNF - driveshaft); 22 Antonio Pizzonia, BR, 1 (DNF - accident damage); 23 Fabrizio Gollin, I, 0 (DNF - driveshaft).
Did not start: David Saelens, B (severe back pain).
Fastest race lap: Pantano, 1m 30.196s, 98.583 mph/158.654 km/h.
Fastest qualifying lap: Wilson, 1m 27.695s, 101.395 mph/ 163.179 km/h.
Championship points: 1 Wilson, 59; 2 Webber, 39; 3 Enge, 36; 4 Bourdais, 25; 5 Pizzonia, 22; 6 Leinders, 14.

FIA INTERNATIONAL FORMULA 3000 CHAMPIONSHIP, Circuit de Spa-Francorchamps, Stavelot, Belgium, 1 September. Round 11. 22 laps of the 4.330-mile/6.968-km circuit, 95.243 miles/ 153.279 km.
1 Ricardo Sperafico, BR, 51m 48.919s, 110.289 mph/177.491 km/h; 2 Justin Wilson, GB, 52m 00.504s; 3 Ricardo Mauricio, BR, 52m 05.901s; 4 Tomas Enge, CZ, 52m 07.171s; 5 Marc Goossens, B, 52m 20.784s; 6 Sébastien Bourdais, F, 52m 21.701s; 7 Bas Leinders, B, 52m 21.792s; 8 Antonio Pizzonia, BR, 52m 22.438s; 9 Derek Hill, USA, 52m 29.078s; 10 Patrick Freisacher, A, 52m 36.668s; 11 Giorgio Pantano, I, 52m 37.632s; 12 Fabrizio Gollin, I, 52m 39.582s; 13 Zsolt Baumgartner, H, 52m 51.809s; 14 Gabriele Lancieri, I, 52m 52.041s; 15 Joël Camathias, CH, 52m 53.149s; 16 Antonio Garcia, E, 52m 53.916s; 17 Enrico Toccacelo, I, 53m 06.424s; 18 Viktor Maslov, RUS, 53m 31.113s; 19 Mario Haberfeld, BR, 53m 31.672s; 20 Norberto Fontana, RA, 11 laps (DNF - gearbox); 21 Darren Manning, GB, 8 (DNF - spin); 22 Andrea Piccini, I, 7 (DNF - accident); 23 David Saelens, B, 7 (DNF - accident); 24 Mark Webber, AUS, 1 (DNF - accident).
Fastest race lap: Haberfeld, 2m 08.781s, 121.035 mph/ 194.786 km/h.
Fastest qualifying lap: Sperafico (Ricardo), 2m 13.129s, 117.082 mph/188.425 km/h.
Championship points: 1 Wilson, 65; 2= Webber, 39; 2= Enge, 39; 4 Bourdais, 26; 5 Pizzonia, 22; 6 Sperafico (Ricardo), 20.

FIA INTERNATIONAL FORMULA 3000 CHAMPIONSHIP, Autodromo Nazionale di Monza, Milan, Italy, 15 September. Round 12. 24 laps of the 3.600-mile/5.793-km circuit, 86.216 miles/ 138.752 km.
1 Giorgio Pantano, I, 43m 58.618s, 117.630 mph/189.307 km/h; 2 Justin Wilson, GB, 43m 59.553s; 3 Ricardo Sperafico, BR, 44m 00.205s; 4 Bas Leinders, B, 44m 03.033s; 5 David Saelens, B, 44m 08.787s; 6 Ricardo Mauricio, BR, 44m 12.150s; 7 Marc Goossens, B, 44m 17.818s; 8 Andrea Piccini, I, 44m 18.216s; 9 Sébastien Bourdais, F, 44m 20.935s; 10 Fabrizio Gollin, I, 44m 24.212s; 11 Antonio Garcia, E, 44m 25.086s; 12 Derek Hill, USA, 44m 26.546s; 13* Mario Haberfeld, BR, 44m 29.181s; 14 Viktor Maslov, RUS, 44m 36.199s; 15 Joël Camathias, CH, 44m 38.203s; 16 Jaroslav Janis, CZ, 44m 39.011s; 17 Zsolt Baumgartner, H, 44m 44.162s; 18 Gabriele Lancieri, I, 21 laps (DNF); 19 Antonio Pizzonia, BR, 19 (DNF - withdrew following penalty); 20 Patrick Freisacher, A, 0 (DNF - accident); 21 Darren Manning, GB, 0 (DNF - accident); 22 Enrico Toccacelo, I, 0 (DNF - accident); 23 Norberto Fontana, RA, 0 (DNF - accident); 24 Mark Webber, AUS, 0 (DNF - spin).
* Haberfeld finished 5th, but was given a 25-second penalty for cutting a corner.
Fastest race lap: Pizzonia, 1m 40.885s, 128.449 mph/206.719 km/h.
Fastest qualifying lap: Pizzonia, 1m 40.033s, 129.543 mph/ 208.479 km/h.

Final Championship points
Drivers
1 Justin Wilson, GB, 71; 2= Mark Webber, AUS, 39; 2= Tomas Enge, CZ, 39; 4 Sébastien Bourdais, F, 26; 5 Ricardo Sperafico, BR, 24; 6 Antonio Pizzonia, BR, 22; 7 Bas Leinders, B, 17; 8 Ricardo Mauricio, BR, 14; 9 Giorgio Pantano, I, 12; 10 David Saelens, B, 10; 11 Darren Manning, GB, 9; 12= Jaime Melo Jr., BR, 8; 12= Patrick Freisacher, A, 8; 14 Stéphane Sarrazin, F, 4; 15 Mario Haberfeld, BR, 3; 16= Joël Camathias, CH, 2; 16= Marc Goossens, B, 2; 18= Fabrizio Gollin, I, 1; 18= Andrea Piccini, I, 1.

Teams
1 Coca-Cola Nordic Racing, 110; 2 Petrobras Junior Team, 46; 3 Super Nova Racing, 42; 4 DAMS, 26; 5 Red Bull Junior Team, 22; 6 KTR (Keerbergs Transport Racing), 19; 7 Team Astromega, 12; 8 European Minardi, 11; 9 Arden Team Russia, 9; 10 Durango Formula, 8; 11 Prost Junior, 4; 12 Coloni, 3.

Euro Formula 3000 Championship

All cars are Lola-Zytek V8

EURO FORMULA 3000 CHAMPIONSHIP, Autodromo di Vallelunga, Campagnano di Roma, Italy, 22 April. Round 1. 44 laps of the 2.002-mile/3.222-km circuit, 88.091 miles/141.768 km.
1 Felipe Massa, BR, 49m 05.454s, 107.666 mph/173.272 km/h; 2 Thomas Biagi, I, 49m 14.253s; 3 Alessandro Piccolo, I, 49m 19.025s; 4 Leopoldo 'Polo' Villaamil, E, 49m 26.962s; 5 Salvatore Tavano, I, 49m 28.061s; 6 Romain Dumas, F, 49m 28.702s; 7 'Babalus', I, 49m 51.565s; 8 Marco Cioci, I, 49m 53.525s; 9 Alexander 'Alex' Müller, D, 49m 57.649s; 10 Armin Pörnbacher, I, 50m 13.640s.
Fastest race lap: Massa, 1m 06.037s, 109.142 mph/175.647 km/h.
Fastest qualifying lap: Massa, 1m 05.637s, 109.807 mph/ 176.717 km/h.

EURO FORMULA 3000 CHAMPIONSHIP, Ente Autodromo di Pergusa, Enna-Pergusa, Sicily, 6 May. Round 2. 21 laps of the 3.076-mile/4.950-km circuit, 64.592 miles/103.950 km.
1 Felipe Massa, BR, 45m 25.500s, 85.316 mph/137.303 km/h; 2 Alessandro Piccolo, I, 45m 31.031s; 3 Thomas Biagi, I, 45m 31.315s; 4 Alexander 'Alex' Müller, D, 45m 40.752s; 5 Salvatore Tavano, I, 45m 56.680s; 6 Michael Bentwood, GB, 46m 13.537s; 7 Massimiliano Busnelli, I, 46m 17.568s; 8 Marco Cioci, I, 46m 22.970s; 9 'Babalus', I, 46m 24.343s; 10 Michele Spoldi, I, 46m 41.551s.
Fastest race lap: Piccolo, 1m 32.609s, 119.565 mph/192.422 km/h.
Fastest qualifying lap: Massa, 1m 42.818s, 107.694 mph/ 173.316 km/h.

EURO FORMULA 3000 CHAMPIONSHIP, Autodromo Nazionale di Monza, Milan, Italy, 24 June. Round 3. 25 laps of the 3.600-mile/5.793-km circuit, 89.990 miles/144.825 km.
1 Felipe Massa, BR, 44m 18.209s, 121.873 mph/196.136 km/h; 2 Alexander 'Alex' Müller, D, 44m 24.151s; 3 Romain Dumas, F, 44m 30.528s; 4 Leopoldo 'Polo' Villaamil, E, 44m 36.090s; 5 Gabriele Gardel, I, 44m 47.747s; 6 Luca Vacis, I, 44m 48.835s; 7 Salvatore Tavano, I, 45m 00.874s; 8 Etienne van der Linde, ZA, 45m 11.784s; 9 'Babalus', I, 45m 20.379s; 10 Valerio Scassellati, I, 45m 39.843s.
Fastest race lap: Massa, 1m 42.783s, 126.077 mph/202.901 km/h.

EURO FORMULA 3000 CHAMPIONSHIP, Donington Park Grand Prix Circuit, Castle Donington, Derbyshire, Great Britain, 12 August. Round 4. 36 laps of the 2.500-mile/4.023-km circuit, 89.992 miles/144.828 km.
1 Thomas Biagi, I, 52m 49.068s, 102.229 mph/164.522 km/h; 2 Salvatore Tavano, I, 53m 13.174s; 3 Etienne van der Linde, ZA, 53m 14.776s; 4 Alexander 'Alex' Müller, D, 53m 15.388s; 5 Romain Dumas, F, 53m 22.886s; 6 Giovanni Montanari, I, 53m 48.584s; 7 Marco Cioci, I, 53m 49.712s; 8 Felipe Massa, BR, 53m 50.280s; 9 Valerio Scassellati, I, 53m 58.688s; 10 Armin Pornbacher, I, 54m 13.097s.
Fastest race lap: Müller, 1m 26.501s, 104.036 mph/167.429 km/h.

EURO FORMULA 3000 CHAMPIONSHIP, Omloop van Zolder, Hasselt, Belgium, 19 August. Round 5. 35 laps of the 2.471-mile/ 3.977-km circuit, 86.492 miles/139.195 km.
1 Salvatore Tavano, I, 50m 53.479s, 101.972 mph/164.109

km/h; **2** Vitor Meira, BR, 50m 54.868s; **3** Alexander 'Alex' Müller, D, 50m 55.461s; **4** Thomas Biagi, I, 50m 55.851s; **5** Alessandro Piccolo, I, 51m 06.978s; **6** Massimiliano Busnelli, I, 51m 07.285s; **7** Gabriele Gardel, I, 51m 15.643s; **8** Yannick Schroeder, F, 51m 18.093s; **9** Etienne van der Linde, ZA, 51m 32.093s; **10** Michael Bentwood, GB, 51m 35.593s.
Fastest race lap: Biagi, 1m 25.919s, 103.543 mph/166.636 km/h.

EURO FORMULA 3000 CHAMPIONSHIP, Autodromo Enzo e Dino Ferrari, Imola, Italy, 26 August. Round 6. 29 laps of the 3.065-mile/4.933-km circuit, 88.891 miles/143.057 km.
1 Felipe Massa, BR, 50m 04.560s, 106.508 mph/171.408 km/h; **2** Thomas Biagi, I, 50m 18.785s; **3** Alexander 'Alex' Müller, D, 50m 24.940s; **4** Massimiliano Busnelli, I, 50m 25.673s; **5** Vitor Meira, BR, 50m 51.199s; **6** Gabriele Gardel, I, 50m 51.480s; **7** Leonardo Nienkotter, BR, 50m 52.006s; **8** Valerio Scassellati, I, 50m 55.432s; **9** Yannick Schroeder, F, 51m 08.340s; **10** Michele Spoldi, I, 51m 30.096s.
Fastest race lap: Massa, 1m 42.799s, 107.344 mph/172.753 km/h.

EURO FORMULA 3000 CHAMPIONSHIP, Nürburgring Grand Prix Circuit, Nürburg/Eifel, Germany, 15 September. Round 7. 31 laps of the 2.831-mile/4.556-km circuit, 87.760 miles/141.236 km.
1 Felipe Massa, BR, 52m 04.674s, 101.110 mph/162.721 km/h; **2** Alexander 'Alex' Müller, D, 52m 11.146s; **3** Vitor Meira, BR, 52m 11.558s; **4** Michael Bentwood, GB, 52m 36.797s; **5** Yannick Schroeder, F, 52m 43.335s; **6** Leonardo Nienkotter, BR, 52m 45.498s; **7** Alessandro Piccolo, I, 52m 55.564s; **8** Luca Vacis, I, 53m 03.705s; **9** Valerio Scassellati, I, 53m 04.199s; **10** Jean de Pourtales, F, 53m 05.203s.
Fastest race lap: Massa, 1m 33.119s, 109.446 mph/176.136 km/h.

EURO FORMULA 3000 CHAMPIONSHIP, Circuit de la Comunitat Valenciana Ricardo Tormo, Cheste, Valencia, Spain, 7 October. Round 8. 35 laps of the 2.490-mile/4.007-km circuit, 87.144 miles/140.245 km.
1 Felipe Massa, BR, 51m 27.597s, 101.606 mph/163.519 km/h; **2** Romain Dumas, F, 52m 05.017s; **3** Vitor Meira, BR, 52m 08.685s; **4** Thomas Biagi, I, 52m 12.167s; **5** Gabriele Gardel, I, 52m 21.757s; **6** Marco Cioci, I, 52m 22.712s; **7** Michael Bentwood, GB, 52m 24.195s; **8** Luca Vacis, I, 52m 26.354s; **9** Leonardo Nienkotter, BR, 52m 27.023s; **10** Valerio Scassellati, I, 34 laps.
Fastest race lap: Massa, 1m 27.209s, 102.781 mph/165.410 km/h.

Final Championship points
1 Felipe Massa, BR, 60; **2** Thomas Biagi, I, 32; **3** Alexander 'Alex' Müller, D, 26; **4** Salvatore Tavano, I, 20; **5** Vitor Meira, BR, 16; **6** Romain Dumas, F, 13; **7** Alessandro Piccolo, I, 12; **8** Leopoldo 'Polo' Villaamil, E, 6; **9** Gabriele Gardel, I, 5; **10=** Etienne van der Linde, ZA, 4; **10=** Massimiliano Busnelli, I, 4; **10=** Michael Bentwood, GB, 4; **13** Yannick Schroeder, F, 2; **14=** Marco Cioci, I, 1; **14=** Giovanni Montanari, I, 1; **14=** Leonardo Nienkotter, BR, 1; **14=** Luca Vacis, I, 1.

Green Flag British Formula 3 Championship

GREEN FLAG BRITISH FORMULA 3 CHAMPIONSHIP, Silverstone International Circuit, Towcester, Northamptonshire, Great Britain, 1 April. Round 1. 2 x 16 laps of the 2.249-mile/3.619-km circuit.
Race 1 (35.984 miles/57.911 km)
1 James Courtney, AUS (Dallara F301-Mugen), 20m 38.613s, 104.587 mph/168.316 km/h; **2** Andy Priaulx, GB (Dallara F301-Mugen), 20m 43.223s; **3** Derek Hayes, GB (Dallara F301-Mugen), 20m 45.052s; **4** Paul Edwards, USA (Dallara F301-Mugen), 20m 51.212s; **5** Gianmaria Bruni, I (Dallara F301-Renault), 20m 51.592s; **6** Matt Davies, GB (Dallara F301-Opel), 20m 52.216s; **7** Anthony Davidson, GB (Dallara F301-Mugen), 20m 53.171s; **8** Nicolas Kiesa, DK (Dallara F301-Opel), 20m 57.385s; **9** Martin O'Connell, GB (Dallara F301-Opel), 21m 01.789s; **10** Atsushi Katsumata, J (Dallara F301-Mugen), 21m 02.338s.
Winner Scholarship Class: Matthew Gilmore, GB (Dallara F398-Opel), 21m 17.049s (15th).
Fastest race lap: Courtney, 1m 15.937s, 106.620 mph/171.588 km/h.
Fastest qualifying lap: Jamie Spence, GB (Dallara F301-Mugen), 1m 26.530s, 93.568 mph/150.582 km/h.

Race 2 (35.984 miles/57.911 km)
1 Matt Davies, GB (Dallara F301-Opel), 20m 44.467s, 104.095 mph/167.524 km/h; **2** Gianmaria Bruni, I (Dallara F301-Renault), 20m 44.613s; **3** Derek Hayes, GB (Dallara F301-Mugen), 20m 46.264s; **4** Takuma Sato, J (Dallara F301-Mugen), 20m 50.931s; **5** Andy Priaulx, GB (Dallara F301-Mugen), 20m 51.910s; **6** Martin O'Connell, GB (Dallara F301-Opel), 20m 55.315s; **7** Nicolas Kiesa, DK (Dallara F301-Opel), 20m 55.594s; **8** James Courtney, AUS (Dallara F301-Mugen), 20m 55.908s; **9** André Lotterer, D (Dallara F301-Mugen), 20m 56.578s; **10** Mark Taylor, GB (Dallara F301-Mugen), 20m 57.244s.
Winner Scholarship Class: Gilmore, 21m 22.775s (18th).
Fastest race lap: Bruni, 1m 16.885s, 105.305 mph/169.472 km/h.
Fastest qualifying lap: Davies, 1m 15.860s, 106.728 mph/171.762 km/h.
Championship points: 1 Davies, 26; **2=** Courtney, 24; **2=** Bruni, 24; **2=** Hayes, 24; **5** Priaulx, 23; **6=** Edwards, 10; **6=** Sato, 10. **Scholarship Class: 1** Gilmore, 42; **2** Mark Mayall, GB, 27; **3** Robert Doornbos, NL, 18.

GREEN FLAG BRITISH FORMULA 3 CHAMPIONSHIP, Snetterton Circuit, Norfolk, Great Britain, 15 April. Round 2. 16 and 17 laps of the 1.952-mile/3.141-km circuit.
Race 1 (31.232 miles/50.263 km)
1 Matt Davies, GB (Dallara F301-Opel), 20m 01.785s, 93.557 mph/150.565 km/h; **2** Derek Hayes, GB (Dallara F301-Mugen), 20m 02.052s; **3** Gianmaria Bruni, I (Dallara F301-Renault), 20m 03.497s; **4** Ryan Dalziel, GB (Dallara F301-Opel), 20m 04.830s; **5** Nicolas Kiesa, DK (Dallara F301-Opel), 20m 05.495s; **6** James Courtney, AUS (Dallara F301-Mugen), 20m 06.873s; **7** André Lotterer, D (Dallara F301-Mugen), 20m 10.005s; **8** Anthony Davidson, GB (Dallara F301-Mugen), 20m 11.311s; **9** Milos Pavlovic, YU (Dallara F301-Opel), 20m 13.430s; **10** Mark Taylor, GB (Dallara F301-Mugen), 20m 13.981s.
Winner Scholarship Class: Robert Doornbos, NL (Dallara F398-Renault), 20m 39.195s (19th).
Fastest race lap: Dalziel, 1m 02.720s, 112.041 mph/180.312 km/h.
Fastest qualifying lap: Davies, 1m 02.247s, 112.892 mph/181.682 km/h.

Race 2 (33.184 miles/53.404 km)
1 Andy Priaulx, GB (Dallara F301-Mugen), 20m 35.129s, 96.721 mph/155.657 km/h; **2** Takuma Sato, J (Dallara F301-Mugen), 20m 35.667s; **3** Paul Edwards, USA (Dallara F301-Mugen), 20m 49.342s; **4** Derek Hayes, GB (Dallara F301-Mugen), 20m 50.556s; **5** Nicolas Kiesa, DK (Dallara F301-Opel), 20m 52.502s; **6** James Courtney, AUS (Dallara F301-Mugen), 20m 52.535s; **7** Ryan Dalziel, GB (Dallara F301-Opel), 20m 57.692s; **8** Matt Davies, GB (Dallara F301-Opel), 21m 02.159s; **9** André Lotterer, D (Dallara F301-Mugen), 21m 02.651s; **10** Gianmaria Bruni, I (Dallara F301-Renault), 21m 04.748s.
Winner Scholarship Class: Robbie Kerr, GB (Dallara F398-Renault), 21m 21.397s (15th).
Fastest race lap: Sato, 1m 11.232s, 98.652 mph/158.765 km/h.
Fastest qualifying lap: Edwards, 1m 12.415s, 97.041 mph/156.172 km/h.
Championship points: 1= Davies, 49; **1=** Hayes, 49; **3** Priaulx, 43; **4** Bruni, 37; **5** Courtney, 36; **6** Sato, 26. **Scholarship Class: 1** Gilmore, 69; **2** Doornbos, 38; **3** Mayall, 35.0

GREEN FLAG BRITISH FORMULA 3 CHAMPIONSHIP, Donington Grand Prix Circuit, Castle Donington, Derbyshire, Great Britain, 29 April. Round 3. 13 and 14 laps of the 2.500-mile/4.023-km circuit.
Race 1 (32.500 miles/52.304 km)
1 Takuma Sato, J (Dallara F301-Mugen), 20m 12.152s, 96.523 mph/155.338 km/h; **2** André Lotterer, D (Dallara F301-Mugen), 20m 13.556s; **3** Gianmaria Bruni, I (Dallara F301-Renault), 20m 17.088s; **4** Derek Hayes, GB (Dallara F301-Mugen), 20m 20.632s; **5** Paul Edwards, USA (Dallara F301-Mugen), 20m 21.585s; **6** Jeffrey Jones, USA (Dallara F301-Mugen), 20m 23.321s; **7** James Courtney, AUS (Dallara F301-Mugen), 20m 24.635s; **8** Anthony Davidson, GB (Dallara F301-Mugen), 20m 25.896s; **9** Jamie Spence, GB (Dallara F301-Mugen), 20m 25.974s; **10** Ryan Dalziel, GB (Dallara F301-Opel), 20m 27.928s.
Winner Scholarship Class: Michael Keohane, IRL (Dallara F398-Toyota), 20m 46.371s (19th).
Fastest race lap: Lotterer, 1m 28.553s, 101.634 mph/163.564 km/h.
Fastest qualifying lap: Lotterer, 1m 28.853s, 101.291 mph/163.012 km/h.

Race 2 (35.000 miles/56.327 km)
1 André Lotterer, D (Dallara F301-Mugen), 20m 52.182s, 100.624 mph/161.939 km/h; **2** James Courtney, AUS (Dallara F301-Mugen), 20m 56.702s; **3** Derek Hayes, GB (Dallara F301-Mugen), 20m 58.330s; **4** Andy Priaulx, GB (Dallara F301-Mugen), 21m 01.822s; **5** Ryan Dalziel, GB (Dallara F301-Opel), 21m 06.650s; **6** Gianmaria Bruni, I (Dallara F301-Renault), 21m 07.176s; **7** Jeffrey Jones, USA (Dallara F301-Mugen), 21m 08.462s; **8** Rob Austin, GB (Dallara F301-Renault), 21m 17.773s; **9** Alex Gurney, USA (Dallara F301-Renault), 21m 19.143s; **10** Tim Spouge, GB (Dallara F301-Renault), 21m 29.653s.
Winner Scholarship Class: Robbie Kerr, GB (Dallara F398-Renault), 21m 34.269s (12th).
Fastest race lap: Mark Taylor, GB (Dallara F301-Mugen), 1m 28.816s, 101.333 mph/163.080 km/h.
Fastest qualifying lap: Lotterer, 1m 28.460s, 101.741 mph/163.736 km/h.
Championship points: 1 Hayes, 71; **2=** Courtney, 55; **2=** Bruni, 55; **4** Priaulx, 53; **5** Davies, 49; **6** Sato, 46. **Scholarship Class: 1** Gilmore, 90; **2** Keohane, 60; **3** Mayall, 54.

GREEN FLAG BRITISH FORMULA 3 CHAMPIONSHIP, Oulton Park International Circuit, Tarporley, Cheshire, Great Britain, 7 May. Round 4. 12 and 15 laps of the 2.775-mile/4.466-km circuit.
Race 1 (33.300 miles/53.591 km)
1 Takuma Sato, J (Dallara F301-Mugen), 18m 18.690s, 109.112 mph/175.598 km/h; **2** Gianmaria Bruni, I (Dallara F301-Renault), 18m 21.079s; **3** Anthony Davidson, GB (Dallara F301-Mugen), 18m 21.494s; **4** Matt Davies, GB (Dallara F301-Opel), 18m 22.566s; **5** Bruce Jouanny, F (Dallara F301-Mugen), 18m 24.344s; **6** Andy Priaulx, GB (Dallara F301-Mugen), 18m 26.361s; **7** James Courtney, AUS (Dallara F301-Mugen), 18m 26.942s; **8** Derek Hayes, GB (Dallara F301-Mugen), 18m 27.188s; **9** Mark Taylor, GB (Dallara F301-Mugen), 18m 28.121s; **10** Milos Pavlovic, YU (Dallara F301-Opel), 18m 29.217s.
Winner Scholarship Class: Robbie Kerr, GB (Dallara F398-Renault), 18m 49.666s (16th).
Fastest race lap: Sato, 1m 30.707s, 110.135 mph/177.245 km/h.
Fastest qualifying lap: Sato, 1m 29.681s, 111.395 mph/179.273 km/h.

Race 2 (41.625 miles/66.989 km)
1 Takuma Sato, J (Dallara F301-Mugen), 25m 34.365s, 97.663 mph/157.173 km/h; **2** Matt Davies, GB (Dallara F301-Opel), 25m 37.766s; **3** Anthony Davidson, GB (Dallara F301-Mugen), 25m 38.108s; **4** Derek Hayes, GB (Dallara F301-Mugen), 25m 38.771s; **5** Jamie Spence, GB (Dallara F301-Mugen), 25m 39.985s; **6** Andy Priaulx, GB (Dallara F301-Mugen), 25m 43.415s; **7** Milos Pavlovic, YU (Dallara F301-Opel), 25m 44.108s; **8** Nicolas Kiesa, DK (Dallara F301-Opel), 25m 44.405s; **9** Gianmaria Bruni, I (Dallara F301-Renault), 25m 46.808s; **10** Mark Taylor, GB (Dallara F301-Mugen), 25m 47.473s.
Winner Scholarship Class: Michael Keohane, IRL (Dallara F398-Toyota), 26m 09.183s (17th).
Fastest race lap: Sato, 1m 30.157s, 110.807 mph/178.326 km/h.
Fastest qualifying lap: Davidson, 1m 29.580s, 111.520 mph/179.475 km/h.
Championship points: 1 Sato, 88; **2** Hayes, 84; **3** Davies, 74; **4** Bruni, 72; **5** Priaulx, 65; **6** Courtney, 59. **Scholarship Class: 1** Gilmore, 107; **2** Kerr, 89; **3** Keohane, 79.

GREEN FLAG BRITISH FORMULA 3 CHAMPIONSHIP, Croft Circuit, Croft-on-Tees, North Yorkshire, Great Britain, 28 May. Round 5. 18 and 12 laps of the 2.127-mile/3.423-km circuit.
Race 1 (38.286 miles/61.615 km)
1 Anthony Davidson, GB (Dallara F301-Mugen), 24m 39.475s, 93.161 mph/149.928 km/h; **2** Andy Priaulx, GB (Dallara F301-Mugen), 24m 43.346s; **3** James Courtney, AUS (Dallara F301-Mugen), 24m 45.716s; **4** Nicolas Kiesa, DK (Dallara F301-Opel), 24m 46.907s; **5** Jeffrey Jones, USA (Dallara F301-Mugen), 24m 48.884s; **6** André Lotterer, D (Dallara F301-Mugen), 24m 49.529s; **7** Paul Edwards, USA (Dallara F301-Mugen), 24m 51.426s; **8** Matt Davies, GB (Dallara F301-Opel), 24m 51.779s; **9** Alex Gurney, USA (Dallara F301-Renault), 24m 52.754s; **10** Ryan Dalziel, GB (Dallara F301-Opel), 24m 58.310s.
Takuma Sato, J (Dallara F301-Mugen) finished 4th in 24m 45.978s and Derek Hayes, GB (Dallara F301-Mugen) finished 10th in 24m 51.869s, but were both disqualified due to their driving behaviour.
Winner Scholarship Class: Mark Mayall, GB (Dallara F398-Mugen), 25m 06.874s (12th).
Fastest race lap: Davidson, 1m 15.105s, 101.953 mph/164.078 km/h.
Fastest qualifying lap: Derek Hayes, GB (Dallara F301-Mugen), 1m 14.610s, 102.630 mph/165.166 km/h.

Race 2 (25.524 miles/41.077 km)
1 Takuma Sato, J (Dallara F301-Mugen), 15m 13.885s, 100.545 mph/161.811 km/h; **2** Jamie Spence, GB (Dallara F301-Mugen), 15m 18.092s; **3** Derek Hayes, GB (Dallara F301-Mugen), 15m 19.097s; **4** Nicolas Kiesa, DK (Dallara F301-Opel), 15m 21.546s; **5** Gianmaria Bruni, I (Dallara F301-Renault), 15m 22.130s; **6** Bruce Jouanny, F (Dallara F301-Mugen), 15m 22.716s; **7** André Lotterer, D (Dallara F301-Mugen), 15m 24.677s; **8** Matt Davies, GB (Dallara F301-Opel), 15m 25.598s; **9** James Courtney, AUS (Dallara F301-Mugen), 15m 26.267s; **10** Paul Edwards, USA (Dallara F301-Mugen), 15m 27.099s.
Winner Scholarship Class: Robbie Kerr, GB (Dallara F398-Renault), 26m 39.155s (14th).
Fastest race lap: Sato, 1m 15.136s, 101.911 mph/164.010 km/h.
Fastest qualifying lap: Hayes, 1m 14.258s, 103.116 mph/165.949 km/h.
Championship points: 1 Sato, 109; **2** Hayes, 96; **3=** Davies, 80; **3=** Bruni, 80; **3=** Priaulx, 80; **6** Courtney, 73. **Scholarship Class: 1** Gilmore, 122; **2** Keohane, 108; **3** Mayall, 101.

GREEN FLAG BRITISH FORMULA 3 CHAMPIONSHIP, Rockingham International Road Course, Corby, Northamptonshire, 10 June. Round 6. 13 and 14 laps of the 2.560-mile/4.120-km circuit.
Race 1 (33.280 miles/53.559 km)
1 Takuma Sato, J (Dallara F301-Mugen), 20m 55.935s, 95.393 mph/153.521 km/h; **2** Andy Priaulx, GB (Dallara F301-Mugen), 20m 58.926s; **3** Derek Hayes, GB (Dallara F301-Mugen), 20m 59.891s; **4** Anthony Davidson, GB (Dallara F301-Mugen), 21m 00.577s; **5** André Lotterer, D (Dallara F301-Mugen), 21m 01.442s; **6** James Courtney, AUS (Dallara F301-Mugen), 21m 07.850s; **7** Bruce Jouanny, F (Dallara F301-Mugen), 21m 20.893s; **8** Ben Collins, GB (Dallara F301-Renault), 21m 22.329s; **9** Jamie Spence, GB (Dallara F301-Mugen), 21m 30.398s; **10** Matt Davies, GB (Dallara F301-Opel), 21m 31.117s.
Winner Scholarship Class: Robbie Kerr, GB (Dallara F398-Renault), 21m 33.576s (13th).
Fastest race lap: Sato, 1m 34.147s, 97.889 mph/157.538 km/h.
Fastest qualifying lap: Hayes, 1m 33.896s, 98.151 mph/157.959 km/h.

Race 2 (35.840 miles/57.679 km)
1 Takuma Sato, J (Dallara F301-Mugen), 25m 31.204s, 84.263 mph/135.608 km/h; **2** Anthony Davidson, GB (Dallara F301-Mugen), 25m 32.427s; **3** André Lotterer, D (Dallara F301-Mugen), 25m 33.865s; **4** James Courtney, AUS (Dallara F301-Mugen), 25m 36.736s; **5** Milos Pavlovic, YU (Dallara F301-Opel), 25m 42.541s; **6** Jeffrey Jones, USA (Dallara F301-Mugen), 25m 42.879s; **7** Derek Hayes, GB (Dallara F301-Mugen), 25m 43.770s; **8** Matt Davies, GB (Dallara F301-Opel), 25m 45.917s; **9** Andy Priaulx, GB (Dallara F301-Mugen), 25m 46.673s; **10** Bruce Jouanny, F (Dallara F301-Mugen), 25m 47.591s.
Winner Scholarship Class: Kerr, 25m 56.986s (11th).
Fastest race lap: Sato, 1m 33.203s, 98.881 mph/159.133 km/h.
Fastest qualifying lap: Davidson, 1m 33.524s, 98.542 mph/158.587 km/h.
Championship points: 1 Sato, 161; **2** Hayes, 112; **3** Priaulx, 96; **4** Courtney, 89; **5** Davies, 84; **6=** Bruni, 80; **6=** Davidson, 80. **Scholarship Class: 1=** Gilmore, 136; **1=** Kerr, 136; **3** Keohane, 135.

GREEN FLAG BRITISH FORMULA 3 CHAMPIONSHIP, Castle Combe Circuit, Wiltshire, 24 June. Round 7. 20 and 23 laps of the 1.850-mile/2.977-km circuit.
Race 1 (37.000 miles/59.546 km)
1 Anthony Davidson, GB (Dallara F301-Mugen), 20m 22.690s, 108.940 mph/175.322 km/h; **2** Takuma Sato, J (Dallara F301-Mugen), 20m 24.555s; **3** James Courtney, AUS (Dallara F301-Mugen), 20m 30.314s; **4** Derek Hayes, GB (Dallara F301-Mugen), 20m 33.674s; **5** Bruce Jouanny, F (Dallara F301-Mugen), 20m 34.623s; **6** André Lotterer, D (Dallara F301-Mugen), 20m 34.909s; **7** Ryan Dalziel, GB (Dallara F301-Mugen), 20m 35.626s; **8** Gianmaria Bruni, I (Dallara F301-Renault), 20m 36.103s; **9** Matt Davies, GB (Dallara F301-Opel), 20m 38.181s; **10** Jamie Spence, GB (Dallara F301-Mugen), 20m 38.944s.
Winner Scholarship Class: Robbie Kerr, GB (Dallara F398-Renault), 20m 54.157s (15th).
Fastest race lap: Sato, 1m 00.040s, 110.926 mph/178.518 km/h.
Fastest qualifying lap: Sato, 59.587s, 111.769 mph/179.875 km/h.

Race 2 (42.550 miles/68.478 km)
1 Anthony Davidson, GB (Dallara F301-Mugen), 25m 19.128s, 100.834 mph/162.277 km/h; **2** Takuma Sato, J (Dallara F301-Mugen), 25m 21.623s
3 James Courtney, AUS (Dallara F301-Mugen), 25m 27.192s; **4** Jamie Spence, GB (Dallara F301-Mugen), 25m 32.390s; **5** Derek Hayes, GB (Dallara F301-Mugen), 25m 33.611s; **6** André Lotterer, D (Dallara F301-Mugen), 25m 34.184s; **7** Ryan Dalziel, GB (Dallara F301-Mugen), 25m 36.368s; **8** Mark Taylor, GB (Dallara F301-Mugen), 25m 38.398s; **9** Matt Davies, GB (Dallara F301-Opel), 25m 40.323s; **10** Bruce Jouanny, F (Dallara F301-Mugen), 25m 41.016s.
Winner Scholarship Class: Matthew Gilmore, GB (Dallara F398-Opel), 25m 55.944s (16th).
Fastest race lap: Davidson, 59.765s, 111.436 mph/179.340 km/h.
Fastest qualifying lap: Davidson, 59.708s, 111.543 mph/179.511 km/h.
Championship points: 1 Sato, 182; **2** Hayes, 130; **3** Davidson, 121; **4** Courtney, 113; **5** Priaulx, 96; **6** Davies, 88. **Scholarship Class: 1** Gilmore, 172; **2** Kerr, 171; **3** Keohane, 135.

GREEN FLAG BRITISH FORMULA 3 CHAMPIONSHIP, Brands Hatch Grand Prix Circuit, Dartford, Kent, Great Britain, 8 July. Round 8. 18 and 15 laps of the 2.6228-mile/4.221-km circuit.
Race 1 (47.210 miles/75.978 km)
1 Derek Hayes, GB (Dallara F301-Mugen), 27m 53.071s, 101.583 mph/163.482 km/h; **2** James Courtney, AUS (Dallara F301-Mugen), 27m 53.727s; **3** André Lotterer, D (Dallara F301-Mugen), 27m 54.155s; **4** Paul Edwards, USA (Dallara F301-Mugen), 27m 58.985s; **5** Anthony Davidson, GB (Dallara F301-Mugen), 27m 59.615s; **6** Mark Taylor, GB (Dallara F301-Mugen), 28m 02.651s; **7** Jamie Spence, GB (Dallara F301-Mugen), 28m 04.356s; **8** Gianmaria Bruni, I (Dallara F301-Renault), 28m 04.892s; **9** Takuma Sato, J (Dallara F301-Mugen), 28m 05.212s; **10** Andy Priaulx, GB (Dallara F301-Mugen), 28m 06.870s.
Winner Scholarship Class: Robbie Kerr, GB (Dallara F398-Renault), 28m 11.797s (11th).
Fastest race lap: Sato, 1m 18.754s, 119.893 mph/192.950 km/h.
Fastest qualifying lap: Sato, 1m 18.634s, 120.076 mph/193.244 km/h.

Race 2 (39.342 miles/63.315 km)
1 Takuma Sato, J (Dallara F301-Mugen), 19m 48.659s, 119.152 mph/191.757 km/h; **2** James Courtney, AUS (Dallara F301-Mugen), 19m 53.224s; **3** Mark Taylor, GB (Dallara F301-Mugen), 20m 02.218s; **4** Paul Edwards, USA (Dallara F301-Mugen), 20m 06.521s; **5** Bruce Jouanny, F (Dallara F301-Mugen), 20m 09.074s; **6** Derek Hayes, GB (Dallara F301-Mugen), 20m 09.451s; **7** André Lotterer, D (Dallara F301-Mugen), 20m 10.307s; **8** Andy Priaulx, GB (Dallara F301-Mugen), 20m 10.625s; **9** Jeffrey Jones, USA (Dallara F301-Mugen), 20m 13.633s; **10** Gianmaria Bruni, I (Dallara F301-Renault), 20m 17.149s.
Winner Scholarship Class: Kerr, 20m 28.184s (11th).
Fastest race lap: Sato, 1m 18.372s, 120.478 mph/193.890 km/h.
Fastest qualifying lap: Courtney, 1m 18.674s, 120.015 mph/193.146 km/h.
Championship points: 1 Sato, 206; **2** Hayes, 156; **3** Courtney, 143; **4** Davidson, 129; **5** Lotterer, 102; **6** Priaulx, 100. **Scholarship Class: 1** Kerr, 213; **2** Gilmore, 197; **3** Keohane, 158.

GREEN FLAG BRITISH FORMULA 3 CHAMPIONSHIP, Donington Grand Prix Circuit, Castle Donington, Derbyshire, Great Britain, 22 July. Round 9. 2 x 15 laps of the 2.500-mile/4.023-km circuit.
Race 1 (37.500 miles/60.350 km)
1 Gianmaria Bruni, I (Dallara F301-Renault), 22m 43.500s, 99.010 mph/159.341 km/h; **2** André Lotterer, D (Dallara F301-Mugen), 22m 44.943s; **3** Derek Hayes, GB (Dallara F301-Mugen), 22m 45.823s; **4** Jeffrey Jones, USA (Dallara F301-Mugen), 22m 47.348s; **5** Mark Taylor, GB (Dallara F301-Mugen), 22m 49.374s; **6** Jamie Spence, GB (Dallara F301-Mugen), 22m 51.149s; **7** Ryan Dalziel, GB (Dallara F301-Mugen), 22m 52.132s; **8** Andy Priaulx, GB (Dallara F301-Mugen), 22m 52.682s; **9** Paul Edwards, USA (Dallara F301-Mugen), 22m 53.219s; **10** Atsushi Katsumata, J (Dallara F300-Mugen), 22m 54.132s.
Winner Scholarship Class: Michael Keohane, IRL (Dallara F398-Toyota), 23m 05.659s (13th).
Fastest race lap: Anthony Davidson, GB (Dallara F301-Mugen), 1m 29.661s, 100.378 mph/161.543 km/h.
Fastest qualifying lap: Takuma Sato, J (Dallara F301-Mugen), 1m 28.262s, 101.969 mph/164.103 km/h.

Race 2 (37.500 miles/60.350 km)
1 Takuma Sato, J (Dallara F301-Mugen), 22m 22.570s, 100.553 mph/161.825 km/h; **2** Matt Davies, GB (Dallara F301-Opel), 22m 33.171s; **3** Bruce Jouanny, F (Dallara F301-Mugen), 22m 34.419s; **4** André Lotterer, D (Dallara F301-Mugen), 22m 35.351s; **5** Anthony Davidson, GB (Dallara F301-Mugen), 22m 38.248s; **6** Derek Hayes, GB (Dallara F301-Mugen), 22m 41.774s; **7** Gianmaria Bruni, I (Dallara F301-Renault), 22m 42.672s; **8** James Courtney, AUS (Dallara F301-Mugen), 22m 46.311s; **9** Jeffrey Jones, USA (Dallara F301-Mugen), 22m 48.486s; **10** Alex Gurney, USA (Dallara F301-Renault), 22m 49.072s.
Winner Scholarship Class: Robbie Kerr, GB (Dallara F398-Renault), 22m 56.595s (15th).
Fastest race lap: Sato, 1m 29.047s, 101.070 mph/162.657 km/h.
Fastest qualifying lap: Sato, 1m 28.427s, 101.779 mph/163.797 km/h.
Championship points: 1 Sato, 237; **2** Hayes, 174; **3** Courtney, 146; **4** Davidson, 138; **5** Lotterer, 125; **6** Bruni, 111. **Scholarship Class: 1** Kerr, 250; **2** Gilmore, 219; **3** Keohane, 193.

GREEN FLAG BRITISH FORMULA 3 CHAMPIONSHIP, Knockhill Racing Circuit, By Dunfermline, Fife, Scotland, 19 August. Round 10. 22 laps of the 1.299-mile/2.090-km circuit.
Race 1 (28.569 miles/45.978 km)
1 Takuma Sato, J (Dallara F301-Mugen), 22m 13.781s, 77.110 mph/124.097 km/h; **2** Anthony Davidson, GB (Dallara F301-Mugen), 22m 15.646s; **3** James Courtney, AUS (Dallara F301-Mugen), 22m 17.557s; **4** Mark Taylor, GB (Dallara F301-Mugen), 22m 26.229s; **5** Derek Hayes, GB (Dallara F301-Mugen), 22m 30.098s; **6** Gianmaria Bruni, I (Dallara F301-Renault), 22m 31.683s; **7** Bruce Jouanny, F (Dallara F301-Mugen), 22m 32.927s; **8** Alex Gurney, USA (Dallara F301-Renault), 22m 33.776s; **9** Ryan Dalziel, GB (Dallara F301-Mugen), 22m 34.563s; **10** Andy Priaulx, GB (Dallara F301-Mugen), 22m 36.383s.
Winner Scholarship Class race (29 laps): Ernani Judice, BR (Dallara F398-Mugen), 29m 49.073s.
Fastest race lap: Sato, 55.707s, 83.921 mph/135.057 km/h.
Fastest qualifying lap: Priaulx, 47.069s, 99.321 mph/159.842 km/h.

Race 2 cancelled due to heavy rain.
Fastest qualifying lap: Davidson, 47.429s, 98.568 mph/158.629 km/h.
Championship points: 1 Sato, 258; **2** Hayes, 182; **3** Courtney, 158; **4** Davidson, 154; **5** Lotterer, 125; **6** Bruni, 117. **Scholarship Class: 1** Kerr, 262; **2** Gilmore, 235; **3** Keohane, 193.

GREEN FLAG BRITISH FORMULA 3 CHAMPIONSHIP, Thruxton Circuit, Andover, Hampshire, Great Britain, 1/2 September. Round 11. 15, 21 and 17 laps of the 2.356-mile/3.792-km circuit.

Race 1 (35.340 miles/56.874 km)

1 Takuma Sato, J (Dallara F301-Mugen), 16m 57.075s, 125.088 mph/201.310 km/h; **2** Anthony Davidson, GB (Dallara F301-Mugen), 16m 57.598s; **3** Andy Priaulx, GB (Dallara F301-Mugen), 17m 00.998s; **4** James Courtney, AUS (Dallara F301-Mugen), 17m 02.528s; **5** Derek Hayes, GB (Dallara F301-Mugen), 17m 03.327s; **6** Bruce Jouanny, F (Dallara F301-Mugen), 17m 03.646s; **7** Mark Taylor, GB (Dallara F301-Mugen), 17m 07.507s; **8** André Lotterer, D (Dallara F301-Mugen), 17m 09.376s; **9** Alex Gurney, USA (Dallara F301-Renault), 17m 09.812s; **10** Matt Davies, GB (Dallara F301-Opel), 17m 11.366s.

Winner Scholarship Class: Robert Doornbos, NL (Dallara F398-Renault), 17m 22.476 (14th).

Fastest race lap: Sato, 1m 07.028s, 126.538 mph/203.643 km/h.

Fastest qualifying lap: Davidson, 1m 06.460s, 127.620 mph/205.384 km/h.

Race 2 (49.476 miles/79.624 km)

1 Anthony Davidson, GB (Dallara F301-Mugen), 27m 39.683s, 107.318 mph/172.711 km/h; **2** Takuma Sato, J (Dallara F301-Mugen), 27m 41.480s; **3** Gianmaria Bruni, I (Dallara F301-Renault), 27m 48.535s; **4** Mark Taylor, GB (Dallara F301-Mugen), 27m 51.953s; **5** James Courtney, AUS (Dallara F301-Mugen), 27m 54.661s; **6** Derek Hayes, GB (Dallara F301-Mugen), 27m 55.128s; **7** Jamie Spence, GB (Dallara F301-Mugen), 27m 57.385s; **8** Ryan Dalziel, GB (Dallara F301-Mugen), 27m 57.834s; **9** Andy Priaulx, GB (Dallara F301-Mugen), 27m 59.200s; **10** Matt Davies, GB (Dallara F301-Opel), 27m 59.830s.

Winner Scholarship Class: Mark Mayall, GB (Dallara F398-Mugen), 28m 14.525s (16th).

Fastest race lap: Davidson, 1m 07.308s, 126.012 mph/202.796 km/h.

Fastest qualifying lap: Davidson, 1m 06.779s, 127.010 mph/204.403 km/h.

Race 3 (40.052 miles/64.457 km)

1 Anthony Davidson, GB (Dallara F301-Mugen), 20m 52.884s, 115.084 mph/185.210 km/h; **2** James Courtney, AUS (Dallara F301-Mugen), 20m 53.136s; **3** Derek Hayes, GB (Dallara F301-Mugen), 20m 55.704s; **4** Mark Taylor, GB (Dallara F301-Mugen), 20m 56.901s; **5** Matt Davies, GB (Dallara F301-Opel), 20m 57.285s; **6** Andy Priaulx, GB (Dallara F301-Mugen), 20m 57.891s; **7** André Lotterer, D (Dallara F301-Mugen), 20m 58.591s; **8** Takuma Sato, J (Dallara F301-Mugen), 20m 59.689s; **9** Ryan Dalziel, GB (Dallara F301-Mugen), 21m 00.197s; **10** Atsushi Katsumata, J (Dallara F300-Mugen), 21m 04.830s.

Winner Scholarship Class: Michael Keohane, IRL (Dallara F398-Toyota), 21m 16.162s (14th).

Fastest race lap: Davidson, 1m 07.367s, 125.901 mph/202.619 km/h.

Fastest qualifying lap: Davidson, 1m 06.779s, 127.010 mph/204.403 km/h.

Championship points: 1 Sato, 297; **2** Davidson, 210; **3** Hayes, 208; **4** Courtney, 191; **5** Lotterer, 132; **6** Bruni, 129. **Scholarship Class: 1** Kerr, 300; **2** Gilmore, 270; **3** Keohane, 232.

GREEN FLAG BRITISH FORMULA 3 CHAMPIONSHIP, Brands Hatch Short Circuit, Dartford, Kent, Great Britain, 16 September. Round 12. 2 x 26 laps of the 1.2262-mile/1.973-km circuit.

Race 1 (31.8812 miles/51.308 km)

1 Anthony Davidson, GB (Dallara F301-Mugen), 18m 32.835s, 103.135 mph/165.980 km/h; **2** Takuma Sato, J (Dallara F301-Mugen), 18m 33.659s; **3** Derek Hayes, GB (Dallara F301-Mugen), 18m 46.105s; **4** Jamie Spence, GB (Dallara F301-Mugen), 18m 48.957s; **5** Matt Davies, GB (Dallara F301-Opel), 18m 49.873s; **6** Ryan Dalziel, GB (Dallara F301-Mugen), 18m 52.069s; **7** Gianmaria Bruni, I (Dallara F301-Renault), 18m 52.946s; **8** Alex Gurney, USA (Dallara F301-Renault), 18m 53.755s; **9** Andy Priaulx, GB (Dallara F301-Mugen), 18m 56.047s; **10** James Courtney, AUS (Dallara F301-Mugen), 18m 56.576s.

Winner Scholarship Class race (26 laps): Matthew Gilmore, GB (Dallara F398-Opel), 18m 53.644s.

Fastest race lap: Davidson, 42.244s, 104.496 mph/168.170 km/h.

Fastest qualifying lap: Davidson, 42.085s, 104.891 mph/168.805 km/h.

Race 2 (31.8812 miles/51.308 km)

1 Takuma Sato, J (Dallara F301-Mugen), 18m 32.534s, 103.163 mph/166.025 km/h; **2** James Courtney, AUS (Dallara F301-Mugen), 18m 38.803s; **3** Anthony Davidson, GB (Dallara F301-Mugen), 18m 39.548s; **4** Mark Taylor, GB (Dallara F301-Mugen), 18m 46.324s; **5** Derek Hayes, GB (Dallara F301-Mugen), 18m 47.398s; **6** André Lotterer, D (Dallara F301-Mugen), 18m 47.845s; **7** Matt Davies, GB (Dallara F301-Opel), 18m 49.257s; **8** Gianmaria Bruni, I (Dallara F301-Renault), 18m 50.693s; **9** Alex Gurney, USA (Dallara F301-Renault), 18m 52.130s; **10** Jamie Spence, GB (Dallara F301-Mugen), 18m 53.825s.

Winner Scholarship Class race (26 laps): Gilmore, 18m 53.323s.

Fastest race lap: Sato, 42.323s, 104.301 mph/167.856 km/h.

Fastest qualifying lap: Courtney, 42.033s, 105.020 mph/169.014 km/h.

Championship points: 1 Sato, 333; **2** Davidson, 243; **3** Hayes, 228; **4** Courtney, 207; **5** Lotterer, 138; **6** Bruni, 136. **Scholarship Class: 1** Kerr, 323; **2** Gilmore, 312; **3** Keohane, 259.

AUTUMN GOLD CUP, Silverstone International Circuit, Towcester, Northamptonshire, Great Britain, 29 September. Round 13. 18 and 20 laps of the 2.249-mile/3.619-km circuit.

Race 1 (40.482 miles/65.149 km)

1 Andy Priaulx, GB (Dallara F301-Mugen), 30m 23.771s, 79.909 mph/128.601 km/h; **2** Anthony Davidson, GB (Dallara F301-Mugen), 30m 25.393s; **3** Mark Taylor, GB (Dallara F301-Mugen), 30m 30.610s; **4** James Courtney, AUS (Dallara F301-Mugen), 30m 32.319s; **5** Gianmaria Bruni, I (Dallara F301-Renault), 30m 33.131s; **6** Bruce Jouanny, F (Dallara F301-Mugen), 30m 34.454s; **7** Ryan Dalziel, GB (Dallara F301-Mugen), 30m 35.324s; **8** Matt Davies, GB (Dallara F301-Opel), 30m 36.716s; **9** Philip Giebler, USA (Dallara F301-Mugen), 30m 37.129s; **10** Rob Austin, GB (Dallara F301-Renault), 30m 40.512s.

Winner Scholarship Class: Michael Keohane, IRL (Dallara F398-Toyota), 30m 44.383s (11th).

Fastest race lap: Takuma Sato, J (Dallara F301-Mugen), 1m 28.627s, 91.354 mph/147.019 km/h.

Fastest qualifying lap: André Lotterer, D (Dallara F301-Mugen), 1m 15.556s, 107.158 mph/172.453 km/h.

Race 2 (44.980 miles/72.388 km)

1 Takuma Sato, J (Dallara F301-Mugen), 25m 34.541s, 105.522 mph/169.821 km/h; **2** Anthony Davidson, GB (Dallara F301-Mugen), 25m 40.072s; **3** Gianmaria Bruni, I (Dallara F301-Renault), 25m 40.727s; **4** James Courtney, AUS (Dallara F301-Mugen), 25m 47.644s; **5** Matt Davies, GB (Dallara F301-Opel), 25m 52.353s; **6** Derek Hayes, GB (Dallara F301-Mugen), 25m 53.500s; **7** Rob Austin, GB (Dallara F301-Renault), 25m 55.722s; **8** André Lotterer, D (Dallara F301-Mugen), 25m 57.270s; **9** Alex Gurney, USA (Dallara F301-Renault), 25m 57.596s; **10** Ryan Dalziel, GB (Dallara F301-Mugen), 26m 02.686s.

Winner Scholarship Class: Matthew Gilmore, GB (Dallara F398-Opel), 26m 21.941s (14th).

Fastest race lap: Sato, 1m 15.944s, 106.610 mph/171.572 km/h.

Fastest qualifying lap: Sato, 1m 27.858s, 92.153 mph/148.306 km/h.

Final Championship points

1 Takuma Sato, J, 355; **2** Anthony Davidson, GB, 273; **3** Derek Hayes, GB, 234; **4** James Courtney, AUS, 227; **5** Gianmaria Bruni, I, 156; **6** Andy Priaulx, GB, 146; **7** André Lotterer, D, 141; **8** Matt Davies, GB, 135; **9** Mark Taylor, GB, 91; **10** Bruce Jouanny, F, 65; **11** Jamie Spence, GB, 63; **12** Paul Edwards, USA, 56; **13** Ryan Dalziel, GB, 54; **14** Nicolas Kiesa, DK, 44; **15** Jeffrey Jones, USA, 36; **16** Alex Gurney, USA, 16; **17** Milos Pavlovic, YU, 15; **18=** Martin O'Connell, GB, 8; **18=** Rob Austin, GB, 8; **20=** Atsushi Katsumata, J, 3; **20=** Ben Collins, GB, 3; **22** Philip Giebler, USA, 2; **23** Tim Spouge, GB, 1.

Scholarship Class

1 Robbie Kerr, GB, 335; **2** Matthew Gilmore, GB, 333; **3** Michael Keohane, IRL, 280; **4** Mark Mayall, GB, 212; **5** Robert Doornbos, NL, 182; **6** Ernani Judice, BR, 164.

French Formula 3 Championship

COUPES DE PAQUES DE NOGARO, Circuit Automobile Paul Armagnac, Nogaro, France, 16 April. Round 1. 2 x 17 laps of the 2.259-mile/3.636-km circuit.

Race 1 (38.408 miles/61.812 km)

1 Tiago Monteiro, P (Dallara F399-Renault), 23m 49.332s, 96.737 mph/155.683 km/h; **2** Bruno Besson, F (Dallara F399-Renault), 23m 54.722s; **3** Renaud Derlot, F (Dallara F399-Renault), 23m 59.863s; **4** Tristan Gommendy, F (Dallara F399-Renault), 24m 01.239s; **5** Mathieu Zangarelli, F (Dallara F399-Renault), 24m 04.802s; **6** Jérôme dalla Lana, F (Martini MK79-Opel), 24m 08.948s; **7** Simon Abadie, F (Martini MK79-Opel), 24m 10.666s; **8** Lucas Lasserre, F (Dallara F399-Renault), 24m 11.983s; **9** Ryo Fukuda, J (Dallara F399-Renault), 24m 12.430s; **10** Jérémie de Souza, F (Dallara F399-Renault), 24m 13.154s.

Fastest race lap: Monteiro, 1m 23.295s, 97.647 mph/157.147 km/h.

Fastest qualifying lap: Monteiro, 1m 21.792s, 99.441 mph/160.035 km/h.

Race 2 (38.408 miles/61.812 km)

1 Ryo Fukuda, J (Dallara F399-Renault), 29m 59.210s, 76.850 mph/123.678 km/h; **2** Renaud Derlot, F (Dallara F399-Renault), 29m 59.805s; **3** Mathieu Zangarelli, F (Dallara F399-Renault), 30m 07.643s; **4** Bruno Besson, F (Dallara F399-Renault), 30m 20.917s; **5** Lucas Lasserre, F (Dallara F399-Renault), 30m 26.828s; **6** Simon Abadie, F (Martini MK79-Opel), 30m 35.687s; **7** Tiago Monteiro, P (Dallara F399-Renault), 31m 12.431s; **8** Kevin Nadin, MC (Dallara F399-Renault), 31m 41.708s; **9** Olivier Pla, F (Dallara F399-Renault), 16 laps; **10** David Moretti, F (Dallara F399-Opel), 16.

Fastest race lap: Fukuda, 1m 43.738s, 78.404 mph/126.179 km/h.

Fastest qualifying lap: Gommendy, 1m 21.473s, 99.831 mph/160.661 km/h.

COUPES DE PRINTEMPS, Circuit de Nimes Lédenon, Remoulins, Nimes, France, 6 May. Round 2. 26 laps of the 1.957-mile/3.150-km circuit, 50.890 miles/81.900 km.

1 Ryo Fukuda, J (Dallara F399-Renault), 34m 55.301s, 87.436 mph/140.714 km/h; **2** Bruno Besson, F (Dallara F399-Renault), 34m 56.985s; **3** Tiago Monteiro, P (Dallara F399-Renault), 34m 59.399s; **4** Mathieu Zangarelli, F (Dallara F399-Renault), 35m 06.072s; **5** Jérôme dalla Lana, F (Martini MK79-Opel), 35m 07.279s; **6** Tristan Gommendy, F (Dallara F399-Renault), 35m 16.559s; **7** Simon Abadie, F (Martini MK79-Opel), 35m 17.080s; **8** Lucas Lasserre, F (Dallara F399-Renault), 35m 26.548s; **9** Jérémie de Souza, F (Dallara F399-Renault), 35m 28.619s; **10** Olivier Pla, F (Dallara F399-Renault), 35m 29.431s.

Fastest race lap: Besson, 1m 19.592s, 88.531 mph/142.477 km/h.

Fastest qualifying lap: Fukuda, 1m 18.532s, 89.726 mph/144.399 km/h.

TROPHÉE ECOSPACE DE PRINTEMPS, Circuit de Nevers, Magny-Cours, France, 20 May. Round 3. 22 laps of the 2.641-mile/4.250-km circuit, 58.112 miles/93.522 km.

1 Ryo Fukuda, J (Dallara F399-Renault), 34m 05.130s, 102.293 mph/164.625 km/h; **2** Tiago Monteiro, P (Dallara F399-Renault), 34m 10.547s; **3** Renaud Derlot, F (Dallara F399-Renault), 34m 13.993s; **4** Lucas Lasserre, F (Dallara F399-Renault), 34m 14.877s; **5** Mathieu Zangarelli, F (Dallara F399-Renault), 34m 17.040s; **6** Bruno Besson, F (Dallara F399-Renault), 34m 23.186s; **7** Olivier Pla, F (Dallara F399-Renault), 34m 32.347s; **8** Jérémie de Souza, F (Dallara F399-Renault), 34m 37.662s; **9** Simon Abadie, F (Martini MK79-Opel), 34m 49.939s; **10** Jérôme dalla Lana, F (Martini MK79-Opel), 34m 53.981s.

Fastest race lap: Fukuda, 1m 32.258s, 103.072 mph/165.878 km/h.

Fastest qualifying lap: Fukuda, 1m 30.610s, 104.947 mph/168.895 km/h.

10th COUPE DU VAL DE VIENNE, Circuit du Val de Vienne, Le Vigeant, France, 24 June. Round 4. 22 laps of the 2.330-mile/3.750-km circuit, 51.263 miles/82.500 km.

1 Tiago Monteiro, P (Dallara F399-Renault), 35m 08.734s, 87.516 mph/140.842 km/h; **2** Bruno Besson, F (Dallara F399-Renault), 35m 14.421s; **3** Ryo Fukuda, J (Dallara F399-Renault), 35m 18.494s; **4** Tristan Gommendy, F (Dallara F399-Renault), 35m 23.308s; **5** Renaud Derlot, F (Dallara F399-Renault), 35m 27.804s; **6** Olivier Pla, F (Dallara F399-Renault), 35m 29.142s; **7** Jérémie de Souza, F (Dallara F399-Renault), 35m 31.517s; **8** Simon Abadie, F (Martini MK79-Opel), 35m 39.954s; **9** Mathieu Zangarelli, F (Dallara F399-Renault), 35m 40.614s; **10** Lucas Lasserre, F (Dallara F399-Renault), 35m 41.530s.

Fastest race lap: Monteiro, 1m 35.170s, 88.142 mph/141.851 km/h.

Fastest qualifying lap: Monteiro, 1m 33.193s, 90.012 mph/144.860 km/h.

RECONTRES PEUGEOT SPORT, Circuit de Spa-Francorchamps, Stavelot, Belgium, 8 July. Round 5. 2 x 10 laps of the 4.330-mile/6.968-km circuit.

Race 1 (43.297 miles/69.680 km)

1 Ryo Fukuda, J (Dallara F399-Renault), 22m 52.134s, 113.597 mph/182.816 km/h; **2** Renaud Derlot, F (Dallara F399-Renault), 22m 54.092s; **3** Tiago Monteiro, P (Dallara F399-Renault), 22m 57.444s; **4** Bruno Besson, F (Dallara F399-Renault), 22m 59.462s; **5** Tristan Gommendy, F (Dallara F399-Renault), 23m 00.874s; **6** Jérôme dalla Lana, F (Martini MK79-Opel), 23m 01.936s; **7** Jérémie de Souza, F (Dallara F399-Renault), 23m 03.163s; **8** Olivier Pla, F (Dallara F399-Renault), 23m 04.730s; **9** Lucas Lasserre, F (Dallara F399-Renault), 23m 10.919s; **10** Mathieu Zangarelli, F (Dallara F399-Renault), 23m 13.954s.

Fastest race lap: Zangarelli, 2m 16.360s, 114.308 mph/183.960 km/h.

Fastest qualifying lap: Zangarelli, 2m 14.577s, 115.822 mph/186.397 km/h.

Race 2 (43.310 miles/69.700 km)

1 Ryo Fukuda, J (Dallara F399-Renault), 22m 40.290s, 114.619 mph/184.460 km/h; **2** Renaud Derlot, F (Dallara F399-Renault), 22m 40.881s; **3** Bruno Besson, F (Dallara F399-Renault), 22m 42.222s; **4** Tiago Monteiro, P (Dallara F399-Renault), 22m 47.798s; **5** Jérémie de Souza, F (Dallara F399-Renault), 22m 48.524s; **6** Tristan Gommendy, F (Dallara F399-Renault), 22m 49.778s; **7** Mathieu Zangarelli, F (Dallara F399-Renault), 22m 53.191s; **8** Lucas Lasserre, F (Dallara F399-Renault), 22m 54.162s; **9** Kevin Nadin, MC (Dallara F399-Renault), 23m 19.164s; **10** Keiko Ihara, J (Dallara F399-Renault), 23m 25.927s.

Fastest race lap: Fukuda, 2m 14.843s, 115.627 mph/186.083 km/h.

Fastest qualifying lap: Fukuda, 2m 36.648s, 99.532 mph/160.180 km/h.

24th GRAND PRIX DU PAS-DE-CALAIS, Circuit Auto-Moto de Croix-en-Ternois, France, 22 July. Round 6. 40 laps of the 1.181-mile/1.900-km circuit, 47.224 miles/76.000 km.

1 Tiago Monteiro, P (Dallara F399-Renault), 33m 52.600s, 83.640 mph/134.605 km/h; **2** Renaud Derlot, F (Dallara F399-Renault), 34m 01.406s; **3** Bruno Besson, F (Dallara F399-Renault), 34m 02.335s; **4** Ryo Fukuda, J (Dallara F399-Renault), 34m 04.262s; **5** Lucas Lasserre, F (Dallara F399-Renault), 34m 05.067s; **6** Simon Abadie, F (Martini MK79-Opel), 34m 14.555s; **7** Olivier Pla, F (Dallara F399-Renault), 34m 16.275s; **8** Jérémie de Souza, F (Dallara F399-Renault), 34m 23.122s; **9** Kevin Nadin, MC (Dallara F399-Renault), 34m 24.010s; **10** Mathieu Zangarelli, F (Dallara F399-Renault), 34m 25.049s.

Fastest race lap: Monteiro, 50.184s, 84.692 mph/136.298 km/h.

Fastest qualifying lap: Monteiro, 49.643s, 85.615 mph/137.783 km/h.

59th GRAND PRIX D'ALBI, Circuit d'Albi, France, 2 September. Round 7. 26 laps of the 2.206-mile/3.551-km circuit, 57.369 miles/92.326 km.

1 Tiago Monteiro, P (Dallara F399-Renault), 42m 01.237s, 81.915 mph/131.829 km/h; **2** Tristan Gommendy, F (Dallara F399-Renault), 42m 01.915s; **3** Ryo Fukuda, J (Dallara F399-Renault), 42m 03.435s; **4** Mathieu Zangarelli, F (Dallara F399-Renault), 42m 10.524s; **5** Bruno Besson, F (Dallara F399-Renault), 42m 12.100s; **6** Olivier Pla, F (Dallara F399-Renault), 42m 21.087s; **7** Simon Abadie, F (Martini MK79-Opel), 42m 27.332s; **8** Keiko Ihara, J (Dallara F399-Renault), 42m 39.549s; **9** Gilles Tinguely, F (Dallara F399-Opel), 42m 40.822s; **10** Robin Longechal, F (Dallara F399-Opel), 42m 41.608s.

Fastest race lap: Monteiro, 1m 09.642s, 114.060 mph/183.561 km/h.

Fastest qualifying lap: Monteiro, 1m 08.693s, 115.636 mph/186.097 km/h.

COUPES D'AUTOMNE, Circuit Le Mans-Bugatti, France, 29 September. Round 8. 21 laps of the 2.675-mile/4.305-km circuit, 56.175 miles/90.405 km.

1 Ryo Fukuda, J (Dallara F399-Renault), 34m 33.042s, 97.552 mph/156.995 km/h; **2** Bruno Besson, F (Dallara F399-Renault), 34m 36.225s; **3** Olivier Pla, F (Dallara F399-Renault), 34m 43.433s; **4** Lucas Lasserre, F (Dallara F399-Renault), 34m 46.195s; **5** Tristan Gommendy, F (Dallara F399-Renault), 34m 48.775s; **6** Tiago Monteiro, P (Dallara F399-Renault), 34m 50.114s; **7** Jérôme dalla Lana, F (Martini MK79-Opel), 34m 53.821s; **8** Renaud Derlot, F (Dallara F399-Renault), 34m 54.491s; **9** Mathieu Zangarelli, F (Dallara F399-Renault), 35m 00.335s; **10** Keiko Ihara, J (Dallara F399-Renault), 35m 20.169s.

Fastest race lap: Fukuda, 1m 37.806s, 98.460 mph/158.456 km/h.

Fastest qualifying lap: Fukuda, 1m 36.822s, 99.461 mph/160.066 km/h.

TROPHÉES D'AUTOMNE, Circuit de Nevers, Magny-Cours, France, 14 October. Round 9. 22 laps of the 2.641-mile/4.251-km circuit, 58.112 miles/93.522 km.

1 Ryo Fukuda, J (Dallara F399-Renault), 34m 01.147s, 102.493 mph/164.946 km/h; **2** Ryan Briscoe, AUS (Dallara F399-Opel), 34m 03.767s; **3** Tristan Gommendy, F (Dallara F399-Renault), 34m 06.719s; **4** Tiago Monteiro, P (Dallara F399-Renault), 34m 08.882s; **5** Bruno Besson, F (Dallara F399-Renault), 34m 10.002s; **6** Mathieu Zangarelli, F (Dallara F399-Renault), 34m 10.931s; **7** Renaud Derlot, F (Dallara F399-Renault), 34m 15.819s; **8** Olivier Pla, F (Dallara F399-Renault), 34m 21.158s; **9** Rob Austin, GB (Dallara F399-Renault), 34m 27.540s; **10** Jérémie de Souza, F (Dallara F399-Renault), 34m 34.011s.

Fastest race lap: Fukuda, 1m 32.098s, 103.251 mph/166.166 km/h.

Fastest qualifying lap: Monteiro, 1m 30.819s, 104.705 mph/168.507 km/h.

Final Championship points

Class A

1 Ryo Fukuda, J, 177; **2** Tiago Monteiro, P, 159; **3** Bruno Besson, F, 129; **4** Renaud Derlot, F, 118; **5** Tristan Gommendy, F, 95; **6** Mathieu Zangarelli, F, 89; **7** Lucas Lasserre, F, 76; **8** Olivier Pla, F, 74; **9** Jérémie de Souza, F, 58; **10** Simon Abadie, F, 55; **11** Jérôme dalla Lana, F, 41; **12** Kevin Nadin, MC, 25; **13** Keiko Ihara, J, 22; **14** Gilles Tinguely, F, 6; **15=** David Moretti, F, 5; **15=** Robin Longechal, F, 5.

'Championnat de France Promotion' (Class B)

1 Philippe Hottinger, F, 145; **2** Olivier Maximin, F, 115; **3** Patrick d'Aubreby, F, 97; **4** Sylvie Valentin, F, 92; **5** Roger Maurice Lemartin, F, 67.

German Formula 3 Championship

INT. AvD/MAC RENNSPORTFESTIVAL, Hockenheimring Short Circuit, Heidelberg, Germany, 21/22 April. 27 and 31 laps of the 1.639-mile/2.638-km circuit.

Round 1 (44.258 miles/71.226 km)

1 Frank Diefenbacher, D (Dallara F301-Opel), 30m 58.803s, 85.715 mph/137.946 km/h; **2** Gary Paffett, GB (Dallara F301-Renault), 31m 05.023s; **3** Tony Schmidt, D (Dallara F301-TOM'S Toyota), 31m 13.209s; **4** Nicolas Stelandre, B (Dallara F399-Opel), 31m 17.584s; **5** Toshihiro Kaneishi, J (Dallara F300-Opel), 31m 19.798s; **6** Tom van Bavel, B (Dallara F399-Opel), 31m 20.532s; **7** Markus Winkelhock, D (Dallara F300-Opel), 31m 30.139s; **8** Laurent Delahaye, F (Dallara F301-Renault), 31m 32.529s; **9** Pierre Kaffer, D (Dallara F300-Mugen), 31m 34.488s; **10** Björn Wirdheim, S (Dallara F301-Opel), 31m 35.273s.

Fastest race lap: Diefenbacher, 1m 07.452s, 87.485 mph/140.793 km/h.

Fastest qualifying lap: Diefenbacher, 57.430s, 102.752 mph/165.363 km/h.

Round 2 (50.814 miles/81.778 km)

1 Frank Diefenbacher, D (Dallara F301-Opel), 30m 42.430s, 99.289 mph/159.789 km/h; **2** Stefan Mücke, D (Dallara F301-Opel), 30m 56.171s; **3** Toshihiro Kaneishi, J (Dallara F300-Opel), 30m 57.129s; **4** Pierre Kaffer, D (Dallara F300-Mugen), 30m 57.457s; **5** Joao Paulo de Oliveira, BR (Dallara F399-Opel), 30m 58.417s; **6** Markus Winkelhock, D (Dallara F300-Opel), 30m 59.434s; **7** Zsolt Baumgartner, H (Dallara F300-Opel), 31m 11.229s; **8** Andrew Kirkcaldy, GB (Dallara F399-Opel), 31m 11.889s; **9** Kimmo Liimatainen, FIN (Dallara F300-Mugen), 31m 12.247s; **10** Björn Wirdheim, S (Dallara F301-Opel), 31m 12.860.

Fastest race lap: Diefenbacher, 58.472s, 100.921 mph/162.416 km/h.

Fastest qualifying lap: Diefenbacher, 57.956s, 101.819 mph/163.862 km/h.

INT. ADAC EIFELRENNEN, Nürburgring Grand Prix Circuit, Nürburg/Eifel, Germany, 5/6 May. 2 x 18 laps of the 2.831-mile/4.556-km circuit.

Round 3 (50.957 miles/82.008 km)

1 Pierre Kaffer, D (Dallara F300-Mugen), 30m 46.499s, 99.348 mph/159.886 km/h; **2** Stefan Mücke, D (Dallara F301-Opel), 30m 48.529s; **3** Markus Winkelhock, D (Dallara F300-Opel), 30m 49.653s; **4** Kousuke Matsuura, J (Dallara F301-Opel), 30m 53.003s; **5** Tom van Bavel, B (Dallara F399-Opel), 30m 54.003s; **6** Toshihiro Kaneishi, J (Dallara F300-Opel), 30m 57.287s; **7** Kimmo Liimatainen, FIN (Dallara F300-Mugen), 31m 01.543s; **8** Gary Paffett, GB (Dallara F301-Renault), 31m 04.548s; **9** Zsolt Baumgartner, H (Dallara F300-Opel), 31m 05.085s; **10** Giuseppe Burlotti, I (Dallara F300-Opel), 31m 05.678s.

Fastest race lap: Kaffer, 1m 35.342s, 106.894 mph/172.029 km/h.

Fastest qualifying lap: Kaffer, 1m 34.224s, 108.162 mph/174.070 km/h.

Round 4 (50.957 miles/82.008 km)

1 Stefan Mücke, D (Dallara F301-Opel), 31m 32.670s, 96.925 mph/155.985 km/h; **2** Toshihiro Kaneishi, J (Dallara F300-Opel), 31m 39.983s; **3** Markus Winkelhock, D (Dallara F300-Opel), 31m 42.460s; **4** Kousuke Matsuura, J (Dallara F301-Opel), 31m 44.210s; **5** Tony Schmidt, D (Dallara F301-TOM'S Toyota), 31m 44.641s; **6** Tom van Bavel, B (Dallara F399-Opel), 31m 53.498s; **7** Pierre Kaffer, D (Dallara F300-Mugen), 31m 54.229s; **8** Zsolt Baumgartner, H (Dallara F300-Opel), 31m 55.942s; **9** Robert Lechner, A (Dallara F301-Opel), 31m 56.595s; **10** Gary Paffett, GB (Dallara F301-Renault), 31m 57.059s.

Fastest race lap: Mücke, 1m 35.109s, 107.156 mph/172.451 km/h.

Fastest qualifying lap: Frank Diefenbacher, D (Dallara F301-Opel), 1m 34.304s, 108.071 mph/173.923 km/h.

INT. ADAC-PREIS DER TOURENWAGEN VON SACHSEN-ANHALT, Motopark Oschersleben, Germany, 19/20 May. 2 x 22 laps of the 2.279-mile/3.667-km circuit.

Round 5 (50.128 miles/80.674 km)

1 Gary Paffett, GB (Dallara F301-Renault), 30m 02.402s, 100.123 mph/161.133 km/h; **2** Toshihiro Kaneishi, J (Dallara F300-Opel), 30m 11.737s; **3** Markus Winkelhock, D (Dallara F300-Opel), 30m 12.920s; **4** Pierre Kaffer, D (Dallara F300-Mugen), 30m 16.932s; **5** Björn Wirdheim, S (Dallara F301-Opel), 30m 17.334s; **6** Tony Schmidt, D (Dallara F301-TOM'S Toyota), 30m 19.259s; **7** Joao Paulo de Oliveira, BR (Dallara F399-Opel), 30m 22.710s; **8** Frank Diefenbacher, D (Dallara F301-Opel), 30m 23.590s; **9** Bernhard Auinger, A (Dallara F399-Opel), 30m 27.814s; **10** Nicolas Stelandre, B (Dallara F399-Opel), 30m 28.082s.

Fastest race lap: Paffett, 1m 21.179s, 101.046 mph/162.618 km/h.

Fastest qualifying lap: Winkelhock, 1m 19.739s, 102.871 mph/165.555 km/h.

Round 6 (50.128 miles/80.674 km)

1 Pierre Kaffer, D (Dallara F300-Mugen), 29m 56.151s, 100.472 mph/161.694 km/h; **2** Toshihiro Kaneishi, J (Dallara F300-Opel),

29m 58.269s; **3** Frank Diefenbacher, D (Dallara F301-Opel), 29m 59.471s; **4** Bernhard Auinger, A (Dallara F399-Opel), 30m 04.563s; **5** Tony Schmidt, D (Dallara F301-TOM'S Toyota), 30m 07.355s; **6** Robert Lechner, A (Dallara F301-Opel), 30m 10.538s; **7** Björn Wirdheim, S (Dallara F301-Opel), 30m 10.818s; **8** Raffaele Giammaria, I (Dallara F301-Opel), 30m 11.241s; **9** Stefan Mücke, D (Dallara F301-Opel), 30m 11.705s; **10** Kimmo Liimatainen, FIN (Dallara F300-Mugen), 30m 12.349s.
Fastest race lap: Kaneishi, 1m 20.998s, 101.272 mph/162.982 km/h.
Fastest qualifying lap: Kaneishi, 1m 19.661s, 102.972 mph/165.717 km/h.

INT. ADAC RUNDSTRECKENRENNEN SACHSENRING, Oberlungwitz, Germany, 16/17 June. 22 and 21 laps of the 2.265-mile/3.645-km circuit.
Round 7 (49.828 miles/80.190 km)
1 Markus Winkelhock, D (Dallara F300-Opel), 31m 06.771s, 96.091 mph/154.643 km/h; **2** Toshihiro Kaneishi, J (Dallara F300-Opel), 31m 10.834s; **3** Frank Diefenbacher, D (Dallara F301-Opel), 31m 11.027s; **4** Hannes Lachinger, A (Dallara F301-TOM'S Toyota), 31m 14.491s; **5** Matteo Grassotto, I (Dallara F301-Opel), 31m 20.645s; **6** Kari Mäenpää, FIN (Dallara F399-Opel), 31m 21.077s; **7** Ronnie Quintarelli, I (Dallara F300-Opel), 31m 23.095s; **8** Tom van Bavel, B (Dallara F399-Opel), 31m 31.757s; **9** Zsolt Baumgartner, H (Dallara F300-Opel), 31m 32.219s; **10** Kousuke Matsuura, J (Dallara F301-Opel), 31m 33.175s.
Fastest race lap: Matsuura, 1m 17.151s, 105.684 mph/170.082 km/h.
Fastest qualifying lap: Kaneishi, 1m 15.151s, 108.497 mph/174.608 km/h.

Round 8 (47.563 miles/76.545 km)
1 Pierre Kaffer, D (Dallara F300-Mugen), 30m 16.912s, 94.240 mph/151.665 km/h; **2** Kari Mäenpää, FIN (Dallara F399-Opel), 30m 17.682s; **3** Matteo Grassotto, I (Dallara F301-Opel), 30m 18.117s; **4** Norbert Siedler, A (Dallara F300-Opel), 30m 37.184s; **5** Gottfried Grasser, A (Dallara F300-Mugen), 30m 42.629s; **6** Zsolt Baumgartner, H (Dallara F300-Opel), 30m 43.570s; **7** Tom van Bavel, B (Dallara F399-Opel), 30m 47.107s; **8** Kimmo Liimatainen, FIN (Dallara F300-Mugen), 30m 50.681s; **9** Marc Caldonazzi, I (Dallara F300-Opel), 30m 52.459s; **10** Marco Schärf, A (Dallara F300-Opel), 31m 15.433s.
Fastest race lap: Kaneishi, 1m 17.520s, 105.181 mph/169.272 km/h.
Fastest qualifying lap: Joao Paulo de Oliveira, BR (Dallara F399-Opel), 1m 15.601s, 107.851 mph/173.569 km/h.

INT. ADAC SPEEDWEEKEND, Norisring, Nürnberg, Germany, 7/8 July. 25 and 35 laps of the 1.429-mile/2.300-km circuit.
Round 9 (35.729 miles/57.500 km)
1 Frank Diefenbacher, D (Dallara F301-Opel), 27m 37.377s, 77.607 mph/124.896 km/h; **2** Tony Schmidt, D (Dallara F301-TOM'S Toyota), 27m 42.421s; **3** Stefan Mücke, D (Dallara F301-Opel), 27m 44.534s; **4** Gary Paffett, GB (Dallara F301-Opel), 27m 45.497s; **5** Nicolas Stelandre, B (Dallara F399-Opel), 27m 57.113s; **6** Toshihiro Kaneishi, J (Dallara F300-Opel), 28m 01.791s; **7** Raffaele Giammaria, I (Dallara F301-Opel), 28m 07.338s; **8** Kousuke Matsuura, J (Dallara F301-Opel), 28m 09.057s; **9** Zsolt Baumgartner, H (Dallara F300-Opel), 28m 10.257s; **10** Matteo Grassotto, I (Dallara F301-Opel), 28m 15.817s.
Fastest race lap: Paffett, 1m 00.184s, 85.487 mph/137.578 km/h.
Fastest qualifying lap: Pierre Kaffer, D (Dallara F300-Mugen), 49.653s, 103.618 mph/166.757 km/h.

Round 10 (50.020 miles/80.500 km)
1 Toshihiro Kaneishi, J (Dallara F300-Opel), 29m 41.193s, 101.097 mph/162.700 km/h; **2** Pierre Kaffer, D (Dallara F300-Mugen), 29m 42.286s; **3** Gary Paffett, GB (Dallara F301-Opel), 29m 46.667s; **4** Frank Diefenbacher, D (Dallara F301-Opel), 29m 49.292s; **5** Kousuke Matsuura, J (Dallara F301-Opel), 29m 55.305s; **6** Björn Wirdheim, S (Dallara F301-Opel), 30m 01.866s; **7** Matteo Grassotto, I (Dallara F301-Opel), 30m 03.675; **8** Hannes Lachinger, A (Dallara F301-TOM'S Toyota), 30m 05.750s; **9** Marco du Pau, NL (Dallara F399-Opel), 30m 07.861s; **10** Nicolas Stelandre, B (Dallara F399-Opel), 30m 09.564s.
Fastest race lap: Kaffer, 49.956s, 102.990 mph/165.746 km/h.
Fastest qualifying lap: Kaffer, 50.072s, 102.751 mph/165.362 km/h.

INT. ADAC PREIS, Hockenheimring Grand Prix Circuit, Heidelberg, Germany, 28/29 July. 2 x 12 laps of the 4.241-mile/6.825-km circuit.
Round 11 (50.890 miles/81.900 km)
1 Joao Paulo de Oliveira, BR (Dallara F399-Opel), 26m 13.580s, 116.426 mph/187.368 km/h; **2** Kousuke Matsuura, J (Dallara F301-Opel), 26m 15.098s; **3** Matteo Grassotto, I (Dallara F301-Opel), 26m 19.260s; **4** Frank Diefenbacher, D (Dallara F301-Opel), 26m 20.002s; **5** Stefan Mücke, D (Dallara F301-Opel), 26m 24.079s; **6** Raffaele Giammaria, I (Dallara F301-Opel), 26m 27.224s; **7** Norbert Siedler, A (Dallara F301-Opel), 26m 28.082s; **8** Pierre Kaffer, D (Dallara F300-Mugen), 26m 28.844s; **9** Tom van Bavel, B (Dallara F399-Opel), 26m 29.512s; **10** Nicolas Kiesa, DK (Dallara F301-TOM'S Toyota), 26m 29.852s.
Fastest race lap: Tony Schmidt, D (Dallara F301-TOM'S Toyota), 2m 09.490s, 117.902 mph/189.744 km/h.
Fastest qualifying lap: de Oliveira, 2m 08.892s, 118.449 mph/190.624 km/h.

Round 12 (50.890 miles/81.900 km)
1 Kousuke Matsuura, J (Dallara F301-Opel), 26m 10.449s, 116.658 mph/187.742 km/h; **2** Joao Paulo de Oliveira, BR (Dallara F399-Opel), 26m 11.385s; **3** Stefan Mücke, D (Dallara F301-Opel), 26m 12.807s; **4** Norbert Siedler, A (Dallara F301-Opel), 26m 15.219s; **5** Pierre Kaffer, D (Dallara F300-Mugen), 26m 18.530s; **6** Matteo Grassotto, I (Dallara F301-Opel), 26m 23.380s; **7** Hannes Lachinger, A (Dallara F301-TOM'S Toyota), 26m 24.001s; **8** Toshihiro Kaneishi, J (Dallara F300-Opel), 26m 26.676s; **9** Raffaele Giammaria, I (Dallara F301-Opel), 26m 27.157s; **10** Frank Diefenbacher, D (Dallara F301-Opel), 26m 27.732s.
Fastest race lap: Mücke, 2m 09.115s, 118.244 mph/190.295 km/h.
Fastest qualifying lap: qualifying not held.

INT. ADAC RUNDSTRECKENRENNEN, EuroSpeedway Lausitz, Klettwitz, Dresden, Germany, 11/12 August. 18 and 17 laps of the 2.817-mile/4.534-km circuit.
Round 13 (50.711 miles/81.612 km)
1 Markus Winkelhock, D (Dallara F300-Opel), 29m 23.001s, 103.551 mph/166.649 km/h; **2** Frank Diefenbacher, D (Dallara F301-Opel), 29m 23.726s; **3** Stefan Mücke, D (Dallara F301-Opel), 29m 25.392s; **4** Toshihiro Kaneishi, J (Dallara F300-Opel), 29m 30.977s; **5** Gary Paffett, GB (Dallara F301-Opel), 29m 34.957s; **6** Pierre Kaffer, D (Dallara F300-Mugen), 29m 37.135s; **7** Hannes Lachinger, A (Dallara F301-TOM'S Toyota), 29m 42.678s; **8** Joao Paulo de Oliveira, BR (Dallara F399-Opel), 29m 43.249s; **9** Zsolt Baumgartner, H (Dallara F300-Opel), 29m 45.981s; **10** Ronnie Quintarelli, I (Dallara F301-Opel), 29m 52.700s.
Fastest race lap: Winkelhock, 1m 36.854s, 104.717 mph/168.526 km/h.
Fastest qualifying lap: Diefenbacher, 1m 35.707s, 105.972 mph/170.546 km/h.

Round 14 (47.894 miles/77.078 km)
1 Frank Diefenbacher, D (Dallara F301-Opel), 27m 49.126s, 103.299 mph/166.243 km/h; **2** Toshihiro Kaneishi, J (Dallara F300-Opel), 27m 53.871s; **3** Stefan Mücke, D (Dallara F301-Opel), 27m 56.436s; **4** Björn Wirdheim, S (Dallara F301-Opel), 27m 57.390s; **5** Nicolas Kiesa, DK (Dallara F301-TOM'S Toyota), 27m 58.941s; **6** Markus Winkelhock, D (Dallara F300-Opel), 27m 59.378s; **7** Tony Schmidt, D (Dallara F301-TOM'S Toyota), 28m 01.694s; **8** Gary Paffett, GB (Dallara F301-Opel), 28m 02.035s; **9** Kousuke Matsuura, J (Dallara F301-Opel), 28m 07.239s; **10** Pierre Kaffer, D (Dallara F300-Mugen), 28m 12.147s.
Fastest race lap: Diefenbacher, 1m 37.129s, 104.421 mph/168.049 km/h.
Fastest qualifying lap: Diefenbacher, 1m 36.399s, 105.211 mph/169.321 km/h.

INT. ADAC GROSSER PREIS DER TOURENWAGEN, Nürburgring Sprint Course, Nürburg/Eifel, Germany, 25/26 August. 2 x 27 laps of the 1.888-mile/3.038-km circuit.
Round 15 (50.969 miles/82.026 km)
1 Björn Wirdheim, S (Dallara F301-Opel), 29m 00.655s, 105.413 mph/169.645 km/h; **2** Joao Paulo de Oliveira, BR (Dallara F399-Opel), 29m 03.590s; **3** Markus Winkelhock, D (Dallara F300-Opel), 29m 05.444s; **4** Kousuke Matsuura, J (Dallara F301-Opel), 29m 11.660s; **5** Pierre Kaffer, D (Dallara F300-Mugen), 29m 14.048s; **6** Hannes Lachinger, A (Dallara F301-TOM'S Toyota), 29m 14.829s; **7** Toshihiro Kaneishi, J (Dallara F300-Opel), 29m 16.284s; **8** Stefan Mücke, D (Dallara F301-Opel), 29m 16.707s; **9** Kari Mäenpää, FIN (Dallara F399-Opel), 29m 17.576s; **10** Laurent Delahaye, F (Dallara F301-Renault), 29m 22.529s.
Fastest race lap: Wirdheim, 1m 03.704s, 106.678 mph/171.682 km/h.
Fastest qualifying lap: Wirdheim, 1m 02.923s, 108.002 mph/173.812 km/h.

Round 16 (50.969 miles/82.026 km)
1 Pierre Kaffer, D (Dallara F300-Mugen), 29m 06.758s, 105.044 mph/169.052 km/h; **2** Markus Winkelhock, D (Dallara F300-Opel), 29m 06.891s; **3** Frank Diefenbacher, D (Dallara F301-Opel), 29m 09.904s; **4** Joao Paulo de Oliveira, BR (Dallara F399-Opel), 29m 10.629s; **5** Hannes Lachinger, A (Dallara F301-TOM'S Toyota), 29m 20.105s; **6** Kari Mäenpää, FIN (Dallara F399-Opel), 29m 21.180s; **7** Stefan Mücke, D (Dallara F301-Opel), 29m 22.027s; **8** Kimmo Liimatainen, FIN (Dallara F300-Mugen), 29m 23.084s; **9** Jaroslav Janis, CZ (Dallara F300-Opel), 29m 26.089s; **10** Zsolt Baumgartner, H (Dallara F300-Opel), 29m 28.212s.
Fastest race lap: Winkelhock, 1m 03.855s, 106.426 mph/171.276 km/h.
Fastest qualifying lap: Kaffer, 1m 03.141s, 107.629 mph/173.212 km/h.

INT. ADAC RUNDSTRECKENRENNEN, A1-Ring, Spielberg, Austria, 8/9 September. 19 and 17 laps of the 2.688-mile/4.326-km circuit.
Round 17 (51.073 miles/82.194 km)
1 Toshihiro Kaneishi, J (Dallara F300-Opel), 28m 30.487s, 107.491 mph/172.991 km/h; **2** Stefan Mücke, D (Dallara F301-Opel), 28m 31.540s; **3** Joao Paulo de Oliveira, BR (Dallara F399-Opel), 28m 32.634s; **4** Gary Paffett, GB (Dallara F301-Opel), 28m 35.123s; **5** Raffaele Giammaria, I (Dallara F301-Opel), 28m 37.413s; **6** Nicolas Kiesa, DK (Dallara F301-TOM'S Toyota), 28m 38.808s; **7** Björn Wirdheim, S (Dallara F301-Opel), 28m 39.325s; **8** Zsolt Baumgartner, H (Dallara F300-Opel), 28m 46.985s; **9** Pierre Kaffer, D (Dallara F300-Mugen), 28m 47.448s; **10** Tony Schmidt, D (Dallara F301-TOM'S Toyota), 28m 49.223s.
Fastest race lap: de Oliveira, 1m 28.410s, 109.456 mph/176.152 km/h.
Fastest qualifying lap: Markus Winkelhock, D (Dallara F300-Opel), 1m 27.707s, 110.333 mph/177.564 km/h.

Round 18 (45.697 miles/73.542 km)
1 Björn Wirdheim, S (Dallara F301-Opel), 31m 30.335s, 87.026 mph/140.055 km/h; **2** Stefan Mücke, D (Dallara F301-Opel), 31m 31.361s; **3** Frank Diefenbacher, D (Dallara F301-Opel), 31m 31.823s; **4** Gary Paffett, GB (Dallara F301-Opel), 31m 32.097s; **5** Joao Paulo de Oliveira, BR (Dallara F399-Opel), 31m 33.220s; **6** Toshihiro Kaneishi, J (Dallara F300-Opel), 31m 34.654s; **7** Kousuke Matsuura, J (Dallara F301-Opel), 31m 36.691s; **8** Kari Mäenpää, FIN (Dallara F399-Opel), 31m 40.220s; **9** Raffaele Giammaria, I (Dallara F301-Opel), 31m 40.853s; **10** Fabrizio del Monte, I (Dallara F300-Mugen), 31m 43.772s.
Fastest race lap: Kaneishi, 1m 29.453s, 108.180 mph/174.098 km/h.
Fastest qualifying lap: Wirdheim, 1m 28.225s, 109.685 mph/176.521 km/h.

INT. DMV-PREIS HOCKENHEIM, Hockenheimring Grand Prix Circuit, Heidelberg, Germany, 7 October. 2 x 12 laps of the 4.241-mile/6.825-km circuit.
Round 19 (50.890 miles/81.900 km)
1 Markus Winkelhock, D (Dallara F300-Opel), 26m 01.091s, 117.357 mph/188.868 km/h; **2** Gary Paffett, GB (Dallara F301-Opel), 26m 01.900s; **3** Stefan Mücke, D (Dallara F301-Opel), 26m 03.053s; **4** Joao Paulo de Oliveira, BR (Dallara F399-Opel), 26m 07.705s; **5** Jaroslav Janis, CZ (Dallara F300-Opel), 26m 08.697s; **6** Raffaele Giammaria, I (Dallara F301-Opel), 26m 09.313s; **7** Toshihiro Kaneishi, J (Dallara F300-Opel), 26m 10.485s; **8** Pierre Kaffer, D (Dallara F300-Mugen), 26m 14.598s; **9** Tony Schmidt, D (Dallara F301-TOM'S Toyota), 26m 18.614s; **10** Bernhard Auinger, A (Dallara F399-Opel), 26m 26.859s.
Fastest race lap: Winkelhock, 2m 08.134s, 119.149 mph/191.752 km/h.
Fastest qualifying lap: Paffett, 2m 06.849s, 120.356 mph/193.695 km/h.

Round 20 (50.890 miles/81.900 km)
1 Stefan Mücke, D (Dallara F301-Opel), 32m 19.225s, 94.446 mph/151.996 km/h; **2** Gary Paffett, GB (Dallara F301-Opel), 32m 30.097s; **3** Kimmo Liimatainen, FIN (Dallara F300-Mugen), 32m 35.244s; **4** Raffaele Giammaria, I (Dallara F301-Opel), 32m 36.225s; **5** Joao Paulo de Oliveira, BR (Dallara F399-Opel), 32m 38.955s; **6** Toshihiro Kaneishi, J (Dallara F300-Opel), 32m 41.711s; **7** Björn Wirdheim, S (Dallara F301-Opel), 32m 43.411s; **8** Tom van Bavel, B (Dallara F399-Opel), 32m 43.600s; **9** Nicolas Kiesa, DK (Dallara F301-TOM'S Toyota), 32m 44.098s; **10** Hannes Lachinger, A (Dallara F301-TOM'S Toyota), 32m 48.000s.
Frank Diefenbacher, D (Dallara F301-Opel), finished 2nd, 31m 31.823s, but was disqualified for passing under yellow flags.
Fastest race lap: Kiesa, 2m 24.753s, 105.439 mph/169.688 km/h.
Fastest qualifying lap: Mücke, 2m 07.165s, 120.022 mph/193.157 km/h.

Final Championship points
1 Toshihiro Kaneishi, J, 182; **2** Stefan Mücke, D, 178; **3** Frank Diefenbacher, D, 172; **4** Pierre Kaffer, D, 156; **5** Markus Winkelhock, D, 141; **6** Gary Paffett, GB, 123; **7** Joao Paulo de Oliveira, BR, 116; **8** Kousuke Matsuura, J, 83; **9** Björn Wirdheim, S, 80; **10** Tony Schmidt, D, 56; **11** Matteo Grassotto, I, 43; **12** Raffaele Giammaria, I, 41; **13** Hannes Lachinger, A, 36; **14=** Kari Mäenpää, FIN, 32; **14=** Tom van Bavel, B, 32; **16=** Kimmo Liimatainen, FIN, 25; **16=** Zsolt Baumgartner, H, 25; **18** Norbert Siedler, A, 24; **19** Nicolas Stelandre, B, 20; **20** Nicolas Kiesa, DK, 17; **21** Bernhard Auinger, A, 13; **22** Jaroslav Janis, CZ, 10; **23=** Gottfried Grasser, A, 8; **23=** Robert Lechner, A, 8; **25** Ronnie Quintarelli, I, 5; **26** Laurent Delahaye, F, 4; **27** Andrew Kirkcaldy, GB, 3; **28=** Marco du Pau, NL, 2; **28=** Marc Caldonazzi, I, 2; **30=** Marco Schärf, A, 1; **30=** Fabrizio del Monte, I, 1; **30=** Giuseppe Burlotti, I, 1.

Italian Formula 3 Championship

GRAN PREMIO CAMPAGNANO - TROFEO IGNAZIO GIUNTI, Autodromo di Vallelunga, Campagnano di Roma, Italy, 1 April. Round 1. 25 laps of the 2.002-mile/3.222-km circuit, 50.051 miles/80.550 km.
1 Lorenzo del Gallo, I (Dallara F300-Fiat), 29m 38.312s, 101.324 mph/163.064 km/h; **2** Gian Paolo Ermolli, I (Dallara F399-Fiat), 29m 52.493s; **3** Stefano Mocellini, I (Dallara F301-Opel), 29m 58.686s; **4** Sergio Ghiotto, I (Dallara F399-Opel), 30m 13.428s; **5** Franco Ghiotto, I (Dallara F399-Opel), 30m 18.306s; **6** Alberto Morelli, I (Dallara F394-Fiat), 30m 51.502s; **7** Wladimiro De Tommaso, I (Dallara F394-Opel), 24 laps; **8** Stefano Comandini, I (Dallara F392-Fiat), 24; **9** Gianpiero Negrotti, I (Dallara F300-Alfa Romeo), 24; **10** Nenad Lazic, I (Dallara F398-Renault), 24.
Fastest race lap: del Gallo, 1m 10.345s, 102.458 mph/164.890 km/h.
Fastest qualifying lap: del Gallo, 1m 09.653s, 103.476 mph/166.528 km/h.

ITALIAN FORMULA 3 CHAMPIONSHIP, Autodromo Santamonica, Misano Adriatico, Rimini, Italy, 22 April. Round 2. 18 laps of the 2.523-mile/4.060-km circuit, 45.410 miles/73.080 km.
1 Lorenzo del Gallo, I (Dallara F300-Fiat), 27m 13.893s, 100.053 mph/161.019 km/h; **2** Stefano Mocellini, I (Dallara F301-Opel), 27m 20.288s; **3** Gian Paolo Ermolli, I (Dallara F399-Fiat), 27m 20.898s; **4** Franco Ghiotto, I (Dallara F399-Opel), 27m 21.794s; **5** Cristiano Citron, I (Dallara F399-Opel), 27m 24.164s; **6** Silvio Alberti, I (Dallara F398-Fiat), 28m 17.227s; **7** Stamatis Katsimis, I (Dallara F396-Fiat), 28m 34.536s; **8** Robert Buonomo, I (Dallara F397-Fiat), 28m 43.153s; **9** Nenad Lazic, I (Dallara F398-Renault), 28m 46.052s; **10** Gianpiero Negrotti, I (Dallara F300-Alfa Romeo), 17 laps.
Fastest race lap: del Gallo, 1m 29.004s, 102.040 mph/164.217 km/h.
Fastest qualifying lap: del Gallo, 1m 27.495s, 103.800 mph/167.049 km/h.

ITALIAN FORMULA 3 CHAMPIONSHIP, Autodromo Enzo e Dino Ferrari, Imola, Italy, 20 May. Round 3. 15 laps of the 3.065-mile/4.933-km circuit, 45.978 miles/73.995 km.
1 Lorenzo del Gallo, I (Dallara F300-Fiat), 27m 04.767s, 101.874 mph/163.950 km/h; **2** Cristiano Citron, I (Dallara F399-Opel), 27m 32.252s; **3** Gian Paolo Ermolli, I (Dallara F399-Fiat), 27m 41.887s; **4** Franco Ghiotto, I (Dallara F399-Opel), 27m 45.898s; **5** Sergio Ghiotto, I (Dallara F398-Fiat), 28m 05.408s; **6** Stefano Mocellini, I (Dallara F301-Opel), 28m 08.016s; **7** Stamatis Katsimis, I (Dallara F396-Fiat), 28m 21.100s; **8** Nino Famá, I (Dallara F394-Opel), 28m 22.234s; **9** Silvio Alberti, I (Dallara F398-Fiat), 28m 47.850s; **10** Gianpiero Negrotti, I (Dallara F300-Alfa Romeo), 14 laps.
Fastest race lap: del Gallo, 1m 47.662s, 102.495 mph/164.949 km/h.
Fastest qualifying lap: del Gallo, 1m 46.750s, 103.371 mph/166.358 km/h.

ITALIAN FORMULA 3 CHAMPIONSHIP, A1-Ring, Spielberg, Austria, 24 June. Round 4. 17 laps of the 2.683-mile/4.318-km circuit, 45.612 miles/73.406 km.
1 Lorenzo del Gallo, I (Dallara F300-Fiat), 26m 28.706s, 103.357 mph/166.338 km/h; **2** Stefano Mocellini, I (Dallara F301-Opel), 26m 46.428s; **3** Gian Paolo Ermolli, I (Dallara F399-Fiat), 26m 46.565s; **4** Sergio Ghiotto, I (Dallara F398-Fiat), 27m 11.841s; **5** Silvio Alberti, I (Dallara F398-Fiat), 27m 18.657s; **6** Stamatis Katsimis, I (Dallara F396-Fiat), 27m 24.205s; **7** Franco Ghiotto, I (Dallara F399-Opel), 27m 30.502s; **8** Robert Buonomo, I (Dallara F397-Fiat), 27m 50.835s; **9** Gianpiero Negrotti, I (Dallara F300-Alfa Romeo), 27m 51.658s; **10** Emanuele Gozzo, I (Dallara F394-Opel), 16 laps.
Fastest race lap: del Gallo, 1m 31.788s, 105.233 mph/169.355 km/h.
Fastest qualifying lap: del Gallo, 1m 31.237s, 105.868 mph/170.378 km/h.

ITALIAN FORMULA 3 CHAMPIONSHIP, Autodromo Santamonica, Misano Adriatico, Rimini, Italy, 29 July. Round 5. 18 laps of the 2.523-mile/4.060-km circuit, 45.410 miles/73.080 km.
1 Massimo Carli, I (Dallara F301-Fiat), 27m 26.499s, 99.287 mph/159.786 km/h; **2** Stefano Mocellini, I (Dallara F301-Opel), 27m 29.202s; **3** Stamatis Katsimis, I (Dallara F396-Fiat), 28m 12.053s; **4** Robert Buonomo, I (Dallara F397-Fiat), 28m 19.708s; **5** Gianpiero Negrotti, I (Dallara F300-Alfa Romeo), 28m 24.672s; **6** Giovanni Rambelli, I (Dallara F393-Fiat), 29m 02.786s; **7** Matteo Meneghello, I (Dallara F395-Renault), 17 laps; **8** Imerio Brigliadori, I (Dallara F394-Fiat), 17; **9** Enrico Forte, I (Dallara F395-Renault), 17; **10** Emanuele Gozzo, I (Dallara F394-Opel), 17.
Fastest race lap: Lorenzo del Gallo, I (Dallara F300-Fiat), 1m 29.552s, 101.416 mph/163.212 km/h.
Fastest qualifying lap: Mocellini, 1m 29.842s, 101.088 mph/162.685 km/h.

ITALIAN FORMULA 3 CHAMPIONSHIP, Autodromo Internazionale del Mugello, Scarperia, Firenze (Florence), Italy, 9 September. Round 6. 15 laps of the 3.259-mile/5.245-km circuit, 48.886 miles/78.675 km.
1 Lorenzo del Gallo, I (Dallara F300-Fiat), 27m 23.710s, 107.069 mph/172.311 km/h; **2** Gian Paolo Ermolli, I (Dallara F399-Fiat), 27m 27.839s; **3** Massimo Carli, I (Dallara F301-Fiat), 27m 49.454s; **4** Stefano Mocellini, I (Dallara F301-Opel), 27m 51.735s; **5** Stamatis Katsimis, I (Dallara F396-Fiat), 27m 54.918s; **6** Sergio Ghiotto, I (Dallara F398-Fiat), 28m 01.646s; **7** Stefano Comandini, I (Dallara F394-Opel), 28m 40.325s; **8** Roberto Petroncini, I (Dallara F394-Fiat), 28m 49.068s; **9** Imerio Brigliadori, I (Dallara F394-Fiat), 28m 49.801s; **10** Nenad Lazic, I (Dallara F398-Renault), 29m 10.828s.
Fastest race lap: del Gallo, 1m 47.557s, 109.084 mph/175.553 km/h.
Fastest qualifying lap: del Gallo, 1m 46.558s, 110.107 mph/177.199 km/h.

40th TROFEO AUTOMOBILE CLUB PARMA, Autodromo Riccardo Paletti, Varano, Parma, Italy, 16 September. Round 7. 39 laps of the 1.118-mile/1.800-km circuit, 43.620 miles/70.200 km.
1 Gian Paolo Ermolli, I (Dallara F399-Fiat), 35m 11.870s, 74.357 mph/119.666 km/h; **2** Sergio Ghiotto, I (Dallara F398-Fiat), 35m 48.848s; **3** Stefano Comandini, I (Dallara F394-Opel), 38 laps; **4** Matteo Meneghello, I (Dallara F395-Renault), 37; **5** Massimo Carli, I (Dallara F301-Fiat), 37; **6** Robert Buonomo, I (Dallara F397-Fiat), 37; **7** Stamatis Katsimis, I (Dallara F396-Fiat), 36; **8** Renato Bicciato, I (Dallara F398-Fiat), 36; **9** Gianpiero Negrotti, I (Dallara F300-Alfa Romeo), 36; **10** Silvio Alberti, I (Dallara F398-Fiat), 35.
Fastest race lap: Stefano Mocellini, I (Dallara F301-Opel), 47.857s, 84.136 mph/135.403 km/h.
Fastest qualifying lap: Ermolli, 44.841s, 89.795 mph/144.510 km/h.

ITALIAN FORMULA 3 CHAMPIONSHIP, Autodromo di Magione, Perugia, Italy, 7 October. Round 8. 30 laps of the 1.558-mile/2.507-km circuit, 46.733 miles/75.210 km.
1 Lorenzo del Gallo, I (Dallara F300-Fiat), 35m 10.474s, 79.717 mph/128.292 km/h; **2** Massimo Carli, I (Dallara F301-Fiat), 35m 36.044s; **3** Stefano Mocellini, I (Dallara F301-Opel), 35m 36.458s; **4** Roberto Petroncini, I (Dallara F394-Fiat), 29 laps; **5** Robert Buonomo, I (Dallara F397-Fiat), 29; **6** Gianpiero Negrotti, I (Dallara F300-Alfa Romeo), 29; **7** Matteo Meneghello, I (Dallara F395-Renault), 29; **8** Renato Bicciato, I (Dallara F398-Fiat), 29; **9** 'J. de Magrys', I (Dallara F395-Renault), 26; **10** Enrico Forte, I (Dallara F395-Renault), 26.
Fastest race lap: del Gallo, 1m 09.293s, 80.932 mph/130.247 km/h.
Fastest qualifying lap: del Gallo, 1m 08.886s, 81.410 mph/131.016 km/h.

Final Championship points
Overall
1 Lorenzo del Gallo, I, 69; **2** Gian Paolo Ermolli, I, 34; **3** Stefano Mocellini, I, 31; **4** Sergio Ghiotto, I, 25; **5** Stamatis Katsimis, I, 21; **6** Massimo Carli, I, 18; **7** Robert Buonomo, I, 17; **8** Imerio Brigliadori, I, 15; **9** Gianpiero Negrotti, I, 14; **10=** Stefano Comandini, I, 13; **10=** Matteo Meneghello, I, 13; **12=** Silvio Alberti, I, 12; **12=** Franco Ghiotto, I, 12; **14** Roberto Petroncini, I, 11; **15** Renato Bicciato, I, 10.

Winner Classe B: Stamatis Katsimis, I; **Winner Classe C:** Matteo Meneghello, I; **Winner Classe D:** Imerio Brigliadori, I.

Major Non-Championship Formula 3 Results

2000 Results

The Macau and Changwon races were run after AUTOCOURSE 2000–2001 went to press

FIA F3 WORLD CUP, 47th MACAU GP, Circuito Da Guia, Macau, 19 November. 2 x 15 laps of the 3.803-mile/6.120-km circuit, 114.084 miles/183.600 km.
Aggregated results from two races
1 Andre Couto, MAC (Dallara F399-Opel), 1h 16m 38.486s, 89.312 mph/143.734 km/h; **2** Paolo Montin, I (Dallara F399-Opel), 30 laps; **3** Ryo Fukuda, J (Dallara F399-Renault), 30; **4** Pierre Kaffer, D (Dallara F300-Opel), 30; **5** Enrico Toccacelo, I (Dallara F300-Opel), 30; **6** Tomas Scheckter, ZA (Dallara F399-Opel), 30; **7** Ben Collins, GB (Dallara F300-Opel), 30; **8** Andy Priaulx, GB (Dallara F300-Mugen), 30; **9** Tiago Monteiro, P (Dallara F399-Renault), 30; **10** Patrick Freisacher, A (Dallara F399-Opel), 30.
Fastest race lap: Narain Karthikeyan, IND (Dallara F300-Mugen), 2m 13.253s, 102.737 mph/165.340 km/h.
Fastest qualifying lap: Karthikeyan, 2m 12.887s, 103.020 mph/165.795 km/h.

KOREA SUPER PRIX, Changwon City Raceway, South Korea, 26 November. 25 laps of the 1.892-mile/3.045-km circuit, 47.302 miles/76.125 km.
Aggregated results from two races
1 Narain Karthikeyan, IND (Dallara F300-Mugen), 30m 05.899s, 94.295 mph/151.753 km/h; **2** Tiago Monteiro, P (Dallara F300-Renault), 30m 08.795s; **3** Gianmaria Bruni, I (Dallara F300-Mugen), 30m 17.682s; **4** Patrick Freisacher, A (Dallara F399-Opel), 30m 22.117s; **5** Peter Sundberg, S (Dallara F300-Opel), 30m 25.749s; **6** Andre Couto, MAC (Dallara F399-Opel), 30m 29.393s; **7** Tomas Scheckter, ZA (Dallara F399-Opel), 30m 30.092s; **8** Takuma Sato, J (Dallara F300-Mugen), 30m 30.644s; **9** Sébastien Philippe, F (Dallara F399-

Renault), 30m 32.729s; **10** Enrico Toccacelo, I (Dallara F300-Opel), 30m 32.909s.
Fastest race lap: Bruni, 1m 11.277s, 95.563 mph/153.794 km/h.
Fastest qualifying lap: Karthikeyan, 1m 10.491s, 96.629 mph/155.509 km/h.

2001 Results

61st GRAND AUTOBILE DE PAU, FIA FORMULA 3 EUROPEAN CUP, Circuit de Pau Ville, France. 4 June. 36 laps of the 1.715-mile/2.760-km circuit, 61.739 miles/99.360 km.
1 Anthony Davidson, GB (Dallara F301-Honda), 43m 38.295s, 84.888 mph/136.614 km/h; **2** Ryo Fukuda, J (Dallara F399-Renault), 43m 45.822s; **3** Björn Wirdheim, S (Dallara F301-Opel), 43m 54.405s; **4** Kousuke Matsuura, J (Dallara F301-Opel), 43m 57.223s; **5** Bruno Besson, F (Dallara F399-Renault), 44m 00.070s; **6** Toshihiro Kaneishi, J (Dallara F300-Opel), 44m 04.556s; **7** Matteo Grassotto, I (Dallara F301-Opel), 44m 07.569s; **8** Mathieu Zangarelli, F (Dallara F399-Renault), 44m 27.041s; **9** Kari Mäenpää, FIN (Dallara F399-Opel), 44m 36.790s; **10** Bernhard Auinger, A (Dallara F301-Opel), 44m 37.109s.
Fastest race lap: Davidson, 1m 11.998s, 85.752 mph/138.003 km/h.
Fastest qualifying lap: Davidson, 1m 10.996s, 86.962 mph/139.951 km/h.

FORMULA 3 INTERNATIONAL INVITATION CHALLENGE, Silverstone Grand Prix Circuit, Towcester, Northamptonshire, Great Britain, 15 July. 15 laps of the 3.194-mile/5.141-km circuit, 47.917 miles/77.115 km.
1 Takuma Sato, J (Dallara F301-Mugen), 25m 56.587s, 110.820 mph/178.348 km/h; **2** Anthony Davidson, GB (Dallara F301-Mugen), 26m 07.812s; **3** Andy Priaulx, GB (Dallara F301-Mugen), 26m 22.903s; **4** Ryan Dalziel, GB (Dallara F301-Mugen), 26m 24.151s; **5** Derek Hayes, GB (Dallara F301-Mugen), 26m 24.769s; **6** André Lotterer, D (Dallara F301-Mugen), 26m 25.513s; **7** Bruce Jouanny, F (Dallara F301-Mugen), 26m 26.036s; **8** Jamie Spence, GB (Dallara F301-Mugen), 26m 27.353s; **9** Mark Taylor, GB (Dallara F301-Mugen), 26m 27.981s; **10** Matt Davies, GB (Dallara F301-Opel), 26m 29.824s.
Fastest race lap: Sato, 1m 42.723s, 111.952 mph/180.170 km/h.
Fastest qualifying lap: Sato, 2m 01.876s, 94.359 mph/151.856 km/h.

11th MARLBORO MASTERS OF FORMULA 3, Circuit Park Zandvoort (Grand Prix Circuit), Holland, 5 August. 25 laps of the 2.672-mile/4.300-km circuit, 66.797 miles/107.500 km.
1 Takuma Sato, J (Dallara F301-Mugen), 39m 58.870s, 100.243 mph/161.326 km/h; **2** André Lotterer, D (Dallara F300-Mugen), 40m 08.098s; **3** Anthony Davidson, GB (Dallara F301-Mugen), 40m 08.557s; **4** Gianmaria Bruni, I (Dallara F301-Mugen), 40m 16.151s; **5** Tiago Monteiro, P (Dallara F300-Renault), 40m 16.908s; **6** Mark Taylor, GB (Dallara F300-Mugen), 40m 19.487s; **7** Toshihiro Kaneishi, J (Dallara F300-Opel), 40m 20.848s; **8** Tony Schmidt, D (Dallara F301-TOM'S Toyota), 40m 21.177s; **9** Ryo Fukuda, J (Dallara F399-Renault), 40m 21.860s; **10** Derek Hayes, GB (Dallara F300-Mugen), 40m 25.155s.
Fastest race lap: Sato, 1m 35.240s, 100.996 mph/162.537 km/h.
Fastest qualifying lap: Sato, 1m 33.677s, 102.681 mph/165.249 km/h.

ELF F3 MASTERS, Circuit de Spa-Francorchamps, Stavelot, Belgium, 23 September. 14 laps of the 4.330-mile/6.968-km circuit, 60.616 miles/97.552 km.
1 Anthony Davidson, GB (Dallara F301-Mugen), 37m 20.724s, 97.387 mph/156.729 km/h; **2** Bruce Jouanny, F (Dallara F301-Mugen), 37m 24.178s; **3** Takuma Sato, J (Dallara F301-Mugen), 37m 25.068s; **4** Stefan Mücke, D (Dallara F301-Opel), 37m 29.450s; **5** Raffaele Giammaria, I (Dallara F301-Opel), 37m 31.623s; **6** Tiago Monteiro, P (Dallara F399-Renault), 37m 34.457s; **7** Frank Diefenbacher, D (Dallara F301-Opel), 37m 35.004s; **8** Milos Pavlovic, YU (Dallara F301-Opel), 37m 39.830s; **9** Hannes Lachinger, A (Dallara F301-TOM'S Toyota), 37m 43.678s; **10** Atsushi Katsumata, J (Dallara F300-Mugen), 37m 45.240s.
Fastest race lap: Sato, 2m 14.810s, 115.622 mph/186.075 km/h.
Fastest qualifying lap: Mark Taylor, GB (Dallara F301-Mugen), 2m 13.302s, 116.930 mph/188.180 km/h.

Results of the Macau and Changwon races will be given in AUTOCOURSE 2002–2003

FIA GT Championship

500 KM DI MONZA, Autodromo Nazionale di Monza, Milan, Italy, 1 April. Round 1. 87 laps of the 3.600-mile/5.793-km circuit, 313.165 miles/503.991 km.
1 Jamie Campbell-Walter/Tom Coronel, GB/NL (Lister Storm GT2), 2h 43m 52.839s, 114.656 mph/184.521 km/h (1st GT class); **2** Christophe Bouchut/Jean-Philippe Belloc, F/F (Chrysler Viper GTS-R), 2h 44m 17.857s; **3** Vincent Vosse/Boris Derichebourg, B/F (Chrysler Viper GTS-R), 2h 45m 46.893s; **4** Didier Defourny/Paul Belmondo, B/F (Chrysler Viper GTS-R), 86 laps; **5** Marc Duez/Günther Blieninger, B/D (Ferrari 550 Maranello), 85; **6** Marco Spinelli/Fabio Villa/Gabriele Sabatini, I/I/I (Porsche 911 GT2), 84; **7** Johnny Cecotto/Philipp Peter, YV/A (Porsche 996 GT3-R), 83 (1st N-GT class); **8** Luca Riccitelli/Dieter Quester, I/A (Porsche 996 GT3-RS), 83; **9** Michel Neugarten/Thierry Perrier, B/F (Porsche 996 GT3-R), 83; **10** Fabio Babini/Luigi Moccia, I/I (Porsche 996 GT3-R), 83.
Fastest race lap: Coronel, 1m 47.545s, 120.494 mph/193.917 km/h.
Pole position: Bouchut, 1m 48.287s, 119.669 mph/192.588 km/h.

FIA GT CHAMPIONSHIP, Automotodrom Brno, Brno, Czech Republic, 16 April. Round 2. 77 laps of the 3.357-mile/5.403-km circuit, 258.510 miles/416.031 km.
1 Christophe Bouchut/Jean-Philippe Belloc, F/F (Chrysler Viper GTS-R), 3h 00m 18.210s, 86.025 mph/138.444 km/h (1st GT class); **2** Vincent Vosse/Boris Derichebourg, B/F (Chrysler Viper GTS-R), 3h 00m 36.973s; **3** Mike Hezemans/Jeroen Bleekemolen, NL/NL (Chrysler Viper GTS-R), 3h 01m 18.837s; **4** Jamie Campbell-Walter/Richard Dean, GB/GB (Lister Storm GT2), 3h 01m 46.889s; **5** Emanuele Naspetti/Domenico 'Mimmo' Schiattarella, I/I (Ferrari 550 Maranello), 76 laps; **6** Marc Duez/Günther Blieninger, B/D (Ferrari 550 Maranello), 75; **7** Didier Defourney/Paul Belmondo, B/F (Chrysler Viper GTS-R), 75; **8** Wim Daems/Tamas Illes, B/H (Chrysler Viper GTS-RS), 75; **9** Luca Riccitelli/Dieter Quester, I/A (Porsche 996 GT3-RS), 75 (1st N-GT class); **10** David Terrien/Christian Pescatori, F/I (Ferrari 360 Modena), 75.
Fastest race lap: Campbell-Walter/Dean, 2m 02.037s, 99.037 mph/159.384 km/h.
Pole position: Emmanuel Clérico/Anthony Kumpen, F/B (Chrysler Viper GTS-R), 2m 02.739s, 98.470 mph/158.473 km/h.

FIA GT CHAMPIONSHIP, Circuit de Nevers, Magny-Cours, France, 1 May. Round 3. 107 laps of the 2.641-mile/4.251-km circuit, 282.635 miles/454.857 km.
1 Jamie Campbell-Walter/Tom Coronel, GB/NL (Lister Storm GT2), 3h 00m 15.125s, 94.080 mph/151.407 km/h (1st GT class); **2** Christophe Bouchut/Jean-Philippe Belloc, F/F (Chrysler Viper GTS-R), 3h 01m 28.759s; **3** Vincent Vosse/Boris Derichebourg, B/F (Chrysler Viper GTS-R), 106 laps; **4** Emanuele Naspetti/Domenico 'Mimmo' Schiattarella, I/I (Ferrari 550 Maranello), 105; **5** Julian Bailey/Nicolaus Springer, GB/D (Lister Storm GT2), 105; **6** Sebastiaan Bleekemolen/Michael Beekemolen, NL/NL (Chrysler Viper GTS-R), 105; **7** Marc Duez/Günther Blieninger, B/D (Ferrari 550 Maranello), 104; **8** Luca Cappellari/Gabriele Matteuzzi, I/I (Chrysler Viper GTS-R), 103; **9** David Terrien/Christian Pescatori, F/I (Ferrari 360 Modena), 102 (1st N-GT class); **10** Luca Riccitelli/Dieter Quester, I/A (Porsche 996 GT3-RS), 102.
Fastest race lap: Mike Hezemans/Jeroen Bleekemolen, NL/NL (Chrysler Viper GTS-R), 1m 36.751s, 98.285 mph/158.175 km/h.
Pole position: Bouchut, 1m 43.570s, 91.814 mph/147.761 km/h.

SILVERSTONE 500, Silverstone Grand Prix Circuit, Towcester, Northamptonshire, Great Britain, 13 May. Round 4. 93 laps of the 3.194-mile/5.141-km circuit, 297.086 miles/478.113 km.
1 Christophe Bouchut/Jean-Philippe Belloc, F/F (Chrysler Viper GTS-R), 3h 00m 37.761s, 98.684 mph/158.816 km/h (1st GT class); **2** Sebastiaan Bleekemolen/Michael Beekemolen, NL/NL (Chrysler Viper GTS-R), 3h 01m 01.409s; **3** Anthony Kumpen/Claudio-Yves Gosselin, B/F (Chrysler Viper GTS-R), 3h 01m 01.918s; **4** Vincent Vosse/Boris Derichebourg, B/F (Chrysler Viper GTS-R), 3h 01m 33.019s; **5** Emanuele Naspetti/Domenico 'Mimmo' Schiattarella, I/I (Ferrari 550 Maranello), 92 laps; **6** Emmanuel Clérico/Didier Defourny, F/B (Chrysler Viper GTS-R), 91; **7** David Terrien/Christian Pescatori, F/I (Ferrari 360 Modena), 91 (1st N-GT class); **8** Luca Cappellari/Gabriele Matteuzzi, I/I (Chrysler Viper GTS-R), 91; **9** Fabio Babini/Luigi Moccia, I/I (Porsche 996 GT3-R), 91; **10** François Lafon/Jean-Pierre Jarier, F/F (Chrysler Viper GTS-R), 90.
Fastest race lap: Jamie Campbell-Walter, GB (Lister Storm GT2), 1m 49.625s, 104.904 mph/168.826 km/h.
Pole position: Mike Hezemans, NL (Chrysler Viper GTS-R), 1m 48.575s, 105.918 mph/170.459 km/h.

ZOLDER 500KM, Omloop van Zolder, Hasselt, Belgium, 20 May. Round 5. 111 laps of the 2.471-mile/3.977-km circuit, 274.302 miles/441.447 km.
1 Christophe Bouchut/Jean-Philippe Belloc, F/F (Chrysler Viper GTS-R), 3h 00m 15.188s, 91.306 mph/146.942 km/h (1st GT class); **2** Mike Hezemans/Jeroen Bleekemolen, NL/NL (Chrysler Viper GTS-R), 3h 00m 32.458s; **3** Marc Duez/Günther Blieninger, B/D (Ferrari 550 Maranello), 3h 00m 35.052s; **4** Claudio-Yves Gosselin/Paul Belmondo, F/F (Chrysler Viper GTS-R), 109 laps; **5** François Lafon/Jean-Pierre Jarier, F/F (Chrysler Viper GTS-R), 109; **6** Luca Cappellari/Gabriele Matteuzzi, I/I (Chrysler Viper GTS-R), 109; **7** Fabio Babini/Luigi Moccia, I/I (Porsche 996 GT3-R), 108 (1st N-GT class); **8** Wolfgang Kaufmann/Stéphane Ortelli, D/MC (Porsche 996 GT3-R), 108; **9** Luca Riccitelli/Andrea Boldrini, I (Porsche 996 GT3-RS), 108; **10** Michel Neugarten/Thierry Perrier, B/F (Porsche 996 GT3-R), 107.
Jamie Campbell-Walter/Tom Coronel, GB/NL (Lister Storm GT2), finished 1st but were disqualified for car failing airbox test.
Fastest race lap: Hezemans/Bleekemolen, 1m 31.348s, 97.389 mph/156.732 km/h.
Pole position: Emanuele Naspetti, I (Ferrari 550 Maranello), 1m 30.994s, 97.768 mph/157.342 km/h.

BUDAPEST 500KM, Hungaroring, Mogyorod, Budapest, Hungary, 1 July. Round 6. 102 laps of the 2.470-mile/3.975-km circuit, 251.935 miles/405.450 km.
1 Mike Hezemans/Jeroen Bleekemolen, NL/NL (Chrysler Viper GTS-R), 3h 01m 18.317s, 83.374 mph/134.177 km/h (1st GT class); **2** Christophe Bouchut/Jean-Philippe Belloc, F/F (Chrysler Viper GTS-R), 3h 02m 39.963s; **3** Sebastiaan Bleekemolen/Michael Beekemolen, NL/NL (Chrysler Viper GTS-R), 101 laps; **4** Nicolaus Springer/Julian Bailey, D/GB (Lister Storm GT2), 101; **5** Vincent Vosse/Boris Derichebourg, B/F (Chrysler Viper GTS-R), 101; **6** Anthony Kumpen/Didier Defourny, B/B (Chrysler Viper GTS-R), 101; **7** David Terrien/Christian Pescatori, F/I (Ferrari 360 Modena), 100 (1st N-GT class); **8** Patrice Goueslard/Sébastien Dumez, F/F (Porsche 996 GT3-RS), 100; **9** François Lafon/Jean-Pierre Jarier, F/F (Chrysler Viper GTS-R), 100; **10** Fabio Babini/Luigi Moccia, I/I (Porsche 996 GT3-R), 99.
Fastest race lap: Springer/Bailey, 1m 39.068s, 89.755 mph/144.446 km/h.
Pole position: Hezemans, 1m 38.186s, 90.561 mph/145.744 km/h.

SPA-FRANCORCHAMPS 24-HOURS, Circuit de Spa-Francorchamps, Stavelot, Belgium, 4-5 August. Round 7. 528 laps of the 4.330-mile/6.968-km circuit, 2286.089 miles/3679.104 km.
1 Christophe Bouchut/Jean-Philippe Belloc/Marc Duez, F/F/B (Chrysler Viper GTS-R), 24h 02m 47.0s, 95.070 mph/153.000 km/h (1st GT class); **2** Sébastien Bourdais/Patrice Goueslard/Sébastien Dumez, F/F/F (Chrysler Viper GTS-R), 523 laps; **3** Eric de Doncker/Vincent Dupont/Robert Dierick, B/B/B (Chrysler Viper GTS-R), 521; **4** Eric Hélary/Vincent Vosse/Emmanuel Clérico, F/B/F (Chrysler Viper GTS-R), 516; **5** Luca Riccitelli/Norman Simon/Dieter Quester/Antonio Garcia, I/D/A/E (Porsche 996 GT3-RS), 511 (1st N-GT class); **6** Stéphane Ortelli/Cyrille Sauvage/Andrea Chiesa, MC/F/CH (Porsche 996 GT3-RS), 508; **7** Michel Neugarten/Thierry Perrier/Kurt Thiers, B/F/MC (Porsche 996 GT3-RS), 502; **8** Claudio-Yves Gosselin/Paul Belmondo/Anthony Kumpen, F/F/B (Chrysler Viper GTS-R), 501; **9** Wim Daems/Bert Longin/Georg Severich, B/B/B (Chrysler Viper GTS-R), 499; **10** Stéphane de Groodt/Markus Paltalla/Philippe Tollenaire, B/FIN/B (Porsche 996 GT3-R) 499 (1st Grp 2). **Fastest race lap:** Mike Hezemans/Thierry Tassin/Jeroen Bleekemolen, NL/B/NL (Chrysler Viper GTS-R), 2m 23.001s, 108.999 mph/175.417 km/h.
Pole position: Hezemans/Tassin/Bleekemolen (Jeroen), 2m 24.053s, 108.203 mph/174.136 km/h.

FIA GT CHAMPIONSHIP, A1-Ring, Spielberg, Austria, 26 August. Round 8. 115 laps of the 2.688-mile/4.326-km circuit, 309.126 miles/497.490 km.
1 Peter Kox/Rickard Rydell, NL/S (Ferrari 550 Maranello), 3h 00m 09.952s, 102.947 mph/165.677 km/h (1st GT class); **2** Mike Hezemans/Jeroen Bleekemolen, NL/NL (Chrysler Viper GTS-R), 3h 00m 58.477s; **3** Sebastiaan Bleekemolen/Michael Beekemolen, NL/NL (Chrysler Viper GTS-R), 3h 01m 04.380s; **4** Julian Bailey/Nicolaus Springer, GB/D (Lister Storm GT2), 3h 01m 41.417s; **5** Christophe Bouchut/Jean-Philippe Belloc, F/F (Chrysler Viper GTS-R), 113 laps; **6** Paul Belmondo/Christophe-Yves Gosselin/Anthony Kumpen, F/F/B (Chrysler Viper GTS-R), 113; **7** Luca Cappellari/Gabriele Matteuzzi, I/I (Chrysler Viper GTS-R), 111; **8** David Terrien/Christian Pescatori, F/I (Ferrari 360 Modena), 110 (1st N-GT class); **9** Stéphane Ortelli/Ni Amorim, MC/P (Porsche 996 GT3-RS), 109; **10** Patrice Goueslard/Sébastien Dumez, F/F (Porsche 996 GT3-RS), 109.
Fastest race lap: Jamie Campbell-Walter/Tom Coronel, GB/NL (Lister Storm GT2), 1m 30.364s, 107.089 mph/172.343 km/h.
Pole position: Rydell, 1m 30.856s, 106.509 mph/171.410 km/h.

FIA GT CHAMPIONSHIP, Nürburgring Grand Prix Circuit, Nürburg/Eifel, Germany, 9 September. Round 9. 97 laps of the 2.831-mile/4.556-km circuit, 274.604 miles/441.932 km.
1 Jamie Campbell-Walter/Mike Jordan, GB/GB (Lister Storm GT2), 3h 00m 19.824s, 91.367 mph/147.041 km/h (1st GT class); **2** Mike Hezemans/Jeroen Bleekemolen, NL/NL (Chrysler Viper GTS-R), 3h 00m 36.464s; **3** Peter Kox/Rickard Rydell, NL/S (Ferrari 550 Maranello), 3h 01m 28.640s; **4** Vincent Vosse/Boris Derichebourg, B/F (Chrysler Viper GTS-R), 96 laps; **5** Paul Belmondo/Christophe-Yves Gosselin/Anthony Kumpen, F/F/B (Chrysler Viper GTS-R), 96; **6** Julian Bailey/Nicolaus Springer, GB/D (Lister Storm GT2), 95; **7** Christophe Bouchut/Jean-Philippe Belloc, F/F (Chrysler Viper GTS-R), 95; **8** François Lafon/Jean-Pierre Jarier, F/F (Chrysler Viper GTS-R), 94; **9** Philipp Peter/Marco Werner, A/D (Porsche 996 GT3-R), 94 (1st N-GT class); **10** Stéphane Ortelli/Robin Liddell, MC/GB (Porsche 996 GT3-RS), 94.
Fastest race lap: Bailey/Springer, 1m 40.252s, 101.659 mph/163.604 km/h.
Pole position: Rydell, 1m 39.651s, 102.272 mph/164.590 km/h.

FIA GT CHAMPIONSHIP, Circuito del Jarama, San Sebastián de los Reyes, Madrid, Spain, 30 September. Round 10. 111 laps of the 2.392-mile/3.850-km circuit, 265.543 miles/427.350 km.
1 Rickard Rydell/Alain Menu, S/CH (Ferrari 550 Maranello), 3h 01m 08.928s, 87.953 mph/141.547 km/h (1st GT class); **2** Vincent Vosse/Boris Derichebourg, B/F (Chrysler Viper GTS-R), 3h 01m 53.304s; **3** Anthony Kumpen/Emmanuel Clérico, B/F (Chrysler Viper GTS-R), 3h 02m 22.277s; **4** Christophe Bouchut/Jean-Philippe Belloc, F/F (Chrysler Viper GTS-R), 3h 02m 25.989s; **5** Julian Bailey/Nicolaus Springer, GB/D (Lister Storm GT2), 110 laps; **6** Paul Belmondo/Christophe-Yves Gosselin, F/F (Chrysler Viper GTS-R), 109; **7** David Terrien/Christian Pescatori, F/I (Ferrari 360 Modena), 109 (1st N-GT class); **8** Luca Riccitelli/Dieter Quester, I/A (Porsche 996 GT3-RS), 109; **9** Wim Daems/Eric Geboers, B/B (Chrysler Viper GTS-R), 108; **10** Fabio Babini/Luigi Moccia, I/I (Porsche 996 GT3-R), 108.
Fastest race lap: Bouchut/Belloc, 1m 32.399s, 93.207 mph/150.002 km/h.
Pole position: Bouchut, 1m 32.630s, 92.974 mph/149.628 km/h.

FIA GT CHAMPIONSIP, Autódromo Fernanda Pires da Silva, Alcabideche, Estoril, Portugal, 21 October. Round 11. 90 laps of the 2.599-mile/4.182-km circuit, 233.872 miles/376.380 km.
1 Mike Hezemans/Jeroen Bleekemolen, NL/NL (Chrysler Viper GTS-R), 3h 01m 09.529s, 77.459 mph/124.657 km/h (1st GT class); **2** Jamie Campbell-Walter/Bobby Verdon-Roe, GB/GB (Lister Storm GT2), 3h 01m 36.899s; **3** Christophe Bouchut/Jean-Philippe Belloc/Tiago Monteiro, F/F/P (Chrysler Viper GTS-R), 3h 03m 02.145s; **4** Sebastiaan Bleekemolen/Michael Beekemolen, NL/NL (Chrysler Viper GTS-R), 89 laps; **5** Oliver Gavin/Peter Kox, GB/NL (Lamborghini Diablo GT), 89; **6** Michel Neugarten/Thierry Perrier, B/F (Porsche 996 GT3-RS), 88 (1st N-GT class); **7** Louis Marques/Claudio-Yves Gosselin, P/F (Chrysler Viper GTS-R), 88; **8** Patrice Goueslard/Sébastien Dumez, F/F (Porsche 996 GT3-RS), 88; **9** David Terrien/Christian Pescatori, F/I (Ferrari 360 Modena), 87; **10** Julian Bailey/Nicolaus Springer, GB/D (Lister Storm GT2), 87.
Fastest race lap: Campbell-Walter/Verdon-Roe, 1m 40.186s, 93.375 mph/150.272 km/h.
Pole position: Antonio Garcia, E (Porsche 996 GT3-R), 1m 45.694s, 88.509 mph/142.441 km/h.

Final Championship points

GT Class
Drivers
1= Christophe Bouchut, F, 77; **1=** Jean-Philippe Belloc, F, 77; **3=** Mike Hezemans, NL, 42; **3=** Jeroen Bleekemolen, NL, 42; **5** Jamie Campbell-Walter, GB, 39; **6** Vincent Vosse, B, 34; **7** Boris Derichebourg, F, 28; **8** Marc Duez, B, 27; **9** Rickard Rydell, S, 24; **10** Tom Coronel, NL, 20; **11=** Michael Beekemolen, NL, 18; **11=** Sebastiaan Bleekemolen, NL, 18; **13=** Anthony Kumpen, B, 16; **13=** Claudio-Yves Gosselin, F, 16; **13=** Peter Kox, NL, 16; **16** Paul Belmondo, F, 14; **17=** Sébastien Bourdais, F, 12; **17=** Patrice Goueslard, F, 12; **17=** Sébastien Dumez, F, 12; **20=** Julian Bailey, GB, 11; **20=** Nicolaus Springer, D, 11; **20=** Emmanuel Clérico, F, 11; **23=** Alain Menu, CH, 10; **23=** Mike Jordan, GB, 10; **25=** Robert Dierick, B, 8; **25=** Eric de Doncker, B, 8; **25=** Vincent Dupont, B, 8; **28=** Emanuele Naspetti, I, 7; **28=** Domenico 'Mimmo' Schiattarella, I, 7; **28=** Günther Blieninger, D, 7.

Teams
1 Larbre Compétition Chereau, F, 89; **2** Team Carsport Holland, NL, 60; **3** Lister Storm Racing, GB, 50; **4** Paul Belmondo Racing, F, 46; **5** Prodrive Allstars, GB, 24; **6** Team Rafanelli, I, 14; **7** Paul Belmondo Compétition, F, 13; **8** Silver Racing, B, 8; **9=** Reiter Engineering, D, 2; **9=** GLPK Racing, B, 2; **9=** Team ART, F, 2; **12=** Racing Box, I, 1; **12=** Redolfi Orlando, I, 1.

N-GT Class
Drivers
1= David Terrien, F, 60; **1=** Christian Pescatori, I, 60; **3** Luca Riccitelli, I, 57; **4** Dieter Quester, A, 52; **5=** Thierry Perrier, F, 36; **5=** Michel Neugarten, B, 36; **7** Stéphane Ortelli, MC, 35; **8** Fabio Babini, I, 33; **9** Sébastien Dumez, F, 28; **10** Luigi Moccia, I, 27.

Teams
1= JMB Compétition, F, 62; **1=** RWS Motorsport, D, 62; **3** Freisinger Motorsport, D, 38; **4** ART Engineering, I, 37; **5** Perspective Racing, F, 36.

Other Sports Car Race

69th 24 HEURES DU MANS, Circuit International Du Mans, Les Raineries, Le Mans, France, 16-17 June. 321 laps of the 8.454-mile/13.605-km circuit, 2713.655 miles/4367.205 km.
1 Frank Biela/Emanuele Pirro/Tom Kristensen, D/I/DK (Audi R8), 23h 59m 06.320s, 113.139 mph/182.080 km/h (1st LMP900 class); **2** Rinaldo Capello/Laurent Aiello/Christian Pescatori, I/F/I (Audi R8), 320 laps; **3** Andy Wallace/Eric van de Poele/Butch Leitzinger, GB/B/USA (Bentley EXP Speed 8), 306 (1st LM-GTP class); **4** Olivier Beretta/Karl Wendlinger/Pedro Lamy, MC/A/P (Chrysler-Mopar LMP), 298; **5** Jordi Gené/Jean-Denis Deletraz/Pascal Fabre, E/CH/F (Reynard 2KQ-Lehmann), 284 (1st LM675 class); **6** Gabrio Rosa/Fabio Babini/Luca Drudi, I/I/I (Porsche 996 GT3-RS), 283 (1st GT class); **7** Gunnar Jeanette/Romain Dumas/Philippe Haezebrouck, USA/F/F (Porsche 996 GT3-RS), 282; **8** Ron Fellows/Johnny O'Connell/Scott Pruett, CDN/USA/USA (Chevrolet Corvette C5-R), 278 (1st GTS class); **9** Thierry Perrier/Michel Neugarten/Nigel Smith, F/B/GB (Porsche 996 GT3-RS), 275; **10** Patrice Goueslard/Jean-Luc Chereau/Sébastien Dumez, F/F/F (Porsche 996 GT3-RS), 274; **11** Hideo Fukuyama/Atsushi Yogo/Kazuyuki Nishizawa, J/J/J (Porsche 996 GT3-RS), 273; **12** Anthony Burgess/Max Cohen-Olivar/Andrew Bagnall, CDN/MC/NZ (Porsche 996 GT3-RS), 272; **13** Sébastien Bourdais/Jean-Christophe Boullion/Laurent Redon, F/F/F (Courage C60-Peugeot), 271; **14** Franck Fréon/Andy Pilgrim/Kelly Collins, F/USA/USA (Chevrolet Corvette C5-R), 271; **15** Wayne Taylor/Max Angelelli/Christophe Tinseau, ZA/I/F (Cadillac Northstar LMP), 270; **16** Mike Youles/David Warnock/Stephen Day, GB/GB/GB (Porsche 996 GT3-RS), 265; **17** Michel Ligonnet/Luc Alphand/Louis Marques, F/F/F (Porsche 996 GT3-R), 265; **18** Oliver Gavin/Franz Konrad/Terry Borcheller, GB/A/USA (Saleen S7R-Ford), 246; **19** Yojiro Terada/Jean-René de Fournoux/Stéphane Daoudi, J/F/F (WR Peugeot LMP), 245; **20** Jean-Philippe Belloc/Christophe Bouchut/Tiago Monteiro, F/F/P (Chrysler Viper GTS-R), 234; **21** Sylvain Noel/Georges Fourgeois/Jean-Luc Maury-Laribière, F/USA/F (Porsche 996 GT3-RS), 193; **22** Seiji Ara/Masahiko Kondo/Ni Amorim, J/J/P (Chrysler-Mopar LMP), 243 (DNF - engine); **23** Johnny Mowlem/Bruno Lambert/Ian McKellar, GB/USA/GB (Saleen S7R-Ford), 175 (DNF - engine); **24** Jan Lammers/Val Hillebrand/Donny Crevels, NL/B/NL (Dome S101-Judd), 156 (DNF - electrics); **25** Werner Lupberger/Ben Collins/Harri Toivonen, ZA/GB/FIN (Ascari A410-Judd), 134 (DNF - fuel pump); **26** Yannick Dalmas/Franck Montagnay/Stéphane Sarrazin, F/F/F (Chrysler-Mopar LMP), 126 (DNF - engine); **27** Vic Rice/Cort Wagner/Bob Mazzuoccola, USA/USA/USA (Callaway C12-R), 98 (DNF - engine); **28** Didier de Radigues/Sascha Maassen/Hideshi Matsuda, B/D/J (Reynard 01Q-Judd), 95 (DNF - fire); **29** Claudia Hürtgen/Rick Fairbanks/Chris Gleason, D/USA/USA (Lola B2K/40-Nissan), 94 (DNF - engine); **30** Mark Blundell/Julian Bailey/Kevin McGarrity, GB/GB/GB (MG-Lola EX257), 92 (DNF - oil leak); **31** Klaus Graf/Jamie Davies/Gary Formato, D/GB/ZA (Panoz LMP07), 86 (DNF - accident); **32** Jan Magnussen/David Brabham/Franck Lagorce, DK/AUS/F (Panoz LMP07), 85 (DNF - gearbox); **33** Johnny Herbert/Ralf Kelleners/Dider Theys, GB/D/B (Audi R8), 81 (DNF - clutch); **34** John Nielsen/Hiroki Katoh/Casper Elgaard, DK/J/DK (Dome S101-Judd), 66 (DNF - electrics); **35** Xavier Pompidou/Scott Maxwell/Klaas Zwart, F/CDN/NL (Ascari A410-Judd), 66 (DNF - accident); **36** Vincent Vosse/Vanina Ickx/Carl Rosenblad, B/B/S (Chrysler Viper GTS-R), 61 (DNF - accident); **37** Martin Brundle/Stéphane Ortelli/Guy Smith, GB/MC/GB (Bentley EXP Speed 8), 56 (DNF - clutch); **38** Eric Bernard/Emmanuele Collard/Marc Goossens/F/F/B (Cadillac Northstar LMP), 56 (DNF - accident); **39** Philippe Gache/Anthony Beltoise/Jérôme Policand, F/F/F (Courage C60-Judd), 51 (DNF - engine); **40** Anthony Kumpen/Jean-Claude Lagniez/Gregoire de Galzain, B/F/F (Chrysler Viper GTS-R), 44 (DNF - accident); **41** Robin Donovan/Chris MacAllister/Tom Lingner, GB/USA/USA (Porsche 996 GT3-R), 44 (DNF - accident); **42** Didier Cottaz/Emmanuel Clérico/Boris Derichebourg, F/F/F (Courage C60-Peugeot), 42 (DNF - accident damage); **43** Stefan Johansson/Patrick Lemarié/Tom Coronel, S/F/NL (Audi R8), 35 (DNF - electrics); **44** Anthony Reid/Warren Hughes/Jonny Kane, GB/GB/GB (MG-Lola EX257), 30 (DNF - engine); **45** John Graham/Milka Duno/David Murry, CDN/YV/USA (Reynard 01Q-Judd), 4 (DNF - accident damage); **46** Walter Brun/Toni Seiler/Charlie Slater, CH/CH/USA (Saleen S7R-Ford), 4 (DNF - accident damage); **47** David Terrien/Jonathan Cochet/Jean-Philippe Dayraut, F/F/F (Chrysler Viper GTS-R), 4 (DNF - accident); **48** Martin O'Connell/Warren Carway/François Migault, GB/IRL/F (Pilbeam MP84-Nissan), 3 (DNF - accident).
Fastest race lap: Aiello, 3m 39.046s, 138.937 mph/223.597 km/h.
Fastest qualifying lap: Capello, 3m 32.429s, 143.264 mph/230.562 km/h.

FedEx CART Championship Series

TECATE TELMEX MONTERREY GRAND PRIX PRESENTED BY HERDEZ, Parque Fundidora, Monterrey, Nuevo Leon, Mexico, 11 March. Round 1. 78 laps of the 2.104-mile/3.386-km circuit, 164.112 miles/264.113 km.
1 Cristiano da Matta, BR (Lola B01/00-Toyota RV8F), 2h 00m

44.856s, 81.548 mph/131.239 km/h; **2** Gil de Ferran, BR (Reynard 01I-Honda HR-1), 2h 00m 46.838s; **3** Paul Tracy, CDN (Reynard 01I-Honda HR-1), 2h 00m 47.658s; **4** Michael Andretti, USA (Reynard 01I-Honda HR-1), 2h 00m 49.781s; **5** Kenny Bräck, S (Lola B01/00-Ford Cosworth XF), 2h 00m 50.261s; **6** Jimmy Vasser, USA (Reynard 01I-Toyota RV8F), 2h 00m 50.560s; **7** Tony Kanaan, BR (Reynard 01I-Honda HR-1), 2h 00m 51.225s; **8** Helio Castroneves, BR (Reynard 01I-Honda HR-1), 2h 00m 52.094s; **9** Dario Franchitti, GB (Reynard 01I-Honda HR-1), 2h 00m 52.430s; **10** Tora Takagi, J (Reynard 01I-Toyota RV8F), 2h 01m 02.307s.
Most laps led: da Matta, 32.
Fastest qualifying lap: Bräck, 1m 15.244s, 100.665 mph/162.004 km/h.
Championship points: **1** da Matta, 21; **2** de Ferran, 16; **3** Tracy, 14; **4** Andretti, 12; **5** Bräck, 11; **6** Vasser, 8.

TOYOTA GRAND PRIX OF LONG BEACH, Long Beach Street Circuit, California, USA, 8 April. Round 2. 82 laps of the 1.968-mile/3.167-km circuit, 161.376 miles/259.709 km.
1 Helio Castroneves, BR (Reynard 01I-Honda HR-1), 1h 52m 17.779s, 86.223 mph/138.763 km/h; **2** Cristiano da Matta, BR (Lola B01/00-Toyota RV8F), 1h 52m 18.313s; **3** Gil de Ferran, BR (Reynard 01I-Honda HR-1), 1h 52m 19.566s; **4** Paul Tracy, CDN (Reynard 01I-Honda HR-1), 1h 52m 20.214s; **5** Jimmy Vasser, USA (Reynard 01I-Toyota RV8F), 1h 52m 21.121s; **6** Dario Franchitti, GB (Reynard 01I-Honda HR-1), 1h 52m 22.634s; **7** Tony Kanaan, BR (Reynard 01I-Honda HR-1), 1h 52m 23.694s; **8** Nicolas Minassian, F (Lola B01/00-Toyota RV8F), 1h 52m 24.528s; **9** Bruno Junqueira, BR (Lola B01/00-Toyota RV8F), 1h 52m 25.344s; **10** Bryan Herta, USA (Reynard 01I-Ford Cosworth XF), 1h 52m 28.948s.
Most laps led: Castroneves, 82.
Fastest qualifying lap: Castroneves, 1m 08.556s, 103.343 mph/166.315 km/h.
Championship points: **1** da Matta, 37; **2** de Ferran, 30; **3** Castroneves, 27; **4** Tracy, 26; **5** Vasser, 18; **6=** Andretti, 12; **6=** Franchitti, 12; **6=** Kanaan, 12.

FIRESTONE FIREHAWK 600 PRESENTED BY PIONEER, Texas Motor Speedway, Fort Worth, Texas, USA, 29 April, Round 3. 1.482-mile/2.385-km circuit.
Race cancelled due to safety concerns.
Fastest qualifying lap: Kenny Bräck, S (Lola B01/00-Ford Cosworth XF), 22.854s, 233.447 mph/375.697 km/h.

LEHIGH VALLEY GRAND PRIX PRESENTED BY TOYOTA, Nazareth Speedway, Pennsylvania, USA, 6 May. Round 4. 225 laps of the 0.946-mile/1.522-km circuit, 212.850 miles/342.549 km.
1 Scott Dixon, NZ (Reynard 01I-Toyota RV8F), 1h 51m 12.419s, 114.840 mph/184.817 km/h; **2** Kenny Bräck, S (Lola B01/00-Ford Cosworth XF), 1h 51m 12.785s; **3** Paul Tracy, CDN (Reynard 01I-Honda HR-1), 1h 51m 13.763s; **4** Jimmy Vasser, USA (Reynard 01I-Toyota RV8F), 1h 51m 14.163s; **5** Christian Fittipaldi, BR (Lola B01/00-Toyota RV8F), 1h 51m 16.644s; **6** Michael Andretti, USA (Reynard 01I-Honda HR-1), 1h 51m 18.820s; **7** Bruno Junqueira, BR (Lola B01/00-Toyota RV8F), 1h 51m 21.612s; **8** Dario Franchitti, GB (Reynard 01I-Honda HR-1), 1h 51m 21.711s; **9** Oriol Servia, E (Lola B01/00-Ford Cosworth XF), 1h 51m 24.740s; **10** Cristiano da Matta, BR (Lola B01/00-Toyota RV8F), 1h 51m 24.976s.
Most laps led: Bräck, 125.
Fastest qualifying lap: Junqueira, 19.700s, 172.873 mph/278.212 km/h.
Championship points: **1=** da Matta, 40; **1=** Tracy, 40; **3=** de Ferran, 30; **3=** Vasser, 30; **5=** Bräck, 29; **5=** Castroneves, 29.

FIRESTONE FIREHAWK 500, Twin Ring Motegi, Haga gun, Japan, 19 May. Round 5. 201 laps of the 1.548-mile/2.491-km circuit, 311.148 miles/500.744 km.
1 Kenny Bräck, S (Lola B01/00-Ford Cosworth XF), 1h 44m 48.888s, 178.113 mph/286.645 km/h; **2** Helio Castroneves, BR (Reynard 01I-Honda HR-1), 1h 44m 52.538s; **3** Tony Kanaan, BR (Reynard 01I-Honda HR-1), 200 laps; **4** Christian Fittipaldi, BR (Lola B01/00-Toyota RV8F), 200; **5** Jimmy Vasser, USA (Reynard 01I-Toyota RV8F), 200; **6** Massimiliano 'Max' Papis, I (Lola B01/00-Ford Cosworth XF), 200; **7** Alex Zanardi, I (Reynard 01I-Honda HR-1), 199; **8** Shinji Nakano, J (Reynard 01I-Honda HR-1), 199; **9** Scott Dixon, NZ (Reynard 01I-Toyota RV8F), 198; **10** Roberto Moreno, BR (Reynard 01I-Toyota RV8F), 198.
Most laps led: Castroneves, 84.
Fastest qualifying lap: Castroneves, 25.849s, 215.591 mph/ 346.959 km/h.
Championship points: **1** Bräck, 49; **2** Castroneves, 47; **3=** da Matta, 40; **3=** Tracy, 40; **3=** Vasser, 40; **6** de Ferran, 30.

MILLER LITE 225, The Milwaukee Mile, Wisconsin State Fair Park, West Allis, Milwaukee, Wisconsin, USA, 3 June. Round 6. 225 laps of the 1.032-mile/1.661-km circuit, 232.200 miles/ 373.690 km.
1 Kenny Bräck, S (Lola B01/00-Ford Cosworth XF), 1h 54m 08.097s, 122.066 mph/196.446 km/h; **2** Michael Andretti, USA (Reynard 01I-Honda HR-1), 1h 54m 09.404s; **3** Scott Dixon, NZ (Reynard 01I-Toyota RV8F), 1h 54m 11.098s; **4** Bruno Junqueira, BR (Lola B01/00-Toyota RV8F), 1h 54m 14.811s; **5** Adrian Fernandez, MEX (Reynard 01I-Honda HR-1), 1h 54m 17.799s; **6** Tony Kanaan, BR (Reynard 01I-Honda HR-1), 1h 54m 18.388s; **7** Gil de Ferran, BR (Reynard 01I-Honda HR-1), 1h 54m 20.918s; **8** Massimiliano 'Max' Papis, I (Lola B01/00-Ford Cosworth XF), 1h 54m 25.877s; **9** Dario Franchitti, GB (Reynard 01I-Honda HR-1), 224 laps; **10** Mauricio Gugelmin, BR (Reynard 01I-Toyota RV8F), 224.
Most laps led: Bräck, 130.
Pole position: Bräck (qualifying rained out).
Championship points: **1** Bräck, 70; **2** Castroneves, 47; **3=** da Matta, 40; **3=** Tracy, 40; **3=** Vasser, 40; **6** Dixon, 38.

TENNECO AUTOMOTIVE GRAND PRIX OF DETROIT, The Raceway on Belle Isle, Detroit, Michigan, USA, 17 June. Round 7. 72 laps of the 2.346-mile/3.776-km circuit, 168.912 miles/271.838 km.
1 Helio Castroneves, BR (Reynard 01I-Honda HR-1), 1h 53m 51.815s, 89.008 mph/143.244 km/h; **2** Dario Franchitti, GB (Reynard 01I-Honda HR-1), 1h 53m 52.517s; **3** Roberto Moreno, BR (Reynard 01I-Toyota RV8F), 1h 53m 54.706s; **4** Michael Andretti, USA (Reynard 01I-Honda HR-1), 1h 53m 55.201s; **5** Christian Fittipaldi, BR (Lola B01/00-Toyota RV8F), 1h 54m 05.280s; **6** Gil de Ferran, BR (Reynard 01I-Honda HR-1), 1h 54m 06.392s; **7** Cristiano da Matta, BR (Lola B01/00-Toyota RV8F), 1h 54m 06.899s; **8** Patrick Carpentier, CDN (Reynard 01I-Ford Cosworth XF), 1h 54m 07.644s; **9** Kenny Bräck, S (Lola B01/00-Ford Cosworth XF), 1h 54m 08.135s; **10** Mauricio Gugelmin, BR (Reynard 01I-Toyota RV8F), 1h 54m 11.490s.
Most laps led: Castroneves, 72.
Fastest qualifying lap: Castroneves, 1m 13.499s, 114.908 mph/184.926 km/h.
Championship points: **1** Bräck, 74; **2** Castroneves, 69; **3** Andretti, 48; **4** da Matta, 46; **5** de Ferran, 44; **6=** Tracy, 40; **6=** Vasser, 40.

FREIGHTLINER/G.I.JOE'S 200 PRESENTED BY TEXACO, Portland International Raceway, Oregon, USA, 24 June. Round 8. 76 laps of the 1.969-mile/3.169-km circuit, 149.644 miles/240.829 km.
Race scheduled for 98 laps but stopped prematurely due to rain and the 2-hour limit.
1 Massimiliano 'Max' Papis, I (Lola B01/00-Ford Cosworth XF), 2h 00m 20.836s, 74.606 mph/120.067 km/h; **2** Roberto Moreno, BR (Reynard 01I-Toyota RV8F), 2h 00m 22.308s; **3** Christian Fittipaldi, BR (Lola B01/00-Toyota RV8F), 2h 00m 24.448s; **4** Max Wilson, BR (Lola B01/00-Ford Cosworth XF), 2h 00m 32.312s; **5** Patrick Carpentier, CDN (Reynard 01I-Ford Cosworth XF), 2h 00m 32.875s; **6** Dario Franchitti, GB (Reynard 01I-Honda HR-1), 2h 00m 33.407s; **7** Scott Dixon, NZ (Reynard 01I-Toyota RV8F), 2h 00m 33.977s; **8** Michael Andretti, USA (Reynard 01I-Honda HR-1), 2h 00m 34.676s; **9** Oriol Servia, E (Lola B01/00-Ford Cosworth XF), 2h 00m 40.012s; **10** Cristiano da Matta, BR (Lola B01/00-Toyota RV8F), 2h 00m 40.454s.
Most laps led: Massimiliano 'Max' Papis, I (Lola B01/00-Ford Cosworth XF), 69.
Fastest qualifying lap: Papis, 57.785s, 122.669 mph/197.416 km/h.
Championship points: **1** Bräck, 76; **2** Castroneves, 69; **3** Andretti, 53; **4** da Matta, 49; **5** Fittipaldi, 46; **6** Franchitti, 45.

MARCONI GRAND PRIX OF CLEVELAND PRESENTED BY FIRSTAR, Burke Lakefront Airport Circuit, Cleveland, Ohio, USA, 1 July. Round 9. 100 laps of the 2.106-mile/3.389-km circuit, 210.600 miles/338.928 km.
1 Dario Franchitti, GB (Reynard 01I-Honda HR-1), 1h 47m 04.723s, 118.007 mph/189.913 km/h; **2** Memo Gidley, USA (Lola B01/00-Toyota RV8F), 1h 47m 05.028s; **3** Bryan Herta, USA (Reynard 01I-Ford Cosworth XF), 1h 47m 12.620s; **4** Gil de Ferran, BR (Reynard 01I-Honda HR-1), 1h 47m 16.793s; **5** Jimmy Vasser, USA (Reynard 01I-Toyota RV8F), 1h 47m 26.021s; **6** Kenny Bräck, S (Lola B01/00-Ford Cosworth XF), 1h 47m 26.784s; **7** Cristiano da Matta, BR (Lola B01/00-Toyota RV8F), 1h 47m 32.262s; **8** Roberto Moreno, BR (Reynard 01I-Toyota RV8F), 1h 47m 32.831s; **9** Alex Tagliani, CDN (Reynard 01I-Ford Cosworth XF), 1h 47m 35.099s; **10** Mauricio Gugelmin, BR (Reynard 01I-Toyota RV8F), 1h 47m 36.561s.
Most laps led: Gidley, 57.
Fastest qualifying lap: Gugelmin, 57.356s, 132.185 mph/212.731 km/h.
Championship points: **1** Bräck, 84; **2** Castroneves, 70; **3** Franchitti, 65; **4** de Ferran, 56; **5** da Matta, 55; **6** Andretti, 53.

MOLSON INDY TORONTO, Canada National Exhibition Place Circuit, Toronto, Ontario, Canada, 15 July. Round 10. 95 laps of the 1.755-mile/2.824-km circuit, 166.725 miles/268.318 km.
1 Michael Andretti, USA (Reynard 01I-Honda HR-1), 1h 59m 58.904s, 83.375 mph/134.179 km/h; **2** Alex Tagliani, CDN (Reynard 01I-Ford Cosworth XF), 2h 00m 01.645s; **3** Adrian Fernandez, MEX (Reynard 01I-Honda HR-1), 2h 00m 03.299s; **4** Alex Zanardi, I (Reynard 01I-Honda HR-1), 2h 00m 03.805s; **5** Scott Dixon, NZ (Reynard 01I-Toyota RV8F), 2h 00m 04.508s; **6** Paul Tracy, CDN (Reynard 01I-Honda HR-1), 2h 00m 05.797s; **7** Mauricio Gugelmin, BR (Reynard 01I-Toyota RV8F), 2h 00m 07.040s; **8** Massimiliano 'Max' Papis, I (Lola B01/00-Ford Cosworth XF), 2h 00m 09.287s; **9** Shinji Nakano, J (Reynard 01I-Honda HR-1), 2h 00m 14.720s; **10** Tony Kanaan, BR (Reynard 01I-Honda HR-1), 94 laps (DNF - mechanical).
Most laps led: Gil de Ferran, BR (Reynard 01I-Honda HR-1), 49.
Fastest qualifying lap: de Ferran, 57.703s, 109.492 mph/176.210 km/h.
Championship points: **1** Bräck, 84; **2** Andretti, 73; **3** Castroneves, 70; **4** Franchitti, 65; **5** de Ferran, 58; **6** da Matta, 55.

HARRAH'S 500 PRESENTED BY TOYOTA, Michigan International Speedway, Brooklyn, Michigan, USA, 22 July. Round 11. 250 laps of the 2.000-mile/3.219-km circuit, 500.000 miles/804.672 km.
1 Patrick Carpentier, CDN (Reynard 01I-Ford Cosworth XF), 2h 54m 55.757s, 171.498 mph/275.999 km/h; **2** Dario Franchitti, GB (Reynard 01I-Honda HR-1), 2h 54m 56.000s; **3** Michel Jourdain Jr., USA (Lola B01/00-Ford Cosworth XF), 2h 54m 56.000s; **4** Cristiano da Matta, BR (Lola B01/00-Toyota RV8F), 2h 54m 56.202s; **5** Bryan Herta, USA (Reynard 01I-Ford Cosworth XF), 2h 54m 56.273s; **6** Alex Tagliani, CDN (Reynard 01I-Ford Cosworth XF), 249 laps; **7** Paul Tracy, CDN (Reynard 01I-Honda HR-1), 249; **8** Helio Castroneves, BR (Reynard 01I-Honda HR-1), 249; **9** Bruno Junqueira, BR (Lola B01/00-Toyota RV8F), 249; **10** Scott Dixon, NZ (Reynard 01I-Toyota RV8F), 248.
Most laps led: Papis, 83.
Fastest qualifying lap: Kenny Bräck, S (Lola B01/00-Ford Cosworth XF), 31.330s, 229.812 mph/369.846 km/h.
Championship points: **1** Bräck, 84; **2** Franchitti, 81; **3** Castroneves, 75; **4** Andretti, 73; **5** da Matta, 67; **6** de Ferran, 58.

TARGET GRAND PRIX PRESENTED BY ENERGIZER, Chicago Motor Speedway, Cicero, Illinois, USA, 29 July. Round 12. 225 laps of the 1.029-miles/1.656-km circuit, 231.525 miles/372.603 km.
1 Kenny Bräck, S (Lola B01/00-Ford Cosworth XF), 1h 45m 12.835s, 132.031 mph/212.483 km/h; **2** Patrick Carpentier, CDN (Reynard 01I-Ford Cosworth XF), 1h 45m 17.315s; **3** Gil de Ferran, BR (Reynard 01I-Honda HR-1), 1h 45m 18.025s; **4** Scott Dixon, NZ (Reynard 01I-Toyota RV8F), 1h 45m 18.398s; **5** Memo Gidley, USA (Lola B01/00-Toyota RV8F), 1h 45m 22.486s; **6** Alex Tagliani, CDN (Reynard 01I-Ford Cosworth XF), 1h 45m 25.872s; **7** Helio Castroneves, BR (Reynard 01I-Honda HR-1), 1h 45m 26.432s; **8** Tony Kanaan, BR (Reynard 01I-Honda HR-1), 1h 45m 27.393s; **9** Alex Zanardi, I (Reynard 01I-Honda HR-1), 1h 45m 29.992s; **10** Adrian Fernandez, MEX (Reynard 01I-Honda HR-1), 1h 45m 33.749s.
Most laps led: Castroneves, 68.
Fastest qualifying lap: Kanaan, 23.145s, 160.052 mph/257.578 km/h.
Championship points: **1** Bräck, 104; **2** Castroneves, 82; **3** Franchitti, 81; **4** Andretti, 73; **5** de Ferran, 72; **6** Dixon, 69.

MILLER LITE 200, Mid-Ohio Sports Car Course, Lexington, Ohio, USA, 12 August. Round 13. 83 laps of the 2.258-mile/3.634-km circuit, 186.450 miles/300.062 km.
1 Helio Castroneves, BR (Reynard 01I-Honda HR-1), 1h 44m 54.931s, 106.629 mph/171.602 km/h; **2** Gil de Ferran, BR (Reynard 01I-Honda HR-1), 1h 44m 55.499s; **3** Patrick Carpentier, CDN (Reynard 01I-Ford Cosworth XF), 1h 44m 57.479s; **4** Paul Tracy, CDN (Reynard 01I-Honda HR-1), 1h 45m 00.257s; **5** Tony Kanaan, BR (Reynard 01I-Honda HR-1), 1h 45m 01.086s; **6** Roberto Moreno, BR (Reynard 01I-Toyota RV8F), 1h 45m 01.634s; **7** Alex Tagliani, CDN (Reynard 01I-Ford Cosworth XF), 1h 45m 02.468s; **8** Christian Fittipaldi, BR (Lola B01/00-Toyota RV8F), 1h 45m 06.252s; **9** Oriol Servia, E (Lola B01/00-Ford Cosworth XF), 1h 45m 09.492s; **10** Cristiano da Matta, BR (Lola B01/00-Toyota RV8F), 1h 45m 10.178s.
Most laps led: Castroneves, 44.
Fastest qualifying lap: de Ferran, 1m 05.442s, 124.214 mph/199.903 km/h.
Championship points: **1** Bräck, 104; **2** Castroneves, 103; **3** de Ferran, 89; **4** Franchitti, 81; **5** Andretti, 73; **6=** da Matta, 70; **6=** Dixon, 70.

MOTOROLA 220, Road America Circuit, Elkhart Lake, Wisconsin, USA, 19 August. Round 14. 45 laps of the 4.048-mile/6.515-km circuit, 182.160 miles/293.158 km.
Race stopped at 2-hour limit.
1 Bruno Junqueira, BR (Lola B01/00-Toyota RV8F), 2h 00m 28.453s, 90.721 mph/146.002 km/h; **2** Michael Andretti, USA (Reynard 01I-Honda HR-1), 2h 00m 31.140s; **3** Adrian Fernandez, MEX (Reynard 01I-Honda HR-1), 2h 00m 38.462s; **4** Scott Dixon, NZ (Reynard 01I-Toyota RV8F), 2h 00m 42.866s; **5** Gil de Ferran, BR (Reynard 01I-Honda HR-1), 2h 00m 43.537s; **6** Cristiano da Matta, BR (Lola B01/00-Toyota RV8F), 2h 00m 44.387s; **7** Helio Castroneves, BR (Reynard 01I-Honda HR-1), 2h 00m 45.392s; **8** Alex Tagliani, CDN (Reynard 01I-Ford Cosworth XF), 2h 00m 46.082s; **9** Patrick Carpentier, CDN (Reynard 01I-Ford Cosworth XF), 2h 00m 46.301s; **10** Oriol Servia, E (Lola B01/00-Ford Cosworth XF), 2h 00m 47.474s.
Most laps led: Castroneves, 24.
Fastest qualifying lap: Kenny Bräck, S (Lola B01/00-Ford Cosworth XF), 2m 03.531s, 117.969 mph/189.852 km/h.
Championship points: **1** Castroneves, 110; **2** Bräck, 105; **3** de Ferran, 99; **4** Andretti, 89; **5** Dixon, 82; **6** Franchitti, 81.

MOLSON INDY VANCOUVER, Vancouver Street Circuit, Concord Pacific Place, Vancouver, British Columbia, Canada, 2 September. Round 15. 98 laps of the 1.781 mile/2.866-km circuit, 174.538 miles/280.892 km.
1 Roberto Moreno, BR (Reynard 01I-Toyota RV8F), 2h 10m 01.276s, 80.543 mph/129.621 km/h; **2** Gil de Ferran, BR (Reynard 01I-Honda HR-1), 2h 10m 05.963s; **3** Michael Andretti, USA (Reynard 01I-Honda HR-1), 2h 10m 08.247s; **4** Tony Kanaan, BR (Reynard 01I-Honda HR-1), 2h 10m 11.775s; **5** Oriol Servia, E (Lola B01/00-Ford Cosworth XF), 2h 10m 14.773s; **6** Michel Jourdain Jr., USA (Lola B01/00-Ford Cosworth XF), 2h 10m 15.126s; **7** Tora Takagi, J (Reynard 01I-Toyota RV8F), 2h 10m 15.796s; **8** Kenny Bräck, S (Lola B01/00-Ford Cosworth XF), 2h 10m 16.088s; **9** Dario Franchitti, GB (Reynard 01I-Honda HR-1), 2h 10m 16.398s; **10** Memo Gidley, USA (Lola B01/00-Toyota RV8F), 2h 10m 17.500s.
Most laps led: Alex Tagliani, CDN (Reynard 01I-Ford Cosworth XF), 68.
Fastest qualifying lap: Tagliani, 1m 00.872s, 105.329 mph/169.511 km/h.
Championship points: **1** de Ferran, 115; **2=** Castroneves, 110; **2=** Bräck, 110; **4** Andretti, 103; **5** Franchitti, 85; **6** Dixon, 82.

THE AMERICAN MEMORIAL, EuroSpeedway Lausitz, Klettwitz, Dresden, Germany, 15 September. Round 16. 154 laps of the 2.023-mile/3.256-km circuit, 311.542 miles/501.378 km.
1 Kenny Bräck, S (Lola B01/00-Ford Cosworth XF), 2h 00m 20.940s, 155.319 mph/249.962 km/h; **2** Massimiliano 'Max' Papis, I (Lola B01/00-Ford Cosworth XF), 2h 00m 21.094s; **3** Patrick Carpentier, CDN (Reynard 01I-Ford Cosworth XF), 2h 00m 23.744s; **4** Michael Andretti, USA (Reynard 01I-Honda HR-1), 2h 00m 25.639s; **5** Oriol Servia, E (Lola B01/00-Ford Cosworth XF), 2h 00m 26.165s; **6** Tora Takagi, J (Reynard 01I-Toyota RV8F), 2h 00m 27.350s; **7** Tony Kanaan, BR (Reynard 01I-Honda HR-1), 2h 00m 27.587s; **8** Gil de Ferran, BR (Reynard 01I-Honda HR-1), 2h 00m 30.202s; **9** Scott Dixon, NZ (Reynard 01I-Toyota RV8F), 2h 00m 30.833s; **10** Paul Tracy, CDN (Reynard 01I-Honda HR-1), 2h 00m 31.264s.
Most laps led: Bräck, 82.
Pole position: de Ferran (qualifying cancelled due to lack of time - grid based on championship placings).
Championship points: **1** Bräck, 131; **2** de Ferran, 120; **3** Andretti, 115; **4** Castroneves, 111; **5** Dixon, 86; **6** Franchitti, 85.

ROCKINGHAM 500, Rockingham Motor Speedway, Corby, Northamptonshire, Great Britain, 22 September. Round 17. 140 laps of the 1.479-mile/2.380-km, 207.060 miles/333.231 km.
Race shortened due to lack of time.
1 Gil de Ferran, BR (Reynard 01I-Honda HR-1), 1h 20m 59.050s, 153.408 mph/246.886 km/h; **2** Kenny Bräck, S (Lola B01/00-Ford Cosworth XF), 1h 20m 59.684s; **3*** Cristiano da Matta, BR (Lola B01/00-Toyota RV8F), 1h 21m 13.713s; **4*** Helio Castroneves, BR (Reynard 01I-Honda HR-1), 1h 21m 05.385s; **5** Michael Andretti, USA (Reynard 01I-Honda HR-1), 1h 21m 16.106s; **6** Paul Tracy, CDN (Reynard 01I-Honda HR-1), 1h 21m 17.969s; **7** Jimmy Vasser, USA (Reynard 01I-Toyota RV8F), 1h 21m 18.110s; **8** Tony Kanaan, BR (Reynard 01I-Honda HR-1), 1h 21m 18.790s; **9** Dario Franchitti, GB (Reynard 01I-Honda HR-1), 1h 21m 19.331s; **10** Oriol Servia, E (Lola B01/00-Ford Cosworth XF), 1h 21m 25.481s.
* Castroneves finished 3rd but was demoted due to pit lane overtaking.
Most laps led: de Ferran, 84.
Fastest qualifying lap: Kanaan, 24.719s, 215.397 mph/346.638 km/h.
Championship points: **1** Bräck, 147; **2** de Ferran, 141; **3** Andretti, 125; **4** Castroneves, 123; **5** da Matta, 92; **6** Franchitti, 89.

TEXACO/HAVOLINE GRAND PRIX OF HOUSTON, Houston Street Circuit, Texas, USA, 7 October. Round 18. 100 laps of the 1.527-mile/2.457-km circuit, 152.026 miles/244.662 km.
1 Gil de Ferran, BR (Reynard 01I-Honda HR-1), 1h 54m 42.336s, 79.521 mph/127.977 km/h; **2** Dario Franchitti, GB (Reynard 01I-Honda HR-1), 1h 54m 45.766s; **3** Memo Gidley, USA (Lola B01/00-Toyota RV8F), 1h 55m 01.183s; **4** Tora Takagi, J (Reynard 01I-Toyota RV8F), 1h 55m 03.230s; **5** Helio Castroneves, BR (Reynard 01I-Honda HR-1), 1h 55m 04.006s; **6** Cristiano da Matta, BR (Lola B01/00-Toyota RV8F), 1h 55m 05.438s; **7** Kenny Bräck, S (Lola B01/00-Ford Cosworth XF), 1h 55m 11.062s; **8** Christian Fittipaldi, BR (Lola B01/00-Toyota RV8F), 1h 55m 16.757s; **9** Massimiliano 'Max' Papis, I (Lola B01/00-Ford Cosworth XF), 1h 55m 20.634s; **10** Patrick Carpentier, CDN (Reynard 01I-Ford Cosworth XF), 1h 55m 21.219s.
Most laps led: de Ferran, 100.
Fastest qualifying lap: de Ferran, 59.421s, 92.513 mph/148.885 km/h.
Championship points: **1** Bräck, 163; **2** de Ferran, 153; **3** Castroneves, 133; **4** Andretti, 125; **5** Franchitti, 105; **6** da Matta, 100.

HONDA GRAND PRIX OF MONTEREY FEATURING THE SHELL 300, Mazda Raceway Laguna Seca, Monterey, California, USA, 14 October. Round 19. 76 laps of the 2.238-mile/3.602-km circuit, 170.088 miles/273.730 km.
1 Massimiliano 'Max' Papis, I (Lola B01/00-Ford Cosworth XF), 2h 00m 10.589s, 84.919 mph/136.664 km/h; **2** Memo Gidley, USA (Lola B01/00-Toyota RV8F), 2h 00m 11.383s; **3** Gil de Ferran, BR (Reynard 01I-Honda HR-1), 2h 00m 12.027s; **4** Scott Dixon, NZ (Reynard 01I-Toyota RV8F), 2h 00m 12.390s; **5** Jimmy Vasser, USA (Reynard 01I-Toyota RV8F), 2h 00m 13.058s; **6** Helio Castroneves, BR (Reynard 01I-Honda HR-1), 2h 00m 15.022s; **7** Bruno Junqueira, BR (Lola B01/00-Toyota RV8F), 2h 00m 16.216s; **8** Tony Kanaan, BR (Reynard 01I-Honda HR-1), 2h 00m 16.681s; **9** Christian Fittipaldi, BR (Lola B01/00-Toyota RV8F), 2h 00m 17.182s; **10** Adrian Fernandez, MEX (Reynard 01I-Honda HR-1), 2h 00m 17.723s.
Most laps led: de Ferran, 36.
Fastest qualifying lap: de Ferran, 1m 08.596s, 117.453 mph/189.022 km/h.
Championship points: **1** de Ferran, 179; **2** Bräck, 153; **3** Castroneves, 141; **4** Andretti, 125; **5** Franchitti, 105; **6** da Matta, 100.

HONDA INDY 300, Surfers Paradise Street Circuit, Southport, Queensland, Australia, 28 October. Round 20. 65 laps of the 2.795-mile/4.498-km circuit, 181.675 miles/292.378 km.
1 Cristiano da Matta, BR (Lola B01/00-Toyota RV8F), 1h 51m 47.260s, 97.511 mph/156.928 km/h; **2** Michael Andretti, USA (Reynard 01I-Honda HR-1), 1h 51m 53.046s; **3** Alex Tagliani, CDN (Reynard 01I-Ford Cosworth XF), 1h 51m 54.786s; **4** Gil de Ferran, BR (Reynard 01I-Honda HR-1), 1h 52m 08.196s; **5** Kenny Bräck, S (Lola B01/00-Ford Cosworth XF), 1h 52m 09.834s; **6** Jimmy Vasser, USA (Reynard 01I-Toyota RV8F), 1h 52m 11.966s; **7** Michel Jourdain Jr., USA (Lola B01/00-Ford Cosworth XF), 1h 52m 26.752s; **8** Christian Fittipaldi, BR (Lola B01/00-Toyota RV8F), 1h 52m 27.727s; **9** Massimiliano 'Max' Papis, I (Lola B01/00-Ford Cosworth XF), 1h 52m 29.825s; **10** Memo Gidley, USA (Lola B01/00-Toyota RV8F), 1h 52m 30.148s.
Most laps led: Moreno, 24.
Fastest qualifying lap: Roberto Moreno, BR (Reynard 01I-Toyota RV8F), 1m 32.095s, 109.257 mph/175.832 km/h.
Championship points: **1** de Ferran, 191; **2** Bräck, 163; **3=** Castroneves, 141; **3=** Andretti, 141; **5** da Matta, 120; **6** Franchitti, 105.

MARLBORO 500 PRESENTED BY TOYOTA, California Speedway, Fontana, California, USA, 4 November. Round 21. 220 laps of the 2.029-mile/3.265-km circuit, 446.380 miles/718.379 km. Race scheduled for 250 laps but shortened due to lack of time.
1 Cristiano da Matta, BR (Lola B01/00-Toyota RV8F), 2h 59m 39.716s, 149.073 mph/239.910 km/h; **2** Massimiliano 'Max' Papis, I (Lola B01/00-Ford Cosworth XF), 2h 59m 39.839s; **3** Alex Tagliani, CDN (Reynard 01I-Ford Cosworth XF), 2h 59m 40.208s; **4** Bruno Junqueira, BR (Lola B01/00-Toyota RV8F), 2h 59m 40.638s; **5** Tony Kanaan, BR (Reynard 01I-Honda HR-1), 2h 59m 40.902s; **6** Gil de Ferran, BR (Reynard 01I-Honda HR-1), 2h 59m 42.847s; **7** Michael Andretti, USA (Reynard 01I-Honda HR-1), 2h 59m 43.564s; **8** Casey Mears, USA (Reynard 01I-Honda HR-1), 2h 59m 43.722s; **9** Alex Barron, USA (Lola B01/00-Ford Cosworth XF), 2h 59m 44.679s; **10** Patrick Carpentier, CDN (Reynard 01I-Ford Cosworth XF), 2h 59m 45.534s.
Most laps led: Papis, 54.
Fastest qualifying lap: Tagliani, 31.935s, 228.727 mph/368.101 km/h.

Final championship points
1 Gil de Ferran, BR, 199; **2** Kenny Bräck, S, 163; **3** Michael Andretti, USA, 147; **4** Helio Castroneves, BR, 141; **5** Cristiano da Matta, BR, 140; **6** Massimiliano 'Max' Papis, I, 107; **7** Dario Franchitti, GB, 105; **8** Scott Dixon, NZ, 98; **9** Tony Kanaan, BR, 93; **10** Patrick Carpentier, CDN, 91; **11** Alex Tagliani, CDN, 80; **12** Jimmy Vasser, USA, 77; **13** Roberto Moreno, BR, 76; **14** Paul Tracy, CDN, 73; **15** Christian Fittipaldi, BR, 70; **16** Bruno Junqueira, BR, 68; **17** Memo Gidley, USA, 65; **18** Adrian Fernandez, MEX, 45; **19** Oriol Servia, E, 42; **20** Michel Jourdain Jr., MEX, 30; **21** Tora Takagi, J, 29; **22** Bryan Herta, USA, 28; **23** Alex Zanardi, I, 24; **24** Mauricio Gugelmin, BR, 17; **25** Max Wilson, BR, 12; **26** Shinji Nakano, J, 11; **27=** Nicolas Minassian, F, 7; **27=** Casey Mears, USA, 7; **29** Alex Barron, USA, 4; **30** Townsend Bell, USA, 1.

Nation's Cup
1 Brazil, 341; 2 United States, 240; 3 Canada, 187; 4 Sweden, 163; 5 Italy, 118; 6 Scotland, 105; 7 New Zealand, 98; 8 Mexico, 75; 9= Japan, 42; 9= Catalonia (Spain), 42; 11 France, 7.

Manufacturer's Cup (engines)
1 Honda, 342; 2 Toyota, 308; 3 Ford Cosworth, 298.

Constructor's Cup
1 Reynard, 378; 2 Lola, 335.

Rookie of the Year
1 Scott Dixon; **2** Bruno Junqueira; **3** Tora Takagi; **4** Max Wilson; **5** Casey Mears; **6** Nicolas Minassian; **7** Townsend Bell.

Indy Car race

85th INDIANAPOLIS 500, Indianapolis Motor Speedway, Speedway, Indiana, USA, 27 May. 200 laps of the 2.500-mile/4.023-km circuit, 500.000 miles/804.672 km.
1 Helio Castroneves, BR (Dallara-Oldsmobile), 3h 31m 54.180s, 141.574 mph/227.842 km/h; **2** Gil de Ferran, BR (Dallara-Oldsmobile), 3h 31m 55.917s; **3** Michael Andretti, USA (Dallara-Oldsmobile), 3h 31m 59.916s; **4** Jimmy Vasser, USA (G-Force-Oldsmobile), 3h 32m 08.165s; **5** Bruno Junqueira, BR (G-Force-Oldsmobile), 3h 32m 21.436s; **6** Tony Stewart, USA (G-Force-Oldsmobile), 3h 32m31.741s; **7** Eliseo Salazar, RCH (Dallara-Oldsmobile), 199 laps; **8** Airton Dare, BR (G-Force-Oldsmobile), 199; **9** Billy Boat, USA (Dallara-Oldsmobile), 199; **10** Felipe Giaffone, BR (G-Force-Oldsmobile), 199;

11 Robby McGehee, USA (Dallara-Oldsmobile), 199; **12** Buzz Calkins, USA (Dallara-Oldsmobile), 198; **13** Arie Luyendyk, NL (G-Force-Oldsmobile), 198; **14** Sam Hornish Jr., USA (Dallara-Oldsmobile), 196; **15** Robbie Buhl, USA (G-Force-Infiniti), 196; **16** Mark Dismore, USA (Dallara-Oldsmobile), 195; **17** Greg Ray, USA (Dallara-Oldsmobile), 192; **18** Buddy Lazier, USA (Dallara-Oldsmobile), 192; **19** Cory Witherill, USA (G-Force-Oldsmobile), 187; **20** Jeret Schroeder, USA (Dallara-Oldsmobile), 187; **21** Robby Gordon, USA (Dallara-Oldsmobile), 184; **22** Jacques Lazier, USA (G-Force-Oldsmobile), 183; **23** Davey Hamilton, USA (Dallara-Oldsmobile), 182 (DNF - engine); **24** Jeff Ward, USA (G-Force-Oldsmobile), 168; **25** Donnie Beechler, USA (Dallara-Oldsmobile), 160 (DNF - oil leak); **26** Eddie Cheever Jr., USA (Dallara-Infiniti), 108 (DNF - electrical); **27** Jon Herb, USA (Dallara-Oldsmobile), 104 (DNF - accident); **28** Stéphan Grégoire, F (G-Force-Oldsmobile), 86 (DNF - oil leak); **29** Nicolas Minassian, F (G-Force-Oldsmobile), 74 (DNF - gearbox); **30** Al Unser Jr., USA (G-Force-Oldsmobile), 16 (DNF - accident); **31** Sarah Fisher, USA (Dallara-Oldsmobile), 7 (DNF - accident); **32** Scott Goodyear, CDN (Dallara-Infiniti), 7 (DNF - accident); **33** Scott Sharp, USA (Dallara-Oldsmobile), 0 (DNF - accident).
Most laps led: Castroneves, 52.
Fastest race lap: Hornish, 40.941s, 219.830 mph/353.780 km/h.
Fastest leading lap: de Ferran, 40.951s, 219.774 mph/353.693 km/h.
Pole position/Fastest qualifying lap: Sharp, 2m 39.266s, 226.037 mph/363.771 km/h (over four laps).

NASCAR Winston Cup

2000 Results

The following races were run after AUTOCOURSE 2000-2001 went to press

PENNZOIL 400 PRESENTED BY KMART, Miami-Dade Homestead Motorsports Complex, Florida, USA, 12 November. Round 33. 267 laps of the 1.500-mile/2.414-km circuit, 400.500 miles/644.542 km.
1 Tony Stewart, USA (Pontiac Grand Prix), 3h 08m 30s, 127.480 mph/205.159 km/h; **2** Jeremy Mayfield, USA (Ford Taurus), 3h 08m 34.561s; **3** Mark Martin, USA (Ford Taurus), 267 laps; **4** Bobby Labonte, USA (Pontiac Grand Prix), 267; **5** Jimmy Spencer, USA (Ford Taurus), 267; **6** Ricky Rudd, USA (Ford Taurus), 267; **7** Jeff Gordon, USA (Chevrolet Monte Carlo), 266; **8** Steve Park, USA (Chevrolet Monte Carlo), 266; **9** Dave Blaney, USA (Pontiac Grand Prix), 265; **10** Casey Atwood, USA (Ford Taurus), 265.
Fastest qualifying lap: Park, 34.518s, 156.440 mph/251.766 km/h.
Championship points: **1** Labonte (Bobby), 4970; **2** Burton (Jeff), 4709; **3** Earnhardt, 4690; **4** Jarrett, 4561; **5** Stewart, 4521; **6** Rudd, 4484.

NAPA 500, Atlanta Motor Speedway, Hampton, Georgia, USA, 20 November. Round 34. 325 laps of the 1.540-mile/2.478-km circuit, 500.500 miles/805.477 km.
Race scheduled for 19 November but postponed due to rain.
1 Jerry Nadeau, USA (Chevrolet Monte Carlo), 3h 32m 32s, 141.296 mph/227.393 km/h; **2** Dale Earnhardt, USA (Chevrolet Monte Carlo), 3h 32m 32.338s; **3** Ward Burton, USA (Pontiac Grand Prix), 325 laps; **4** Jeff Gordon, USA (Chevrolet Monte Carlo), 325; **5** Bobby Labonte, USA (Pontiac Grand Prix), 325; **6** Mike Skinner, USA (Chevrolet Monte Carlo), 325; **7** Rusty Wallace, USA (Ford Taurus), 325; **8** Sterling Marlin, USA (Chevrolet Monte Carlo), 325; **9** Matt Kenseth, USA (Ford Taurus), 324; **10** Johnny Benson Jr., USA (Pontiac Grand Prix), 324.
Fastest qualifying lap: Gordon, 28.537s, 194.274 mph/312.654 km/h.

Final Championship points
Drivers
1 Bobby Labonte, 5130; **2** Dale Earnhardt, 4865; **3** Jeff Burton, USA, 4836; **4** Dale Jarrett, USA, 4684; **5** Ricky Rudd, USA, 4575; **6** Tony Stewart, USA, 4570; **7** Rusty Wallace, USA, 4544; **8** Mark Martin, USA, 4410; **9** Jeff Gordon, USA, 4361; **10** Ward Burton, USA, 4152; **11** Steve Park, USA, 3934; **12** Mike Skinner, USA, 3898; **13** Johnny Benson Jr., USA, 3716; **14** Matt Kenseth, USA, 3711; **15** Joe Nemechek, USA, 3534; **16** Dale Earnhardt Jr., USA, 3516; **17** Terry Labonte, USA, 3433; **18** Ken Schrader, USA, 3398; **19** Sterling Marlin, USA, 3363; **20** Jerry Nadeau, USA, 3273; **21** Bill Elliott, USA, 3267; **22** Jimmy Spencer, USA, 3188; **23** John Andretti, USA, 3169; **24** Jeremy Mayfield, USA, 3156; **25** Robert Pressley, USA, 3055; **26** Kenny Wallace, USA, 2874; **27** Michael Waltrip, USA, 2797; **28** Kevin Lepage, USA, 2795; **29** Elliott Sadler, USA, 2762; **30** Bobby Hamilton, USA, 2715.

Raybestos Rookie of the Year: Matt Kenseth.
Bud Pole Award Winner: Rusty Wallace.

Manufacturers
1 Ford; **2** Pontiac; **3** Chevrolet.

2001 Results

DAYTONA 500, Daytona International Speedway, Daytona Beach, Florida, USA, 18 February. Round 1. 200 laps of the 2.500-mile/4.023-km circuit, 500.000 miles/804.672 km.
1 Michael Waltrip, USA (Chevrolet Monte Carlo), 3h 05m 26s, 161.783 mph/260.365 km/h; **2** Dale Earnhardt Jr., USA (Chevrolet Monte Carlo), 3h 05m 26.124s; **3** Rusty Wallace, USA (Ford Taurus), 200 laps; **4** Ricky Rudd, USA (Ford Taurus), 200; **5** Bill Elliott, USA (Dodge Intrepid), 200; **6** Mike Wallace, USA (Ford Taurus), 200; **7** Sterling Marlin, USA (Dodge Intrepid), 200; **8** Bobby Hamilton, USA (Chevrolet Monte Carlo), 200; **9** Jeremy Mayfield, USA (Ford Taurus), 200; **10** Stacy Compton, USA (Dodge Intrepid), 200.
Fastest qualifying lap: Elliott, 49.029s, 183.565 mph/295.419 km/h.
Drivers Championship points: **1** Waltrip, 180; **2** Earnhardt Jr., 175; **3** Wallace (Rusty), 165; **4=** Rudd, 160; **4=** Elliott, 160; **6** Marlin, 151.

DURA-LUBE 400, North Carolina Motor Speedway, Rockingham, North Carolina, USA, 25-26 February. Round 2. 393 laps of the 1.017-mile/1.637-km circuit, 399.681 miles/643.224 km.
Race stopped by rain after 52 laps and continued the following day.
1 Steve Park, USA (Chevrolet Monte Carlo), 3h 34m 21s, 111.877 mph/180.049 km/h; **2** Bobby Labonte, USA (Pontiac Grand Prix), 3h 34m 21.138s; **3** Jeff Gordon, USA (Chevrolet Monte Carlo), 393 laps; **4** Tony Stewart, USA (Pontiac Grand Prix), 393; **5** Ricky Craven, USA (Ford Taurus), 393; **6** Johnny Benson Jr., USA (Pontiac Grand Prix), 393; **7** Rusty Wallace, USA (Ford Taurus), 393; **8** Sterling Marlin, USA (Dodge Intrepid), 393; **9** Dave Blaney, USA (Dodge Intrepid), 393; **10** Dale Jarrett, USA (Ford Taurus), 393.
Fastest qualifying lap: Gordon, 23.401s, 156.455 mph/251.790 km/h.
Drivers Championship points: **1** Wallace (Rusty), 311; **2** Marlin, 298; **3** Waltrip, 291; **4** Hamilton, 266; **5** Park, 255; **6** Elliott, 254.

UAW-DAIMLER CHRYSLER 400, Las Vegas Motor Speedway, Nevada, USA, 4 March. Round 3. 267 laps of the 1.500-mile/2.414-km circuit, 400.500 miles/644.542 km.
1 Jeff Gordon, USA (Chevrolet Monte Carlo), 2h 57m 17s, 135.546 mph/218.140 km/h; **2** Dale Jarrett, USA (Ford Taurus), 2h 57m 18.477s; **3** Sterling Marlin, USA (Dodge Intrepid), 267 laps; **4** Johnny Benson Jr., USA (Pontiac Grand Prix), 267; **5** Todd Bodine, USA (Ford Taurus), 267; **6** Mark Martin, USA (Ford Taurus), 267; **7** Steve Park, USA (Chevrolet Monte Carlo), 267; **8** Kevin Harvick, USA (Chevrolet Monte Carlo), 267; **9** Ron Hornaday, USA (Pontiac Grand Prix), 267; **10** Jimmy Spencer, USA (Ford Taurus), 267.
Fastest qualifying lap: Jarrett, 31.376s, 172.106 mph/276.978 km/h.
Drivers Championship points: **1** Marlin, 468; **2** Gordon, 433; **3** Waltrip, 415; **4** Jarrett, 411; **5** Park, 401; **6** Benson Jr., 394.

CRACKER BARREL OLD COUNTRY STORE 500, Atlanta Motor Speedway, Hampton, Georgia, USA, 11 March. Round 4. 325 laps of the 1.540-mile/2.478-km circuit, 500.500 miles/805.477 km.
1 Kevin Harvick, USA (Chevrolet Monte Carlo), 3h 29m 36s, 143.273 mph/230.575 km/h; **2** Jeff Gordon, USA (Chevrolet Monte Carlo), 3h 29m 36.006s; **3** Jerry Nadeau, USA (Chevrolet Monte Carlo), 325 laps; **4** Dale Jarrett, USA (Ford Taurus), 325; **5** Terry Labonte, USA (Chevrolet Monte Carlo), 325; **6** Ricky Rudd, USA (Ford Taurus), 325; **7** Johnny Benson Jr., USA (Pontiac Grand Prix), 325; **8** Ken Schrader, USA (Pontiac Grand Prix), 325; **9** Mike Skinner, USA (Chevrolet Monte Carlo), 325; **10** Kurt Busch, USA (Ford Taurus), 324.
Fastest qualifying lap: Jarrett, 28.763s, 192.748 mph/310.197 km/h.
Drivers Championship points: **1** Gordon, 613; **2** Jarrett, 576; **3** Benson Jr., 540; **4** Marlin, 531; **5** Waltrip, 509; **6** Elliott, 495.

CAROLINA DODGE DEALERS 400, Darlington Raceway, South Carolina, USA, 18 March. Round 5. 293 laps of the 1.366-mile/2.198-km circuit, 400.238 miles/644.121 km.
1 Dale Jarrett, USA (Ford Taurus), 3h 09m 45s, 126.557 mph/203.675 km/h; **2** Steve Park, USA (Chevrolet Monte Carlo), 3h 09m 45.527s; **3** Jeremy Mayfield, USA (Ford Taurus), 293 laps; **4** Jimmy Spencer, USA (Ford Taurus), 293; **5** Sterling Marlin, USA (Dodge Intrepid) 293; **6** John Andretti, USA (Dodge Intrepid) 293; **7** Johnny Benson Jr., USA (Pontiac Grand Prix) 293; **8** Ricky Rudd, USA (Ford Taurus) 293; **9** Bobby Hamilton, USA (Chevrolet Monte Carlo) 293; **10** Rusty Wallace, USA (Ford Taurus) 293.
Fastest qualifying lap: none due to inclement weather.
Pole position: Jeff Gordon, USA (Chevrolet Monte Carlo).
Drivers Championship points: **1** Jarrett, 756; **2=** Marlin, 691; **2=** Benson Jr., 691; **4** Gordon, 661; **5** Park, 615; **6** Rudd, 609.

FOOD CITY 500, Bristol Motor Speedway, Tennessee, USA, 25 March. Round 6. 500 laps of the 0.533-mile/0.858-km circuit, 266.500 miles/428.890 km.
1 Elliott Sadler, USA (Ford Taurus), 3h 03m 54s, 86.949 mph/139.932 km/h; **2** John Andretti, USA (Dodge Intrepid), 3h 03m 54.426s; **3** Jeremy Mayfield, USA (Ford Taurus), 500 laps; **4** Jeff Gordon, USA (Chevrolet Monte Carlo), 500; **5** Ward Burton, USA (Dodge Intrepid), 500; **6** Terry Labonte, USA (Chevrolet Monte Carlo), 500; **7** Rusty Wallace, USA (Ford Taurus), 500; **8** Bobby Hamilton, USA (Chevrolet Monte Carlo), 500; **9** Steve Park, USA (Chevrolet Monte Carlo), 500; **10** Ricky Rudd, USA (Ford Taurus), 500.
Fastest qualifying lap: Mark Martin, USA (Ford Taurus), 15.192s, 126.303 mph/203.265 km/h.
Drivers Championship points: **1** Jarrett, 871; **2** Gordon, 826; **3** Marlin, 823; **4** Benson Jr., 776; **5** Park, 758; **6** Wallace (Rusty), 752.

HARRAH'S 500, Texas Motor Speedway, Fort Worth, Texas, USA, 1 April. Round 7. 334 laps of the 1.500-mile/2.414-km circuit, 501.000 miles/806.281 km.
1 Dale Jarrett, USA (Ford Taurus), 3h 31m 59s, 141.804 mph/228.211 km/h; **2** Steve Park, USA (Chevrolet Monte Carlo), 3h 31m 59.703s; **3** Johnny Benson Jr., USA (Pontiac Grand Prix), 334 laps; **4** Kurt Busch, USA (Ford Taurus), 334; **5** Jeff Gordon, USA (Chevrolet Monte Carlo), 334; **6** Dave Blaney, USA (Dodge Intrepid), 334; **7** Kevin Harvick, USA (Chevrolet Monte Carlo), 334; **8** Dale Earnhardt Jr., USA (Chevrolet Monte Carlo), 334; **9** Mark Martin, USA (Ford Taurus), 334; **10** Ken Schrader, USA (Pontiac Grand Prix), 334.
Fastest qualifying lap: Earnhardt Jr., 28.320s, 190.678 mph/306.866 km/h.
Drivers Championship points: **1** Jarrett, 1051; **2** Gordon, 981; **3** Benson Jr., 946; **4** Park, 933; **5** Marlin, 889; **6** Wallace (Rusty), 879.

VIRGINIA 500, Martinsville Speedway, Virginia, USA, 8 April. Round 8. 500 laps of the 0.526-mile/0.847-km circuit, 263.000 miles/423.257 km.
1 Dale Jarrett, USA (Ford Taurus), 3h 42m 53s, 70.799 mph/113.941 km/h; **2** Ricky Rudd, USA (Ford Taurus), 3h 42m 54.388s; **3** Jeff Burton, USA (Ford Taurus), 500 laps; **4** Bobby Hamilton, USA (Chevrolet Monte Carlo), 500; **5** Sterling Marlin, USA (Dodge Intrepid), 500; **6** Matt Kenseth, USA (Ford Taurus), 500; **7** Tony Stewart, USA (Pontiac Grand Prix), 500; **8** Bobby Labonte, USA (Pontiac Grand Prix), 500; **9** Jimmy Spencer, USA (Ford Taurus), 500; **10** Jerry Nadeau, USA (Chevrolet Monte Carlo), 500.
Fastest qualifying lap: Jeff Gordon, USA (Chevrolet Monte Carlo), 20.126s, 94.087 mph/151.419 km/h.
Drivers Championship points: **1** Jarrett, 1236; **2** Gordon, 1113; **3=** Benson Jr., 1049; **3=** Marlin, 1049; **5** Park, 1039; **6** Wallace (Rusty), 1008.

TALLADEGA 500, Talladega Superspeedway, Alabama, USA, 22 April. Round 9. 188 laps of the 2.660-mile/4.281-km circuit, 500.080 miles/804.801 km.
1 Bobby Hamilton, USA (Chevrolet Monte Carlo), 2h 43m 04s, 184.003 mph/296.125 km/h; **2** Tony Stewart, USA (Pontiac Grand Prix), 2h 43m 04.183s; **3** Kurt Busch, USA (Ford Taurus), 188 laps; **4** Mark Martin, USA (Ford Taurus), 188; **5** Bobby Labonte, USA (Pontiac Grand Prix), 188; **6** Joe Nemechek, USA (Chevrolet Monte Carlo), 188; **7** Johnny Benson Jr., USA (Pontiac Grand Prix), 188; **8** Dale Earnhardt Jr., USA (Chevrolet Monte Carlo), 188; **9** Mike Wallace, USA (Ford Taurus), 188; **10** Jeff Burton, USA (Ford Taurus), 188.
Fastest qualifying lap: Stacy Compton, USA (Dodge Intrpid), 51.801s, 184.861 mph/297.505 km/h.
Drivers Championship points: **1** Jarrett, 1345; **2** Gordon, 1200; **3** Benson Jr., 1195; **4** Hamilton, 1175; **5** Marlin, 1153; **6** Wallace (Rusty), 1137.

NAPA AUTO PARTS 500, California Speedway, Fontana, California, USA, 29 April. Round 10. 250 laps of the 2.000-mile/3.219-km circuit, 500.000 miles/804.672 km.
1 Rusty Wallace, USA (Ford Taurus), 3h 29m 37s, 143.118 mph/230.327 km/h; **2** Jeff Gordon, USA (Chevrolet Monte Carlo), 3h 29m 37.270s; **3** Dale Earnhardt Jr., USA (Chevrolet Monte Carlo), 250 laps; **4** Tony Stewart, USA (Pontiac Grand Prix), 250; **5** Jeremy Mayfield, USA (Ford Taurus), 250; **6** Ricky Rudd, USA (Ford Taurus), 250; **7** Jimmy Spencer, USA (Ford Taurus), 250; **8** Jerry Nadeau, USA (Chevrolet Monte Carlo), 250; **9** Sterling Marlin, USA (Dodge Intrepid), 250; **10** Robert Pressley, USA (Ford Taurus), 250.
Fastest qualifying lap: Bobby Labonte, USA (Pontiac Grand Prix), 39.423s, 182.635 mph/293.922 km/h.
Drivers Championship points: **1** Jarrett, 1441; **2** Gordon, 1375; **3** Benson Jr., 1330; **4** Wallace (Rusty), 1322; **5** Marlin, 1291; **6** Rudd, 1251.

PONTIAC EXCITEMENT 400, Richmond International Raceway, Virginia, USA, 5 May. Round 11. 400 laps of the 0.750-mile/1.207-km circuit, 300.000 miles/482.803 km.
1 Tony Stewart, USA (Pontiac Grand Prix), 3h 07m 45s, 95.872 mph/154.291 km/h; **2** Jeff Gordon, USA (Chevrolet Monte Carlo), 3h 07m 45.372s; **3** Rusty Wallace, USA (Ford Taurus), 400 laps; **4** Steve Park, USA (Chevrolet Monte Carlo), 400; **5** Ricky Rudd, USA (Ford Taurus), 400; **6** Johnny Benson Jr., USA (Pontiac Grand Prix), 400; **7** Dale Earnhardt Jr., USA (Chevrolet Monte Carlo), 400; **8** Matt Kenseth, USA (Ford Taurus), 400; **9** Ken Schrader, USA (Pontiac Grand Prix), 400; **10** Bobby Labonte, USA (Pontiac Grand Prix), 400.
Fastest qualifying lap: Mark Martin, USA (Ford Taurus), 21.667s, 124.613 mph/200.546 km/h.
Drivers Championship points: **1** Jarrett, 1559; **2** Gordon, 1545; **3** Wallace (Rusty), 1497; **4** Benson Jr., 1480; **5** Martin, 1421; **6** Rudd, 1411.

COCA-COLA 600, Lowe's Motor Speedway, Concord, North Carolina, USA, 27 May. Round 12. 400 laps of the 1.500-mile/2.414-km circuit, 600.000 miles/965.606 km.
1 Jeff Burton, USA (Ford Taurus), 4h 20m 40s, 138.107 mph/222.262 km/h; **2** Kevin Harvick, USA (Chevrolet Monte Carlo), 4h 20m 43.190s; **3** Tony Stewart, USA (Pontiac Grand Prix), 400 laps; **4** Mark Martin, USA (Ford Taurus), 400; **5** Bobby Labonte, USA (Pontiac Grand Prix), 400; **6** Jimmy Spencer, USA (Ford Taurus), 400; **7** Ricky Rudd, USA (Ford Taurus), 400; **8** Dale Jarrett, USA (Ford Taurus), 400; **9** Ward Burton, USA (Dodge Intrpid), 400; **10** Jeremy Mayfield, USA (Ford Taurus), 400.
Fastest qualifying lap: Ryan Newman, USA (Ford Taurus), 29.155s, 185.217 mph/298.078 km/h.
Drivers Championship points: **1** Jarrett, 1701; **2** Gordon, 1626; **3** Wallace (Rusty), 1623; **4** Benson Jr., 1583; **5** Rudd, 1557; **6** Stewart, 1552.

MBNA PLATINUM 400, Dover Downs International Speedway, Dover, Delaware, USA, 3 June. Round 13. 400 laps of the 1.000-mile/1.609-km circuit, 400.000 miles/643.738 km.
1 Jeff Gordon, USA (Chevrolet Monte Carlo), 3h 19m 24s, 120.361 mph/193.702 km/h; **2** Steve Park, USA (Chevrolet Monte Carlo), 3h 19m 24.828s; **3** Dale Earnhardt Jr., USA (Chevrolet Monte Carlo), 400 laps; **4** Ricky Craven, USA (Ford Taurus), 400; **5** Dale Jarrett, USA (Ford Taurus), 400; **6** Sterling Marlin, USA (Dodge Intrepid), 400; **7** Tony Stewart, USA (Pontiac Grand Prix), 400; **8** Kevin Harvick, USA (Chevrolet Monte Carlo), 400; **9** Mark Martin, USA (Ford Taurus), 400; **10** Ricky Rudd, USA (Ford Taurus), 400.
Fastest qualifying lap: none due to inclement weather.
Pole position: Jarrett.
Drivers Championship points: **1** Jarrett, 1861; **2** Gordon, 1811; **3** Wallace (Rusty), 1728; **4** Stewart, 1703; **5** Marlin, 1699; **6** Rudd, 1691.

KMART 400, Michigan International Speedway, Brooklyn, Michigan, USA, 10 June. Round 14. 200 laps of the 2.000-mile/3.219-km circuit, 400.000 miles/643.738 km.
1 Jeff Gordon, USA (Chevrolet Monte Carlo), 2h 58m 50s, 134.203 mph/215.979 km/h; **2** Ricky Rudd, USA (Ford Taurus), 2h 58m 50.085s; **3** Sterling Marlin, USA (Dodge Intrepid), 200 laps; **4** Jeremy Mayfield, USA (Ford Taurus), 200; **5** Ryan Newman, USA (Ford Taurus), 200; **6** Hut Stricklin, USA (Ford Taurus), 200; **7** Jeff Burton, USA (Ford Taurus), 200; **8** Dave Blaney, USA (Dodge Intrepid), 200; **9** Bill Elliott, USA (Dodge Intrepid), 200; **10** Kevin Harvick, USA (Chevrolet Monte Carlo), 200.
Fastest qualifying lap: Gordon, 38.247s, 188.250 mph/302.959 km/h.
Drivers Championship points: **1** Gordon, 1996; **2** Jarrett, 1970; **3** Marlin, 1869; **4** Rudd, 1866; **5** Stewart, 1791; **6** Wallace (Rusty), 1768.

POCONO 500, Pocono Raceway, Long Pond, Pennsylvania, USA, 17 June. Round 15. 200 laps of the 2.500-mile/4.023-km circuit, 500.000 miles/804.672 km.
1 Ricky Rudd, USA (Ford Taurus), 3h 43m 14s, 134.389 mph/216.277 km/h; **2** Jeff Gordon, USA (Chevrolet Monte Carlo), 3h 43m 15.119s; **3** Dale Jarrett, USA (Ford Taurus), 200 laps; **4** Sterling Marlin, USA (Dodge Intrepid), 200; **5** Mark Martin, USA (Ford Taurus), 200; **6** Matt Kenseth, USA (Ford Taurus), 200; **7** Tony Stewart, USA (Pontiac Grand Prix), 200; **8** Bobby Labonte, USA (Pontiac Grand Prix), 200; **9** Ken Schrader, USA (Pontiac Grand Prix), 200; **10** Jeff Burton, USA (Ford Taurus), 200.
Fastest qualifying lap: Rudd, 52.785s, 170.503 mph/274.398 km/h.
Drivers Championship points: **1** Gordon, 2176; **2** Jarrett, 2140; **3** Rudd, 2046; **4** Marlin, 2029; **5** Stewart, 1937; **6** Wallace (Rusty), 1883.

DODGE/SAVE MART 350, Sears Point Raceway, Sonoma, California, USA, 24 June. Round 16. 112 laps of the 2.000-mile/3.219-km circuit, 224.000 miles/360.493 km.
1 Tony Stewart, USA (Pontiac Grand Prix), 2h 57m 06s, 75.889 mph/122.132 km/h; **2** Robby Gordon, USA (Ford Taurus), 2h 57m 07.746s; **3** Jeff Gordon, USA (Chevrolet Monte Carlo), 112 laps; **4** Ricky Rudd, USA (Ford Taurus), 112; **5** Rusty Wallace, USA (Ford Taurus), 112; **6** Ward Burton, USA (Dodge Intrepid), 112; **7** Bobby Labonte, USA (Pontiac Grand Prix), 112; **8** Jeff Burton, USA (Ford Taurus), 112; **9** Bill Elliott, USA (Dodge Intrepid), 112; **10** Mark Martin, USA (Ford Taurus), 112.
Fastest qualifying lap: Gordon (Jeff), 1m 16.842s, 93.699 mph/150.794 km/h.
Drivers Championship points: **1** Gordon (Jeff), 2351; **2** Jarrett, 2225; **3** Rudd, 2206; **4** Stewart, 2117; **5** Marlin, 2108; **6** Wallace (Rusty), 2038.

PEPSI 400, Daytona International Speedway, Daytona Beach, Florida, USA, 7 July. Round 17. 160 laps of the 2.500-mile/4.023-km circuit, 400.000 miles/643.738 km.
1 Dale Earnhardt Jr., USA (Chevrolet Monte Carlo), 2h 32m 17s, 157.601 mph/253.634 km/h; **2** Michael Waltrip, USA (Chevrolet Monte Carlo), 2h 32m 17.123s; **3** Elliott Sadler, USA (Ford Taurus), 160 laps; **4** Ward Burton, USA (Dodge Intrepid), 160; **5** Bobby Labonte, USA (Pontiac Grand Prix), 160; **6** Jerry Nadeau, USA (Chevrolet Monte Carlo), 160; **7** Rusty Wallace, USA (Ford Taurus), 160; **8** Jeff Burton, USA (Ford Taurus), 160; **9** Brett Bodine, USA (Ford Taurus), 160; **10** Mike Wallace, USA (Ford Taurus), 160.
Fastest qualifying lap: Sterling Marlin, USA (Dodge Intrepid), 48.972s, 183.778 mph/295.763 km/h.
Drivers Championship points: **1** Gordon (Jeff), 2403; **2** Jarrett, 2355; **3** Rudd, 2327; **4** Stewart, 2202; **5** Wallace (Rusty), 2184; **6** Marlin, 2159.

TROPICANA 400, Chicagoland Speedway, Chicago, Illinois, USA 15 July. Round 18. 267 laps of the 1.500-mile/2.414-km circuit, 400.500 miles/644.542 km.
1 Kevin Harvick, USA (Chevrolet Monte Carlo), 3h 18.16s, 121.200 mph/195.053 km/h; **2** Robert Pressley, USA (Ford Taurus), 3h 18m 16.649s; **3** Ricky Rudd, USA (Ford Taurus), 267 laps; **4** Dale Jarrett, USA (Ford Taurus), 267; **5** Jimmy Spencer, USA (Ford Taurus), 267; **6** Mark Martin, USA (Ford Taurus), 267; **7** Matt Kenseth, USA (Ford Taurus), 267; **8** Kurt Busch, USA (Ford Taurus), 267; **9** Sterling Marlin, USA (Dodge Intrepid), 267; **10** Bill Elliott, USA (Dodge Intrepid), 267.
Fastest qualifying lap: Todd Bodine, USA (Ford Taurus), 29.393s, 183.717 mph/295.664 km/h.
Drivers Championship points: **1=** Gordon (Jeff), 2515; **1=** Jarrett, 2515; **3** Rudd, 2497; **4** Wallace (Rusty), 2308; **5** Marlin, 2297; **6** Stewart, 2266.

NEW ENGLAND 300, New Hampshire International Speedway, Loudon, New Hampshire, USA, 22 July. Round 19. 300 laps of the 1.058-mile/1.703-km circuit, 317.400 miles/510.806 km.
1 Dale Jarrett, USA (Ford Taurus), 3h 06m 28s, 102.131 mph/164.364 km/h; **2** Jeff Gordon, USA (Chevrolet Monte Carlo), 3h 06m 28.659s; **3** Ricky Rudd, USA (Ford Taurus), 300 laps; **4** Mark Martin, USA (Ford Taurus), 300; **5** Tony Stewart, USA (Pontiac Grand Prix), 300; **6** Steve Park, USA (Chevrolet Monte Carlo), 300; **7** Bobby Labonte, USA (Pontiac Grand Prix), 300; **8** Kevin Harvick, USA (Chevrolet Monte Carlo), 300; **9** Dale Earnhardt Jr., USA (Chevrolet Monte Carlo), 300; **10** Mike Wallace, USA (Ford Taurus), 300.
Fastest qualifying lap: Gordon (Jeff), 28.905s, 131.770 mph/212.063 km/h.
Drivers Championship points: **1=** Jarrett, 2695; **1=** Gordon (Jeff), 2695; **3** Rudd, 2667; **4** Stewart, 2421; **5** Marlin, 2414; **6** Wallace (Rusty), 2342.

PENNSYLVANIA 500, Pocono Raceway, Long Pond, Pennsylvania, USA, 29 July. Round 20. 200 laps of the 2.500-mile/4.023-km circuit, 500.000 miles/804.672 km.
1 Bobby Labonte, USA (Pontiac Grand Prix), 3h 42m 54s, 134.590 mph/216.601 km/h; **2** Dale Earnhardt Jr., USA (Chevrolet Monte Carlo), 3h 42m 55.680s; **3** Tony Stewart, USA (Pontiac Grand Prix), 200 laps; **4** Bill Elliott, USA (Dodge Intrepid), 200; **5** Johnny Benson Jr., USA (Pontiac Grand Prix), 200; **6** Rusty Wallace, USA (Ford Taurus), 200; **7** Mark Martin, USA (Ford Taurus), 200; **8** Jeff Gordon, USA (Chevrolet Monte Carlo), 200; **9** Robert Pressley, USA (Ford Taurus), 200; **10** Ricky Craven, USA (Ford Taurus), 200.
Fastest qualifying lap: Todd Bodine, USA (Ford Taurus), 52.840s, 170.326 mph/274.112 km/h.
Drivers Championship points: **1** Gordon (Jeff), 2847; **2** Rudd, 2802; **3** Jarrett, 2740; **4** Stewart, 2586; **5** Marlin, 2529; **6** Wallace (Rusty), 2492.

BRICKYARD 400, Indianapolis Motor Speedway, Speedway, Indiana, USA, 5 August. Round 21. 160 laps of the 2.500-mile/4.023-km circuit, 400.000 miles/643.738 km.
1 Jeff Gordon, USA (Chevrolet Monte Carlo), 3h 03m 30s, 130.790 mph/210.486 km/h; **2** Sterling Marlin, USA (Dodge Intrepid), 3h 03m 30.943s; **3** Johnny Benson Jr., USA (Pontiac Grand Prix), 160 laps; **4** Rusty Wallace, USA (Ford Taurus), 160; **5** Kurt Busch, USA (Ford Taurus), 160; **6** Ward Burton, USA (Dodge Intrepid), 160; **7** Steve Park, USA (Chevrolet Monte Carlo), 160; **8** Bill Elliott, USA (Dodge Intrepid), 160; **9** Ricky Craven, USA (Ford Taurus), 160; **10** Dale Earnhardt Jr., USA (Chevrolet Monte Carlo), 160.
Fastest qualifying lap: Jimmy Spencer, USA (Ford Taurus), 50.093s, 179.666 mph/289.144 km/h.
Drivers Championship points: **1** Gordon (Jeff), 3027; **2** Jarrett, 2867; **3** Rudd, 2848; **4** Marlin, 2704; **5** Stewart, 2703; **6** Wallace (Rusty), 2652.

GLOBAL CROSSING @ THE GLEN, Watkins Glen International, New York, USA, 12 August. Round 22. 90 laps of the 2.450-mile/3.943-km circuit, 220.500 miles/354.860 km.
1 Jeff Gordon, USA (Chevrolet Monte Carlo), 2h 28m 31s, 89.081 mph/143.362 km/h; **2** Jeff Burton, USA (Ford Taurus), 2h 28m 31.172s; **3** Jeremy Mayfield, USA (Ford Taurus), 90 laps; **4** Ricky Rudd, USA (Ford Taurus), 90; **5** Todd Bodine, USA (Ford Taurus), 90; **6** Jerry Nadeau, USA (Chevrolet

Monte Carlo), 90; **7** Kevin Harvick, USA (Chevrolet Monte Carlo), 90; **8** Boris Said, USA (Ford Taurus), 90; **9** Bobby Labonte, USA (Pontiac Grand Prix), 90; **10** Steve Park, USA (Chevrolet Monte Carlo), 90.
Fastest qualifying lap: Jarrett, 1m 11.884s, 122.698 mph/197.463 km/h.
Drivers Championship points: 1 Gordon (Jeff), 3207; **2** Rudd, 3013; **3** Jarrett, 2939; **4** Marlin, 2792; **5** Stewart, 2788; **6** Earnhardt Jr., 2719.

PEPSI 400 PRESENTED BY MEIJER, Michigan International Speedway, Brooklyn, Michigan, USA, 19 August. Round 23. 162 laps of the 2.000-mile/3.219-km circuit, 324.000 miles/521.427 km.
Race scheduled for 200 laps but stopped prematurely due to rain.
1 Sterling Marlin, USA (Dodge Intrepid), 2h 18m 21s, 140.513 mph/226.134 km/h (under caution); **2** Ricky Craven, USA (Ford Taurus), 162 laps; **3** Bill Elliott, USA (Dodge Intrepid), 162; **4** Matt Kenseth, USA (Ford Taurus), 162; **5** Johnny Benson Jr., USA (Pontiac Grand Prix), 162; **6** Dave Blaney, USA (Dodge Intrepid), 162; **7** Jeff Gordon, USA (Chevrolet Monte Carlo), 162; **8** Mark Martin, USA (Ford Taurus), 162; **9** Steve Park, USA (Chevrolet Monte Carlo), 162; **10** Casey Atwood, USA (Dodge Intrepid), 162.
Fastest qualifying lap: Craven, 38.272s, 188.127 mph/302.761 km/h.
Drivers Championship points: 1 Gordon (Jeff), 3353; **2** Rudd, 3055; **3** Jarrett, 2999; **4** Marlin, 2972; **5** Stewart, 2870; **6** Earnhardt Jr., 2846.

SHARPIE 500, Bristol Motor Speedway, Tennessee, USA, 25 August. Round 24. 500 laps of the 0.533-mile/0.858-km circuit, 266.500 miles/428.890 km.
1 Tony Stewart, USA (Pontiac Grand Prix), 3h 07m 53s, 85.106 mph/136.965 km/h; **2** Kevin Harvick, USA (Chevrolet Monte Carlo), 3h 07m 53.487s; **3** Jeff Gordon, USA (Chevrolet Monte Carlo), 500 laps; **4** Ricky Rudd, USA (Ford Taurus), 500; **5** Rusty Wallace, USA (Ford Taurus), 500; **6** Dale Jarrett, USA (Ford Taurus), 500; **7** Steve Park, USA (Chevrolet Monte Carlo), 500; **8** Bobby Labonte, USA (Pontiac Grand Prix), 500; **9** Sterling Marlin, USA (Dodge Intrepid), 500; **10** Terry Labonte, USA (Chevrolet Monte Carlo), 500.
Fastest qualifying lap: Jeff Green, USA (Chevrolet Monte Carlo), 15.515s, 123.674 mph/199.034 km/h.
Drivers Championship points: 1 Gordon (Jeff), 3528; **2** Rudd, 3220; **3** Jarrett, 3149; **4** Marlin, 3110; **5** Stewart, 3050; **6** Earnhardt Jr., 2967.

MOUNTAIN DEW SOUTHERN 500, Darlington Raceway, South Carolina, USA, 2 September. Round 25. 367 laps of the 1.366-mile/2.198-km circuit, 501.322 miles/806.800 km.
1 Ward Burton, USA (Dodge Intrepid), 4h 05m 00s, 122.773 mph/197.584 km/h (under caution); **2** Jeff Gordon, USA (Chevrolet Monte Carlo), 367 laps; **3** Bobby Labonte, USA (Pontiac Grand Prix), 367; **4** Tony Stewart, USA (Pontiac Grand Prix), 367; **5** Bill Elliott, USA (Dodge Intrepid), 367; **6** Jeff Burton, USA (Ford Taurus), 367; **7** Ricky Rudd, USA (Ford Taurus), 367; **8** Kevin Harvick, USA (Chevrolet Monte Carlo), 367; **9** Jerry Nadeau, USA (Chevrolet Monte Carlo), 367; **10** Ken Schrader, USA (Pontiac Grand Prix), 367.
Fastest qualifying lap: Kurt Busch, USA (Ford Taurus), 29.263s, 168.048 mph/270.448 km/h.
Drivers Championship points: 1 Gordon (Jeff), 3708; **2** Rudd, 3366; **3** Marlin, 3230; **4** Jarrett, 3215; **5** Stewart, 3210; **6** Labonte (Bobby), 3117.

CHEVROLET MONTE CARLO 400 WITH LOONEY TUNES, Richmond International Raceway, Virginia, USA, 8 September. Round 26. 400 laps of the 0.750-mile/1.207-km circuit, 300.000 miles/482.803 km.
1 Ricky Rudd, USA (Ford Taurus), 3h 09m 11s, 95.146 mph/153.122 km/h; **2** Kevin Harvick, USA (Chevrolet Monte Carlo), 3h 09m 11.833s; **3** Dale Earnhardt Jr., USA (Chevrolet Monte Carlo), 400 laps; **4** Dale Jarrett, USA (Ford Taurus), 400; **5** Rusty Wallace, USA (Ford Taurus), 400; **6** Bobby Labonte, USA (Pontiac Grand Prix), 400; **7** Tony Stewart, USA (Pontiac Grand Prix), 400; **8** Jimmy Spencer, USA (Ford Taurus), 400; **9** Jeff Burton, USA (Ford Taurus), 400; **10** Johnny Benson Jr., USA (Pontiac Grand Prix), 400.
Fastest qualifying lap: Jeff Gordon, USA (Chevrolet Monte Carlo), 21.617s, 124.902 mph/201.010 km/h.
Drivers Championship points: 1 Gordon (Jeff), 3768; **2** Rudd, 3546; **3** Jarrett, 3375; **4** Stewart, 3356; **5** Marlin, 3302; **6** Labonte (Bobby), 3267.

MBNA CAL RIPKEN JR. 400, Dover Downs International Speedway, Dover, Delaware, USA, 23 September. Round 27. 400 laps of the 1.000-mile/1.609-km circuit, 400.000 miles/643.738 km.
1 Dale Earnhardt Jr., USA (Chevrolet Monte Carlo), 3h 56m 19s, 101.559 mph/163.443 km/h; **2** Jerry Nadeau, USA (Chevrolet Monte Carlo), 3h 56m 20.576s; **3** Ricky Rudd, USA (Ford Taurus), 400 laps; **4** Jeff Gordon, USA (Chevrolet Monte Carlo), 400; **5** Tony Stewart, USA (Pontiac Grand Prix), 400; **6** Kevin Harvick, USA (Chevrolet Monte Carlo), 400; **7** Joe Nemechek, USA (Chevrolet Monte Carlo), 400; **8** Sterling Marlin, USA (Dodge Intrepid), 400; **9** Casey Atwood, USA (Dodge Intrepid), 400; **10** Bobby Hamilton, USA (Chevrolet Monte Carlo), 400.
Fastest qualifying lap: Dale Jarrett, USA (Ford Taurus), 23.238s, 154.919 mph/249.317 km/h.
Drivers Championship points: 1 Gordon (Jeff), 3928; **2** Rudd, 3716; **3** Stewart, 3516; **4** Jarrett, 3507; **5** Marlin, 3444; **6** Earnhardt Jr., 3429.

PROTECTION ONE 400, Kansas Speedway, Kansas City, Kansas, 30 September. Round 28. 267 laps of the 1.500-mile/2.414-km circuit, 400.500 miles/644.542 km.
1 Jeff Gordon, USA (Chevrolet Monte Carlo), 3h 37m 19s, 110.576 mph/177.955 km/h; **2** Ryan Newman, USA (Ford Taurus), 3h 37m 19.413s; **3** Ricky Rudd, USA (Ford Taurus), 267 laps; **4** Rusty Wallace, USA (Ford Taurus), 267; **5** Sterling Marlin, USA (Dodge Intrepid), 267; **6** Mark Martin, USA (Ford Taurus), 267; **7** Robert Pressley, USA (Ford Taurus), 267; **8** Tony Stewart, USA (Pontiac Grand Prix), 267; **9** Kurt Busch, USA (Ford Taurus), 267; **10** Dave Blaney, USA (Dodge Intrepid), 267.
Fastest qualifying lap: Jason Leffler, USA (Dodge Intrepid), 30.595s, 176.499 mph/284.048 km/h.
Drivers Championship points: 1 Gordon (Jeff), 4108; **2** Rudd, 3886; **3** Stewart, 3658; **4** Marlin 3604; **5** Jarrett, 3580; **6** Wallace (Rusty), 3525.

UAW-GM QUALITY 500, Lowe's Motor Speedway, Concord, North Carolina, USA, 7 October. Round 29. 334 laps of the 1.500-mile/2.414-km circuit, 501.000 miles/806.281 km.
1 Sterling Marlin, USA (Dodge Intrepid), 3h 36m 15s, 139.006 mph/223.708 km/h; **2** Tony Stewart, USA (Pontiac Grand Prix), 3h 36m 21.002s; **3** Ward Burton, USA (Dodge Intrepid), 334 laps; **4** Dale Earnhardt Jr., USA (Chevrolet Monte Carlo), 334; **5** Jeff Burton, USA (Ford Taurus), 334; **6** Dale Jarrett, USA (Ford Taurus), 334; **7** Rusty Wallace, USA (Ford Taurus), 334; **8** Kevin Harvick, USA (Chevrolet Monte Carlo), 334; **9** Mark Martin, USA (Ford Taurus), 334; **10** Bobby Labonte, USA (Pontiac Grand Prix), 334.
Fastest qualifying lap: Jimmy Spencer, USA (Ford Taurus), 29.166s, 185.147 mph/297.965 km/h.
Drivers Championship points: 1 Gordon (Jeff), 4223; **2** Rudd, 3986; **3** Stewart, 3833; **4** Marlin, 3789; **5** Jarrett, 3730; **6** Wallace (Rusty), 3671.

OLD DOMINION 500, Martinsville Speedway, Virginia, USA, 15 October. Round 30. 500 laps of the 0.526-mile/0.847-km circuit, 263.000 miles/423.257 km.
Race scheduled for 14 October but postponed due to rain.
1 Ricky Craven, USA (Ford Taurus), 3h 28m 19s, 75.750 mph/ 121.908 km/h; **2** Dale Jarrett, USA (Ford Taurus), 3h 28m 19.141s; **3** Ward Burton, USA (Dodge Intrepid), 500 laps; **4** Bobby Labonte, USA (Pontiac Grand Prix), 500; **5** Jeff Burton, USA (Ford Taurus), 500; **6** Johnny Benson Jr., USA (Pontiac Grand Prix), 500; **7** Mark Martin, USA (Ford Taurus), 500; **8** Mike Wallace, USA (Ford Taurus), 500; **9** Jeff Gordon, USA (Chevrolet Monte Carlo), 500; **10** Sterling Marlin, USA (Dodge Intrepid), 500.
Fastest qualifying lap: Todd Bodine, USA (Ford Taurus), 20.204s, 93.724 mph/150.834 km/h.
Drivers Championship points: 1 Gordon (Jeff), 4366; **2** Rudd, 4032; **3** Marlin, 3923; **4** Jarrett, 3905; **5** Stewart, 3873; **6** Wallace (Rusty), 3789.

EA SPORTS 500 PRESENTED BY DODGE, Talladega Superspeedway, Alabama, USA, 21 October. Round 31. 188 laps of the 2.660-mile/4.281-km circuit, 500.080 miles/804.801 km.
1 Dale Earnhardt Jr., USA (Chevrolet Monte Carlo), 3h 02m 45s, 164.185 mph/264.230 km/h; **2** Tony Stewart, USA (Pontiac Grand Prix), 3h 02m 45.388s; **3** Jeff Burton, USA (Ford Taurus), 188 laps; **4** Matt Kenseth, USA (Ford Taurus), 188; **5** Bobby Hamilton, USA (Chevrolet Monte Carlo), 188; **6** Kenny Wallace, USA (Chevrolet Monte Carlo), 188; **7** Jeff Gordon, USA (Chevrolet Monte Carlo), 188; **8** Joe Nemechek, USA (Chevrolet Monte Carlo), 188; **9** Mark Martin, USA (Ford Taurus), 188; **10** Kevin Lepage, USA (Ford Taurus) 188.
Fastest qualifying lap: Stacy Compton, USA (Dodge Intrepid), 51.695s, 185.240 mph/298.115 km/h.
Drivers Championship points: 1 Gordon (Jeff), 4512; **2** Rudd, 4117; **3** Stewart, 4043; **4** Marlin, 4040; **5** Jarrett, 3998; **6** Earnhardt Jr., 3925.

CHECKER AUTO PARTS 500 PRESENTED BY PENNZOIL, Phoenix International Raceway, Arizona, USA, 28 October. Round 32. 312 laps of the 1.000-mile/1.609-km circuit, 312.000 miles/502.115 km.
1 Jeff Burton, USA (Ford Taurus), 3h 02m 26s, 102.613 mph/165.139 km/h; **2** Mike Wallace, USA (Ford Taurus), 3h 02m 28.245s; **3** Ricky Rudd, USA (Ford Taurus), 312 laps; **4** Matt Kenseth, USA (Ford Taurus), 312; **5** Tony Stewart, USA (Pontiac Grand Prix), 312; **6** Jeff Gordon, USA (Chevrolet Monte Carlo), 312; **7** Robby Gordon, USA (Chevrolet Monte Carlo), 312; **8** Ricky Craven, USA (Ford Taurus), 312; **9** Dale Jarrett, USA (Ford Taurus), 312; **10** Johnny Benson Jr., USA (Pontiac Grand Prix), 312.
Fastest qualifying lap: Casey Atwood, USA (Dodge Intrepid), 27.419s, 131.296 mph/211.300 km/h.
Drivers Championship points: 1 Gordon (Jeff), 4662; **2** Rudd, 4282; **3** Stewart, 4198; **4** Jarrett, 4136; **5** Marlin, 4101; **6** Wallace (Rusty), 4027.

POP SECRET MICROWAVE POPCORN 400, North Carolina Motor Speedway, Rockingham, North Carolina, USA, 4 November. Round 33. 393 laps of the 1.017-mile/1.637-km circuit, 399.681 miles/643.224 km.
1 Joe Nemechek, USA (Chevrolet Monte Carlo), 3h 05m 59s, 128.941 mph/207.510 km/h; **2** Kenny Wallace, USA (Chevrolet Monte Carlo), 3h 06m 05.285s; **3** Johnny Benson Jr., USA (Pontiac Grand Prix), 393 laps; **4** Dale Jarrett, USA (Ford Taurus), 393; **5** Jerry Nadeau, USA (Chevrolet Monte Carlo), 393; **6** Ward Burton, USA (Dodge Intrepid), 393; **7** Tony Stewart, USA (Pontiac Grand Prix), 393; **8** Ricky Rudd, USA (Ford Taurus), 393; **9** Bobby Labonte, USA (Pontiac Grand Prix), 393; **10** Matt Kenseth, USA (Ford Taurus), 393.
Fastest qualifying lap: Wallace (Kenny), 23.668s, 154.690 mph/248.949 km/h.
Drivers championship points: 1 Gordon (Jeff), 4750; **2** Rudd, 4424; **3** Stewart, 4349; **4** Jarrett, 4296; **5** Marlin, 4231; **6** Wallace (Rusty), 4118.

PENNZOIL FREEDOM 400, Miami-Dade Homestead Motorsports Complex, Florida, USA, 11 November. Round 34. 267 laps of the 1.500-mile/2.414-km circuit, 400.500 miles/644.542 km.
1 Bill Elliott, USA (Dodge Intrepid), 3h 24m 36s, 117.449 mph/189.015 km/h; **2** Michael Waltrip, USA (Chevrolet Monte Carlo), 3h 24m 37.420s; **3** Casey Atwood, USA (Dodge Intrepid), 267 laps; **4** Jeff Burton, USA (Ford Taurus), 267; **5** Sterling Marlin, USA (Dodge Intrepid), 267; **6** Dave Blaney, USA (Dodge Intrepid), 267; **7** Kevin Harvick, USA (Chevrolet Monte Carlo), 267; **8** Bobby Labonte, USA (Pontiac Grand Prix), 267; **9** Jeff Green, USA (Chevrolet Monte Carlo), 267; **10** Jason Leffler, USA (Dodge Intrepid), 267.
Fastest qualifying lap: Elliott, 34.788s, 155.226 mph/249.812 km/h.

Provisional championship points
Drivers
1 Jeff Gordon, USA, 4829; **2** Ricky Rudd, USA, 4524; **3** Tony Stewart, USA, 4465; **4** Sterling Marlin, USA, 4391; **5** Dale Jarrett, USA, 4336; **6** Rusty Wallace, USA, 4245; **7** Dale Earnhardt Jr., USA, 4213; **8** Bobby Labonte, USA, 4211; **9** Kevin Harvick, USA, 4151; **10** Jeff Burton, USA, 4143; **11** Johnny Benson Jr., USA, 3931; **12** Mark Martin, USA, 3860; **13** Matt Kenseth, USA, 3710; **14** Ward Burton, USA, 3654; **15** Jimmy Spencer, USA, 3618; **16** Bill Elliott, USA, 3606; **17** Bobby Hamilton, USA, 3417; **18** Ken Schrader, USA, 3364; **19** Jerry Nadeau, USA, 3360; **20** Ricky Craven, USA, 3276; **21** Elliott Sadler, USA, 3274; **22** Terry Labonte, USA, 3131; **23** Dave Blaney, USA, 3128; **24** Michael Waltrip, USA, 3031; **25** Kurt Busch, USA, 2981; **26** Casey Atwood, USA, 2914; **27** Robert Pressley, USA, 2910; **28** Steve Park, USA, 2859; **29** Joe Nemechek, USA, 2845; **30** John Andretti, USA, 2800.

Rookie of the Year: Kevin Harvick.

Manufacturers
1 Chevrolet, 235; **2** Ford, 211; **3** Pontiac, 156; **4** Dodge, 146.

Results of the Atlanta and New Hampshire races will be given in AUTOCOURSE 2002–2003

Other NASCAR races

THE BUDWEISER SHOOTOUT, Daytona International Speedway, Daytona Beach, Florida, USA, 11 February. 70 laps of the 2.500-mile/4.023-km circuit, 175.000 miles/281.635 km.
1 Tony Stewart, USA (Pontiac Grand Prix), 57m 59.975s, 181.036 mph/291.349 km/h; **2** Dale Earnhardt, USA (Chevrolet Monte Carlo), 58m 00.120s; **3** Rusty Wallace, USA (Ford Taurus), 58m 00.250s; **4** Dale Jarrett, USA (Ford Taurus), 58m 00.360s; **5** Jeff Burton, USA (Ford Taurus), 58m 00.431s; **6** Dale Earnhardt Jr., USA (Chevrolet Monte Carlo), 58m 00.523s; **7** Bobby Labonte, USA (Pontiac Grand Prix), 58m 00.565s; **8** Mark Martin, USA (Ford Taurus), 58m 00.680s; **9** Ricky Rudd, USA (Ford Taurus), 58m 00.737s; **10** Mike Skinner, USA (Chevrolet Monte Carlo), 58m 00.849s.
Fastest race lap: Jarrett, 47.844s, 188.111 mph/302.736 km/h.
Fastest qualifying lap: Ken Schrader, USA (Pontiac Grand Prix).

THE WINSTON, Lowe's Motor Speedway, Concord, North Carolina, USA, 19 May. 70 laps of the 1.500-mile/2.414-km circuit, 105.000 miles/168.981 km.
Run over three segments (30, 30 and 10 laps). Aggregate results given.
1 Jeff Gordon, USA (Chevrolet Monte Carlo); **2** Dale Jarrett, USA (Ford Taurus); **3** Tony Stewart, USA (Pontiac Grand Prix); **4** Bobby Labonte, USA (Pontiac Grand Prix); **5** Jerry Nadeau, USA (Chevrolet Monte Carlo); **6** Ward Burton, USA (Dodge Intrepid); **7** Dale Earnhardt Jr., USA (Chevrolet Monte Carlo); **8** Todd Bodine, USA (Ford Taurus); **9** Jonny Benson Jr., USA (Pontiac Grand Prix); **10** Bobby Hamilton, USA (Chevrolet Monte Carlo).
Fastest race lap: Rusty Wallace, USA (Ford Taurus), 46.819s, 115.337 mph/185.618 km/h.
Pole position: Terry Labonte, USA (Chevrolet Monte Carlo).

Dayton Indy Lights Championship

All cars are Lola T97/20-Dayton

MONTERREY INDY LIGHTS RACE, Parque Fundidora, Monterrey, Nuevo Leon, Mexico, 11 March. Round 1. 35 laps of the 2.104-mile/3.386-km circuit, 73.640 miles/118.512 km
1 Derek Higgins, GB, 54m 48.128s, 80.625 mph/129.753 km/h; **2** Townsend Bell, USA, 54m 48.307s; **3** John Fogarty, USA, 54m 53.927s; **4** Mario Dominguez, MEX, 54m 54.462s; **5** Dan Wheldon, GB, 54m 57.565s; **6** Kristian Kolby, DK, 54m 58.025s; **7** Damien Faulkner, IRL, 55m 01.103s; **8** Rudy Junco Jr., MEX, 55m 11.456s; **9** Cory Witherill, USA, 55m 36.123s; **10** Rolando Quintanilla, MEX, 56m 13.419s.
Most laps led: Higgins, 35
Fastest qualifying lap: Higgins, 1m 25.345s, 88.750 mph/142.830 km/h.

LONG BEACH INDY LIGHTS RACE, Long Beach Street Circuit, California, USA, 8 April. Round 2. 38 laps of the 1.968-mile/3.167-km circuit, 74.784 miles/120.353 km.
1 Townsend Bell, USA, 57m 13.430s, 78.412 mph/126.192 km/h; **2** Dan Wheldon, GB, 57m 17.205s; **3** Derek Higgins, GB, 57m 18.772s; **4** Mario Dominguez, MEX, 57m 19.292s; **5** Kristian Kolby, DK, 57m 25.756s; **6** Andy Booth, USA, 57m 32.333s; **7** Cory Witherill, USA, 57m 32.912s; **8** Rudy Junco Jr., MEX, 57m 37.253s; **9** Luis Diaz, MEX, 58m 05.463s; **10** Larry Mason, USA, 36 laps.
Most laps led: Wheldon, 32.
Fastest qualifying lap: Damien Faulkner, IRL, 1m 18.516s, 90.234 mph/145.217 km/h.

TEXAS INDY LIGHTS RACE, Texas Motor Speedway, Fort Worth, Texas, USA, 28 April. Round 3. 67 laps of the 1.482-mile/2.385-km circuit, 99.294 miles/159.798 km.
1 Damien Faulkner, IRL, 39m 35.283s, 150.491 mph/242.192 km/h; **2** Derek Higgins, GB, 39m 35.632s; **3** Kristian Kolby, DK, 39m 35.812s; **4** Luis Diaz, MEX, 39m 36.020s; **5** Rolando Quintanilla, MEX, 39m 36.410s; **6** Mario Dominguez, MEX, 66 laps; **7** Rudy Junco Jr., MEX, 66; **8** Townsend Bell, USA, 65; **9** Jon Fogarty, USA, 53; **10** Dan Wheldon, GB, 52.
Most laps led: Faulkner, 65.
Fastest qualifying lap: Faulkner, 29.060s, 183.593 mph/295.464 km/h.

MILWAUKEE INDY LIGHTS RACE, The Milwaukee Mile, Wisconsin State Fair Park, West Allis, Milwaukee, Wisconsin, USA, 3 June. Round 4. 100 laps of the 1.032-mile/1.661-km circuit, 103.200 miles/166.084 km.
1 Townsend Bell, USA, 43m 27.503s, 142.481 mph/229.301 km/h; **2** Mario Dominguez, MEX, 99 laps; **3** Dan Wheldon, GB, 98; **4** Luis Diaz, MEX, 98; **5** Rudy Junco Jr., MEX, 97; **6** Kristian Kolby, DK, 96; **7** Damien Faulkner, IRL, 95; **8** Rolando Quintanilla, MEX, 95; **9** Matthew Halliday, NZ, 95; **10** Jon Fogarty, USA, 80.
Most laps led: Bell, 100.
Fastest qualifying lap: Bell, 24.256s, 153.166 mph/246.497 km/h.

SPIRIT MOUNTAIN CASINO CHALLENGE, Portland International Raceway, Oregon, USA, 24 June. Round 5. 38 laps of the 1.969-mile/3.169-km circuit, 74.822 miles/120.414 km.
1 Damien Faulkner, IRL, 58m 58.791s, 76.116 mph/122.497 km/h; **2** Rudy Junco Jr., MEX, 59m 14.925s; **3** Derek Higgins, GB, 59m 19.292s; **4** Matthew Halliday, NZ, 59m 27.727s; **5** Rolando Quintanilla, MEX, 59m 57.179s; **6** Townsend Bell, USA, 1h 00m 15.203s; **7** Cory Witherill, USA, 1h 00m 23.856s; **8** Kristian Kolby, DK, 36 laps; **9** Luis Diaz, MEX, 36; **10** Dan Wheldon, GB, 2.
Most laps led: Faulkner, 22.
Fastest qualifying lap: Bell, 1m 04.991s, 109.067 mph/175.527 km/h.

KANSAS INDY LIGHTS RACE, Kansas Speedway, Kansas City, Kansas, USA, 8 July. Round 6. 67 laps of the 1.520-mile/2.446-km circuit, 101.840 miles/163.896 km.
1 Kristian Kolby, DK, 40m 25.322s, 151.165 mph/243.277 km/h; **2** Damien Faulkner, IRL, 40m 25.323s; **3** Dan Wheldon, GB, 40m 25.535s; **4** Matthew Halliday, NZ, 40m 26.071s; **5** Townsend Bell, USA, 40m 26.339s; **6** Cory Witherill, USA, 40m 26.542s; **7** Luis Diaz, MEX, 40m 26.672s; **8** Rolando Quintanilla, MEX, 65 laps; **9** Rudy Junco Jr., MEX, 58; **10** Mario Dominguez, MEX, 43.
Most laps led: Bell, 27.
Fastest qualifying lap: Dominguez, 30.252s, 180.881 mph/291.099 km/h.

TORONTO INDY LIGHTS RACE, Canada National Exhibition Place Circuit, Toronto, Ontario, Canada, 15 July. Round 7. 43 laps of the 1.755-mile/2.824-km circuit, 75.465 miles/121.449 km.
1 Townsend Bell, USA, 51m 18.593s, 88.246 mph/142.018 km/h; **2** Mario Dominguez, MEX, 51m 25.595s; **3** Damien Faulkner, IRL, 51m 26.158s; **4** Matthew Halliday, NZ, 51m 26.926s; **5** Luis Diaz, MEX, 51m 29.251s; **6** Geoff Boss, USA, 51m 30.615s; **7** Dan Wheldon, GB, 51m 53.894s; **8** Rolando Quintanilla, MEX, 51m 03.240s; **9** Derek Higgins, GB, 42 laps; **10** Kristian Kolby, DK, 24.
Most laps led: Bell, 43.
Fastest qualifying lap: Bell, 1m 04.202s, 98.408 mph/158.373 km/h.

MID-OHIO INDY LIGHTS RACE, Mid-Ohio Sports Car Course, Lexington, Ohio. 12 August. Round 8. 34 laps of the 2.258-mile/3.634-km circuit, 75.808 miles/122.001 km.
1 Townsend Bell, USA, 50m 19.940s, 90.369 mph/145.435 km/h; **2** Dan Wheldon, GB, 50m 20.175s; **3** Damien Faulkner, IRL, 50m 20.406s; **4** Kristian Kolby, DK, 50m 22.088s; **5** Matthew Halliday, NZ, 50m 22.711s; **6** Mario Dominguez, MEX, 50m 23.056s; **7** Rudy Junco Jr., MEX, 50m 24.023s; **8** Cory Witherill, USA, 50m 24.686s; **9** Rolando Quintanilla, MEX, 50m 25.597s; **10** Geoff Boss, USA, 31 laps.
Most laps led: Bell, 34.
Fastest qualifying lap: Bell, 1m 13.809s, 110.133 mph/177.242 km/h.

GATEWAY INDY LIGHTS RACE, Gateway International Raceway, Madison, Illinois, 26 August. Round 9. 80 laps of the 1.270-mile/2.044-km circuit, 101.600 miles/163.509 km.
1 Dan Wheldon, GB, 43m 31.081s, 140.080 mph/225.437 km/h; **2** Mario Dominguez, MEX, 43m 54.903s; **3** Matthew Halliday, NZ, 43m 55.654s; **4** Derek Higgins, GB, 79 laps; **5** Damien Faulkner, IRL, 79; **6** Luis Diaz, MEX, 79; **7** Rudy Junco Jr., MEX, 78; **8** Rolando Quintanilla, MEX, 78; **9** Townsend Bell, USA, 70; **10** Cory Witherill, USA, 13.
Most laps led: Bell, 69.
Fastest qualifying lap: Bell, 29.942s, 152.695 mph/245.739 km/h.

AUDI PETIT LE MANS, Road Atlanta Motor Sports Center, Braselton, Georgia, 6 October. Round 10. 29 laps of the 2.540-mile/4.088-km circuit, 73.660 miles/118.544 km.
1 Dan Wheldon, GB, 42m 57.299s, 102.889 mph/165.584 km/h; **2** Townsend Bell, USA, 42m 57.555s; **3** Damien Faulkner, IRL, 42m 59.835s; **4** Mario Dominguez, MEX, 43m 02.079s; **5** Jon Fogarty, USA, 43m 03.090s; **6** Derek Higgins, GB, 43m 06.242s; **7** Luis Diaz, MEX, 43m 13.226s; **8** Matthew Halliday, NZ, 43m 15.362s; **9** Rolando Quintanilla, MEX, 28 laps; **10** Cory Witherill, USA, 20.
Most laps led: Bell, 28.
Fastest qualifying lap: Bell, 1m 14.711s, 122.392 mph/196.970 km/h.

YAHOO! SPORTS MONTEREY CHALLENGE, Mazda Raceway Laguna Seca, Monterey, California, USA, 14 October. Round 11. 34 laps of the 2.238-mile/3.602-km circuit, 76.092 miles/122.458 km.
1 Townsend Bell, USA, 44m 34.521s, 102.423 mph/164.833 km/h; **2** Jon Fogarty, USA, 44m 36.484s; **3** Luis Diaz, MEX, 44m 44.495s; **4** Damien Faulkner, IRL, 44m 50.954s; **5** Dan Wheldon, GB, 44m 52.053s; **6** Derek Higgins, GB, 45m 05.393s; **7** Matthew Halliday, NZ, 45m 07.956s; **8** Rolando Quintanilla, MEX, 45m 13.851s; **9** Rudy Junco Jr., MEX, 45m 26.224s; **10** Mario Dominguez, MEX, 45m 44.462s.
Most laps led: Bell, 34.
Fastest qualifying lap: Bell, 1m 16.313s, 105.576 mph/169.908 km/h.

FONTANA INDY LIGHTS RACE, California Speedway, Fontana, California, USA, 4 November. Round 12. 44 laps of the 2.029-mile/3.265-km circuit, 89.276 miles/143.675 km.
Race scheduled for 50 laps but shortened due to rain.
1 Townsend Bell, USA, 29m 22.667s, 182.334 mph/ 293.438 km/h; **2** Dan Wheldon, GB, 29m 22.718s; **3** Matthew Halliday, NZ, 29m 40.021s; **4** Derek Higgins, IRL, 29m 40.023s; **5** Mario Dominguez, MEX, 29m 40.028s; **6** Luis Diaz, MEX, 29m 40.098s; **7** Damien Faulkner, IRL, 29m 40.114s; **8** Rudy Junco Jr., MEX, 29m 40.376s; **9** Rolando Quintanilla, MEX, 29m 51.009s; **10** Cory Witherill, USA, 38 laps.
Most laps led: Bell, 44.
Fastest qualifying lap: Bell, 39.098s, 186.823 mph/300.662 km/h.

Final championship points
1 Townsend Bell, USA, 193; **2** Dan Wheldon, GB, 149; **3** Damien Faulkner, IRL, 141; **4** Mario Dominguez, MEX, 120; **5** Derek Higgins, IRL, 113; **6** Matthew Halliday, NZ, 89; **7** Luis Diaz, MEX, 88; **8** Kristian Kolby, DK, 80; **9** Rudy Junco Jr., MEX, 67; **10** Rolando Quintanilla, MEX, 62; **11** Jon Fogarty, USA, 48; **12** Cory Witherill, USA, 44; **13** Geoff Boss, USA, 11; **14** Andy Booth, USA, 8; **15** Larry Mason, USA, 3; **16** Nilton Rossoni, BR, 1.

Nation's Cup
1 United States, 193; **2** Ireland, 179; **3** Mexico, 152; **4** England, 150; **5** New Zealand, 97; **6** Denmark, 80; **7** Brazil, 1.

Rookie of the year
1 Dan Wheldon, GB, 149; **2** Damien Faulkner, IRL, 141; **3** Matthew Halliday, NZ, 89; **4** Kristian Kolby, DK, 80; **5** Jon Fogarty, USA, 48; **6** Andy Booth, USA, 8; **7** Larry Mason, USA, 3; **8** Nilton Rossoni, BR, 1.